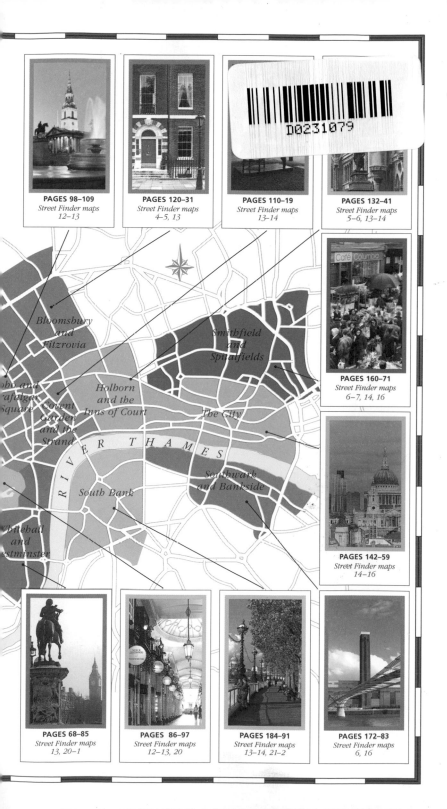

PAGES 98–109
Street Finder maps
12–13

PAGES 120–31
Street Finder maps
4–5, 13

PAGES 110–19
Street Finder maps
13–14

PAGES 132–41
Street Finder maps
5–6, 13–14

PAGES 160–71
Street Finder maps
6–7, 14, 16

PAGES 142–59
Street Finder maps
14–16

Bloomsbury
and
Fitzrovia

Smithfield
and
Spitalfields

Soho and
Trafalgar
Square

Holborn
and the
Inns of Court

Covent
Garden
and the
Strand

The City

RIVER THAMES

South Bank

Southwark
and Bankside

Whitehall
and
Westminster

PAGES 68–85
Street Finder maps
13, 20–1

PAGES 86–97
Street Finder maps
12–13, 20

PAGES 184–91
Street Finder maps
13–14, 21–2

PAGES 172–83
Street Finder maps
6, 16

EYEWITNESS TRAVEL
LONDON

EYEWITNESS TRAVEL

LONDON

Main contributor: MICHAEL LEAPMAN

DK

LONDON, NEW YORK,
MELBOURNE, MUNICH AND DELHI
www.dk.com

PROJECT EDITOR Jane Shaw
ART EDITOR Sally Ann Hibbard
EDITOR Tom Fraser
DESIGNERS Pippa Hurst, Robyn Tomlinson
DESIGN ASSISTANT Clare Sullivan

First published in Great Britain in 1993
by Dorling Kindersley Limited
80 Strand, London WC2R 0RL

**Reprinted with revisions 1994, 1995, 1996, 1997, 1999,
2000 (twice), 2001, 2002, 2003, 2004, 2005, 2006, 2007**

Copyright 1993, 2007 © Dorling Kindersley Limited, London
A Penguin Company

Front cover main image: Houses of Parliament

CONTENTS

HOW TO USE
THIS GUIDE **6**

Portrait of Sir Walter Raleigh (1585)

INTRODUCING
LONDON

FOUR GREAT DAYS IN
LONDON **10**

PUTTING LONDON
ON THE MAP **12**

THE HISTORY OF
LONDON **16**

LONDON
AT A GLANCE **36**

LONDON THROUGH
THE YEAR **56**

A RIVER VIEW
OF LONDON **60**

Bedford Square doorway (1775)

LONDON AREA BY AREA

WHITEHALL AND
WESTMINSTER **68**

PICCADILLY AND
ST JAMES'S **86**

SOHO AND
TRAFALGAR SQUARE **98**

COVENT GARDEN AND
THE STRAND **110**

The Broadwalk at Hampton Court (c.1720)

SHOPS AND
MARKETS **320**

ENTERTAINMENT IN
LONDON **342**

CHILDREN'S
LONDON **356**

Bandstand in St James's Park

Beefeater at the Tower of London

BLOOMSBURY AND
FITZROVIA **120**

HOLBORN AND THE
INNS OF COURT **132**

THE CITY **142**

SMITHFIELD AND
SPITALFIELDS **160**

SOUTHWARK AND
BANKSIDE **172**

SOUTH BANK **184**

CHELSEA **192**

SOUTH KENSINGTON
AND KNIGHTSBRIDGE **198**

KENSINGTON AND
HOLLAND PARK **214**

REGENT'S PARK AND
MARYLEBONE **220**

HAMPSTEAD **228**

GREENWICH AND
BLACKHEATH **236**

FURTHER AFIELD **244**

SIX GUIDED
WALKS **262**

Houses of Parliament

SURVIVAL GUIDE

PRACTICAL
INFORMATION **362**

GETTING TO
LONDON **372**

GETTING AROUND
LONDON **378**

LONDON
STREET FINDER **386**

GENERAL INDEX **424**

ACKNOWLEDGMENTS **446**

St Paul's Church: Covent Garden

TRAVELLERS' NEEDS

WHERE TO STAY **278**

RESTAURANTS AND
PUBS **292**

HOW TO USE THIS GUIDE

This eyewitness travel guide helps you get the most from your stay in London with the minimum of practical difficulty. The opening section, *Introducing London,* locates the city geographically, sets modern London in its historical context and describes the regular highlights of the London year. *London at a Glance* is an overview of the city's specialities. *London Area by Area* takes you round the city's areas of interest. It describes all the main sights with maps, photographs and detailed illustrations. In addition, six planned walking routes take you to parts of London you might otherwise miss.

Well-researched tips on where to stay, eat, shop, and on entertainments are in *Travellers' Needs. Children's London* lists highlights for young visitors, and *Survival Guide* tells you how to do anything from posting a letter to using the Underground.

LONDON AREA BY AREA

The city has been divided into 16 sightseeing areas, each with its own section in the guide. Each section opens with a portrait of the area, summing up its character and history and listing all the sights to be covered. Sights are numbered and clearly located on an *Area Map.* After this comes a large-scale *Street-by-Street Map* focusing on the most interesting part of the area. Finding your way about the area section is made simple by the numbering system. This refers to the order in which sights are described on the pages that complete the section.

1 The Area Map

For easy reference, the sights in each area are numbered and located on an Area Map. *To help the visitor, the map also shows Underground and main-line stations.*

Photographs of facades and distinctive details of buildings help you to locate the sights.

Colour-coding on each page makes the area easy to find in the book.

2 The Street-by-Street Map

This gives a bird's-eye view of the heart of each sight-seeing area. The most important buildings are picked out in stronger colour, to help you spot them as you walk around.

A locator map shows you where you are in relation to surrounding areas. The area of the *Street-by-Street Map* is shown in red.

Sights at a Glance lists the sights in the area by category: Historic Streets and Buildings, Churches, Museums and Galleries, Monuments, Parks and Gardens.

The area covered in greater detail on the *Street-by-Street Map* is shaded red.

Numbered circles pinpoint all the listed sights on the area map. St Margaret's Church, for example, is ❻

Travel tips help you reach the area quickly by public transport.

St Margaret's Church is shown on this map as well.

A suggested route for a walk takes in the most attractive and interesting streets in the area.

Stars indicate the sights that no visitor should miss.

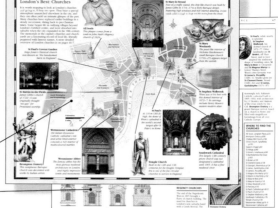

LONDON AT A GLANCE

Each map in this section concentrates on a specific theme: *Remarkable Londoners, Museums and Galleries, Churches, Parks and Gardens, Ceremonies.* The top sights are shown on the map; others are described on the following two pages and cross-referenced to their full entries in the *Area by Area* section.

Each sightseeing area is colour-coded.

The theme is explored in greater detail on the pages following the map.

3 Detailed information on each sight
All important sights in each area are described in depth in this section. They are listed in order, following the numbering on the Area Map. *Practical information is also provided.*

PRACTICAL INFORMATION
Each entry provides all the information needed to plan a visit to the sight. The key to the symbols is inside the back cover.

Telephone number

Address

Map reference to Street Finder at back of book

St Margaret's Church 6 — Sight Number

Parliament Sq SW1. **Map** 13 B5.
Tel 020-7654 4840. ⊖ *Westminster.*
Open 9:30am–3:45pm Mon–Fri,
9:30am –1:45pm Sat, 2–5pm Sun.
🕇 11am Sun. ∅ 🕭 *Concerts.*

Opening hours

Services and facilities available

Nearest Underground station

4 London's major sights
These are given two or more full pages in the sightseeing area in which they are found. Historic buildings are dissected to reveal their interiors; museums and galleries have colour-coded floor plans to help you find important exhibits.

The Visitors' Checklist provides the practical information you will need to plan your visit.

The façade of each major sight is shown to help you spot it quickly.

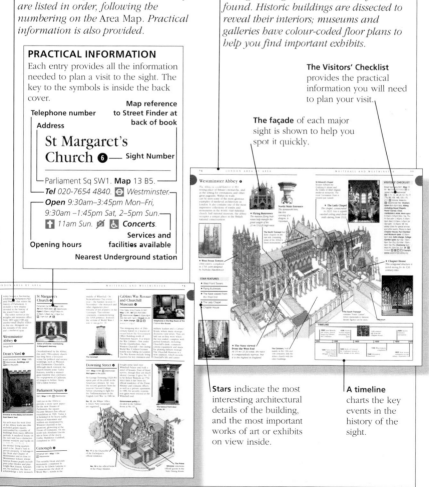

Stars indicate the most interesting architectural details of the building, and the most important works of art or exhibits on view inside.

A timeline charts the key events in the history of the sight.

INTRODUCING LONDON

FOUR GREAT DAYS 10–11
PUTTING LONDON ON THE MAP 12–15
THE HISTORY OF LONDON 16–35
LONDON AT A GLANCE 36–55
LONDON THROUGH THE YEAR 56–59
A RIVER VIEW OF LONDON 60–65

FOUR GREAT DAYS IN LONDON

For things to see and do, visitors to London are spoiled for choice. Whether here for a short stay or just wanting a flavour of this great city, you need to make the most of your time. So here are ideas for four days of sightseeing and fun. You'll find

Chinatown dragon

suggestions on what to see, how to get about and where to eat. Each of these four itineraries follows a theme and sights are reachable using public transport. Prices include travel, food and admission. Family prices are for two adults and two children.

Café at the National Portrait Gallery with a view of Trafalgar Square

HISTORY AND CULTURE

- **Art at the National Gallery**
- **Coffee with a view**
- **Houses of Parliament**
- **Buckingham Palace**

TWO ADULTS allow at least £70

Morning
Start the day by 10am in **Trafalgar Square** *(see p102)*. This is when the **National Gallery** *(see p104)* opens. Give yourself an hour and a half. The gallery is free, but visitors are encouraged to make a donation. After, go for a coffee at the Portrait Restaurant on the top floor of the neighbouring **National Portrait Gallery** *(see p102)*, which has a great view over Trafalgar Square and Nelson's column. Set off down Whitehall to Parliament Square, a 15-minute walk that may be extended by the passing distractions of Horse Guard's Parade, **Banqueting House** *(see p80)* and **Downing Street** *(see p75)*. See the **Houses of Parliament** *(see pp72–3)* before visiting the next highlight, the

fabulous **Westminster Abbey** *(see pp76–7)*. There are a number of inexpensive lunch spots around St James's Park tube station, such as Fuller's Ale and Pie House, 33 Tothill Street. Or go to the more pricey but attractive Inn the Park (must book; 020 7451 9999) by the lake in **St James's Park** *(see p93)*.

Afternoon
On the far side of St James's Park is **Buckingham Palace** *(see p94–5)*. The Queen's Gallery has changing exhibitions and you can buy regal souvenirs in its shop. For tea, head up past St James's Palace to Piccadilly. You may not feel you can afford a £70 tea for two at the Palm Court at the **Ritz** *(see p91)* but there are several cafés and patisseries nearby, such as Richoux at 172 Piccadilly. For the best evening entertainment, get tickets for a West End play or show. These should be booked in advance *(see p343)*, although last-minute tickets are sometimes on sale at the theatre box offices.

SHOPPING IN STYLE

- **St James's – shopping with history**
- **Old Bond Street for style**
- **Browse in trendy Covent Garden and the Piazza**

TWO ADULTS allow at least £55

Morning
Start in Piccadilly and **St James's Street**, *(see pp88–9)*, home of suppliers to royalty and historic fashion leaders: John Lobb, the bootmaker is at No. 9 and Lock the hatter at 6. Turn right into Jermyn Street for high-class men's tailors such as Turnbull & Asser and New Lingwood, outfitters to Eton College. Floris the perfumer at 89 was founded in 1730 and the cheese shop Paxton & Whitfield at 93 has been here since 1740. Walk through Piccadilly Arcade to **Fortnum & Mason** *(see p313)*, where the Fountain Tea Room can provide refreshment before

Historic shopping mall at the Burlington Arcade, Piccadilly

The Queen's House, Greenwich

buying souvenirs. Stop in at **The Royal Academy** *(see p90)* and the **Burlington Arcade** *(see p91)*, before heading up **Old** and **New Bond** streets *(see p322)*, the smartest shopping address in town, with art galleries, antiques and designer shops. Try South Molton Street for women's fashion and Oxford Street for **Selfridge's** massive department store *(see p321)*.

Afternoon
Head to **Covent Garden** *(see p114)* and wander the Piazza and streets to the north; Floral Street is renowned for high fashion. Check out alternative lifestyles in **Neal's Yard** *(see p115)*. The **Photographers' Gallery** *(see p116)* offers exhibitions and a shop. Stop for tea in Paul Bakery and Café at 29 Bedford Street.

THE GREAT OUTDOORS

- **Sail to the Cutty Sark**
- **Ponds and a memorial in the Palace gardens**
- **Tea at Kensington Palace**

TWO ADULTS allow at least £50

Morning
Take a one-hour boat trip from Westminster Millennium Pier to **Greenwich** *(see pp238–43)*. A morning is easily passed at this UNESCO World Heritage Site. There's the Maritime Museum, Royal Observatory, Queen's House, and Cutty Sark. Have a snack

lunch overlooking the river at the historic **Trafalgar Tavern** *(see p242)*.

Afternoon
Return by boat and head to **Kensington Gardens** *(see p210)*. Admire the boats on the Round Pond, and see what's on at the **Serpentine Gallery** *(see p210)*. Beyond this is the **Princess Diana Memorial Fountain** *(see p219)*. By the Long Water is the delightful statue of Peter Pan. Visit **Kensington Palace** *(see p210)*, Princess Diana's former home. Have tea in the Palace's Orangery Tea Room.

A FAMILY FUN DAY

- **Take the kids to the Tower**
- **Messing about in boats**
- **Enjoy the undersea world**
- **Hit Chinatown**

FAMILY OF 4 allow at least £200.

Predators at the London Aquarium

Morning
Head to the **Tower of London** *(see pp154-7)*, London's top visitor attraction and an

established family favourite. Book tickets to avoid the queue. The fascinating castle and Crown Jewels will take at least a couple of hours to explore. For lunch, head across Tower Bridge to **St Katherine's Dock** *(see p158)* where, among an eclectic collection of boats, there are several attractive places to eat, including the Dickens Inn for snacks or a full meal.

Afternoon
The **British Airways London Eye** is a thrilling trip above the city on the South Bank *(see p189; phone bookings can be made on: 0870 5000 600)*.

Nearby there is plenty of other entertainment, especially in the former **County Hall** *(see p188)*. This leisure complex has the London Aquarium. Younger people will enjoy the video games and simulators, bowling alley and bumper cars in the Namco Station. Afterwards, take the tube to **Chinatown** *(see p108)*, situated in and around Gerrard Street, which with its many superb restaurants, colourful shops and vibrant streetlife, is always lively and interesting. Go for an early Chinese supper of *dim sum*, or small dishes. If the kids are still up for entertainment, end the day at a film in one of the many luxurious cinemas around Leicester Square.

The gracious sweep of the Diana Memorial Fountain, Hyde Park

Putting London on the Map

London, the capital of the United
Kingdom, is a city of seven million
people covering 620 sq miles (1,606 sq
km) of southeast England. It is built on
the River Thames and is at the centre of
the UK road and rail networks. From
London visitors can easily reach the
country's other main tourist attractions.

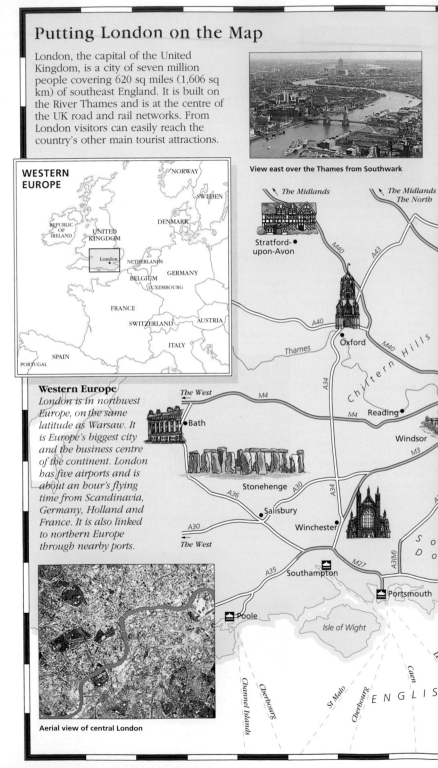

View east over the Thames from Southwark

**WESTERN
EUROPE**

NORWAY

SWEDEN

REPUBLIC
OF
IRELAND

UNITED
KINGDOM

DENMARK

London

NETHERLANDS

GERMANY

BELGIUM

LUXEMBOURG

FRANCE

SWITZERLAND

AUSTRIA

ITALY

SPAIN

PORTUGAL

The Midlands

The Midlands
The North

Stratford-
upon-Avon

M40

A43

A40

Oxford

M40

C h i l t e r n   H i l l s

Thames

A34

Western Europe

*London is in northwest
Europe, on the same
latitude as Warsaw. It
is Europe's biggest city
and the business centre
of the continent. London
has five airports and is
about an hour's flying
time from Scandinavia,
Germany, Holland and
France. It is also linked
to northern Europe
through nearby ports.*

The West

M4

Bath

M4

Reading

Windsor

M3

Stonehenge

A30

A34

A36

Salisbury

Winchester

A30

The West

A3

S
O
D
O

A35

M27

Southampton

A3(M)

Portsmouth

Poole

Isle of Wight

Channel Islands

Cherbourg

St Malo

Cherbourg

Caen

Ie

E N G L I S

Aerial view of central London

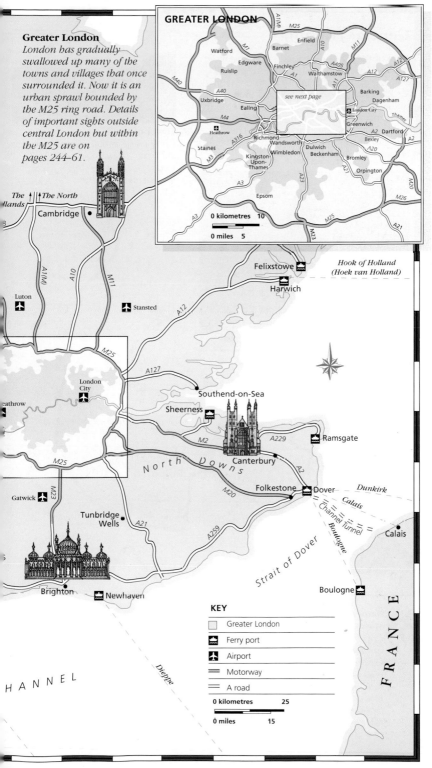

Greater London

London has gradually swallowed up many of the towns and villages that once surrounded it. Now it is an urban sprawl bounded by the M25 ring road. Details of important sights outside central London but within the M25 are on pages 244–61.

GREATER LONDON

Watford
Enfield
Barnet
Edgware
Ruislip
Finchley
Walthamstow
Uxbridge
Ealing
see next page
Barking
Dagenham
London City
Greenwich
Heathrow
Richmond
Wandsworth
Wimbledon
Dulwich
Beckenham
Bexley
Dartford
Kingston-Upon-Thames
Bromley
Orpington
Epsom

0 kilometres 10
0 miles 5

The North
lands
Cambridge
Luton
Stansted

Felixstowe
Harwich

Hook of Holland
(Hoek van Holland)

London City

athrow

Southend-on-Sea
Sheerness
Ramsgate
Canterbury
North Downs
Folkestone
Dover
Dunkirk
Calais
Channel Tunnel
Boulogne
Calais
Gatwick
Tunbridge Wells
Strait of Dover
Brighton
Newhaven
Boulogne

F R A N C E

KEY

	Greater London
	Ferry port
	Airport
	Motorway
	A road

0 kilometres 25
0 miles 15

H A N N E L

Dieppe

Central London

Most of the sights described in this book lie within 14 areas of central London, plus two outlying districts of Hampstead and Greenwich. Each area has its own chapter. If time is short, you may decide to restrict yourself to the five areas that contain most of London's famous sights: Whitehall and Westminster, The City, Bloomsbury and Fitzrovia, Soho and Trafalgar Square, and South Kensington.

Tower of London
For much of its 900-year history the Tower was an object of fear. Its bloody past and the Crown Jewels make it a major attraction (see pp154–7).

National Gallery
This gallery has over 2,300 paintings, and the collection is particularly strong on Dutch, early Renaissance Italian and 17th-century Spanish painting (see pp104–7).

Natural History Museum
Life on earth and the earth itself are vividly explored at the museum, through a combination of interactive techniques and traditional displays (see pp208–9).

KEY

■	Major sight
Ⓔ	Underground Station
▤	Railway Station
▨	River Boat Pier
ℹ	Tourist information

0 kilometres 1

0 miles 0.5

Buckingham Palace
The office and home of the monarchy, the palace is also used for state occasions. The State Rooms open to the public in the summer (see pp94–5).

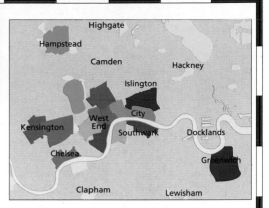

Museum of London
This museum, on the edge of the Barbican complex in the City, provides a lively account of London life from prehistoric times to the outbreak of World War I (see pp166–7).

Houses of Parliament
The Palace of Westminster has been the seat of the two Houses of Parliament, called the Lords and the Commons, since 1512 (see pp72–3).

THE HISTORY OF LONDON

The dragon: the City of London's symbol

In 55 BC, Julius Caesar's Roman army invaded England, landed in Kent and marched north-west until it reached the broad River Thames at what is now Southwark. There were a few tribesmen living on the opposite bank but no major settlement. However, by the time of the second Roman invasion 88 years later, a small port and mercantile community had been established here. The Romans bridged the river and built their administrative headquarters on the north bank, calling it Londinium – a version of its old Celtic name.

LONDON AS CAPITAL

London was soon the largest city in England and, by the time of the Norman Conquest in 1066, it was the obvious choice for national capital.

Settlement slowly spread beyond the original walled city, which was virtually wiped out by the Great Fire of 1666. The post-Fire rebuilding formed the basis of the area we know today as the City but, by the 18th century, London enveloped the settlements around it. These included the royal city of Westminster which had long been London's religious and political centre. The explosive growth of commerce and industry during the 18th and 19th centuries made London the biggest and wealthiest city in the world, creating a prosperous middle class who built the fine houses that still grace parts of the capital. The prospect of riches also lured millions of the dispossessed from the countryside and from abroad. They crowded into insanitary dwellings, many just east of the City, where docks provided employment.

By the end of the 19th century, 4.5 million people lived in inner London and another 4 million in its immediate vicinity. Bombing in World War II devastated many central areas and led to substantial rebuilding in the second half of the 20th century, when the docks and other Victorian industries disappeared.

The following pages illustrate London's history by giving snapshots of significant periods in its evolution.

A map of 1580 showing the City of London and, towards the lower left corner, the City of Westminster

◁ A 15th-century manuscript showing the Tower of London with London Bridge in the background

Roman London

1st-century Roman coin

When the Romans invaded Britain in the 1st century AD, they already controlled vast areas of the Mediterranean, but fierce opposition from local tribes (such as Queen Boadicea's Iceni) made Britain difficult to control. The Romans persevered however, and had consolidated their power by the end of the century. Londinium, with its port, developed into a capital city; by the 3rd century, there were some 50,000 people living here. But, as the Roman Empire crumbled in the 5th century, the garrison pulled out, leaving the city to the Saxons.

EXTENT OF THE CITY

◼ 125 AD   ☐ Today

Public Baths
Bathing was an important part of Roman life. This pocket-sized personal hygiene kit (including a nail pick) and bronze pouring dish date from the 1st century.

Site of present-day Museum of London

Roman fort

Site of present-day St Paul's

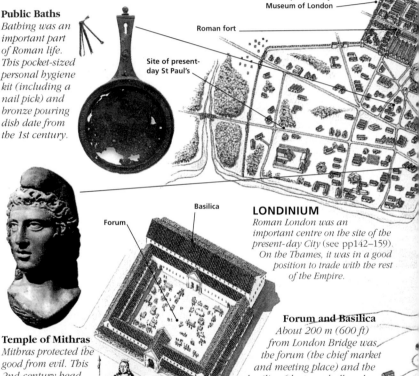

Basilica

Forum

LONDINIUM
Roman London was an important centre on the site of the present-day City (see pp142–159). On the Thames, it was in a good position to trade with the rest of the Empire.

Temple of Mithras
Mithras protected the good from evil. This 2nd-century head was in his temple.

Forum and Basilica
About 200 m (600 ft) from London Bridge was the forum (the chief market and meeting place) and the basilica (the town hall and court of justice).

TIMELINE

55 BC Julius Caesar invades Britain		**200** City wall built	**410** Roman troops begin to leave
	AD 61 Boadicea attacks		
100	200	300	400
	AD 43 Claudius establishes Roman London and builds the first bridge		

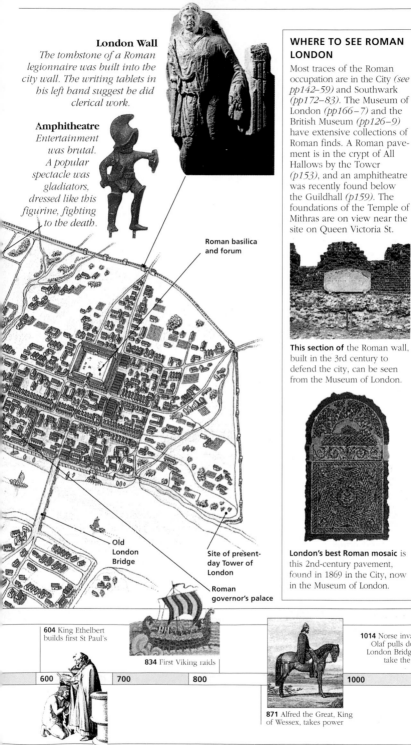

London Wall
The tombstone of a Roman legionnaire was built into the city wall. The writing tablets in his left hand suggest he did clerical work.

Amphitheatre
Entertainment was brutal. A popular spectacle was gladiators, dressed like this figurine, fighting to the death.

Roman basilica and forum

Old London Bridge

Site of present-day Tower of London

Roman governor's palace

WHERE TO SEE ROMAN LONDON

Most traces of the Roman occupation are in the City *(see pp142–59)* and Southwark *(pp172–83)*. The Museum of London *(pp166–7)* and the British Museum *(pp126–9)* have extensive collections of Roman finds. A Roman pavement is in the crypt of All Hallows by the Tower *(p153)*, and an amphitheatre was recently found below the Guildhall *(p159)*. The foundations of the Temple of Mithras are on view near the site on Queen Victoria St.

This section of the Roman wall, built in the 3rd century to defend the city, can be seen from the Museum of London.

London's best Roman mosaic is this 2nd-century pavement, found in 1869 in the City, now in the Museum of London.

604 King Ethelbert builds first St Paul's

834 First Viking raids

600   700   800   1000

871 Alfred the Great, King of Wessex, takes power

1014 Norse invader Olaf pulls down London Bridge to take the city

Medieval London

The historic division between London's centres of
commerce (the City) and government (Westminster)
started in the mid-11th century when Edward the
Confessor established his court and sited his
abbey *(see pp76–9)* at Westminster. Mean-
while, in the City, tradesmen set up their own
institutions and guilds, and London appointed
its first mayor. Disease was rife and the population never rose much above its Roman
peak of 50,000. The Black Death (1348)
reduced the population by half.

EXTENT OF THE CITY
☐ 1200   ☐ Today

LONDON BRIDGE
*The first stone bridge was built in 1209
and lasted 600 years. It was the only
bridge across the Thames in London
until Westminster Bridge (1750).*

**The Chapel of St
Thomas**, erected the
year the bridge was
completed,
was one of its
first buildings.

St Thomas à Becket
*As Archbishop of Canterbury
he was murdered in 1170,
at the prompting of
Henry II with whom
he was quarrelling.
Thomas was made
a saint and
pilgrims visited his
Canterbury shrine.*

**Iron
railings**

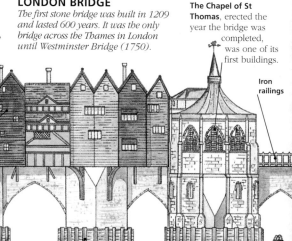

Houses and shops
projected over both
sides of the bridge.
Shopkeepers made
their own merchan-
dise on the premises
and lived above their
shops. Apprentices
did the selling.

THE CORPORATION OF
THE HOUSE OF
RICHARD
WHITTINGTON
MAYOR OF LONDON
STOOD ON THIS SITE
1423
THE CITY OF LONDON

The piers were
made from wooden
stakes rammed into
the river bed and
filled with rubble.

Dick Whittington
*The 15th-century trader
was thrice mayor of
London (see p39).*

Stag Hunting
*Such sports were the
chief recreation of
wealthy landowners.*

The arches ranged
from 4.5 m (15 ft) to
10 m (35 ft) in width.

TIMELINE

1042 Edward the Confessor becomes king	**1086** Domesday Book, England's first survey, published		**1191** Henry Fitzalwin becomes London's first mayor	**1215** King John's Magna Carta gives City more powers
1050	**1100**	**1150**	**1200**	**125**
	1066 William I crowned in Abbey		**1176** Work starts on the first stone London Bridge	**1240** First parliament sits at Westminster
	1065 Westminster Abbey completed			

Chivalry

Medieval knights were idealized for their courage and honour. Edward Burne-Jones (1833–98) painted George, patron saint of England, rescuing a maiden from this dragon.

Geoffrey Chaucer

The poet and customs controller (see p39), is best remembered for his Canterbury Tales *which creates a rich picture of 14th-century England.*

WHERE TO SEE MEDIEVAL LONDON

There were only a few survivors of the Great Fire of 1666 (*see pp24–5*) – the Tower (*pp154–7*), Westminster Hall (*p72*) and Westminster Abbey (*pp76–9*), and a few churches (*p46*). The Museum of London (*pp166–7*) has artifacts, while Tate Britain (*pp82–5*) and the National Gallery (*pp104–7*) have paintings. Manuscripts, including the Domesday Book, are found at the British Library (*p125*).

The Tower of London was started in 1078 and became one of the few centres of royal power in the largely self-governing City.

A 14th-century rose window is all that remains of Winchester Palace near the Clink (*see p182*).

Plan of the Bridge

The bridge had 19 arches to span the river making it, for many years, the longest stone bridge in England.

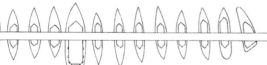

Many 13th-century pilgrims went to Canterbury.

	1348 Black Death kills thousands	**1394** Westminster Hall remodelled by Henry Yevele	*The Great Seal of Richard I shows us what medieval kings looked like.*
	1350	**1400**	**1450**
	1381 Peasants' Revolt defeated	**1397** Richard Whittington becomes mayor	**1476** William Caxton sets up first printing press at Westminster

Elizabethan London

In the 16th century the monarchy was stronger than ever before. The Tudors established peace throughout England, allowing art and commerce to flourish. This renaissance reached its zenith under Elizabeth I as explorers opened up the New World, and English theatre, the nation's most lasting contribution to world culture, was born.

Curtain

SHAKESPEARE'S GLOBE

Elizabethan theatres were built of wood and only half covered, so plays had to be cancelled in bad weather.

EXTENT OF THE CITY

☐ 1561   ☐ Today

A balcony on the stage was part of the scenery.

The apron stage had a trap door for special effects.

Death at the Stake

The Tudors dealt harshly with social and religious dissent. Here Bishops Latimer and Ridley die for so-called heresy in 1555, when Elizabeth's sister, Mary I, was queen. Traitors could expect to be hung, drawn and quartered.

In the pit, below the level of the stage, commoners stood to watch the play.

Hunting and Hawking

Popular 16th-century pastimes are shown on this cushion cover.

TIMELINE

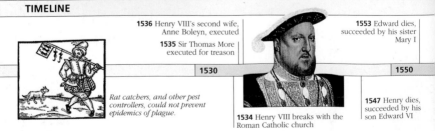

1536 Henry VIII's second wife, Anne Boleyn, executed

1535 Sir Thomas More executed for treason

1553 Edward dies, succeeded by his sister Mary I

1530

1550

Rat catchers, and other pest controllers, could not prevent epidemics of plague.

1534 Henry VIII breaks with the Roman Catholic church

1547 Henry dies, succeeded by his son Edward VI

he galleries
ere for rich
heatre-goers
ho could watch
om the comfort
f seats.

Elizabeth I
The "Virgin Queen" sat for this portrait to celebrate victory over the Spanish in 1588.

Tilting Spurs
The aim of this high-speed sport, popular among noblemen, was to knock opponents off their horses.

Steps allowed tiered seating.

Astronomical Clock
Made in 1540 at Hampton Court, it shows the sun moving round the earth.

Audience entrance

WHERE TO SEE ELIZABETHAN LONDON

The Great Fire of 1666 wiped out the City. Fortunately, Middle Temple Hall *(see p139)*, Staple Inn *(p141)* and the Lady Chapel inside Westminster Abbey *(pp76–9)* were beyond its reach. The Museum of London *(pp166–7)*, Victoria and Albert *(pp202–5)*, and Geffrye Museums *(p248)* have fine furniture and artefacts. Further afield are Hampton Court *(pp254–7)* and Sutton House *(p248)*.

Elizabeth I watched *Twelfth Night* by Shakespeare under the hammerbeam roof of Middle Temple Hall in 1603.

The Parr Pot, now in the Museum of London, was made by Venetian craftsmen in London in 1547.

Plague
s Europe

1570 Francis Drake makes first voyage to the West Indies

1584 Walter Raleigh's first attempt to colonize America

1588 Drake defeats Spanish Armada

1591 First play by Shakespeare produced

| 1560 | 1570 | 1580 | 1590 |

Mary I's death
s Elizabeth queen

Gloves made from imported silk and velvet

1603 Elizabeth dies, James I accedes

Restoration London

Civil War had broken out in 1642 when the mercantile class demanded that some of the monarch's power be passed to Parliament. The subsequent Commonwealth was dominated by Puritans under Oliver Cromwell. The Puritans outlawed simple pleasures, such as dancing and theatre, so it was small wonder that the restoration of the monarchy under Charles II in 1660 was greeted with rejoicing and the release of pent-up creative energies. The period was, however, also marked with two major tragedies: the Plague (1665) and the Great Fire (1666).

EXTENT OF THE CITY

■ 1680   □ Today

St Paul's was destroyed in the fire that raged as far west as Fetter Lane (*map 14 E1*).

London Bridge itself survived, but many of the buildings on it were burned down.

Oliver Cromwell
He led the Parlia-mentarian army and was Lord Protector of the Realm from 1653 until his death in 1658. At the Restoration, his body was dug up and hung from the gallows at Tyburn, near Hyde Park (see p207).

Charles I's Death
The king was beheaded for tyranny on a freezing day (30 January 1649) outside Banqueting House (see p80).

Charles I
His belief in the Divine Right of Kings angered Parliament and was one of the causes of civil war.

TIMELINE

1623 Shakespeare's First Folio published

1625 James I dies, succeeded by his son Charles I

1642 Civil war starts when Parliament defies king

| 1620 | 1640 | 1650 |

1605 Guy Fawkes leads failed attempt to blow up the King and Parliament

Feathered belmet worn by Royalist cavaliers

1649 Charles I executed, Commonwealth established

Newton's Telescope
Physicist and astronomer Sir Isaac Newton (1642–1727) discovered the law of gravity.

Samuel Pepys
His exuberant diaries tell us much about courtly life of the time.

The Tower of London was just out of the fire's reach.

WHERE TO SEE RESTORATION LONDON

Wren's churches and his St Paul's Cathedral *(see p47 and pp148–51)* are, with Inigo Jones's Banqueting House *(p80)*, London's most famous 17th-century buildings. On a more modest scale are Lincoln's Inn *(p136)* and Cloth Fair *(p165)*. There is a fine period interior at the Museum of London *(pp166–7)*. The British Museum *(pp126–9)* and the Victoria and Albert *(pp202–205)* have pottery, silver and textile collections.

Ham House *(p252)* was built in 1610 but much enlarged later in the century. It has the finest interior of its time in England.

THE GREAT FIRE OF 1666
An unidentified Dutch artist painted this view of the fire that burned for 5 days, destroying 13,000 houses.

The Plague
During 1665, carts collected the dead and took them to communal graves outside the city.

Peter Paul Rubens painted the ceiling in 1636 for Inigo Jones's Banqueting House *(p80)*. This is one of its panels.

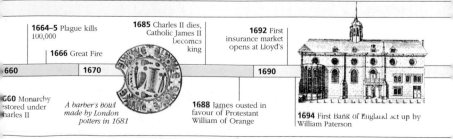

1664–5 Plague kills 100,000

1666 Great Fire

1685 Charles II dies, Catholic James II becomes king

1692 First insurance market opens at Lloyd's

660   1670   1690

1660 Monarchy restored under Charles II

A barber's bowl made by London potters in 1681

1688 James ousted in favour of Protestant William of Orange

1694 First Bank of England set up by William Paterson

Georgian London

George I
(reigned
1714–27)

The foundation of the Bank of England in 1694 spurred the growth of London and, by the time George I came to the throne in 1714, it had become an important financial and commercial centre. Aristocrats with West End estates began laying out elegant squares and terraces to house newly-rich merchants. Architects such as the Adam brothers, John Soane and John Nash developed stylish medium-scale housing. They drew inspiration from the great European capitals, as did English painters, sculptors, composers and craftsmen.

EXTENT OF THE CITY

☐ *1810*   ☐ *Today*

Manchester Square
was laid out in
1776–8.

Portman Square was on the town's outskirts when it was started in 1764.

Great Cumberland Place
Built in 1790, it was named after a royal duke and military commander.

Grosvenor Square
Few of the original houses remain on one of the oldest and largest Mayfair squares (1720).

Docks
Purpose-built docks handled the growth in world trade.

TIMELINE

1714 George I becomes king

1727 George II becomes king

1759 Kew Gardens established

1768 Royal Academy of Art established

1720

1740

1760

1717 Hanover Square built, start of West End development

1729 John Wesley (1703–91) founds the Methodist Church

1760 George III becomes king

John Nash
Stylish Nash shaped 18th-century London with variations on Classical themes, such as this archway in Cumberland Terrace, near Regent's Park.

GEORGIAN LONDON

The layout of much of London's West End has remained very similar to how it was in 1828, when this map was published.

WHERE TO SEE GEORGIAN LONDON

The portico of the Theatre Royal Haymarket *(see pp344–5)* gives a taste of the style of fashionable London in the 1820s. In Pall Mall *(p92)* Charles Barry's Reform and Travellers' Clubs are equally evocative. Most West End squares have some Georgian buildings, while Fournier Street *(p170)* has good small-scale domestic architecture. The Victoria and Albert Museum (V&A, *pp202–5*) has silver, as do the London Silver Vaults *(p141)*, where it is for sale. Hogarth's pictures, at Tate Britain *(pp82–5)* and Sir John Soane's Museum *(pp136–7)*, show the social conditions.

This English long-case clock (1725), made of oak and pine with Chinese designs, is in the V&A.

Captain Cook
This Yorkshire-born explorer discovered Australia during a voyage round the world in 1768–71.

Berkeley Square
Built in the 1730s and 1740s in the grounds of the former Berkeley House, several characteristic original houses remain on its west side.

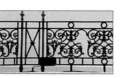

Ironwork
Crafts flourished. This ornate railing is on Manchester Square.

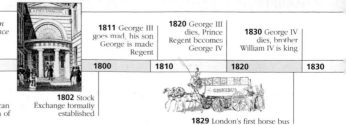

Signatories of the American Declaration of Independence

1776 Britain loses American colonies with Declaration of Independence

1802 Stock Exchange formally established

1811 George III goes mad, his son George is made Regent

1820 George III dies, Prince Regent becomes George IV

1830 George IV dies, brother William IV is king

1829 London's first horse bus

| 1800 | 1810 | 1820 | 1830 |

Victorian London

Much of London today is Victorian. Until the early 19th century, the capital had been confined to the original Roman city, plus Westminster and Mayfair to the west, ringed by fields and villages such as Brompton, Islington and Battersea. From the 1820s these green spaces filled rapidly with terraces of houses for the growing numbers attracted to London by industrialization. Rapid expansion brought challenges to the city. The first cholera epidemic broke out in 1832, and in 1858 came the Great Stink, when the smell from the Thames became so bad that Parliament had to go into recess. But Joseph Bazalgette's sewerage system (1875), involving banking both sides of the Thames, eased the problem.

Queen Victoria in her coronation year (1838)

EXTENT OF THE CITY

▨ 1900   ☐ Today

The building was 560 m (1,850 ft) long and 33 m (110 ft) high.

Nearly 14,000 exhibitors came from all over the world, bringing more than 100,000 exhibits.

Pantomime
The traditional family Christmas entertainment – still popular today (see p344) *– started in the 19th century.*

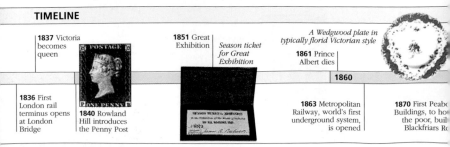

Soldiers marched and jumped on the floor to test its strength before the exhibition opened.

Massive elm trees growing in Hyde Park were left standing and the exhibition was erected around them.

The Crystal Fountain was 8 m (27 ft) high.

Carpets and stained glass were hung from the galleries.

TIMELINE

1837 Victoria becomes queen

1836 First London rail terminus opens at London Bridge

1840 Rowland Hill introduces the Penny Post

1851 Great Exhibition

Season ticket for Great Exhibition

A Wedgwood plate in typically florid Victorian style

1861 Prince Albert dies

1860

1863 Metropolitan Railway, world's first underground system, is opened

1870 First Peabody Buildings, to house the poor, built Blackfriars Road

Railways

By 1900 fast trains, such as this Scotch Express, *were crossing the country.*

WHERE TO SEE VICTORIAN LONDON

Grandiose buildings best reflect the spirit of the age, notably the rail termini, the Kensington Museums (see pp198–213) and the Royal Albert Hall (p207). Leighton House (p218) has a well-preserved interior. Pottery and fabrics are in the Victoria and Albert Museum, and London's Transport Museum (p114) has buses, trams and trains.

Telegraph

Newly invented communications technology, like this telegraph from 1840, made business expansion easier.

Crystal Palace

Between May and October 1851, six million people visited Joseph Paxton's superb feat of engineering. In 1852 it was dismantled and reassembled in south London where it remained until destroyed by fire in 1936.

The Victorian Gothic style suited buildings like the Public Record Office in Chancery Lane.

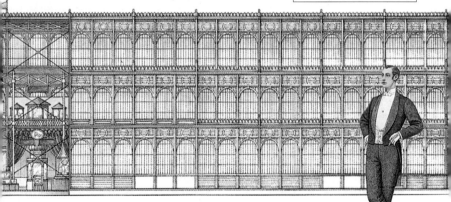

THE GREAT EXHIBITION OF 1851

The exhibition, held in the Crystal Palace in Hyde Park, celebrated industry, technology and the expanding British Empire.

Formal Dress

Under Victoria, elaborate men's attire was replaced by more restrained evening wear.

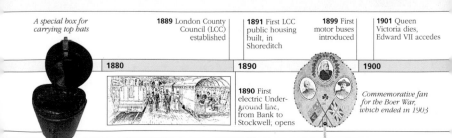

A special box for carrying top hats

1889 London County Council (LCC) established

1891 First LCC public housing built, in Shoreditch

1899 First motor buses introduced

1901 Queen Victoria dies, Edward VII accedes

1880

1890

1900

1890 First electric Underground line, from Bank to Stockwell, opens

Commemorative fan for the Boer War, which ended in 1903

London Between the World Wars

Art Deco china by Clarice Cliff

The society that emerged from World War I grasped eagerly at the innovations of early 20th-century London – the motor car, the telephone, commuter transport. The cinema brought transatlantic culture, especially jazz and swing music. Victorian social restraints were discarded as people flocked to dance in restaurants, clubs and dance halls. Many left the crowded inner city for new suburban estates. Then came the 1930s global Depression, whose effects had barely worn off when World War II began.

EXTENT OF THE CITY

■ *1938*   □ *Today*

METRO-LAND

Formal evening wear, including hats for both sexes, was still compulsory when going to smart West End night spots.

Commuting
London's new outer suburbs were made popular by the under-ground railway. In the north was "Metroland", named after the Metro-politan line which penetrated Hertfordshire.

High Fashion
The sleek flowing new styles contrasted with the fussy elaboration of the Victorians and Edwardians. This tea gown is from the 1920s.

A LONDON STREET SCENE
Maurice Greiflenhagen's painting (1926) captures the bustle of London after dark.

TIMELINE

Medals, like this from 1914, were struck during the campaign for women's votes.

1910

1921 North Circular Road links northern suburbs

1922 First BBC national radio broadcast

1920

1910
George V succeeds Edward VII

Cavalry was still used in the Middle Eastern battles of World War I (1914–18).

Early Cinema

London-born Charlie Chaplin (1889–1977), seen here in City Lights, *was a popular star of both silent and talking pictures.*

Seven new theatres were built in central London from 1924 to 1931.

WORLD WAR II AND THE BLITZ

World War II saw large-scale civilian bombing for the first time, bringing the horror of war to Londoners' doorsteps. Thousands were killed in their homes. Many people took refuge in Underground stations and children were evacuated to the safety of the country.

WOMEN OF BRITAIN
COME INTO THE FACTORIES

As in World War I, women were recruited for factory work formerly done by men who were away fighting.

George VI
Oswald Birley painted this portrait of the king who became a model for wartime resistance and unity.

Early motor buses had open tops, like the old horse-drawn buses.

Communications
The radio provided home entertainment and information. This is a 1933 model.

Throughout the period newspaper circulations increased massively. In 1930 *The Daily Herald* sold 2 million copies a day.

Bombing raids in 1940 and 1941 (the Blitz) caused devastation all over the city.

1929 US stock market crash brings world Depression

1939 World War II begins

1930

1927 First talking pictures

1936 Edward VIII abdicates to marry US divorcée Wallis Simpson. George VI accedes

1940 Winston Churchill becomes Prime Minister

Postwar London

Much of London was flattened by World War II bombs. Afterwards, the chance for imaginative rebuilding was missed – some badly designed postwar developments are already being razed. But, by the 1960s, London was such a dynamic world leader in fashion and popular music that *Time* magazine dubbed it "swinging London". Skyscrapers sprang up, but some stayed empty as 1980s boom gave way to 1990s recession.

EXTENT OF THE CITY

▨ 1959　　□ Today

The Beatles
The Liverpool pop group, pictured in 1965, had rocketed to stardom two years earlier with songs of appealing freshness and directness. The group symbolized carefree 1960s London.

Festival of Britain
After wartime, the city's morale was lifted by the Festival, marking the 1851 Great Exhibition's centenary (see pp28–9).

Margaret Thatcher
Britain's first woman Prime Minister (1979–90) promoted the market-led policies that fuelled the 1980s boom.

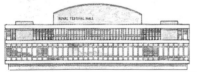

The Royal Festival Hall (1951) was the Festival's centrepiece and is still a landmark *(see p188).*

Telecom Tower (1964), at 189 m (620 ft) high, dominates the Fitzrovia skyline.

The Lloyd's Building (1986) is Richard Rogers' Post-Modernist emblem *(see p159).*

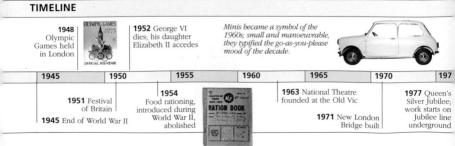

TIMELINE

1948 Olympic Games held in London

1952 George VI dies; his daughter Elizabeth II accedes

Minis became a symbol of the 1960s; small and manoeuvrable, they typified the go-as-you-please mood of the decade.

| 1945 | 1950 | 1955 | 1960 | 1965 | 1970 | 197 |

1951 Festival of Britain

1945 End of World War II

1954 Food rationing, introduced during World War II, abolished

1963 National Theatre founded at the Old Vic

1971 New London Bridge built

1977 Queen's Silver Jubilee; work starts on Jubilee line underground

Docklands Light Railway
In the 1980s, new, driverless trains started to transport people to the developing Docklands.

POST-MODERN ARCHITECTURE

The new wave of architects since the 1980s are reacting against the bleak and stark shapes of the Modernists. Some, like Richard Rogers, are masters of high-tech, emphasizing structural features in their designs. Others, Terry Farrell for example, adopt a more playful approach using pastiches of Classical features such as columns.

YOUTH CULTURE

With their new mobility and spending power, young people began to influence the development of British popular culture in the years after World War II. Music, fashion and design were increasingly geared to their rapidly changing tastes.

Punks were a phenomenon of the 1970s and 1980s. Their clothes, music, hair and habits were designed to shock.

The Prince of Wales
As heir to the throne, he is outspokenly critical of much of London's recent architecture. He prefers Classical styles.

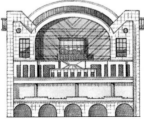

Canada Tower (1991) is London's tallest building. It was designed by César Pelli *(see p249).*

Charing Cross (1991) has Terry Farrell's glasshouse on top of the Victorian station *(see p119).*

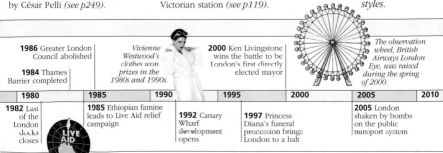

1986 Greater London Council abolished

1984 Thames Barrier completed

Vivienne Westwood's clothes won prizes in the 1980s and 1990s.

2000 Ken Livingstone wins the battle to be London's first directly elected mayor

The observation wheel, British Airways London Eye, was raised during the spring of 2000.

1980	1985	1990	1995	2000	2005	2010

1982 Last of the London docks closes

1985 Ethiopian famine leads to Live Aid relief campaign

1992 Canary Wharf development opens

1997 Princess Diana's funeral procession brings London to a halt

2005 London shaken by bombs on the public transport system

Kings and Queens in London

London has been the royal capital of England since 1066, when William the Conqueror began a tradition of holding coronations in Westminster Abbey. Since then, successive kings and queens have left their mark on London and many of the places described in this book have royal associations: Henry VIII hunted at Richmond, Charles I was executed on Whitehall and the young Queen Victoria rode on Queensway. Royalty is also celebrated in many of London's traditional ceremonies – for more details on these turn to pages 52–5.

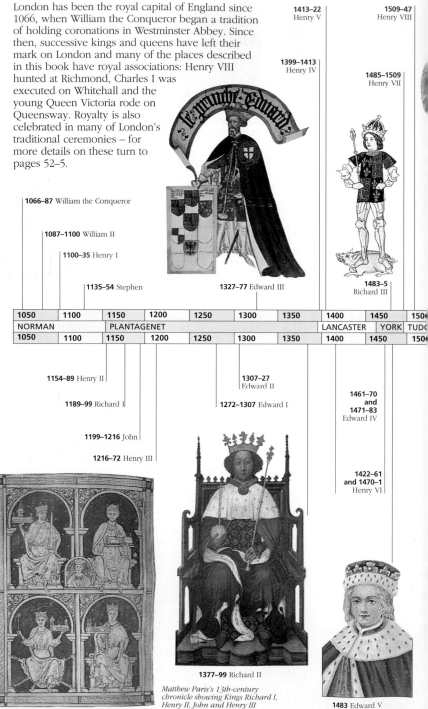

1413–22 Henry V

1509–47 Henry VIII

1399–1413 Henry IV

1485–1509 Henry VII

1066–87 William the Conqueror

1087–1100 William II

1100–35 Henry I

1135–54 Stephen

1327–77 Edward III

1483–5 Richard III

1050	1100	1150	1200	1250	1300	1350	1400	1450	150
NORMAN		PLANTAGENET					LANCASTER	YORK	TUDO
1050	1100	1150	1200	1250	1300	1350	1400	1450	150

1154–89 Henry II

1189–99 Richard I

1199–1216 John

1216–72 Henry III

1307–27 Edward II

1272–1307 Edward I

1461–70 and 1471–83 Edward IV

1422–61 and 1470–1 Henry VI

1377–99 Richard II

Matthew Paris's 13th-century chronicle showing Kings Richard I, Henry II, John and Henry III

1483 Edward V

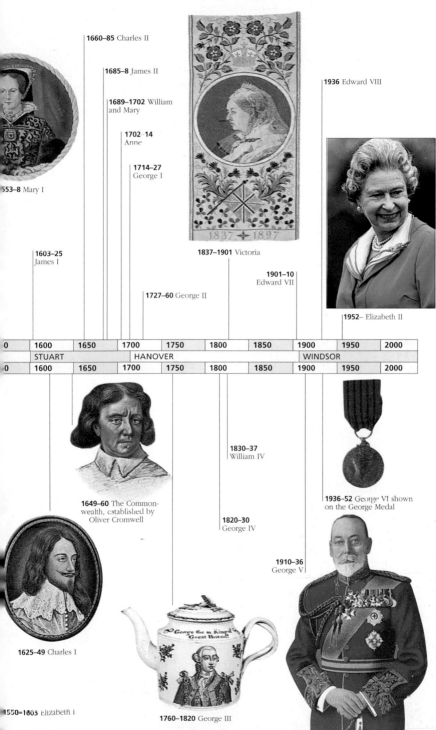

1660–85 Charles II

1685–8 James II

1689–1702 William and Mary

1702–14 Anne

1714–27 George I

1936 Edward VIII

553–8 Mary I

1603–25 James I

1837–1901 Victoria

1901–10 Edward VII

1727–60 George II

1952– Elizabeth II

0	1600	1650	1700	1750	1800	1850	1900	1950	2000
	STUART		HANOVER				WINDSOR		
0	1600	1650	1700	1750	1800	1850	1900	1950	2000

1830–37 William IV

1649–60 The Commonwealth, established by Oliver Cromwell

1936–52 George VI shown on the George Medal

1820–30 George IV

1910–36 George V

1625–49 Charles I

1550–1603 Elizabeth I

1760–1820 George III

7–53 Edward VI

LONDON AT A GLANCE

There are nearly 300 places of interest described in the Area by Area section of this book. These range from the magnificent National Gallery *(see pp104–7)* to gruesome Old St Thomas' Operating Theatre *(p176)*, and from ancient Charterhouse *(p164)* to modern Canary Wharf *(p249)*. To help you make the most of your stay, the following 18 pages are a time-saving guide to the best London has to offer. Museums and galleries, churches, and parks and gardens each have a section, and there are guides to remarkable Londoners and ceremonies in London. Each sight mentioned is cross-referenced to its own full entry. Below are the ten top tourist attractions to start you off.

LONDON'S TOP TEN TOURIST ATTRACTIONS

St Paul's
See pp148–51.

Hampton Court
See pp254–7.

Changing of the Guard
Buckingham Palace, see pp94–5.

British Museum
See pp126–9.

National Gallery
See pp104–7.

Westminster Abbey
See pp76–9.

Madame Tussaud's
See p224.

Houses of Parliament
See pp72–3.

Tower of London
See pp154–7.

Victoria and Albert Museum
See pp202–5.

◁ Big Ben and the British Airways London Eye

Remarkable Londoners

London has always been a gathering place for the most prominent and influential people of their times. Some of these figures have come to London from other parts of Britain or from countries further afield; others have been Londoners, born and bred. All of them have left their mark on London, by designing great and lasting buildings, establishing institutions and traditions, and by writing about or painting the city they knew. Most of them have also had an influence on their times that spread out from London to the rest of the world.

Caricature of the Duke of Wellington

Venus Venticordia by Dante Gabriel Rossetti

ARCHITECTS AND ENGINEERS

John Nash's Theatre Royal Haymarket (1821)

A number of people who built London still have works standing. Inigo Jones (1573–1652), London-born, was the father of English Renaissance architecture. He was also a landscape painter and a stage designer. Jones lived and worked at Great Scotland Yard, Whitehall, then the residence of the royal architect – the post in which he was later succeeded by Sir Christopher Wren (1632–1723).

Wren's successors as the prime architects of London were his protégé Nicholas Hawksmoor (1661–1736) and James Gibbs (1682–1754). Succeeding generations each produced architects who were to stamp their genius on the city: in the 18th century the brothers Robert (1728–92) and James Adam (1730–94), then John Nash (1752–1835), Sir Charles Barry (1795–1860), Decimus Burton (1800–81), and the Victorians Alfred Waterhouse (1830–1905),

Norman Shaw (1831–1912) and Sir George Gilbert Scott (1811–78). The engineer Sir Joseph Bazalgette (1819–91) built London's sewer system and the Thames Embankment.

ARTISTS

Painters in London, as elsewhere, often lived in enclaves, for mutual support and because they shared common priorities. During the 18th century, artists clustered around the court at St James's to be near their patrons. Thus both William Hogarth (1697–1764) and Sir Joshua Reynolds (1723–92) lived and worked in Leicester Square, while Thomas Gainsborough (1727–88) lived in Pall Mall. (Hogarth's Chiswick house was his place in the country.)

Later, Cheyne Walk in Chelsea, with its river views, became popular with artists, including the masters J M W Turner (1775–1851), James McNeill Whistler (1834–1903), Dante Gabriel Rossetti (1828–82), Philip Wilson Steer (1860–1942) and the sculptor

HISTORIC LONDON HOMES

Dickens Museum

Four writers' homes that have been recreated are those of the romantic poet **John Keats** (1795–1821); the historian **Thomas Carlyle** (1795–1881); the lexicographer **Dr Samuel Johnson** (1709–84); and the prolific and popular novelist **Charles Dickens** (1812–70). The house that the architect **Sir John Soane** (1753–1837) designed for himself remains largely as it was when he died, as does the house where the psychiatrist **Sigmund Freud** (1856–1939) settled after fleeing from the Nazis before World War II.

Apsley House, on Hyde Park Corner, was the residence of the **Duke of Wellington** (1769–1852), hero of the Battle of Waterloo. The life and music of Baroque composer **George Frideric Handel** (1685–1759) are on show at his former home in Mayfair. Finally, the rooms of Sir Arthur Conan Doyle's fictional detective **Sherlock Holmes** have been created in Baker Street.

Carlyle's House

PLAQUES

All over London the former homes of well-known figures are marked by plaques. Look out for these, especially in Chelsea, Kensington and Mayfair, and see how many names you recognize.

No. 3 Sussex Square, Kensington

No. 27b Canonbury Square, Islington

No. 56 Oakley Street, Chelsea

Sir Jacob Epstein (1880–1959). Augustus John (1879–1961) and John Singer Sargent (1856–1925) had studios in Tite Street. John Constable (1776–1837) is best known as a Suffolk painter but lived for a while at Hampstead, from where he painted many fine views of the heath.

WRITERS

Geoffrey Chaucer (c.1345–1400), author of *The Canterbury Tales*, was born in Upper Thames Street, the son of an innkeeper. Both the playwrights William Shakespeare (1564–1616) and Christopher Marlowe (1564–93) were associated with the theatres in Southwark, and may have lived nearby.

The poets John Donne (1572–1631) and John Milton (1608–74) were both born in Bread Street in the City. Donne, after a profligate youth, became Dean of St Paul's. The diarist Samuel Pepys (1633–1703) was born off Fleet Street.

The young novelist Jane Austen (1775–1817) lived briefly off Sloane Street, near the Cadogan Hotel, where the flamboyant Oscar Wilde (1854–1900) was arrested in 1895 for homosexuality. Playwright George Bernard Shaw (1856–1950) lived at No. 29 Fitzroy Square in Bloomsbury. Later the same house was home to Virginia Woolf (1882–1941) and

George Bernard Shaw

became a meeting place for the Bloomsbury Group of writers and artists, which included Vanessa Bell, John Maynard Keynes, E M Forster, Roger Fry and Duncan Grant.

LEADERS

In legend, a penniless boy named Dick Whittington came to London with his cat seeking streets paved with gold, and later became Lord Mayor. In fact, Richard Whittington (1360?–1423), Lord Mayor three times between 1397 and 1420 and one of London's most celebrated early politicians, was the son of a noble. Sir Thomas More (1478–1535), a Chelsea resident, was Henry VIII's chancellor until they quarrelled over the king's break with the Catholic church and Henry ordered More's execution. More was canonized in 1935. Sir Thomas Gresham (1519?–79) founded the Royal Exchange. Sir Robert Peel (1788–1850) started the London police force, who were known as "bobbies" after him.

ACTORS

Nell Gwynne (1650–87) won more fame as King Charles II's mistress than as an actress. However, she did appear on stage at Drury Lane Theatre; she also sold oranges there. The Shakespearean actor Edmund Kean (1789–1833) and the great tragic actress

Sarah Siddons (1755–1831) were more distinguished players at Drury Lane. So were Henry Irving (1838–1905) and Ellen Terry (1847–1928), whose stage partnership lasted 24 years. Charlie Chaplin (1889–1977), born in Kennington, had a poverty-stricken childhood in the slums of London.

In the 20th century, a school of fine actors blossomed at the Old Vic, including Sir John Gielgud (1904–2001), Sir Ralph Richardson (1902–83), Dame Peggy Ashcroft (1907–91) and Laurence (later Lord) Olivier (1907–89), who was appointed the first director of the National Theatre.

Laurence Olivier

WHERE TO FIND HISTORIC LONDON HOMES

Thomas Carlyle *p196*
Charles Dickens *p125*
Sigmund Freud *p246*
George Frideric Handel *p349*
William Hogarth *p259*
Sherlock Holmes *p226*
Dr Samuel Johnson *p140*
John Keats *p233*
Sir John Soane *p136*
The Duke of Wellington *p97*

London's Best: Museums and Galleries

London's museums are filled with an astonishing diversity of treasures from all over the world. This map highlights 15 of the city's most important galleries and museums whose exhibits cater to most interests. Some of these collections started from the legacies of 18th- and 19th-century explorers, traders and collectors. Others specialize in one aspect of art, history, science or technology. A more detailed overview of London's museums and galleries is on pages 42–3.

British Museum
This Anglo-Saxon helmet is part of a massive collection of antiquities.

Wallace Collection
Frans Hals's Laughing Cavalier *is a star attraction in this museum of art, furniture, armour and* objets d'art.

Regent's Park and Marylebone

Royal Academy of Arts
Major international art exhibitions are held here, and the renowned Summer Exhibition, when works are on sale, takes place every year.

Kensington and Holland Park

South Kensington and Knightsbridge

Piccac and St Jam

Science Museum
Newcomen's steam engine of 1712 is just one of many exhibits that cater for both novice and expert.

Chelsea

Natural History Museum
All of life is here, with vivid displays on everything from dinosaurs (like this Triceratops *skull) to butterflies.*

Victoria and Albert
It is the world's largest museum of decorative arts. This Indian vase is 18th century.

0 kilometres   1

0 miles   0.5

National Portrait Gallery
Important British figures are documented in paintings and photographs. This is Vivien Leigh, by Angus McBean (1954).

National Gallery
The world-famous paintings in its collection are mainly European and date from the 15th to the 19th centuries.

Museum of London
London's history is told through fascinating objects such as this 15th-century reliquary.

Tower of London
The Crown Jewels and a vast collection of arms and armour are here. This armour was worn by a 14th-century Italian knight.

Bloomsbury and Fitzrovia

Smithfield and Spitalfields

Holborn and the Inns of Court

The City

Soho and Trafalgar Square

Covent Garden and the Strand

Design Museum
The changing exhibitions here showcase all aspects of design from household prototypes to high fashion garments.

Southwark and Bankside

South Bank

Whitehall and Westminster

Tate Modern
Works of the 20th century, such as Dali's Lobster Telephone, *are celebrated here.*

Tate Britain
Formerly the Tate Gallery, this museum showcases an outstanding collection of British art covering the 16th century to the present.

Imperial War Museum
It uses displays, film and special effects to recreate 20th-century battles. This is one of the earliest tanks.

Courtauld Gallery
Well-known works, such as Manet's Bar at the Folies-Bergère, *line its galleries.*

Exploring Museums and Galleries

Austin Mini, exhibited at the Design Museum

London boasts astonishingly rich and diverse museums, the product, in part, of centuries at the hub of worldwide trade and a far-flung Empire. The world-renowned collections cannot be missed, but do not neglect the city's range of smaller museums. From buses to fans, these cover every imaginable speciality and are often more peaceful than their grander counterparts.

Geffrye Museum: Art Nouveau Room

ANTIQUITIES AND ARCHAEOLOGY

Some of the most celebrated artifacts of ancient Asia, Egypt, Greece and Rome are housed in the **British Museum**. Other antiquities, including books, manuscripts, paintings, busts and gems, are displayed in **Sir John Soane's Museum**, which is one of the most idiosyncratic to be found in London.

The **Museum of London** contains much of archaeological interest from all periods of the city's history.

FURNITURE AND INTERIORS

The Museum of London recreates typical domestic and commercial interiors from the Roman period right up to the present day. The **Victoria and Albert Museum** (or V&A) contains complete rooms rescued from now vanished buildings, plus a magnificent collection of furniture ranging from the 16th century to work by contemporary designers.

Design Museum display of chairs

Eclectic collection at Sir John Soane's Museum

On a more modest scale, the **Geffrye Museum** consists of fully-furnished period rooms dating from 1600 to the 1990s. Writers' houses, such as the **Freud Museum**, give insights into the furniture of specific periods, while the **Linley Sambourne House** offers visitors a perfectly preserved example of a late Victorian interior.

COSTUME AND JEWELLERY

The **V&A's** vast collections include English and European clothes of the last 400 years, and some stunning jewellery from China, India and Japan. The priceless Crown Jewels, at the **Tower of London**, should also not be missed. **Kensington Palace's** Court Dress Collection opens a window on Court uniforms and protocol from about 1750. The **Theatre Museum** has displays of costumes, props and other memorabilia, while the **British Museum** displays ancient Aztec, Mayan and African costume.

CRAFTS AND DESIGN

Once again, the **Victoria and Albert Museum** (V&A) is the essential first port of call; its collections in these fields remain unrivalled. The **William Morris Gallery** shows every aspect of the 19th-century designer's work within the Arts and Crafts movement. The **Design Museum** focuses on modern design including products and fashion, while the **Crafts Council Gallery** displays (and sometimes sells) contemporary British craftwork.

MILITARY ARTIFACTS

The **National Army Museum** uses vivid models and displays to narrate the history of the British Army from the reign of Henry VII to the present. The crack regiments of Foot Guards, who are the elite of the British Army, are the main focus of the **Guards Museum**. The **Tower of London** holds part of the national collection of arms and armour; the **Wallace Collection** also has a large and impressive display. The **Imperial War Museum** has recreations of World War I trenches and the 1940 Blitz. The **Florence Nightingale Museum** illustrates the hardships of 19th-century warfare.

TOYS AND CHILDHOOD

Teddy bears, toy soldiers and dolls' houses are some of the toys that can be seen in **Pollock's Toy Museum**. The collection includes Eric, "the oldest known teddy-bear". The **Bethnal Green Museum of Childhood** and the **Museum of London** are a little more formal, but still fun, and illustrate aspects of the social history of childhood with the former offering some interesting children's activities.

SCIENCE AND NATURAL HISTORY

Computers, electricity, space exploration, industrial processes and transport can all be studied at the **Science Museum**. Transport enthusiasts are also catered for at **London's Transport Museum**. There are other specialized museums such as the **Faraday Museum** concerning the development of electricity, and the **Kew Bridge Steam Museum**, focusing on water power. The **National Maritime Museum** and the **Royal Observatory** in Greenwich chart both maritime history and the creation of GMT, by which the world still sets its clocks.

Samson and Delilah (1620) by Van Dyck at the Dulwich Picture Gallery

The **Natural History Museum** mixes displays of animal and bird life with ecological exhibits. The **Museum of Garden History** is devoted to the favourite British pastime.

Imperial War Museum

VISUAL ARTS

The particular strengths of the **National Gallery** are early Renaissance Italian and 17th-century Spanish painting and a wonderful collection of Dutch masters. **Tate Britain** specializes in British paintings spanning all periods, while **Tate Modern** has displays of international modern art from 1900 to the present day. The **V&A** is strong on European art from 1500–1900 and British art of 1700–1900. The **Royal Academy** and the **Hayward Gallery** specialize in

Stone Dancer (1913) by Gaudier-Brzeska at Tate Britain

major temporary exhibitions. The **Courtauld Institute of Art Gallery** contains Impressionist and Post-Impressionist works, while the **Wallace Collection** has 17th-century Dutch and 18th-century French paintings. The **Dulwich Picture Gallery** includes works by Rembrandt, Rubens, Poussin and Gainsborough, while **Kenwood House** is home to paintings by Reynolds, Gainsborough and Rubens in fine Adam interiors. The **Saatchi Gallery** is devoted to contemporary, mainly British, art.

WHERE TO FIND THE COLLECTIONS

Bethnal Green Museum of Childhood *p248*
British Museum *pp126–9*
Courtauld Institute of Art Gallery *p117*
Crafts Council Gallery *p247*
Design Museum *p183*
Dulwich Picture Gallery *p250*
Faraday Museum *p97*
Florence Nightingale Museum *p185*
Freud Museum *p246*
Geffrye Museum *p248*
Guards Museum *p81*
Hayward Gallery *p184*
Imperial War Museum *p186*
Kensington Palace *p210*
Kenwood House *p234*
Kew Bridge Steam Museum *p258*
Linley Sambourne House *p218*
London's Transport Museum *p114*
Museum of Garden History *p185*
Museum of London *pp166–7*
National Army Museum *p197*
National Gallery *pp104–7*
National Maritime Museum *p240*
Natural History Museum *pp208–9*
Pollock's Toy Museum *p131*
Royal Academy of Arts *p90*
Saatchi Gallery *pp196–7*
Science Museum *pp212–13*
Sir John Soane's Museum *p136*
Tate Britain *pp82–5*
Tate Modern *pp178–81*
Theatre Museum *p115*
Tower of London *pp154–7*
Victoria and Albert Museum *pp202–5*
Wallace Collection *p226*
William Morris Gallery *p249*

London's Best: Churches

It is worth stopping to look at London's churches and going in, if they are open. They have a special atmosphere unmatched elsewhere in the city, and they can often yield an intimate glimpse of the past. Many churches have replaced earlier buildings in a steady succession, dating back to pre-Christian times. Some began life in outlying villages beyond London's fortified centre, and were absorbed into suburbs when the city expanded in the 18th century. The memorials in the capital's churches and church-yards are a fascinating record of local life, liberally peppered with famous names. A more detailed overview of London churches is on pages 46–7.

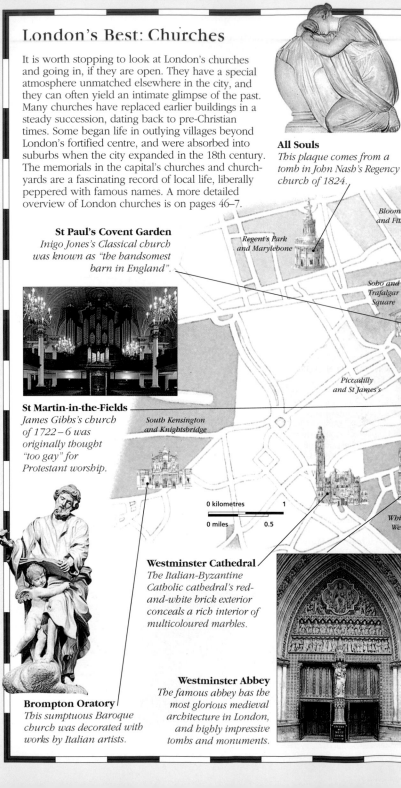

All Souls
This plaque comes from a tomb in John Nash's Regency church of 1824.

Bloomsbury and Fitzrovia

St Paul's Covent Garden
Inigo Jones's Classical church was known as "the handsomest barn in England".

Regent's Park and Marylebone

Soho and Trafalgar Square

Piccadilly and St James's

St Martin-in-the-Fields
James Gibbs's church of 1722–6 was originally thought "too gay" for Protestant worship.

South Kensington and Knightsbridge

0 kilometres   1

0 miles   0.5

Whitehall Westminster

Westminster Cathedral
The Italian-Byzantine Catholic cathedral's red-and-white brick exterior conceals a rich interior of multicoloured marbles.

Westminster Abbey
The famous abbey has the most glorious medieval architecture in London, and highly impressive tombs and monuments.

Brompton Oratory
This sumptuous Baroque church was decorated with works by Italian artists.

St Mary-le-Strand
Now on a traffic island, this ship-like church was built by James Gibbs in 1714–17 to a lively Baroque design. Featuring high windows and rich interior detailing, it was made solid enough to keep out the noise from the street.

St Mary Woolnoth
The jewel-like interior of Nicholas Hawksmoor's small Baroque church (1716–27) appears larger than the outside.

Smithfield and Spitalfields

Holborn and the Inns of Court

Covent Garden and the Strand

RIVER THAMES

The City

South Bank

Southwark and Bankside

St Stephen Walbrook
Wren was at his best with this domed interior of 1672–7. Its carvings include Henry Moore's austere modern altar.

St Paul's
At 110 m (360 ft) high, the dome of Wren's cathedral is the world's second largest after St Peter's in Rome.

Southwark Cathedral
This largely 13th-century priory church was not designated a cathedral until 1905. It has a fine medieval choir.

Temple Church
Built in the 12th and 13th centuries for the Knights Templar, this is one of the few circular churches to survive in England.

Exploring Churches

The church spires that puncture London's skyline span nearly a thousand years of the city's history. They form an index to many of the events that have shaped the city – the Norman Conquest (1066); the Great Fire of London (1666); the great restoration, led by Wren, that followed it; the Regency period; the confidence of the Victorian era; and the devastation of World War II. Each has had its effect on the churches, many designed by the most influential architects of their times.

St Paul's, Covent Garden

MEDIEVAL CHURCHES

The most famous old church to survive the Great Fire of 1666 is the superb 13th-century **Westminster Abbey**, the church of the Coronation, with its tombs of British monarchs and heroes. Less well known are the well-hidden Norman church of **St Bartholomew-the-Great**, London's oldest church, (1123), the circular **Temple Church** founded in 1160 by the Knights Templar and **Southwark Cathedral**, set amid Victorian railway lines and warehouses. **Chelsea Old Church** is a charming village church near the river.

CHURCHES BY JONES

Inigo Jones (1573–1652) was Shakespeare's contemporary, and his works were almost as revolutionary as the great dramatist's. Jones's Classical churches of the 1620s and 1630s shocked a public used to conservative Gothic finery. By far the best-known is **St Paul's Church** of the 1630s, the centrepiece of Jones's Italian-style piazza in Covent Garden. **Queen's Chapel, St James's** was built in 1623 for Queen Henrietta Maria, the Catholic wife of Charles I. It was the first Classical church in England and has a magnificent interior but is, unfortunately, usually closed to the public.

CHURCHES BY HAWKSMOOR

Nicholas Hawksmoor (1661–1736) was Wren's most talented pupil, and his churches are among the finest

Spires
Look out for London's richly decorated church steeples. Here are four of the city's most distinctive to get you started.

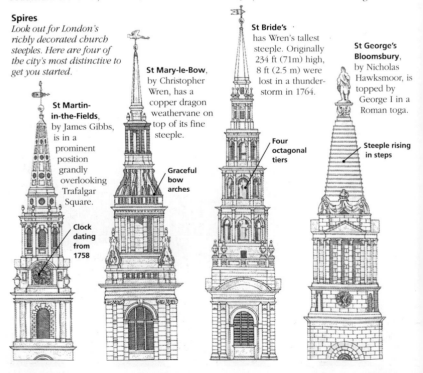

St Martin-in-the-Fields, by James Gibbs, is in a prominent position grandly overlooking Trafalgar Square.

Clock dating from 1758

St Mary-le-Bow, by Christopher Wren, has a copper dragon weathervane on top of its fine steeple.

Graceful bow arches

St Bride's has Wren's tallest steeple. Originally 234 ft (71m) high, 8 ft (2.5 m) were lost in a thunderstorm in 1764.

Four octagonal tiers

St George's Bloomsbury, by Nicholas Hawksmoor, is topped by George I in a Roman toga.

Steeple rising in steps

Baroque buildings to be found in Britain.

St George's, Bloomsbury (1716–31) has an unusual centralized plan and a pyramid steeple topped by a statue of King George I. **St Mary Woolnoth** is a tiny jewel of 1716–27, and further east **Christ Church, Spitalfields** is a Baroque tour-de-force of 1714–29, now being restored.

Among Hawksmoor's East End churches are the stunning **St Anne's, Limehouse** and **St Alfege**, of 1714–17, which is across the river in Greenwich. The tower on this temple-like church was added later by John James in 1730.

St Anne's, Limehouse

CHURCHES BY GIBBS

James Gibbs (1682–1754) was more conservative than his Baroque contemporaries such as Hawksmoor, and he also kept his distance from the Neo-Classical trend so popular after 1720. His idiosyncratic London churches were enormously influential. **St Mary-le-Strand** (1714–17) is an island church which appears to be sailing down the Strand. The radical design of **St Martin-in-the-Fields** (1722–6) predates its setting, Trafalgar Square, by a hundred years.

REGENCY CHURCHES

The end of the Napoleonic Wars in 1815 brought a flurry of church building. The need for churches in London's new suburbs fused with a Greek Revival. The

CHRISTOPHER WREN

Sir Christopher Wren (1632–1723) was leader among the many architects who helped restore London after the Great Fire of London. He devised a new city plan, replacing the narrow streets with wide avenues radiating from piazzas. His plan was rejected, but he was commissioned to build 52 new churches; 31 have survived various threats of demolition and the bombs of World War II, although six are shells. Wren's great masterpiece is the massive **St Paul's**, while nearby is splendid **St Stephen Walbrook**, his domed church of 1672–77. Other landmarks are **St Bride's**, off Fleet Street, said to have inspired the traditional shape of wedding cakes, **St Mary-le-Bow** in Cheapside and **St Magnus Martyr** in Lower Thames Street. Wren's own favourite was **St James's, Piccadilly** (1683–4). Smaller gems are **St Clement Danes**, Strand (1680–82) and **St James, Garlickhythe** (1674–87).

results may lack the exuberance of Hawksmoor, but they have an austere elegance of their own. **All Souls, Langham Place** (1822–4), at the north end of Regent Street, was built by the Prince Regent's favourite, John Nash, who was ridiculed at the time for its unusual combination of design styles. Also worth visiting is **St Pancras**, Greek Revival church of 1819–22, which is typical of the period.

VICTORIAN CHURCHES

London has some of the finest 19th-century churches in Europe. Grand and colourful, their riotous decoration is in marked contrast to the chaste Neo-Classicism of the preceding Regency era. Perhaps the best of the capital's late Victorian churches is **Westminster Cathedral**, a

stunningly rich, Italianate Catholic cathedral built in 1895–1903, with architecture by J F Bentley and *Stations of the Cross* reliefs by Eric Gill. **Brompton Oratory** is a grand Baroque revival, based on a church in Rome and filled with magnificent furnishings from all over Catholic Europe.

WHERE TO FIND THE CHURCHES

All Souls, Langham Place *p225*
Brompton Oratory *p206*
Chelsea Old Church *p196*
Christ Church, Spitalfields *p170*
Queen's Chapel *p93*
St Alfege *p240*
St Anne's, Limehouse *p249*
St Bartholomew-the-Great *p165*
St Bride's *p139*
St Clement Danes *p138*
St George's, Bloomsbury *p124*
St James, Garlickhythe *p144*
St James's, Piccadilly *p90*
St Magnus the Martyr *p152*
St Martin-in-the-Fields *p102*
St Mary-le-Bow *p147*
St Mary-le-Strand *p118*
St Mary Woolnoth *p145*
St Pancras *p130*
St Paul's Cathedral *pp148-51*
St Paul's Church *p114*
St Stephen Walbrook *p146*
Southwark Cathedral *p176*
Temple Church *p139*
Westminster Abbey *pp76-9*
Westminster Cathedral *p81*

Brompton Oratory

London's Best: Parks and Gardens

Since medieval times London has had large expanses of green. Some of these, such as Hampstead Heath, were originally common land, where small-holders could graze their animals. Others, such as Richmond Park and Holland Park, were royal hunting grounds or the gardens of large houses; several still have formal features dating from those times. Today you can cross much of central London by walking from St James's Park in the east to Kensington Gardens in the west. Purpose-built parks, like Battersea, and botanical gardens, like Kew, appeared later.

Hampstead Heath
This breezy, open space is located in the midst of north London. Nearby Parliament Hill offers views of St Paul's, the City and the West End.

Kensington Gardens
This plaque is from the Italian Garden, one of the features of this elegant park.

Kensington and Holland Park

Kew Gardens
The world's premier botanic garden is a must for anyone with an interest in plants, exotic or mundane.

Holland Park
The former grounds of one of London's grandest homes are now its most romantic park.

0 kilometres 1

0 miles 0.5

Richmond Park
The biggest Royal Park in London remains largely unspoiled, with deer and magnificent river views.

Regent's Park

In this Park, surrounded by fine Regency buildings, you can stroll around the rose garden, visit the open-air theatre, or simply sit and admire the view.

Hyde Park

The Serpentine is one of the highlights of a park which also boasts restaurants, an art gallery and Speakers' Corner.

Greenwich Park

Its focal point is the National Maritime Museum, well worth a visit for its architecture as well as its exhibits. There are also fine views.

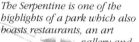

nt's
and
rlebone

Bloomsbury and Fitzrovia

Holborn and the Inns of Court

Smithfield and Spitalfields

Soho and Trafalgar Square

The City

Piccadilly

South Bank

Southwark and Bankside

Whitehall and Westminster

RIVER THAMES

Greenwich and Blackheath

Green Park

Its leafy paths are favoured by early-morning joggers from the Mayfair hotels.

Battersea Park

Visitors can hire a rowing boat for the best view of the ictorian landscaping around the lake.

St James's Park

People come here to feed the ducks, or watch the pelicans. A band plays throughout the summer.

Exploring Parks and Gardens

London has one of the the world's greenest city centres, full of tree-filled squares and grassy parks. From the intimacy of the Chelsea Physic Garden to the wild, open spaces of Hampstead Heath, every London park has its own charm and character. For those looking for a specific outdoor attraction – such as sports, wildlife or flowers – here are some of the most interesting London parks.

Camilla japonica

FLOWER GARDENS

The British are famed for their gardens and love of flowers and this is reflected in several of London's parks. Really keen gardeners will find all they ever wanted to know at **Kew Gardens** and the **Chelsea Physic Garden**, which is especially strong on herbs. Closer to the centre of town, **St James's Park** boasts some spectacular flower beds, filled with bulbs and bedding plants, which are changed every season. **Hyde Park** sports a magnificent show of daffodils and crocuses in the spring and London's best rose garden is Queen Mary's in

Regent's Park. Kensington Gardens' flower walk has an exemplary English mixed border, and there is also a delightful small 17th-century garden at the **Museum of Garden History**.

Battersea Park also has a charming flower garden, and indoor gardeners should head to the **Barbican Centre**'s well-stocked conservatory.

FORMAL GARDENS

The most spectacular formal garden is at **Hampton Court**, which has a network of gardens from different periods, starting with Tudor. The gardens at **Chiswick**

Sunken garden at Kensington Palace

Embankment Gardens

House remain dotted with their 18th-century statuary and pavilions. Other restored gardens include 17th-century **Ham House**, and **Osterley Park**, whose 18th-century layout was retraced through the art of dowsing. **Fenton House** has a really fine walled garden; **Kenwood** is less formal, with its woodland area. **The Hill** is great in summer. The sunken garden at **Kensington Palace** has a formal layout and **Holland Park** has flowers around its statues.

RESTFUL CORNERS

London's squares are cool, shady retreats but, sadly, many are reserved for key-holders, usually residents of the surrounding houses. Of those open to all, **Russell Square** is the largest and most secluded. **Berkeley Square** is open but barren. **Green Park**, with its shady trees and deck chairs, offers a cool picnic spot right in central London. The Inns of Court provide some really pleasant havens: **Gray's Inn** gardens, **Middle Temple**

GREEN LONDON

In Greater London there are 1,700 parks covering a total of 67 sq miles (174 sq km). This land is home to some 2,000 types of plant and 100 bird species that breed in the trees. Trees help the city to breathe, manufacturing oxygen from the polluted air. Here are some of the species you are most likely to see in London.

The London plane, now the most common tree in London, grows along many streets.

The English oak grows all over Europe. The Royal Navy used to build ships from it.

gardens and **Lincoln's Inn Fields**. **Soho Square**, which is surrounded by streets, is more urban and animated.

MUSIC IN SUMMER

Stretching out on the grass or in a deck chair to listen to a band is a British tradition. Military and other bands give regular concerts throughout the summer at **St James's** and **Regent's Parks** and also at **Parliament Hill Fields**. The concert schedule will usually be found posted up close to the bandstand in the park.

Open-air festivals of classical music are held in the summer in several parks (see p349).

WILDLIFE

There is a large and well-fed collection of ducks and other water birds, even including a few pelicans, in **St James's Park**. Duck lovers will also appreciate **Regent's, Hyde** and **Battersea Parks**, as well as **Hampstead Heath**. Deer roam in **Richmond** and **Greenwich Parks**. For a wide variety of captive animals, **London Zoo** is in **Regent's Park** and there are aviaries or aquariums at several parks and gardens, including **Kew Gardens** and **Syon House**.

Geese in St James's Park

HISTORIC CEMETERIES

In the late 1830s a ring of private cemeteries was established around London to ease the pressure on the monstrously overcrowded and unhealthy burial grounds of the inner city. Today some of these (notably **Highgate Cemetery** and Kensal Green – Harrow Road W10) are worth visiting for their air of repose and their Victorian monuments. **Bunhill Fields** is earlier; it was first used during the plague of 1665.

Kensal Green cemetery

Boating pond at Regent's Park

SPORTS

Cycling is not universally encouraged in London's parks, and footpaths tend to be too bumpy to allow much rollerskating. However, most parks have tennis courts, which normally have to be reserved in advance with the attendant. Rowing boats may be hired at **Hyde, Regent's** and **Battersea Parks**, among others. Athletics tracks are at both Battersea Park and also **Parliament Hill**. The public may swim at the ponds on **Hampstead Heath** and in the Serpentine in Hyde Park. Hampstead Heath is also ideal kite-flying territory.

WHERE TO FIND THE PARKS

Barbican Centre p165
Battersea Park p251
Berkeley Square p270
Bunhill Fields p168
Chelsea Physic Garden p197
Chiswick House pp259
Fenton House p233
Gray's Inn p141
Green Park p97
Greenwich Park p243
Ham House p252
Hampstead Heath p234
Hampton Court pp254–7
Highgate Cemetery p246
The Hill p235
Holland Park p218
Hyde Park p211
Kensington Gardens pp210–11
Kensington Palace p210
Kenwood House pp234–5
Kew Gardens pp260–61
Lincoln's Inn Fields p137
London Zoo p227
Middle Temple p139
Museum of Garden History p185
Osterley Park p253
Parliament Hill Fields pp234–5
Regent's Park p224
Richmond Park p252
Russell Square p125
St James's Park p93
Soho Square p108
Syon House p253

The common beech has a close relation, the copper beech, with reddish purple leaves.

The horse chestnut's hard round fruits are used by children for a game called conkers.

London's Best: Ceremonies

Much of London's rich inheritance of
tradition and ceremony centres on
royalty. Faithfully enacted today,
some of these ceremonies date back
to the Middle Ages, when the ruling
monarch had absolute power and had
to be protected from opponents. This
map shows the venues for some of
the most important ceremonies in
London. For more details on these
and other ceremonies please turn to
pages 54–5; information on all sorts
of events taking place in London
throughout the year can be found
on pages 56–9.

**St James's Palace
and Buckingham
Palace**
*Members of the
Queen's Life
Guard stand at
the gates of these
two palaces.*

Bloomsb
and Fitzr

Soho and
Trafalgar
Square

South Kensington
and Knightsbridge

Piccadilly and
St James's

Hyde Park
*Royal Salutes are fired by
guns of the King's Troop
Royal Horse Artillery on
royal anniversaries and
ceremonial occasions.*

Whitehall and
Westminster

Chelsea

Chelsea Hospital
*In 1651 Charles II hid
from parliamentary
forces in an oak tree. On
Oak Apple Day, Chelsea
Pensioners decorate his
statue with oak leaves
and branches.*

Horse Guards
*At Trooping the
Colour, the most
elaborate of
London's royal
ceremonies, the
Queen salutes as
a battalion of
Foot Guards
parades its colours
before her.*

The City and Embankment
At the Lord Mayor's Show, pikemen and musketeers escort the newly elected Lord Mayor through the City in a gold state coach.

Holborn and the
Inns of Court

The City

*ent
n and
rand*

R I V E R   T H A M E S

South Bank

Southwark and
Bankside

The Cenotaph
On Remembrance Sunday the Queen pays homage to the nation's war dead.

Tower of London
In the nightly Ceremony of the Keys, a Yeoman Warder locks the gates. A military escort ensures the keys are not stolen.

0 kilometres   1

0 miles   0.5

Houses of Parliament
Each autumn the Queen goes to Parliament in the Irish State Coach to open the new parliamentary session.

Attending London's Ceremonies

Royalty and commerce provide the two principal sources of London's rich calendar of ceremonial events. Quaint and old-fashioned these events may be, but what may seem arcane ritual has real historical meaning – many of the capital's ceremonies originated in the Middle Ages.

ROYAL CEREMONIES

Although the Queen's role is now largely symbolic, the Guard at Buckingham Palace still patrols the palace grounds. The impressive ceremony of the **Changing of the Guard** – dazzling uniforms, shouted commands, military music – consists of the Old Guard, which forms up in the palace forecourt, going off duty and handing over to the New Guard. The Guard consists of three officers and 40 men when the Queen is in residence, but only three officers and 31 men when she is away. The ceremony takes place in front of the palace. In another changeover ceremony, the Queen's Life Guards travel daily from Hyde Park Barracks to Horse Guards' Parade.

A Queen's Guard in winter

One of the Queen's Life Guards

The **Ceremony of the Keys** at the Tower of London is one of the capital's most timeless ceremonies. After each of the Tower gates has been locked, the last post is sounded by a trumpeter before the keys are secured in the Queen's House.

The Tower of London and Hyde Park are also the scene of **Royal Salutes** which take place on birthdays and other occasions throughout the year. At such times 41 rounds are fired in Hyde Park at noon, and 62 rounds at the Tower at 1pm. The spectacle in Hyde Park is a stirring one as 71 horses and six 13-pounder cannons swirl into place and the roar of the guns begins.

The combination of pageantry, colour and music makes the annual **Trooping the Colour** the high point of London's ceremonial year. The Queen takes the Royal Salute, and after her troops have marched past, she leads them to Buckingham Palace where a second march past takes place. The best place to watch this spectacle is from the Horse Guards Parade side of St James's Park.

Bands of the Household Cavalry and the Foot Guards stage the ceremony of **Beating the Retreat** at Horse Guards Parade. This takes place three or four evenings a week in the fortnight leading up to Trooping the Colour.

The spectacular **State Opening of Parliament**, when the Queen opens the annual parliamentary session in the House of Lords – usually in November – is not open to the general public, although it is now televised. The huge royal procession, which moves from Buckingham Palace to Westminster, is, however, a magnificent sight, with the Queen travelling in the highly ornate Irish State Coach drawn by four horses.

MILITARY CEREMONIES

The cenotaph in Whitehall is the setting for a ceremony held on **Remembrance Sunday**, to give thanks to those who died fighting in the two World Wars.

National **Navy Day** is commemorated by a parade down the Mall, followed by a service held at Nelson's Column in Trafalgar Square.

Royal salute, Tower of London

Trooping the Colour

Silent Change ceremony at Guildhall for the new Lord Mayor

CEREMONIES IN THE CITY

November is the focus of the City of London's ceremonial year. At the **Silent Change** in Guildhall, the outgoing Lord Mayor hands over symbols of office to the new Mayor in a virtually wordless ceremony. The following day sees the rumbustious **Lord Mayor's Show**. Accompanying the Lord Mayor in his gold state coach a procession of bands, decorated floats and military detachments makes its way through the City from Guildhall past the Mansion House to the Law Courts, and back again along the Embankment.

Lord Mayor's chain of office

Many of the ceremonies that take place in the City are linked to the activities of the Livery Companies *(see p152)*. These include the Worshipful Companies of **Vintners' and Distillers'** annual celebration of the wine harvest and the Stationers' **Cakes and Ale Sermon**, held in St Paul's. Cakes and ale are provided according to the will of a 17th-century stationer.

NAME-DAY CEREMONIES

Every 21 May **King Henry VI**, who was murdered in the Tower of London in 1471, is still remembered by the members of his two famous foundations, Eton College and King's College, Cambridge,

who meet for a ceremony at the Wakefield Tower where he was killed. **Oak Apple Day** commemorates King Charles II's lucky escape from the Parliamentary forces of Oliver Cromwell in 1651. The King managed to conceal himself in a hollow oak tree, and today Chelsea Pensioners honour his memory by decorating his statue at Chelsea Royal Hospital with oak leaves and branches. On 18 December, the lexicographer **Dr Johnson** is commemorated in an annual service held at Westminster Abbey.

INFORMAL CEREMONIES

Each July, six guildsmen from the Company of Watermen compete for the prize in **Doggett's Coat and Badge Race**. In autumn, the **Pearly Kings and Queens**, representatives of east London's traders, meet at St Martin-in-the-Fields. In March children are given oranges and lemons at the **Oranges and Lemons service** at St Clement Danes Church. In February, clowns take part in a service for **Joseph Grimaldi** (1779–1837) at the Holy Trinity Church in Dalston E8.

Pearly Queen

WHERE TO FIND THE CEREMONIES

Beating the Retreat
Horse Guards *p80*, date arranged during first two weeks of June.
Cakes and Ale Sermon
St Paul's *pp148–51*, Ash Wed.
Ceremony of the Keys
Tower of London *pp154–7*, 9.30pm daily. Tickets from the Tower, but book well in advance.
Changing of the Guard
Buckingham Palace *pp94–5*, Apr–Jul: 11.30am daily; Aug–Mar: alternate days. Horse Guards, Whitehall *p80*, 11am Mon–Sat, 10am Sun. For details call the London Tourist Board Information Line on 0906 866 3344.
Doggett's Coat and Badge Race
From London Bridge to Cadogan Pier, Chelsea *pp192–7*, July.
Dr Johnson Memorial
Westminster Abbey *pp76–9*, 18 Dec.
Joseph Grimaldi Memorial
Holy Trinity Church, Dalston E8, 7 Feb.
King Henry VI Memorial
Wakefield Tower, Tower of London *pp154–7*, 21 May.
Lord Mayor's Show
The City *pp143–53*, second Sat Nov.
Navy Day
Trafalgar Sq *p102*, 21 Oct.
Oak Apple Day
Royal Hospital *p197*, Thu after 29 May.
Oranges and Lemons Service
St Clement Danes *p138*, March.
Pearly Kings and Queens Harvest Festival
St Martin-in-the-Fields *p102*, autumn.
Remembrance Sunday
Cenotaph *p74*, Sun nearest 11 Nov.
Royal Salutes
Hyde Park *p211*, royal anniversaries and other state occasions.
Silent Change
Guildhall *p159*, second Fri Nov.
State Opening of Parliament
Houses of Parliament *pp72–3*, Oct–Nov. Procession from Buckingham Palace to Westminster.
Trooping the Colour
Horse Guards *p80*, 2nd Sat Jun (rehearsals on previous two Sats). Tickets from Household Division, Horse Guards.
Vintners' and Distillers' Wine Harvest
St Olave's Church, Hart St EC3, second Tue Oct.

LONDON THROUGH THE YEAR

Springtime in London carries an almost tangible air of a city waking up to longer days and outdoor pursuits. The cheerful yellow of daffodils studs the parks, and less hardy Londoners turn out for their first jog of the year to find themselves puffing in the wake of serious runners training for the Marathon. As spring turns into summer, the royal parks reach their full glory, and in Kensington Gardens

nannies gather to chat under venerable chestnut trees. As autumn takes hold, these same trees are ablaze with red and gold, and Londoners' thoughts turn to afternoons in museums, followed by tea in a café. The year closes with Guy Fawkes and Christmas shopping. The official visitor organization, Visit London, www.visitlondon.com *(p363)*, and the listings magazines *(p342)* have details of seasonal events.

SPRING

The weather during the spring months may be raw, and an umbrella is a necessary precaution. Druids celebrate the Spring Equinox in a subdued ceremony on Tower Hill. Painters compete to have their works accepted by the Royal Academy. Footballers close their season in May with the FA Cup Final, while cricketers don their sweaters to begin theirs. Oxford and Cambridge Universities row their annual boat race along the Thames, and Marathon runners pound the streets.

MARCH

Chelsea Antiques Fair *(2nd week, also Sep)*, Chelsea Old Town Hall, King's Rd SW3.
Ideal Home Exhibition *(second week)*, Earl's Court, Warwick Rd SW5. It is a long-established show with the latest in domestic gadgetry and state-of-the-art technology.
Oranges and Lemons Service, St Clement Danes *(p55)*. Service for school-children; each child is given an orange and a lemon.
Oxford v Cambridge boat race *(Sat before Easter, or Easter)*, Putney to Mortlake *(p355)*.
Spring Equinox celebration *(21 Mar)*, Tower Hill EC3. Historic pagan ceremony with modern-day druids.

EASTER

Good Fri and following Mon are public holidays.
Easter parades, Battersea Park *(p251)*.

Runners in the London Marathon passing Tower Bridge

Kite flying, Blackheath *(p243)*.
Easter Kite Festival Hampstead Heath *(p234)*.
Easter procession and hymns *(Easter Mon)*, Westminster Abbey *(pp76–9)*. One of London's most evocative religious celebrations.
International Model Railway Exhibition *(Easter weekend)*, Royal Horticultural Hall, Vincent Sq SW1. Of real interest to everyone.

A London park in the spring

APRIL

London Harness Horse Parade *(early Apr)*, Battersea Park *(p251)*.
Queen's Birthday gun salutes *(21 Apr)*, Hyde Park, Tower of London *(p54)*.
London Marathon *(Sun in Apr or May)*, champions and novices run from Greenwich to Westminster *(p355)*.

MAY

First and last Mon are public holidays.
FA Cup Final, football season's climax *(p354)*.
Henry VI Memorial *(p55)*.
Beating the Bounds *(Ascension Day)*, throughout the City. Young boys from the City parish beat buildings that mark the parish boundaries.
Oak Apple Day, at the Royal Hospital, Chelsea *(p55)*.
Funfairs *(late May public hol weekend)*, various commons.
Chelsea Flower Show *(late May)*, Royal Hospital, Chelsea.
Beating the Retreat *(p54)*.

AVERAGE DAILY HOURS OF SUNSHINE

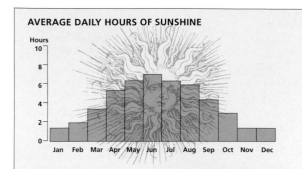

Sunshine Chart
London's longest and hottest days fall between May and August. In the height of summer, daylight hours can extend from well before 5am to after 9pm. Daytime is much shorter in the winter, but London can be stunning in the winter sunshine.

SUMMER

London's summer season is packed full of indoor and outdoor events. The weather is very unreliable, even at the height of summer, but unless you are notably unlucky there should be enough fine days to sample what is on offer.

The selection includes many traditional events, such as the Wimbledon tennis champion-ships and the cricket test matches at Lord's and the Oval. Well out of view from the general public and prying photographers, the Queen holds garden parties for favoured subjects in the splendid grounds of Buckingham Palace. The summer public holiday is also marked with funfairs in some of London's parks.

JUNE

Coronation Day gun salutes *(2 Jun)*, Hyde Park and Tower of London *(p54)*.
International Ceramics Fair, Park Lane Hotel, Park Lane W1.
Fine Art and Antiques fair, Olympia, Olympia Way W14.
Trooping the Colour, Horse Guards Parade *(p54)*.
Duke of Edinburgh's Birthday gun salutes *(10 Jun)*, Hyde Park and Tower of London *(p54)*.
Covent Garden Flower Festival *(mid-Jun)*, Covent Garden WC2 *(pp111–119)*. Floral installations, street performers and fashion shows. Free entry to all.
Wimbledon Lawn Tennis Championships *(two weeks in late Jun; p354)*.
Cricket test match, Lord's Cricket Ground *(p354)*.

Revellers at Notting Hill Carnival

Open-air theatre season *(throughout the summer)*, Regent's Park and Holland Park. Shakespeare, Shaw and others offer the perfect op-portunity for a picnic *(p344)*.
Open-air concerts, Kenwood, Hampstead Heath, Crystal Palace, Marble Hill, St James's Park *(p349)*.
Summer festivals *(late Jun)*, Spitalfields and Primrose Hill. Contact Visit London *(p363)* or see the listings magazines *(p342)* for times and venues of all these events and see July, below.
City of London Festival *(late Jun–mid-July)*, various City venues *(p143)*. Arts and music festival taking place in some of London's most beautiful historic churches.

JULY

Summer festivals Greenwich and Docklands, Regent's Park, Richmond and Soho.
Sales. Price reductions across London's shops *(p321)*.
Doggett's Coat and Badge Race *(p55)*.
Hampton Court Flower Show, Hampton Court Palace *(pp254–7)*.
Capital Radio Jazz Festival, Royal Festival Hall *(p188)*.
Henry Wood Promenade Concerts *(late Jul–Sep)*, Royal Albert Hall *(p207)*.
Royal Academy Summer Exhibition *(Jun–Aug)*, Piccadilly *(p90)*.

AUGUST

Last Monday in August is a public holiday.
Notting Hill Carnival *(late Aug holiday weekend)*. An internationally famous and well attended Caribbean carnival organized by the area's various ethnic communities *(p219)*.
Funfairs *(Aug holiday)*. These tend to run throughout London's parks during the summer months.

Regimental band, St James's Park

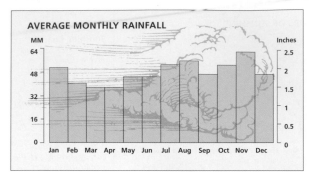

AVERAGE MONTHLY RAINFALL

AUTUMN

There is a sense of purpose about London in autumn. The build-up to the busiest shopping season, the start of the academic year, and the new parliamentary session, opened by the Queen, inject some life into the colder months. The cricket season ends in mid-September, while food-lovers may be interested in the spectacular displays of fresh fish that are laid out in the vestry of St Mary-at-Hill, celebrating the harvest of this island nation.

Memories of a more turbulent opening of Parliament are revived on 5 November, when there are bonfires and fireworks to commemorate the failure of a conspiracy led by Guy Fawkes to blow up the Palace of Westminster in 1605. A few days later the dead of two World Wars are commemorated at a ceremony held in Whitehall.

Pearly Kings gathering for the harvest festival at St Martin-in-the-Fields

London-to-Brighton veteran car run

SEPTEMBER

Mayor Thames Festival, *(mid-Sep)*. Entertainment by and on the river between Westminster Bridge and Southwark Cathedral.
Great River Race, Thames.
Last Night of the Proms *(mid-Sep)*, Royal Albert Hall *(p207)*. Rousing classical hits.
Spitalfields Show *(mid-Sep)*, Old Spitalfields Market *(p170)*.

OCTOBER

Pearly Harvest Festival *(first Sun)*, St Martin-in-the-Fields.
Punch and Judy Festival Covent Garden WC2. Celebration of puppet duo.
Harvest of the Sea *(second Sun)*, St Mary-at-Hill Church *(p152)*.
Horse of the Year Show Wembley Arena *(p353)*.
Vintners' and Distillers' Wine Harvest *(p55)*.
Navy Day *(p54)*.

NOVEMBER

State Opening of Parliament *(p54)*.
Guy Fawkes Night *(5 Nov)*. Listings magazines give details of firework displays *(p342)*.
Remembrance Day Service *(p54)*.
Silent Change *(p55)*.
Lord Mayor's Show *(p55)*.
London to Brighton veteran car rally *(first Sun)*.
Christmas lights *(late Nov–6 Jan)*. The West End *(p323)*, especially Regent's Street, lights up for the festive season.

Autumn colours in a London park

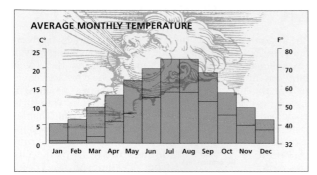

AVERAGE MONTHLY TEMPERATURE

Temperature Chart
The chart shows the average minimum and maximum temperatures for each month. Top temperatures averaging 22° C (75° F) belie London's reputation for year-round chilliness, although November through to February can be icy.

WINTER

Some of the most striking images of London are drawn from winter: paintings of frost fairs in the 17th and 18th centuries, when the River Thames froze over completely; and Claude Monet's views of the river and its bridges.

For centuries thick "pea-souper" fogs were an inevitable part of winter, until the Clean Air Act of 1956 barred coal-burning in open grates.

Christmas trees and lights twinkle everywhere – from the West End shopping streets to construction sites. The scent of roasting chestnuts pervades as street pedlars sell them from glowing mobile braziers.

Seasonal menus feature roast turkey, mince pies and rich, dark Christmas pudding. Traditional fare in theatres includes colourful family pantomimes (where the customary cross-dressing between the sexes baffles many visitors – *p344*) and popular ballets such as *Swan Lake* or *The Nutcracker*.

Skaters use the open-air rink at the Broadgate Centre in the City, and at Somerset House (*see p117*). It is rarely safe to use the parks' frozen lakes.

Winter in Kensington Gardens

DECEMBER

Oxford v Cambridge rugby union match Twickenham (*p355*).
International Showjumping Championships (*late Dec*), Olympia. Equestrian competition featuring the cream of riders from around the world.

CHRISTMAS, NEW YEAR

25–26 Dec and **1 Jan** are public hols. There is no train service on Christmas Day.

Carol services (*leading up to Christmas*), Trafalgar Square (*p102*), St Paul's (*pp148–51*), Westminster Abbey (*pp76–9*) and other churches.
Turkey auction (*24 Dec*), Smithfield Market (*p164*).
Christmas Day swim Serpentine, Hyde Park (*p211*).
New Year's Eve celebrations (*31 Dec*), Trafalgar Square, St Paul's.

JANUARY

Sales (*p321*).
New Year's Day Parade starts at Parliament Sq (*p74*).
International Boat Show, Earl's Court, Warwick Rd SW5.
International Mime Festival (*mid Jan–early Feb*), various venues.
Charles I Commemoration (*last Sun*), procession from St James's Palace (*p91*) to Banqueting House (*p80*).
Chinese New Year (*late Jan–mid-Feb*), Chinatown (*p108*) and Soho (*p109*).

FEBRUARY

Queen's Accession gun salutes (*6 Feb*), 41 gun salute Hyde Park; 62-gun salute Tower of London (*p54*).
Pancake races (*Shrove Tue*), Lincoln's Inn Fields (*p137*) and Covent Garden (*p112*).

PUBLIC HOLIDAYS

New Year's Day (1 Jan); **Good Friday; Easter Monday; May Day** (first Monday in May); **Whit Monday** (last Monday in May); **August Bank Holiday** (last Monday in August); **Christmas** (25–26 December).

Christmas illuminations in Trafalgar Square

A RIVER VIEW OF LONDON

Cruising down the Thames is one of the most interesting ways to experience London. As the country's main commercial artery from the Roman invasion to well into the 1950s, the river is packed with historical references, including the reconstruction of the Elizabethan Globe Theatre, royal palaces and parks, numerous storied bridges and decommissioned power stations. Now the river is the city's foremost leisure amenity, with the banks accessible via

Decoration on Chelsea Bridge

the Thames Path, numerous riverside pubs and commuters as well as tourists sailing the river.

Passenger boat services cover about 50 kilometres (30 miles) of the Thames, from Hampton Court in the west to the Thames Barrier in the east. The most popular and best served section runs through the heart of the city from Westminster to Tower Bridge. Often accompanied by interesting and witty commentary, a cruise along this fascinating stretch of the Thames should not be missed.

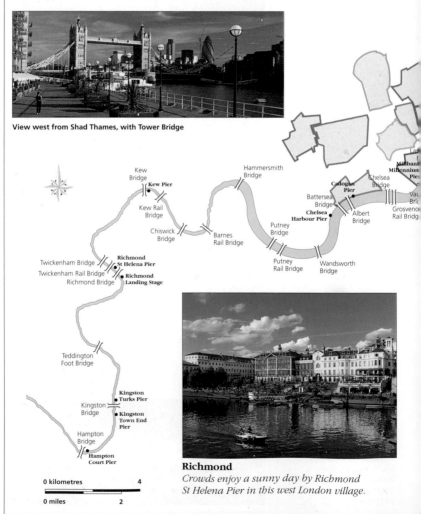

View west from Shad Thames, with Tower Bridge

Kew Bridge
Kew Pier
Kew Rail Bridge
Chiswick Bridge
Barnes Rail Bridge
Hammersmith Bridge
Putney Bridge
Putney Rail Bridge
Wandsworth Bridge
Battersea Bridge
Chelsea Harbour Pier
Albert Bridge
Cadogan Pier
Chelsea Bridge
Millennium Pier
Grosvenor Rail Bridge
Vau
Bri
Twickenham Bridge
Twickenham Rail Bridge
Richmond Bridge
Richmond St Helena Pier
Richmond Landing Stage
Teddington Foot Bridge
Kingston Turks Pier
Kingston Bridge
Kingston Town End Pier
Hampton Bridge
Hampton Court Pier

0 kilometres   4
0 miles   2

Richmond
Crowds enjoy a sunny day by Richmond St Helena Pier in this west London village.

The Thames Barrier
Completed in 1982, the world's largest moveable flood barrier protects London from rising water levels. The massive steel gates have been raised over 60 times.

Riverside pubs
Beautifully preserved pubs, such as the Prospect of Whitby in Wapping, hug the river's banks.

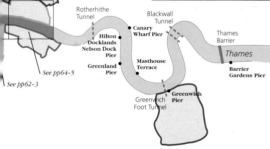

Rotherhithe Tunnel
Blackwall Tunnel
Canary Wharf Pier
Hilton Docklands Nelson Dock Pier
Thames Barrier
Greenland Pier
Masthouse Terrace
Thames
Barrier Gardens Pier
See pp64-5
See pp62-3
Greenwich Foot Tunnel
Greenwich Pier

CRUISE OPERATORS

Bateaux London
Tel 020-7925 2215.
www.bateauxlondon.com

Campion Launches
Tel 020-8305 0300.

Catamaran Cruisers
Tel 020-7987 1185.
www.catamarancruisers.co.uk

City Cruises
Tel 020-7740 0400.
www.citycruises.com

Crown River Cruises
Tel 020-7936 2033.
www.crownriver.com

Thames Clippers
Tel 0870-781 5049.
www.thamesclippers.com

Thames Executive Charters
Tel 01342-322440
www.thamesexecutivecharters.com

Thames River Services
Tel 020-7930 4097.
www.westminsterpier.co.uk

Turks Launches
Tel 020-8546 2434.
www.turks.co.uk

Westminster Passenger Service Association (Upriver) Ltd
Tel 020-7930 2062
or 020-7930 4721.
www.wpsa.co.uk

CRUISE HIGHLIGHTS

Most regular services run from April through September, with some routes having winter schedules. During the summer, sailing times are frequent from Westminster and Embankment to Greenwich, with a boat arriving between every half hour and every hour. Commuter river services link Canary Wharf and Chelsea Harbour with some of the city's main termini. Numerous operators cover a variety of routes and a River Thames Boat Service Guide is available at tube stations. Most operators give a third off the ticket price to Travelcard holders *(see p378).*

GREENWICH *(see pp236–43)*
Blessed with frequent service, accessing this area steeped in shipping lore by boat gives a day trip a fitting nautical spin.
Operators: Catamaran Cruisers, City Cruises, Thames River Services.
Piers: Westminster, Waterloo, Embankment, Bankside, Tower.
Duration: 1 hr (Westminster).

THAMES BARRIER *(see p249)*
Sail between the nine massive piers that raise the steel gates. Cruises to the barrier also pass the shell of the striking Millennium Dome and numerous industrial sites.
Operator: Thames River Services.
Piers: Westminster, Greenwich.
Duration: 30 min (Greenwich).

KEW *(see pp260–61)*
A cruise to Kew leaves the city behind after passing the Battersea Power Station and sailing through Hammersmith.
Operator: WPSA (upriver only).
Piers: Westminster.
Duration: 1.5 hrs (Westminster).

HAMPTON COURT *(see pp254–7)* Arrive at Hampton Court in regal style, but be aware that the round trip from Westminster can take up to eight hours. Consider sailing from one of the piers upriver.
Operator: WPSA (upriver only), Turks Launches.
Piers: Kew, all Richmond and Kingston piers.
Duration: 2 hrs (Kew).

Westminster Bridge to Blackfriars Bridge

Until World War II, this stretch of the Thames marked the division between rich and poor London. On the north bank were the offices, shops, luxury hotels and apartments of Whitehall and the Strand, the Inns of Court and the newspaper district. To the south were smoky factories and slum dwellings. After the war, the Festival of Britain in 1951 started the revival of the South Bank *(see pp184–91)*, which now has some of the capital's most interesting modern buildings.

Savoy Hotel
This hotel is on the site of a medieval palace (p116).

Somerset House, built in 1786, houses three art galleries *(p117)*.

Shell Mex House
Once offices for the oil company, they were built in 1931 on the site of the vast Cecil Hotel.

Cleopatra's Needle was made in ancient Egypt and given to London in 1819 *(p118)*.

Embankment Gardens is the site of many open-air concerts held in the bandstand during the summer months *(p118)*.

Charing Cross

Savoy Pier

Waterloo Bridge

Festival Pier

Embankment

Embankment Pier

The **South Bank** was the site of the 1951 Festival of Britain and is London's most important arts complex. It is dominated by the Royal Festival Hall, the National Theatre and the Hayward Gallery *(pp184–91)*.

Charing Cross
The rail terminus is encased in a Post-Modernist office complex with many shops (p119).

Hungerford Railway Bridge

Waterloo Millennium Pier

British Airways London Eye offers breathtaking views over London *(p189)*.

The Banqueting House is one of Inigo Jones's finest works, built as part of Whitehall Palace *(p80)*.

The Ministry of Defence is a bulky white fortress completed in the 1950s.

Westminster Pier

Westminster

Westminster Bridge

County Hall
This is now home to the state-of-the-art London Aquarium and its 350 species of fish.

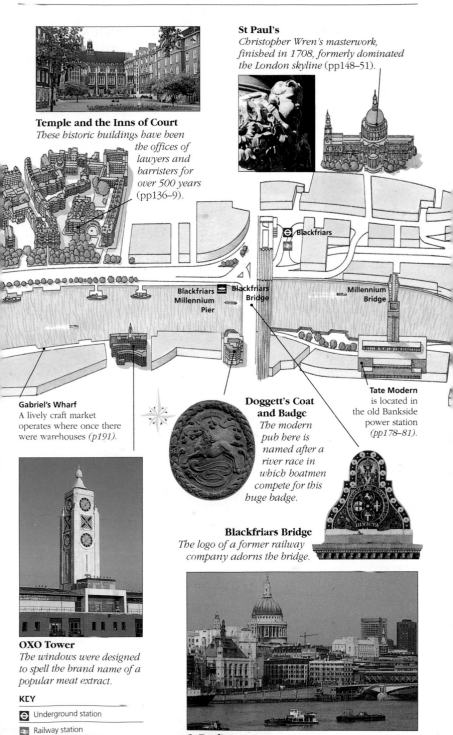

Temple and the Inns of Court
These historic buildings have been the offices of lawyers and barristers for over 500 years (pp136–9).

St Paul's
Christopher Wren's masterwork, finished in 1708, formerly dominated the London skyline (pp148–51).

Blackfriars

Blackfriars Millennium Pier

Blackfriars Bridge

Millennium Bridge

Gabriel's Wharf
A lively craft market operates where once there were warehouses *(p191)*.

Doggett's Coat and Badge
The modern pub here is named after a river race in which boatmen compete for this huge badge.

Tate Modern
is located in the old Bankside power station *(pp178–81)*.

Blackfriars Bridge
The logo of a former railway company adorns the bridge.

OXO Tower
The windows were designed to spell the brand name of a popular meat extract.

KEY

🔵 Underground station

🚆 Railway station

🛥 River boat boarding point

St Paul's
The cathedral dominates views from the South Bank.

Southwark Bridge to St Katharine's Dock

For centuries the stretch just east of London Bridge was the busiest part of the Thames, with ships of all sizes jostling for position to unload at the wharves on both banks. Then, in the 19th century, the construction of the docks to the east eased congestion. Today most landmarks on this section hark back to that commercial past.

Old Billingsgate
Note the flying fish weather vanes on what was London's main fish market (p152).

Fishmongers' Hall
The hall (1834) of this ancient City guild dominates the view north from London Bridge (p152).

Monument
The Great Fire of 1666 started near this spot (p152).

A Custom House has been here since 1272. This version dates from 1825.

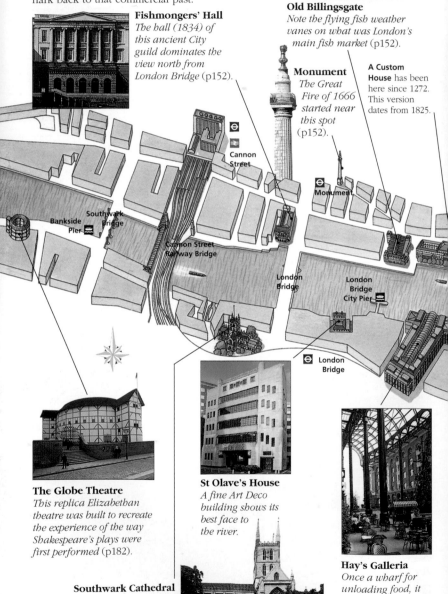

Cannon Street

Monument

Bankside Pier

Southwark Bridge

Cannon Street Railway Bridge

London Bridge

London Bridge City Pier

London Bridge

The Globe Theatre
This replica Elizabethan theatre was built to recreate the experience of the way Shakespeare's plays were first performed (p182).

St Olave's House
A fine Art Deco building shows its best face to the river.

Hay's Galleria
Once a wharf for unloading food, it has been covered to house shops and restaurants.

Southwark Cathedral
Parts of this building date from the 12th century. It contains memorials to Shakespeare (p176).

Southwark Wharves
Now there are walkways with river views where ships used to dock.

Tower Bridge
It still opens to let tall ships pass, but not as often as it did when cargo vessels came through (p153).

Tower of London
Look out for Traitors' Gate, where prisoners would be taken into the Tower by boat (pp154–7).

St Katharine's Dock
The former dock is now a lively attraction for visitors. Its yacht marina is a highlight (p158).

Tower Millennium Pier

Tower Bridge

St Katharine's Pier

A stunning new building, City Hall, houses the Mayor and the governing offices.

Victorian warehouses on Butlers Wharf have been converted into apartments.

HMS Belfast
This World War II cruiser has been a museum since 1971 (p183).

Design Museum
Opened in 1989, this ship-like building is a shining example of Docklands' renaissance (p183).

LONDON AREA BY AREA

WHITEHALL AND WESTMINSTER 68–85
PICCADILLY AND ST JAMES'S 86–97
SOHO AND TRAFALGAR SQUARE 98–109
COVENT GARDEN AND THE STRAND 110–19
BLOOMSBURY AND FITZROVIA 120–31
HOLBORN AND THE INNS OF COURT 132–41
THE CITY 142–59
SMITHFIELD AND SPITALFIELDS 160–71
SOUTHWARK AND BANKSIDE 172–83
SOUTH BANK 184–91
CHELSEA 192–7
SOUTH KENSINGTON
AND KNIGHTSBRIDGE 198–213
KENSINGTON AND HOLLAND PARK 214–19
REGENT'S PARK AND MARYLEBONE 220–27
HAMPSTEAD 228–35
GREENWICH AND BLACKHEATH 236–43
FURTHER AFIELD 244–61
SIX GUIDED WALKS 262–75

WHITEHALL AND WESTMINSTER

Whitehall and Westminster have been at the centre of political and religious power in England for a thousand years. King Canute, who ruled at the beginning of the 11th century, was the first monarch to have a palace on what was then an island in the swampy meeting point of the Thames and its vanished tributary, the Tyburn. Canute built his palace beside the church that, some 50 years later, Edward the Confessor would enlarge into England's greatest abbey, giving the area its name (a minster is an abbey church). Over the following centuries the offices of state were established in the vicinity. All this is still reflected in Whitehall's heroic statues and massive government buildings. But, to its north, Trafalgar Square marks the start of the West End entertainment district.

Horse Guard on Whitehall

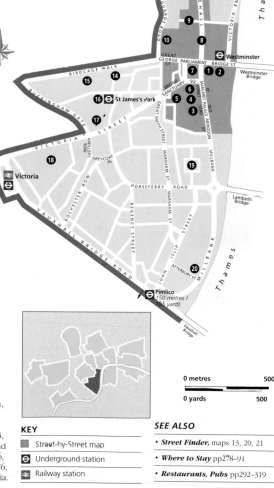

SIGHTS AT A GLANCE

Historic Streets and Buildings
Houses of Parliament pp72–3 **1**
Big Ben **2**
Jewel Tower **3**
Dean's Yard **5**
Parliament Square **7**
Downing Street **9**
Cabinet War Rooms and Churchill Museum **10**
Banqueting House **11**
Horse Guards Parade **12**
Queen Anne's Gate **14**
St James's Park Station **16**
Blewcoat School **17**

Churches, Abbeys and Cathedrals
Westminster Abbey pp76–9 **4**
St Margaret's Church **6**
Westminster Cathedral **18**
St John's, Smith Square **19**

Museums and Galleries
Guards' Museum **15**
Tate Britain pp82–5 **20**

Theatres
Whitehall Theatre **13**

Monuments
Cenotaph **8**

GETTING THERE
Rail services and the Victoria, Jubilee, District and Circle lines all serve the area. Bus numbers 3, 11, 12, 24, 29, 53, 77, 77A, 88, 109, 159, 170 and 184 go to Whitehall; 2, 2B, 16, 25, 36A, 38, 39, 52, 52A, 73, 76, 135, 507 and 510 serve Victoria.

KEY
■ Street-by-Street map
🚇 Underground station
🚆 Railway station

SEE ALSO
- *Street Finder,* maps 13, 20, 21
- *Where to Stay* pp278–91
- *Restaurants, Pubs* pp292–319

0 metres 500
0 yards 500

◁ Looking down Whitehall towards Big Ben

Street-by-Street: Whitehall and Westminster

Compared with many capital cities, London has little monumental architecture designed to overawe with pomp. Here, at the historic seat both of the government and of the established church, it most closely approaches the broad, stately avenues of Paris, Rome and Madrid. On weekdays the streets are crowded with members of the civil service, as most of their work is based in this area. At weekends, however, it is popular with tourists visiting some of London's most famous sights.

Earl Haig, the British World War I chief, was sculpted by Alfred Hardiman in 1936.

Downing Street. *British Prime Ministers have lived here since 1732* **9**

Central Hall is a florid example of the Beaux Arts style, built in 1911 as a Methodist meeting hall. In 1946 the first General Assembly of the United Nations was held here.

★ **Cabinet War Rooms and Churchill Museum**
The War Rooms were Winston Churchill's World War II headquarters **10**

★ **Westminster Abbey**
The Abbey is London's oldest and most important church **4**

The Sanctuary was a medieval safe place for those escaping the law.

Dean's Yard
Westminster School was founded here in 1540 **5**

Richard I's Statue, by Carlo Marochetti (1860), depicts the 12th-century *Coeur de Lion* (Lionheart).

Jewel Tower
Kings once stored their most valuable possessions here **3**

The Burghers of Calais is a cast of Auguste Rodin's original in Paris.

KING CHARLES

STOREY'S GATE

GREAT GEORGE STREET

BROAD SANCTUARY PARLIAMENT S

ST MARGARET STREET

GREAT COLLEGE STREET

ABINGDON STREET

★ **Horse Guards**
A mounted guard is ceremonially changed here twice a day **12**

To Trafalgar Square

Dover House, a stately mansion dating from 1787, now houses the Scottish Office.

LOCATOR MAP
See Central London Map pp14–15

★ **Banqueting House**
Inigo Jones designed this elegant building, which has a Rubens ceiling, in 1622 **11**

Cenotaph
Edwin Lutyens's war memorial dates from 1920 **8**

Richmond House is William Whitfield's prize-winning 1980s building for the Department of Health.

The Treasury is where the nation's finances are administered.

Norman Shaw Buildings, the Victorian site of New Scotland Yard, the Metropolitan Police headquarters.

Westminster Pier is a starting point for river excursions.

Westminster station

Boadicea, the British queen who resisted the Romans, was portrayed by Thomas Thornycroft in the 1850s.

STAR SIGHTS

★ Westminster Abbey

★ Houses of Parliament and Big Ben

★ Banqueting House

★ Cabinet War Rooms and Churchill Museum

★ Horse Guards

Parliament Square
Statues of famous statesmen, such as Benjamin Disraeli and Sir Winston Churchill, stand here **7**

★ **Houses of Parliament and Big Ben**
These were designed by Barry in 1834 when the Palace of Westminster burned down **1 2**

St Margaret's Church
Society weddings often take place here, in Parliament's church **6**

KEY

– – – Suggested route

0 metres   100
0 yards   100

Houses of Parliament ①

Since 1512 the Palace of Westminster has been the seat of the two Houses of Parliament, called the Lords and the Commons. The Commons is made up of elected Members of Parliament (MPs) of different political parties; the party with the most MPs forms the Government, and its leader becomes Prime Minister. MPs from other parties make up the Opposition. Commons' debates can become heated and are impartially chaired by an MP designated as Speaker. The Government formulates legislation which is first debated in both Houses before becoming law.

The mock-Gothic building was designed by Victorian architect Sir Charles Barry. Victoria Tower, on the left, contains 1.5 million Acts of Parliament passed since 1497.

★ Commons' Chamber
The room is upholstered in green. The Government sits on the left, the Opposition on the right, and the Speaker presides from a chair between them.

Big Ben
The vast bell was hung in 1858 and chimes on the hour; four smaller ones ring on the quarter hours (see p74).

Members' entrance

STAR FEATURES

★ Westminster Hall

★ Lords' Chamber

★ Commons' Chamber

★ Westminster Hall
The only surviving part of the original Palace of Westminster, it dates from 1097; its hammerbeam roof is 14th century.

Peers are members of the House of Lords – many receive their titles for services to their country. This is their lobby.

Central Lobby
People who come to meet their MP wait here under a ceiling of rich mosaics.

Royal Gallery
The Queen passes through here at the State Opening. It is lined with peers' desks.

St Stephen's entrance

★ Lords' Chamber
At the State Opening of Parliament (see pp54–5) the Queen delivers a speech from the throne of the House of Lords, which outlines the Government's plans.

TIMELINE

1042 Work starts on first palace for Edward the Confessor	**1547** St Stephen's chapel becomes first Chamber of the House of Commons	**1642** Charles I tries to arrest five MPs but is forced to withdraw by the Speaker	**1941** Chamber of House of Commons destroyed by World War II bomb

1000	1200	1400	1600	1800	2000

1087–1100 Westminster Hall built	**1512** After a fire, palace stops being a royal residence		**1870** Present building completed
The Mace: symbol of royal authority in the Commons	**1605** Guy Fawkes and others try to blow up the king and Houses of Parliament	**1834** Palace destroyed by fire; only Westminster Hall and the Jewel Tower survive	

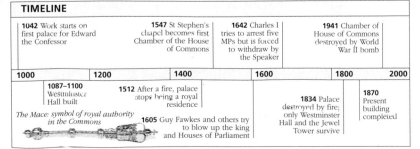

Houses of Parliament ❶

See pp72–3.

Big Ben ❷

Bridge St SW1. **Map** 13 C5.
🚇 Westminster.
Not open to the public.

To be pedantic, Big Ben is not the name of the world-famous four-faced clock in the 106-m (320-ft) tower that rises above the Houses of Parliament, but of the resonant 14-tonne bell on which the hours are struck. It was named after Sir Benjamin Hall, Chief Commissioner of Works when the bell was hung in 1858. Cast at Whitechapel, it was the second giant bell made for the clock, the first having become cracked during a test ringing. (The present bell also has a slight crack.) The clock is the largest in Britain, its four dials 7.5 m (23 ft) in diameter and the minute hand 4.25 m (14 ft) long, made in hollow copper for lightness. It has kept exact time for the nation more or less continuously since it was first set in motion in May 1859. The deep chimes have become a symbol of Britain all over the world and are broadcast daily on BBC radio.

Jewel Tower ❸

Abingdon St SW1. **Map** 13 B5.
Tel 020-7222 2219. 🚇 Westminster.
Open Apr–Oct: 10am–5pm;
Nov–Mar: 10am–4pm daily. **Closed**
24–26 Dec, 1 Jan. **Adm charge.** 📷
♿ ground floor only. 📖
www.english-heritage.org.uk

This and Westminster Hall *(see p72)* are the only vestiges of the old Palace of Westminster. The tower was built in 1365 as a stronghold for Edward III's treasure and today houses a fascinating exhibition, *Parliament Past and Present*, that relates the history of Parliament. It includes a new display devoted to the history of the Jewel Tower itself.

The tower served as the weights and measures office from 1869 until 1938 and another small display relates to that era. Alongside are the remains of the moat and a medieval quay.

Westminster Abbey ❹

See pp76–9.

Dean's Yard ❺

Broad Sanctuary SW1. **Map** 13 B5.
🚇 *Westminster.* **Buildings not open** to the public.

Entrance to the Abbey and cloisters from Dean's Yard

An arch near the west door of the Abbey leads into this secluded grassy square, surrounded by a jumble of buildings from many different periods. A medieval house on the east side has a distinctive dormer window and backs on to Little Dean's Yard, where the monks' living quarters used to be. Dean's Yard is private property. It belongs to the Dean and Chapter of Westminster and is close to Westminster School, whose famous former pupils include poet John Dryden and playwright Ben Jonson. Scholars are, by tradition, the first to acknowledge a new monarch.

St Margaret's Church ❻

Parliament Sq SW1. **Map** 13 B5.
Tel 020-7654 4840. 🚇 *Westminster.*
Open 9.30am–3.45pm Mon–Fri,
9.30am–1.45pm Sat, 2–5pm Sun.
⛪ 11am Sun. 📷 ♿

Statue of Charles I overlooking St Margaret's doorway

Overshadowed by the Abbey, this early 15th-century church has long been a favoured venue for political and society weddings, such as Winston and Clementine Churchill's. Although much restored, the church retains some Tudor features, notably a stained-glass window that celebrates the engagement of Catherine of Aragon to Arthur, Henry VIII's eldest brother.

Parliament Square ❼

SW1. **Map** 13 B5. 🚇 *Westminster.*

Laid out in the 1840s to provide a more open aspect for the new Houses of Parliament, the square became Britain's first official roundabout in 1926. Today it is hemmed in by heavy traffic. Statues of statesmen and soldiers are dominated by Winston Churchill in his greatcoat, glowering at the House of Commons. On the north side Abraham Lincoln sits in front of the mock-Gothic Middlesex Guildhall, completed in 1913.

Cenotaph ❽

Whitehall SW1. **Map** 13 B4.
🚇 *Westminster.*

This suitably bleak and pale monument, completed in 1920 by Sir Edwin Lutyens to commemorate the dead of World War I, stands in the middle of Whitehall. On Remembrance Day every year – the Sunday nearest 11 November – the monarch and other dignitaries place wreaths of red poppies on the Cenotaph. This solemn ceremony, commemorating the 1918 armistice, honours the victims of World Wars I and II *(see pp54–5).*

The Cenotaph

Cabinet War Rooms and Churchill Museum ❿

Clive Steps, King Charles St SW1.
Map 13 B5. *Tel* 020-7930 6961.
🚇 *Westminster.* **Open** 9.30am–6pm daily (last adm: 5pm). **Closed** 24–26 Dec. **Adm charge.** 🔣 ▢ ▢
www.iwm.org.uk

This intriguing slice of 20th-century history is a warren of rooms below the Government Office Building north of Parliament Square. It is where the War Cabinet – first under Neville Chamberlain, then Winston Churchill – met during World War II when German bombs were falling on London. The War Rooms include living quarters for key ministers and

Telephones in the Map Room of the Cabinet War Rooms

military leaders and a Cabinet Room, where many strategic decisions were taken. They are laid out as they were when the war ended, complete with period furniture, including Churchill's desk, communications equipment and maps for plotting military strategy. The Churchill Museum is a new addition, which records Churchill's life and career.

Downing Street ❾

SW1. **Map** 13 B4. 🚇 *Westminster.* **Not open** to the public.

Sir George Downing (1623–84) spent part of his youth in the American colonies. He was the second graduate from the nascent Harvard College before returning to fight for the Parliamentarians in the English Civil War. In 1680 he

bought some land near Whitehall Palace and built a street of houses. Four of these survive, though they are much altered. George II gave No. 10 to Sir Robert Walpole in 1732. Since then it has been the official residence of the Prime Minister and contains offices as well as a private apartment. In 1989, for security reasons, iron gates were erected at the Whitehall end.

Government policy is decided in the Cabinet Room at No. 10.

The famous front door of No. 10

No. 12, the Whips' Office, is where Party campaigns are organized.

No. 11 is the Chancellor of the Exchequer's official residence.

No. 10 is the official home of the Prime Minister.

The Prime Minister entertains official guests in the State Dining Room.

Westminster Abbey ④

The Abbey is world-famous as the resting-place of Britain's monarchs, and as the setting for coronations and other great pageants. Within its walls can be seen some of the most glorious examples of medieval architecture in London. It also contains one of the most impressive collections of tombs and monuments in the world. Half national church, half national museum, the abbey occupies a unique place in the British national consciousness.

★ **Flying Buttresses**
The massive flying buttresses help transfer the great weight of the 31-m (102-ft) high nave.

Main Entrance
The stonework here, like this carving of a dragon, is Victorian.

The North Transept has three chapels on the east side containing some of the Abbey's finest monuments.

★ **West Front Towers**
These towers, completed in 1745, were designed by Nicholas Hawksmoor.

STAR FEATURES

★ West Front Towers

★ Flying Buttresses

★ The Nave viewed from the West End

★ The Lady Chapel

★ Chapter House

★ **The Nave viewed from the West End**
At 10 m (35 ft) wide, the nave is comparatively narrow, but it is the highest in England.

The Cloisters, built mainly in the 13th and 14th centuries, link the Abbey church with the other buildings.

St Edward's Chapel
houses Edward the
Confessor's shrine and
the tombs of other English
medieval monarchs. The
royal Coronation Chair is
located just outside.

★ The Lady Chapel
*The chapel, consecrated
in 1519, has a superb
vaulted ceiling and choir
stalls dating from 1512.*

VISITORS' CHECKLIST

Broad Sanctuary SW1. **Map** 13
B5. **Tel** 020-7222 5152. 🚇 St
James's Park, Westminster.
🚌 3, 11, 12, 24, 29, 53, 70, 77,
77a, 88, 109, 148, 159, 170,
211. 🚆 Victoria, Waterloo.
🚢 Westminster Pier. **Cloisters**
open 8am–6pm daily. **Abbey,
including Royal Chapels,
Poets' Corner, Choir,
Statesmen's Aisle, Nave open**
9.30am–3.45pm Mon, Tue, Thu,
Fri (last adm: 3.45pm), 9.30am–
6pm Wed, 9.30am–1.45pm Sat
(last adm: 12.45pm). NB: the
abbey closes for special services
and other events. Phone to check.
**Chapter House, Pyx Chamber
and Museum open** 10.30am–
4pm daily. **Adm charge. College
Garden open** Apr–Sep: 10am–
6pm Tue–Thu; Oct–Mar: 10am–
4pm Tue–Thu. **Evensong** 5pm
Mon–Fri, 3pm Sat, Sun. 🚫 ♿
limited. 📷 🍴 🏪 🏪 **Concerts.**
www.westminster-abbey.org

★ Chapter House
*This octagonal structure is
worth seeing for its 13th-
century tiles.*

The South Transept
contains "Poets' Corner",
where memorials to famous
literary figures can be seen.

Museum

TIMELINE

1050 New Benedic-tine abbey church begun by Edward the Confessor	**1376** Henry Yevele begins rebuilding the nave	*13th-century tile from the Chapter House*		**1838** Queen Victoria's coronation	
1000	1200	1400	1600	1800	2000
	1245 New church begun to the designs of Henry of Rheims	**1269** Body of Edward the Confessor moved to new shrine in the abbey	**1540** Monastery dissolved	**1745** West towers completed	**1953** Most recent coronation in the abbey: Elizabeth II's

A Guided Tour of Westminster Abbey

The abbey's interior presents an exceptionally diverse array of architectural and sculptural styles. These range from the austere French Gothic of the nave to the stunning complexity of Henry VII's Tudor chapel and the riotous invention of the later 18th-century monuments. Many British monarchs were buried here; some of their tombs are deliberately plain, while others are lavishly decorated. At the same time, there are monuments to a number of Britain's greatest public figures – ranging from politicians to poets – crowded into the aisles and transepts.

HISTORICAL PLAN OF THE ABBEY

The first abbey church was established as early as the 10th century, when St Dunstan brought a group of Benedictine monks to the area. The present structure dates largely from the 13th century; the new, French-influenced design was begun in 1245 at the behest of Henry III. Because of its unique role as the royal coronation church, the abbey survived Henry VIII's mid-16th-century onslaught on Britain's monastic buildings.

KEY

- ☐ Built between 1055–1350
- ☐ Added from 1350–1420
- ☐ Built between 1500–1512
- ☐ Towers completed 1745
- ☐ Restored after 1850

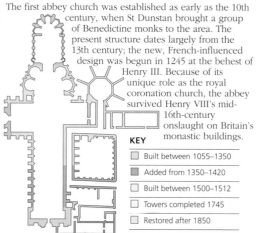

② **Nightingale Memorial**
The North Transept chapels contain some of the abbey's finest monuments – this one, by Roubiliac, is for Lady Elizabeth Nightingale (1761).

Main entrance

① **The Nave**
The nave is 10.5 m (35 ft) wide and 31 m (102 ft) high. It took 150 years to build.

The Choir houses a gilded 1840s screen, which contains remnants of the 13th-century original.

The Jericho Parlour, added in the early 16th century, contains some fine panelling.

The Jerusalem Chamber has a 17th-century fireplace, fine tapestries and an interesting painted ceiling. It is closed to the public.

The Deanery, home of the Dean of Westminster, was once the monastic abbot's house. It is closed to the public.

⑧ **Grave of the Unknown Warrior**
The body of an unknown soldier was brought from the battlefields of World War I and buried here in 1920. His grave commemorates all who have lost their lives in war. It is closed to the public.

CORONATION
The abbey has been the fittingly sumptuous setting for all royal coronations since 1066. The last occupant of the Coronation Chair was the present monarch, Elizabeth II. She was crowned in 1953 in the first televised coronation.

The Chapel of St John the Baptist is full of tombs dating from the 14th to the 19th centuries.

St Faith Chapel contains works of art that date back to the 13th century.

③ **Coronation Chair**
Constructed in 1301, this is the chair on which monarchs have been crowned since 1308.

④ **Tomb of Elizabeth I**
Inside Henry VII's Chapel you will find Elizabeth I's (reigned 1558–1603) huge tomb. It also houses the body of her sister, "Bloody" Mary I.

⑤ **Henry VII Chapel**
The undersides of the choir stalls, dating from 1512, are beautifully carved with exotic and fantastic creatures.

⑥ **St Edward's Chapel**
The shrine of the Saxon king Edward the Confessor and the tombs of many medieval monarchs are here.

The Pyx Chamber's gaunt columns date from the 11th century.

⑦ **Poets' Corner**
Take time to explore the memorials to countless literary giants, such as Shakespeare and Dickens, which are gathered here.

Dean's Yard entrance

KEY
- - - Tour route

Banqueting House ⓫

Whitehall SW1. **Map** 13 B4. **Tel** 020-7839 8918. Ⓔ *Charing Cross, Embankment, Westminster.* **Open** *10am–5pm Mon–Sat (last adm 4.30pm).* **Closed** *Sun, public hols, 24 Dec–1 Jan; for functions (phone first).* **Adm charge.** 🎥 🖫 www.hrp.org.uk

This delightful building is of great architectural importance. It was the first in central London to embody the Classical Palladian style that designer Inigo Jones brought back from his travels in Italy. Completed in 1622, its disciplined stone facade marked a startling change from the Elizabethans' fussy turrets and unrestrained external decoration. It was the sole survivor of the fire that destroyed most of the old Whitehall Palace in 1698.

The ceiling paintings by Rubens, a complex allegory on the exaltation of James I, were commissioned by his son, Charles I, in 1630. This blatant glorification of royalty was despised by Oliver Cromwell and the Parliamentarians, who executed King Charles I on a scaffold outside Banqueting House in 1649. Ironically, Charles II celebrated his restoration to the throne here 11 years later. The building is occasionally used for official functions.

Mounted sentries stationed outside Horse Guards Parade

Horse Guards Parade ⓬

Whitehall SW1. **Map** 13 B4. **Tel** 0870-588 7711. Ⓔ *Westminster, Charing Cross, Embankment.* **Open** *8am–6pm daily.* **Changing the Guard** *11.30am Mon–Sat, 10am Sun.* **Dismounting Ceremony** *4pm daily. Times for both are subject to change (phone for details).* **Trooping the Colour** *see* **Ceremonial London** *pp52–5.*

Once Henry VIII's tiltyard (tournament ground), nowadays the Changing of the Guard takes place here every morning. The elegant buildings, completed in 1755, were designed by William Kent. On the left is the Old Treasury, also by Kent, and Dover House, completed in 1758 and now used as the Scottish Office.

Nearby is a trace of the "real tennis" court where Henry VIII is said to have played the ancient precursor of modern lawn tennis. On the opposite side, the view is dominated by the ivy-covered Citadel. This is a bomb-proof structure that was erected in 1940 beside the Admiralty. During World War II it was used as a communications headquarters by the Navy.

Whitehall Theatre ⓭

Whitehall SW1. **Map** 13 B3. **Tel** 0870-060 6632. Ⓔ *Charing Cross.* **Open** *for performances only. See* **Entertainment** *pp344–5.*

Detail of a Whitehall Theatre box

Built in 1930, the plain white front seems to emulate the Cenotaph *(see p74)* at the other end of the street but, inside, the theatre boasts fine Art Deco detailing. The theatre now comprises two new intimate spaces, now housing the Trafalgar Studios.

Queen Anne's Gate ⓮

SW1. **Map** 13 A5. Ⓔ *St James's Park.*

The spacious terraced houses at the west end of this well-preserved enclave date from 1704 and are notable for the ornate canopies over their front doors. At the other end are houses built some 70 years later, sporting blue plaques that record former residents, such as Lord Palmerston, the Victorian Prime Minister. Until recently, the British Secret Service, MI5, was allegedly based in this unlikely spot. A small statue of Queen Anne stands in front of the wall separating Nos. 13 and 15. To the west, situated at the corner of Petty France, Sir Basil Spence's Home Office building (1976)

Panels from the Rubens ceiling, Banqueting House

is an architectural incongruity. Cockpit Steps, leading down to Birdcage Walk, mark the site of a 17th-century venue for the popular, yet blood-thirsty, sport of cockfighting.

Guards Museum **⑮**

Birdcage Walk SW1. **Map** 13 A5. **Tel** 020-7414 3428. ⊖ St James's Park. **Open** 10am– 4pm daily (last adm: 3.30pm). **Closed** Christmas, ceremonies. **Adm charge** (free for under-16s). ⬛ ♿ ⬛ www.armymuseums.org.uk

Entered from Birdcage Walk, the museum is under the parade ground of Wellington Barracks, headquarters of the five Guards regiments. A must for military buffs, the museum uses tableaux and dioramas to illustrate various battles in which the Guards have taken part, from the English Civil War (1642–8) to the present. Weapons and row after row of colourful uniforms are on display, as well as a fascin-ating collection of models.

St James's Park Station **⑯**

55 Broadway SW1. **Map** 13 A5. ⊖ St James's Park.

Epstein sculpture outside St James's Park Station

The station is built into Broadway House, Charles Holden's 1929 headquarters for London Transport. It is notable for its sculptures by Jacob Epstein and reliefs by Henry Moore and Eric Gill.

Blewcoat School **⑰**

23 Caxton St SW1. **Map** 13 A5. **Tel** 020- 7222 2877. ⊖ St James's Park. **Open** 10am –5.30pm Mon– Wed, Fri, 10am –7pm Thu. ⬛

Statue of a Blewcoat pupil above the Caxton Street entrance

A red-brick gem hemmed in by the office towers of Victoria Street, it was built in 1709 as a charity school to teach pupils how to "read, write, cast accounts and the catechism". It remained as a school until 1939, then became an army store during World War II and was bought by the National Trust in 1954. The beautifully proportioned interior now serves as a National Trust gift shop.

Westminster Cathedral **⑱**

Ashley Place SW1. **Map** 20 F1. **Tel** 020-7798 9055. ⊖ Victoria. **Open** 7am–7pm Mon–Fri, 8am–7pm Sat & Sun. **Adm charge** for bell tower lift (Apr–Nov: 9am–5pm daily. Dec–Mar: 9am–5pm Thu–Sun). ✝ 5.30pm Mon–Fri, 10.30am Sat & Sun, sung Mass. ♿ ⬛ ⬛ www.westminstercathedral.org.uk

One of London's rare Byzantine buildings, it was designed by John Francis Bentley for the Catholic diocese and completed in 1903 on the site of a former prison. Its 87-m (285-ft) high, red-brick tower, with horizontal stripes of white stone, stands out on the skyline in sharp contrast to the Abbey nearby. A restful piazza on the north

side provides a good view of the cathedral from Victoria Street. The rich interior decor-ation, with marble of varying colours and intricate mosaics, makes the domes above the nave seem incongruous. They were left bare because the project ran out of money.

Eric Gill's dramatic reliefs of the 14 Stations of the Cross, created during World War I, adorn the pier of the nave, which is the widest in Britain. The organ is one of the finest in Europe, and there are free recitals every Sunday afternoon at 4.45pm.

St John's, Smith Square **⑲**

Smith Sq SW1. **Map** 21 B1. **Tel** 020-7222 1061. ⊖ Westminster. Box office open 10am–5pm Mon–Fri. Not open to public except for concerts. ⬛ ♿ phone first. ⬛ www.sjss.org.uk

Baroque interior of St John's, Smith Square

Described by artist and art historian Sir Hugh Casson as one of the masterpieces of English Baroque architecture, Thomas Archer's plump church, with its turrets at each corner, looks as if it is trying to burst from the confines of the square, and rather over-powers the pleasing 18th-century houses on its north side. Today it is principally a concert hall. It has an accident-prone history: com-pleted in 1728, it was burned down in 1742, struck by light-ning in 1773 and destroyed by a World War II bomb in 1941. There is a reasonably priced basement restaurant that is open daily for lunch and on concert evenings.

Tate Britain **⑳**

See pp82–5.

Tate Britain ⓴

Formerly the Tate Gallery, Tate Britain displays the world's largest collection of British art from the 16th to the 21st century. The international modern art once housed here is now held at Tate Modern *(see pp178–181)*. In the Clore Galleries is the magnificent Turner Bequest, left to the nation by the great landscape artist J M W Turner in 1851. The Clore Galleries have their own entrance, giving direct access to the Turner Collection and allowing a full appreciation of Sir James Stirling's Post-Modernist design for the building.

Loan exhibitions
covering aspects of British art will be installed here and on the lower floor during 2007.

Main floor

Lower floor

Manton St entrance

The Saltonstall Family *(1637)*
David des Granges's life-size family portrait includes the dead first Lady Saltonstall as the second shows off her new baby.

★ **Ophelia** *(1851–2)*
Taken from Shakespeare's play Hamlet, *the scene of the drowning of Ophelia by Pre-Raphaelite John Millais is one of the most famous – and popular – . paintings at Tate Britain.*

GALLERY GUIDE

The permanent collection displays occupy three quarters of the main floor. Starting in the northwest corner, the displays follow a broad chronological sweep from the early 16th century to the present. Each room explores an historical theme or is devoted to a major artist. Major loan exhibitions are installed in the remaining quarter of the main floor and in the lower-floor galleries.

KEY TO FLOORPLAN

- ☐ 1500–1800
- ☐ 1800–1900
- ☐ 1900–1960
- ☐ 1960 to present
- ☐ Duveen Sculpture Gallery
- ☐ Clore Galleries
- ☐ Loan Exhibitions
- ☐ Non-exhibition space

Carnation, Lily, Lily, Rose *(1885–6)*
John Singer Sargent (1856–1925) moved to Britain from Paris in 1885 and adopted some of the Impressionist techniques established by his peronal friend, Claude Monet. The title of this work is taken from a popular song of the time.

THE ART OF GOOD FOOD

On the lower floor Tate Britain boasts a café and an espresso bar, as well as a restaurant. Celebrated murals by Rex Whistler adorn the walls of the restaurant, telling the tale of the mythical inhabitants of Epicuriana and their expedition in search of rare foods. The extensive wine list has won awards and is known for its fair pricing. Open for lunch only.

VISITORS' CHECKLIST

Millbank SW1. **Map** 21 B2.
Tel *020-7887 8000.* 020-7887 8008. Pimlico.
C10, 36, 77a, 88, 159, 185, 507.
Victoria, Vauxhall. **Open**
10am–5.50pm daily. **Closed**
24–26 Dec. **Adm charge** for
special exhibitions only.
Atterbury St.
Lectures, film presentations, exhibitions, children's activities. www.tate.org.uk

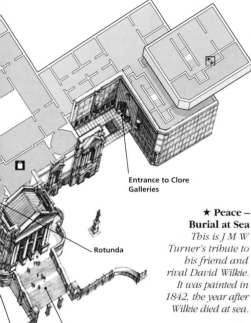

Entrance to Clore Galleries

Rotunda

Millbank entrance

Stairs to lower floor

Lady of Shalott *(1888)*
J W Waterhouse's work reflects the Pre-Raphaelite fascination with Arthurian myth.

★ **Peace – Burial at Sea**
This is J M W Turner's tribute to his friend and rival David Wilkie. It was painted in 1842, the year after Wilkie died at sea.

★ **Three Studies for Figures at the Base of a Crucifixion**
(1944, detail)
Francis Bacon's famous triptych encapsulates an anguished vision of human existence. When first displayed, its savagery deeply shocked audiences.

STAR PAINTINGS

★ Peace – Burial at Sea by Turner

★ Ophelia by John Millais

★ Three Studies for Figures at the Base of a Crucifixion by Bacon

Exploring Tate Britain

Tate Britain draws its displays from the massive Tate Collection. The variety of works on show, coupled with a rigorous programme of loan exhibitions, results in a selection to suit all tastes – from Elizabethan portraiture to cutting-edge installation. The gallery has recently undergone major renovation, to stunning effect. The displays are changed frequently to explore many different aspects of the history and art of Britain.

The Cholmondeley Sisters (c. 1600–10), British School

1500–1800

This group of galleries covers a period of dramatic change in British history, from the Tudors and Stuarts through to the age of Thomas Gainsborough. "Hogarth and the Art of Conversation" includes important works by one of Britain's greatest painters, known for his biting satire on the lifestyle and beliefs of his contemporaries. By contrast, "The Grand Manner" shows dramatic large-scale paintings by artists such as Joshua Reynolds, the head of the newly established Royal Academy. Landscape painting lies at the heart of the revolution in British painting during the nineteenth century, and "British Landscape" shows how images of the countryside changed ideas not only about art, but about what it means to be British. The last room in this section is devoted to a series of changing displays about the poet and artist William Blake.

Satan Smiting Job with Sore Boils (c.1826) by William Blake

1800–1900

The end of the eighteenth century and the first half of the nineteenth saw dramatic expansion and change in the arts in Britain. New themes began to emerge, and artists started working on a much larger scale as they competed with each other for attention on the walls of public exhibitions. "Romantic Painting" includes monumental canvases by John Martin, Thomas Lawrence and John Singleton Copley, as well as celebrated works by David Wilkie. This is followed by a series of three rooms that tell the story of Victorian art. Storytelling was at the heart of the Victorians' belief in the power of art to convey moral messages, and "Victorian Narrative" includes such important works as William Powell Frith's *The Derby Day*, as well as Augustus Egg's series *Past and Present*. "The Pre-Raphaelite Brotherhood" brings together work by perhaps the most popular group of artists at Tate Britain: it includes John Everett Millais's *Ophelia* and William Holman Hunt's *Awakening Conscience*. The last in this sequence of three rooms, "Victorian Spectacle", is a dramatic display of painting and sculpture from the late Victorian period, including John Singer Sargent's haunting evocation of young girls in a garden at twilight in *Carnation, Lily, Lily, Rose*.

TURNER AT THE CLORE GALLERIES

The Turner Bequest comprises some 300 oil paintings and about 20,000 watercolours and drawings received by the nation from the great landscape painter J M W Turner after his death in 1851. Turner's will had specified that a gallery be built to house his pictures and this was finally done in 1987 with the opening of the Clore Galleries. Most of the oil paintings are on view in the main galleries, while the watercolours are the subject of changing displays.

The Scarlet Sunset: A Town on a River (c. 1830–40)

Mr. and Mrs. Clark and Percy (1970–1) by David Hockney

1900–1960

The modern section of the gallery begins with the early twentieth century. "Modern Figures" looks at artists' fascination with modern cities: cosmopolitan, noisy places with crowded streets, continually changing architecture and fast, mechanized transport, as well as new places of entertainment. It includes Jacob Epstein's *Torso in Metal from "The Rock Drill"*, a machine-like robot, visored and menacing, that became a symbol of the new age, as well as the work of Wyndham Lewis and his Vorticist group, who saw the artist at the still centre of the vortex of modern life.

Work by celebrated British sculptors, such as Barbara Hepworth and Henry Moore, can also be seen in this section. Paintings by two of the most famous, and disturbing, modern British artists are also on display here: Francis Bacon, whose *Three Studies for Figures at the Base of a Crucifixion* depicts three mutant organisms in agony, confined in an apparently hostile and godless world; and Lucian Freud, whose works at Tate Britain include his portrait of *Francis Bacon*.

Recumbent Figure (1938) by Henry Moore

1960 TO PRESENT

From the 1960s, Tate's funding for the purchase of works began to increase substantially, while artistic activity continued to pick up speed, encouraged by public funding. As a result, the Tate Collection is particularly rich on this time period, which means that the frequent rotation of displays is necessary.

There is, however, one room devoted to "Pop", one of the liveliest developments of British art in the 1960s, which focuses in particular on the beginnings of the movement through iconic works by artists such as Peter Blake, the early work of David Hockney, and Richard Hamilton.

A revolt against this movement took place at the end of the 1960s, with the emergence of Conceptual artists such as Gilbert and George, known as the Living Sculptures, and Richard Long, who created a whole new approach to landscape painting by importing the land itself into the gallery.

Conceptual art in turn was rejected at the start of the 1980s by the School of London painters, including Howard Hodgkin, Frank Auerbach and R B Kitaj, while Tony Cragg, Richard Deacon and Antony Gormley pioneered a new kind of sculpture.

The 1990s saw a new surge in British art. Most recent British movements are well represented at Tate Britain. These include the work of the so-called Young British Artists (YBAs), who include Damian Hirst, perhaps the most notorious, as well as Tracey Emin and Sarah Lucas. Cornelia Parker brings a more thoughtful and poetic approach to the YBAs' characteristic use of found objects, as in her work *Cold Dark Matter: An Exploded View*. Many contemporary British artists, including Tacita Dean, Douglas Gordon, Sam Taylor-Wood, Steve McQueen and the Wilson twins, use film and video as their medium – a major development of recent years and the subject of a number of special displays at Tate Britain recently.

The frequently changing displays at Tate Britain include wider surveys as well as rooms devoted to single artists, and feature important works newly acquired by Tate. Special ArtNow space is devoted to new work by the latest up-and-coming artists.

Cold Dark Matter: An Exploded View (1991) by Cornelia Parker

LONDON AREA BY AREA

PICCADILLY AND ST JAMES'S

Piccadilly is the main artery of the West End. Once called Portugal Street, it acquired its present name from the ruffs, or pickadills, worn by 17th-century dandies. St James's still bears traces of the 18th century, when it surrounded the royal residences, and denizens of the court and society shopped and disported

Buckingham Palace decorative lock

themselves here. Two shops in St James's Street – James Lock the hatter and Berry Bros. & Rudd vintners – recall that era. Fortnum and Mason, on Piccadilly, has served high-quality food for nearly 300 years. Mayfair to the north is still the most fashionable address in London, while Piccadilly Circus marks the start of Soho.

SIGHTS AT A GLANCE

Historic Streets and Buildings
Piccadilly Circus ❶
Albany ❸
Burlington Arcade ❺
Ritz Hotel ❻
Spencer House ❼
St James's Palace ❽
St James's Square ❾
Royal Opera Arcade ❿
Pall Mall ⓫
The Mall ⓮
Marlborough House ⓯
Clarence House ⓱
Lancaster House ⓲
Buckingham Palace pp94–5 ⓳
Royal Mews ㉑
Wellington Arch ㉒
Shepherd Market ㉔

Museums and Galleries
Royal Academy of Arts ❹
Institute of Contemporary Arts ⓬
Queen's Gallery ⑳
Royal Mews ㉑
Apsley House ㉓
Faraday Museum ㉖

Churches
St James's Church ❷
Queen's Chapel ⓰

Parks and Gardens
St James's Park ⓭
Green Park ㉕

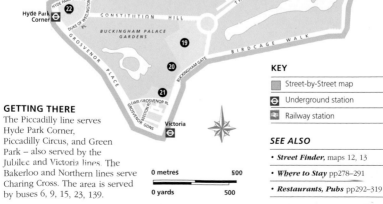

KEY

▨	Street-by-Street map
⊖	Underground station
⇄	Railway station

SEE ALSO

- *Street Finder,* maps 12, 13
- *Where to Stay* pp278–291
- *Restaurants, Pubs* pp292–319

GETTING THERE

The Piccadilly line serves Hyde Park Corner, Piccadilly Circus, and Green Park – also served by the Jubilee and Victoria lines. The Bakerloo and Northern lines serve Charing Cross. The area is served by buses 6, 9, 15, 23, 139.

0 metres 500
0 yards 500

◁ **Piccadilly Arcade with its many fine shops**

Street-by-Street: Piccadilly and St James's

As soon as Henry VIII built St James's Palace in the 1530s, the area around it became the centre of fashionable London, and it has remained so ever since. The most influential people in the land strut importantly along its historic streets as they press on with the vital business of lunching in their clubs, discussing matters of pith and moment and brandishing their gold cards in the capital's most exclusive stores, or paying a visit to one of the many art galleries.

★ Royal Academy of Arts
Sir Joshua Reynolds founded the Academy in 1768. Now it mounts large popular exhibitions **4**

★ Burlington Arcade
Uniformed beadles discourage unruly behaviour in this 19th-century mall **5**

The Ritz Hotel
Named after César Ritz, and opened in 1906, it still lives up to his name **6**

Albany
This has been one of London's smartest addresses since it opened in 1803 **3**

Fortnum and Mason
was founded in 1707 by one of Queen Anne's footmen (*see p321*).

Spencer House
An ancestor of Princess Diana built this house in 1766 **7**

St James's Palace
This Tudor palace is still the Court's official headquarters **8**

REGEN

SACKVILLE STREET

OLD BOND STREET

PICCADILLY

JERMYN

ST JAMES'S

STREET

RYDER ST

KING

ST JAMES'S PLACE

CATHERINE WHEEL YARD

STABLE YARD

To The Mall

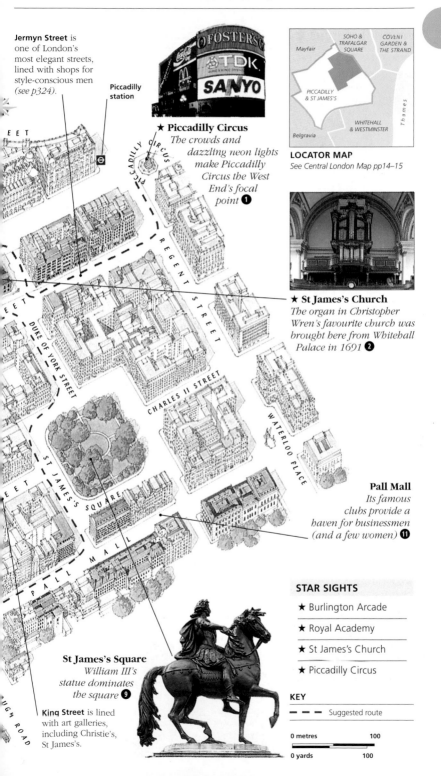

Jermyn Street is one of London's most elegant streets, lined with shops for style-conscious men *(see p324).*

Piccadilly station

★ **Piccadilly Circus**
The crowds and dazzling neon lights make Piccadilly Circus the West End's focal point ❶

LOCATOR MAP
See Central London Map pp14–15

★ **St James's Church**
The organ in Christopher Wren's favourite church was brought here from Whitehall Palace in 1691 ❷

Pall Mall
Its famous clubs provide a haven for businessmen (and a few women) ⓫

St James's Square
William III's statue dominates the square ❾

King Street is lined with art galleries, including Christie's, St James's.

STAR SIGHTS

★ Burlington Arcade

★ Royal Academy

★ St James's Church

★ Piccadilly Circus

KEY

– – – Suggested route

0 metres   100

0 yards   100

Piccadilly Circus ❶

W1. **Map** 13 A3. ⊖ *Piccadilly Circus*

Alfred Gilbert's statue of Eros

For years people have congregated beneath the symbolic figure of Eros, originally intended as an angel of mercy but renamed after the Greek god of love. Poised delicately with his bow, Eros has become almost a trade mark for the capital. It was erected in 1892 as a memorial to the Earl of Shaftesbury, the Victorian philanthropist. Part of Nash's master plan for Regent Street, Piccadilly Circus has been considerably altered in recent years and consists for the most part of shopping malls. One of them can be found behind the façade of the London Pavilion (1885), once a popular music hall.
The circus has London's gaudiest array of neon advertising signs marking the entrance to the city's lively entertainment district with cinemas, theatres, night clubs, restaurants and pubs.

St James's Church ❷

197 Piccadilly W1. **Map** 13 A3. **Tel** *020-7734 4511.* ⊖ *Piccadilly Circus.* **Open** *8am–6.30pm daily.* **Craft market** *9am–6pm Wed–Sat,* **antiques market** *9am–6pm Tue.* ♿ *access from Jermyn St.* ▢ **Concerts, talks, events.** www.st-james-piccadilly.org

Among the many churches Wren designed *(see p47)*, this is said to be one of his favourites. It has been altered over the years and was half wrecked by a bomb in 1940, but it maintains its essential features from 1684 – the tall, arched windows, thin spire (a 1966 fibreglass replica of the original) and a light, dignified interior. The ornate screen behind the altar is one of the finest works of the 17th-century master carver Grinling Gibbons, who also made the exquisite marble font, with a scene depicting Adam and Eve standing by the Tree of Life. Artist and poet William Blake and Prime Minister Pitt the Elder were both baptized here. More of Gibbons's carvings can be seen above the grandiose organ, made for Whitehall Palace chapel but installed here in 1691. Today the church has a full calendar of events, and houses a popular café.

Albany ❸

Albany Court Yard, Piccadilly W1. **Map** 12 F3. ⊖ *Green Park, Piccadilly Circus.* **Closed** *to the public.*

These desirable and discreet bachelor apartments, half hidden through an entrance off Piccadilly, were built in 1803 by Henry Holland. Notable residents have included the poet Lord Byron, novelist Graham Greene, two Prime Ministers (William Gladstone and Edward Heath) and the actor Terence Stamp. Married men were admitted in 1878 but could not bring their wives to live with them until 1919. Women are now allowed to live here in their own right.

Byron lived in The Albany

Royal Academy of Arts ❹

Burlington House, Piccadilly W1. **Map** 12 F3. **Tel** *020-7300 8000.* ⊖ *Piccadilly Circus, Green Park.* **Open** *10am–6pm Sun–Thu, 10am–10pm Fri & Sat.* **Closed** *24–25 Dec.* **Adm charge.** ⊘ ♿ 🖉 *by appt.* 🕭 🍴 🖥 📷 www.royalacademy.org.uk

Michelangelo's Madonnna and Child

The courtyard in front of Burlington House, one of the West End's few surviving mansions from the early 18th century, is often crammed with people waiting to get into one of the prestigious visiting art exhibitions on show at the Royal Academy (founded 1768). The famous annual summer exhibition, which has now been held for over 200 years, comprises around 1,200 new works by both established and unknown artists. Any artist, regardless of background or talent, may submit work.
The airy Sackler Galleries (1991), designed by Norman Foster, show visiting exhibitions. There are permanent items in the sculpture promenade outside the galleries, notably a Michelangelo relief of the Madonna and Child (1505). The exceptional permanent collection (not all on display) includes one work by each current and former Academician; the newly restored Madejski Rooms display the highlights. There is a good shop on the first floor selling cards and other items that are designed by Academy members for the RA.

Burlington Arcade **5**

Piccadilly W1. **Map** 12 F3. ⊖ *Green Park, Piccadilly Circus. See **Shops and Markets** p328.*

This is one of four 19th-century arcades of small shops which sell traditional British luxuries. (The Princes and Piccadilly Arcades are on the south side of Piccadilly, while the Royal Opera Arcade is off Pall Mall.) It was built for Lord Cavendish in 1819 to stop rubbish being thrown into his garden. The arcade is still patrolled by beadles who make sure an atmosphere of refinement is maintained. They have authority to eject anyone who sings, whistles, runs or opens an umbrella; those powers are infrequently invoked now, perhaps because the dictates of commerce take precedence over those of decorum.

Ritz Hotel **6**

Piccadilly W1. **Map** 12 F3. **Tel** 020-7493 8181. ⊖ *Green Park.* **Open** *to non-residents for tea or restaurant (book ahead).* ♿ *(See p287.)* www.theritzlondon.com

Cesar Ritz, the famed Swiss hotelier who inspired the adjective "ritzy", had virtually retired by the time this hotel was built and named after him in 1906. The colonnaded frontal aspect of the imposing château-style building was meant to suggest Paris, where the very grandest and most fashionable hotels were to be

The exquisite Palm Room of Spencer House

found around the turn of the century. It maintains its Edwardian air of opulence and is a popular stop, among those who are suitably dressed (no jeans or trainers; jacket and tie for men), for afternoon tea, with daily servings in the Palm Court at 11.30am, 1.30, 3.30 and 5.30pm. Champagne tea is served at 7.30pm.

Spencer House **7**

27 St James's Pl SW1. **Map** 12 F4. **Tel** 020-7499 8620. ⊖ *Green Park.* **Open** *10.30am–5.45pm Sun (last adm: 4.45pm). Garden open one Sunday in June 2pm–5pm.* **Closed** *Jan & Aug.* **Adm charge. Children** *not under 10.* ⊘ ♿ 📷 *compulsory.* www.spencerhouse.co.uk

This Palladian palace, built in 1766 for the first Earl Spencer, an ancestor of the late Princess of Wales, has been completely restored to its 18th-century splendour (thanks to an £18

million renovation project). It contains some wonderful paintings and contemporary furniture; one of the highlights is the beautifully decorated Painted Room. The house is open to the public for guided tours, receptions and meetings.

St James's Tudor gatehouse

St James's Palace **8**

Pall Mall SW1. **Map** 12 F4. ⊖ *Green Park.* **Not open** *to the public.*

Built by Henry VIII in the late 1530s on the site of a former leper hospital, it was a primary royal residence only briefly, mainly during the reign of Elizabeth I and during the late 17th and early 18th centuries. In 1952 Queen Elizabeth II made her first speech as queen here, and foreign ambassadors are still officially accredited to the Court of St James's. Its northern gatehouse, seen from St James's Street, is one of London's most evocative Tudor landmarks. Behind it the palace buildings are now occupied by privileged Crown servants.

Afternoon tea served in the opulent Palm Court of the Ritz

Royal Opera Arcade

St James's Square ❾

SW1. **Map** 13 A3. 🚇 *Green Park, Piccadilly Circus.*

One of London's earliest squares, it was laid out in the 1670s and lined by exclusive houses for those whose business made it vital for them to live near St James's Palace. Many of the buildings date from the 18th and 19th centuries and have had many illustrious residents. During World War II Generals Eisenhower and de Gaulle both had headquarters here.

Today No. 10 on the north side is Chatham House (1736), home of the Royal Institute for International Affairs and, in the northwest corner, can be found the London Library (1896), a private lending library founded in 1841 by historian Thomas Carlyle *(see p196)* and others. The lovely gardens in the middle contain an equestrian statue of William III, here since 1808.

Royal Opera Arcade ❿

SW1. **Map** 13 A3. 🚇 *Piccadilly Circus.*

London's first shopping arcade was designed by John Nash and completed in 1818, behind the Haymarket Opera House (now called Her Majesty's Theatre). It beat the Burlington Arcade *(see p91)* by a year or so. The traditional shops that used to be based here have recently

moved on: Farlows, selling shooting and fishing equipment, and the famous Hunter's green Wellington boots, are now nearby, at No. 9 Pall Mall.

Pall Mall ⓫

SW1. **Map** 13 A4. 🚇 *Charing Cross, Green Park, Piccadilly Circus.*

The Duke of Wellington (1842): a frequent visitor to Pall Mall

This dignified street is named from the game of palle-maille, a cross between croquet and golf, which was played here in the early 17th century. For more than 150 years Pall Mall has been at the heart of London's clubland. Here exclusive gentlemen's clubs were formed to provide members with a refuge from their womenfolk.

The clubhouses now amount to a text book of the most fashionable architects of the era. From the east end, on the left is the colonnaded entrance to No. 116, Nash's United Services Club (1827). This was the favourite club of the Duke of Wellington and

now houses the Institute of Directors. Facing it, on the other side of Waterloo Place, is the Athenaeum (No. 107), designed three years later by Decimus Burton, and long the power house of the British establishment. Next door are two clubs by Sir Charles Barry, architect of the Houses of Parliament *(see pp72–3)*; the Travellers' is at No. 106 and the Reform at No. 104. The clubs' stately interiors are well preserved but only members and their guests are admitted.

Institute of Contemporary Arts ⓬

The Mall SW1. **Map** 13 B3. **Tel** 020-7930 3647. 🚇 *Charing Cross, Piccadilly Circus.* **Open** *noon–10.30pm Sun, noon–11pm Mon, noon–1am Tue–Sat. (Exhibition space closes 7.30pm, bookshop 9pm.)* **Closed** *24–26, 31 Dec, 1 Jan, public hols.* **Adm charge.** 🔊 *(cinema and lower gallery) phone first.* ▢ 🔢 ▢ **Concerts, theatre, dance, lectures, films, exhibitions. See Entertainment** *pp350–51.* **www**.ica.org.uk

The Institute (ICA) was established in 1947 in an effort to offer British artists some of the facilities which were available to artists at The Museum of Modern Art in New York. Originally on Dover Street, it has been situated in John Nash's Classical Carlton House Terrace (1833) since 1968. With its entrance on The Mall, this extensive warren contains a cinema, auditorium, bookshop, art gallery, bar and restaurant. It also offers plays, concerts and lectures. Non-members pay a charge.

Institute of Contemporary Arts, Carlton House Terrace

St James's Park ⓭

SW1. **Map** 13 A4. **Tel** 020-7298
2000. 🚇 *St James's Park.* **Open**
dawn to dusk daily. 🍴 **Open** *daily.*
♿ **Concerts** *twice daily on summer
weekends in good weather.* **Bird
collection.** **www.**royalparks.org.uk

In summer office workers
sunbathe between the dazzling
flower beds of this, the
capital's most ornamental park.
In winter overcoated civil
servants discuss affairs of state
as they stroll by the lake and
eye its ducks, geese and
pelicans. Originally a marsh,
the park was drained by Henry
VIII and incorporated into his
hunting grounds. Later Charles
II redesigned it for pedestrian
pleasures, with an aviary along
its southern edge (hence
Birdcage Walk, the street
where the aviary was). It is
still a popular place to take
the air, with an appealing
view of Whitehall rooftops. In
the summer there are concerts
on the bandstand.

The Mall ⓮

SW1. **Map** 13 A4. 🚇 *Charing
Cross, Green Park, Piccadilly Circus.*

This broad triumphal approach
to Buckingham Palace was
created by Aston Webb when
he redesigned the front of the
palace and the Victoria Monument in 1911 *(see picture
p96)*. It follows the course of
the old path at the edge of St
James's Park, laid out in the
reign of Charles II when it
became London's most
fashionable promenade. On
the flagpoles down both sides
of The Mall fly national flags
of foreign heads of state
during official visits.

Marlborough
House ⓯

Pall Mall SW1. **Map** 13 A4. **Tel** 020-
7747 6491. 🚇 *St James's Park, Green
Park.* **Open** *one Sat in Sep only (phone
for details).* 📷 *By appointment.*

Marlborough House was
designed by Christopher
Wren *(see p47)* for the
Duchess of Marlborough, and

finished in 1711. It was
substantially enlarged in the
19th century and used by
members of the Royal Family.
From 1863 until he became
Edward VII in 1901, it was the
home of the Prince and
Princess of Wales and the
social centre of London. An
Art Nouveau memorial in the
Marlborough Road wall of the
house commemorates
Edward's queen, Alexandra.
The building now houses the
Commonwealth Secretariat.

Queen's Chapel ⓰

Marlborough Rd SW1. **Map** 13 A4.
Tel 020-7930 4832. 🚇 *Green Park.*
Open *Easter–July. Sun, Saints' Days.*

This exquisite work of the
architect Inigo Jones was built
for Charles I's French wife,
Henrietta Maria, in 1627, and
was the first Classical church
in England. It was initially
intended to be part of St

Queen's Chapel

James's Palace but is now
separated from it by
Marlborough Gate. George III
married his queen, Charlotte
of Mecklenburg-Strelitz (who
was to bear him 15 children),
here in 1761.
The interior of the chapel,
with its wonderful Annibale
Carracci altarpiece and glorious
17th-century fittings is open to
both regular worshippers and
visitors during the spring and
early summer.

Early summer in St James's Park

Buckingham Palace ⓳

Buckingham Palace is both office and home to the British monarchy. It is also used for ceremonial state occasions such as banquets for visiting heads of state. About 300 people work at the palace, including officers of the Royal Household and domestic staff.

John Nash converted the original Buckingham House into a palace for George IV (reigned 1820–30). Both he and his brother, William IV (reigned 1830–37), died before work was completed, and Queen Victoria was the first monarch to live at the palace. The present east front, facing The Mall, was added to Nash's conversion in 1913. The State Rooms are now open to the public in summer.

Music Room
State guests are presented and royal christenings take place in this room, which boasts a beautiful, original parquet floor by Nash.

The State Dining Room is where meals that are less formal than state banquets are held.

Kitchen and staff quarters

State Ballroom
The Edwardian French-style ballroom is used for state banquets and investitures.

Blue Drawing Room
Imitation onyx columns, created by John Nash, decorate this room.

Private post office

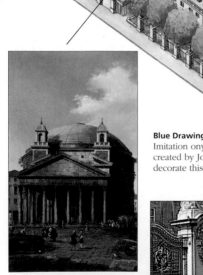

The Queen's Gallery
Artworks from the Queen's Collection (see p96), such as Canaletto's Rome: The Pantheon, *are often on display.*

Changing of the Guard
During the summer the palace guard is changed regularly in a colourful and musical military ceremony (see pp52–5).

VISITORS' CHECKLIST

SW1. Map 12 F5. Tel 020-7766
7300. ⊖ St James's Park, Victoria.
🚌 2B, 11, 16, 24, 25, 36, 38, 52,
73, 135, C1. 🚊 Victoria. State
rooms open Aug–Sep: 9.30am–
5.30pm daily. Adm charge. 📷
Changing of the Guard:
Apr–Jul: 11.30am daily; Aug–Mar:
alternate days. Tel 0906 866
3344 (Visit London). Tickets in
advance from www.royal.gov.uk

The garden is a haven for wild-life and is overlooked by most of the lavishly decorated state rooms at the back of the palace.

The White Drawing Room is where the Royal Family assemble before passing into the State Dining Room or Ball Room.

A swimming pool lies in the palace grounds, as does a private cinema.

The Throne Room is illuminated by seven magnificent chandeliers.

The Green Drawing Room is the first of the state rooms entered by guests at royal functions.

Queen's Audience Chamber
This is one of the Queen's 12 private rooms on the first floor of the palace.

The Royal Standard flies when the Queen is in residence.

View over The Mall
Traditionally, the Royal Family waves to crowds from the balcony.

WHO LIVES IN BUCKINGHAM PALACE?

The palace is the London residence of the Queen and her husband, the Duke of Edinburgh. Prince Edward also has an apartment here, as do Princess Anne and the Duke of York. About 50 domestic staff have rooms in the palace. There are more staff homes situated in the Royal Mews (see p96).

Clarence House ⑰

Stable Yard SW1. **Map** 12 F4. **Tel**
020-7766 7303. 🚇 *Green Park, St
James's Park.* **Open** *Aug–mid-Oct:
9am–7pm (book ahead).* 🔴 📷 📹
mandatory. **www**.royal.collection.org

Designed by John Nash for
William IV in 1827, this is
Prince Charles's London home.
Once a year, the public has
access to the opulent ground
floor – booking essential.

Lancaster House ⑱

Stable Yard SW1. **Map** 12 F4.
🚇 *Green Park, St James's Park.*
Not open to the public.

Lancaster House

This royal residence was built
for the Duke of York by
Benjamin Wyatt, architect of
Apsley House, in 1825. In
1848 Chopin played here for
Queen Victoria, Prince Albert
and the Duke of Wellington.
It is now a conference centre.

Buckingham Palace ⑲

See pp94–5.

Queen's Gallery ⑳

Buckingham Palace Rd SW1.
Map 12 F5. **Tel** *020-7766 7301.* 🚇
St James's Park, Victoria. **Open**
*10am–5.30pm daily (last adm:
4.30pm).* **Closed** *25 & 26 Dec.* **Adm
charge.** 🚫 **www**.royal.collection.org

The Queen possesses one
of the finest and most
valuable art collections in the
world, rich in the work of Old

Masters, including Vermeer
and Leonardo. The galleries
have been expanded in the
most extensive addition to
Buckingham Palace in 150
years. There is now three
and a half times more display
space and an impressive new
entrance gallery with a
striking columned portico.
  Among the gallery's seven
rooms, one is dedicated to a
permanent display of some of
the royal collection's masterpieces. Changing exhibitions
will be able to call on an
array of works, from fine art
to jewels, porcelain, furniture,
books and manuscripts.

Royal Mews ㉑

Buckingham Palace Rd SW1. **Map**
12 E5. **Tel** *020-7766 7302.* 🚇 *St
James's Park, Victoria.* **Open**
*Mar–Oct: 11am–4pm daily (last adm:
3.15pm). Subject to closure at short
notice (phone first).* **Adm charge.**
🔴 📷 📹 **www**.royal.collection.org

Although open for only a few
hours each day, the
Mews is worth catching
for all lovers of horses
and of royal pomp. The
stables and coach
houses, designed by
Nash in 1825,
accommodate the
horses and coaches
used by the Royal
Family on state
occasions. The star
exhibit is the gold
state coach, built
for George III in
1761, with fine
panels by Giovanni
Cipriani. Among the
other vehicles are the
Irish state

Fabergé egg, Queen's Gallery

coach, bought by Queen
Victoria for the State Opening
of Parliament; the open-
topped royal landau; and the
glass coach which was used
for royal weddings and for
transporting foreign ambassadors. The elaborate horses'
harnesses are also on display,
and so are some of the fine
animals that wear them. The
Mews has a new
exhibition that
explains its history and
current workings.
  Visitors may see carriages
being prepared for use or
limousines in action. A new
guided route around
the mews includes a
chance to view the
18th-century riding
school where the
horses are put
through their paces.
There is also a shop
here selling a range
of royal merchandise
and souvenirs, open
daily from 9.30am
until 5pm.

The Victoria Monument outside Buckingham Palace

Wellington Arch ㉒

SW1. **Map** 12 D4. **Tel** 020-7930
2726. Hyde Park Corner. **Open**
Mar–Oct: 10am–5pm Wed–Sun &
bank hols; Nov–Mar: 10am–4pm
Wed–Sun. **Closed** 24–26 Dec, 1 Jan.
Adm charge.
www.english-heritage.org.uk

After nearly a century of
debate about what to do with
the patch of land in front of
Apsley House, Wellington Arch,
designed by Decimus Burton,
was erected in 1828. The
sculpture, by Adrian Jones, was
added in 1912. Before it was
installed Jones seated three
people for dinner in the body
of one of the horses.

A recent conservation project
restored the arch. The public
now has access to exhibitions
in the inner rooms. A viewing
platform beneath the sculpture
has great views over London.

Interior of Apsley House

Wellington Arch

Apsley House ㉓

Hyde Park Corner W1. **Map** 12 D4.
Tel 020-7499 5676. Hyde Park
Corner. **Open** Mar–Oct: 10am–5pm
Tue–Sun & bank hols; Nov–Mar: 10am–
4pm Tue–Sun & bank hols. **Closed**
24–26 Dec, 1 Jan, Good Fri, May Day.
pre-booked groups only.
www.english-heritage.org.uk

Apsley House, on the southeast corner of Hyde Park, was
completed by Robert Adam
for Baron Apsley in 1778.
Fifty years later it was
enlarged and altered by the
architect Benjamin Dean
Wyatt, to provide a grand
home for the Duke of
Wellington. His dual career as
soldier and politician brought
him victory against Napoleon
at Waterloo (1815), and two
terms as prime minister (1828-
30, 1834). Against a sumptuous

background of silk hangings
and gilt decoration hangs the
duke's fine art collection.
Paintings by Goya, Velázquez,
Brueghel and Rubens stand
alongside displays of porcelain,
silver and furniture. The
duke's memorabilia includes
swords and medals, but is
dominated by Canova's
colossal statue of Napoleon,
who was Wellington's arch-
enemy, wearing only a fig leaf.

Shepherd Market ㉔

W1 **Map** 12 E4. Green Park.

This attractive and bijou
pedestrianized enclave of
small shops, restaurants, and
outdoor cafés, between
Piccadilly and Curzon Street,
was named after Edward
Shepherd, who built it in the
middle of the 18th century.
During the 17th century the
annual 15-day May Fair (from
which the name of the area is
derived) took place on this
site, and today Shepherd
Market is still very much the
centre of Mayfair.

Green Park ㉕

SW1. **Map** 12 E4. **Tel** 020-7298
2000. Green Park, Hyde Park
Corner. **Open** 5am–midnight daily.
www.royalparks.org.uk

Once part of Henry VIII's
hunting ground, it was, like St
James's Park, adapted for
public use by Charles II in the
1660s and is a natural,
undulating landscape of grass

and trees (with a good spring
show of daffodils). It was a
favourite site for duels during
the 18th century; in 1771 the
poet Alfieri was wounded
here by his mistress's
husband, Viscount Ligonier,
but then rushed back to the
Haymarket Theatre in time
to catch the last act of a
play. Today the park is
popular with guests staying
at the Mayfair hotels as a
place to jog.

Faraday Museum ㉖

The Royal Institution, 21 Albemarle
St W1. **Map** 12 F3. **Tel** 020-7409
2992. Green Park. **Open**
10am–5.30pm Mon–Fri. **Closed** 24
Dec–3 Jan. **Adm charge.**
phone first. **Lectures.** www.rigb.org

Michael Faraday was a 19th-
century pioneer of the uses of
electricity. His laboratory has
been reconstructed in the
basement here, and is on
display along with a recently
refurbished museum showing
some of Faraday's scientific
apparatus and personal effects.

Michael Faraday

SOHO AND TRAFALGAR SQUARE

S oho has been renowned for pleasures of the table, the flesh and the intellect ever since it was first developed in the late 17th century. For its first century the area was one of London's most fashionable, and Soho residents of the time have gone down in history for their extravagant parties.

During the later part of the 20th century, Soho consolidated its reputation as a centre for entertainment. With a

Clock on Liberty department store

cosmopolitan mix of people, visitors here enjoy the many pleasant bars, restaurants and cafés – popular with everyone from tourists to locals, office workers and London's gay community.

Soho is one of London's most multi-cultural districts. The first immigrants were 18th-century Huguenots from France (*see Christ Church, Spitalfields p170*). Soho is also famous as a Chinatown; Gerrard Street is lined with Chinese restaurants.

SIGHTS AT A GLANCE

Historic Streets and Buildings
Trafalgar Square ❶
Admiralty Arch ❷
Leicester Square ❻
Shaftesbury Avenue ❽
Chinatown ❾
Charing Cross Road ❿
Soho Square ⓬
Carnaby Street ⓮

Shops and Markets
Berwick Street Market ⓭
Liberty ⓯

Churches
St Martin-in-the-Fields ❹

Museums and Galleries
National Gallery pp104–7 ❸
National Portrait Gallery ❺

Theatres
Palace Theatre ⓫
Theatre Royal Haymarket ❼

GETTING THERE
This area is served by the Central, Piccadilly, Bakerloo, Victoria and Northern lines. Many buses pass through Trafalgar Square and Piccadilly Circus. Rail services run from Charing Cross.

KEY

▦	Street-by-Street map
⊖	Underground station
⇌	Railway station

SEE ALSO

• **Street Finder,** maps 11, 12, 13

• **Where to Stay** pp278–291

• **Restaurants, Pubs** pp292–319

◁ **St Martin-in-the-Fields and Trafalgar Square**

Street-by-Street: Trafalgar Square

This area buzzes both day and night
with crowds enjoying the numerous
restaurants, cinemas and nightclubs.
Broad avenues lined with regal office
buildings converge at Trafalgar Square.
Some of the roads that ring the square
have now been pedestrianized, making
this already popular meeting place far
more accessible.

**To Tottenham Court
Road station**

**Charing
Cross Road**
*The shops here
are a feast for
booklovers* ⑩

Shaftesbury Avenue
*Theatreland's main
artery is lined with
announcements for
current shows* ⑧

★ **Chinatown**
*An area of Chinese restaurants
and shops, this is home to many
Chinese-speaking people* ⑨

The Blue Posts pub stands
on the site of a pick-up
point for sedan chairs in
the 18th century.

The Trocadero's
neon and laser beam
decorations attract a
youthful crowd to the
floors of games, cafés,
shops and cinemas.

STAR SIGHTS

★ National Gallery

★ National Portrait
Gallery

★ St Martin-in-
the-Fields

★ Chinatown

★ Trafalgar Square

Leicester Square
*Film pioneer Charlie
Chaplin stands in the
traffic-free square* ⑥

KEY

– – – Suggested route

0 metres   100

0 yards   100

**Theatre Royal
Haymarket**
*It is graced by a John
Nash portico* ⑦

Notre Dame, once a theatre, was converted into a church in 1855. The Jean Cocteau murals inside date from 1960.

LOCATOR MAP
See Central London Map pp14–15

The Hippodrome, a disco and nightclub *(see pp352–3)*, was once a variety theatre.

Cecil Court is lined with shops selling old books and prints.

★ **National Gallery**
The national collection of art is housed in these buildings ❸

★ **St Martin-in-the-Fields**
James Gibbs's masterpiece set the US "colonial" style ❹

★ **National Portrait Gallery**
Portraits of prominent Britons from Tudor times to the present day adorn the walls here ❺

Leicester Square station

Charing Cross station

Admiralty Arch
The entrance to the Mall was designed in 1911 ❷

★ **Trafalgar Square**
Millions of tourists come here to admire the statues and the fountains ❶

Nelson's Column

Trafalgar Square ❶

WC2. **Map** 13 B3. 🚇 *Charing Cross.*

London's main venue for rallies and outdoor public meetings was conceived by John Nash and was mostly constructed during the 1830s. The 50-m (165-ft) column commemorates Admiral Lord Nelson, Britain's most famous sea lord, who died heroically at the Battle of Trafalgar against Napoleon in 1805. It dates from 1842; 14 stonemasons held a dinner on its flat top before the statue of Nelson was finally installed. Edwin Landseer's four lions were added to guard its base 25 years later. The north side of the square is now taken up by the National Gallery and its annexe *(see pp104–7)*, with Canada House on the west side, and South Africa House on the east. The restored Grand Buildings on the south side, with their fine arcade, were built in 1880 as the Grand Hotel. The square has recently been partially pedestrianized, with the refurbishments including an enlarged central staircase descending from the National Gallery.

Nelson's statue over-looking the square

Admiralty Arch ❷

The Mall SW1. **Map** 13 B3. 🚇 *Charing Cross.*

Designed in 1911, this triple archway was part of Aston Webb's scheme to rebuild The Mall as a grand processional route honouring Queen Victoria. The arch effectively seals the eastern end of The Mall, although traffic passes through the smaller side gates, and separates courtly London from the hurly-burly of Trafalgar Square. The central gate is opened only for royal processions, making a fine setting for the coaches and horses trotting through.

Filming *Howard's End* at Admiralty Arch

National Gallery ❸

See pp104–7.

St Martin-in-the-Fields ❹

Trafalgar Sq WC2. **Map** 13 B3. **Tel** 020-7766 1100. 🚇 *Charing Cross.* **Open** *8am–6.30pm daily.* ✝ *8am, 10am, noon, 5pm, 6.30pm Sun (phone for other days).* ♿ 🔲 📷 **London Brass Rubbing Centre Tel** 020-7930 9306. **Open** *10am–7pm Mon–Wed, 10am–10pm Thu–Sat, noon–7pm Sun (last brass rubbing entry 1 hr before close).* **Concerts** see **Entertainment** pp348–9. **www**.smif.org

There has been a church on this site since the 13th century. Many famous people were buried here, including Charles II's mistress, Nell Gwynne, and the painters William Hogarth and Joshua Reynolds. The present church was designed by James Gibbs and completed in 1726. In architectural terms it was one of the most influential ever built; it was much copied in the United States, where it became a model for the Colonial style of church-building. An unusual feature of St Martin's spacious interior is the royal box at gallery level on the left of the altar.

From 1914 until 1927 the crypt was used as a shelter for homeless soldiers and down-and-outs; during World War II it was used as an air-raid shelter. Today it helps the homeless by providing a lunchtime soup kitchen for them. It also has a café and a religious bookshop as well as the London Brass Rubbing Centre. There is a craft market in the yard *(see p325)* and concerts are held in the church.

National Portrait Gallery ❺

2 St Martin's Place WC2. **Map** 13 B3. **Tel** 020-7306 0055. 🚇 *Leicester Sq, Charing Cross.* **Open** *10am–6pm Sat–Wed, 10am–9pm Thu–Fri.* **Closed** *Good Fri, 24–26 Dec, 1 Jan.* 🔲 ♿ *Orange St entrance.* 📷 🍽 🔲 📷 **Lectures. www**.npg.org.uk

Too often ignored in favour of the National Gallery next door, this fascinating museum recounts Britain's development through portraits of its main characters, giving faces to names which are familiar from the history books. There are pictures of kings, queens, poets, musicians, artists,

William Shakespeare portrait on display in the Ondaatje Wing

thinkers, heroes and villains from all periods since the late 14th century. The oldest works, on the fourth floor, include a Hans Holbein cartoon of Henry VIII and paintings of several of his wives.

The National Portrait Gallery's millennium development project, the new Ondaatje Wing, opened in May 2000, allowing it 50 per cent more exhibition and public space. It includes a Tudor Gallery, displaying some of the earliest and most important paintings, including one of Shakespeare (by John Taylor in 1651), and the Ditchley portrait of Elizabeth I. A new balcony provides an extra display area for portraits from the 1960s to the 1990s.

The gallery has a new rooftop restaurant, and the spacious lecture theatre in the basement that is also used for drama and film events.

The gallery also houses temporary exhibitions and has an excellent shop selling books on art and literature, as well as an extensive range of cards, prints and posters featuring pictures from the main collection.

Leicester Square ❻

WC2. **Map** 13 B2. ⊖ *Leicester Sq, Piccadilly Circus.*

It is hard to imagine that this, the perpetually animated heart of the West End entertainment district, was once a fashionable place to live. Laid out in 1670 south of Leicester House, a long-gone royal residence, the square's occupants included the scientist Isaac Newton and the artists Joshua Reynolds and William Hogarth. Reynolds made his fortune painting high society in his elegant salon at No. 46. Hogarth's house, in the south-east corner, became the Hôtel de la Sablionère in 1801, probably the area's first public restaurant.

In Victorian times several of London's most popular music halls were established here, including the Empire (today

the cinema on the same site perpetuates the name) and the Alhambra, replaced in 1937 by the Art Deco Odeon. A useful booth selling cut-price theatre tickets *(see p344)* sits in the square. There is also a statue of Charlie Chaplin (by John Doubleday), which was unveiled in 1981. The Shakespeare fountain dates from an earlier renovation in 1874.

Theatre Royal Haymarket ❼

Haymarket SW1. **Map** 13 A3. *Tel* 020-7930 8890. ⊖ *Piccadilly Circus.* **Open** *performances and guided tours (phone to check).* ♿ **www**.trh.co.uk

The fine frontage of this theatre, with its portico of six Corinthian columns, dates from 1821, when John Nash designed it as part of his plan for a stately route from Carlton House to Regent's Park. The interior is equally grand.

Shaftesbury Avenue ❽

W1. **Map** 13 A2. ⊖ *Piccadilly Circus, Leicester Sq.*

The main artery of London's theatreland, Shaftesbury Avenue has six theatres and two cinemas, all on its north side. This street was cut through an area of terrible slums between 1877 and 1886 in order to improve communications across the city's busy West End; it follows the route of a much earlier highway. It is named after the Earl of Shaftesbury (1801–85), whose attempts to improve housing conditions had helped some of the local poor. (The Earl is also commemorated by the Eros statue in Piccadilly Circus – *see p90.*) The Lyric Theatre, which was designed by C J Phipps, has been open for almost the same length of time as the avenue.

London's West End: the façade of the Gielgud Theatre

National Gallery ❸

Trafalgar Square façade

The National Gallery has flourished since its inception in the early 19th century. In 1824 George IV persuaded a reluctant government to buy 38 major paintings, including works by Raphael and Rembrandt, and these became the start of a national collection. The collection grew over the years as rich benefactors contributed works and money. The main gallery building was designed in Neo-Classical style by William Wilkins and built in 1834–8. To its left lies the Sainsbury Wing, financed by the grocery family and completed in 1991.

GALLERY GUIDE

Most of the collection is housed on one floor divided into four wings. The paintings hang chronologically, with the earliest works (1250–1500) in the Sainsbury Wing. The North, West and East Wings cover 1500–1600, 1600–1700 and 1700–1900. Lesser paintings of all periods are on the lower floor.

Stairs and lift to lower galleries

Education centre entrance

Stairs to lower floor

Link to main building

Stairs to lower floors

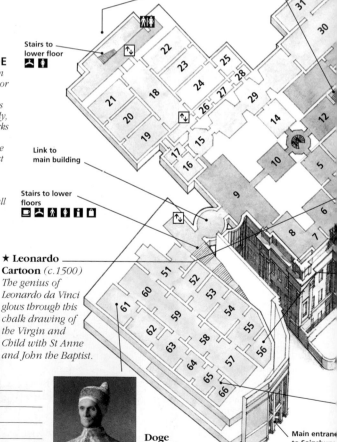

★ **Leonardo Cartoon** *(c.1500)* *The genius of Leonardo da Vinci glows through this chalk drawing of the Virgin and Child with St Anne and John the Baptist.*

KEY TO FLOORPLAN

- ☐ Painting 1250–1500
- ☐ Painting 1500–1600
- ☐ Painting 1600–1700
- ☐ Painting 1700–1900
- ☐ Special exhibitions
- ☐ Non-exhibition space

Doge Leonardo Loredan *(1501)* *Giovanni Bellini portrays this Venetian head of state as a serene father figure.*

Main entrance to Sainsbury Wing

★ Rokeby Venus *(1649)*
Diego Velázquez painted it to match a lost Venetian nude.

★ The Hay-Wain *(1821)*
John Constable brilliantly caught the effect of distance and the changing light and shadow of a typically English cloudy summer day in this famous classic.

VISITORS' CHECKLIST

Trafalgar Sq WC2. **Map** 13 B3.
Tel 020-7747 2885. ⊖ Charing Cross, Leicester Sq, Piccadilly Circus. ▦ 3, 6, 9, 11, 12, 13, 15, 23, 24, 29, 53, 77a, 88, 91, 94, 109, 139, 159, 176.
⊟ Charing Cross. **Open** 10am–6pm daily (9pm Wed). **Closed** 24–26 Dec, 1 Jan. 🖉
🖐 Sainsbury Wing entrance.
▨ 🖶 ▣ 🍴 ▣ ⤢
Lectures, film presentations, exhibitions, special events.
www.nationalgallery.org.uk

33
32
34
37
35
36
41
38
43
42
39
44
45
46
1

ℹ
🚹

Sir Paul Getty Entrance

Trafalgar Square entrance

Bathers at Asnières *(1884)*
Georges Seurat experiments here with millions of little dots of colour, to create a Neo-Classical portrayal of modern urban life.

★ The Ambassadors
The strange shape in the foreground of this Hans Holbein portrait (1533) is a foreshortened skull, a symbol of mortality.

★ Baptism of Christ
Piero della Francesca painted this tranquil masterpiece (1450s) of early Renaissance perspective for a church in his native Umbria.

Arnolfini Portrait
The woman in Jan van Eyck's famous painting (1434) is not pregnant – her rotund shape conforms to contemporary ideas of female beauty.

STAR PAINTINGS

★ Baptism of Christ by Piero della Francesca

★ 'The Cartoon' by Leonardo da Vinci

★ Rokeby Venus by Diego Velázquez

★ The Ambassadors by Hans Holbein

★ The Hay-Wain by John Constable

Exploring the National Gallery

The National Gallery has over 2,300 paintings, most kept on permanent display. The collection ranges from early works by Cimabue, in the 13th century, to 19th-century Impressionists, but its particular strengths are in Dutch, early Renaissance Italian and 17th-century Spanish painting. The bulk of the British collections are housed in Tate Britain *(see pp82–5)* while Tate Modern specializes in international modern art *(pp178–81)*.

The Adoration of The Kings (1564) by Pieter Brueghel the Elder

EARLY RENAISSANCE (1250–1500): ITALIAN AND NORTHERN PAINTING

Three lustrous panels from the *Maestà*, Duccio's great altarpiece in Siena cathedral, are among the earliest paintings here. Other Italian works of the period include his outstanding *Madonna*.

The fine *Wilton Diptych* portraying England's Richard II is probably by a French artist. It displays the lyrical elegance of the International Gothic style that swept Europe.

Italian masters of this style include Pisanello and Gentile da Fabriano, whose *Madonna* often hangs beside another, by Masaccio – both date from 1426. Also shown are works by Masaccio's pupil, Fra Filippo Lippi, as well as Botticelli and Uccello. Umbrian paintings include Piero della Francesca's *Nativity* and *Baptism*, and an excellent collection of Mantegna, Bellini and other works from the Venetian and Ferrarese schools. Antonello da Messina's *St Jerome in his Study* has been mistaken for a van Eyck; it is not hard to see why, when you compare it with van Eyck's *Arnolfini Portrait*. Important

Netherlandish pictures, including some by Rogier van der Weyden and his followers, are also here, in the Sainsbury Wing.

HIGH RENAISSANCE (1500–1600): ITALIAN, NETHERLANDISH AND GERMAN PAINTING

Christ Mocked (1490–1500) by Hieronymus Bosch

Sebastiano del Piombo's *The Raising of Lazarus* was painted, with Michelangelo's assistance, to rival Raphael's great *Transfiguration*, which hangs in the Vatican in Rome.

These and other well-known names of the High (or Late) Renaissance are extremely well represented, often with massive works. Look out for Parmigianino's *Madonna and Child with Saints*, Leonardo da Vinci's charcoal cartoon of the *Virgin and Child* (a full-sized drawing used for copying as a painting), and his second version of the *Virgin of the Rocks*. There are also tender and amusing works by Piero di Cosimo, and several Titians, including *Bacchus and Ariadne* – which the public found too bright and garish when it was first cleaned by the gallery in the 1840s.

The Netherlandish and German collections are weaker. Even so, they include *The Ambassadors*, a fine double portrait by Holbein; and Altdorfer's superb *Christ Taking Leave of his Mother*, bought by the gallery in 1980. There is also an Hieronymus Bosch of *Christ Mocked* (sometimes known as *The Crowning with Thorns*), and an excellent Brueghel, *The Adoration of the Kings*.

The Annunciation (c. late 1450s) by Fra Filippo Lippi

THE SAINSBURY WING

Plans for this new wing, opened in 1991, provoked a storm of dissent. An incensed Prince Charles dubbed an early design "a monstrous carbuncle on the face of a much-loved friend". The final building, by Venturi, has drawn criticism from other quarters for being a derivative compromise.

This is where major changing exhibitions are held. It also houses the Micro Gallery, a computerized database of the Collection.

DUTCH, ITALIAN, FRENCH AND SPANISH PAINTING (1600–1700)

The superb Dutch collection gives two entire rooms to Rembrandt. There are also works by Vermeer, Van Dyck (among them his equestrian portrait of King Charles I) and Rubens (including the popular *Chapeau de Paille*).

From Italy, the works of Carracci and Caravaggio are strongly represented, and Salvatore Rosa has a glowering self-portrait.

French works on show include a magnificent portrait of Cardinal Richelieu by Philippe de Champaigne. Claude's seascape, *The Embarkation of the Queen of Sheba*, hangs beside Turner's rival painting *Dido Building Carthage*, as Turner himself had instructed.

The Spanish school has works by Murillo, Velázquez, Zurbarán and others.

Young Woman Standing at a Virginal (1670) by Jan Vermeer

The Scale of Love (1715–18) by Jean-Antoine Watteau

VENETIAN, FRENCH AND ENGLISH PAINTING (1700–1800)

One of the gallery's most famous 18th century works is Canaletto's *The Stone-Mason's Yard*. Other Venetians here are Longhi and Tiepolo.

The French collection includes Rococo masters such as Chardin, Watteau and Boucher, as well as landscapists and portraitists.

Gainsborough's early work *Mr and Mrs Andrews* and *The Morning Walk* are favourites with visitors; his rival, Sir Joshua Reynolds, is represented by some of his most Classical work and by more informal portraits.

ENGLISH, FRENCH AND GERMAN PAINTING (1800–1900)

The great age of 19th-century landscape painting is amply represented here, with fine works by Constable and Turner, including

Constable's *The Hay-Wain* and Turner's *The Fighting Temeraire*, as well as works by the French artists Corot and Daubigny.

Of Romantic art, there is Géricault's vivid work, *Horse Frightened by Lightning*, and several interesting paintings by Delacroix. In contrast, the society portrait of *Mme Moitessier* by Ingres, though still Romantic, is more restrained and Classical.

Impressionists and other French avant-garde artists are well represented. Among the highlights are *Waterlilies* by Monet, Renoir's *At the Theatre*, Van Gogh's *Sunflowers*, not to mention Rousseau's *Tropical Storm with Tiger*. In Seurat's *Bathers at Asnières* he did not originally use the pointillist technique he was later to invent, but subsequently reworked areas of the picture using dots of colour.

At the Theatre (1876–7) by Pierre-Auguste Renoir

Chinatown

Streets around Gerrard St W1.
Map 13 A2. 🚇 *Leicester Sq,
Piccadilly Circus.*

There has been a Chinese
community in London since the
19th century. Originally it was
concentrated around the East
End docks at Limehouse,
where the opium dens of
Victorian melodrama were
sited. As the number of
immigrants increased in the
1950s, many moved into Soho
where they created an ever-
expanding Chinatown. It
contains scores of restaurants,
and mysterious aroma-filled
shops selling oriental produce.
Three Chinese arches straddle
Gerrard Street, where a vibrant,
colourful street festival, held in
late January, celebrates Chinese
New Year *(see p59).*

Charing Cross Road ❿

WC2. **Map** 13 B2. 🚇 *Leicester Sq.*
See **Shops and Markets** *pp318–19.*

**Antiquarian books from the
shops on Charing Cross Road**

The road is a mecca for book-
lovers, with a row of second-
hand bookshops south of
Cambridge Circus and, north of
these, a clutch of shops that,
between them, should be able
to supply just about any recent
volume. Visit the giants: huge
Foyle's and busy Waterstones,
and the smaller, specialist
shops: try Shipley's *(pp318–19)*
for art books and Sportspages
for sports. Sadly, huge rent
rises have put this unique mix
under threat. At the junction
with New Oxford Street rises
the 1960s skyscraper, Centre-
point. It lay empty for nearly
ten years after it was built, its
owners finding this more
profitable than renting it out.

At the Palace Theatre in 1898

Palace Theatre ⓫

Shaftesbury Ave W1. **Map** 13 B2. **Tel
Box office** *0870-264 3333.* 🚇
Leicester Sq. **Open** *for performances
only. See* **Entertainment** *pp344–5.*
www.rutheatres.com

Most West End theatres are
disappointingly unassertive.
This one, which dominates
the west side of Cambridge
Circus, is a splendid
exception, with its sparkling
terracotta exterior and
opulent furnishings.
Completed as an opera house
in 1891, it became a music
hall the following year. The
ballerina Anna Pavlova made
her London debut here in
1910. Now the theatre, owned
by Andrew Lloyd Webber
whose own musicals are all
over London, stages hit shows
such as *The Woman in White.*

Soho Square ⓬

W1. **Map** 13 A1. 🚇 *Tottenham
Court Rd.*

Soon after it was laid out in
1681 this Square enjoyed a
brief reign as the most
fashionable address in London.
Originally it was called King
Square, after Charles II, whose
statue was erected in the
middle. The square went out
of fashion by the late 18th
century and is now surrounded by bland office buildings.
The mock-Tudor garden shed
in the centre was added much
later in Victorian times.

Berwick Street Market ⓭

W1. **Map** 13 A1. 🚇 *Piccadilly
Circus.* **Open** *9am–6pm Mon–Sat.
See* **Shops and Markets** *p324.*

There has been a market here
since the 1840s. Berwick
Street trader Jack Smith
introduced grapefruit to
London in 1890. Today this is
the West End's best street
market, at its cheeriest and
most crowded during the
lunch hour. The freshest and
least expensive produce for
miles around is to be had
here. There are also some
interesting shops, including
Borovick's, which sells
extraordinary fabrics, and a
growing number of cafés and
restaurants. At its southern
end the street narrows into an
alley on which Raymond's
Revue Bar (the comparatively
respectable face of Soho
sleaze) has presented its
festival of erotica since 1958.

Some of London's cheapest produce at Berwick Street Market

Carnaby Street ⑭

W1. **Map** 12 F2. ⊖ *Oxford Circus.*
www.carnaby.co.uk

During the 1960s this street was so much the centre of swinging London that the Oxford English Dictionary recognized the term "Carnaby Street" as meaning "fashionable clothing for young people". After many years of neglect, the street is once again gaining a reputation for cutting-edge fashion; nearby streets such as Newburgh Street, Kingly Court and Fouberts Place also have some interesting young designers' clothing shops. England's oldest pipe maker, Inderwick's, founded in 1797, is situated at No. 45.

Liberty's mock-Tudor façade

Liberty ⑮

Regent St W1. **Map** 12 F2. ⊖ *Oxford Circus. See **Shops and Markets** p313.*

Arthur Lasenby Liberty opened his first shop, selling oriental silks, on Regent Street in 1875. Among his first customers were the artists Ruskin, Rossetti and Whistler. Soon Liberty prints and designs, by artists such as William Morris, epitomized the Arts and Crafts movement of the late 19th and early 20th centuries. They are still very fashionable today.

The present mock-Tudor building with its country-house feel dates from 1925, and was built specifically to house the store.

Today the shop maintains its strong links with crafts people of all kinds, including potters, jewellers and furniture designers. This is reflected in the high quality and originality of much of the goods on sale. The top floor houses period Art Nouveau, Art Deco and Arts and Crafts furniture.

The Heart of Soho

Old Compton Street is Soho's High Street. Its shops and restaurants reflect the variety of people who have lived in the area over the centuries. These include many great artists, writers and musicians.

Maison Bertaux is known for producing delicious croissants and coffee and wonderful cakes as good as those found in Paris.

Ronnie Scott's opened in 1959, and nearly all the big names of jazz have played here *(see pp351–3).*

Bar Italia is a coffee shop situated under the room where John Logie Baird first demonstrated television in 1926. As a child, Mozart stayed next door with his family in 1764 and 1765.

The Coach and Horses pub has been a centre of bohemian Soho since the 1950s and is still popular.

Algerian Coffee Stores is one of Soho's oldest shops. Delicious aromas of the world's coffees fill the shop.

Patisserie Valerie is a Hungarian-owned café serving delicious pastries *(see pp312–15).*

St Anne's Church Tower is all that remains after a bomb destroyed the church in 1940.

The French House was frequented by Maurice Chevalier and General de Gaulle.

The Palace Theatre has hosted many successful musicals.

COVENT GARDEN AND THE STRAND

The open-air cafés, street entertainers, stylish shops and markets make this area a magnet for visitors. At its centre is the Piazza, which sheltered a wholesale market until 1974. Since then, the pretty Victorian buildings here and in the surrounding streets have been converted into one of the city's liveliest districts. In medieval times the area was occupied by a convent garden that supplied Westminster Abbey with produce. Then in the 1630s, Inigo Jones laid out the Piazza as London's first square, with its west side dominated by his St Paul's Church.

The Piazza was commissioned as a residential development by the Earl of Bedford, owner of one of the mansions that lined the Strand. Before the Embankment was built, the Strand ran along the river.

Dried flowers from the Piazza

SIGHTS AT A GLANCE

Historic Streets and Buildings
The Piazza and Central Market **1**
Neal Street and Neal's Yard **7**
Savoy Hotel **13**
Somerset House **15**
Roman Bath **17**
Bush House **18**
Adelphi **21**
Charing Cross **22**

Museums and Galleries
London's Transport Museum **3**
Theatre Museum **4**
Photographers' Gallery **11**

Churches
St Paul's Church **2**
Savoy Chapel **14**
St Mary-le-Strand **16**

Monuments and Statues
Seven Dials **9**
Cleopatra's Needle **19**

Famous Theatres
Theatre Royal Drury Lane **5**
Royal Opera House **6**
Adelphi Theatre **12**
The London Coliseum **23**

Parks and Gardens
Victoria Embankment Gardens **20**

Historic Pubs, Shopping Arcades
Lamb and Flag **10**
Thomas Neal's **8**

```
0 metres        500
0 yards         500
```

GETTING THERE
Covent Garden, Leicester Square and Charing Cross Underground stations are all nearby. There are frequent buses: 9, 11, 15 and 30 to the Strand or 14, 19, 22b, 24, 29, 38 and 176 to Shaftesbury Avenue. Charing Cross rail station is a short walk.

SEE ALSO
• *Street Finder,* maps 13, 14
• *Where to Stay* pp278–291
• *Restaurants, Pubs* pp292–319

KEY
■ Street-by-Street map
◎ Underground station
⇌ Railway station

◁ **Enzo Piazotta's statue *The Young Dancer* (1988), opposite the Royal Opera House**

Street-by-Street: Covent Garden

Once an area of decaying streets and warehouses, Covent Garden came alive only after dark when the fruit and vegetable market traders went about their business. Now it is completely revitalized. Day and night, visitors, residents and street-entertainers of every vocation throng the Piazza, much as they would have done several centuries ago.

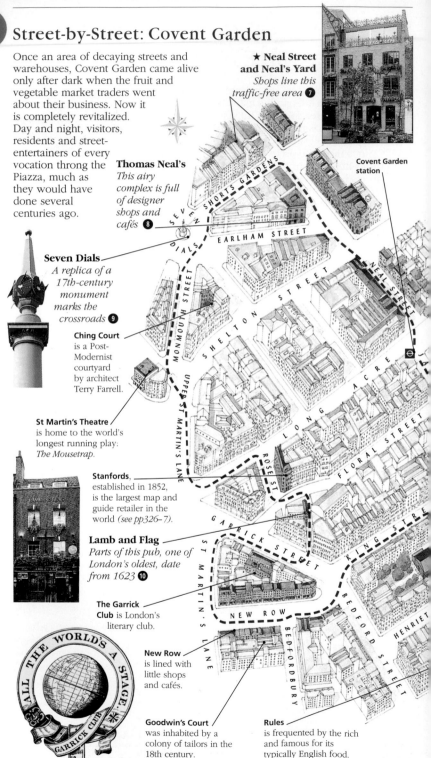

★ **Neal Street and Neal's Yard**
Shops line this traffic-free area 7

Covent Garden station

Thomas Neal's
This airy complex is full of designer shops and cafés 8

Seven Dials
A replica of a 17th-century monument marks the crossroads 9

Ching Court
is a Post-Modernist courtyard by architect Terry Farrell.

St Martin's Theatre
is home to the world's longest running play: The Mousetrap.

Stanfords,
established in 1852, is the largest map and guide retailer in the world (see pp326–7).

Lamb and Flag
Parts of this pub, one of London's oldest, date from 1623 10

The Garrick Club is London's literary club.

New Row
is lined with little shops and cafés.

Goodwin's Court
was inhabited by a colony of tailors in the 18th century.

Rules
is frequented by the rich and famous for its typically English food.

★ The Piazza and Central Market
Performers of all kinds – jugglers, clowns, acrobats and musicians – entertain the crowds in the square ❶

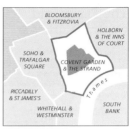

LOCATOR MAP
See Central London Map pp14–15

Royal Opera House
Most of the world's greatest singers and dancers have appeared on its stage ❻

Bow Street Police Station
housed London's first police force, the Bow Street Runners, in the 18th century. It closed in 1992.

★ Theatre Museum
A collection of theatrical memorabilia is housed here ❹

Theatre Royal Drury Lane
The old theatre shows extravagant musicals ❺

Boswells, now a coffee house, is where Dr Johnson first met his biographer, Boswell.

Jubilee Market sells clothes and bric-à-brac.

★ St Paul's Church
Despite appearances, Inigo Jones's church faces away from the Piazza – the entrance is through the churchyard ❷

★ London's Transport Museum
The history of the city's tube and buses is brought to life in this museum ❸

STAR SIGHTS

★ The Piazza and Central Market

★ St Paul's Church

★ London's Transport Museum

★ Theatre Museum

★ Neal Street and Neal's Yard

KEY

– – – Suggested route

0 metres	100
0 yards	100

The Piazza and Central Market **❶**

Covent Garden WC2. **Map** 13 C2.
🚇 *Covent Garden*. 🚻 *but cobbled streets*. **Street performers** *10am–dusk daily. See **Shops and Markets** p333.*

The 17th-century architect Inigo Jones originally planned this area to be an elegant residential square, modelled on the piazza at Livorno, northern Italy. Today the buildings on and around the Piazza are almost entirely Victorian. The covered central market was designed by Charles Fowler in 1833 for fruit and vegetable whole-salers, the glass and iron roof anticipating the giant rail termini built later in the century – for instance, St Pancras *(see p130)* and Waterloo *(see p191)*. It now makes a magnificent shell for an array of small shops selling designer clothes, books, arts, crafts, decorative items and antiques, all surrounded by bustling market stalls that continue south in the neighbouring Jubilee Hall, which was built in 1903.

The colonnaded Bedford Chambers, on the north side, give a hint of Inigo Jones's plan, although even they are not original: they were rebuilt and partially modified in 1879.

Street entertainment is a well-loved and now expected tradition of the area; in 1662, diarist Samuel Pepys wrote of watching a Punch and Judy show under the portico of St Paul's Church.

West entrance to St Paul's

St Paul's Church **❷**

Bedford St WC2. **Map** 13 C2. **Tel** *020-7836 5221.* 🚇 *Covent Garden.* **Open** *8.30am–4.30pm Mon–Fri, 9am–1pm Sun.* 🕆 *11am Sun, 2nd Sun of the month 4pm evensong.* 🚻

Inigo Jones built this church (completed in 1633) with the altar at the west end, so as to allow his grand portico, with its two square and two round columns, to face east into the Piazza. Clerics objected to this unorthodox arrangement, and the altar was moved to its conventional position at the east end. Jones went ahead with his original exterior design. Thus the church is entered from the west, and the east portico is a fake door, used now as an impromptu stage for street entertainers. In 1795 the interior was destroyed by fire but was rebuilt in Jones's airy, uncomplicated style. Today the church is all that is left of Jones's original plan for the Piazza. St Paul's has long been called "the actors' church" and plaques commem-orate distinguished men and women of the theatre. A 17th-century carving by Grinling Gibbons, on the west screen, is a memorial to the architect.

Punch and Judy performer

London's Transport Museum **❸**

The Piazza WC2. **Map** 13 C2.
Tel *020-7379 6344.* 🚇 *Covent Garden.* **Open** *opening times may be limited due to refurbishment – phone to check.* **Adm charge.** 📷 💻 🚻 🚻
www.ltmuseum.co.uk

London's Transport Museum

You do not have to be a train spotter or a collector of bus numbers to enjoy this museum. The intriguing collection is housed in the picturesque Victorian Flower Market, which was built in 1872, and features public transport from the past and present.

The history of London's transport is in essence a social history of the capital. Bus, tram and underground route patterns first reflected the city's growth and then promoted it: the northern and western suburbs began to develop only after their tube connections were built. The museum houses a fine collection of 20th-century commercial art. London's bus and train companies have been, and still are, prolific patrons of contemporary artists, and copies of some of the finest posters on display can be bought at the well-stocked museum shop. They include the innovative Art Deco designs of E McKnight Kauffer, as well as work by renowned artists of the 1930s, such as Graham Sutherland and Paul Nash.

This museum is excellent for children. There are plenty of hands-on exhibits, and these include the opportunity for children to put themselves in the driver's seat of a London bus, or a train from the underground system.

A mid-18th-century view of the Piazza

Theatre Museum ❹

7 Russell St WC2. **Map** 13 C2.
Tel 020-7943 4700. 🖰 *Covent Garden*. **Open** *10am–6pm Tue–Sun (last adm: 5.30pm).* **Closed** *25 & 26 Dec, 1 Jan & public hols.*
🖰 🖰 🖰
www.theatremuseum.org

A journey into the Theatre Museum's subterranean galleries with their fascinating collection of theatrical memorabilia is one not to be missed. The displays include playbills, programmes, props and costumes from historic productions, bits of interior decor from theatres that have long since vanished, as well as paintings of actors and scenes from plays. The main gallery illustrates the way in which theatre has evolved from Shakespeare's time to the present day and uses models of auditoriums through the ages. Exhibitions and interactive theatre activities are held at the

Theatre Royal Drury Lane ❺

Catherine St WC2. **Map** 13 C2. **Tel** 0870-264 3333. 🖰 *Covent Garden, Holborn.* **Open** *for performances and guided tours (phone to check).* **Adm charge.** *See* **Entertainment** *pp344–5.* **www**.rutheatres.com

The first theatre on this site was built in 1663 as one of only two venues in London where drama could legally be staged. Nell Gwynne acted here. Three of the theatres built here since then burned down, including one designed by Sir Christopher Wren *(see p47).* The present one, by Benjamin Wyatt, was completed in 1812 and has one of the city's largest auditoriums. In the 1800s it was famous for pantomimes – now it stages block-buster musicals. It is called the Theatre Royal Drury Lane even though its entrance is on Catherine Street.

The glass Floral Hall, part of the recently reopened Royal Opera House

Royal Opera House ❻

Covent Garden WC2. **Map** 13 C2. **Tel** 020-7304 4000. 🖰 *Covent Garden.* **Open** *for performances and guided tours (phone to check). See* **Entertainment** *p348.* 🖰
www.royaloperahouse.org

The first theatre on this site was built in 1732, and staged plays as well as concerts. However, like its neighbour the Theatre Royal Drury Lane, it proved prone to fire and was destroyed in 1808 and again in 1856. The present opera house was designed in 1858 by E M Barry. John Flaxman's portico frieze, depicting tragedy and comedy, survived from the previous building of 1809.

The Opera House has had both high and low points during its history. In 1892, the first British performance of Wagner's Ring was conducted here by Gustav Mahler. Later, during World War I, the opera house was used as a storehouse by the government. The building is home to the Royal Opera and Royal Ballet Companies – the best tickets can cost over £100. After two years of extensive renovation the building reopened in time for the new millennium, complete with a second auditorium and new

rehearsal rooms for its Royal Opera and Royal Ballet companies. Backstage tours are available, and once a month visitors can watch the Royal Ballet attending its daily class.

Neal Street and Neal's Yard ❼

Covent Garden WC2. **Map** 13 B1. 🖰 *Covent Garden. See* **Shops and Markets** *pp322–3.*

A specialist shop on Neal Street

In this attractive street, former warehouses from the 19th century can be identified by the hoisting mechanisms high on their exterior walls. The buildings have been converted into a number of shops, art galleries and restaurants. Off Neal Street in Short's Gardens is Neal's Yard Dairy, one of London's best cheese shops, which also sells delicious fresh-baked breads. Brainchild of the late Nicholas Saunders, it remains an oasis of alternative values amid the growing commercialism of the area.

Café at Thomas Neal's

Thomas Neal's ❽

Earlham St WC2. **Map** 13 B2.
🚇 Covent Garden. ♿ ground floor only.

Opened in the early 1990s, this upmarket shopping complex offers an interesting range of shops, selling designer clothes and cosmetics, jewellery and accessories, antique clothing and lace. There is a coffee shop and restaurant on the lower floor. The Donmar Warehouse theatre *(see p346)* is also part of the complex, staging must-see productions such as The Blue Room.

Seven Dials ❾

Monmouth St WC2. **Map** 13 B2.
🚇 Covent Garden, Leicester Sq.

The pillar at this junction of seven streets incorporates six sundials (the central spike acted as a seventh). It was installed in 1989 and is a copy of a 17th-century monument. The original was removed in the 19th century because it had become a notorious meeting place for criminals.

Lamb and Flag ❿

33 Rose St WC2. **Map** 13 B2.
Tel 020-7497 9504. 🚇 Covent Garden, Leicester Sq. **Open** 11am–11pm Mon–Thu, 11am–10.45pm Fri & Sat, noon–10.30pm Sun. See **Restaurants and Pubs** p317.

There has been an inn here since the 16th century. The cramped bars are still largely unmodernized. A plaque

concerns satirist John Dryden, attacked in the alley outside in 1679 after lampooning the Duchess of Portsmouth (one of Charles II's mistresses).

Photographers' Gallery ⓫

5 & 8 Great Newport St WC2. **Map** 13 B2. **Tel** 020-7831 1772. 🚇 Leicester Sq. **Open** 11am–6pm Mon–Sat (to 8pm Thu), noon–6pm Sun. ♿ 🖥 📷 www.photonet.org.uk

This enterprising gallery is London's leading venue for photographic exhibitions. There are regular lectures and theatrical events, as well as an excellent photographic book and print shop and a café. The plaque on the outside commemorates Sir Joshua Reynolds, the founder of the Royal Academy *(see p90)*, who lived here in the 18th century.

Adelphi Theatre ⓬

Strand WC2. **Map** 13 C3.
Tel 0870-403 0303. 🚇 Charing Cross, Embankment.
Open for performances only.
See **Entertainment** pp344–5.

Built in 1806, the Adelphi was opened by John Scott, a wealthy tradesman, who was helping to launch his daughter on the stage. It was remodelled in 1930 in Art Deco style. Note the highly distinctive lettering on the frontage, and the well-kept lobby and auditorium, with their stylized motifs.

Savoy Hotel ⓭

Strand WC2. **Map** 13 C2.
Tel 020-7836 4343. 🚇 Charing Cross, Embankment. See **Where to Stay** p290.

Pioneer of en-suite bathrooms and electric lighting, the grand Savoy was built in 1889 on the site of the medieval Savoy Palace. The forecourt is the only street in Britain where traffic drives on the right. Attached to the hotel are the Savoy Theatre built for D'Oyly Carte opera, Simpson's English restaurant *(see p302)*, and the Savoy Taylor's Guild with its Art Nouveau shop front. Next door is Shell Mex House, which replaced the Cecil Hotel while keeping its Strand façade.

Front entrance to the Savoy Hotel

Savoy Chapel ⓮

Strand WC2. **Map** 13 C2. **Tel** 020-7836 7221. 🚇 Charing Cross, Embankment. **Open** 11.30am–3.30pm Tue–Fri. **Closed** Aug–Sep. 🕚 11am Sun. 🚫 📷 phone to book.

The first Savoy Chapel was founded in the 16th century as the chapel for the hospital established by Henry VII on the site of the old Savoy Palace. Parts of the outside walls date from 1512, but most of the present building dates from the mid-19th century. In 1890 it was London's first church to be electrically lit. It became the chapel of the Royal Victorian Order in 1937, and is now a private chapel of the Queen. Nearby on Savoy Hill were the first studios of the BBC from 1922 until 1932.

Somerset House ⑮

Strand WC2. **Map** 14 D2. **Tel** 020-7845 4600. ⊖ *Temple*. **Open** 10am–6pm daily (last adm to galleries: 5.15pm). **Closed** 1 Jan, 24–26 Dec. **Ice rink:** open two months in winter. **Adm charge**. ⬜ **Courtauld Institute of Art Gallery Tel** 020-7848 2526. ⬜ 🔲 **Gilbert Collection Tel** 020-7420 9400. 🔲 🔲 **Hermitage Rooms Tel** 020-7845 4630. 🔲 ⬜ 🔲 **Adm charge** all galleries. ♿ all galleries. **Admiralty Restaurant Tel** 020-7845 4646 for reservations. **www**.somerset-house.org.uk

This elegant Georgian building was the creation of Sir William Chambers. It was erected in the 1770s after the first Somerset House, a Renaissance palace built for the Duke of Somerset in the mid-16th century, was pulled down following years of neglect. The replacement was the first major building to be designed for use as offices and has served to house the Navy Board (note that the classical grandeur of the Seamen's Waiting Hall and Nelson's Staircase are not to be missed), a succession of Royal Societies and, for a substantial amount of time, the Inland Revenue. Today it is home to three collections of art – the Courtauld Institute, the Gilbert Collection and the Hermitage Rooms. The courtyard of Somerset House was closed to the public for nearly a century, but has recently been cleared, as part of a £48-million restoration scheme, to create an attractive piazza with a 55-jet fountain, the occasional classical music concert and, for a few weeks in winter, an ice rink. From the courtyard visitors can stroll through the South Building, where the highly regarded Admiralty Restaurant overlooks the Thames, on to a new riverside development, that includes an open-air summer café and a restaurant, and which has pedestrian access to Waterloo Bridge and the South Bank.

Located in Somerset House, but famous in its own right, is the small but spectacular **Courtauld Institute of Art**

Partridge by Gorg Ruel (c.1600), Gilbert Collection

Gallery. Its exquisite collection of paintings has been displayed here since 1990 and owes its existence to the bequest of textile magnate and philanthropist Samuel Courtauld. On display are works by Botticelli, Brueghel, Bellini and Rubens (including one of his early masterpieces *The Descent from the Cross*), but it is the Courtauld's collection of Impressionist and Post-Impressionist paintings that draws the most attention. As well as works by Monet, Gauguin, Pissarro, Renoir and Modigliani, visitors can gaze captivated on Manet's *A Bar at the Folies-Bergères*, Van Gogh's *Self-Portrait with Bandaged Ear*, Cézanne's *The Card Players* and some evocative studies of dancers by Degas. In addition to its permanent collection, the Courtauld Institute now hosts a series of world-class temporary exhibitions that take place throughout the year.

Another treasure is London's recently acquired museum of decorative arts. Housed in the South Building, the **Gilbert Collection** was given to the nation by the London-born property tycoon Arthur Gilbert. The bequest of this collection was the catalyst that brought about the revival of Somerset House. It is made up of 800 pieces, including an astonishing array of gold snuff boxes, Italian *pietra dura* (hard stone) mosaics, enamelled portrait miniatures and European silverware dating from the 16th century.

The **Hermitage Rooms** recreate, in miniature, the imperial splendour of the Winter Palace and its various wings, which now make up the State Hermitage Museum in St Petersburg. Rotating exhibitions are mounted from the collections of the Museum along with other Hermitage-related activities.

Van Gogh's *Self-Portrait with Bandaged Ear* (1889) at the Courtauld

St Mary-le-Strand ⑯

Strand WC2. **Map** 14 D2. **Tel** 020-
7836 3126. ⊖ Temple. **Open**
11am–4pm Mon–Fri, 10am–2pm
Sun. 🕇 11am Sun, 1.05pm Tue &
Thu. ⚲ 🔲
www.stmarylestrand.org

Now beached on a road island
at the east end of the Strand,
this pleasing church was
consecrated in 1724. It was
the first public building by
James Gibbs, who designed
St-Martin-in-the-Fields (see
p102). Gibbs was influenced
by Christopher Wren, but the
exuberant external decorative
detail here was inspired by the
Baroque churches of Rome,
where Gibbs studied. Its multi-
arched tower is layered like a
wedding cake, and culminates
in a cupola and lantern. St-
Mary-le-Strand is now the
official church of the Women's
Royal Naval Service.

St-Mary-le-Strand

Roman Bath ⑰

5 Strand Lane WC2. **Map** 14 D2.
Tel 020-7641 5264. ⊖ Temple,
Embankment, Charing Cross.
Open summer: 2–4pm most Wed;
phone to book. ⚿ via Temple Pl.

This little bath and its
surround may be seen from a
full-length window on Surrey
Street, by pressing a light
switch on the outside wall. It
is almost certainly not Roman,
for there is no other evidence

Bush House from Kingsway

of Roman habitation in the
immediate area. It is more
likely to have been part of
Arundel House, one of
several palaces which stood
on the Strand from Tudor
times until the 17th century,
when they were demolished
for new building. In the 19th
century the bath was open to
the public for cold plunges,
believed to be healthy.

Bush House ⑱

Aldwych WC2. **Map** 14 D2.
⊖ Temple, Holborn. **Not open** to
the public.

Situated at the centre of the
Aldwych crescent, this Neo-
Classical building was first
designed as manufacturers'
showrooms by an American,
Irving T Bush, and completed
in 1935. It appears especially
imposing when viewed from
Kingsway, its dramatic north
entrance graced with various
statues symbolizing Anglo-
American relations. Since
1940 it has been used as radio
studios, and is the head-
quarters of the BBC World
Service, which is due to be
relocated to West London
within a few years.

Cleopatra's Needle ⑲

Embankment WC2. **Map** 13 C3.
⊖ Embankment, Charing Cross.

Erected in Heliopolis in about
1500 BC, this incongruous
pink granite monument is
much older than London
itself. Its inscriptions celebrate

the deeds of the pharaohs of
ancient Egypt. It was
presented to Britain by the
then Viceroy of Egypt,
Mohammed Ali, in 1819 and
erected in 1878, shortly after
the Embankment was built.
It has a twin in New York's
Central Park, behind the
Metropolitan Museum of Art.
The bronze sphinxes, added
in 1882, are not Egyptian.
  In its base is a Victorian
time capsule of artifacts of the
day, such as the day's
newspapers, a rail timetable
and photographs of 12
contemporary beauties.

Victoria Embankment Gardens ⑳

WC2. **Map** 13 C3. ⊖
Embankment, Charing Cross. **Open**
7.30am–dusk daily. ⚿ 🔲

This narrow sliver of a public
park, created when the
Embankment was built,
boasts well-maintained flower
beds, a clutch of statues of
British worthies (including the
Scottish poet Robert Burns)
and, in summer, a season of
concerts. Its main historical
feature is the water gate at its
northwest corner, which was
built as a triumphal entry to
the Thames for the Duke of
Buckingham in 1626. It is a
relic of York House, which
used to stand on this site and
was the home first of the
Archbishops of York and then
of the Duke. It is still in its
original position and although
the water used to lap against
it, because of the Thames's
Embankment the gate is now
a good 100 m (330 ft) from
the river's edge.

Victoria Embankment Gardens

The new shopping and office block above Charing Cross

Adelphi ㉑

Strand WC2. **Map** 13 C3. **Tel** 020-7451 6845. ◉ *Embankment, Charing Cross.* **Not open** to the public.

John Adam Street, Adelphi

Adelphi is a pun on *adelphoi*, the Greek word for brothers – this area was once an elegant riverside residential development designed in 1772 by brothers Robert and John Adam. The name now refers to the Art Deco office block, its entrance adorned with N A Trent's heroic reliefs of workers at toil, which in 1938 replaced the Adams' much admired Palladian-style apartment complex. That destruction is now viewed as one of the worst acts of 20th-century official vandalism. A number of the Adams' surrounding buildings survive, notably No. 8, the ornate Royal Society for the encouragement of Arts, Manufactures & Commerce

just opposite (open first Sunday of the month, 10am–12.30pm, not January). In the same exuberant idiom are Nos. 1–4 Robert Street, where Robert Adam lived for a time, and No. 7 Adam Street.

Charing Cross ㉒

Strand WC2. **Map** 13 C3. ◉ *Charing Cross, Embankment.*

The name derives from the last of the 12 crosses erected by Edward I to mark the funeral route in 1290 of his wife, Eleanor of Castile, from Nottinghamshire to Westminster Abbey. Today a 19th-century replica stands in the forecourt of Charing Cross station. Both the cross and the Charing Cross Hotel, built into the station frontage, were designed in 1863 by E M Barry, architect of the Royal Opera House *(see p115)*.

Above the station platforms has risen an assertive shopping centre and office block, completed in 1991. Designed by Terry Farrell it resembles a giant ocean liner, with portholes looking on to Villiers Street. The new building is best seen from the river, where it dominates its neighbours. The railway arches at the rear of the station

have been modernized as a suite of small shops and cafés, as well as a new venue for the Players Theatre, the last repository of Victorian music hall entertainment.

The London Coliseum ㉓

St Martin's Lane WC2. **Map** 13 B3. **Tel** 020-7632 8300. ◉ *Leicester Sq, Charing Cross.* **Open** performances ♿ ▯ 🍸 **Lectures.** See **Entertainment** pp348–9. **www**.eno.org

London's largest theatre and one of its most elaborate, this flamboyant building, topped with a large globe, was designed in 1904 by Frank Matcham and was equipped with London's first revolving stage. It was also the first theatre in Europe to have lifts. A former variety house, today it is the home of the English National Opera, and well worth visiting, if only for the Edwardian interior with its gilded cherubs and heavy purple curtains. In 2003, the original glass roof was restored, providing dramatic views over Trafalgar Square.

London Coliseum

BLOOMSBURY AND FITZROVIA

Since the beginning of the 20th century, Bloomsbury and Fitzrovia have been synonymous with literature, art and learning. The Bloomsbury Group of writers and artists were active from the early 1900s until the 1930s; the name Fitzrovia was invented by writers such as Dylan

Carving in Russell Square

Thomas who drank in the Fitzroy Tavern. Bloomsbury still boasts the University of London, the British Museum and many fine Georgian squares. But it is now also noted for its Charlotte Street restaurants and the furniture and competitively priced electrical shops lining Tottenham Court Road.

SIGHTS AT A GLANCE

Historic Streets and Buildings
Bloomsbury Square ②
Russell Square ④
Queen Square ⑤
British Library ⑧
St Pancras International ⑨
Woburn Walk ⑪
Fitzroy Square ⑬
Charlotte Street ⑮

Museums
British Museum pp126–9 ①
Charles Dickens Museum ⑥

Foundling Museum ⑦
Percival David Foundation of Chinese Art ⑫
Pollock's Toy Museum ⑯

Churches
St George's, Bloomsbury ③
St Pancras Parish Church ⑩

Pubs
Fitzroy Tavern ⑭

SEE ALSO

• *Street Finder,* maps 4, 5, 6, 13
• *Where to Stay* pp278–291
• *Restaurants, Pubs* pp292–319

KEY

▢ Street-by-Street map
🚇 Underground station
🚉 Railway station

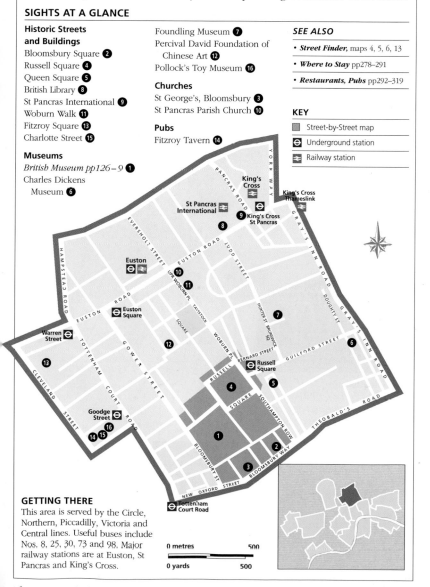

GETTING THERE

This area is served by the Circle, Northern, Piccadilly, Victoria and Central lines. Useful buses include Nos. 8, 25, 30, 73 and 98. Major railway stations are at Euston, St Pancras and King's Cross.

0 metres	500
0 yards	500

◁ **A grand Georgian house in Bedford Square**

Street-by-Street: Bloomsbury

The British Museum dominates Bloomsbury. Its earnestly intellectual atmosphere spills over into the surrounding streets, and to its north lies the main campus of London University. The area has been home to writers and artists, and is a traditional centre of the book trade. Most of the publishers have left, but there are still many bookshops around.

The Senate House (1932) is the administrative headquarters of the University of London. It holds a priceless library.

Bedford Square is one of London's most complete Georgian squares. Its uniform doorways are fringed in artificial stone.

★ British Museum
Designed in the mid-19th century, it is extremely popular and attracts some five million visitors a year ❶

STAR SIGHTS

★ British Museum

★ Russell Square

KEY

– – – Suggested route

0 metres   100

0 yards   100

Museum Street is lined with small cafés and shops selling old books, prints and antiques.

Pizza Express occupies a charming and little-altered Victorian dairy.

The Duke of Bedford's statue commemorates the fifth duke, Francis Russell (1765–1805). An avid farmer, he is shown with sheep and a plough.

LOCATOR MAP
See Central London Map pp14–15

★ **Russell Square**
It was once part of the Duke of Bedford's estate, and is now a shady retreat on a hot day ❹

Bloomsbury Square
Laid out in 1661, it is graced by a statue of states-man Charles James Fox (1749–1806) ❷

To Holborn station

St George's, Bloomsbury
The tower on this typically flamboyant Hawksmoor church is modelled on the tomb of King Mausolus ❸

Sicilian Avenue is a small and unexpected pedestrian precinct from 1905, where colonnades evoke Roman architecture.

British Museum ❶

See pp126–9.

Bloomsbury Square ❷

WC1. **Map** 5 C5. Ⓔ *Holborn.*

This is the oldest of the Bloomsbury squares. It was laid out in 1661 by the Earl of Southampton, who owned the land. None of the original buildings survives and its shaded garden is encircled by a busy one-way traffic system. (Unusually for central London, you can nearly always find a space in the car park under the square.)

The square has had many famous residents; a plaque commemorates members of the literary and artistic Bloomsbury Group, who lived in the area during the early years of the last century. The group included novelist Virginia Woolf, biographer Lytton Strachey, and artists Vanessa Bell, Duncan Grant and Dora Carrington. Look out for their individual plaques throughout the area.

A plaque commemorating famous Bloomsbury residents

St George's, Bloomsbury ❸

Bloomsbury Way WC1. **Map** 13 B1. **Tel** 020-7405 3044. Ⓔ *Holborn, Tottenham Court Rd.* **Open** 10am–5.30pm Mon–Fri. ⬆ 1.10pm Wed & Fri, 10.30am Sun. **Recitals.** ♿ **www**.stgeorgesbloomsbury.org.uk

A slightly eccentric church, St George's was designed by Nicholas Hawksmoor, Wren's pupil, and completed in 1730. It was built as a place of

The flamboyant Russell Hotel on Russell Square

worship for the prosperous residents of newly-developed, fashionable Bloomsbury. The layered tower, modelled on the tomb of King Mausolus (the original mausoleum in Turkey) and topped by a statue of George I, was for a long time an object of derision – the king was thought to be presented too heroically. In 1913, the funeral of Emily Davison, the suffragette who threw herself under King George V's horse, was held here. The church has recently been fully restored.

Russell Square ❹

WC1. **Map** 5 B5. Ⓔ *Russell Sq.* ⬛ *opening hours flexible.*

One of London's largest squares, Russell Square is a lively place, with a fountain, café and traffic roaring around its perimeter. The east side boasts perhaps the best of the Victorian grand hotels to survive in the capital. Charles Doll's Russell Hotel, which was opened in 1900, is a wondrous confection of red terracotta,

with colonnaded balconies and prancing cherubs beneath the main columns. The exuberance is continued in the lobby, faced with marble of many colours.

Poet T S Eliot worked at the west corner of the square, from 1925 until 1965, in what were the offices of publishers Faber and Faber.

Queen Square ❺

WC1. **Map** 5 C5. Ⓔ *Russell Sq.*

In spite of being named after Queen Anne, this square contains a statue of Queen Charlotte. Her husband, George III, stayed at the house of a doctor here when he became ill with the hereditary disease that drove him mad before his death in 1820. Originally, the north side of the square was left open so that inhabitants had a clear view of Hampstead and Highgate. Today the square is almost completely surrounded by hospital buildings, with early Georgian houses on the west side.

Queen Charlotte's statue in Queen Square

Charles Dickens Museum ⑥

48 Doughty St WC1. **Map** 6 D4. **Tel** 020-7405 2127. ⊖ Chancery Lane, Russell Sq. **Open** 10am–5pm Mon– Sat (last adm: 4.30pm), 11am– 5pm Sun. **Adm charge.** ♿ ground floor. ✗ 🖥 www.dickensmuseum.com

The novelist Charles Dickens lived in this early 19th-century terraced house for three of his most productive years (from 1837 to 1839). The popular works *Oliver Twist* and *Nicholas Nickleby* were entirely written here, and *Pickwick Papers* was finished. Although Dickens had many London homes throughout his lifetime, this is the only one to have survived. In 1923 it was acquired by the Dickens Fellowship and it is now a well-conceived museum with some of the principal rooms laid out exactly as they were in Dickens's time. Others have been adapted to display a varied collection of articles associated with him. The exhibits include papers, portraits and pieces of furniture taken from his other homes as well as first editions of many of his best-known works. The most moving mementos are of Mary Hogarth, the author's sister-in-law, who died, aged 17, a month after the family moved here.

Portrait of Captain Coram (1740) by William Hogarth

Nautical publisher's trade sign, Dickens Museum

Foundling Museum ⑦

40 Brunswick Square WC1. **Map** 5 C4. **Tel** 020-7841 3600. ⊖ Russell Square. ⊙ 10am–6pm Tue–Sat, 12– 6pm Sun. **Adm charge.** ✗ ♿ 📷 book ahead. 🖥 🍴 **Coram's Fields** Guilford St WC1. ⊙ 8am–dusk. www.foundlingmuseum.org.uk

In 1722, Captain Thomas Coram, a retired sailor and ship-builder recently returned from the Americas, vowed to establish a refuge for abandoned children. Horrified by the poverty on London streets, Coram was determined to alter the fate of the city's foundlings by housing, educating and placing them in private homes. Assisted by his friend, the artist William Hogarth, Coram worked tirelessly to raise funds for the refuge. Finally in 1739, after much petitioning of George II, he was granted a Royal Charter to establish a Foundling Hospital. Hogarth donated numerous paintings to the hospital and other artists followed suit, effectively creating the first art gallery in Britain. The wealthy were encouraged to view the works of art and the children at the hospital, in the hope that they would contribute to the charity.

The original hospital located at the end of Lambs Conduit Street was demolished in the 1920s, but the interiors of two of the 18th-century rooms were saved and relocated to 40 Brunswick Square, the current location of the museum. On the ground floor, the story of the thousands of children who were cared for in the Foundling Hospital since its establishment is told. The nationally important collection of 18th-century paintings, sculpture, furniture and interiors is displayed on the first floor.

Adjacent to the museum, with its entrance on Guilford Street, is **Coram's Fields**, a favourite central London playground with lots of space. It's highly popular with children and a convenient pace changer for families visiting the museums. Dogs are not allowed, and all adults must be accompanied by children.

British Library ⑧

96 Euston Rd NW1. **Map** 5 B3. **Tel** 020-7412 7332. ⊖ King's Cross St Pancras. **Open** 9.30am–6pm Mon– Fri (8pm Tue), 9.30am–5pm Sat, 11am–5pm Sun. **Regular events.** ♿ ✗ 🖥 🍴 📷 www.bl.uk

London's most important building from the late 20th century houses the national collection of books, manuscripts and maps, as well as the British Library Sound Archive. Designed in red brick by Sir Colin St John Wilson, it opened in 1997 after nearly 20 years under construction, involving controversial cost over-runs, but is now widely admired.

A copy of nearly every printed book in the United Kingdom is held here – more than 16 million – and can be consulted by those with a reader's ticket. There are also exhibition galleries open to everyone. Visitors may view some of the Library's most precious items, including the Lindisfarne Gospels, with the Turning the Pages system which shows each page on a monitor. Other volumes include a Gutenberg Bible and Shakespeare's First Folio. Running through six floors is a spectacular glass tower holding George III's library.

Page from the Lindisfarne Gospels

British Museum ❶

The oldest public museum in the world, the British Museum was established in 1753 to house the collections of the physician Sir Hans Sloane (1660–1753), who also helped create the Chelsea Physic Garden *(see p197)*. Sloane's

The innovatively designed Great Court

artefacts have been added to by gifts and purchases from all over the world, and the museum now contains innumerable items stretching from the present day to prehistory. Robert Smirke designed the main part of the building (1823–50), but the architectural highlight is Norman Foster's Great Court, with the world-famous Reading Room at its centre.

Upper floor   94
90
91
67
66
63
62
57
61   58
59   57
73
72

★ Egyptian Mummies

The ancient Egyptians preserved their dead in expectation of an afterlife. Animals that were believed to have sacred powers were also often mummified. This cat comes from Abydos on the Nile and dates from about 30 BC.

Montague Place entrance

34
35

Main floor

33
24
26

★ Parthenon Sculptures

These reliefs were brought to England by Lord Elgin from the Parthenon in Athens. The British government purchased them from him in 1816.

Lower floor

25
21
20
9
19   22   4
8
77
78
79
86
80   87
81   82   88
85   89
83
84

35

17
18   16
10
15

KEY TO FLOORPLAN

☐ Asian collection

☐ Enlightenment

☐ Coins, medals, prints and drawings

☐ Greek and Roman collection

☐ Egyptian collection

☐ Ancient Near Eastern collection

☐ Europe collection

☐ Temporary exhibitions

☐ Non-exhibition space

☐ World Collection

☐ Special Exhibitions

Lower floor

Main floor

Numerous large-scale sculptures are featured in the Concourse Gallery of the Great Court.

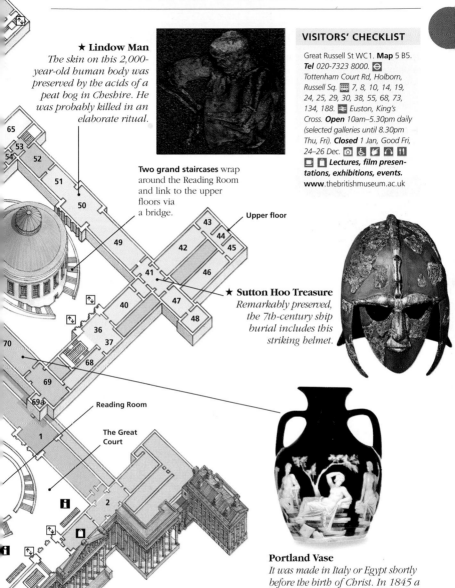

★ Lindow Man
The skin on this 2,000-year-old human body was preserved by the acids of a peat bog in Cheshire. He was probably killed in an elaborate ritual.

Two grand staircases wrap around the Reading Room and link to the upper floors via a bridge.

Upper floor

★ Sutton Hoo Treasure
Remarkably preserved, the 7th-century ship burial includes this striking helmet.

Reading Room

The Great Court

Main entrance

Portland Vase
It was made in Italy or Egypt shortly before the birth of Christ. In 1845 a visitor smashed it into 200 pieces, since when it has been reassembled.

VISITORS' CHECKLIST

Great Russell St WC1. **Map** 5 B5.
Tel 020-7323 8000.
Tottenham Court Rd, Holborn,
Russell Sq. 7, 8, 10, 14, 19,
24, 25, 29, 30, 38, 55, 68, 73,
134, 188. Euston, King's
Cross. **Open** 10am–5.30pm daily
(selected galleries until 8.30pm
Thu, Fri). **Closed** 1 Jan, Good Fri,
24–26 Dec. **Lectures, film presentations, exhibitions, events.**
www.thebritishmuseum.ac.uk

GALLERY GUIDE

The Greek and Roman and Ancient Near Eastern collections are found on all three levels of the museum, predominantly on the west side. The African collection is located on the lower floor, while Asian exhibits are found on the main and upper floors on the north side of the Museum. The Americas collection is located in the northeast corner of the main floor. Egyptian artifacts are found west of the Great Court and on the upper floors.

STAR EXHIBITS

★ Parthenon Sculptures

★ Lindow Man

★ Egyptian Mummies

★ Sutton Hoo Treasure

Exploring the British Museum's Collections

The Museum's immense hoard of treasure spans two million years of history and culture. The 94 galleries, which stretch 2.5 miles (4 km), cover civilisations from ancient Egypt and Assyria to modern Japan.

Ornamental detail from a Sumerian Queen's lyre

PREHISTORIC AND ROMAN BRITAIN

1st-century BC bronze helmet dredged up from the Thames

Relics of prehistoric Britain are on display in six separate galleries. The most impressive items include the gold "Mold Cape", a ceremonial bronze-age cape found in Wales; an antlered headdress worn by hunter-gatherers some 9000 years ago; and "Lindow Man", a 1st-century AD sacrificial victim who lay preserved in a bog until 1984. Some superb Celtic metalwork is also on show, alongside the silver Mildenhall Treasure and other Roman pieces. The Hinton St. Mary mosaic (4th century AD) features a roundel containing the earliest known British depiction of Christ.

EUROPE

The spectacular Sutton Hoo ship treasure, the burial hoard of a 7th-century Anglo-Saxon king, is on display in Room 41. This superb find, made in 1939, revolutionized our understanding of Anglo-Saxon life and ritual. The artifacts include a helmet and shield, Celtic hanging bowls, the remains of a lyre, and gold and garnet jewellery.

Adjacent galleries contain a collection of clocks, watches and scientific instruments. Some exquisite timepieces are on view, including a 400-year-old clock from Prague,

designed as a model galleon; in its day it pitched, played music, and even fired a cannon. Also nearby are the famous 12th-century Lewis chessmen, and a gallery housing Baron Ferdinand Rothschild's (1839–98) remarkably varied treasures.

The museum's modern collection includes some Wedgwood pottery, glassware, and a series of Russian revolutionary plates.

Gilded brass late-16th-century ship clock from Prague

ANCIENT NEAR EAST

There are numerous galleries devoted to the Western Asian collections, covering 7,000 years of history. The most famous items are the 7th-century BC Assyrian reliefs from King Ashurbanipal's palace at Nineveh, but of equal interest are two large human-headed bulls from 7th-century BC Khorsabad, and an inscribed Black Obelisk of Assyrian King Shalmaneser III. The upper floors contain pieces from ancient Sumeria, part of the Oxus Treasure (which lay buried for over 2,000 years), and the museum's collection of clay

cuneiform tablets. The earliest of these are inscribed with the oldest known pictographs (c.3300 BC). Also of interest is a skull discovered in Jericho in the 1950s; augmented with shells and lime plaster, the skull belonged to a hunter who lived in the area some 7,000 years ago.

EGYPT

The British Museum's Egyptian sculptures can be found in Room 4. These include a fine red granite head of a king, thought to depict Amenophis III, and a colossal statue of King Rameses II. Also on show is the Rosetta Stone, which was used by Jean-François Champollion (1790–1832) as a primer for deciphering Egyptian hieroglyphs. An extraordinary array of mummies, jewellery and Coptic art can also be found upstairs. The various instruments that were used by embalmers to preserve bodies before entombment are all displayed.

Part of a colossal granite statue of Rameses II, the 13th-century BC Egyptian monarch

GREECE AND ROME

The Greek and Roman collections include the museum's most famous treasure, the Parthenon sculptures. These 5th-century BC reliefs were once part of a marble frieze that decorated the Parthenon, Athena's temple on the Acropolis in Athens. Much of it was ruined in battle in 1687, and most of what survived was removed between 1801 and 1804 by the British diplomat Lord Elgin, and sold to the British nation. Other highlights include the Nereid Monument

Ancient Greek vase illustrating the mythical hero Hercules's fight with a bull

and sculptures and friezes from the Mausoleum at Halicarnassus. The beautiful 1st-century BC cameo-glass Portland Vase is located in the Roman Empire section.

ASIA

The Chinese collection is noted for its fine porcelain and ancient Shang bronzes (c.1500–1050 BC). Particularly impressive are the ceremonial ancient Chinese bronze vessels, with their enigmatic animal-head shapes.

The fine Chinese ceramics range from delicate tea bowls to a model pond, which is almost a thousand years old.

Adjacent to these is one of the finest collections of Asian religious sculpture outside India. A major highlight is an assortment of sculpted reliefs, which once covered the walls of the Buddhist temple at Amaravati, and which recount stories from the life of the Buddha. A Korean section contains some gigantic works of Buddhist art.

The museum's collection of Islamic art, including a stunning jade terrapin found

Statue of the Hindu God Shiva Nataraja, also known as the Lord of the Dance (11th century AD)

in a water tank, can be found in Room 34. Rooms 92 to 94 house the Japanese galleries, with a Classical teahouse in Room 92.

AFRICA

An interesting collection of African sculptures, textiles and graphic art can also be found in Room 25 on the lower floor of the museum. Famous bronzes from the Kingdom of Benin stand alongside modern African prints, paintings, drawings and colourful fabrics.

THE GREAT COURT AND THE READING ROOM

Surrounding the Reading Room of the former British Library, the £100-million Great Court opened to coincide with the new millennium. Designed by Sir Norman Foster, the Court is covered by a wide-span, lightweight roof, creating London's first indoor public square. The Reading Room has been restored to its original design, so visitors can sample the atmosphere which Karl Marx, Mahatma Gandhi and George Bernard Shaw found

so agreeable. From the outside, however, it is scarcely recognizable; it is housed in a multi-level construction which partly supports the roof, and which also contains a Centre for Education, temporary exhibition galleries, bookshops, cafés and restaurants. Part of the Reading Room also serves as a study suite where those wishing to learn more about the Museum's collections have access to information.

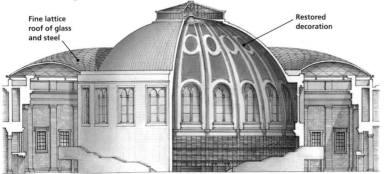

Fine lattice roof of glass and steel

Restored decoration

The massive former Midland Grand Hotel above St Pancras Station

St Pancras International ⑨

Euston Rd NW1. **Map** 5 B2.
Tel 08705 186186 ⊖ *King's Cross, St Pancras.* **Open** *5am–11pm daily.*
See **Getting to London** *pp376–7.*
www.eurostar.com

Easily the most spectacular of the three rail termini along Euston Road, its extravagant frontage, in red-brick gingerbread Gothic, is technically not part of the station. It was really Sir George Gilbert Scott's Midland Grand Hotel, opened in 1874 as one of the most sumptuous hotels of its time. From 1935 until the early 1980s the building was used as offices; it is now being lavishly restored. Extensive work has been under way to make the station

Figures on St Pancras Church

the main London terminal for international Eurostar services to Europe; it is due to open in summer 2007. St Pancras International will have six platforms for use solely by Eurostar services.

St Pancras Parish Church ⑩

Euston Rd NW1. **Map** 5 B3.
Tel 020-7388 1461. ⊖
Euston. **Open** *Mon–Fri
(phone to check).* ⊤ *8am,
10am Sun.* ♿ **Recitals**
*1.15pm Thu, evensong 6pm
Sun.* **www.**stpancraschurch.org

This is a stately Greek revival church of 1822 by William Inwood and his son Henry, both great enthusiasts for Athenian architecture. The design is based on the Erectheum on the Acropolis in Athens, and even the wooden pulpit stands on miniature Ionic columns of its own. The long, galleried interior has a dramatic severity appropriate to the church's style. The female figures on the northern outer wall were originally taller than they are now; a chunk had to be taken out of the middle of each to make them fit under the roof they were meant to be supporting.

Woburn Walk ⑪

WC1. **Map** 5 B4. ⊖ *Euston, Euston Sq.*

A well-restored street of bow-fronted shops, it was designed by Thomas Cubitt in 1822. The high pavement on the east side was to protect shop fronts from the mud thrown up by carriages. The poet W B Yeats lived at No. 5 from 1895 until 1919.

Percival David Foundation of Chinese Art ⑫

53 Gordon Sq WC1. **Map** 5 B4. *Tel*
020-7387 3909. ⊖ *Russell Sq, Euston
Sq, Goodge St.* **Open** *10.30am–5pm
Mon–Fri.* **Closed** *public hols.* ♿
limited. ⊡ **www.**pdfmuseum.org.uk

Particularly fascinating to those with a specialized interest in Chinese porcelain, but attractive also to the non-specialist, this is an important collection of exquisite wares made between the 10th and 18th centuries. Percival David presented his fine collection to the University of London in 1950, and it is now administered by the School of Oriental and African Studies. The foundation includes a research library and, as well as the permanent collection, houses occasional special exhibitions of east Asian art.

Blue temple vase from David's collection

Fitzroy Square ⑬

W1. **Map** 4 F4. ⊖ *Warren St, Great Portland St.*

Designed by Robert Adam in 1794, the square's south and east sides survive in their original form, in dignified

Portland stone. Blue plaques record the homes of many artists, writers and statesmen: George Bernard Shaw and Virginia Woolf both lived at No. 29 – although not at the same time. Shaw gave money to the artist Roger Fry to establish the Omega workshop at No. 33 in 1913. Here young artists were paid a fixed wage to produce Post-Impressionist furniture, pottery, carpets and paintings for sale to the public.

No. 29 Fitzroy Square

Fitzroy Tavern ⓮

16 Charlotte St W1. **Map** 4 F5.
Tel 020-7580 3714. 🚇 *Goodge St.*
Open *11am–11pm Mon–Sat,*
noon–10.30pm Sun. 🚻 *See **Pubs**
pp316–19.*

This traditional pub was a meeting place between World Wars I and II for a group of writers and artists who dubbed the area around Fitzroy Square and Charlotte Street "Fitzrovia". A basement "Writers and Artists Bar" contains pictures of former customers, including the writers Dylan Thomas and George Orwell, and the artist Augustus John.

Charlotte Street ⓯

W1. **Map** 5 A5. 🚇 *Goodge St.*

As the upper classes moved west from Bloomsbury in the early 19th century, a flood of artists and European immigrants moved in, turning the area into a northern appendage to Soho *(see pp98–109)*. The artist John Constable lived and worked for many years at No. 76. Some of the new residents established small workshops

to service the clothing shops on Oxford Street and the furniture stores on Tottenham Court Road. Others set up reasonably-priced restaurants. The street still boasts a great variety of eating places. It is overshadowed from the north by the 189 m (620-ft) Telecom Tower, built in 1964 as a vast TV, radio and telecommunications aerial (see p32).

Pollock's Toy Museum ⓰

1 Scala St W1. **Map** 5 A5.
Tel 020-7636 3452. 🚇 *Goodge St.*
Open *10am–5pm Mon–Sat.* **Adm**
charge. 🚻
www.pollockstoymuseum.com

Benjamin Pollock was a renowned maker of toy theatres in the late 19th and

Telecom Tower

early 20th centuries – the novelist Robert Louis Stevenson was an enthusiastic customer. The museum opened in 1956 and the final room is devoted to stages and puppets from Pollock's theatres, together with a reconstruction of his workshop. This is a child-sized museum created in two largely unaltered 18th-century houses. The small rooms have been filled with a fascinating assortment of historic toys from all over the world. There are dolls, puppets, trains, cars, construction sets, a fine rocking horse and a splendid collection of mainly Victorian doll's houses. Puppet shows are held here during school holidays: but parents should beware – the exit leads you through a very tempting toyshop.

Pearly king and queen dolls from Pollock's Toy Museum

HOLBORN & THE INNS OF COURT

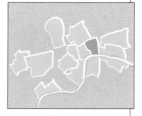

This area is traditionally home to the legal and journalistic professions. The law is still here, in the Royal Courts of Justice and the Inns of Court, but most national newspapers left Fleet Street in the 1980s. Several buildings here predate the Great Fire of 1666 *(see pp24–5)*. These include the

Royal crest at Lincoln's Inn

superb façade of Staple Inn, Prince Henry's Room, and the interior of Middle Temple Hall. Holborn used to be one of the capital's main shopping districts. Times have changed the face of the area, but the jewellery and diamond dealers of Hatton Garden are still here, as are the London Silver Vaults.

SIGHTS AT A GLANCE

Historic Buildings, Sights and Streets
Lincoln's Inn ❷
Old Curiosity Shop ❹
Law Society ❺
Royal Courts of Justice ❼
Fleet Street ❾
Prince Henry's Room ❿
Temple ⓫
Dr Johnson's House ⓮
Holborn Viaduct ⓰
Hatton Garden ⓲
Staple Inn ⓳
Gray's Inn ㉑

Museums and Galleries
Sir John Soane's Museum ❶

Churches
St Clement Danes ❻
St Bride's ⓬
St Andrew, Holborn ⓯
St Etheldreda's Chapel ⓱

Monuments
Temple Bar Memorial ❽

Parks and Gardens
Lincoln's Inn Fields ❸

Pubs
Ye Olde Cheshire Cheese ⓭

Shops
London Silver Vaults ⓴

KEY

▮	Street-by-Street map
🚇	Underground station
🚆	Railway station

GETTING THERE
This area is served by the Circle, Central, District, Metropolitan and Piccadilly lines. Buses 17, 18, 45, 46, 171, 243 and 259 are among many in the area, and trains run from a number of mainline stations inside or close to the area.

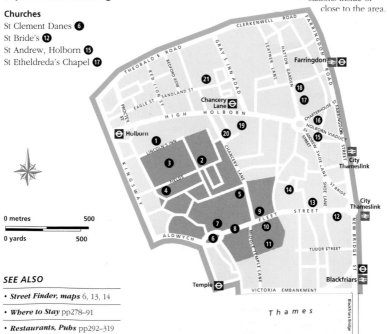

SEE ALSO

- *Street Finder, maps* 6, 13, 14
- *Where to Stay* pp278–91
- *Restaurants, Pubs* pp292–319

◁ **The Royal Courts of Justice on the Strand**

Street-by-Street: Lincoln's Inn

This is calm, dignified, legal London, packed with history and interest. Lincoln's Inn, adjoining one of the city's first residential squares, has buildings dating from the late 15th century. Dark-suited lawyers carry bundles of briefs between their offices here and the Neo-Gothic Law Courts. Nearby is the Temple, another historic legal district with a famous 13th-century round church.

★ Sir John Soane's Museum
The Georgian architect made this his London home and left it, with his collection, to the nation ❶

To Kingsway

★ Lincoln's Inn Fields
The mock-Tudor archway, leading to Lincoln's Inn and built in 1845, overlooks the Fields ❸

Old Curiosity Shop
This is a rare 17th-century, pre-Great Fire building which is now a shop ❹

The Royal College of Surgeons was designed in 1836 by Sir Charles Barry. Inside there are laboratories for research and teaching as well as a museum of anatomical specimens.

STAR SIGHTS

- ★ Sir John Soane's Museum
- ★ Temple
- ★ Lincoln's Inn Fields
- ★ Lincoln's Inn

KEY

– – – Suggested route

0 metres	100
0 yards	100

Twinings has been selling tea from here since 1706. The doorway dates from 1787 when the shop was called the Golden Lion.

The Gladstone Statue was erected in 1905 to commemorate William Gladstone, the Victorian statesman who was Prime Minister four times.

★ Lincoln's Inn
The Court of Chancery sat here, in Old Hall, from 1835 until 1858. Sir John Taylor Coleridge, nephew of the poet, was a well-known judge of the time **2**

LOCATOR MAP
See Central London Map pp14–15

Royal Courts of Justice
The country's main court for civil cases and appeals was built in 1882. It is made out of 35 million bricks faced with Portland stone **7**

Law Society
Look for the gold lions on the railings of this superb building **5**

Fleet Street
For two centuries this was the centre of the national press. Today the newspaper offices are gone **9**

El Vino is a venerable wine bar, where journalists still mingle with lawyers.

Prince Henry's Room
There is an authentic 17th-century room in this former gatehouse **10**

St Clement Danes
Designed by Wren (1679), it is the Royal Air Force church **6**

Temple Bar Memorial
A dragon marks where the City of London meets Westminster **8**

★ Temple
It was built for the Knights Templar in the 13th century, but today lawyers stroll here **11**

Wigged barristers on their way to their offices in Lincoln's Inn

Lincoln's Inn ❷

WC2. **Map** 14 D1. **Tel** 020-7405 6360. ⊖ Holborn, Chancery Lane. **Grounds open** 7am–7pm Mon–Fri. **Chapel open** 12.30–2pm Mon–Fri. **Hall** not open to the public. ♿

Some of the buildings in Lincoln's Inn, the best-preserved of London's Inns of Court, go back to the late 15th century. The coat of arms above the arch of the Chancery Lane gatehouse is Henry VIII's, and the heavy oak door is of the same vintage. Shakespeare's contemporary, Ben Jonson, is believed to have laid some of the bricks of Lincoln's Inn during the reign of Elizabeth I. The chapel is early 17th-century Gothic. Women were not allowed to be buried here until 1839, when the grieving Lord Brougham petitioned to have the rule changed so that his beloved daughter could be interred in the chapel, to wait for him to join her.

Lincoln's Inn has its share of famous alumni. Oliver Cromwell and John Donne,

Sir John Soane's Museum ❶

13 Lincoln's Inn Fields WC2. **Map** 14 D1. **Tel** 020-7405 2107. ⊖ Holborn. **Open** 10am–5pm Tue–Sat, 6–9pm first Tue of month. **Closed** 24–26 Dec, 1 Jan, Easter, public hols. ♿ limited – phone first. 📷 Sat 2.30pm; groups book ahead. 🚻 www.soane.org

One of the most surprising museums in London, this house was left to the nation by Sir John Soane in 1837, with a far-sighted stipulation that nothing at all should be changed. One of Britain's leading 19th-century architects, responsible for designing the Bank of England, Soane was the son of a bricklayer. After prudently marrying the niece of a wealthy builder, whose fortune he inherited, he bought and reconstructed No. 12 Lincoln's Inn Fields. In 1813 he and his wife moved into No. 13 and later, in 1824, he rebuilt No. 14, due to re-open to the public in 2006.

Today, true to Soane's wishes, the collections are much as he left them – an eclectic gathering of beautiful, peculiar and often instructional objects.

The building itself abounds with architectural surprises and illusions. In the main ground floor room, with its deep red and green colouring, cunningly placed mirrors play tricks with light and space. The picture gallery is lined with layers of folding panels to increase its capacity. The panels open out to reveal galleried extensions to the room itself. Among other works here are many of Soane's own exotic designs, including those for Pitzhanger Manor (see p258) and the Bank of England (see p147). Here also is William Hogarth's *Rake's Progress* series.

In the centre of the low-ceilinged basement an atrium stretches up to the roof. A glass dome lights galleries, on every floor, that are laden with Classical statuary.

A glass dome allows light into the basement.

A vast sarcophagus stands on the floor of the basement.

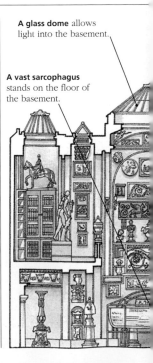

the 17th-century poet, were both students here, as was William Penn, founder of the US state of Pennsylvania.

Lincoln's Inn Fields ❸

WC2. **Map** 14 D1. 🚇 *Holborn.* **Open** *dawn–dusk daily.* **Public tennis courts.**

This used to be a public execution site. Under the Tudors and the Stuarts, many religious martyrs, and those suspected of treachery to the Crown, perished here.

When the developer William Newton wanted to build here in the 1640s, students at Lincoln's Inn and other residents made him undertake that the land in the centre would remain a public area for ever. Thanks to this early protest, lawyers today play tennis here throughout the summer, or read their briefs in the fresh air. In recent years it has also become the site of an evening soup kitchen for some of London's homeless.

Old Curiosity Shop sign

Old Curiosity Shop ❹

13–14 Portsmouth St WC2. **Map** 14 D1. 🚇 *Holborn.*

Whether it is or is not the original for Charles Dickens's novel of the same name, this is a genuine 17th-century building and almost certainly the oldest shop in central London. With its overhanging first floor, it gives a rare impression of a London streetscape from before the Great Fire of 1666.

The Old Curiosity Shop maintains its retailing tradition, and currently operates as a shoe shop. A preservation order guarantees the long-term future of the building.

Law Society ❺

113 Chancery Lane WC2. **Map** 14 E1. **Tel** 020-7242 1222. 🚇 *Chancery Lane.* **Not open** to the public.

The headquarters of the solicitors' professional body is, architecturally, one of the most interesting buildings in the legal quarter. The main part, dominated by four Ionic columns, was completed in 1832. More significant is the northern extension, an early work of Charles Holden, an Arts and Crafts enthusiast who later made his name as a designer of London Underground stations. In his window arches the four seated figures depict truth, justice, liberty and mercy.

The building is on the corner of Carey Street, the site of the bankruptcy court whose name, corrupted to "Queer Street", entered the language to describe a state of destitution.

Every wall is covered, and every room filled, with artifacts from Soane's massive collection.

In the picture gallery, panels covered with paintings unfold to reveal more works of art behind them.

The Monk's Parlour is full of grotesque, Gothic casts.

St Clement Danes ❻

Strand WC2. **Map** 14 D2. **Tel** 020-7242 8282. 🚇 Temple. **Open** 9am–4pm Mon–Fri, 9.30am–3pm Sat & Sun. **Closed** noon 25 Dec–27 Dec, public hols. 🕇 12.30am Wed & Fri, 11am Sun. 🔊 See **Ceremonial London** p55.

Christopher Wren designed this wonderful church in 1680. Its name derives from an earlier church built here by the descendants of Danish invaders whom Alfred the Great had allowed to remain in London in the 9th century. From the 17th to 19th centuries many people were buried here, and their restplates are now in the crypt. The chain now hanging on the crypt wall was probably used to secure coffin lids against body snatchers who stole fresh corpses and sold them to the teaching hospitals.

St Clement Danes sits proudly isolated on a traffic island. It is now the Royal Air Force (RAF) church, and the interior

Clock at the Victorian law courts

is dominated by RAF symbols, memorials and monuments. Outside, to the east, is a statue (1910) of Dr Johnson *(see p140)*, who often came to services here. The church bells ring to the tune of the English nursery rhyme Oranges and Lemons at 9am, noon, 3pm and 6pm Mon–Sat, and there is an annual oranges and lemons service in March.

Royal Courts of Justice (the Law Courts) ❼

Strand WC2. **Map** 14 D2. **Tel** 020-7947 6000. 🚇 Holborn, Temple, Chancery Lane. **Open** 9am–4.30pm Mon–Fri. **Closed** public hols. 🔊 ⬜ 🖥 www.courtservice.gov.uk

Knots of demonstrators and television cameras can often be seen outside this sprawling and fanciful Victorian Gothic building, waiting for the result of a contentious case. These are the nation's main civil courts, dealing with such matters as divorce, libel, civil liability and appeals. Criminals are dealt with at the Old Bailey *(see p147)*, ten minutes' walk to the east. The public are admitted to all the court rooms and a list tells you which case is being heard in which court. The massive Gothic building was completed in 1882. It is said to contain 1,000 rooms and 5.6 km (3.5 miles) of corridors.

Temple Bar Memorial ❽

Fleet St EC4. **Map** 14 D2. 🚇 Holborn, Temple, Chancery Lane.

The monument in the middle of Fleet Street, outside the Law Courts, dates from 1880 and marks the entrance to the City of London. On state occasions it is a long-standing tradition for the monarch to have to pause here and ask permission of the Lord Mayor to enter. Temple Bar, a huge archway designed by Wren, used to stand here. You can see what it used to look like from one of the four reliefs that surround the base of the present monument.

Fleet Street ❾

EC4. **Map** 14 E1. 🚇 Temple, Blackfriars, St Paul's.

England's first printing press was set up here in the late 15th century by William Caxton's assistant, and Fleet

The dragon, symbol of the City, at the entrance to the City at Temple Bar

William Capon's engraving of Fleet Street in 1799

Street has been a centre of London's publishing industry ever since. Playwrights Shakespeare and Ben Jonson were patrons of the old Mitre tavern, now No. 37 Fleet Street. In 1702 the first newspaper, *The Daily Courant*, was issued from Fleet Street – conveniently placed for the City and Westminster which were the main sources of news. Later the street became synonymous with the Press.

The printing presses underneath the newspaper offices were abandoned in 1987, when new technology made it easy to produce papers away from the centre of town in areas such as Wapping and the Docklands. Today the newspapers have left their Fleet Street offices and only the agencies, Reuters and the Press Association, remain.

El Vino wine bar, at the western end opposite Fetter Lane, is a traditional haunt of journalists and lawyers.

Prince Henry's Room ❿

17 Fleet St EC4. **Map** 14 E1. *Tel* 020-7936 2710. ⊖ Temple, Chancery Lane. **Open** 11am–2pm Mon–Sat. **Closed** public hols. 🖾 **www**.cityoflondon.gov.uk

Built in 1610 as part of a Fleet Street tavern, this gets its name from the Prince of Wales's coat of arms and the initials PH in the centre of the ceiling. They were probably put there to mark the investiture as Prince of Wales of Henry, James I's eldest son who died before he became king.

The fine half-timbered front, alongside the gateway to Inner Temple, is original and so is some of the room's oak panelling. It contains an exhibition about the diarist Samuel Pepys.

Temple ⓫

Inner Temple, King's Bench Walk EC4. **Map** 14 E2. *Tel* 020-7797 8250. ⊖ Temple. **Open** 12.30pm–3pm Mon–Fri (grounds only). 🖾 **Middle Temple Hall**, Middle Temple Lane EC4. *Tel* 020-7427 4800. **Open** 10am–11.30, 3–4pm Mon–Fri. **Closed** at short notice for functions. 🖾 📷 book ahead. 🚇 **Temple Church** *Tel* 020-7353 3470. **Open** Wed–Fri; call for times & services. **www**.templechurch.com

This embraces two of the four Inns of Court, the Middle Temple and the Inner Temple. (The other two are Lincoln's and Gray's Inns, *pp136, 141.*) The name derives from the

Knights Templar, a chivalrous order which used to protect pilgrims to the Holy Land. The order was based here until it was suppressed by the Crown because its power was viewed as a threat. Initiations probably took place in the crypt of Temple Church and there are 13th-century effigies of Knights Templar in the nave.

Among some other ancient buildings is the Middle Temple Hall. Its fine Elizabethan interior survives – Shakespeare's *Twelfth Night* was performed here in 1601. Behind Temple, peaceful lawns stretch lazily down towards the Embankment.

St Bride's ⓬

Fleet St EC4. **Map** 14 F2. *Tel* 020-7427 0133. ⊖ Blackfriars. **Open** 8am–6.30pm Mon–Fri, 11am–3pm Sat, 10am–1pm, 5–7.30pm Sun. **Closed** public hols. 🖾 ✝ 11am & 6.30pm Sun. **Concerts** Check website for details. **www**.stbrides.com

St Bride's, church of the Press

St Bride's is one of Wren's best-loved churches. Its position just off Fleet Street has made it the traditional venue for memorial services to departed journalists. Wall plaques commemorate Fleet Street journalists and printers.

The marvellous octagonal layered spire has been the model for tiered wedding cakes since shortly after it was added in 1703. Bombed in 1940, the interior was faithfully restored after World War II. The fascinating crypt contains remnants of earlier churches on the site, and a section of Roman pavement.

Effigies in Temple Church

Ye Olde Cheshire Cheese ⑬

145 Fleet St EC4. **Map** 14 E1.
Tel 020-7353 6170. 🚇 *Blackfriars.*
Open 11am–11pm Mon–Sat,
noon–3pm Sun. See **Pubs**
pp316–19.

There has been an inn here
for centuries; parts of this
building date back to 1667,
when the Cheshire Cheese
was rebuilt after the Great
Fire. The diarist Samuel Pepys
often drank here in the 17th
century, but it was Dr Samuel
Johnson's association with
"the Cheese" that made it
a place of pilgrimage for 19th-
century literati. These
included novelists Mark
Twain and Charles Dickens.
   This is one of the few pubs
to have kept the 18th-century
arrangement of small rooms
with fireplaces, tables and
benches, instead of knocking
them into larger bars.

Dr Johnson's House ⑭

17 Gough Sq EC4. **Map** 14 E1. **Tel**
020-7353 3745. 🚇 *Blackfriars,
Chancery Lane, Temple.* **Open** May–
Sep: 11am–5.30pm Mon–Sat; Oct–
Apr: 11am–5pm Mon–Sat. **Closed**
public hols. **Adm charge.** 📷 *small
charge.* 🎫 *book ahead.* 📖
www.drjohnsonshouse.org

Dr Samuel Johnson was an
18th-century scholar famous
for the many witty (and often
contentious) remarks that his
biographer, James Boswell,

**Schoolgirl figure mounted on the
façade of St Andrew church**

recorded and published.
Johnson lived here from 1748
to 1759. He compiled the first
definitive English dictionary
(1755) in the attic, where six
scribes and assistants stood all
day at high desks.
   The house, built before 1700,
is furnished with 18th-century
pieces and a small collection
of exhibits relating to Johnson
and the times in which he
lived. These include a tea set
belonging to his friend Mrs
Thrale and pictures of Johnson
and his contemporaries. A
recent addition is a selection
of replica Georgian costumes
for children to try on.

Reconstructed interior of Dr Johnson's house

St Andrew, Holborn ⑮

Holborn Circus EC4. **Map** 14 E1. **Tel**
020-7583 7394. 🚇 *Chancery Lane.*
Open 9am–5pm Mon–Fri. 📷 ♿

The medieval church here
survived the Great Fire of
1666. In 1686 Christopher
Wren was, however, asked to
redesign it, and the lower part
of the tower is virtually all
that remains of the earlier
church. One of Wren's most
spacious churches, it was
gutted during World War II
but faithfully restored as the
church of the London trade
guilds. Benjamin Disraeli, the
Jewish-born Prime Minister,
was baptized here in 1817, at
the age of 12. In the 19th
century a charity school was
attached to the church.

Holborn Viaduct ⑯

EC1. **Map** 14 F1. 🚇 *Farringdon,
St Paul's, Chancery Lane.*

Civic symbol on Holborn Viaduct

This piece of Victorian
ironwork was erected in the
1860s as part of a much-
needed traffic scheme. It is
best seen from Farringdon
Street which is linked to the
bridge by a staircase. Climb
up and see the statues of City
heroes and bronze images of
Commerce, Agriculture,
Science and Fine Arts.

St Etheldreda's Chapel ⑰

14 Ely Place EC1. **Map** 6 E5. **Tel**
020-7405 1061. 🚇 *Farringdon.*
Open 8am–6.30pm daily. 📷 🖥
noon–2pm.

This is a rare 13th-century
survivor, the chapel and crypt
of Ely House, where the
Bishops of Ely lived until the

Reformation. Then it was acquired by an Elizabethan courtier, Sir Christopher Hatton, whose descendants demolished the house but kept the chapel and turned it into a Protestant church. It passed through various hands and, in 1874, reverted to the Catholic faith.

Hatton Garden

EC1. **Map** 6 E5. ⊖ *Chancery Lane, Farringdon.*

Built on land that used to be the garden of Hatton House, this is London's diamond and jewellery district. Gems ranging from the priceless to the mundane are traded from scores of small shops with sparkling window displays, and even from the pavements. One of the city's few remaining pawnbrokers is here – look for its traditional sign of three brass balls above the door.

Staple Inn

Holborn WC1. **Map** 14 E1.
⊖ *Chancery Lane.* **Courtyard open** *9am–5pm Mon–Fri.*

This building was once the wool staple, where wool was weighed and taxed. The frontage overlooks Holborn and is the only real example of Elizabethan half-timbering left in central London. Although now much restored, it would still be recognizable by someone who had known it in 1586, when it was built. The shops at street level have the feel of the 19th century, and there are some 18th-century buildings in the courtyard.

London Silver Vaults

53–64 Chancery Lane WC2.
Map 14 D1. ⊖ *Chancery Lane, Holborn.*

These silver vaults originate from the Chancery Lane Safe Deposit Company, established in 1885. After descending a

Staple Inn, a survivor from 1586

staircase you pass through formidable steel security doors and reach a nest of underground shops sparkling with antique and modern silverware. London silver makers have been renowned for centuries, reaching their peak in the Georgian era. The best examples sell for many thousands of pounds but most shops also offer modest pieces at realistic prices.

Coffee pot (1716): Silver Vaults

Gray's Inn

Gray's Inn Rd WC1. **Map** 6 D5. **Tel** *020-7458 7800.* ⊖ *Chancery Lane, Holborn.* **Grounds open** *noon–2.30pm Mon–Fri.* ask first. &

This ancient legal centre and law school goes back to the 14th century. Like many of the buildings in this area, it was badly damaged by World War II bombs but much of it has been rebuilt. At least one of Shakespeare's plays (*A Comedy of Errors*) was first performed in Gray's Inn hall in 1594. The hall's 16th-century interior screen still survives.

More recently, the young Charles Dickens was employed as a clerk here in 1827–8. Today the garden, once a convenient site for staging duels, is open to lunchtime strollers for part of the year, and typifies the cloistered calm of the four Inns of Court. The buildings may be visited only by prior arrangement.

THE CITY

Traditional bank sign on Lombard Street

London's financial district is built on the site of the original Roman settlement. Its full title is the City of London, but it is usually referred to as the City. Most traces of the early City were obliterated by the Great Fire of 1666 and World War II (see pp24–5 and 33). Today glossy modern offices stand among a plethora of banks, with marbled halls and stately pillars. It is the contrast between dour, warren-like Victorian buildings and shiny new ones that gives the City its distinctive character. Though it hums with activity in business hours, few people have lived here since the 19th century, when it was one of London's main residential centres. Today only the churches, many of them by Christopher Wren (see p47), are a reminder of those past times.

SIGHTS AT A GLANCE

Historic Streets and Buildings
Mansion House ❶
Royal Exchange ❸
Old Bailey ❼
Apothecaries' Hall ❽
Fishmongers' Hall ❾
Tower of London pp154–7 ⓰
Tower Bridge ⓱
Stock Exchange ⓲
Lloyd's of London ㉓

Museums and Galleries
Bank of England Museum ❹
Guildhall Art Gallery ㉔

Historic Markets
Billingsgate ⓬
Leadenhall Market ㉒

Monuments
Monument ⓫

Churches and Cathedrals
St Stephen Walbrook ❷
St Mary-le-Bow ❺
St Paul's Cathedral pp148–51 ❻
St Magnus the Martyr ❿
St Mary-at-Hill ⓭
St Margaret Pattens ⓮
All Hallows by the Tower ⓯
St Helen's Bishopsgate ⓴
St Katharine Cree ㉑

Docks
St Katharine's Dock ⓲

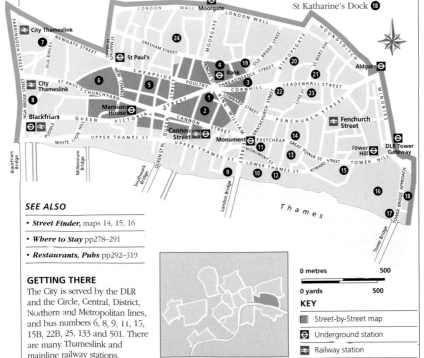

SEE ALSO

• *Street Finder,* maps 14, 15, 16

• *Where to Stay* pp278–291

• *Restaurants, Pubs* pp292–319

GETTING THERE

The City is served by the DLR and the Circle, Central, District, Northern and Metropolitan lines, and bus numbers 6, 8, 9, 11, 15, 15B, 22B, 25, 133 and 501. There are many Thameslink and mainline railway stations.

0 metres 500
0 yards 500

KEY

▨ Street-by-Street map

⊖ Underground station

⊠ Railway station

◁ St Paul's Cathedral with Tower 42, formerly NatWest Tower (1980), to its left

Street-by-Street: The City

This is the business centre of London, home to
vast financial institutions such as the Stock
Exchange and the Bank of England. But in
contrast to these 19th- and 20th-century buildings
are the older survivors. A walk through the City
is in part a pilgrimage through the architectural
visions of Christopher Wren, England's most
sublime and probably most prolific architect.
After the Great Fire of 1666 he supervised the
rebuilding of 52 churches within the area, and
enough survive to testify to his genius.

St Mary-le-Bow
*Anyone born within earshot
of the bells of this Wren
church (the historic Bow
Bells) is said to be a true
Londoner or Cockney* ❺

The Temple of Mithras is
an important Roman
relic whose foundations
were revealed by a
World War II bomb.

★ **St Paul's**
*Wren's masterpiece
still dominates
the City skyline* ❻

St Paul's station

NEW CHANGE

WATLING STREET

BREAD STREET

ST PAUL'S CHURCHYARD

CANNON STREET

FRIDAY ST

QUEEN VICTORIA

QUEEN

**Mansion
House
station**

COLLEGE · OF · ARMS

The College of Arms received its
royal charter in 1484 from Richard
III. Still active today, it assesses
who has a legitimate claim to a
British family coat of arms.

St Nicholas Cole Abbey
was the first church
Wren built in the City
(in 1677). Like many
others, it had to be
restored after World
War II bomb damage.

St James Garlickhythe
contains unusual sword rests
and hat stands, beneath
Wren's elegant spire of 1717.

STAR SIGHTS

★ St Paul's

★ St Stephen Walbrook

★ Bank of England
  Museum

KEY

– – – Suggested route

0 metres   100

0 yards   100

Skinners' Hall is the Italianate
18th-century guild hall for the
leather trade.

Mansion House
The official home of the City of London's Lord Mayor contains a small prison ❶

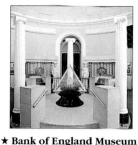

★ **Bank of England Museum**
The intriguing story of England's financial system is vividly displayed here ❹

LOCATOR MAP
See Central London Map pp14–15

SMITHFIELD & SPITALFIELDS

THE CITY

Thames

SOUTHWARK & BANKSIDE

KING ST

IRONMONGER LANE

OLD JEWRY

PRINCE'S STREET

THREADNEEDLE STREET

STREET

STREET

Bank station

CORNHILL

WALBROOK

LOMBARD ST

ST SWITHIN'S

KING WILLIAM STREET

CANNON STREET

Royal Exchange
Since its foundation in Tudor times, this has been at the heart of London's commerce ❸

Lombard Street
is named after Italian bankers who settled here from Lombardy in the 13th century. It is still a banking centre.

St Mary Woolnoth is a characteristically powerful work by Wren's pupil, Nicholas Hawksmoor.

St Mary Abchurch
owes its unusually spacious feel to Wren's large dome. The altar carving is by Grinling Gibbons.

★ **St Stephen Walbrook**
Experimenting for St Paul's, Wren created its unique dome. The interior contains original features, such as this font ❷

Mansion House ❶

Walbrook EC4. **Map** 15 B2.
Tel 020-7626 2500. 🚇 *Bank, Mansion House.* **Open** *to group tours only by appt.* www.cityoflondon.gov.uk

The official residence of the Lord Mayor, it was completed in 1753 to the design of George Dance the Elder, whose designs are now in John Soane's Museum *(see pp136–7)*. The Palladian front with its six large Corinthian columns is one of the most familiar City landmarks. The state rooms have a dignity appropriate to the office of mayor, one of the most spectacular being the 27-m (90-ft) Egyptian Hall.

Formerly located here, and now in the Museum of London *(see pp166–7)*, were 11 holding cells, a reminder of the building's other function as a magistrate's court; the Mayor is chief magistrate of the City during his year of office. Emmeline Pankhurst, who campaigned for women's suffrage in the early 20th century, was once held here.

Egyptian Hall in Mansion House

St Stephen Walbrook ❷

39 Walbrook EC4. **Map** 15 B2. *Tel* 020-7626 8242. 🚇 *Bank, Cannon St.* **Open** *10am–4pm Mon–Thu, 10am–3pm Fri.* ✝ *12.45pm Thu, sung Mass.* 📷 **Organ recitals** *Fri.*

The Lord Mayor's parish church was built by Christopher Wren in 1672–9. Architectural writers consider it to be the finest of his City churches *(see p47)*. The deep, coffered dome, with its ornate plasterwork, was a forerunner of St Paul's. St Stephen's airy columned interior comes as a surprise after its plain exterior. The font cover and pulpit canopy are decorated with exquisite carved figures that contrast strongly with the stark simplicity of Henry Moore's massive white stone altar (1987).

However, perhaps the most moving monument of all is a telephone in a glass box. This is a tribute to Rector Chad Varah who, in 1953, founded the Samaritans, a voluntarily staffed telephone help-line for people in emotional need.

The Martyrdom of St Stephen, which hangs on the north wall, is by American painter Benjamin West, who became a Royal Academician *(see p90)* in 1768.

The spire was added in 1717.

The dome makes this small church light and airy.

Wren's original altar and screen are still here.

Wren's pulpit has a delicate canopy.

Henry Moore's polished stone altar was added in 1987.

Royal Exchange ❸

EC3. **Map** 15 C2. **Tel** 020-7623 0444.
🚇 Bank. **Not open** to the public.

Sir Thomas Gresham, the Elizabethan merchant and courtier, founded the Royal Exchange in 1565 as a centre for commerce of all kinds. The original building was centred on a vast courtyard where merchants and tradesmen did business. Queen Elizabeth I gave it its Royal title and it is still one of the sites from which new kings and queens are announced. Dating from 1844, this is the third splendid building on the site since Gresham's.

Britain's first public lavatories were built in the forecourt here in 1855. Exclusively for male use, they symbolized the era's unenlightened attitudes.

The façade of William Tite's Royal Exchange of 1844

Bank of England Museum ❹

Bartholomew Lane EC2. **Map** 15 B1. **Tel** 020-7601 5545. 🚇 Bank. **Open** 10am–5pm Mon–Fri, Lord Mayor's Show (p55). **Closed** public hols. ♿ phone first. 📷 📖 **Films, lectures.** www.bankofengland.co.uk/museum

The Duke of Wellington (1884) opposite the Bank of England

The Bank of England was set up in 1694 to raise money for foreign wars. It grew to become Britain's central bank, and also issues currency notes. Sir John Soane (see pp136–7) was the architect of the 1788 bank building on this site, but only the exterior wall of his design has survived. The rest was destroyed in the 1920s and 1930s when the Bank was enlarged. There is now a

reconstruction of Soane's stock office of 1793.

Glittering gold bars, silver plated decoration and a Roman mosaic floor, discovered during the rebuilding, are among the items on display. The museum illustrates the work of the Bank and the financial system. The gift shop sells paperweights which are made out of used banknotes.

St Mary-le-Bow ❺

(Bow Church) Cheapside EC2. **Map** 15 A2. **Tel** 020-7248 5139. 🚇 St Paul's, Mansion Hse. **Open** 6.30am– 6pm Mon–Thu, 6.30am–4pm Fri. ✝ 7.30am Tue, 1pm Wed & Fri, 6pm Thu. 🕚 www.stmarylebow.co.uk

The church takes its name from the bow arches in the Norman crypt. When Wren rebuilt the church (in 1670– 80) after the Great Fire, he continued this architectural pattern through the graceful arches on the steeple. The weathervane, dating from 1674, is an enormous dragon.

The church was bombed in 1941 leaving only the steeple and two outer walls standing. It was restored in 1956–62 when the bells were recast and rehung. Bow bells are important to Londoners: traditionally only those born within their sound can claim to be true Cockneys.

St Paul's ❻

See pp148–51.

Old Bailey ❼

EC4. **Map** 14 F1. **Tel** 020-7248 3277. 🚇 St Paul's. **Open** 10am–1pm, 2–5pm Mon–Fri (but opening hours vary from court to court). **Closed** Christmas, New Year, Easter, public hols. 📷 www.cityoflondon.gov.uk

Old Bailey's rooftop Justice

This short street has a long association with crime and punishment. The new Central Criminal Courts opened here in 1907 on the site of the notorious and malodorous Newgate prison (on special days in the legal calendar judges still carry small posies to court as a reminder of those times). Across the road, the Magpie and Stump served "execution breakfasts" until 1868, when mass public hangings outside the prison gates were stopped.

Today, when the courts are in session, they are open to members of the public.

St. Paul's Cathedral ❻

Following the Great Fire of London in 1666, the medieval cathedral of St. Paul's was left in ruins. The authorities turned to Christopher Wren to rebuild it, but his ideas met with considerable resistance from the conservative Dean and Chapter. Wren's 1672 Great Model plan was not at all popular with them, and so a watered-down plan was finally agreed in 1675. Wren's determination paid off though, as can be witnessed from the grandeur of the present cathedral.

Stone statuary outside the South Transept

★ The Dome
At 360 ft (110 m) high, the dome at St. Paul's is the second biggest in the world after St. Peter's in Rome, as spectacular from inside as outside.

The balustrade along the top was added in 1718 against Wren's wishes.

The pediment carvings, dating from 1706, show the Conversion of St. Paul.

★ The West Front and Towers
The towers were not on Wren's original plan – he added them in 1707, when he was 75 years old. Both were designed to have clocks.

Flying buttresses support the nave walls and the dome.

STAR SIGHTS

★ West Front and Towers

★ Dome

★ Whispering Gallery

The West Portico comprises two tiers of columns rather than the single colonnade that Wren intended.

The West Porch, approached from Ludgate Hill, is the main entrance to St. Paul's.

Queen Anne's Statue
An 1886 copy of Francis Bird's 1712 original now stands on the forecourt.

The lantern weighs a massive 850 tons.

The golden gallery lies at the highest point of the dome.

The brick cone located inside the outer dome supports the heavy lantern.

The oculus is an opening through which the lantern can be seen.

The stone gallery offers a splendid view over London.

A false upper story masks the huge flying buttresses.

The North and South Transepts cross the nave in a medieval style that contrasts with Wren's original plan *(see p150)*.

★ **Whispering Gallery**
The unusual acoustics here cause whispers to echo around the dome.

South Porch
Wren took the idea of a semicircular porch from a Baroque church in Rome.

TIMELINE

Detail on Tijou gate (see p151)

604 Bishop Mellitus builds the first St. Paul's. It burned down in 1087				**1666** St. Paul's reduced to a burnt ruin after the Great Fire	**1708** Wren's son Christopher lays the last stone on the lantern		
600	800	1000	1200	1400	1600	1800	2000
	1087 Bishop Maurice begins Old St. Paul's: a Norman cathedral of stone			**1675** Foundation stone of Wren's design laid	**1940–1** Slight bomb damage to the cathedral	**1981** Prince Charles marries Lady Diana Spencer	

A Guided Tour of St Paul's

The visitor to St Paul's will be immediately impressed by its cool, beautifully ordered and extremely spacious interior. The nave, transepts and choir are arranged in the shape of a cross, as in a medieval cathedral, but Wren's Classical vision shines through this conservative floor plan, forced on him by the cathedral authorities. Aided by some of the finest craftsmen of his day, he created an interior of grand majesty and Baroque splendour, a worthy setting for the many great ceremonial events that have taken place here. These include the funeral of Winston Churchill in 1965 and

the wedding of Prince Charles and Lady Diana Spencer in 1981.

The mosaics on the choir ceiling were completed in the 1890s by William Richmond.

① The Nave
Take in the full glory of the massive arches and the succession of saucer domes that open out into a huge space below the main dome.

② The North Aisle
As you walk along the North Aisle, look above: the aisles are vaulted with small domes mimicking those of the nave ceiling.

⑨ South Aisle
From here the brave can ascend the 259 steps to the Whispering Gallery and test the acoustics.

Entrance to Whispering Gallery

⑧ Florence Nightingale's Tomb
Famous for her pioneering work in nursing standards, Florence Nightingale was the first woman to receive the Order of Merit.

Main entrances

The **Geometrical Staircase** is a spiral of 92 stone steps giving access to the cathedral library.

⑦ Wren's Tomb
Wren's burial place is marked by a slab. The inscription states: "Reader, if you seek a monument look around you."

KEY

– – – Tour route

③ The Crossing
The climax of Wren's interior is this great open space. The vast dome is decorated with monochrome frescoes by Sir James Thornhill, the leading architectural painter of Wren's time.

Entrance to crypt

④ The Choir
Jean Tijou, a Huguenot refugee, created much of the cathedral's fine wrought ironwork, such as these screens in the choir aisles.

John Donne's memorial, from 1631, was the only monument to survive the Great Fire of 1666. The poet posed for it in his lifetime.

⑤ The High Altar
The canopy over the altar was replaced after World War II. It is based on Wren's original Baroque drawings.

Grinling Gibbons's work can be found on the choir stalls, with typically intricate carvings of cherubs, fruits and garlands.

T E Lawrence, or Lawrence of Arabia, the British World War I hero who earned his nickname by fighting alongside Arab tribes in their resistance to Turkish rule in 1915, is commemorated by this bust in the crypt.

⑥ The Crypt
The tombs of famous figures and such popular heroes as Lord Nelson, can be seen in the crypt.

Apothecaries' Hall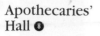

Blackfriars Lane EC4. **Map** 14 F2.
Tel *020-7236 1189.* ⊖ *Blackfriars.*
Courtyard open *9am–5pm Mon–Fri.*
Closed *public hols, end Aug.* **Phone Hall** *for appt to visit (groups only).* ⟁

Apothecaries' Hall, rebuilt in 1670

London has had livery companies, or guilds, to protect and regulate specific trades since early medieval times. The Apothecaries' Society was founded in 1617 for those who prepared, prescribed or sold drugs. It has some surprising alumni, including Oliver Cromwell and the poet John Keats. Now nearly all the members are physicians or surgeons.

Fishmongers' Hall ❾

London Bridge EC4. **Map** 15 B3.
Tel *020-7626 3531.* ⊖ *Monument.*
Not open *to the public. Limited tours by appt only.* **www.**fishhall.co.uk

This is one of the oldest livery companies, established in 1272. Lord Mayor Walworth, a member of the Fishmongers' Company, killed Wat Tyler, leader of the Peasants' Revolt, in 1381 *(see p162).* Today it still fulfils its original role; all the fish sold in the City must be inspected by Company officials.

St Magnus the Martyr ❿

Lower Thames St EC3. **Map** 15 C3.
Tel *020-7626 4481.* ⊖ *Monument.*
Open *10am–4pm Tue–Fri, 10am–1pm Sun.* ⛪ *11am Sun.* ⟁
www.stmagnusmartyr.org.uk

There has been a church here for over 1,000 years. Its patron saint, St Magnus, Earl of the Orkney Islands and a renowned Norwegian Christian leader, was brutally murdered in 1110.

When Christopher Wren built this church in 1671–6, it was at the foot of old London Bridge, until 1738 the only bridge across the River Thames in London. Anyone going south from the city would have passed under Wren's magnificent arched porch spanning the flagstones leading to the old bridge.

Highlights of St Magnus the Martyr include the carved musical instruments that decorate the organ case. Wren's pulpit, with its slender supporting stem, was restored in 1924.

Monument ⓫

Monument St EC3. **Map** 15 C2.
Tel *020-7626 2717.* ⊖ *Monument.*
Open *9.30am–5pm daily.* **Closed** *1 Jan, 24–26 Dec.* **Adm charge.** 📷
www.towerbridge.org.uk

The column, designed by Christopher Wren to commemorate the Great Fire of London which devastated the original walled city in September 1666, is the tallest isolated stone column in the world. It is 62 m (205 ft) high and is said to be 62 m west of where the fire started in Pudding Lane. It was sited on the direct approach to old London Bridge, which was a few steps downstream from the present one. Reliefs around the column's base

The altar of St Magnus the Martyr

show Charles II restoring the city. The 311 steps to the top lead to a viewing platform. In 1842 this was enclosed with railings after a suicide. The views are spectacular.

Billingsgate ⓬

Lower Thames St EC3. **Map** 15 C3.
⊖ *Monument.* **Not open** *to the public.*

Fish weathervane at Billingsgate

London's main fish market was based here for 900 years, on one of the city's earliest quays. During the 19th and early 20th centuries 400 tonnes of fish were sold here every day, much of it delivered by boat. It was London's noisiest market, renowned, even in Shakespeare's day, for foul language. In 1982 the market moved from this building (1877) to the Isle of Dogs.

St Mary-at-Hill ⓭

Lovat Lane EC3. **Map** 15 C2. **Tel** *020-7626 4184.* ⊖ *Monument.* **Concerts. Open** *10am–3pm Mon–Fri.* ⛪ *1pm Wed.*

The interior and east end of St Mary-at-Hill were Wren's first church designs (1670–76). The Greek cross design was a prototype for his St Paul's proposals. Ironically, the delicate plasterwork and rich 17th-century fittings, which had survived both the Victorian mania for refurbishment and the bombs of World War II, were lost in a fire in

1988. The building was then restored to its original appearance, only to be damaged again by an IRA bomb in 1992.

St Margaret Pattens ⓴

Rood Lane and Eastcheap EC3. **Map** 15 C2. **Tel** 020-7623 6630. ⊖ Monument. **Open** 8am–4pm Mon–Fri. **Closed** Christmas week. 🕇 1.15pm Thu, 10.30am Sun. ♿

Wren's church of 1684–7 was named after a type of overshoe made near here. Its rendered brickwork and Portland stone contrast with the Georgian stucco shopfront in the forecourt. The interior retains 17th-century canopied pews and an ornate font.

All Hallows by the Tower ⓯

Byward St EC3. **Map** 16 D3. **Tel** 020-7481 2928. ⊖ Tower Hill. **Open** 9am–5.30pm Mon–Fri, 10am–5pm Sat & Sun. **Closed** 26 Dec–2 Jan. 🕇 11am Sun. ♿ 🛗 🍴 🛈 **Adm charge** undercroft museum. **www**.allhallowsbythetower.org.uk

The first church on this site was Saxon. The arch in the southwest corner, which contains Roman tiles, dates from that period, as do some crosses in the crypt. There is a Roman pavement in the crypt. William Penn, founder of Pennsylvania, was baptized here in 1644. Most of the interior has been altered, but a limewood font cover, carved by Grinling Gibbons in 1682, survives. John

Roman tile from All Hallows

Quincy Adams married here in 1797 before he was US president. Samuel Pepys watched the Great Fire from the church tower. There are a small museum, brass rubbing centre, concerts and a bookstall.

Tower of London ⓰

See pp154–7.

Tower Bridge ⓱

SE1. **Map** 16 D3. **Tel** 020-7403 3761. ⊖ Tower Hill. **The Tower Bridge Exhibition Open** Apr–Sep: 10am–6.30pm daily (last adm: 5.30pm); Oct–Mar: 9.30am–6pm daily (last adm: 5pm). **Closed** 24 & 25 Dec. **Adm charge.** 📷 🛗 ♿ 🛈 **www**.towerbridge.org.uk

Completed in 1894, this flamboyant piece of Victorian engineering quickly became a symbol of London. Its pinnacled towers and linking catwalk support the mechanism for raising the roadway when big ships have to pass through, or for special and historic occasions.

The bridge now houses The Tower Bridge Exhibition, with interactive displays bringing the bridge's history to life, river views from the catwalk and a close-up look at the steam engine which powered the lifting machinery until 1976, when the system was electrified.

The walkways, which are now open to the public, afford stunning views along the river.

When raised, the bridge is 40 m (135 ft) high and 60 m (200 ft) wide. In its heyday it was opened five times a day.

There are nearly 300 stairs to the top of the towers.

The Victorian winding machinery was powered by steam until 1976.

Tower of London ⑯

For much of its 900-year history the Tower was an object of fear. Those who had committed treason or threatened the throne were held within its dank walls. A lucky few lived in comparative comfort, but the majority had to put up with appalling conditions. Many did not get out alive, and some were tortured before meeting violent deaths on nearby Tower Hill.

★ **The White Tower**
When it was finished, c.1097, it was the tallest building in London – 30 m (90 ft) high.

★ **The Jewel House** is where the magnificent Crown Jewels are housed *(see p156).*

"Beefeaters"
Thirty-six Yeoman Warders guard the Tower and live here.

Beauchamp Tower
Many high-ranking prisoners were held here, often with their own retinues of servants.

Tower Green was where the aristocratic prisoners were executed, away from the ghoulish crowds on Tower Hill. But only seven people died here – including two of Henry VIII's six wives – hundreds had to bear public executions on Tower Hill.

STAR BUILDINGS

★ White Tower

★ Jewel House

★ Chapel of St. John

★ Traitors' Gate

Main entrance

THE RAVENS

The Tower's most celebrated residents are a colony of seven ravens. It is not known when they first settled here, but there is a legend that should they desert the Tower, the kingdom will fall. In fact the birds have part of their wings clipped on one side, making flight impossible. The Ravenmaster, one of the Yeoman Warders, looks after the birds.

A memorial in the moat commemorates some of the ravens who have died at the Tower since the 1950s.

Queen's House
This is the official residence of the Tower's governor.

★ Chapel of St John
Stone for this austerely beautiful Romanesque chapel was brought from France.

Wakefield Tower, part of the medieval Palace, has been carefully refurbished to match its original appearance in the 13th century.

VISITORS' CHECKLIST

Tower Hill EC3. **Map** 16 D3. **Tel** 0870-756 6060 (info); 0870-756 7070 (advance booking). 🚇 Tower Hill. 🚌 RV1, 15, X15, 25, 42, 78, 100. 🚉 Fenchurch Street. **Docklands Light Railway** Tower Gateway. **Open** Mar–Oct: 9am–6pm Mon–Sat, 10am–6pm Sun; Nov–Feb: 9am–5pm Tue–Sat, 10am–5pm Sun & Mon. **Tower closed** 1 Jan, 24–26 Dec. **Adm charge**. Ceremony of the Keys 9.30pm daily (book ahead). See pp53–5. 🚻 🍴 📷 📖 www.historicroyalpalaces.org.

The Bloody Tower is associated with the legend of the two princes and other deaths (*see p157*).

★ Traitors' Gate
Prisoners, many on their way to die, entered the Tower by boat here.

Medieval Palace
This was created by Henry III in 1220. It was enlarged by his son, Edward I, who added Traitors' Gate.

TIMELINE

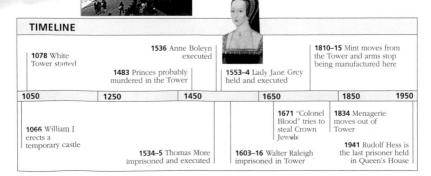

1078 White Tower started	**1536** Anne Boleyn executed	**1810–15** Mint moves from the Tower and arms stop being manufactured here
	1483 Princes probably murdered in the Tower	**1553–4** Lady Jane Grey held and executed

1050	1250	1450	1650	1850	1950

1066 William I erects a temporary castle	**1671** "Colonel Blood" tries to steal Crown Jewels	**1834** Menagerie moves out of Tower
1534–5 Thomas More imprisoned and executed	**1603–16** Walter Raleigh imprisoned in Tower	**1941** Rudolf Hess is the last prisoner held in Queen's House

Inside the Tower

The Tower has been a tourist attraction since the reign of Charles II (1660–85), when both the Crown Jewels and the collection of armour were first shown to the public. They remain powerful reminders of royal might and wealth.

The Orb, symbolizing the power and Empire of Christ the Redeemer

THE CROWN JEWELS

The Crown Jewels comprise the regalia of crowns, sceptres, orbs and swords used at coronations and other state occasions. They are impossible to price but their worth is irrelevant beside their enormous significance in the historical and religious life of the kingdom. Most of the Crown Jewels date from 1661, when a new set was made for the coronation of Charles II; Parliament had destroyed the previous crowns and sceptres after the execution of Charles I in 1649. Only a few pieces survived, hidden by the clergy of Westminster Abbey until the Restoration.

The Coronation Ceremony
Many elements in this solemn and mystical ceremony date from the days of Edward the Confessor. The king or queen proceeds to Westminster Abbey, accompanied by objects of the regalia, including the State Sword which represents the monarch's own sword. He or she is then anointed with holy oil, to signify divine approval, and invested with ornaments and royal robes. Each of the jewels represents

an aspect of the monarch's role as head of the state and church. The climax comes when St Edward's Crown is placed on the sovereign's head; there is a cry of "God Save the King" (or Queen), the trumpets sound, and guns at the Tower are fired. The last coronation was Elizabeth II's in 1953.

The Imperial State Crown, containing more than 2,800 diamonds, 273 pearls as well as other gems

The crowns
There are 10 crowns on display at the Tower. Many of these have not been worn for years, but the Imperial State Crown is in frequent use. The Queen wears it at the Opening of Parliament (see p73). The crown was made in 1937 for George VI, and is similar to the one made for Queen Victoria. The sapphire set in the cross is said to have been worn in a ring by Edward the Confessor (ruled 1042–66).

The most recent crown is not at the Tower, however. It was made for Prince Charles's investiture as Prince of Wales at Caernarvon Castle in north Wales in 1969, and is kept at the Museum of Wales in Cardiff. The Queen Mother's

crown was made for the coronation of her husband, George VI, in 1937. It is the only one to be made out of platinum – all the other crowns on display at the Tower are made of gold.

Other regalia
Apart from the crowns, there are other pieces of the Crown Jewels that are essential to coronations. Among these are three Swords of Justice, symbolizing mercy, spiritual and temporal justice. The orb is a hollow gold sphere encrusted with jewels and weighing about 1.3 kg (3 lbs). The Sceptre with the Cross contains the biggest cut diamond in the world, the 530-carat First Star of Africa. The rough stone it comes from weighed 3,106 carats.

The Sovereign's Ring, sometimes referred to as "the wedding ring of England"

Plate Collection
The Jewel House also holds a collection of elaborate gold and silver plate. The Maundy Dish is still used on Maundy Thursday when the monarch distributes money to selected old people. The Exeter Salt (a very grand salt cellar from the days when salt was a valuable commodity) was given by the citizens of Exeter, in west England, to Charles II; during the 1640s' Civil War Exeter was a Royalist stronghold.

The Sceptre with the Cross (1660), rebuilt in 1910 after Edward VII was presented with the First Star of Africa diamond

The hilt and solid-gold scabbard of the jewelled State Sword, one of the most valuable swords in the world

THE WHITE TOWER

This is the oldest surviving
building in the Tower of
London, begun by William I in
c.1070 and completed before
1100. For centuries it served as
an armoury, and much of the
national collection of arms and
armour was held here. In the
1990s many exhibits moved to
the Royal Armouries' other
museums in Leeds or Portsmouth, but some of the most
historic items, especially those
connected with the Tower,
have remained. The extra
space allows the exhibits to be
displayed more effectively,
and highlights architectural
features of the building itself.

The Royal Castle and
Armour Gallery

These two chambers on the
first floor were the main ceremonial rooms of the original
Norman castle. The first one,
to the east, is the smaller,
probably an antechamber to
the Banqueting Hall beyond,
and contains exhibits setting
out the history of the White
Tower. It adjoins St John's
Chapel, a rare surviving early
Norman chapel virtually intact,
a powerfully solid interior with
little ornamentation. Originally
the two main rooms were
twice their present height; a
pitched roof was removed in
1490 to allow extra floors to be
built on top. Suits of armour
from Tudor and Stuart times
are here, including three made
for Henry VIII, one covering
his horse as well. A suit made
in Holland for Charles I is
decorated in gold leaf.

**Japanese armour presented
to James I in 1613**

The Ordnance Gallery

This and the temporary exhibition gallery next door were
chambers created in 1490 when
the roof was raised. They were
used chiefly for storage and in
1603 a new floor was installed
to allow gunpowder to be
kept here: by 1667 some
10,000 barrels of it were
stored in the Tower. Among
the displays are gilt panels
and ornament from the barge
of the Master of the Ordnance
built in 1700.

The Small Armoury
and Crypt

The westerly room on the
ground floor may originally
have been a living area, and
has traces of the oldest fireplaces known in England.
Pistols, muskets, swords,
pikes and bayonets are

mounted on the walls and panels in elaborate symmetrical
patterns based on displays in
the Tower armouries in the
18th and 19th centuries. They
were shown in the Grand
Storehouse until it burned
down in 1841. A collection of
weapons taken from the men
who planned to assassinate
William III in 1696 is on
show, and next door is a
wooden block made in 1747
for the execution of Lord
Lovat – the last public
beheading in England. The
crypt now houses a shop.

The Line of Kings

The Line of Kings, ten life-
size carvings of prominent
English Monarchs, wearing
armour and seated on horse-
back, originated in Tudor
times, when eight such figures
adorned the royal palace at
Greenwich. Two more had
been added by the time they
first appeared in the Tower in
1660, celebrating the Restoration of Charles II. In 1688,
17 new horses and heads
were commissioned, some
from the great carver Grinling
Gibbons (the third from the
left is reputed to be his work).

**Henry VIII's
armour
(1540)**

THE PRINCES IN
THE TOWER

Now explored in a display in
the Bloody Tower, one of
the Tower's darkest mysteries
concerns two boy princes,
sons and heirs of Edward IV.
They were put into the
Tower by their uncle, Richard
of Gloucester, when their
father died in 1483. Neither
was seen again and Richard
was crowned later that year.
In 1674 the skeletons of two
children were found nearby.

The yacht haven of the restored St Katharine's Dock

St Katharine's Dock ⓲

E1. **Map** 16 E3. **Tel** 020-7481 8350.
🚇 Tower Hill. ♿ 🍴 💻 🏪
www.stkaths.co.uk

This most central of all London's docks was designed by Thomas Telford and opened in 1828 on the site of St Katharine's hospital. Commodities as diverse as tea, marble and live turtles (turtle soup was a Victorian delicacy) were unloaded here.

During the 19th and early 20th centuries the docks flourished, but by the mid-20th century cargo ships were delivering their wares in massive containers. The old docks became too small and new ones had to be built downstream. St Katharine's closed in 1968.

St Katharine's is now one of London's most successful developments, with its commercial, residential and entertainment facilities, including a hotel and a yacht haven. Old warehouse buildings have shops and restaurants on their ground floors, and offices above.

On the north side of the dock is LIFFE Commodity Products, trading in commodities such as coffee, sugar and oil. There is no public gallery but, if you ask at the door, you may be able to look down from the glass-walled reception area on to the frenzied trading floors. The dock is worth wandering through after visiting the Tower or Tower Bridge *(see pp154–7 and p153)*.

Stock Exchange ⓳

Old Broad St EC4. **Map** 15 B1.
🚇 Bank. **Not open** to the public.

The first Stock Exchange was established in Threadneedle Street in 1773 by a group of stockbrokers who previously met and did business in nearby City coffee houses. By the 19th century the rules of exchange were laid down, and for a hundred years London's was the biggest stock exchange in the world. Nevertheless, the rise of the American and Japanese economies during the 20th century gradually challenged London's dominance, and today its exchange is third in size after Tokyo and New York. Unlike most exchanges, however, London's is free from government legislation.

The present building, which dates from 1969, used to house the frenzied trading floor, but in 1986 the business was computerized and the floor made redundant. The former public viewing gallery stayed open for a while, but was closed after a terrorist bomb attempt.

St Helen's Bishopsgate ⓴

Great St Helen's EC3. **Map** 15 C1. **Tel** 020-7283 2231. 🚇 Liverpool St, Bank. **Open** 9.30am–5pm Mon–Fri (phone to check). 🕇 12.35pm, 1.15pm Tue, 1pm Thu, 10.15am, 7pm Sun. 📷 ♿
www.st-helens.org.uk

The curious appearance of this 13th-century church is due to its origins as two places of worship: one a parish church, the other the chapel of a long-gone nunnery next door. (The medieval nuns of St Helen's were notorious for their "secular kissing".)

Among its monuments is the tomb of Sir Thomas Gresham, who founded the Royal Exchange *(see p147)*.

St Katharine Cree ㉑

86 Leadenhall St EC3. **Map** 16 D1. **Tel** 020-7283 5733. 🚇 Aldgate, Tower Hill. **Open** 10.30am–4pm Mon–Thu, 10.30am–2pm Fri. 🕇 1.10pm Wed.
www.stkatharinecree.org

The organ at St Katharine Cree

A rare pre-Wren 17th-century church with a medieval tower, this was one of only eight churches in the City to survive the fire of 1666. Some of the elaborate plasterwork on and beneath the high ceiling of the nave portrays the coats of arms of the guilds, with which the church has special links. The 17th-century organ, supported on magnificent carved wooden columns, was played by both Purcell and Handel.

St Helen's Bishopsgate

Leadenhall Market ㉒

Whittington Ave EC3. **Map** 15 C2.
🚇 *Bank, Monument.* **Open**
*7am–4pm Mon–Fri. See **Shops and Markets** pp332–41.*

There has been a food market here, on the site of the Roman forum *(see pp18–19),* since the Middle Ages. Its name is derived from a lead-roofed mansion that stood nearby in the 14th century. The ornate, Victorian covered shopping precinct of today was designed in 1881 by Sir Horace Jones, the architect of Billings-gate fish market *(see p152).*

Essentially a food market, offering traditional game, poultry, fish, and meat, Leadenhall also has a number of independent shops, which offer all kinds of fare from chocolates to wine. The area is busiest during breakfast and lunch hours, and is best seen at Christmas when all the stores are decorated. It is particularly popular among local City workers, many of whom work in the adjacent Lloyd's of London building.

Lloyd's of London ㉓

1 Lime St EC3. **Map** 15 C2.
Tel 020-7327 1000. 🚇 *Bank, Monument, Liverpool St, Aldgate.*
Not open to the public.

Lloyd's was founded in the late 17th century and takes its name from the coffee house where underwriters and shipowners used to meet to arrange marine insurance contracts. Lloyd's soon became the world's main insurers, issuing policies on everything from oil tankers to Betty Grable's legs.

The present building, by Richard Rogers, dates from 1986 and is one of the most interesting modern buildings in London *(see p32).* Its exaggerated stainless steel external piping and high-tech ducts echo Rogers' forceful Pompidou Centre in Paris. Lloyd's is a far more elegant building and particularly worth seeing floodlit at night.

Leadenhall Market in 1881

Guildhall Art Gallery ㉔

Guildhall Yard EC2. **Map** 15 B1. **Tel**
020-7332 3700. 🚇 *St Paul's.* **Open**
*10am–5pm Mon–Sat, noon–4pm
Sun (last adm: 30 mins prior).* **Closed**
1 Jan, 25 & 26 Dec. **Adm charge.** 🅿
♿ 🚇 **Guildhall** Gresham St EC2.
Tel 020-7606 3030. **Open** phone to
check **www**.cityoflondon.gov.uk

The Guildhall Art Gallery was built in 1885 to house the art collection of the Corporation of London, but was destroyed in World War II. The present gallery houses the studio collection of 20th-century artist Sir Matthew Smith, portraits from the 16th century to the present day, a gallery of 18th-century works, including John Singleton Copley's *Defeat of the Floating Batteries at Gibraltar,* and numerous Victorian works.

In 1988, the foundations of a Roman amphitheatre were discovered beneath the gallery. Built in 70 AD and capable of holding about 6000 spectators, the arena would have featured animal hunts, executions and gladiatorial combat. Access to the atmospheric ruins is included with gallery admission.

The adjacent Guildhall itself has been the administrative centre of the City for at least 800 years. For centuries the hall was used for trials and many people were condemned to death here, including Henry Garnet, one of the Gunpowder Plot conspirators *(see p24).* Today, a few days after the Lord Mayor's parade *(see pp54–5),* the Prime Minister addresses a banquet here.

Richard Rogers' Lloyd's building illuminated at night

SMITHFIELD AND SPITALFIELDS

The areas just north of the City walls have always been a refuge for those who did not want to come under its jurisdiction, or were not welcome there. These included Huguenots in the 17th century and, in later times, other immigrants from Europe and then Bengal. They founded small industries and brought with them their restaurants and places of worship. The name Spitalfields comes from the medieval priory of St Mary Spital. Middlesex Street became known as Petticoat Lane in the 16th century, for its clothing stalls; it is still the hub of a popular Sunday morning street market that spreads as far east as Brick Lane, today lined with aromatic Bengali food shops. London's meat market is at Smithfield, and nearby is the Barbican, a late 20th-century residential and arts complex.

Stone dragon in Smithfield Market

SIGHTS AT A GLANCE

Historic Streets and Buildings
Charterhouse ④
Cloth Fair ⑤
Barbican ⑦
Whitbread's Brewery ⑨
Wesley's Chapel–Leysian
Mission ⑪
Broadgate Centre ⑫
Petticoat Lane ⑬
Fournier Street ⑰
Spitalfields Centre Museum of
Immigration & Diversity ⑲
Brick Lane ⑳
Dennis Severs House ㉑

Museums and Galleries
Museum of London
pp166 – 7 ③
Whitechapel Gallery ⑭

Churches and Mosques
St Botolph, Aldersgate ②
St Bartholomew-
the-Great ⑥
St Giles, Cripplegate ⑧
Christ Church, Spitalfields ⑯
London Jamme Masjid ⑱

Cemeteries
Bunhill Fields ⑩

Markets
Smithfield Market ①
Old Spitalfields Market ⑮
Columbia Road Market ㉒

0 metres 500

0 yards 500

GETTING THERE
This area is served by the Northern, Hammersmith and City, Central and Circle Underground lines and by rail. The Nos. 8, 15 and many other buses run close by.

SEE ALSO

- *Street Finder,* maps 6, 7, 8, 15, 16

- *Where to Stay* pp278–91

- *Restaurants, Pubs* pp292–319

KEY

■ Street-by-Street map

⊖ Underground station

⊠ Railway station

◁ **Columbia Road flower and plant market**

Street-by-Street: Smithfield

This area is among the most historic in London. It contains one of the capital's oldest churches, some rare Jacobean houses, vestiges of the Roman wall (near the Museum of London) and central London's only surviving wholesale food market.

Smithfield's long history is also bloody. In 1381 the rebel peasant leader, Wat Tyler, was killed here by an ally of Richard II as he presented the king with demands for lower taxes. Later, in the reign of Mary I (1553–8), scores of Protestant religious martyrs were burned at the stake here.

The Fat Boy: the Great Fire ended here

The Fox and Anchor pub is open from 7am for hearty breakfasts, washed down with ale by the market traders of Smithfield.

CHARTERHOUSE STREET

LON

WEST SMITHFIELD

★ Smithfield Market
A contemporary print shows Horace Jones's stately building for the meat market when it was completed in 1867 ❶

Fat Boy

SMITHFIELD STREET

THE CORPORATION OF

SITE OF THE
SARACEN'S HEAD
INN
DEMOLISHED
1868

THE CITY OF LONDON

The Saracen's Head, an historic inn, stood on this site until the 1860s when it was demolished to make way for Holborn Viaduct *(see p140)*.

COCK LANE

SNOW HILL

GILTSPUR STREET

St Bartholomew-the-Less has a 15th-century tower and vestry. Its links to the hospital are shown by this early 20th-century stained glass of a nurse; a gift of the Worshipful Company of Glaziers.

St Bartholomew's Hospital has stood on this site since 1123. Some of the existing buildings date from 1759.

KEY

– – – Suggested route

0 metres   100

0 yards   100

Charterhouse
The square contains the remnants of a medieval monastery and a school where John Wesley (see p168) studied ❹

Barbican station

See Central London Map pp14–15

LOCATOR MAP

Hackney

Islington

SMITHFIELD & SPITALFIELDS

THE CITY

★ **Barbican**
World War II bombs flattened this immense site, which was rebuilt as a housing development in the 1960s. It contains the famous Barbican Centre ❼

CHARTERHOUSE SQUARE

CARTHUSIAN ST

BEECH STREET

ALDERSGATE STREET

NE

TH FAIR

LONDON WALL

LITTLE BRITAIN

Cloth Fair
Two of its houses are survivors of the 1666 Great Fire ❺

St Bartholomew-the-Great
It has the best-preserved medieval interior of any London church ❻

★ **Museum of London**
The city's history is told vividly through fascinating and colourful exhibits ❸

Christ Church tower is all that remains of one of Wren's most splendid churches (1704).

To St Paul's station

STAR SIGHTS
★ Museum of London
★ Barbican
★ Smithfield Market

Smithfield Market, now officially known as London Central Markets

Smithfield Market **1**

Charterhouse St EC1. **Map** 6 F5.
⊝ *Farringdon, Barbican.* **Open**
5–9am Mon–Fri.

Animals have been traded here since the 12th century, but the spot was granted its first official charter in 1400. In 1648 it was officially established as a cattle market and live cattle continued to be sold here until the mid-19th century. It now confines itself to wholesale trading in dead meat and poultry. It was originally sited in Smithfield outside the city walls, London's main location for public executions. Although moved to its present location in Charterhouse Street in the 1850s and called the London Central Meat Market, the original name stuck. The old buildings are by Horace Jones, the Victorian architect, but there are 20th-century additions. Some pubs in the area keep market hours and, from dawn, serve hearty breakfasts. The meat market is currently threatened with being moved out of central London.

St Botolph, Aldersgate **2**

Aldersgate St EC1. **Map** 15 A1.
Tel *020-7606 0684.* ⊝ *St Paul's, Barbican, Moorgate.* ✝ *1pm Tue–Thu.* ♿

A modest late Georgian exterior (completed in the late 18th century) conceals a flamboyant, well-preserved interior which has a finely decorated plaster ceiling, a rich brown wooden organ case and galleries, as well as an oak pulpit resting on a carved palm tree. The original box pews have been kept in the galleries rather than in the body of the church. Some of the memorials come from a 14th-century church that originally existed on the site.

The former church-yard alongside was converted in 1880 into a relaxing green space known as Postman's Park, because it was used by workers from the nearby Post Office head-quarters. In the late 19th century, the Victorian artist G F Watts dedicated one of the walls to a quirky collection of plaques that commemorate acts of bravery and self-sacrifice by ordinary people. Some of these plaques are still here and can be viewed. There are three St Botolph churches in the City; the other two can be found at Aldgate and in Bishopsgate.

Museum of London **3**

See pp166–7.

Charterhouse **4**

Charterhouse Sq EC1. **Map** 6 F5.
Tel *020-7253 9503.* ⊝ *Barbican.*
Open *for* 🔲 *only; book well ahead.*
Tel *020-7251 5002.*

The Tudor gateway on the north side of the square leads to the site of a former Carthusian monastery which was dissolved under Henry VIII. In 1611 the buildings were converted into a hospital for poor pensioners, and a charity school – called Charterhouse – whose pupils included John Wesley *(see p168)*, writer William Thackeray and Robert Baden-Powell, founder of the Boy Scouts. In 1872 the school, which is now a top boarding school, relocated to Godalming in Surrey. Part of the original site was subsequently taken over by St Bartholomew's Hospital medical school. Some of the old buildings survived. These include the chapel and part of the cloisters. Today Charterhouse is still home to over 40 pensioners, supported by the charitable foundation.

Charterhouse: stone carving

Cloth Fair ❺

EC1. **Map** 6 F5. 🚇 *Barbican.*

This pretty street is named after the notoriously rowdy Bartholomew Fair, which was the main cloth fair in medieval and Elizabethan England, held annually at Smithfield until 1855. Nos. 41 and 42 are fine 17th-century houses and have distinctive two-storeyed wooden bay windows, although their ground floors have since been modernized. The former poet laureate John Betjeman, who died in 1984, lived in No. 43 for most of his life. It has now been turned into a wine bar named after him.

17th-century houses: Cloth Fair

St Bartholomew-the-Great ❻

West Smithfield EC1. **Map** 6 F5. **Tel** *020-7606 5171.* 🚇 *Barbican.* **Open** *8.30am–5pm (4pm in winter) Tue–Fri, 10.30am–1.30pm Sat, 8.30am–1pm & 2.30–8pm Sun.* 🕈 *9am, 11am, 6.30pm Sun.* ♿ 🎦 *by appt.* 📷 **Concerts.** www.greatstbarts.com

One of London's oldest churches was founded in 1123 by the monk Rahere, whose tomb is inside. He was Henry I's courtier and had a dream in which St Bartholomew saved him from a winged monster.
The 13th-century arch used to be the door to the church until the nave of that earlier building was pulled down when Henry VIII dissolved the priory. Today the arch leads from West Smithfield to the

burial ground – the gatehouse above it is from a later period. The present building retains the crossing and chancel of the original, with its round arches and other fine Norman detailing. There are also some fine Tudor monuments. The painter William Hogarth was baptized here in 1697.
Parts of the church have been used for secular purposes. In 1725 US statesman Benjamin Franklin worked for a printer in the Lady Chapel. The church also featured in the films *Four Weddings and a Funeral* and *Shakespeare in Love.*

Barbican ❼

Silk St EC2. **Map** 7 A5. **Tel** *020-7638 8891.* 🎦 *020-7638 4141.* 🚇 *Barbican, Moorgate.* **Barbican Centre open** *9am–10.30pm Mon–Sat, noon–11pm Sun, public hols.* 📷 💻 🍴 🎦 📷 ♿ *induction loop.* See **Entertainment** *pp342–53.* www.barbican.org.uk

An ambitious piece of 1960s city planning, this large residential, commercial and arts complex was begun in 1962 on a site devastated by World War II bombs, and not completed for nearly 20 years. Tall residential tower blocks surround the Barbican Centre, the arts complex, which also includes an ornamental lake and fountains.
The old city wall turned a corner here and substantial remains are still clearly visible (particularly so from the Museum of London – *see pp166–7*). The word barbican means a defensive tower over

St Bartholomew's gatehouse

a gate – perhaps the architects were trying to live up to the name when they designed this self-sufficient community with formidable defences against the outside world. Obscure entrances and raised walkways remove pedestrians from the cramped bustle of the City, but, in spite of the signposts, and yellow lines on the pavement, the complex can be difficult to navigate.
As well as two theatres and a concert hall, the Barbican Centre has two cinemas, two galleries, one of which is for major exhibitions, an excellent library with children's and music sections, and a surprising conservatory. The Guildhall School of Music and Drama is also located in the Barbican.

The well-stocked conservatory at the Barbican Centre

Museum of London ❸

Opened in 1976 on the edge of the Barbican, this museum provides a lively account of London life from prehistoric times to the outbreak of World War I. Reconstructed interiors and street scenes are alternated with displays of original domestic artifacts and items found in the museum's archaeological digs. Look out for the new Medieval gallery and a model of the Great Fire of 1666, accompanied by Samuel Pepys's eyewitness account.

★ Marble Head of Serapis
This statue of the Egyptian god of the underworld (2nd–3rd century) was discovered in the temple of Mithras (see p144).

Great Fire of London Experience

Ramp to lower level

Leather Shoes
These remarkably well-preserved shoes (13th and 14th centuries) illustrate changing fashion in Medieval London.

Boy's Leather Jerkin
This practical sleeveless jacket (c.1560), decorated with punched hearts and stars, would have been worn over a doublet for extra warmth.

Main entrance

GALLERY GUIDE
The galleries are laid out chronologically, starting on the entrance level with prehistory and finishing on the lower floor with World City (1789–1914). Special exhibitions are also held on the lower level.

Flint Hand Axe
Thousands of these cutting tools (c.350,000–120,000 BC) have been found in the gravels beneath modern London.

STAR EXHIBITS

- ★ Marble Head of Serapis
- ★ Lord Mayor's Coach
- ★ Tobacconist, Victorian Walk

KEY TO FLOORPLAN

☐ London before London	☐ Late Stuart London
☐ Roman London	☐ 18th Century London
☐ Dark Age and Saxon London	☐ World City 1789–1914
☐ Medieval London	☐ Victorian Walk
☐ Tudor London	☐ Temporary exhibitions
☐ Early Stuart London	☐ Non-exhibition space

★ Tobacconist
The Victorian Walk uses several original shop fronts and objects to recreate the atmosphere of late 19th-century London.

VISITORS' CHECKLIST

London Wall EC2. **Map** 15 A1.
Tel 0870 444 3851.
🄴 Barbican, St Paul's, Moorgate.
🚌 4, 8, 25, 56, 100, 172, 242, 501, 521. 🚆 City Thameslink, Moorgate. **Open** 10am–5.50pm Mon–Sat, noon–5.50pm Sun. **Closed** 24–26 Dec, 1 Jan.
♿ Induction loops fitted.
🅿 🎥 **Lectures, film presentations.**
www.museumoflondon.org.uk

Motor Goggles and Licence
Goggles such as these (c.1912) were necessary to drive early open-top cars on London's dusty roads.

Ramp to entrance level

18th-Century Dresses
These dresses are made from printed linen, an alternative to expensive woven silk.

★ Lord Mayor's Coach
Finely carved and painted, this gilded coach (c.1757) is paraded once a year during the Lord Mayor's Show (see p55).

Late Stuart Interior
This reconstruction of a wealthy merchant's parlour is made up of features from several grand houses of the late 17th century.

St Giles, Cripplegate ❽

Fore St EC2. **Map** 7 A5. **Tel** 020-7638 1997. ⊖ *Barbican, Moorgate.* **Open** *10am–4pm Mon–Fri.* ✝ *Sun: 8am, 10am, 6pm Easter–Sep, 4pm Oct–Easter Sun (family service 11.30am 3rd Sun of month).* 📷 *2–4.40pm Tue.* ⚘ **www**.stgilescripplegate.com

Completed in 1550, this church survived the ravages of the Great Fire in 1666, but was so badly damaged by a World War II bomb that only the tower survived. St Giles was refurbished during the 1950s to serve as the parish church of the Barbican, and now stands awkwardly amidst the stark modernity of the Barbican.

Oliver Cromwell married Elizabeth Bourchier here in 1620 and the poet John Milton was buried here in 1674. Well-preserved remains of London's Roman and medieval walls can be seen to the south.

Whitbread's Brewery ❾

Chiswell St EC1. **Map** 7 B5. ⊖ *Barbican, Moorgate.* **Not open** to public.

In 1736, when he was aged just 16, Samuel Whitbread became an apprentice brewer in Bedford. By the time of his death in 1796, his Chiswell Street brewery (which he had bought in 1750) was brewing

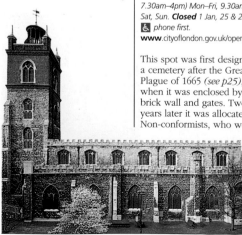
St Giles, Cripplegate

Blake's gravestone at Bunhill Fields

909,200 litres (200,000 gal) a year. The building has not been used as a brewery since 1976 when it was converted into rooms hired out for private functions – they are no longer open to the public. The Porter Tun room, which is now used as a banqueting suite, boasts the largest timber post roof in Europe, and has a huge span of 18 m (60 ft).

The street's 18th-century buildings are well-preserved examples of their period, and are worth a look from the outside. A plaque on one commemorates a visit to the brewery in 1787 by George III and Queen Charlotte.

Bunhill Fields ❿

City Rd EC1. **Map** 7 B4. **Tel** 020-7374 4127. ⊖ *Old St.* **Open** *Apr–Sep: 7.30am–7pm or dusk (Oct–Mar: 7.30am–4pm) Mon–Fri, 9.30am–4pm Sat, Sun.* **Closed** *1 Jan, 25 & 26 Dec.* ⚘ *phone first.* **www**.cityoflondon.gov.uk/openspaces

This spot was first designated a cemetery after the Great Plague of 1665 (see p25), when it was enclosed by a brick wall and gates. Twenty years later it was allocated to Non-conformists, who were

banned from being buried in churchyards because of their refusal to use the Church of England prayer book. The cemetery is situated on the edge of the City, and shaded by large plane trees. There are monuments to the well-known writers Daniel Defoe, John Bunyan and William Blake, as well as to members of the Cromwell family. John Milton wrote his epic poem *Paradise Lost* while he lived in Bunhill Row, located on the west side of the cemetery.

The website has further information on the burial records of Bunhill Fields.

Wesley's Chapel–Leysian Mission ⓫

49 City Rd EC1. **Map** 7 B4.**Tel** 020-7253 2262. ⊖ *Old St.* **Open** *10am–4pm Mon–Sat, 12.30–1.45pm Sun.* ⚘ *not house.* ✝ *9.45am (not 1st Sun of month), 11am Sun, 12.45pm Thu.* 📷 *groups book ahead.* 📷 **www**.wesleyschapel.org.uk

Wesley's Chapel

John Wesley, the founder of the Methodist church, laid the chapel's foundation stone in 1777. He preached here until his death in 1791, and is buried behind the chapel. Next door is the house where he lived, and today some of his furniture, books and other assorted possessions can be seen on display there.

The chapel, adorned in a spartan style, in accordance with Wesley's austere religious principles, has columns made from ships' masts. Beneath it is a small museum that explores the history of the Methodist church. Baroness Thatcher, the first British woman Prime Minister, in office from 1979 to 1990, was married in the chapel.

Broadgate Centre ⑫

Exchange Sq EC2. **Map** 7 C5. **Tel** 020-7505 4068 (ice arena; see pp354–5). ⊖ Liverpool St. 🚻 🚍 📷 🚻

Broadgate Centre skating rink

Situated around Liverpool Street station, the terminus for trains to eastern England, this is one of the most successful recent (1985–91) shop and office developments. Each of the squares has its own distinctive character. Broadgate Arena emulates New York's Rockefeller Center, doubling as a skating rink until the end of March (depending on the weather) and a venue for entertainment in summer.

Among the many sculptures in the complex are George Segal's *Rush Hour Group*, and Barry Flanagan's *Leaping Hare on Crescent and Bell*. Don't miss the spectacular view of Liverpool Street station and its glass-roofed train shed, seen from Exchange Square to the north.

Petticoat Lane ⑬

Middlesex St E1. **Map** 16 D1. ⊖ Aldgate East, Aldgate, Liverpool St. **Open** 9am–2pm Sun. See **Shops and Markets** pp332–41.

In Queen Victoria's prudish reign the name of this street, long famous for its market, was changed to the respectable but colourless Middlesex Street. That is still its official designation, but the old name, derived from its many years as a centre of the clothing trade, has stuck, and

is now applied to the market held every Sunday morning in this and the surrounding streets. Numerous attempts were made to stop the market, but it was allowed by Act of Parliament in 1936. A great variety of goods is sold but there is still a bias towards clothing, especially leather coats. The atmosphere is noisy and cheerful, with Cockney stall-holders making use of their wit to attract custom. There are scores of snack bars, and many of these sell traditional Jewish food such as salt beef sandwiches and bagels with smoked salmon.

Whitechapel Art Gallery ⑭

Whitechapel High St E1. **Map** 16 E1. **Tel** 020-7522 7888. ⊖ Aldgate East, Aldgate. **Open** 11am–6pm Tue–Sun, (to 9pm Thu). **Closed** 1 Jan, 25 & 26 Dec. **Occasional adm charge for exhibitions.** 🚻 📷 📷 📷 **Wide range of talks & events.** www.whitechapel.org

A striking Art Nouveau façade by C Harrison Townsend fronts this light, airy gallery,

Entrance to Whitechapel Gallery

which was founded in 1901, and is situated close to Brick Lane and the burgeoning art scene in the area. This independent gallery's aim is to bring art to the people of East London. Today it enjoys an excellent international reputation for high-quality shows of major contemporary artists. In the 1950s and 1960s the likes of Jackson Pollock, Robert Rauschenberg, Anthony Caro and John Hoyland all displayed their work here. In 1970 David Hockney's first exhibition was held here.

The gallery also has a well-stocked arts bookshop, and there is a café here, serving a range of appetizing and healthy wholefoods in a relaxed atmosphere.

Bustling Petticoat Lane Market

18th-century Fournier Street

Old Spitalfields Market **⑮**

Commercial St E1. **Map** 8 E5. ⊖ *Liverpool St.* **Open** *11am–3pm Mon–Fri, 9.30am–5.30pm Sun. See* **Shops and Markets** *pp332–41.*

One of the oldest markets in London, Spitalfields started life as a produce market in 1682. Today good quality food, including organic fruit and vegetables, breads and preserves, can still be purchased here. Although open during the week it is on Sundays that hundreds of people throng the market in search of vintage clothing, bric-a-brac, crafts and especially innovative fashion by young designers.

Christ Church, Spitalfields **⑯**

Commercial St E1. **Map** 8 E5. **Tel** *020-7377 6793.* ⊖ *Liverpool St.* **Open** *11am–4pm Tue, 1–4pm Sun during services.* ✝ *10.30am & 7pm Sun.* **Concerts** ♿ 📷 *book ahead.* **www**.*spitalfieldsvenue.org*

The finest of Nicholas Hawksmoor's six London churches, completed in 1729, was mauled by Victorian alterations. Christ Church still dominates the surrounding streets, however. Its portico and spire are best seen from the far end of Brushfield Street.

Christ Church was commissioned by parliament in the Fifty New Churches Act of 1711. The act's purpose was to combat the threat of Non-conformism (to the established Church of England) and the church needed to make a strong statement here, in an area that was fast becoming a Huguenot stronghold. The Protestant Huguenots had fled from religious persecution in Catholic France and came to Spitalfields to work in the local silkweaving industry.

The church's impression of size and strength is reinforced inside by the high ceiling, the sturdy wooden canopy over the west door and the gallery. It has recently been fully restored to its former glory.

Fournier Street **⑰**

E1. **Map** 8 E5. ⊖ *Aldgate East, Liverpool Street.*

The 18th-century houses on the north side of this street have attics with broad windows that were designed to give maximum light to the silkweaving French Huguenot community who lived here. Even now, the textile trade lives on, in this and nearby streets, still dependent on immigrant labour. Today it is Bengalis who toil at sewing machines in workrooms that are as cramped as they were when the Huguenots used them. Working conditions are improving, however, and many of the sweatshops have been converted into showrooms for companies which now have modern factories away from the town centre.

Christ Church, Spitalfields

Bengali sweet factory: Brick Lane

London Jamme Masjid **⑱**

Brick Lane E1. **Map** 8 E5. ⊖ *Liverpool St, Aldgate East.*

Muslims now worship here, in a building whose life story as a religious site reflects the fascinating history of immigration in the area. Built in 1743 as a Huguenot chapel, it was a synagogue in the 19th century, a Methodist chapel in the early 20th century, and is now a mosque. A sundial at the entrance reads *Umbra sumus*, "we are shadows".

Spitalfields Centre Museum of Immigration & Diversity **⑲**

19 Princelet St E1. **Map** 8 E5. **Tel** *020-7247 5352.* ⊖ *Liverpool St.* **Open** *some days & by appt (phone to check).* **www**.*19princeletstreet.org.uk*

A little Victorian synagogue hidden behind a 1719 Huguenot silk merchant's house mounts exhibitions celebrating the Jewish and other peoples who arrived as immigrants and settled in London's East End.

Brick Lane **⑳**

E1. **Map** 8 E5. ⊖ *Liverpool St, Aldgate East, Shoreditch.* **Market open** *dawn–noon Sun. See* **Shops and Markets** *pp332–41.*

Once a lane running through brickfields, this is now the busy centre of London's

The grand bedroom of Dennis Severs House

Bengali district. Its shops and houses, some dating from the 18th century, have seen waves of immigrants of many nationalities, and most now sell food, spices, silks and sarees. The first Bengalis to live here were sailors who came in the 19th century. In those days it was a predominantly Jewish quarter, and a few Jewish shops remain, including a 24-hour bagel shop at No. 159.

On Sundays a large market is held here and in the surrounding streets, complementing Petticoat Lane (*see p169*). At the northern end of Brick Lane is the former Black Eagle Brewery, a medley of 18th- and 19th-century industrial architecture, now reflected in, and set off by, a sympathetic mirror-glassed extension.

18th-century portrait: Dennis Severs House

Dennis Severs House ㉑

18 Folgate St E1. **Map** 8 D5. **Tel** 020-7247 4013. Liverpool St. **Open** Mon after dark (book ahead); 2–5pm 1st & 3rd Sun of month and noon–2pm Mon following those Sundays. Private and group bookings welcome. **Adm charge**. www.dennissevershouse.co.uk

At No. 18 Folgate Street, built in 1724, the late designer and performer Dennis Severs has recreated a historical interior that takes you on a journey from the 17th to the 19th centuries. It offers what he called "an adventure of the imagination … a visit to a time-mode rather than … merely a look at a house". The rooms are like a series of *tableaux vivants*, as if the occupants had simply left for a moment. There is broken bread on the plates, wine in the glasses, fruit in the bowl; the candles flicker and horses' hooves clatter on the cobbles outside. This highly theatrical experience is far removed from more usual museum recreations and is not suitable for the under-12s. Praised by many, including artist David Hockney, it is truly unique. The house's motto is "you either see it or you don't". Around the corner on Elder Street are two of London's earliest surviving terraces, where many of the Georgian red-brick houses have been carefully restored.

Columbia Road Market ㉒

Columbia Rd E2. **Map** 8 D3. Liverpool St, Old St, Bethnal Green. **Open** 8.30am–1pm Sun. See **Shops and Markets** pp332–41.

A visit to this flower and plant market is one of the most delightful things to do on a Sunday morning in London, whether you want to take advantage of the exotic species on offer there or not. Set in a well-preserved street of small Victorian shops, it is a lively, sweet-smelling and colourful event. Apart from the stalls, there are several shops selling, among other things, home-made bread and farmhouse cheeses, antiques and interesting objects, many of them flower-related. There is also a Spanish delicatessen and an excellent snack bar that sells bagels and welcome mugs of hot chocolate on chilly winter mornings.

Columbia Road flower market

SOUTHWARK AND BANKSIDE

Southwark once offered an escape route from the City, where many forms of entertainment were banned. Borough High Street was lined with taverns: the medieval courtyards that still run off it mark where they stood. The George survives as the only galleried London inn. Among the illicit pleasures that thrived here were brothels that occupied houses by the river, as well as theatres and bear and cock

Shakespeare window, Southwark Cathedral

pits, which were established in the late 16th century. Shakespeare's company was based at the Globe Theatre, which has now been rebuilt close to its original site. Today the south bank of the river has undergone extensive renovation. Southwark's riverside attractions range from the Design Museum and Tate Modern, next to the bladelike Millennium Bridge, to historic pubs and Southwark Cathedral.

SIGHTS AT A GLANCE

Historic Streets and Areas
Hop Exchange ❷
The Old Operating Theatre ❺
Cardinal's Wharf ❼
Bermondsey ⓭

Museums and Galleries
Shakespeare's Globe ❻
Bankside Gallery ❽
Tate Modern ❾
Vinopolis ⓫
Clink Prison Museum ⓬

London Dungeon ⓮
Design Museum ⓯

Cathedrals
Southwark Cathedral ❶

Pubs
George Inn ❹
The Anchor ❿

Markets
Borough Market ❸

Historic Ships
HMS Belfast ⓰

| 0 metres | 500 |
| 0 yards | 500 |

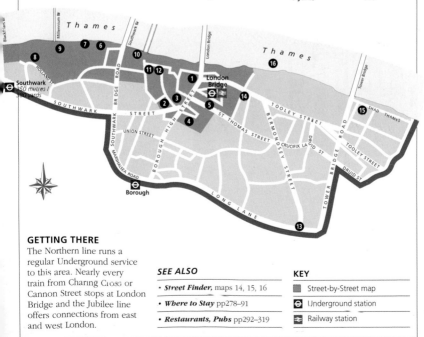

GETTING THERE
The Northern line runs a regular Underground service to this area. Nearly every train from Charing Cross or Cannon Street stops at London Bridge and the Jubilee line offers connections from east and west London.

SEE ALSO
- **Street Finder,** maps 14, 15, 16
- **Where to Stay** pp278–91
- **Restaurants, Pubs** pp292–319

KEY
■ Street-by-Street map
◉ Underground station
⇄ Railway station

◁ **The Millennium Bridge located opposite Tate Modern**

Street-by-Street: Southwark

From medieval times until the 18th century, Southwark
was a venue for the pursuit of illicit pleasures. Located
south of the Thames, it was out of the jurisdiction of the
City authorities. The 18th and 19th centuries brought
docks, warehouses and factories. Now Southwark is once
again one of London's most exciting boroughs, with the
arrival of Tate Modern, a regenerated Borough Market and
the stunning recreation of Shakespeare's Globe Theatre.

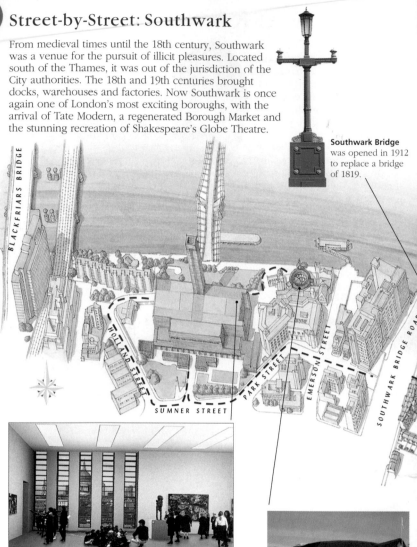

Southwark Bridge
was opened in 1912
to replace a bridge
of 1819.

★ **Tate Modern**
*The former Bankside Power Station is now a
powerhouse of contemporary art, its spectacular
open spaces showing off exhibits to perfection* ❾

★ **Shakespeare's Globe**
*This brilliant recreation of an
Elizabethan theatre has open-
air performances in the
summer months* ❻

STAR SIGHTS

★ Southwark
  Cathedral

★ Tate Modern

★ Shakespeare's
  Globe

0 metres   100

0 yards   100

KEY

– – – Suggested route

Southwark Quayside

LOCATOR MAP
See Central London Map pp14–15

The Anchor
For centuries it has been a favourite riverside pub with fine views ⑩

Vinopolis
This attraction is a city of wine on the banks of the river ⑪

Clink Prison Museum
This museum, on the site of the notorious old prison, looks back at Southwark's colourful past ⑫

Rose window

Replica of Sir Francis Drake's *Golden Hind*

★ **Southwark Cathedral**
Despite major alterations, it still contains medieval elements ❶

London Bridge, in its various forms, was the only river crossing in London from Roman times until 1750. The present bridge, completed in 1972, replaced the one of 1831 now in the US.

Borough Market
There has been a market on or near this site since 1276. Now it is a flourishing fine food market ❸

The War Memorial, commemorating soldiers who fell in World War I, was erected in 1924 on Borough High Street where it has become a powerful landmark.

George Inn
This is London's only surviving traditional, galleried inn ❹

Southwark Cathedral ❶

Montague Close SE1. **Map** 15 B3.
Tel 020-7367 6700. 🚇 *London Bridge*. **Open** *8am–6pm daily.* 🚻 *daily (phone to check).* ♿ 📷 📧 🎵 *Concerts.*
www.southwark.anglican/cathedral

This church did not become a cathedral until 1905. However, some parts of it date back to the 12th century, when the building was attached to a priory, and many of its medieval features remain. The memorials are fascinating, including a late 13th-century wooden effigy of a knight. John Harvard, who went on to found Harvard University, was baptized here in 1607 and there is a chapel named after him.

The cathedral has now been restored in a multi-million pound restoration programme. This includes the addition of new buildings, which house a shop and a café. The exterior has been landscaped to create a herb garden and an attractive Millennium Courtyard that leads to the riverside.

Shakespeare Window in Cathedral

Hop Exchange ❷

Southwark St SE1. **Map** 15 B4. 🚇 *London Bridge.* **Not open** *to the public.*

Southwark, with its easy access to Kent where hops are grown, was a natural venue for brewing beer and trading hops. In 1866 this building was constructed as the centre of that trade. Now

The George Inn, now owned by the National Trust

offices, it retains its original pediment complete with carved scenes showing the hop harvest, and iron gates with a hop motif.

Borough Market ❸

8 Southwark St SE1. **Map** 15 B4. 🚇 *London Bridge.* **Retail market open** *Fri noon–6pm, Sat 9am–4pm.*

Borough Market was until recently an exclusively wholesale fruit and vegetable market, which had its origins in medieval times, and moved to its current atmospheric position beneath the railway tracks in 1756. A popular fine food market has now been introduced, selling gourmet foods from Britain and Europe, as well as quality fruit and vegetables, to locals and tourists alike.

George Inn ❹

77 Borough High St SE1. **Map** 15 B4.
Tel 020-7407 2056. 🚇 *London Bridge, Borough.* **Open** *11am–11pm Mon–Sat, noon–10.30pm Sun.* 🍴
See **Restaurants and Pubs** *pp316–19.*

Dating from the 17th century, this building is the only example of a traditional galleried coaching inn left in London and is mentioned by Dickens in *Little Dorrit*. It was rebuilt after the Southwark fire of 1676 in a style that dates back to the Middle Ages.

Originally there would have been three wings around a courtyard where plays were staged in the 17th century. In 1889 the north and east wings were demolished, so there is only one wing remaining.

The inn, now owned by the National Trust, is still a restaurant. Perfect on a cold wet day, the pub has a well-worn, comfortable atmosphere. In the summer, the yard fills with picnic tables and patrons are occasionally entertained by actors and morris dancers.

The Old Operating Theatre ❺

9a St Thomas St SE1. **Map** 15 B4.
Tel 020-7955 4791. 🚇 *London Bridge.* **Open** *10.30am–5pm daily.* **Closed** *15 Dec–5 Jan.* **Adm charge.**
📷 **www**.thegarret.org.uk

St. Thomas' Hospital, one of the oldest in Britain, stood here from its foundation in the 12th century until it was moved west in 1862. At this time nearly all of its buildings were demolished in order to make way for the railway. The women's operating

19th-century surgical tools

theatre (The Old Operating Theatre Museum and Herb Garret) survived only because it was located away from the main buildings, in a garret over the hospital church. The UK's oldest operating theatre, it dates back to 1822, lay, bricked up and forgotten, until the 1950s. It has now been fitted out just as it would have been in the early 19th century, before the discovery of either anaesthetics or antiseptics. The display shows how patients were blindfolded, gagged and bound to the wooden operating table, while a box of sawdust underneath was used to catch the blood.

Shakespeare's Henry IV (performed at the Globe Theatre around 1600)

Shakespeare's Globe ❻

New Globe Walk SE1. **Map** 15 A3. *Tel* 020-7902 1400. *Tel* box office 020-7401 9919. Ⓔ *Southwark, London Bridge.* **Exhibition open** *May–Sep: 9am–5pm; Oct–Apr: 10am– 5pm daily.* **Adm charge**. ☑ *every 30 mins. (Rose Theatre tours for groups of 15 or more by appt only.)* **Performances** *mid-May–Sep.* ☒ ☐ ⅱ ☐ www.shakespeares-globe.org

Built on the banks of the Thames, Shakespeare's Globe is an impressive recon-struction of the Elizabethan theatre where many of his plays were first performed. The wooden, circular struc-ture is open in the middle, leaving some of the audience exposed to the elements. Those holding seat tickets have a roof over their heads. The performances operate only in summer, and seeing a

play here is a thrilling experi-ence, with top-quality acting. There is an informative tour for visitors, and groups may book to see the foundations of the nearby Rose Theatre. Beneath the theatre, and open all year round, is Shakespeare's Globe Exhibition, which brings his work and times to life.

Cardinal's Wharf ❼

SE1. **Map** 15 A3. Ⓔ *London Bridge.*

A small group of 17th-century houses still survives here in the shadow of Tate Modern art gallery *(see pp178–81).* A plaque com-memorates Christopher Wren's stay here while St Paul's Cathedral *(see pp148–51)* was being built. He would have had a particu-larly fine view of the works. It is thought that the wharf got its name from Cardinal Wolsey who was Bishop of Winchester in 1529.

Bankside Gallery ❽

48 Hopton St SE1. **Map** 14 F3. *Tel* 020-7928 7521. Ⓔ *Blackfriars, Southwark.* **Open** *11am–6pm daily.* **Closed** *25 Dec–1 Jan.* ☒ ☐ *Lectures.* www.banksidegallery.com

This modern riverside gallery is the headquarters of two historic British societies, namely the Royal Watercolour Society and the Royal Society of Painter-Printmakers. The

View from the Founders' Arms

members of these societies are elected by their peers in a tradition that dates back over 200 years. Their work embraces both established and experimental practices. The gallery's permanent collection is not on show here but there are constantly changing temporary displays of contemporary water colours and original artists' prints. The exhibitions feature the work of both societies and many of the pieces on display are for sale. There is also a superb specialist art shop that sells both books and materials.

There is an unparalleled view of St Paul's Cathedral from the nearby pub, the Founders' Arms – built on the site of the foundry where the cathedral's bells were cast. South of here, on Hopton Street, is a series of alms-houses dating from 1752.

Row of 17th-century houses on Cardinal's Wharf

Tate Modern ❾

Looming over the southern bank of the Thames, Tate Modern occupies the converted Bankside power station, a dynamic space for one of the world's premier collections of contemporary art. Up until 2000, the Tate collection was shown at three galleries: Tate St Ives, Tate Liverpool and the Tate Gallery, now Tate Britain *(see pp82–85)*. When Tate Modern joined this family of galleries, space was made for an ever-expanding collection of contemporary art. Tate Modern has had its first major re-hang since it opened, so works and exhibitions may change from those described here.

★ **Composition (Man and Woman)** *(1927)*
Alberto Giacometti's sculpture portrays the human form trapped in urban life.

Britain Seen from the North *(1981)*
Tony Cragg's mixed media work was inspired by a trip the artist made from Germany, where he lived, back to his native Britain.

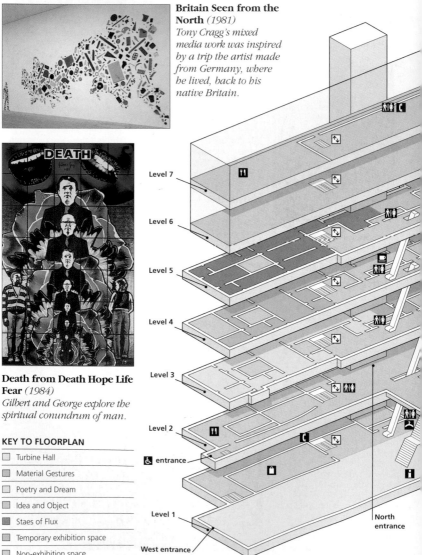

Death from Death Hope Life Fear *(1984)*
Gilbert and George explore the spiritual conundrum of man.

KEY TO FLOORPLAN

☐	Turbine Hall
☐	Material Gestures
☐	Poetry and Dream
☐	Idea and Object
■	Staes of Flux
☐	Temporary exhibition space
☐	Non-exhibition space

Level 7

Level 6

Level 5

Level 4

Level 3

Level 2

♿ entrance

Level 1

West entrance

North entrance

★ Scrapheap Services
(1995)
This video and mixed media installation by Michael Landy consists of mannequin cleaners sweeping up tiny human figures – made from tin cans and paper wrappers – which are then fed into a shredder.

VISITORS' CHECKLIST

Holland St, SE1. **Map** 14 F3, 15 A3. **Tel** 020-7887 8000. Ⓔ *Blackfriars, Mansion House, Southwark.* 🚌 45, 63, 100, 344, 381. **Open** Sun–Thu 10am–6pm, Fri–Sat 10am–10pm. **Closed** 24–26 Dec. **Adm charge** for special exhibitions only. 🚻 🖥 🚫 🅿 ♿ 🚹
www.tate.org.uk

The "light beam", a two-storey glass box, allows light to filter into the upper galleries.

A balcony gives great views of St Paul's Cathedral *(pp148–51)* across the river.

Soft Drainpipe – Blue (Cool) Version *(1967)*
An advert for drainpipes was the inspiration for this sculpture by Pop artist Claes Oldenburg. Like many of his pieces, Soft Drainpipe uses pliable material to represent hard surfaces, and thus renders a familiar object strange.

GALLERY GUIDE
The main west entrance opens into the expansive, sloped Turbine Hall. From here, a flight of stairs leads to the café and foyer of level 2, or an escalator whisks visitors straight up to gallery level 3. Temporary exhibitions are on level 4, while level 5 is again devoted to galleries. Level 6 is members' access only, but a superb restaurant and spectacular city views can be found on level 7.

★ Light Red Over Black
(1957)
This moody painting of blurred rectangles on a vertical back drop is typical of Mark Rothko's later work.

STAR EXHIBITS

- ★ Composition by Giacometti
- ★ Light Red Over Black by Rothko
- ★ Scrapheap Services by Landy

The Turbine Hall
The massive scale of this space – it covers 3,300 sq m (35,520 sq ft) – presents an unusual challenge for the artists who install pieces here.

Exploring Tate Modern

Tate Modern organizes its displays by theme rather than chronology or school, placing modern artists such as Patrick Caulfield and Jackson Pollock alongside figures like Claude Monet. Four themes based on traditional genres (Material Gestures; Poetry and Dream; Nude/Action/Body; History/Memory/Society) reveal how traditions have been challenged by modern artists. The displays are changed regularly.

After Lunch (1975) by Patrick Caulfield

MATERIAL GESTURES

The Material Gestures wing is centred around a room committed to painting and sculpture from the 1940s and 1950s which demonstrates how new forms of abstraction and expressive figuration arrived in America and Europe in the aftermath of the Second World War.

The pieces that occupy the surrounding rooms seek to relate the innovative artists of this post-war period to their predecessors, whilst also illustrating how their ideas have influenced modern artists and inspired the further development of art.

Pieces by Anish Kapoor and Barnett Newman are brought together as an introduction to the wing. A frequent feature of Newman's paintings is a vertical line representative of a column of light. Kapoor has adapted this concept to real space in *Ishi's Light* (2003), a sculptural installation which viewers are able to enter, only to find themselves standing within the ray of light generated at the centre of the piece.

Subsequent rooms in the wing focus on Mark Rothko, Expressionism, Picasso and Matisse, the resurgence of painting since the 1990s and the work of contemporary artist Tacita Dean. However, the most visually arresting room in Material Gestures is perhaps that which brings together works by Claude Monet with pieces by Jackson Pollock, Mark Rothko and Joan Mitchell.

POETRY AND DREAM

The central concept of Poetry and Dream is the process by which modern and contemporary art develops out of what has gone before, whilst also fuelling our understanding of these past movements. Poetry and Dream illustrates this primary concept using the key artists of the Surrealist movement, including Salvador Dalí, René Magritte and Pablo Picasso. After identifying key Surrealist themes, techniques and principles, the wing invites visitors to examine works by more modern figures such as Cindy Sherman, Louise Bourgeois and Francis Bacon and illustrates how these artists invoke the legacy of their Surrealist predecessors. Further rooms focus on the use of film as a Surrealist medium, Cy Twombly and Joseph Beuys, Susan Hiller and her installation piece *From the Freud Museum* (1991-6), and the survival of Realism alongside the burgeoning Surrealist movement using works by André Derain, Christian Schad and Diego Rivera.

NUDE/ACTION/BODY

From Greek Art onwards, the human figure has been a central preoccupation of western art. Tate Modern has assembled 20th-century artists who have attempted to re-shape the body. Among the paintings and sculpture on

BANKSIDE POWER STATION

This forbidding fortress was designed in 1947 by Sir Giles Gilbert Scott, the architect of Battersea Power Station, Waterloo Bridge and London's famous red telephone boxes. The power station is of a steel-framed brick skin construction, comprising over 4.2 million bricks. The Turbine Hall was designed to accommodate huge oil-burning generators and three vast oil tanks are still in situ, buried under the ground just south of the building. The tanks are to be employed in a future stage of Tate Modern development. The power station itself was converted by Swiss architects Herzog and de Meuron who designed the two-storey glass box, or lightbeam, which runs the length of the building. This serves to flood the upper galleries with light and also provides wonderful views of London.

The façade, chimney and light beam of Tate Modern

Summertime: Number 9A (1948) by Jackson Pollock

display is 'Lovis Corinth's powerful *Magdalen with Pearls in her Hair*. Stanley Spencer and Christian Schad's candidly honest depictions of their own bodies are shown alongside other nudes by Walker Sickert and Pablo Picasso. Another room explores the influence of tribal art on imagery of the human form by artists such as Henry Moore and Modigliani. In *The Bath*, Pierre Bonnard has created a sensual yet sad depiction of his wife in the bath, her body constrained by the geometric composition.

Beginning in the 1960s, Performance art used the artist's own body as the central means of expression, and often involved photography or film. A room is devoted to Robert Morris, whose films show how he used his body to interact with a set of objects. The weird and wonderful world of film-maker Matthew Barney and the highly decorative portraits of Chris Ofili's can also be found in these rooms.

HISTORY/MEMORY/SOCIETY

Taking its cue from a genre that covers ancient myth, literature and historical events, this suite of rooms collects together a number of 20th-century artists who engage with the moral, social or political world. Umberto Boccioni's striding figure *Unique Forms of Continuity in Space* embodies speed, strength and mechanization – virtues idealized by the Futurist movement. A room called *Shattered Visions* looks at artists who have responded to social and political

Unique Forms of Continuity in Space (1913) by Umberto Boccioni

upheavals in the first half of the 20th century, expressed through the anarchic imagery of Picasso's *Three Dancers* and the bleak image of murder and prostitution in George Grosz's painting about Weimar Germany. In contrast, *Utopia* shows work by the artists of De Stijl ("Style" or "The Way"), a Dutch group that sought to create a purely abstract, essential art that

would lead to a more harmonious society. The best known artist of this group is Piet Mondrian, whose grids of colour are shown alongside the delicate sculpture of Naum Gabo. Some artists used their work to celebrate ideologies or as political propaganda. *Soviet Graphics* displays different posters from the Soviet era. Andy Warhol's familiar images of icons that reflect on the cult of celebrity appear here. In *England*, Gilbert and George mock the idea of nationalism by photographing themselves as gargoyles.

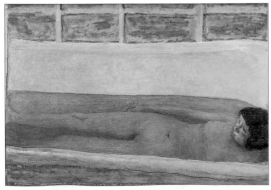

Maman (2000) by Louise Bourgeois

SPECIAL EXHIBITIONS

To complement its permanent collection, Tate Modern presents a programme of exhibitions including three large shows a year (retrospectives of modern masters or surveys of important movements). Smaller-scale projects are dotted around, and occasionally outside, the gallery. Once a year Tate Modern challenges an artist to create a work capable of occupying the vast Turbine Hall. Louise Bourgeois was the first artist to install here, with works that included her sculpture *Maman*. Recently, Olafur Eliasson's *The Weather Project* lit the Turbine Hall with a giant glowing sun.

The Bath (1925) by Pierre Bonnard

The Anchor ⑩

34 Park St SE1. **Map** 15 A3.
Tel 020-7407 1577. 🚇 London
Bridge. **Open** 11am–11pm
Mon–Sat, noon–10.30pm Sun.
♿ 🍴

This is one of London's most
famous riverside pubs. It
dates from after the Southwark
fire of 1676, which devastated
the area (see pp24–5). The
present building is 18th-
century, but traces of much
earlier hostelries have been
found beneath it. The inn was
once connected with a
brewery across the road that
belonged to Henry Thrale, a
close friend of Dr Johnson
(see p140). When Thrale died
in 1781, Johnson went to the
brewery sale and encouraged
the bidders with a phrase that
has passed into the English
language: "The potential of
growing rich beyond the
dreams of avarice."

Pub sign at the Anchor Inn

Vinopolis ⑪

1 Bank End SE1. **Map** 15 B3. **Tel**
0870-241 4040. 🚇 London Bridge.
Open noon–9pm Mon, Fri & Sat,
noon–6pm Tue–Thu & Sun (bank
hols: phone to check); last adm: 2 hrs
before close. **Closed** 25 & 26 Dec,
1 Jan. Adm charge. ♿ 🍴 📷 🎧
🅿 www.vinopolis.co.uk

Vinopolis is a unique attraction
devoted to the enjoyment of
wine. Its blend of interactive
fun and educational exhibits
has made it a popular destination for anyone who
wishes to know more about
making and drinking wine.
Set within cavernous Victorian
railway arches, Vinopolis

explores the history of
the grape from earliest
times and illuminates
the process of wine-
making from planting
the vines through to
labelling the bottles.
"Tasting stations" pro-
vide an opportunity to
savour the subject
matter along the way.
A selection of choice
vintages can be pur-
chased from the wine
warehouse after the
tour, while the shop
has a vast assortment
of wine-related
merchandise. Cantina
Vinopolis offers good
food, great service,
and, unsurprisingly,
high-quality wines.

Clink Prison Museum ⑫

1 Clink St SE1. **Map** 15 B3.
Tel 020-7403 0900. 🚇 London
Bridge. **Open** 10am–6pm Mon–Fri,
10am–9pm Sat & Sun. **Closed**
25 Dec. **Adm charge.** 📷 📱
🎧 for groups (phone first).
www.clink.co.uk

Now a macabre museum, the
prison that was once located
here first opened in the 12th
century. It was owned by
successive Bishops of
Winchester, who lived in the
adjoining palace just east of
the museum, of which all that
now remains is a lovely rose
window. During the 15th
century, the prison became
known as the "Clink", and
finally closed in 1780.
The museum illustrates the
history of the prison. Tales of
the inmates are told, including
those of the numerous

Antiques stall at Bermondsey Market

prostitutes, debtors and priests
that were incarcerated here.
Hands-on displays of
instruments of torture leave
little to the imagination and
are not for the faint-hearted.

Bermondsey ⑬

SE1. **Map** 15 C5. 🚇 London
Bridge, Borough. **Market Open**
5am–3pm Fri, starts closing noon.
Fashion and Textile Museum 83
Bermondsey St SE1. **Tel** 020-7407
8664. **Open** 10am–4pm daily (last
adm: 3.30pm). **Adm charge.**
♿ phone first. 📱 📷
www.ftmlondon.co.uk

Bermondsey's winding streets
still hold traces of its historic
past in the form of medieval,
18th-century and Victorian
buildings. Today it is famous
for its antique market. Each
Friday at dawn, seriously
committed antiques dealers
trade their latest acquisitions
at Bermondsey. There are
occasional press reports about
long-lost masterpieces changing hands here for a song,
and optimists are welcome to
try their luck and test their
judgment. However, trading
starts at the crack of dawn,
and the best bargains tend to
go before most people are
even awake.
The Fashion and Textile
Museum in Bermondsey
Street opened in 2003, and
contains the best of British and
international fashion,
including the collection of
designer Zandra Rhodes, from
the 1950s to the present day.

**Replica of Civil
War trooper's helmet
made in the Clink**

London Dungeon ⑭

Tooley St SE1. **Map** 15 C3. ☎ *020-7403 7221.* ⊖ *London Bridge.* **Open** *Jul–Sep 9.30am–6pm daily, Sep–Oct 10am–5.30pm, Nov–Easter 10.30am–5pm, Easter–Jun 10am–5.30pm.* **Closed** *25 Dec.* **Adm charge.** ♿ ▢ ▯ **www.**thedungeons.com

In effect a much-expanded version of the chamber of horrors at Madame Tussaud's *(see p224)*, this museum is a great hit with children. It illustrates the most blood-thirsty events in British history, and its activities include live actors and special effects. It is played strictly for terror, and screams abound with experiences such as Gruesome Goings-on, which includes live actors, a ride and shows; the Great Plague; the Torture Chamber; and Jack the Ripper.

Eduardo Paolozzi sculpture outside the Design Museum

Design Museum ⑮

Butlers Wharf, Shad Thames SE1. **Map** 16 E4. **Tel** *0870-833 9955.* ⊖ *Tower Hill, London Bridge.* **Open** *10am–5.45pm daily (last adm: 5.15pm).* **Closed** *25 & 26 Dec.* **Adm charge.** 🍽 **Blueprint Café** *020-7378 7031 (booking advised).* ▢ ▯ 🔼 ♿ **www.**designmuseum.org

This museum was the first in the world to be devoted solely to modern and contemporary design when it was founded in 1989. A frequently changing programme of exhibitions explores landmarks in modern design history and the most exciting innovations in contemporary design set against the context of social, cultural, economic

Spooky London Dungeon logo, an indication of the gruesome displays

and technological changes. The Design Museum embraces every area of design, from furniture and fashion, to household products, cars, graphics, websites and architecture in exhibitions and new design commissions. Each spring the museum hosts Designer of the Year, a national design prize, with an exhibition at which the public can vote for the winner.

The museum is arranged over three floors, with major exhibitions on the first floor. There is a choice of smaller displays on the second, which also houses an Interaction Space, where visitors can play vintage video games and learn about the designers featured in the museum in the Design at the Design Museum online research archive. The shop and café are on the ground floor. On the first floor is the **Blueprint Café** restaurant, which has stunning views of the Thames.

HMS Belfast ⑯

Morgan's Lane, Tooley St SE1. **Map** 16 D3. ☎ *020-7940 6300.* ⊖ *London Bridge, Tower Hill.* **Open** *Mar–Oct: 10am–6pm daily; Nov–Feb: 10am–5pm daily (last adm: 45 mins before closing).* **Closed** *24–26 Dec.* **Adm charge.** ♿ *limited.* ▢ ▯ **www.**iwm.org.uk

Originally launched in 1938 to serve in World War II, HMS *Belfast* was instrumental in the destruction of the German battle cruiser, *Scharnhorst*, in the battle of North Cape, and also played an important role in the Normandy Landings.

After the war, the battle cruiser, designed for offensive action and for supporting amphibious operations, was sent to work for the United Nations in Korea. The ship remained in service with the British navy until 1965.

Since 1971, the cruiser has been used as a floating naval museum. Part of it has been recreated to show what the ship was like in 1943, when it participated in sinking the German battle cruiser. Other displays portray life on board during World War II and there are also exhibits relating to the history of the Royal Navy.

As well as being a great family day out, it is also possible for children to take part in educational activity weekends on board the ship.

The now familiar sight of the naval gunship HMS *Belfast* on the Thames

SOUTH BANK

Following the Festival of Britain in 1951, the South Bank arts centre grew up around the newly erected Royal Festival Hall. The architecture has been criticized over the years, especially the chunky concrete Hayward Gallery, but now appears to be valued as an important part of London's river frontage. The area functions well, and is crowded with culture-seekers most evenings and afternoons. As well as the Royal National Theatre and the Old Vic theatre, concert halls and galleries, the South Bank has the National Film Theatre and London's most striking cinema, the IMAX *(see p347)*. In keeping with Festival of Britain tradition, the South Bank was a focal point for the new millennium, with the raising of the world's highest observation wheel, the London Eye.

SIGHTS AT A GLANCE

Historic Streets and Buildings
Lambeth Palace ⑧
Gabriel's Wharf ⑪
Waterloo Station ⑫

Museums and Galleries
Hayward Gallery ②
Florence Nightingale Museum ⑥
Museum of Garden History ⑦
Imperial War Museum ⑨

Attractions
County Hall ④
British Airways London Eye ⑤

Theatres and Concert Halls
Royal National Theatre ①
Royal Festival Hall ③
The Old Vic ⑩

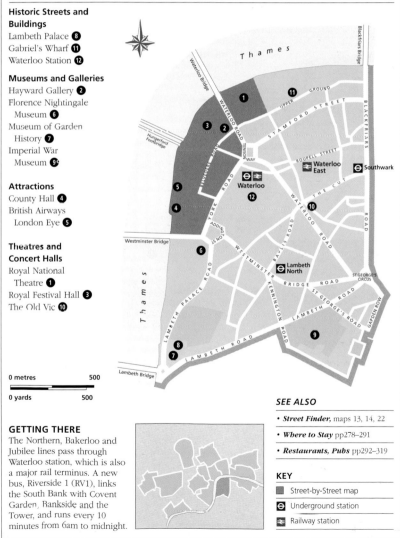

0 metres   500
0 yards   500

GETTING THERE

The Northern, Bakerloo and Jubilee lines pass through Waterloo station, which is also a major rail terminus. A new bus, Riverside 1 (RV1), links the South Bank with Covent Garden, Bankside and the Tower, and runs every 10 minutes from 6am to midnight.

SEE ALSO

- *Street Finder,* maps 13, 14, 22
- *Where to Stay* pp278–291
- *Restaurants, Pubs* pp292–319

KEY

▮ Street-by-Street map
🚇 Underground station
🚉 Railway station

◁ Thameside promenade on the South Bank

Street-by-Street: South Bank Centre

Originally this was an area of wharves and
factories which was much damaged by bombing
during World War II. It was chosen as the site
of the 1951 Festival of Britain *(see p32)*,
celebrating the centenary of the Great
Exhibition *(see pp28–9)*. The Royal Festival
Hall is the only building from 1951 to remain,
but since then London's main arts centre has
been created around it, including the national
showplaces for theatre, music and film, and a
major art gallery.

**Memorial to the
International Brigade of
the Spanish Civil War**

To the Strand

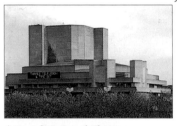

★ Royal National Theatre
*Its three auditoriums offer a
choice of plays ranging
from the classics to the
sharpest modern writing* ❶

The National Film Theatre was
established in 1953 to show
historic films *(see p347)*.

Festival Pier

The Queen Elizabeth Hall
stages more intimate
concerts than the Festival
Hall. The adjoining Purcell
Room is for chamber music
(see pp348–9).

Hayward Gallery
*The concrete interior of
this venue for important
exhibitions is well suited to
many modern works* ❷

★ Royal Festival Hall
*The London Philharmonic
is one of many world-class
orchestras to perform here
in the focal point of the
South Bank Centre* ❸

Hungerford Bridge
was built in 1864 to
carry both trains
and pedestrians to
Charing Cross. It
also now includes
two footbridges.

STAR SIGHTS

- ★ British Airways
  London Eye

- ★ Royal National
  Theatre

- ★ Royal Festival Hall

KEY

– – – Suggested route

0 metres   100

0 yards   100

**★ British Airways
London Eye**
*The world's largest obser-
vation wheel offers a
unique view of London* ❺

Waterloo Bridge was completed in 1945 to Sir Giles Gilbert Scott's design. It replaced Rennie's bridge of 1817.

LOCATOR MAP
See Central London Map pp14–15

The Struggle is My Life is a bronze of Nelson Mandela, the South African leader. Made by Ian Walters, it was unveiled here in 1985.

The Shell Building, head-quarters of the international oil company, was completed in 1963. Its architectural merit is still hotly debated.

County Hall
This is now home to the London Aquarium, art galleries, as well as a leisure complex ❹

CONCERT HALL APPROACH

BELVEDERE ROAD

CHICHELEY STREET

WESTMINSTER BRIDGE ROAD

UPPER GROUND

Jubilee Gardens were laid out in 1977 to celebrate the Silver Jubilee of Queen Elizabeth II.

To Westminster station

The new façade of the Hayward Gallery

Royal National Theatre ❶

South Bank SE1. **Map** 14 D3. 🎫 020-7452 3000. 🚇 Waterloo. **Open** 10am–11pm Mon–Sat. **Closed** 24, 25 Dec, Good Fri. 🚫 during performances. 🍴 🖥 📷 ♿ 🎁 **Concerts** at 6pm, **exhibitions**. See **Entertainment** pp342–3. **www**.nationaltheatre.org.uk

Even if you don't want to see a play, this well-appointed complex is worth a visit. Sir Denys Lasdun's building was opened in 1976 after 200 years of debate about whether there should be a national theatre and where it should be sited. The company was formed in 1963, under Laurence (later Lord) Olivier, Britain's leading 20th-century actor. The largest of the three theatres is named after him – the others, the Cottesloe and the Lyttleton, commemorate administrators.

Festival of Britain: symbol of 1951

Hayward Gallery ❷

South Bank SE1. **Map** 14 D3. **Tel** 020-7921 0813. 🚇 Waterloo. **Open** 10am–6pm Mon, Thu, Sat & Sun, 10am–8pm Tue & Wed, 10am–9pm Fri. **Closed** 1 Jan, 24–26 Dec, between exhibitions. **Adm charge.** ♿ 🖥 📷 **www**.hayward.org.uk

The Hayward Gallery is one of London's main venues for large art exhibitions. Its slabby grey concrete exterior is too starkly modern for some tastes, but it is also considered by many as an icon of 1960s "Brutalist" architecture. The new foyer by Dan Graham, completed in 2003, shows a selection of cartoons and artists' videos.

Hayward exhibitions cover classical and contemporary art, but the work of British contemporary artists is particularly well represented.

Royal Festival Hall ❸

South Bank SE1. **Map** 14 D4. **Tel** 0870-380 0400. 🚇 Waterloo. **Open** 10am–10pm daily. **Closed** 25 Dec. 🚫 during performances. 🍴 🖥 📷 ♿ **Pre-concert talks, exhibitions, free concerts.** See **Entertainment** p346. **www**.rfh.org.uk

This was the only structure in the 1951 Festival of Britain (see p32) designed for permanence. Sir Robert Matthew and Sir Leslie Martin's concert hall was the first major public building in London following World War II. It has stood the test of time so well that many of the capital's major arts institutions have gathered round it. Festival Riverside on level 1 opened in 2004, with new restaurants and retail, community and visitors facilities. Phase II of the redevelopment began in 2005 and will be completed in 2007. The stage has hosted renowned musicians, including the cellist Jacqueline du Pré and the conductor Georg Solti. The organ was installed in 1954. There are cafés and book stalls on the lower floors.

County Hall ❹

Westminster Bridge Rd SE1. **Map** 13 C4. **Aquarium Tel** 020-7967 8010. 🚇 Waterloo. **Open** 10am–6pm daily. **Adm charge.** ♿ 🖥 📷 **www**.londonaquarium.co.uk **Dali Universe Tel** 020-7620 2720.

Shark in a scenic tank at the London Aquarium

Once the home of London's elected government, this imposing building now houses a leisure complex. The London Aquarium, a Salvador Dalí exhibition, *Dali Universe*, and *Namco Station*, a computer games hall, occupy the space alongside two hotels, several restaurants and a health club.

The Aquarium's glass walls hold over 350 aquatic species from the Atlantic and Pacific Oceans. Witness the spectacular Atlantic Feed, where divers hand-feed various rays and native British sharks. There is also a touch pool.

British Airways London Eye ⑤

The London Eye is a 135-m (443-ft) high observation wheel. Erected in 2000 as part of London's millennium celebrations, it immediately became one of the city's most recognizable landmarks, notable not only for its size, but for its circularity amid the block-shaped buildings flanking it. Thirty-two capsules, each holding up to 25 people, take a gentle 30-minute round trip. On a clear day, the Eye affords a unique 40-km (25-mile) view which sweeps over the capital in all directions and on to the countryside and hills beyond.

The glass capsules are mounted on the outside of the rim, allowing unobstructed 360-degree views.

80 spokes made from 6 km (3.7 miles) of cable hold the structure in tension, strengthening the wheel.

Houses of Parliament
Seventeen minutes into the flight, the spectacular aerial view of Westminster should not be missed.

Battersea Power Station
After 15 minutes, the distinctive white smokestacks of this old power station are visible.

Two cables, 60 metres (197 feet) in length, support the entire structure from concrete bases in Jubilee Gardens.

The wheel rim was floated down the Thames in sections and then assembled on site.

Buckingham Palace
Ten minutes into the journey, the Queen's official residence glides into view.

The Eye turns continuously and moves slowly enough that the capsules are boarded here while moving. The wheel is halted for those requiring assistance.

Florence Nightingale Museum ❻

2 Lambeth Palace Rd SE1. **Map** 14
D5. **Tel** 020-7620 0374. ⊖
Waterloo, Westminster. **Open**
10am–5pm Mon– Fri, 10am–4.30pm
Sat, Sun & public hols (last adm one
hour before closing). **Closed** 24
Dec–2 Jan, Good Fri, Easter Sun.
Adm charge. ⊘ 🅿 ♿ **Videos,
lectures.**
www.florence-nightingale.co.uk

This determined woman
captured the nation's
imagination as the "Lady of
the Lamp", who nursed the
wounded soldiers of the
Crimea War (1853 – 6). She
also founded Britain's first
school of nursing at old St
Thomas' Hospital in 1860.

Obscurely sited near the
entrance to the new St
Thomas' Hospital, the
museum is worth finding. It
gives a fascinating
account of Nightingale's
career through displays of
original documents and
personal memorabilia.
They illustrate her life
and the developments
she pioneered in health
care, until her death
in 1910, aged 90.

Florence Nightingale

Museum of Garden History ❼

Lambeth Palace Rd SE1. **Map** 21 C1.
Tel 020-7401 8865. ⊖ Waterloo,
Lambeth North, Westminster.
Open 10.30am–5pm daily. **Closed**
mid-Dec–early Jan. ♿ 🖥 🅿
**Library by appt, lectures,
filmshows.**
www.museumgardenhistory.org

The world's first museum of
garden history is housed in
the restored church of St Mary
of Lambeth Palace. In the
grounds are the tombs of
John Tradescant, father and
son who, as well as being
gardeners to Charles I and
Charles II, were also adventurous plant hunters and
collectors of curiosities. The
tomb of William Bligh of *The
Bounty* can also be seen here.

The Museum of Garden
History consists of a history of

gardening in Britain,
illustrated by a selection of
historic garden tools, artifacts
and curiosities. It also runs a
programme of exhibitions,
events, lectures and
educational activities.

There is a shop with a stock
of garden-related items for
freshly inspired gardeners.

Lambeth Palace ❽

SE1. **Map** 21 C1. ⊖ Lambeth
North, Westminster, Waterloo,
Vauxhall. **Not open** to the public.

This has been the London
base of the Archbishop of
Canterbury, the senior cleric
in the Church of England, for
800 years. The chapel and its
undercroft contain elements
from the 13th century, but a
large part of the rest of the
building is far more
recent. It has been
frequently restored,
most recently by
Edward Blore in 1828.
The Tudor gatehouse,
however, dates from
1485 and is one of
London's most
pleasing and
familiar riverside
landmarks.

Until the first
Westminster
Bridge was built,
the horse ferry that operated
between here and Millbank
was a principal river crossing.
The revenues from it went to
the Archbishop, who received
compensation for loss of
business when the bridge
opened in 1750.

The Tudor gatehouse

Imperial War Museum ❾

Lambeth Rd SE1. **Map** 22 E1.
Tel 020-7416 5000. 🎬 020-7416
5320. ⊖ Lambeth North, Elephant
& Castle. **Open** 10am–6pm daily.
Closed 24–26 Dec. 📷 ♿ 🍴
🖥 🅿 **Filmshows, lectures.**
www.iwm.org.uk

In spite of the two colossal
guns that point up the drive
from the main entrance, this
is not just a display of the
engines of modern warfare.
Massive tanks, artillery, bombs
and aircraft are on show, yet
some of the most fascinating
exhibits in the museum relate
more to the impact on the lives
of people at home than to the
business of fighting. There are
displays about food rationing,
air raid precautions, censor-
ship and morale-boosting.

The arts are well represented,
with extracts from wartime
films, radio programmes and
literature, plus many
hundreds of photographs,
paintings by Graham

The machinery of war through the ages

Sutherland and Paul Nash, and sculpture by Jacob Epstein. Henry Moore did some evocative drawings of life during the Blitz of 1940, when many Londoners slept in Underground stations in order to protect themselves from falling bombs. There is also a library with a fascinating archive. The Holocaust exhibition is a major permanent display, using historical material and original artifacts to tell its story.

The museum is housed in part of what used to be the Bethlehem Royal Hospital for the Insane ("Bedlam"), built in 1811. In the 19th century, visitors would come for the afternoon to enjoy the antics of the patients. The hospital moved out to new premises in Surrey in 1930, leaving this vast building empty. Its two large, flanking wings were pulled down and this central block converted into the museum which moved here from its former South Kensington site in 1936.

The Old Vic's façade from 1816

The Old Vic ❿

Waterloo Rd SE1. **Map** 14 E5.
Tel 0870-060 6628. 🔁 Waterloo.
Open for performances only. ♿ 🍴
📺 See **Entertainment** pp344–5.
www.oldvictheatre.com

This splendid building dates back to 1818, when it was opened as the Royal Coburg Theatre. In 1833 the name was changed to the Royal Victoria, in honour of the future queen. Shortly after this the theatre became a centre for "music hall", the immensely popular Victorian entertainment which included singers,

comedians and other acts. In 1912 Lillian Baylis became manager and from 1914 to 1923 she staged all of Shakespeare's plays here. In the 1960s the National Theatre (see p188) was founded and based at this site.

In 1997, Sally Greene, with the director Stephen Daldry and others, set up a charitable trust to secure the theatre's future. The Trust set up The Old Vic Theatre Company as a resident company in 2003, with Kevin Spacey as Artistic Director. There are cheap seats for younger people and pantomimes at Christmas.

Gabriel's Wharf ⓫

56 Upper Ground SE1. **Map** 14 E3.
🔁 Waterloo. See **Shops and Markets** pp332–41.

This pleasant enclave of boutiques, craft shops and cafés was the product of a long and stormy debate over the future of what was once an industrial riverside area. Residents of Waterloo strongly opposed various schemes for office developments before a community association was able to acquire the site in 1984 and build co-operative housing around the wharf.

Adjoining the market is a small garden and a riverside walkway with marvellous views to the north of the City. The OXO Tower to the east, built in 1928 surreptitiously to advertise a meat extract by means of its window shapes, is now the setting for a fine restaurant (see p302).

The memorial to the dead of World War I at Waterloo Station

Waterloo Station ⓬

York Rd SE1. **Map** 14 D4.
Tel 08457 484950. 🔁 Waterloo.
See **Getting to London** pp374–5.

The terminus for trains to southwest England, Waterloo station was originally built in 1848 but completely remodelled in the early 20th century, with the addition of a grand formal entrance on the northeast corner. Today the spacious concourse, lined with shops, cafés and bars, makes it one of the most practical of the London rail terminals

Towards the end of the 20th century the station was enlarged again to serve as London's first Channel Tunnel rail link to Europe. In summer 2007, the Eurostar terminal will move from Waterloo station to its new home at St Pancras International.

The area around Waterloo has a great community feel and it is worth passing down Lower Marsh with its shops, eateries and street market.

Illusionistic painting on the buildings around Gabriel's Wharf

CHELSEA

The showy young shoppers who paraded along the King's Road from the 1960s until the 1980s have more or less gone, along with Chelsea's reputation for extreme behaviour established by the bohemian Chelsea Set of writers and artists in the 19th century. Formerly a riverside village, Chelsea became fashionable in Tudor times. Henry VIII liked it so much that he built a small palace (long vanished) here. Artists, including Turner, Whistler and Rossetti, were attracted by the river views from

Cow's head outside the Old Dairy on Old Church Street

Cheyne Walk. The historian Thomas Carlyle and the essayist Leigh Hunt arrived in the 1830s and began a literary tradition continued by writers such as the poet Swinburne. Yet Chelsea has always had a raffish element, too: in the 18th century the pleasure gardens were noted for beautiful courtesans and the Chelsea Arts Club has had riotous balls for nearly a century. Chelsea is too expensive for most artists now, but the artistic connection is maintained by many galleries and antique shops.

SIGHTS AT A GLANCE

Historic Streets and Buildings
King's Road ❶
Carlyle's House ❷
Cheyne Walk ❺
Royal Hospital ❽
Sloane Square ❿

Museums
National Army Museum ❼
Saatchi Gallery ❾

Churches
Chelsea Old Church ❸

Gardens
Roper's Garden ❹
Chelsea Physic Garden ❻

GETTING THERE
The District and Circle Underground lines serve Sloane Square; the Piccadilly line passes just outside this area, through South Kensington. Buses 11, 19 and 22 all stop on the King's Road.

SEE ALSO

- *Street Finder,* maps 19, 20

- *Where to Stay* pp278–91

- *Restaurants, Pubs* pp292–319

- *Chelsea and Battersea Walk* pp266–7

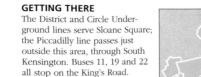

KEY

▨	Street-by-Street map
⊖	Underground station

0 metres 500
0 yards 500

◁ **Picturesque Chelsea residences in a cul-de-sac off the King's Road**

Street-by-Street: Chelsea

Once a peaceful riverside village,
Chelsea has been fashionable since
Tudor times when Sir Thomas More,
Henry VIII's Lord Chancellor, lived here.
Artists, including Turner, Whistler and
Rossetti, were attracted by the views
from Cheyne Walk, before a busy main
road disturbed its peace. Chelsea's
artistic connection
is maintained by
its galleries and
antique shops,
while enclaves of
18th-century
houses preserve
its old village
atmosphere.

King's Road
*In the 1960s and
1970s it was the
boutique-lined
centre of fashionable
London, and is still
a main shopping
street* ❶

The Old Dairy, at 46 Old
Church Street, was built in
1796, when cows still
grazed in the surrounding
fields. The tiling is original.

To King's
Road

Carlyle's House
*The historian and philosopher
lived here from 1834 until his
death in 1882* ❷

Chelsea Old Church
*Although severely
damaged during
World War II, it still
holds some fine Tudor
monuments* ❸

Roper's Garden
*It includes a sculpture
by Jacob Epstein who
had a studio here* ❹

Thomas More, sculpted in 1969
by L Cubitt Bevis, gazes
calmly across the river near
where he lived.

STAR SIGHTS

★ Chelsea Physic
  Garden

KEY

– – –   Suggested route

| 0 metres | 100 |
| 0 yards | 100 |

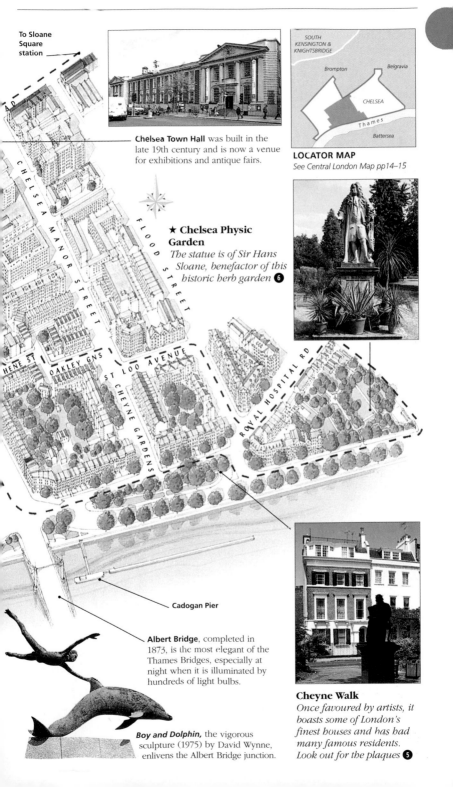

To Sloane
Square
station

Chelsea Town Hall was built in the
late 19th century and is now a venue
for exhibitions and antique fairs.

★ **Chelsea Physic
Garden**
*The statue is of Sir Hans
Sloane, benefactor of this
historic herb garden* ❻

Cadogan Pier

Albert Bridge, completed in
1873, is the most elegant of the
Thames Bridges, especially at
night when it is illuminated by
hundreds of light bulbs.

Boy and Dolphin, the vigorous
sculpture (1975) by David Wynne,
enlivens the Albert Bridge junction.

Cheyne Walk
*Once favoured by artists, it
boasts some of London's
finest houses and has had
many famous residents.
Look out for the plaques* ❺

The Pheasantry, King's Road

King's Road ❶

SW3 and SW10. **Map** 19 B3.
🚇 *Sloane Square. See **Shops and Markets** pp332–41.*

This is Chelsea's central artery, with its wealth of small fashion shops packed with young people looking for designer fashions. The mini-skirt revolution of the 1960s began here and so have many subsequent style trends, perhaps the most famous of them being punk.

Look out for the Pheasantry at No. 152, with its columns and statuary. It was built in 1881 as the shop-front of a furniture maker's premises but now conceals a modern restaurant. Antique-lovers will find three warrens of stalls on the south side of the King's Road: Antiquarius at No. 137, the Chenil Galleries at Nos. 181–3 and the Chelsea Antiques Market at No. 253.

Carlyle's House ❷

24 Cheyne Row SW3. **Map** 19 B4.
Tel *020-7352 7087.* 🚇 *Sloane Square, South Kensington.* **Open** *Apr–Oct: 2–5pm Wed–Fri, 11am–5pm Sat, Sun & public hols (last adm: 4.30pm).* **Adm charge.** 🚫 📷 *by appt.*
www.nationaltrust.org.uk

The historian and founder of the London Library (*see St James's Square p92*), Thomas Carlyle moved into this modest 18th-century house in 1834, and wrote many of his

best-known books here, notably *The French Revolution* and *Frederick the Great*. His presence made Chelsea more fashionable and the house became a mecca for some great literary figures. The novelists Charles Dickens and William Thackeray, poet Alfred Lord Tennyson and naturalist Charles Darwin were all regular visitors here. The house has been restored and looks as it did during Carlyle's lifetime.

Chelsea Old Church ❸

Cheyne Walk SW3. **Map** 19 A4. **Tel** *020-7795 1019.* 🚇 *Sloane Sq, South Kensington.* **Open** *times vary – phone to check.* ♿ 📷 *by appt.* 🕐 *8am, 10am, 11am, 12.15pm, 6pm Sun.*
www.chelseaoldchurch.org.uk

Chelsea Old Church in 1860

Rebuilt after World War II, this square-towered building does not look old from the outside. However, early prints confirm that it is a careful replica of the medieval church that was destroyed by World War II bombs.

The glory of this church is its Tudor monuments. One to Sir Thomas More, who built a chapel here in 1528, contains an inscription he wrote (in Latin), asking to be buried next to his wife. Among other monuments is a chapel to Sir Thomas Lawrence, who was an Elizabethan merchant, and a 17th-century memorial to Lady Jane Cheyne, after whose husband Cheyne Walk was named. Outside the church is a statue in memory of Sir Thomas More, "statesman, scholar, saint", gazing piously across the river.

Roper's Garden ❹

Cheyne Walk SW3. **Map** 19 A4.
🚇 *Sloane Square, South Kensington.*

This is a small park outside Chelsea Old Church. It is named after Margaret Roper, Thomas More's daughter, and her husband William, who wrote More's biography. The sculptor Jacob Epstein worked at a studio on the site between 1909 and 1914, and there is a stone carving by him commemorating the fact. The park also contains a figure of a nude woman by Gilbert Carter.

Cheyne Walk ❺

SW3. **Map** 19 B4. 🚇 *Sloane Square, South Kensington.*

Until Chelsea Embankment was constructed in 1874, Cheyne Walk was a pleasant riverside promenade. Now it overlooks a busy road that has destroyed much of its charm. Many of the 18th-century houses remain, though, bristling with blue plaques celebrating some of the famous people who have lived in them. Most were writers and artists, including J M W Turner who lived incognito at No. 119, George Eliot who died at No. 4 and a clutch of writers (Henry James, T S Eliot and Ian Fleming) in Carlyle Mansions.

Thomas More on Cheyne Walk

Chelsea Physic Garden ❻

66 Royal Hospital Road SW3. **Map** 19 C4. **Tel** 020-7352 5646. ⊖ *Sloane Square.* **Open** *Apr–Oct: noon–5pm Wed, noon–6pm Sun; Jul–Sept: noon–5pm Tue and Thur; noon–5pm Mon–Fri during Chelsea Flower Show in May, see p56.* **Adm charge**. ♿ 🖻 🛉 **Gardening school**. www.chelseaphysicgarden.co.uk

Established by the Society of Apothecaries in 1673 to study plants for medicinal use, this garden was saved from closure in 1722 by a gift from Sir Hans Sloane, whose statue adorns it. Many new varieties have been nurtured in its glasshouses, including cotton sent to the plantations of the southern United States. Visitors can see ancient trees and one of Britain's first rock gardens, installed in 1772.

National Army Museum ❼

Royal Hospital Rd SW3. **Map** 19 C4. **Tel** 020-7730 0717. ⊖ *Sloane Square.* **Open** *10am–5.30pm daily.* **Closed** *1 Jan, Good Fri, May Day, 24–26 Dec.* ♿ 🖻 🛉 www.national-army-museum.ac.uk

A lively account of the history of British land forces from 1485 to the present can be found here. Tableaux, dioramas, archive film and interactive displays illustrate major engagements and give a taste of life behind the lines. There are fine paintings of battle scenes and portraits of soldiers. The shop sells a range of books and model soldiers.

Royal Hospital ❽

Royal Hospital Rd SW3. **Map** 20 D3. **Tel** 020-7881 5204. ⊖ *Sloane Sq.* **Open** *10am–noon, 2–4pm Mon–Sat, 2–4pm Sun.* **Closed** *Sun Oct–Mar, public hols, functions (check first).* ♿ limited. 🛉 www.chelsea-pensioners.co.uk

This graceful complex was commissioned by Charles II

Chelsea Physic Garden in autumn

from Christopher Wren in 1682 as a retirement home for old or wounded soldiers, who have been known as Chelsea Pensioners ever since. The hospital opened ten years later and is still home to about 330 retired soldiers, whose distinctive uniforms of scarlet coats and tricorne hats date from the 17th century. Flanking the northern entrance are Wren's two main public rooms: the chapel, notable for its wonderful simplicity, and the panelled Great Hall, still used as the dining room. A small museum explains the history of the Pensioners. A statue of Charles II by Grinling Gibbons is to be found on the terrace outside, and there is a fine view of the remains of Battersea Power Station across the river.

A Chelsea Pensioner in uniform

Saatchi Gallery ❾

Duke of York's HQ, King's Road Chelsea **Map** 19 C3. ⊖ *Sloane Square.* **Open** *Due to re-open early 2007* 🛉 🖻 www.saatchi-gallery.co.uk

The Saatchi Gallery is famous for presenting the best in contemporary art and has seen an astonishing rise in interest since it opened twenty years ago. The gallery now receives over 600,000 visitors each year. Many of

the featured artists are unknown when first exhibited at the gallery but often rise to fame as a result. Recently relocated from the South Bank, the Saatchi Gallery's new location at the Duke of York's HQ offers an ideal environment in which to view contemporary art. Admire pieces by established names such as Tracy Emin and Jenny Saville while also keeping an eye open for up-and-coming new talent.

Sloane Square ❿

SW1. **Map** 20 D2. ⊖ *Sloane Square.*

Sloane Square fountain

This pleasant small square (rectangle to be precise) has a paved centre with a flower stall and fountain depicting Venus. Laid out in the late 18th century, it was named after Sir Hans Sloane, the wealthy physician and collector who bought the manor of Chelsea in 1712. Opposite Peter Jones, the 1936 department store on the square's west side, is the Royal Court Theatre, which for over a century has fostered new drama.

SOUTH KENSINGTON AND KNIGHTSBRIDGE

Bristling with embassies and consulates, South Kensington and Knightsbridge are among London's most desirable, and expensive, areas. The proximity of Kensington Palace, a royal residence, means they have remained fairly unchanged.

The prestigious shops of Knightsbridge serve their wealthy residents. With Hyde Park to the north, and museums that celebrated Victorian learning at its heart, visitors to this part of London can expect to find a unique combination of the serene and the grandiose.

SIGHTS AT A GLANCE

Historic Streets and Buildings
Royal College of Music **5**
Royal College of Art **7**
Kensington Palace **10**
Speakers' Corner **13**

Churches
Brompton Oratory **4**

Museums and Galleries
Natural History Museum pp208–9 **1**
Science Museum pp212–13 **2**
Victoria and Albert Museum pp202–5 **3**

Serpentine Gallery **9**

Parks and Gardens
Kensington Gardens **11**
Hyde Park **12**

Monuments
Albert Memorial **8**
Marble Arch **14**

Concert Halls
Royal Albert Hall **6**

Shops
Harrods **15**

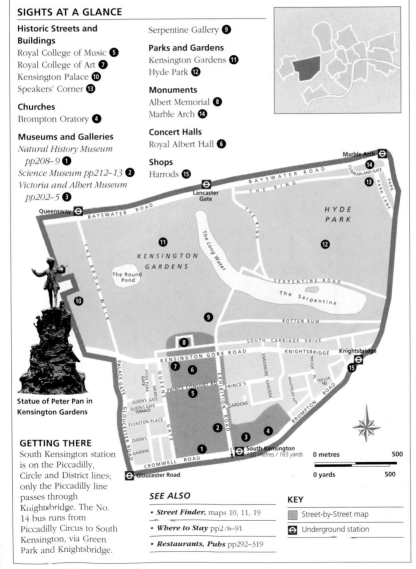

Statue of Peter Pan in Kensington Gardens

GETTING THERE
South Kensington station is on the Piccadilly, Circle and District lines; only the Piccadilly line passes through Knightsbridge. The No. 14 bus runs from Piccadilly Circus to South Kensington, via Green Park and Knightsbridge.

SEE ALSO

• *Street Finder,* maps 10, 11, 19

• *Where to Stay* pp278–91

• *Restaurants, Pubs* pp292–319

KEY
  Street-by-Street map
  Underground station

◁ The Albert Memorial, opposite the Royal Albert Hall

Street-by-Street: South Kensington

A clutch of museums and colleges provide this area with its dignified character. The Great Exhibition of 1851 in Hyde Park was so successful that in the following years smaller exhibitions were held here, just to its south. By the end of the 19th century some of these had become permanent museums, housed in grandiose buildings celebrating Victorian self-confidence.

Royal College of Art
David Hockney and Peter Blake are among the great artists who trained here **7**

The Royal College of Organists was decorated by F W Moody in 1876.

★ **Royal Albert Hall**
Opened in 1870, the Hall was partly funded by selling seats on a 999-year lease **6**

Royal College of Music
Historic musical instruments, like this harpsichord (1531), are exhibited here **5**

★ **Natural History Museum**
The dinosaur exhibits are one of the museum's most popular attractions **1**

★ **Science Museum**
Visitors here can experiment with the interactive displays **2**

The Albert Hall Mansions, built by Norman Shaw in 1879, started a fashion for red brick.

Albert Memorial
This memorial was built to commemorate Queen Victoria's consort 8

LOCATOR MAP
See Central London Map pp14–15

KEY

– – – Suggested route

0 metres	100
0 yards	100

The Royal Geographical Society was founded in 1830. Scottish missionary and explorer David Livingstone (1813–73) was a member.

Imperial College, part of London University, is one of the country's leading scientific institutions.

★ Victoria and Albert Museum
A range of objects and a stunning photo gallery illustrate the nation's history of design and decoration 3

Brompton Oratory
The Oratory was built during the 19th-century Catholic revival 4

Brompton Square, begun in 1821, established this as a fashionable residential area.

Holy Trinity church dates from the 19th century and is located in a calm backwater among cottages.

To Knightsbridge station

STAR SIGHTS

★ Victoria and Albert Museum

★ Natural History Museum

★ Science Museum

★ Royal Albert Hall

Victoria and Albert Museum ❸

The Glass Gallery

The Victoria and Albert Museum (the V&A) contains one of the world's widest collections of art and design, ranging from early Christian devotional objects to cutting-edge furniture design. Originally founded in 1852 as the Museum of Manufactures to inspire design students, it was renamed by Queen Victoria in 1899 in memory of Prince Albert. The museum is undergoing a dramatic redisplay of much of its collection, including the redesign of the garden, sculpture galleries and main shop. To find out if a particular gallery will be open, call the bookings office on 020-7942 2211.

British Galleries (1760–1900)
This charming sweet box (1770) is one of many pieces on display that were crafted in the workshops of Britain.

Silver galleries
Radiant pieces such as the Burgess Cup (Britain, 1863) fill these stunning galleries.

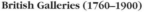

★ Fashion gallery
In this gallery, European clothing from the mid-1500s to the present day is displayed, such as these famous Vivienne Westwood shoes.

★ British Galleries (1500–1760)
Displays of evocative objects, such as this writing desk from King Henry VIII's court, illustrate Britain's fascinating history.

Exhibition
Road entrance

KEY TO FLOORPLAN

- ☐ Level 0
- ☐ Level 1
- ☐ Level 2
- ☐ Level 3
- ☐ Level 4
- ☐ Level 6
- ☐ Henry Cole Wing
- ☐ Non-exhibition space

GALLERY GUIDE

The V&A has a 7-mile (11-km) layout spread over six levels. The main floor, level 1, houses the China, Japan and South Asia galleries, as well as the Fashion gallery and the Cast Courts. The British Galleries are on levels 2 and 4. Level 3 contains the 20th Century galleries and displays of silver, ironwork, paintings and works of 20th-century design. The textile galleries are in the far north-eastern corner of this floor. The glass display is also on level 4. The Henry Cole Wing houses the Education Centre, RIBA Architecture Study Rooms and the Prints and Drawings Study Rooms.

VISITORS' CHECKLIST

Cromwell Rd SW7. **Map** 19 A1.
Tel 020-7942 2000.
South Kensington. 14,
74, 414, C1. **Open** 10am–
5.45pm daily (10am–10pm Wed
and last Fri of every month).
Closed 24–26 Dec. **Lectures,
presentations, tours,
exhibitions, events.**
www.vam.ac.uk

★ Architecture gallery
*This features highlights
from the world-class
collection of drawings,
models, photographs and
architectural fragments
of the V&A.*

China gallery
*This magnificent
ancestor portrait
is among the
many exquisite
pieces on show
in this gallery.*

★ South Asia gallery
*Considered the greatest collection
outside India, it includes Tippoo's
Tiger (1795), a pump organ in
the form of a man being mauled
by a tiger.*

Aston Webb's façade
(1909) is decorated
with 32 sculptures
of English craftsmen
and designers.

Main entrance

STAR EXHIBITS

★ British Galleries

★ Fashion gallery

★ Architecture gallery

★ South Asia
gallery

Exploring the V&A's Collections

The sheer size of the V&A means you should plan your visit carefully to avoid missing a highlight or an area of particular interest. One of the joys of the V&A, however, is stumbling across unexpected treasures. Be sure to visit the museum's original refreshment rooms off rooms 13 and 15 (one of which was designed by the then unknown William Morris), now being used once again for their original purpose as a café. The Photography Gallery (room 38a) displays the national collection of 300,000 photographs from 1856 to the present.

present, the impressive collection includes a giant Buddha's head from 700–900 AD, a huge yet elegant Ming canopied bed, and rare jade and ceramics.

Japanese art is concentrated in the Japan Gallery in room 45, and is particularly notable for lacquer, Samurai armour and woodblock prints.

Gilt copper ice chest (Qing Dynasty 1700s), room 44

BRITISH GALLERIES

A sequence of grand rooms starting on level 2 and continuing on level 4 are devoted to the luxurious British Galleries. By presenting design and decorative arts from 1500 to 1900, the galleries chart Britain's rise from obscure island to "workshop of the world". The galleries present the evolution of British high design and the numerous influences, whether technological or aesthetic, absorbed from all over the world.

Beautiful textiles, furniture, costumes and household objects illustrate the tastes and lifestyles of Britain's ruling classes. Among the highlights are James II's wedding suit, the opulent State Bed from Melville House, and a number of carefully preserved period rooms, including the stunning Rococo Norfolk House Music Room. Discovery Areas give visitors a

chance to delve even deeper into the past by sporting a Tudor ruff or viewing 3-D images through a Victorian stereoscope.

CHINA, JAPAN AND SOUTH ASIA

The evocative South Asia Gallery in room 41 forms the centrepiece of the museum's extensive collection of Indian art from 1550 to 1900. The Mughal tent of hanging painted cotton (1640) decorated with birds, trees and a double-headed eagle is a highlight of the collection.

Art from Syria, Iraq, Iran, Turkey and Egypt is found in room 42. Beautifully crafted textiles and ceramics illustrate Islamic influence on fine and decorative arts.

A dramatic arc of burnished steel fins, representing the spine of a Chinese dragon, spans the China Gallery (room 44). Covering the millennia from 3000 BC to the

ARCHITECTURE GALLERY

The Architecture Gallery features highlights from the world-class collections of drawings, models, photographs and architectural fragments of the V&A and the Royal Institute of British Architects (RIBA).

The gallery explores the architecture that shapes our world through five themes. "The Art of Architecture" explores the history and ideas behind architectural styles. A superb collection of artifacts and illustrations is on display, grouped by period and spanning world cultures, including Asian, Spanish Islamic, Classical, Gothic and Modernist.

"The Function of Buildings" looks at the way in which the design of a building is

Embroidered jacket (1610) in room 56

THE GREAT BED OF WARE

Made in about 1590 of oak with inlaid and painted decoration, the Great Bed of Ware measures some 3.6 by 3.6 m (12 by 12 ft) and is 2.6 m (8 ft 9 inches) high. It is the V&A's most celebrated piece of furniture. Elaborately carved and decorated, the bed is a superb example of the art of the English woodworker. Its name derives from the town of Ware in Hertfordshire, about a day's ride north of London, where it resided in a number of inns. The Great Bed's enormous size made it an early tourist attraction, and no doubt interest was boosted by Shakespeare's reference to it in *Twelfth Night*, which he wrote in 1601.

Recently redecorated and refurbished, the bed is located in room 57.

One of four Hunting Tapestries in room 94 woven in Flanders between 1425 and 1450

informed by its function and the demands of climate.

"Architects and Architecture" examines the team effort involved in designing a building, and how this has evolved over the centuries. A huge range of sketches, models and drawings used by architects supports the theme.

"Structures" examines the different structures needed to create different buildings, from chunky low-rise to tall buildings.

"Buildings in Context" takes the construction of London's Trafalgar Square, from original maps in 1730 to the present day, to explore the relationship between a building and its surroundings.

TWENTIETH CENTURY

Since its foundation in 1852, the V&A has collected examples of contemporary art and design. Two galleries show works exclusively from the 20th century. Art and design are in rooms 70 to 74, and a 20th-century study gallery in rooms 103 to 106 shows the development of furniture design, as well as ceramics, glass, metalwork and radios. Displays include objects by C R Mackintosh, Charles and Ray Eames and Marcel Breuer.

TEXTILES AND FASHION

Covering 400 years of high fashion, the Fashion Gallery in room 40 includes 18th-century courtly dress and 20th-century couturiers, such as Dior and Alexander McQueen.

Four huge medieval tapestries, among the museum's greatest treasures, dominate room 94 on level 3. Striking in their detail and depiction of courtly pastimes, they are known as the Devonshire Hunts, despite being made in Flanders.

The extensive textile collection continues in rooms 95 to 101. The museum's collection of Asian and Middle Eastern carpets is justifiably renowned.

Necklace of silver, steel, gold and mother of pearl (1983)

METALWORK

This group of galleries is located on level 3. In the Silver Galleries, 3500 pieces from 1400 to the present day are displayed in the beautifully refurbished Victorian rooms 65 to 69. Arms and armour, European metalwork from the 1500s to the present, and Islamic brass and bronze are located in rooms 81, 82 and 87 to 89. The Church Plate galleries in rooms 83 and 84 display reliquaries, chalices and other devotional treasures. A

dizzying collection of all manner of metal adornment is shown in the Jewellery Galleries in rooms 91 to 93. The highlight of the ironwork galleries, rooms 113 to 114e, is the dazzling Hereford Screen designed by Sir George Gilbert Scott in 1862. The screen was given to the V&A in the 1980s in fragmented, rusty condition and became the V&A's largest conservation project to date.

GLASS AND CERAMICS

Examples of 2,000 years of glass are exhibited across galleries on level 4. These contain a stunning balustrade by glass artist Danny Lane in room 131. Displays of international contemporary glass are exhibited in this room as well as in room 129.

The V&A's world-renowned collection of ceramics is currently undergoing a dramatic redisplay and will eventually be on show in newly refurbished galleries within the museum.

Stained glass roundel entitled Susanna and the Elders (c. 1520)

Natural History Museum ❶

See pp208–9.

Relief: Natural History Museum

Science Museum ❷

See pp212–13.

Victoria and Albert Museum ❸

See pp202–205.

Brompton Oratory ❹

Brompton Rd SW7. **Map** 19 A1. *Tel*
020-7808 0900. ⊖ *South Kensing-ton.* **Open** *6.30am–8pm daily.* 🕆
11am Sun sung Latin Mass. 🕭 📷
www.bromptonoratory.com

The Italianate Oratory is a
rich (some think a little too
rich) monument to the
English Catholic revival of the

late 19th century. The Oratory
was established by John Henry
Newman (who later became
Cardinal Newman). Father
Frederick William Faber (1814–
63) had already founded a
London community of priests
at Charing Cross. The group
had moved to Brompton, then
an outlying London district,
and this was to be its oratory.
Newman and Faber (both
Anglican converts to
Catholicism) were following
the example of St Philip Neri,
who set up a community of
secular priests living without
vows and based in cities.

The present church was
opened in 1884. Its facade
and dome were added in the
1890s, and the interior has
been progressively enriched
ever since. Herbert Gribble,
the architect, who was yet
another Catholic convert,
was only 29 when he
triumphed in the
highly prestigious
competition to design
it. Inside, all the most
eye-catching treasures
predate the church –
many of them were
transported here
from Italian churches.
Giuseppe Mazzuoli
carved the huge
marble figures of the 12
apostles for Siena
Cathedral in the
late 17th century.
The beautiful Lady
Altar was originally created in
1693 for the Dominican
church in Brescia, and the
18th-century altar in St

Wilfrid's Chapel was actually
imported from a church in
Rochefort, Belgium.

The Oratory has always
been famous for its splendid
musical tradition.

Royal College of Music ❺

Prince Consort Rd SW7. **Map** 10 F5.
Tel 020-7589 3643. ⊖ *Knights-bridge, South Kensington.* **Museum
of Instruments** *Tel* 020-7591
4842. **Open** *2–4.30pm Wed & Thu
in term-time or by appointment.*
Adm charge. 🕭 *limited.* 📷
📷 www.rcm.ac.uk

Sir Arthur Blomfield
designed the turreted Gothic
palace, with Bavarian
overtones, that has housed
this distinguished institution
since 1894. The college was
founded in 1882 by
George Grove, who
also compiled the
famous *Dictionary of
Music;* pupils have
included English
composers Benjamin
Britten and Ralph
Vaughan Williams.
The Museum of
Musical Instruments
has limited opening
hours; if you do
manage to get
inside, you will see
instruments from
the earliest times
and from many parts of the
world. Some of the exhibits
were played by such greats
as Handel and Haydn.

**17th-century viol at the
Royal College of Music**

The sumptuous interior of Brompton Oratory

Joseph Durham's statue of Prince Albert (1858) by the Royal Albert Hall

Royal Albert Hall ❻

Kensington Gore SW7. **Map** 10 F5. *Tel* 020-7589 8212. 🚇 *High St Kensington, South Kensington.* **Open** *for performances.* 🌐 📷 *10am–3.30pm Fri–Tue.* ♿ 🍴 💺 *See Entertainment pp348–9.* **www.**royalalberthall.com

Designed by an engineer, Francis Fowke, and completed in 1871, this huge concert hall was modelled on Roman amphitheatres and is easier on the eye than most Victorian structures. On the red-brick exterior the only ostentation is a pretty frieze symbolizing the triumph of arts and science. In plans the building was called the Hall of Arts and Science but Queen Victoria changed it to the Royal Albert Hall, in memory of her husband, when she laid the foundation stone in 1868.

The hall is often used for Classical concerts, most famously the "Proms", but it also accommodates other large gatherings, such as tennis matches, comedy shows, rock concerts, circus shows and major business conferences.

Royal College of Art ❼

Kensington Gore SW7. **Map** 10 F5. *Tel* 020-7590 4444. 🚇 *High St Kensington, South Kensington.* **Open** *10am–6pm Mon–Fri (phone first).* ♿ 💺 📷 *Lectures, events, film presentations, exhibitions.* **www.**rca.ac.uk

Sir Hugh Casson's mainly glass-fronted building (1962) is in stark contrast to the Victoriana around it. The college was founded in 1837 as a school of design and practical art for the manufacturing industries. It became noted for modern art in the 1950s and 1960s when David Hockney, Peter Blake and Eduardo Paolozzi were there.

Albert Memorial ❽

South Carriage Drive, Kensington Gdns SW7. **Map** 10 F5. 🚇 *High St Kensington, South Kensington.*

This grandiose but dignified memorial to Queen Victoria's beloved consort was completed in 1876, 15 years after his death. Albert was a German prince and a cousin of Queen Victoria's. When he died from typhoid in 1861 he was only 41 and they had been happily married for 21 years, producing nine children. It is fitting that the monument is near the site of the 1851 Exhibition (*see pp28–9*), for Prince Albert was closely identified with the Exhibition itself and with the scientific advances it celebrated. The larger than life statue, by John Foley, shows him with an exhibition catalogue on his knee.

The desolate Queen chose Sir George Gilbert Scott to design the monument which stands 55 m (175 ft) high. It is loosely based on a medieval market cross – although many times more elaborate, with a black and gilded spire, multi-coloured marble canopy, stones, mosaics, enamels, wrought iron and nearly 200 sculpted figures. In October 1998 the re-gilded statue was unveiled by Elizabeth II, it had not been gilded since 1915 when it was painted black to avoid attracting attention during World War I.

Victoria and Albert at the Great Exhibition opening (1851)

Natural History Museum ●

Life on Earth and the Earth itself are vividly
explained at the Natural History Museum.
Combining the latest interactive techniques with
traditional displays, the exhibits tackle fundamental
issues, such as the origin of species and how
human beings evolved. The vast, cathedral-like
museum building is a masterpiece in itself. It
opened in 1881 and was designed by Alfred
Waterhouse using revolutionary Victorian
building techniques. It is built on an iron and
steel framework concealed behind arches and
columns, richly decorated with sculptures
of plants and animals.

Spirit Collection
*Over 22 million specimens
are preserved in
450,000 jars.*

Ground floor

★ Dinosaurs
*T Rex, one of the
museum's impressively
life-like animatronic
models, lurches and roars
in this hugely popular
gallery. More traditional
exhibits of fossilized
skeletons and eggs are
also on display.*

GALLERY GUIDE

*The museum is divided into
three sections, the Blue Zone,
the Green Zone and the Red
Zone.*

*A 26-m (85-ft) skeleton of
the dinosaur Diplodocus
dominates the central
hall in the Blue Zone –
Human Biology, together
with Mammals and
Dinosaurs, are to the left
of the hall, while Creepy
Crawlies and Ecology are to
the right. On the first floor are
found Origin of Species and
Minerals and Meteorites.*

*The giant escalator in
Visions of Earth leads through
a stunning globe to Green
Zone highlights The Power
Within and Earth's Treasury.*

Cromwell Road
entrance – Life
Galleries

Access to
basement

Creepy Crawlies
*Eight out of ten animal
species are arthropods –
insects, crustaceans,
centipedes and spiders, like
this tarantula.*

KEY TO FLOORPLAN

- Blue Zone
- Green Zone
- Red Zone

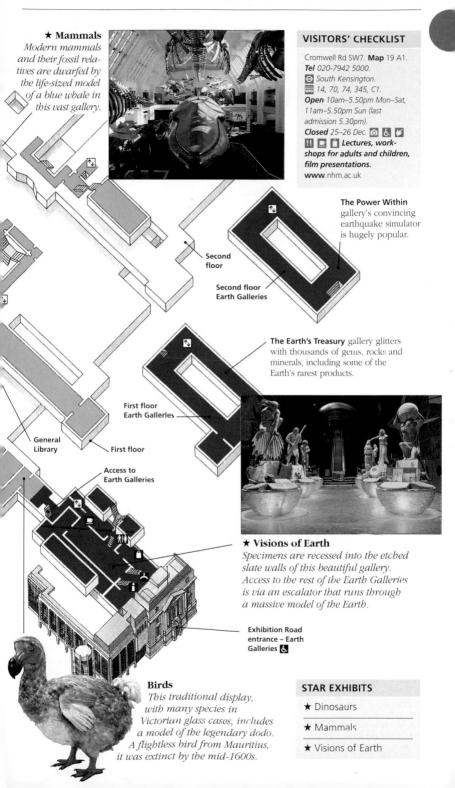

★ Mammals
Modern mammals and their fossil relatives are dwarfed by the life-sized model of a blue whale in this vast gallery.

VISITORS' CHECKLIST

Cromwell Rd SW7. **Map** 19 A1.
Tel 020-7942 5000.
South Kensington.
14, 70, 74, 345, C1.
Open 10am–5.50pm Mon–Sat,
11am–5.50pm Sun (last admission 5.30pm).
Closed 25–26 Dec.
Lectures, workshops for adults and children, film presentations.
www.nhm.ac.uk

The Power Within gallery's convincing earthquake simulator is hugely popular.

Second floor

Second floor Earth Galleries

The Earth's Treasury gallery glitters with thousands of gems, rocks and minerals, including some of the Earth's rarest products.

First floor Earth Galleries

First floor

General Library

Access to Earth Galleries

★ Visions of Earth
Specimens are recessed into the etched slate walls of this beautiful gallery. Access to the rest of the Earth Galleries is via an escalator that runs through a massive model of the Earth.

Exhibition Road entrance – Earth Galleries

Birds
This traditional display, with many species in Victorian glass cases, includes a model of the legendary dodo. A flightless bird from Mauritius, it was extinct by the mid-1600s.

STAR EXHIBITS

★ Dinosaurs

★ Mammals

★ Visions of Earth

Statue of young Queen Victoria by her daughter Princess Louise outside Kensington Palace

Serpentine Gallery ❾

Kensington Gdns W2. **Map** 11 A4. **Tel** 020-7402 6075. ⊖ *Lancaster Gate, South Kensington.* **Open** *10am–6pm daily.* **Closed** *25 & 26 Dec & between exhibitions.* **Lectures.** ♿ 🖥 *summer only.* 🛈 *art bookshop.* **www**.serpentinegallery.org

In the southeast corner of Kensington Gardens is the Serpentine Gallery, which houses temporary exhibitions of major contemporary artists' work. Past exhibitions have shown Gilbert & George, Rachel Whiteread and Felix Gonzalez-Torres. This exciting gallery transforms its space to suit the exhibits, sometimes spilling out into the park. An architectural commission is erected every summer, where the café is located.

Kensington Palace ❿

Kensington Palace Gdns W8. **Map** 10 D4. **Tel** 0870-451 5170. ⊖ *High St Kensington, Queensway, Notting Hill Gate.* **Open** *Mar–Oct: 10am–6pm daily; Nov–Feb: 10am–5pm daily (last adm: 1 hr earlier).* **Closed** *24–26 Dec.* **Adm charge.** 🛈 🖥 🛈 ♿ *ground floor only.* **Exhibitions.** **www**.historicroyalpalaces.org

Half of this spacious palace is used as lavish royal apartments; the other half, which includes the 18th-century state rooms, is open to the public. When William III

and his wife Mary came to the throne in 1689 they bought a mansion, dating from 1605, and commissioned Christopher Wren to convert it into a royal palace. He created separate suites of rooms for the king and queen, and today visiting members of public use the queen's entrance.

Highlights include the finely decorated state rooms. There are no labels in these rooms, but the free audio guide evokes the atmosphere of 17th- and 18th-century court life that was once conducted here. On the ground floor, an exhibition of court dress from 1760 to the present, includes items worn by Queen Elizabeth II. There is also a permanent display of Princess Diana's dresses.

The palace has seen some important royal events. In 1714 Queen Anne died here from a fit of apoplexy brought on by over-eating and, on 20 June 1837, Princess Victoria of Kent was woken at 5am to be told that her uncle William IV had died and she was now queen – the start of her 64-year reign. After the death in 1997 of Diana, Princess of Wales, the William gates became a focal point for mourners in their thousands, who turned the surrounding area into a field of bouquets.

Kensington Gardens ⓫

W8. **Map** 10 E4. **Tel** 020-7298 2000. ⊖ *Bayswater, High St Kensington, Queensway, Lancaster Gate.* **Open** *dawn–dusk daily.* 🖥 **www**.royalparks.gov.uk

The former grounds of Kensington Palace became a public park in 1841. A small part of it has been dedicated as a memorial playground to Diana, Princess of Wales *(see p219).* The gardens are full of charm, starting with Sir George Frampton's statue (1912) of J M Barrie's fictional Peter Pan, the boy who never grew up, playing his pipes to the bronze fairies and animals that cling to the column below. Often surrounded by parents, nannies and their charges, the statue stands near the west bank of the Serpentine, not far from where Harriet, wife of the poet Percy Bysshe Shelley, drowned herself in 1816. Just north of here (in Hyde Park) are the ornamental fountains and statues, including Jacob Epstein's *Rima*, at the lake's head. George Frederick Watts's statue of a muscular horse and rider, *Physical Energy*, stands to the south. Not far away is a summer house designed by William Kent in 1735, and the Serpentine Gallery.

Detail of the Coalbrookdale gate, Kensington Gardens

The Round Pond, created in 1728 just east of the palace, is often packed with model boats navigated by children and older enthusiasts. In winter it is occasionally fit for skating. In the north, near Lancaster Gate, is a dogs' cemetery, started in 1880 by the Duke of Cambridge while mourning one of his pets.

Hyde Park **⓬**

W2. **Map** 11 B3. **Tel** 020-7298 2000. ⊖ Hyde Park Corner, Knightsbridge, Lancaster Gate, Marble Arch. **Open** 5am–midnight daily. 🔲 **Sporting facilities**. www.royalparks.org.uk

Riding on Rotten Row, Hyde Park

The ancient manor of Hyde was part of the lands of Westminster Abbey seized by Henry VIII at the Dissolution of the Monasteries in 1536. It has remained a royal park ever since. Henry used it for hunting but James I opened it to the public in the early 17th century, and it became one of the city's most prized public spaces. The Serpentine, an artificial lake used for boating and bathing, was created when Caroline, George II's queen, dammed the flow of the Westbourne River in 1730.

In its time the park has been a venue for duelling, horse racing, highwaymen, demonstrations, music and parades. The 1851 Exhibition was held here in a vast glass palace (see pp28–9). The aristocracy drove their carriages on the outer roads. The Princess Diana Memorial fountain is to the south of the Serpentine.

Speakers' Corner **⓭**

Hyde Park W2. **Map** 11 C2. ⊖ Marble Arch.

An 1872 law made it legal to assemble an audience and address them on whatever topic you chose; since then this corner of Hyde Park has become the established venue for budding orators and a fair number of eccentrics. It is well worth spending time here on a Sunday: speakers from fringe groups and one-member political parties reveal their plans for the betterment of mankind while the assembled onlookers heckle them without mercy.

Marble Arch **⓮**

Park Lane W1. **Map** 11 C2. ⊖ Marble Arch.

John Nash designed the arch in 1827 as the main entrance to Buckingham Palace. It was, however, too narrow for the grandest coaches and was moved here in 1851. Now, only senior members of the Royal Family and one of the royal artillery regiments are allowed to pass under it.

The arch stands near the site of the old Tyburn gallows (marked by a plaque), where until 1783 the city's most notorious criminals were hanged in front of crowds of bloodthirsty spectators.

An orator at Speakers' Corner

Harrods **⓯**

Knightsbridge SW1. **Map** 11 C5. **Tel** 020-7730 1234. ⊖ Knightsbridge. **Open** 10am–7pm Mon–Sat, noon–6pm Sun. 🚫 🍴 🔲 🔵 See **Shops and Markets** p321. www.harrods.com

London's most famous department store began in 1849 when Henry Charles Harrod opened a small grocery shop nearby on Brompton Road. By concentrating on good quality and impeccable service (rather than on low prices) the store was soon popular enough to expand over the surrounding area.

It used to be claimed that Harrods could supply anything from a packet of pins to an elephant – not quite true today, but the range of stock is still phenomenal.

Harrods at night, lit by 11,500 lights

Science Museum ❷

Centuries of continuing scientific and technological development lie at the heart of the Science Museum's massive collections. The hardware displayed is magnificent: from steam engines to aero-engines; spacecraft to the very first mechanical computers. Equally important is the social context of science – what discoveries and inventions mean for day-to-day life – and the process of discovery itself. The high-tech Wellcome Wing has many interactive displays, an IMAX Cinema and a SimEx simulator.

★ Science and Art of Medicine
A 17th-century Italian vase for storing snake bite treatment is part of this interesting collection.

Science in the 18th Century
The original orrery, a mechanical model of the solar system, is one of many beautiful scientific instruments in this gallery.

Computing
Babbage's Difference Engine No. 1 (1832), the first automatic calculator and a magnificent example of precision engineering, is a highlight of this gallery.

Energy: Fuelling the Future is a new gallery that explores how energy powers every aspect of our lives.

Challenge of Materials
Our expectations of materials are confounded with exhibits such as a bridge made of glass and this steel wedding dress.

Stairs to lower level

KEY TO FLOORPLAN

- ☐ Basement
- ☐ Ground floor
- ☐ First floor
- ☐ Second floor
- ☐ Third floor
- ☐ Fourth floor
- ☐ Fifth floor
- ☐ Wellcome Wing

★ The Energy Hall
Dedicated to steam power, this gallery includes the still-operational Harle Syke Mill Engine (1903).

Main entrance

★ **Flight**
This gallery is packed with early flying contraptions, fighter planes and aeroengines, many of them suspended as if in mid-flight.

VISITORS' CHECKLIST

Exhibition Rd SW7. **Map** 19 A1.
Tel 0870-870 4868. ⊖ *South Kensington.* 🚌 *9, 10, 49, 52, 74, 345, C1. **Open** 10am–6pm daily. **Closed** 24–26 Dec. **Adm charge** for some exhibitions, IMAX cinema and simulators.* ♿ **Lectures, films, workshops.** 🖥️ 📷
www.sciencemuseum.org.uk

Marine Engineering
The display of navigational equipment includes this ornately decorated circumferentor (1676) by the architect Joannes Macarius.

★ **Wellcome Wing**
The highlight of the Wellcome Wing is the 'Who Am I?' exhibition, where interactive games allow visitors to explore the science of what it is to be human.

Escalator to
Imax Cinema

★ **Making the Modern World**
Apollo 10 took US astronauts around the moon in May 1969, and now forms part of this stunning gallery of museum highlights.

The hands-on galleries,
including The Launch Pad and
Garden, prove very popular
with children.

GALLERY GUIDE

The Science Museum is spread over seven floors, balconies and mezzanine levels. The Wellcome Wing, offering four floors of interactive technology, is at the west end of the museum and is accessible from the ground floor and third floor of the main building. Power dominates the ground floor; here too are Space and Making the Modern World. The first floor has the Challenge of Materials gallery as well as Weather and Agriculture. On the second floor is a range of such diverse galleries as shipping, mathematics and computing. The third floor includes Flight and Health Matters. The fourth and fifth floors (accessible by only one of the lifts) house the medical history galleries.

STAR EXHIBITS

★ Flight

★ Science and Art of Medicine

★ Making the Modern World

★ The Energy Hall

★ Wellcome Wing

KENSINGTON AND HOLLAND PARK

The western and northern perimeters of Kensington Gardens are a rich residential area and include many foreign embassies. The shops on Kensington High Street are almost as smart as those in Knightsbridge, and Kensington Church Street is a good source of quality antiques. Around Holland Park are some magnificent late Victorian houses, two of them open to the public. But as you cross into Bayswater and Notting Hill you enter a more vibrant, cosmopolitan part of London. Its stucco terraces are lined with medium-priced hotels and inexpensive restaurants. Westbourne Grove has become increasingly popular with the young, designer-clad

Tiled crest from Holland House

crowd. Whiteleys, in Queensway, is one of the many historic buildings in the area. Built in 1912 by Belcher and Joass as a fashionable department store, it was converted in the 1980s into a vibrant shopping centre. To the west, Portobello Road is a popular street market selling anything from food to antiques. Notting Hill is known for its flamboyant Caribbean carnival, which took to the streets in 1965 and has been staged every year since, on the last weekend in August (*see p57*).

SIGHTS AT A GLANCE

Historic Streets and Buildings
Holland House ②
Leighton House ③
Linley Sambourne House ④
Kensington Square ⑥
Kensington Palace
  Gardens ⑦
Queensway ⑨

Parks and Gardens
Holland Park ①
Kensington Roof
  Gardens ⑤
The Diana, Princess
  of Wales Memorial
  Playground ⑧

Markets
Portobello Road ⑩

Historic Areas
Notting Hill ⑪

GETTING THERE
The District, Circle and Central lines serve the area. Bus numbers C1, 9, 10, 27, 28, 31, 49, 52, 70, 73 stop on Kensington High Street; 12, 27, 28, 31, 52, 70, 94 go to Notting Hill Gate; and 7, 12, 15, 23, 27, 36, 70, 94 cross Bayswater.

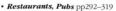

KEY

| | Street-by-Street map |
| | Underground station |

0 metres 500
0 yards 500

SEE ALSO
• **Street Finder**, maps 9, 17
• **Where to Stay** pp278–91
• **Restaurants, Pubs** pp292–319

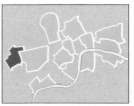

◁ **Entrance to a house in Edwardes Square, Kensington**

Street-by-Street: Kensington and Holland Park

Although now part of central London, as recently as the 1830s this was a country village of market gardens and mansions. Outstanding among these was Holland House; part of its grounds are now Holland Park. The area grew up rapidly in the mid-19th century and most of its buildings date from then – mainly expensive apartments, mansion flats and fashionable shops.

Holland House
The rambling Jacobean mansion, started in 1605 and pictured here in 1795, was largely demolished in the 1950s ❷

★ Holland Park
Parts of the old formal gardens of Holland House have been retained to grace this delightful public park ❶

The Orangery, now a gallery showing temporary exhibitions, has parts that date from the 1630s when it was in the grounds of Holland House.

Melbury Road is lined with large, Victorian houses. Many were built for fashionable artists of the time.

The Victorian letter box on the High Street is one of the oldest in London.

★ Leighton House
It is preserved as it was when the Victorian painter, Lord Leighton, lived here. He had a passion for Middle Eastern tiles ❸

PHILL

ILCHESTER PLACE

MELBURY ROAD

EDWARDES SQUA

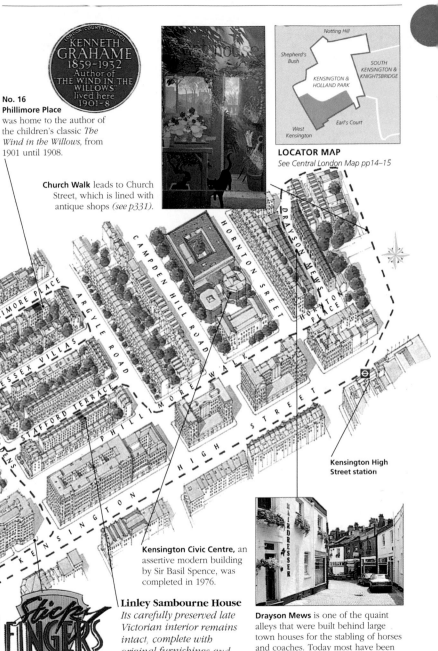

No. 16 Phillimore Place was home to the author of the children's classic *The Wind in the Willows,* from 1901 until 1908.

KENNETH GRAHAME 1859–1932 Author of 'THE WIND IN THE WILLOWS' lived here 1901–8

LOCATOR MAP
See Central London Map pp14–15

Notting Hill

Shepherd's Bush

SOUTH KENSINGTON & KNIGHTSBRIDGE

KENSINGTON & HOLLAND PARK

West Kensington

Earl's Court

Church Walk leads to Church Street, which is lined with antique shops *(see p331).*

Kensington High Street station

Kensington Civic Centre, an assertive modern building by Sir Basil Spence, was completed in 1976.

Linley Sambourne House
Its carefully preserved late Victorian interior remains intact, complete with original furnishings and draperies ❹

Drayson Mews is one of the quaint alleys that were built behind large town houses for the stabling of horses and coaches. Today most have been converted into small houses.

Sticky Fingers, a lively café on the corner of Phillimore Gardens, is owned by Bill Wyman, former guitarist with the *Rolling Stones* rock group.

STAR SIGHTS

★ Holland Park

★ Leighton House

KEY

– – – Suggested route

0 metres   100

0 yards   100

Holland Park ❶

Abbotsbury Rd W14. **Map** 9 B4.
Tel 020-7602 2226. ⊖ Holland
Park, High St Kensington, Notting Hill
Gate. **Open** dawn–dusk daily (hours
are flexible depending on light).
Closed 25 Dec. 🍴 ☐ **Open-air
opera, theatre, dance**. Tel 020-
7602 7856. **Art exhibitions** Apr–Oct.
See **Entertainment** pp344–5.

This small but delightful park,
more wooded and intimate
than the large royal parks to its
east (Hyde Park and
Kensington Gardens,
see pp206–7), was opened in
1952 on what remained of the
grounds of Holland House –
the rest had been sold off in
the late 19th century for the
construction of large houses
and terraces to the north and
west. The park still contains
some of the formal gardens,
laid out in the early 19th
century for Holland House.
There is also a Japanese
garden, created for the 1991
London Festival of Japan. The
park has an abundance of
wildlife, including peacocks.

Holland House ❷

Holland Park W8. **Map** 9 B5.
Youth Hostel Tel 020-7937 0748.
⊖ Holland Park, High Street
Kensington. ♿

Original tiling in Holland House

During its heyday in the 19th
century, this was a noted
centre of social and political
intrigue. Statesmen such as
Lord Palmerston mixed here
with the likes of the poet
Byron. The remains of the
house are now used
as a youth hostel.
   The outhouses are put to
various uses: exhibitions
are held in the orangery and
the ice house (a forerunner of
the fridge), and the old Garden
Ballroom is now a restaurant.

The café in Holland Park

Leighton House ❸

12 Holland Park Rd W14. **Map** 17 B1.
Tel 020-7602 3316. ⊖ High St Kensington. **Open** 11am–5.30pm Wed–
Mon. **Closed** 1 Jan, 25 & 26 Dec.
Adm charge 📷 2.30pm Wed–Thu
or by appt for groups. 🎵 **Concerts,
exhibitions**. www.rbkc.gov.uk/
leightonhousemuseum

Built for respected Victorian
painter Lord Leighton in
1864–79, the house has been
preserved with its opulent
decoration as an extraordinary monument to Victorian
aesthetics. The highlight is the
Arab hall, added in 1879 to
house Leighton's collection of
Islamic tiles, some of which
are inscribed with pieces from
the Koran. The best paintings
include some by Edward
Burne-Jones, John Millais,
G F Watts and many works
by Leighton himself.

Linley Sambourne House ❹

18 Stafford Terrace W8. **Map** 9 C5.
Tel 020-7602 3316. ⊖ High St
Kensington. **Open** for guided tours
only – phone to book tour; Sat & Sun:
tours at 10am, 11.15am, 1pm,
2.15pm & 3.30pm; weekdays by appt.
Closed mid-Dec–Feb. **Adm charge**.
📷 mandatory. 🎵 www.rbkc.
gov.uk/linleysambournehouse

The house, built in about
1870, has received a facelift,
but remains much as Linley
Sambourne decorated and
furnished it, in the Victorian
manner, with china ornaments
and heavy velvet drapes.

Sambourne was a cartoonist
for the satirical magazine Punch
and drawings cram the walls.
Some rooms have William
Morris wallpaper (see p249).

Kensington Roof Gardens ❺

99 High Street W8 (entrance in Derry
Street). **Map** 10 D5. **Tel** 020-7937
7994. **Open** 9am–5pm daily (but call
ahead, as sometimes closed for
private functions). 🍴

A hundred feet above the
bustle of Kensington High
Street is one of London's best-
kept secrets – a 6,000 square-
metre roof garden. First
planted in the 1930s by the
owners of Derry and Toms
department store below (now
houses many different stores),
the themed gardens are a
lavish flight of fancy and

**Logo for Punch magazine
(1841–1992)**

feature a woodland garden, a Spanish garden (with palm trees) and a formal English garden (with a pond, live ducks and a pair of pink flamingos). Best of all, it's free to wander round, though there is no access when the gardens have been booked for events.

Kensington Square **6**

W8. **Map** 10 D5. 🚇 *High St Kensington.*

This is one of London's oldest squares. It was laid out in the 1680s, and a few early 18th-century houses still remain. (Nos. 11 and 12 are the oldest.) The renowned philosopher John Stuart Mill lived at No. 18, and the Pre-Raphaelite painter and illustrator Edward Burne-Jones at No.41.

Resident's plaque in Kensington Square

> LCC
> JOHN STUART MILL
> 1806-1873
> Philosopher
> Lived Here

Kensington Palace Gardens **7**

W8. **Map** 10 D3. 🚇 *High St Kensington, Notting Hill Gate, Queensway.*

This private road of luxury mansions occupies the site of the former kitchen gardens of Kensington Palace *(see p210).* It changes its name half-way down; the southern part is known as Palace Green. It is open to pedestrians but closed to cars, unless they have specific business here. Most of the houses are occupied by embassies and their staff. At cocktail hour, you can watch black limousines with diplomatic number plates sweep beneath the raised barriers at each end of the road.

Queensway shop front

The Diana, Princess of Wales Memorial Playground **8**

Kensington Gardens. **Map** 10 E3. **Tel** 020 7298 2141. 🚇 *Bayswater, Queensway. Open* 10am–4.45pm (3.45 in winter) daily. 🚻 🅿

The newest of Kensington Gardens' three playgrounds was opened in 2000 and is dedicated to the memory of the late Princess Diana. Located close to the Bayswater Road (Peter Pan's creator, J M Barrie, funded the first playground to be built here), this innovative new adventure playground takes the boy who didn't want to grow up as its theme and is packed with novel ideas and activities including a beach cove with a 50-ft pirates' galleon, a tree house with walkways and ramps and a half-submerged slumbering crocodile (careful not to rouse him!). Though all children up to the age of twelve must be accompanied by an adult, staff are on hand to make sure the children are safe. Many features of the playground, such as the musical garden, have been specially designed to be accessible to children with special needs.

Queensway **9**

W2. **Map** 10 D2. 🚇 *Queensway, Bayswater.*

One of London's most cosmopolitan streets, Queensway has the heaviest concentration of eating places outside Soho. Newsagents are abundantly stocked with foreign newspapers. At the northern end is Whiteley's shopping centre. Founded by William Whiteley, who was born in Yorkshire in 1863, it was probably the world's first department store. The present building dates from 1911.
   The street is named after Queen Victoria, who rode here as a princess.

Portobello Road **10**

W11. **Map** 9 C3. 🚇 *Notting Hill Gate, Ladbroke Grove. Antiques market open* 9.30am–4pm Fri, 8am–5pm Sat. See also *Shops and Markets p333.*

There has been a market here since 1837. These days the southern end consists almost exclusively of stalls that sell antiques, jewellery, souvenirs and many other collectables. The market is extremely popular with tourists and tends to be very crowded on summer weekends. However, it is well worth visiting just to experience its bustling and cheerful atmosphere even if you don't intend to buy anything. If you do decide to buy, be warned – you are unlikely to get a real bargain, since the stallholders have a sound idea of the value of what they are selling.

Antique shop on Portobello Road

Notting Hill **11**

W11. **Map** 9 C3. 🚇 *Notting Hill Gate.*

Now the home of Europe's biggest street carnival, most of this area was farmland until the 19th century.
   In the 1950s and 1960s Notting Hill became a centre for the Caribbean community, many of whom lived here when they first arrived in Britain. The carnival started in 1966 and takes over the area every August over the holiday weekend *(see p57)* when costumed parades flood through the streets.

REGENT'S PARK AND MARYLEBONE

The area south of Regent's Park, incorporating the medieval village of Marylebone, has London's highest concentration of quality Georgian housing. It was developed by Robert Harley, Earl of Oxford, as London shifted west in the 18th century. Terraces by John Nash adorn the southern edge of Regent's Park, the busiest of the Royal Parks, while to its northwest lies St John's Wood, a smart inner suburb.

GETTING THERE

Regent's Park and Baker Street are the nearest tube stations. Marylebone is served by tube and rail. Buses 13, 139 and 159 run from Trafalgar Square to near Baker Street, and numerous buses run along Oxford St, Baker St and Gloucester Pl.

0 metres   500
0 yards   500

SIGHTS AT A GLANCE

Historic Streets and Buildings

Harley Street **4**
Portland Place **5**
Broadcasting House **6**
Cumberland Terrace **15**

Museums and Galleries

Wallace Collection **10**
Sherlock Holmes Museum **11**

Churches and Mosques

St Marylebone Parish Church **3**
All Souls, Langham Place **7**
London Central Mosque **12**

Parks and Gardens

Regent's Park **2**

Entertainment

Madame Tussauds and the Planetarium **1**
Wigmore Hall **9**
London Zoo **14**

Historic Hotels

Langham Hotel **8**

Historic Waterways

Regent's Canal **13**

Map labels: PRINCE ALBERT ROAD · OUTER CIRCLE · REGENT'S PARK · QUEEN MARY'S GARDENS · INNER CIRCLE · CHESTER ROAD · PARK ROAD · PRINCE ALBERT ROAD · Baker Street · MARYLEBONE ROAD · Regent's Park · PARK CRESCENT · BAKER STREET · GLOUCESTER PLACE · PADDINGTON STREET · MARYLEBONE HIGH STREET · WIMPOLE STREET · HARLEY STREET · PORTLAND PLACE · LANGHAM · THAYER ST · CAVENDISH SQ · WIGMORE STREET · PORTMAN SQUARE

SEE ALSO

- **Street Finder**, maps 3, 4, 12
- **Where to Stay** pp278–91
- **Restaurants, Pubs** pp292–319
- **Regent's Canal Walk** pp264–5

KEY

▢ Street-by-Street map

Ⓔ Underground station

◁ St Andrew's Place, Regent's Park

Street-by-Street: Marylebone

South of Regent's Park lies the medieval village of Marylebone (originally Maryburne, the stream by St Mary's church). Until the 18th century it was surrounded by fields, but these were built over as fashionable London drifted west. In the mid-19th century, professional people, especially doctors, used the spacious houses to receive wealthy clients. The area has maintained its medical connection and its elegance. Marylebone High Street is full of interesting, high-quality food and clothes shops, bookshops and cafés.

Tiananmen Square memorial: Portland Place

★ Regent's Park
John Nash laid out the royal park in 1812 as a setting for classically designed villas and terraces ❷

The Royal Academy of Music, England's first music academy, was founded in 1774. The present brick building, with its own concert hall, is from 1911.

★ Madame Tussauds and the Planetarium
The wax museum of famous people, historical and contemporary, is one of London's most popular attractions. Next door, a planetarium shows models of the sky at night ❶

To Regent's Park

YORK BRIDGE

CIRCLE

YORK TERRACE EAST

YORK GATE

OUTER

YORK TERRACE WEST

MARYLEBONE

MARYLEBONE HIGH STREET

ALLSOP PLACE

NOTTINGHAM PLACE

LUXBOROUGH STREET

St Marylebone Parish Church
Poets Robert Browning and Elizabeth Barrett married in this church ❸

NOTTINGHAM STREET

BAKER STREET

KEY

– – – Suggested route

Baker Street station

0 metres   100

0 yards   100

Park Crescent's breathtaking façades by Nash have been preserved, although the interiors were rebuilt as offices in the 1960s. The crescent seals the north end of Nash's ceremonial route from St James's to Regent's Park, via Regent Street and Portland Place.

LOCATOR MAP
See Central London Map pp14–15

The London Clinic is one of the best-known private hospitals in this medical district.

Regent's Park station

Portland Place
In the centre of this broad street stands a statue of Field Marshal Sir George Stuart White, who won the Victoria Cross for gallantry in the Afghan War of 1879 ❺

The Royal Institute of British Architects is housed in a striking Art Deco building designed by Grey Wornum in 1934.

Harley Street
Consulting rooms of eminent medical specialists have been here for more than a century ❹

№ 90ᴬ
HARLEY
STREET

STAR SIGHTS

★ Madame Tussauds and the Planetarium

★ Regent's Park

Mme Tussauds and the Planetarium ❶

Marylebone Rd NW1. **Map** 4 D5.
📞 0870-400 3000. ⊖ Baker St.
Open 9am–6pm daily. **Closed**
25 Dec. **Adm charge.** 📷 💻 🎫
♿ phone first.
www.madame-tussauds.com

Madame Tussaud began her wax-modelling career rather morbidly, taking death masks of many of the best-known victims of the French Revolution. In 1835 she set up an exhibition of her work in Baker Street, not far from the collection's present site.

The collection still uses traditional wax-modelling techniques to recreate politicians, film and television actors, rock stars and sporting heroes.

The main sections of the exhibition are "Blush", where visitors get to feel what it is like to be at a celebrity "A-list" party; "Premier Night", devoted to the giants of the entertainment world; and the "World Stage", containing a

Traditional wax-modelling at Madame Tussauds

collection of royalty, statesmen and world leaders, writers and artists. Where else could Lenin, Martin Luther King, Shakespeare and Kylie Minogue all rub shoulders?

The Chamber of Horrors is the most renowned part of Madame Tussauds. It includes recreations of the most gruesome episodes in the grim catalogue of crime and punishment: the murderer Dr Crippen; Vlad the impaler; and the chill gloom of an east

London Victorian street during Jack the Ripper's time in the late 19th century.

The "Spirit of London" is the finale. Visitors travel in stylized London taxi-cabs and participate in momentous events of the city, from the Great Fire of 1666 to 1960s Swinging London.

Next door, and part of the same complex, is the London Planetarium (now called Tussauds Auditorium), where a spectacular star show explores and reveals some of the mysteries of the planets and the solar system. There is an interactive exhibition that contains many detailed models of the planets, satellites and spacecraft.

Waxwork of Elizabeth II

Tulip time at Queen Mary's Gardens in Regent's Park

Regent's Park ❷

NW1. **Map** 3 C2. **Tel** 020-7298 2000.
⊖ Regent's Park, Baker St, Great
Portland St. **Open** 5am–dusk daily.
♿ 💻 **Open air theatre** see **Entertainment** pp344–5. **Zoo** see p227.
Sports facilities.
www.royalparks.org.uk

This area of land became enclosed as a park in 1812. John Nash designed the scheme and originally envisaged a kind of garden suburb,

dotted with 56 villas in a variety of Classical styles, with a pleasure palace for the Prince Regent. In the event only eight villas – but no palace – were built inside the park (three survive round the edge of the Inner Circle).

The boating lake, which has many varieties of water birds, is marvellously romantic, especially when music drifts across from the bandstand in the distance. Queen Mary's Gardens are a mass of

wonderful sights and smells in summer, when visitors can enjoy Shakespeare productions at the **Open Air Theatre** nearby.

Nash's master plan for the park continues just beyond its northeastern edge in Park Village East and West. These elegant stucco buildings date from 1828.

The park is also renowned for its excellent sports facilities.

St Marylebone Parish Church ❸

Marylebone Rd NW1. **Map** 4 D5. **Tel**
020-7935 7315. ⊖ Regent's Park.
Open phone to check. ♿ 🕆 11am
Sun. 💻 **www**.stmarylebone.org

This is where the poets Robert Browning and Elizabeth Barrett were married in 1846 after eloping from her strict family home on nearby Wimpole Street. The large, stately church by Thomas Hardwick was consecrated in 1817 after the former church, where Lord Byron was christened in 1778, had become too small. Hardwick was determined that the same should not happen to his new church – so everything is on a grand scale.

Commemorative window in St Marylebone Parish Church

Harley Street ④

W1. **Map** 4 E5. ⊖ *Regent's Park, Oxford Circus, Bond St, Great Portland St.*

The large houses on this late 18th-century street were popular with successful doctors and specialists in the middle of the 19th century when it was a rich residential area. The doctors' practices stayed and lend the street an air of hushed order, unusual in central London. There are very few private houses or apartments here now, but William Gladstone lived at No. 73 from 1876 to 1882.

Portland Place ⑤

W1. **Map** 4 E5. ⊖ *Regent's Park, Oxford Circus.*

The Adam Brothers, Robert and James, laid this street out in 1773. Only a few of the original houses remain, the best being 27 to 47 on the west side, south of Devonshire Street. John Nash added the street to his processional route from Carlton House to Regent's Park and sealed its northern end with Park Crescent.

The building of the Royal Institute of British Architects (1934) at No. 66 is adorned with symbolic statues and reliefs. Its bronze front doors depict London's buildings and the River Thames.

Broadcasting House ⑥

Portland Place W1. **Map** 12 E1. ⊖ *Oxford Circus.* **Not open** *to the public.* **BBC Backstage Tours** BBC Television Centre, Wood Lane. **Tel** 0870-603 0304. ⊖ *White City.* **Adm charge.** ♿ 🎥 *mandatory, call to book. No children under 10.*

Broadcasting House was built in 1931 as a suitably modern Art Deco headquarters for the brand-new medium of broadcasting. Its front, curving with the street, is dominated by Eric Gill's stylized relief of Prospero and Ariel. As the invisible spirit of the air, Shakespeare's Ariel was considered an appropriate personification of broadcasting. The character appears in two other sculptures on the western frontage, and again over the eastern entrance in "Ariel Piping to Children". Leslie French, who was playing Ariel in the Old Vic's presentation of *The Tempest* at the time, acted as Gill's model for the reliefs.

Broadcasting House is now occupied by management, as some radio studios moved to west London in the 1990s. Fascinating tours of the BBC TV Centre in White City are available. Each tour is unique, as the itinerary depends on programming and events of the day.

Relief on the Royal Institute of British Architects on Portland Place

All Souls, Langham Place ⑦

Langham Place W1. **Map** 12 F1. **Tel** 020-7580 3522. ⊖ *Oxford Circus.* **Open** *9.30am–6pm Mon–Fri, 9am–9pm Sun.* 🕐 *9.30, 11.30am, 6.30pm Sun.* ♿ 📷 *Sun.* www.allsouls.org

John Nash designed this church in 1824. Its quirky round frontage is best seen from Regent Street. When it was first built, the spire was ridiculed as it appeared too slender and flimsy.

The only Nash church in London, it had close links with the BBC, based opposite at Broadcasting House, and ten years ago used to double as a recording studio for the daily broadcast church service.

Langham Hotel ⑧

1 Portland Place W1. **Map** 12 E1. **Tel** 020-7636 1000. ⊖ *Oxford Circus. See* **Where to Stay** *p288.* www.langhamhotels.com

This was London's grandest hotel after opening in 1865. The writers Oscar Wilde and Mark Twain, and composer Antonin Dvořák were among its many distinguished guests. It was, for a time, used by the BBC, but has since been restored behind its original facade. Its marble-lined entrance hall leads into the Palm Court, where there is piano music at tea-time. Colonial days are recalled in the Memories restaurant and the Chukka bar.

All Souls, Langham Place (1824)

Wigmore Hall 🟢

36 Wigmore St W1. **Map** 12 E1. *Tel* 020-7935 2141. 🚇 *Bond St, Oxford Cir.* 🚻 🔢 🍸 *See* **Entertainment** *p349.* **www**.wigmore-hall.org.uk

This appealing little concert hall for chamber music was designed by T E Collcutt, architect of the Savoy Hotel (*see p290*), in 1900. At first it was called Bechstein Hall because it was attached to the Bechstein piano showroom: the area used to be the heart of London's piano trade. Opposite is the Art Nouveau emporium built in 1907 as Debenham and Freebody's department store – now Debenham's on Oxford Street.

Wallace Collection 🔟

Hertford House, Manchester Sq W1. **Map** 12 D1. 📠 020-7563 9500. 🚇 *Bond St.* **Open** *10am–5pm daily.* **Closed** *24–26 Dec.* **Lectures.** 🚻 🔢 🔢 🔢
www.wallacecollection.org

Late 18th-century Sèvres porcelain vase at the Wallace Collection

This is one of the world's finest private collections of art. It has remained intact since it was bequeathed to the government in 1897 with the stipulation that it should go on permanent public display with nothing added or taken away. The product of passionate collecting for four generations of the Hertford family, it is a

The Mosque on the edge of Regent's Park

must for anyone with even a passing interest in the progress of European art up to the late 19th century. In June 2000 four new galleries were opened so that even more of the collection may be shown.

Among the 70 master works are Frans Hals's *The Laughing Cavalier*, Titian's *Perseus and Andromeda* and Rembrandt's *Titus*. There are superb portraits by Reynolds, Gainsborough and Romney. Other highlights include Sèvres porcelain and sculpture by Houdon and Roubiliac. The fine European and Oriental armour collection is the second largest in the UK.

Sherlock Holmes Museum 🟦

221b Baker St NW1. **Map** 3 C5. *Tel* 020-7935 8866. 🚇 *Baker St.* **Open** *9.30am–6pm daily.* **Closed** *25 Dec.* **Adm charge.** 🔢
www.sherlock-holmes.co.uk

Sir Arthur Conan Doyle's fictional detective lived at 221b Baker Street. This building, dating from 1815, has been converted to resemble Holmes's flat, and is furnished exactly as described in the books. Visitors are greeted by Holmes's "housekeeper" and shown to his recreated rooms on the first floor. The shop sells the novels and deerstalker hats.

London Central Mosque 🟦

146 Park Rd NW8. **Map** 3 B3. *Tel* 020-7724 3363. 🚇 *Marylebone, St John's Wood, Baker St.* **Open** *dawn–dusk daily.* 🚻 🔢 **Lectures.**

Surrounded by trees on the edge of Regent's Park, this large, golden-domed mosque was designed by Sir Frederick Gibberd and completed in 1978. Built to cater for the increasing number of Muslim residents and visitors in London, the mosque is capable of holding 1,800 worshippers. The main hall of worship is a plain square chamber with a domed roof and a magnificent carpet. Visitors must remove their shoes before entering the mosque, and women should remember to cover their heads.

Conan Doyle's Sherlock Holmes

Regent's Canal ⑬

NW1 & NW8. **Map** 3 C1. **Tel** 020-7482 2660 (waterbus). Ⓔ Camden Town, St John's Wood, Warwick Ave. **Canal towpaths open** dawn–dusk daily. See **Six Guided Walks** pp264–5.

A boat trip on Regent's Canal

John Nash was extremely enthusiastic about this waterway, opened in 1820 to link the Grand Junction Canal, which ended at Little Venice in Paddington in the west, with the London docks at Limehouse in the east. He saw it as an added attraction for his new Regent's Park, and originally wanted the canal to run through the middle of that park. He was persuaded out of that by those who thought that the bargees' bad language would offend the genteel residents of the area. Perhaps this was just as well – the steam tugs that hauled the barges were dirty and sometimes dangerous.

In 1874 a barge carrying gunpowder blew up in the cutting by London Zoo, killing the crew, destroying a bridge and terrifying the populace, and the animals. After an initial period of prosperity the canal began to be hit by increasing competition from the new railways and so gradually slipped into decline.

Today it has been revived as a leisure amenity; the towpath is paved as a pleasant walkway and short boat trips are offered between Little Venice and Camden Lock, where there is a thriving crafts market. Visitors to the zoo can use the landing stage that is situated alongside it.

London Zoo ⑭

Regent's Park NW1. **Map** 4 D2. 🄵 020-7722 3333. Ⓔ Camden Town **Open** 10am–5.30pm (4pm Nov–Feb) daily. **Closed** 25 Dec. ♿ ▢ ⬚ **Adm charge. www.**zsl.org

Opened in 1828, the zoo has been one of London's biggest tourist attractions ever since, and is also a major research and conservation centre. London Zoo has over 600 species of animal, from Sumatran tigers and sloth bears to Mexican red-kneed bird-eating spiders. One of

London Zoo's aviary designed by Lord Snowdon (1964)

the newest exhibits is the astonishing Web of Life which takes you through the vast range of life forms found in Earth's major habitats.

Cumberland Terrace ⑮

NW1. **Map** 4 E2. Ⓔ Great Portland St, Regent's Park, Camden Town.

James Thomson is credited with the detailed design of this, the longest and most elaborate of the Nash terraces around Regent's Park. Its imposing central block of raised Ionic columns is topped with a decorated triangular pediment. Completed in 1828, it was designed to be visible from the palace Nash planned for the Prince Regent (later George IV). The palace was never built because the Prince was too busy with his plans for Buckingham Palace (see pp94–5).

Nash's Cumberland Terrace, dating from 1828

HAMPSTEAD

Hampstead has always stayed aloof from London, looking down from its site on the high ridge north of the metropolis. Today it is essentially a Georgian village. The heath separating Hampstead from Highgate reinforces its appeal, isolating it further from the hurly-burly of the modern city. A stroll around the charming village streets, followed by a tramp across the Heath, makes for one of the finest walks in London.

SIGHTS AT A GLANCE

Historic Streets and Buildings
Flask Walk and Well Walk ①
Church Row ⑤
Downshire Hill ⑥
Vale of Health ⑬

Museums and Galleries
Burgh House ②
Fenton House ④
Keats House ⑦
Kenwood House ⑩

Parks and Gardens
Hampstead Heath ⑧
Parliament Hill ⑨
The Hill Garden ⑫

Pubs and Restaurants
Old Bull and Bush ③
Spaniards Inn ⑪

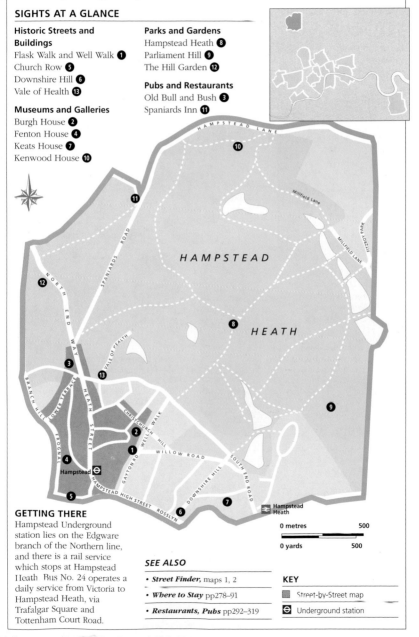

GETTING THERE

Hampstead Underground station lies on the Edgware branch of the Northern line, and there is a rail service which stops at Hampstead Heath. Bus No. 24 operates a daily service from Victoria to Hampstead Heath, via Trafalgar Square and Tottenham Court Road.

SEE ALSO

• *Street Finder,* maps 1, 2

• *Where to Stay* pp278–91

• *Restaurants, Pubs* pp292–319

KEY

▓ Street-by-Street map

🚇 Underground station

0 metres 500
0 yards 500

◁ **View across Hampstead Heath towards Highgate**

Street-by-Street: Hampstead

Perched awkwardly on a hilltop, with its broad
heath to the north, Hampstead has kept its
villagey atmosphere and sense of being aloof from
urban pressures. This has attracted artists and
writers since Georgian times and made it one of
London's most desirable residential areas.
Its mansions and town houses are perfectly
maintained and a stroll through
Hampstead's narrow
streets is one of
London's quieter
pleasures.

Old Bull and Bush
*This pub on the edge of the Heath
was a former haunt for writers
and artists* ❸

★ Hampstead Heath
*A welcome retreat from the
city, its broad open spaces
include bathing ponds,
meadows and lakes* ❽

Whitestone Pond takes its
name from the old white
milestone nearby. It is 4.5
miles (7 km) from Holborn
(see pp132–41).

Grove Lodge was home to
novelist John Galsworthy
(1867–1933), author of the
Forsyte Saga, for the last 15
years of his life.

Admiral's House dates from
about 1700. Built for a sea
captain, its name derives
from its external maritime
motifs. No admiral ever
actually lived in it.

STAR SIGHTS

★ Burgh House

★ Hampstead Heath

★ Fenton House

★ Church Row

KEY

– – – Suggested route

0 metres   100

0 yards   100

★ Fenton House
*Summer visitors should seek
out this late 17th-century
house and its exquisite
walled garden, which are
well hidden in the jumble of
streets near the Heath* ❹

★ Burgh House
Built in 1702 but much altered since, the house contains an intriguing local history museum and a café overlooking the small garden ②

LOCATOR MAP
See Central London Map pp14–15

The New End Theatre
produces rare but significant work. The building used to be a morgue.

CANNON PLACE

HAMPSTEAD SQUARE

CHRISTCHURCH HILL

NEW END SQUARE

WELL WALK

No. 40 Well Walk is where artist John Constable lived while working on his many Hampstead pictures.

NEW END

STREET

STREATLEY PLACE

BACK LANE

FLASK WALK

Flask Walk and Well Walk
An alley of charming specialist shops broadens into a residential village street ①

HOLLY HILL

HAMPSTEAD HIGH ST

Hampstead station

The Everyman Cinema has been an art cinema since 1933.

CHURCH ROW

★ Church Row
The tall houses are rich in original detail. Notice the superb iron-work on what is probably London's finest Georgian street ⑤

Old Bull and Bush in 1900

Flask Walk and Well Walk ❶

NW3. **Map** 1 B5. 🅔 *Hampstead.*

Flask Walk is named after the Flask pub. Here, in the 18th century, therapeutic spa water from what was then the separate village of Hampstead was put into flasks and sold to visitors or sent to London. The water, rich in iron salts, came from nearby Well Walk where a disused fountain now marks the site of the well. The Wells Tavern, almost opposite the spring, used to be a hostelry that specialized in accommodating those who engaged in the illicit liaisons for which the spa became notorious.

In later times, there have been many notable residents of Well Walk including artist John Constable (at No. 40), novelists D H Lawrence and J B Priestley and the poet John Keats, before he moved to his better-known house in what is now Keats Grove.

Site of the well on Well Walk

At the High Street end, Flask Walk is narrow and lined with old shops. Beyond the pub (note the Victorian tiled panels outside) it broadens into a row of Regency houses, one of which used to belong to the novelist Kingsley Amis.

Burgh House ❷

New End Sq NW3. **Map** 1 B4. *Tel 020-7431 0144.* 🅔 *Hampstead.* **Open** *noon–5pm Wed–Fri & Sun (Sat by appt), 2–5pm public hols.* **Closed** *Christmas week.* 📷 ♿ 🍴 🛍 **Music recitals.**
www.burghhouse.org.uk

The last private tenant of Burgh House was the son-in-law of the writer Rudyard Kipling, who visited here occasionally in the last years of his life until 1936. After a period under the ownership of Hampstead Borough Council, the house was let to the independent Burgh House Trust. Since 1979 the Trust has run it as the Hampstead Museum, which illustrates the history of the area and concentrates on some of its most celebrated residents.

One room is devoted to the life of John Constable, who painted an extraordinary series of studies of clouds from Hampstead Heath. The house also has sections on Lawrence, Keats, the artist Stanley Spencer and others who lived and worked in the area. There is a display about Hampstead as a spa in the 18th and 19th centuries, which is also worth a visit. Burgh House often has exhibitions by contemporary local artists.

The house itself was built in 1703 but is named after a 19th-century resident, the Reverend Allatson Burgh. It has been much altered inside, and today the marvellously carved staircase is a highlight of the interior. Also worth seeing is the music room which was reconstructed in 1920, but contains good 18th-century pine panelling from another house. In the 1720s Dr William Gibbons, chief physician to the then thriving Hampstead spa, lived here.

There is a basement café, with a terrace that overlooks the house's pretty garden.

Burgh House staircase

Old Bull and Bush ❸

North End Rd NW3. **Map** 1 A2. *Tel 020-8905 5456.* 🅔 *Golders Green.* **Open** *noon–11pm Mon–Sat, noon–10.30pm Sun.* ♿ 🍴

This pub, one of London's oldest and most famous, dates back to 1645, when it was a farmhouse. It received its licence to sell ale in 1721 and quickly became a haunt for artists and literary figures, including the famous artist William Hogarth *(see p259)* and the writer Austin Dobson. It is reputed that Hogarth planted a tree in the pub's garden. Located next to Hampstead Heath, the pub serves food at lunchtime and in the evening, and has barbecues in the summer in the garden. The interior is comfortably furnished.

Fenton House ❹

20 Hampstead Grove NW3. **Map** 1
A4. **Tel** 020-7435 3471. 🚇 Hampstead. **Open** Apr–Oct: 2–5pm Wed–Fri,
11am–5pm Sat & Sun, public hols.
Adm charge. ♿ ground floor only.
📷 book ahead. **Concerts** 8pm Thu &
Sun. **www**.nationaltrust.org.uk

Built in 1686, this splendid
William and Mary house is
the oldest mansion in
Hampstead. It contains two
specialized exhibitions that
are open to the public during
the summer: the Benton-
Fletcher collection of early
keyboard instruments, which
includes a harpsichord dating
from 1612, said to have been
played by Handel; and a fine
collection of porcelain. The
instruments are kept in full
working order and are
actually used for concerts
held in the house. The
porcelain collection was
largely accumulated by
Lady Binning who, in
1952, bequeathed the
house and its contents
to the National Trust.

Church Row ❺

NW3. **Map** 1 A5. 🚇 Hampstead.

The row is one of the most
complete Georgian streets in
London. Much of its original
detail has survived, notably
the ironwork.
    At the west end is St John's,
Hampstead's parish church,
built in 1745. The iron gates
are earlier and come from
Canons Park in Edgware.
Inside the church is a bust of
John Keats. John Constable's
grave is in the churchyard,
and many Hampstead
luminaries are buried in the
adjoining cemetery.

Downshire Hill ❻

NW3. **Map** 1 C5. 🚇 Hampstead.

A beautiful street of mainly
Regency houses, it lent its
name to a group of artists,
including Stanley Spencer and
Mark Gertler, who would
gather at No. 47 between the
two World Wars. That same

house had been the meeting-
place of Pre-Raphaelite artists,
among them Dante Gabriel
Rossetti and Edward Burne-
Jones. A more recent resident,
at No. 5, was the late Jim
Henson, the creator of the television puppets, *The Muppets*.
    The church on the corner
(the second Hampstead church
to be called St John's) was
built in 1823 to serve the
Hill's residents. Inside, it still
has its original box pews.

Keats House ❼

Keats Grove NW3. **Map** 1 C5.
📞 020-7435 2062. 🚇 Hampstead,
Belsize Park. **Open** 1–5pm Tue–Sun.
Closed 24–28 Dec.
♿ ground floor only.
📖 **Poetry readings, talks,
lectures**.
www.cityoflondon.gov.uk/keats

Lock of Fanny Brawne's hair

Originally two semi-
detached houses built in
1816, the smaller one became
Keats's home in 1818 when
a friend persuaded him to

St John's, Downshire Hill

move in. Keats spent two
productive years here: *Ode to
a Nightingale*, perhaps his
most celebrated poem, was
written under a plum tree in
the garden. The Brawne
family moved into the larger
house a year later and Keats
became engaged to their
daughter, Fanny. However,
the marriage never took
place because Keats died of
consumption in Rome before
two years had passed. He
was only 25 years old.
    A copy of one of Keats's
love letters to Fanny, the
engagement ring he offered
her, and a lock of her hair are
among the mementos that are
exhibited at the house – it
was first opened to the public
in 1925. Visitors are also able
to see facsimiles of some of
Keats's manuscripts, part of a
collection that serves as an
evocative and memorable
tribute to his life and work.

Fenton House's 17th-century façade

View over London from Hampstead Heath

Hampstead Heath **8**

NW3. **Map** 1 C2. **Tel** 020-7485 4491.
🚇 Belsize Park, Hampstead. **Open**
24hrs daily. **Special walks** on Sundays. ♿ phone for disability buggies.
🅿 **Concerts, some children's
activities** in summer. **Sports
facilities, bathing ponds. Sports
bookings Tel** 020-7284 3648.

The best time to stride across
these broad 3 sq miles (8 sq
km) is Sunday afternoon,
when the local residents walk
off their roast beef lunches,
discussing the contents of the
Sunday papers. Separating the
hilltop villages of Hampstead

and Highgate (see p246), the
Heath was made from the
grounds of several, formerly
separate, properties and
embraces a variety of land-
scapes – woods, meadows,
hills, ponds and lakes. It
remains uncluttered by the
haphazard buildings and
statues that embellish the
central London parks, and its
open spaces have become
increasingly precious to
Londoners as the areas around
it get more crowded. There
are ponds for bathing and
fishing and, on three holiday
weekends – Easter, late spring
and late summer – the southern part of the Heath is taken
over by a funfair (see pp56–9).

Parliament Hill **9**

NW5. **Map** 2 E4. **Tel** 020-7485
4491. 🚇 Belsize Park, Hampstead.
♿ **Concerts, children's activities**
in summer. **Sporting facilities.** 🅿

An unlikely but romantic
explanation for the area's
name is that it is where Guy
Fawkes's fellow-plotters
gathered on 5 November 1605
in the vain hope of watching
the Houses of Parliament
blow up after they had
planted gunpowder there (see
p24). More probably it was a
gun emplacement for the
Parliamentary side during the
Civil War 40 years later. The
gunners would have enjoyed

Kenwood House **10**

Hampstead Lane NW3. **Map** 1 C1. **Tel**
020-8348 1286. 🚇 Highgate, Archway. **Open** Apr–Oct: 10am–5pm daily
(from 10.30am Wed & Fri); Nov–Mar:
10am–4pm daily (from 10.30am Wed
& Fri). **Closed** 1 Jan, 24–26 Dec. 🅿
Lakeside concerts in summer.
Regular events. ♿ ground floor.
🅿 🎟 See **Entertainment** pp348–9.
www.english-heritage.org.uk

This is a magnificent Adam
mansion, filled with Old
Master paintings, including
works by Vermeer, Turner and
Romney (who lived in
Hampstead). It is situated in
landscaped grounds high on
the edge of Hampstead Heath.
There has been a house here

since 1616 – the present one
was remodelled by Robert
Adam in 1764 for the Earl of
Mansfield. Adam refitted
existing rooms and added to
the original building. Most of
his work has survived, the
highlight being the library. A
Rembrandt self-portrait is the
star attraction of the collection,
and there are also works by
Van Dyck, Hals and Reynolds.

The orangery is
now used for
occasional concerts
and recitals.

a broad view across London: even today, when tall buildings intervene, it provides one of the most spectacular views over the capital. From here the dome of St Paul's is prominent. Parliament Hill is also a popular place for flying kites and sailing model boats on the boating pond.

Spaniards Inn ⓫

Spaniards Rd NW3. **Map** 1 B1.
Tel 020-8731 6571. ⊜ *Hampstead, Golders Green.* **Open** *11am–11pm Mon–Sat, noon–10.30pm Sun.* & *See* **Restaurants and Pubs** *pp292–319.*

The historic Spaniards Inn

Dick Turpin, the notorious 18th-century highwayman, is said to have frequented this pub. When he wasn't holding up stage-coaches on their way to and from London, he stabled his horse, Black Bess, at the Kenwood stables. The building certainly dates from Turpin's

time and, although the bar downstairs has been altered frequently, the small upstairs Turpin Bar is original. A pair of guns over the bar were reputedly taken from anti-Catholic rioters, who came to Hampstead to burn the Lord Chancellor's house at Kenwood during the Gordon Riots of 1780. The landlord detained them by offering pint after pint of free beer and, when they were drunk, disarmed them.

Among the pub's noted patrons have been the poets Shelley, Keats and Byron, the actor David Garrick and the artist Sir Joshua Reynolds.

The toll house has been restored; it juts into the road so that, in the days when tolls were levied, traffic could not race past without paying.

The Hill Garden ⓬

North End Way NW3. **Map** 1 A2
Tel 020-8455 5183. ⊜ *Hampstead, Golders Green.* **Open** *9am–one hour before dusk daily.*

This charming garden was created by the Edwardian soap manufacturer and patron of the arts, Lord Leverhulme. It was originally the grounds to his house, and is now part of Hampstead Heath. It boasts a pergola walkway, best seen in summer when the plants are in flower; the garden also has a beautiful formal pond.

Pergola walk at The Hill Garden

Vale of Health ⓭

NW3. **Map** 1 B4. ⊜ *Hampstead.*

This area was famous as a distinctly unhealthy swamp before it was drained in 1770; until then it was known as Hatches Bottom. Its newer name may derive from people fleeing here from cholera in London at the end of the 18th century. Alternatively, the name could have been the hype of a property developer, when it was first recorded in 1801.

The poet James Henry Leigh Hunt put it on the literary map when he moved here in 1815, and played host to Coleridge, Byron Shelley and Keats.

D H Lawrence lived here briefly and Stanley Spencer painted in a room above the Vale of Health Hotel, demolished in 1964.

Adam redesigned the façade of the old building.

Adam furnished these older rooms.

Lord Mansfield, who lived here from 1754 until 1793, had his dressing room here.

The ante-room was designed at the same time as the library.

The Adam library has a spectacularly curved, painted ceiling.

GREENWICH AND BLACKHEATH

Best known as the place from which the world's time is measured, Greenwich marks the historic eastern approach to London by land and water. Home to the National Maritime Museum and the Queen's House, Greenwich remains an elegant oasis of bookshops, antique shops and markets. Blackheath lies just to the south.

SIGHTS AT A GLANCE

Historic Streets and Buildings
Queen's House ❷
Old Royal Naval College ❼
Royal Observatory
  Greenwich ❾
Croom's Hill ⓬

Museums
National Maritime Museum ❶
Fan Museum ⓭

Wernher Collection ❹

Churches
St Alfege Church ❸

Parks and Gardens
Greenwich Park ❿
Blackheath ⓫

Walkway
Greenwich Foot
  Tunnel ❻

Pubs and Restaurants
Trafalgar Tavern ❽

Ships
Cutty Sark ❺

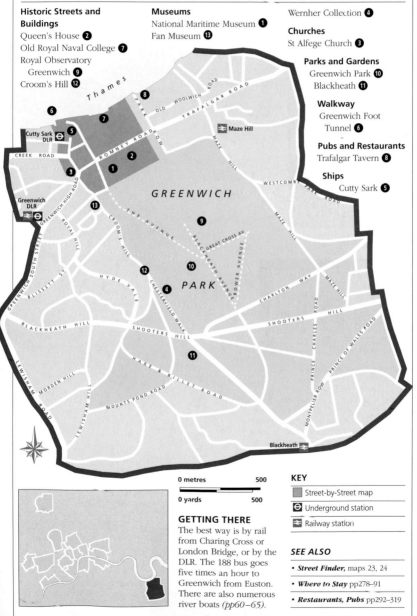

KEY

▨ Street-by-Street map

⊖ Underground station

⊯ Railway station

0 metres   500
0 yards   500

GETTING THERE
The best way is by rail from Charing Cross or London Bridge, or by the DLR. The 188 bus goes five times an hour to Greenwich from Euston. There are also numerous river boats *(pp60–65)*.

SEE ALSO

• *Street Finder*, maps 23, 24

• *Where to Stay* pp278–91

• *Restaurants, Pubs* pp292–319

◁ **View north across the Thames from Greenwich Park, overlooking Queen's House**

Street-by-Street: Greenwich

This historic town marks the eastern approach to
London and is best visited by river *(see pp60–5)*. In
Tudor times it was the site of a palace much enjoyed
by Henry VIII, near a fine hunting ground and his naval
base. The old palace is gone, leaving Inigo Jones's
exquisite Queen's House, built for James I's wife.
Museums, book and antique shops, markets, Wren's
architecture and the magnificent park make Greenwich
an enjoyable day's excursion. Greenwich has also
been awarded the status of a World Heritage Site.

Greenwich Foot Tunnel
*Leading to the Isle of Dogs,
this is one of two tunnels built
solely for pedestrians* ❻

Greenwich Pier provides a
boarding point for boat
services to Westminster
and the Thames Barrier.

Cutty Sark
*Majestic clipper
ships, such as this,
once traded across
the oceans* ❺

To Cutty ←
Sark DLR

Goddard's Pie and Eel House is a rare
survivor of a London tradition.

Greenwich Market
sells crafts, antiques
and books at week-
ends. It is especially
popular on Sundays.

St Alfege Church
*There has been a church
here since 1012* ❸

Spread Eagle Yard was a
stopping point for horse-drawn
carriages. The ticket office is
now a second-hand book shop.

LOCATOR MAP
See Greater London Map pp12–13

★ **Old Royal Naval College**
Wren's stately structure was built in two halves so that the Queen's House would keep its river view **7**

The George II Statue was sculpted by John Rysbrack in 1735 and depicts the king as a Roman emperor.

The Painted Hall contains 18th-century murals by Sir James Thornhill, who painted the interior of the dome at St Paul's Cathedral.

O M N E Y   R O A D

★ **Queen's House**
On his return from Italy, this was the first building Inigo Jones designed in the Palladian style **2**

STAR SIGHTS

★ Royal Naval College

★ Queen's House

National Maritime Museum
Real and model boats, paintings and instruments, like this 18th-century compass, illustrate naval history **1**

KEY

– – – Suggested route

0 metres	100
0 yards	100

National Maritime Museum ❶

Romney Rd SE10. **Map** 23 C2.
Tel 020-8312 6565. ⊖ *Cutty
Sark DLR.* ⊒ *Greenwich.* **Open**
*Sep–Jun: 10am–5pm daily; Jul &
Aug: 10am–6pm daily (last adm:
30 mins before close).* **Closed** *24–26
Dec.* **Adm charge** *special
exhibitions.* Ø ⛐ ⛁ ⛒
Lectures. www.nmm.ac.uk

The sea has always played an
extremely important role in
British history as a means of
both defence and expansion,
and this museum celebrates
the "island nation's" seafaring
heritage. Exhibits tell the story
of explorers, from early
Elizabethan times through the
development of passenger
lines to the modern day.
There are sections devoted to
trade and empire, the
exploratory expeditions
of Captain Cook and Sir
Ernest Shackleton, and the
Napoleonic Wars.

One of the star exhibits is
the uniform that Lord Horatio
Nelson was wearing when he
was shot at the Battle of
Trafalgar in October 1805:
you can easily see the bullet
hole and the bloodstains.

Rather more spectacular,
however, is the royal barge
that was built for Prince
Frederick in 1732, decorated
with gilded mermaids, shells,
garlands and his Prince of
Wales's feathers on the stern.
Throughout the museum,
(built in the 19th century
as a school for sailors'
children), are scores of finely
crafted models of ships and
historic paintings.

St Alfege's altar with rails attributed to Jean Tijou

Queen's House ❷

Romney Rd SE10. **Map** 23 C2. **Tel**
020-8312 6565. ⊖ *Cutty Sark DLR.*
⊒ *Greenwich.* **Open** *10am–5pm
daily (last adm: 4.30pm). Closes early
some Fri & Sat for special events –
phone to check.* **Closed** *24–26 Dec.*
Ø ⛐ ⛘ ⛁ ⛒ www.nmm.ac.uk

The house was
designed by Inigo
Jones and was com-
pleted in 1637. It was
originally meant to be
the home of Anne of
Denmark, wife of James I,
but she died while it was
still being built and it was
finished for Charles I's
queen, Henrietta Maria. She
fell in love with it and called
it her house of delights. After
the Civil War it was briefly
occupied by Henrietta as
dowager queen, but was not
much used by the royal
family after that.

The building has been
refurbished, and in 2001 the
house opened with galleries
displaying the art collection of
the National Maritime
Museum. On the ground floor
is a permanent exhibition,
Historic Greenwich, which
includes two models showing
how the house looked in
17th-century Greenwich. The
paintings on show include
early views of Greenwich and
portraits of historical figures
associated with the house,
including Inigo Jones. Visitors
can also see the spiral "tulip
staircase", which curves
sinuously upwards without a
central support.

St Alfege Church ❸

Greenwich Church St SE10.
Map 23 B2. **Tel** 020-8293 5595.
⊖ *Cutty Sark DLR.* **Open** *phone
to check.* ⛘ *9.30am Sun.* ⛐
phone ahead. **Concerts.**
www.st-alfege.org

This is one of Nicholas
Hawksmoor's most distinctive
and powerful designs, with its
gigantic columns and

**Prince Frederick's barge at the
National Maritime Musueum**

pediments topped by urns. It was completed in 1714 on the site of an older church which marked the martyrdom of St Alfege, the then Archbishop of Canterbury, killed on this spot by Danish invaders in 1012. A second church here was the site of Henry VIII's baptism in 1491 and of 16th-century composer and organist Thomas Tallis's burial in 1585. Today a stained-glass window commemorates Thomas Tallis.

Some of the carved wood inside is by Grinling Gibbons, but much of it was badly damaged by a World War II bomb and has been restored. The wrought iron of the altar and gallery rails is original, attributed to Jean Tijou.

Wernher Collection ❹

Ranger's House, Chesterfield Walk, Greenwich Park SE10. **Map** 23 C4. *Tel* 020-8853 0035. ❺ *Cutty Sark DLR.* ➽ *Blackheath.* **Open** *Apr–Sep: 10am–5pm Wed–Sun & bank hols; Oct–Dec & Mar: Tue & Thu for groups only (book ahead).* **Closed** *22 Dec–Feb.* **Adm charge.** ▨ *by appt.* ▣ ▯ www.english-heritage.org.uk

Opal-set lizard pendant at the Wernher Collection

The Wernher Collection is located in Ranger's House (1688), an elegant building southeast of Greenwich Park *(see p243)*. It is an enchanting array of over 650 pieces accumulated by South African mine owner Sir Julius Wernher in the late 19th century. The collection is displayed in 12 rooms and includes paintings, jewellery, furniture and porcelain. Highlights include Renaissance masterworks by Hans Memling and Filippo Lippi, over 100 Renaissance jewels, and an opal-set lizard pendant jewel. Other curiosities include enamelled skulls.

The domed terminal of the Greenwich Foot Tunnel

Cutty Sark ❺

King William Walk SE10. **Map** 23 B2. *Tel* 020-8858 2698. ❺ *Cutty Sark DLR.* ➽ *Greenwich Pier.* **Open** *10am–5pm daily.* **Closed** *24–26 Dec.* **Adm charge.** ▣ *restricted.* ▨ *phone to check times as conservation work 2007–09.* ▯ www.cuttysark.org.uk

This majestic vessel is a survivor of the clippers that crossed the Atlantic and Pacific Oceans in the 19th century. Launched in 1869 as a tea carrier, it was something of a speed machine in its day, winning the annual clippers' race from China to London in 1871 in a time of 107 days. It made its final voyage in 1938 and was put on display here in 1957. On board you can see where the seamen slept, ate, worked and pursued their interests. Exhibits show the history of sailing and of trade in the Pacific and there is also an interesting collection of old carved ships' figureheads.

Greenwich Foot Tunnel ❻

Between Greenwich Pier SE10 and Isle of Dogs E14. **Map** 23 B1. ❺ *Island Gardens, Cutty Sark DLR.* ➽ *Greenwich Pier.* **Open** *24hrs daily.* **Lifts open** *5am–9pm daily.* ▣ ♿ *when lifts open.*

This 370-m (1,200-ft) long tunnel was opened in 1902 to allow south London labourers to walk to work in Millwall

Docks. Today it is worth crossing for the wonderful views, across the river, of Christopher Wren's Royal Naval College and of Inigo Jones's Queen's House.

Matching round red-brick terminals, with glass domes, mark the top of the lift shafts on either side of the river. The tunnel is about 2.5 m (9 ft) high and is lined with 200,000 tiles. Both ends of the tunnel are close to stations on the Docklands Light Railway (DLR), with trains to Canary Wharf *(see p249)*, Limehouse, East London, Tower Hill and Lewisham. Although there are security cameras, the tunnel can be eerie at night.

A late 19th-century figurehead in the Cutty Sark

Old Royal Naval College ❼

Greenwich SE10. **Map** 23 C2. 🄵 *020-8269 4791.* 🔵 *Cutty Sark, Greenwich.* 🚆 *Greenwich, Maze Hill.* **Open** *10am–5pm daily.* **Grounds open** *8am–6pm daily.* **Chapel open** *10am–5pm Mon–Sat, 12.30am–5pm Sun.* 🄾 ☑ 🄶 🄸 ☐ 🄳 **www.**greenwichfoundation.org.uk

These ambitious buildings by Christopher Wren were built on the site of the old 15th-century royal palace, where Henry VIII, Mary I and Elizabeth I were born. Only the chapel, the hall and the visitors' centre are open to the public. The west front was completed by Vanbrugh.

Wren's chapel was destroyed by fire in 1779. The present Greek Revival interior, by James Stuart, is light and airy, with dainty plasterwork decorations. The Painted Hall was opulently decorated by Sir James Thornhill in the early 18th century. The ceiling paintings are supported by his illusionistic pillars and friezes. At the foot of one of his paintings, the artist himself is shown, apparently extending his hand for more money.

Trafalgar Tavern ❽

Park Row SE10. **Map** 23 C1. **Tel** *020-8858 2909.* 🔵 *Greenwich.* **Open** *noon–11pm Mon–Sat, noon–10.30pm Sun.* 🄶 *See* **Restaurants and Pubs** *pp315–19.*

This charming panelled pub was built in 1837 and quickly became established, along with other waterside inns in

Thornhill's painting of King William III in the Hall of the Naval College

Greenwich, as a venue for "whitebait dinners". Government ministers, legal luminaries and the like would arrive from Westminster and Charing Cross by water on celebratory occasions and feast on the tiny fish. The last such meeting of government ministers was held here in 1885. Whitebait still features, when they are in season, on the menu at the pub's restaurant, although they are no longer fished from the Thames.

This was another of Charles Dickens's haunts. He drank here with one of his novels' most famous illustrators, George Cruickshank.

In 1915 the pub became an institution for old merchant seamen. It was restored in 1965 after a spell of being used as a social club for working men.

Royal Observatory Greenwich ❾

Greenwich Park SE10. **Map** 23 C3. **Tel** *020-8312 6565.* 🔵 *Cutty Sark DLR.* 🚆 *Greenwich.* **Open** *10am–5pm daily (last adm: 4.30pm).* **Closed** *24–26 Dec.* **Adm charge** *for Planetarium shows.* 🄾 🄶 🄳 **www.**rog.nmm.ac.uk

The meridian (0° longitude) that divides the Earth's eastern and western hemispheres passes through here, and millions of visitors have taken the opportunity of being photographed standing with a foot on either side of it. In 1884, Greenwich Mean Time became the basis of time measurement for most of the world, following an important international agreement.

The original building, still standing, is the recently refurbished Flamsteed House, designed by Christopher Wren. It has an octagonal room at the top, hidden by square outer walls and crowned with two turrets. Above one of them is a ball on a rod which has dropped at 1pm every day since 1833, so that sailors on the Thames, and makers of chronometers (navigators' clocks), could set their clocks by it. The house now contains a display of John Harrison's marine timekeepers and an intriguing exhibition about

Trafalgar Tavern viewed from the Thames

Greenwich Mean Time. Flamsteed was the first Astronomer Royal, appointed by Charles II, and this was the official government observatory from 1675 until 1948, when the lights of London became too bright and the astronomers moved to darker Sussex.

A rare 24-hour clock at the Royal Observatory Greenwich

Greenwich Park ❿

SE10. **Map** 23 C3. **Tel** 020 8858 2000. ⬤ ⮐ *Greenwich, Blackheath, Maze Hill.* **Open** *6am–dusk daily.* ▢ ♿ *Children's shows, sports facilities.* **Ranger's House**, Chesterfield Walk, Greenwich Park SE10. **Map** 23 C4. **www**.english-heritage.co.uk *see also* **Wernher Collection**, *p241.*

Originally the grounds of a royal palace and still a Royal Park, the park was enclosed in 1433 and its brick wall built in the reign of James I. Later, in the 17th century, the French royal landscape gardener André Le Nôtre, who laid out the gardens at Versailles, was invited to design one at Greenwich. The broad avenue, rising south up the hill, was part of his plan.

There are great river views from the hilltop and on a fine day most of London can be seen.

To the southeast of the park, and on the edge of the park's rose garden, is the Ranger's House (1688), which now houses the Wernher Collection *(see p241).*

From here the walk to the charming village of Blackheath is flat, compared with the steep walk down to the village of Greenwich at the bottom of the hill.

Blackheath ⓫

SE3. **Map** 24 D5. ⮐ *Blackheath.*

This open heath used to be a rallying point for large groups who were entering London from the east, including Wat Tyler's band of rebels at the time of the Peasants' Revolt in 1381.

Blackheath is also the place where King James I of England (who was also King James VI of Scotland) introduced the game of golf from his native Scotland, to the then largely sceptical English.

Today the heath is well worth exploring for the stately Georgian houses and terraces that surround it. In the prettily-named Tranquil Vale to the south, there are shops selling books, prints and antiques.

Ranger's House in Greenwich Park

Croom's Hill ⓬

SE10. **Map** 23 C3. ⮐ *Greenwich.*

This is one of the best kept 17th- to early 19th-century streets in London. The oldest buildings are at the southern end, near Blackheath: the original Manor House of 1695; near it, No. 68, from about the same date; and No. 66 the oldest of all. Famous residents of Croom's Hill include Irish actor Daniel Day Lewis.

Fan Museum ⓭

12 Croom's Hill SE10. **Map** 23 B3. **Tel** 020-8858 7879. ⮐ *Greenwich.* **Open** *11am–5pm Tue–Sat, noon–5pm Sun.* **Adm charge.** ▢ *no flash.* 📷 *by appt.* ▢ ♿ **Lectures, fan-making workshops** *first Sat of the month.* **www**.fan-museum.org

One of London's most unlikely museums – the only one of its kind in the world – was opened here in 1991. It owes its existence and appeal to the enthusiasm of Helene Alexander, whose personal collection of 2,000 fans from the 17th century onwards has been augmented by gifts from others, including several fans that were made for the stage. If there, Mrs Alexander will act as a guide.

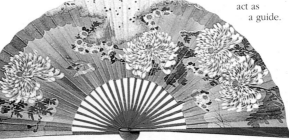

Stage fan used in a D'Oyly Carte operetta

FURTHER AFIELD

M any of the great houses originally built as country retreats for London's high and mighty were overrun by sprawling suburbs in the Victorian era. Fortunately several have survived as museums in these now less-rustic surroundings. Most are less than an hour's journey from central London. Richmond Park and Wimbledon Common give a taste of the country, while a trip to the Thames Barrier is an adventure.

SIGHTS AT A GLANCE

Historic Streets and Buildings
Sutton House **11**
Charlton House **19**
Eltham Palace **20**
Hampton Court pp254–5 **28**
Ham House **29**
Orleans House Gallery **30**
Marble Hill House **31**
Syon House **33**
Osterley Park House **35**
PM Gallery and House **36**
Strand on the Green **39**
Chiswick House **40**
Fulham Palace **42**

Churches
St Mary, Rotherhithe **13**
St Anne's, Limehouse **14**
St Mary's, Battersea **24**

Markets
Camden Market **2**

Museums and Galleries
Lord's Cricket Ground **1**
Freud Museum **3**
The Jewish Museum **6**
St John's Gate **7**
Crafts Council Gallery **8**
Geffrye Museum **10**
Bethnal Green Museum
of Childhood **12**
William Morris Gallery **16**
Horniman Museum **21**
Dulwich Picture Gallery **22**
Wimbledon Lawn Tennis
Museum **25**
Wimbledon Windmill
Museum **26**
Musical Museum **34**
Kew Bridge Steam
Museum **37**
Hogarth's House **41**

Parks and Gardens
Battersea Park **23**
Richmond Park **27**
Kew Gardens pp260–61 **38**

Cemeteries
Highgate Cemetery **5**

Modern Architecture
Canary Wharf **15**
The Dome **18**
Chelsea Harbour **43**

Historic Districts
Highgate **4**
Islington **9**
Richmond **32**

Modern Technology
Thames Barrier **17**

All the sights in this section lie inside
the M25 motorway *(see pp12–13).*

KEY
Main sightseeing areas
Motorway

0 kilometres 5
0 miles 3

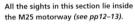

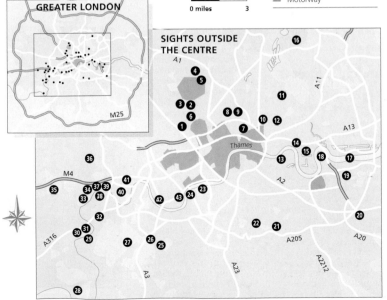

GREATER LONDON

M25

SIGHTS OUTSIDE
THE CENTRE

Thames

North of the Centre

Lord's Cricket Ground **1**

NW8. **Map** 3 A3. **Tel** 020-7289 1611. 🚇 St John's Wood. **Open** for guided tours and ticket-holders to matches only. **Closed** 25 Dec. **Adm charge.** ♿ 📷 noon, 2pm (also 10am mid-Apr–mid-Sep); groups pre-book on 020-7616 8595. 📱 See **Entertainment** pp354–5. www.lords.org

The headquarters of Britain's chief summer sport contains a museum, including a stuffed sparrow killed by a cricket ball as well as the Ashes (burned wood in an urn), the object of ferocious competition between the English and Australian national teams. The museum explains the history of the game, while paintings and mementos of notable cricketers make it a place of pilgrimage for devotees of the sport.

Cricket pioneer Thomas Lord moved his ground here in 1814. The Pavilion (1890), from which women were excluded until 1999, is late Victorian. There are tours of Lord's even when there is no game being played.

The Ashes at Lord's

Camden Market **2**

NW1. 🚇 Camden Town, Chalk Farm. **Open** noon–6pm daily.

Camden Market is really six markets located close to each other along Chalk Farm Road and Camden High Street. Packed with shoppers at the weekends, most of the shops and some of the stalls are open on weekdays. Many units are housed in restored Victorian buildings alongside Camden Lock and the canal. The first market here was a crafts market at Camden Lock, in 1975. Today all the markets sell a wide range of exciting goods, from arts and crafts and street fashion, to new age remedies and body piercing.

Sigmund Freud's famous couch

Freud Museum **3**

20 Maresfield Gdns NW3. **Tel** 020-7435 2002. 🚇 Finchley Rd. **Open** noon–5pm Wed–Sun. **Closed** 24–26 Dec. **Adm charge.** 📷 no flash. ♿ limited. 📱 **Events.** www.freud.org.uk

In 1938 Sigmund Freud, the founder of psychoanalysis, fled from Nazi persecution in Vienna to this Hampstead house. Making use of the possessions he brought with him, his family recreated the atmosphere of his Vienna consulting rooms. After Freud died in 1939 his daughter Anna (who was a pioneer of child psychoanalysis) kept the house as it was. In 1986 it was opened as a museum dedicated to Freud. The most famous item is the couch on which patients lay for analysis. A series of 1930s home movies shows cheerful moments with his dog as well as scenes of Nazi attacks on his apartment. The bookshop has a large collection of his works.

Highgate **4**

N6. 🚇 Highgate.

There has been a settlement here since at least the early Middle Ages, when an important staging post on the Great North Road from London was established with a gate to control access. Like Hampstead across the Heath (see pp234–5), it soon became fashionable for its unpolluted air, and noblemen built country houses here. It still has an exclusive feel, with a Georgian High Street and expensive houses. It was on Highgate Hill in medieval times, that Dick Whittington (a poor young lad) and his pet cat were persuaded to turn back, and try their fortune in the city, by the sound of Bow Bells. He went on to become Lord Mayor of London. A statue of a black cat marks the spot of his epiphany (see p39).

Highgate Cemetery **5**

Swain's Lane N6. **Tel** 020-8340 1834. 🚇 Archway. **Eastern Cemetery open** Apr–Oct: 10am–5pm Mon–Fri, 11am–4pm Sat–Sun; Nov–Mar: 10am–4pm daily. **Western Cemetery open** 📷 **only** Mar–Oct: 2pm Mon–Fri, 11am–4pm Sat, Sun; Nov–Feb: 11am–3pm Sat, Sun. **Closed** 25–26 Dec, during funerals – phone to check. **Adm charge.** ♿ Eastern only. www.highgate-cemetery.org

The western part of this early Victorian gem opened in 1839. Its graves and tombs perfectly reflect high Victorian taste. For many years it lay neglected until a voluntary group, the Friends of Highgate Cemetery, stepped in to save it from further decline. They have restored the Egyptian Avenue, a street of family vaults built in a style based on ancient Egyptian tombs, and the Circle of Lebanon, more vaults in a ring, topped by a cedar tree. In the eastern section lies Karl Marx, beneath a huge black bust of his image, and novelist George Eliot (real name, Mary Anne Evans).

George Wombwell's memorial at Highgate Cemetery

Jewish Bakers' Union banner, c.1926, Jewish Museum, Camden

The Jewish Museum ❻

Camden branch 129–31 Albert Street, NW1. **Map** 4 E1. **Tel** 020-7284 1997. Camden Town. **Open** 10am–4pm Mon–Thu, 10am–5pm Sun. **Closed** Jewish hols. **Adm charge.** ♿ 🅿
Sternberg Centre 80 East End Road, Finchley N3. **Tel** 020-8349 1143. Finchley Central. **Open** 10.30am–5pm Mon–Thu, 10.30am–4.30pm Sun. **Closed** Jewish & public hols, 24 Dec–4 Jan. **Adm charge.** ♿ limited. 🅿 www.jewishmuseum.org.uk

London's Jewish Museum was founded in 1932. Today it is spread across two sites. The Camden branch has three galleries celebrating Jewish life in this country from the Middle Ages. The museum is packed with memorabilia and interactive displays and has important collections of Jewish ceremonial art, including Hanukkah lamps, a collection of Jewish marriage rings and some illuminated marriage contracts. The highlight of this collection is a 16th-century Venetian synagogue ark.

The Finchley site houses the museum's social history collections which feature taped and photographic archives as well as reconstructions of East End tradesmen's workshops and a Holocaust exhibition.

St John's Gate ❼

St John's Lane EC1. **Map** 6 F4. **Tel** 020-7324 4005. Farringdon. **Museum Tel** 020-7324 4070. **Open** 10am–5pm Mon–Fri, 10am–4pm Sat. **Adm** donation. 📷 11am, 2.30pm Tue, Fri, Sat. 🅿 ♿ limited. www.sja.org.uk/museum

The Tudor gatehouse and parts of the 12th-century church are all that remain of the priory of the Knights of St John, which flourished here for 400 years and was the precursor of the St John Ambulance. Over the years, the priory buildings have had many uses, such as offices for Elizabeth I's Master of the Revels, a pub, and a coffee shop run by the artist William Hogarth's father. A museum of the order's history is open daily, but to see the rest of the building, join a guided tour.

The Crafts Council Gallery

Crafts Council Gallery ❽

44a Pentonville Rd N1. **Map** 6 D2. **Tel** 020-7278 7700. Angel. **Open** 11am–5.45pm Tue–Sat, 2–5.45pm Sun. **Closed** 25 Dec–1 Jan. ♿ 🅿 **Lectures.** www.craftscouncil.org.uk

The Crafts Council is the national agency for promoting the creation and appreciation of contemporary crafts in the UK. It has a collection of contemporary British crafts, some of which are displayed here, along with special exhibitions. There is a library, an information service and a bookshop which also sells good contemporary crafts.

Islington ❾

N1. **Map** 6 E1. Angel, Highbury & Islington.

Islington was once a highly fashionable spa, but the rich began to move out in the late 18th century, and the area deteriorated rapidly. During the 20th century, writers such as Evelyn Waugh, George Orwell and Joe Orton lived here. Now Islington has again returned to fashion as one of London's first areas to become "gentrified", with many young professionals buying and refurbishing old houses.

An older relic is Canonbury Tower, the remains of a medieval manor house converted into apartments in the 18th century. Writers such as Washington Irving and Oliver Goldsmith lived here and today it houses the Tower Theatre. On Islington Green there is a statue of Sir Hugh Myddleton, who built a canal through Islington in 1613 to bring water to London from Hertfordshire; today a pleasant landscaped walk along its banks runs between Essex Road and Canonbury stations. There are two markets, Chapel Market and Camden Passage, close to the Angel station (see p332), as well as a shopping and cinema complex, the N1 Centre.

St John's Priory: today, only the gatehouse remains intact

East of the Centre

Geffrye Museum's Georgian Room

Geffrye Museum ⑩

Kingsland Rd E2. *Tel* 020-7739 9893.
🚇 *Liverpool St, Old St.* **Open** 10am–
5pm Tue–Sat, noon–5pm Sun & bank
hols. **Closed** 1 Jan, Good Fri, 24–26
Dec. **Garden open** Apr–Oct. 🚻 🖵
🎨 *Special exhibitions & events.*
www.geffrye-museum.org.uk

This delightful museum is
housed in a set of almshouses,
one of which has been
recently restored. They were
built in 1715 on land
bequeathed by Sir Robert
Geffrye, a 17th-century Lord
Mayor of London who made
his fortune through trade.
Inside, a series of rooms
have been decorated in
different period styles, each
one providing an insight into
the domestic interiors of the
urban middle classes. The
historic room settings begin
with Elizabethan (which
contains magnificent
panelling) and run through
various major styles,
including High Victorian,
while an attractive extension
houses more modern
settings, such as an example
of 1990s "loft living".
Each room contains superb
examples of British furniture
of the period. Outside, there
is a series of garden "rooms"
that show the designs and
planting schemes popular in
urban gardens between the
16th and 20th centuries.
There is a good café which
has a children's menu.

Sutton House ⑪

2–4 Homerton High St E9. *Tel* 020-
8986 2264. 🚇 *Bethnal Green then
bus 253.* **Open** Feb–Dec:
12.30–4.30pm Thurs–Sun. **Adm
charge.** 🚻 limited. 📷 *phone first.*
🖵 🎨 *Regular events.*
www.nationaltrust.org.uk

One of the few London
Tudor merchants' houses to
survive in something like its
original form. Built in 1535
for Ralph Sadleir, a courtier to
Henry VIII, it was owned by
several wealthy families before
becoming a girls' school in
the 17th century. In the 18th
century the front was altered,
but the Tudor fabric remains
surprisingly intact, with much
original brickwork, large fireplaces and linenfold panelling.

Bethnal Green Museum of Childhood ⑫

Cambridge Heath Rd E2. *Tel* 020-
8983 5200. 🚇 *Bethnal Green.* **Open**
10am–5.50pm Sat–Thu. **Closed**
24–26 Dec, 1 Jan. 📷 🚻 🖵 🎨
Workshop, children's activities.
www.museumofchildhood.org.uk

This recently refurbished
branch of the Victoria and
Albert Museum *(see pp202–5)*
has the largest collection of
childhood-related objects in
the UK. Its array of toys,
games, lavish dolls' houses,
model trains, theatres and
costumes dates from the 16th
century to the present day, and
is well explained and enticingly
displayed. The upper floor

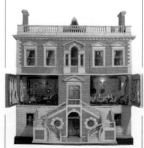

Tate "Baby" house made in 1760

has lots of fun activities, such
as dressing up, a playable
jukebox and wobbly mirror.
The shop is excellent.
The purpose-built museum
building was originally erected
on the V&A site. In 1872, it
was dismantled and reassembled here to bring the light of
learning to the East End. The
toy collection began in the
early 20th century and Bethnal
Green became a dedicated
museum of childhood in 1974.

St Mary, Rotherhithe ⑬

St Marychurch St SE16. *Tel* 020-7231
2465. 🚇 *Rotherhithe.* **Open**
7.30am–6pm daily. 🔔 9.30am, 6pm
Sun. 📷 *with permission.* 🚻
www.stmaryrotherhithe.org

St Mary, Rotherhithe

This church was built in 1715
on the site of a medieval
church. It has nautical conno-
tations, most notably a memorial to Christopher Jones,
captain of the *Mayflower*, on
which the Pilgrim Fathers
sailed to North America. The
communion table is made
from the timbers of the
Temeraire, a warship whose
final journey to the breaker's
yard at Rotherhithe was
evocatively recorded in
Turner's painting at the
National Gallery *(see pp104–7)*.
The church also contains a fine
example of 18th-century organ
building by John Byfield.

William Morris tapestry (1885)

St Anne's, Limehouse ⑭

Commercial Rd E14. *Tel* 020-7515 0977. ⊝ *Westferry (DLR).* **Open** 2–4pm Mon–Fri, 2.30–5pm Sat, Sun (viewing by appointment only). 🚻 10.30am, 6pm Sun. 📷 📷 **Concerts, lectures.**

This is one of a group of East End churches designed by Nicholas Hawksmoor; it was completed in 1724. Its 40-m (130-ft) tower very soon became a landmark for ships using the East End docks – St Anne's still has the highest church clock in London. The church was damaged by fire in 1850 and its interior was subsequently Victorianized. It was bombed in World War II and is today in need of further restoration.

Canary Wharf ⑮

E14. ⊝ *Canary Wharf.* 🚻 🚻 📷 🚻 **Information centre, concerts.** **Museum in Docklands** No. 1 Warehouse, West India Quay E14 *Tel* 0870-444 3857. **Open** 10am–6pm daily. **Closed** 1 Jan, 24–26 Dec. 🚻 🚻 📷 www.museumindocklands.org.uk

London's most ambitious commercial development opened in 1991, when the first tenants moved into the 50-storey Canada Tower,

designed by Argentine architect César Pelli. At 250 m (800 ft), it dominates the city's eastern skyline. The tower stands on what was the West India Dock, closed, like all the London docks, between the 1960s and the 1980s, when trade moved to the modern port down river at Tilbury. Today, Canary Wharf is thriving. A major shopping complex, as well as offices and restaurants, is located in and around Canada Tower. The **Museum in Docklands**, occupying a late Georgian warehouse, tells the story of the Port of London from Roman times to the present.

William Morris Gallery ⑯

Lloyd Park, Forest Rd E17. *Tel* 020-8527 3782. ⊝ *Walthamstow Central.* **Open** 10am–1pm, 2–5pm Tue–Sat, 10am–1pm, 2–5pm first Sun of month. **Closed** 24–26 Dec and public hols. 🚻 *ground floor.* 📷 **Lectures.** www.lbwf.gov.uk/wmg

The most influential designer of the Victorian era, born in 1834, lived in this imposing 18th-century house as a youth. It is now a beguiling and well-presented museum giving a full account of William Morris the artist, designer, writer, craftsman and socialist. It has choice examples of his work and that of other members of the Arts and Crafts movement that he inspired – furniture by A H Mackmurdo, Kelmscott Press books, tiles by William de Morgan, and paintings by members of the Pre-Raphaelite Brotherhood.

Canada Tower at Canary Wharf

Thames Barrier ⑰

Unity Way SE18. *Tel* 020-8305 4188. 🚆 *Charlton, Silvertown.* **Open** Apr–Sep: 10.30am–4.30pm daily; Oct–Mar: 11am–3.30pm. **Closed** 24 Dec–2 Jan. **Adm charge.** 🚻 📷 🚻 *exhibition.* www.environment-agency.gov.uk

In 1236 the Thames rose so high that people rowed across Westminster Hall; London flooded again in 1663, 1928 and in 1953. Something had to be done, and in 1965 the Greater London Council invited proposals. The Thames Barrier was completed in 1984 and is 520 m (1,700 ft) across. Its 10 gates, which pivot from being flat on the river bed, swing up to 1.6 m (6 ft) above the level reached by the tide in 1953. The barrier was raised 19 times in 2003, and can be visited by boat in summer.

Unique structure of the Dome

The Dome ⑱

North Greenwich SE10. ⊝ *North Greenwich/The Dome (Jubilee Line).* **Closed** to the public.

The Dome was the focal point of Britain's celebration of the year 2000. Controversial from its earliest days, it is nonetheless a spectacular feat of engineering. Its base is ten times that of St Paul's Cathedral, and Nelson's Column could stand beneath its roof. Its canopy is made from 100,000 sq m (109,000 sq yards) of Teflon-coated spun glass-fibre, and is held by over 70 km (43 miles) of steel cable rigged to twelve 100-m (328-ft) masts.

The intention is currently to develop the area as "mixed use" – including residential, hotel, office, retail and entertainment facilities – and use part or all of the Dome as an arena for sports, entertainment and exhibitions.

South of the Centre

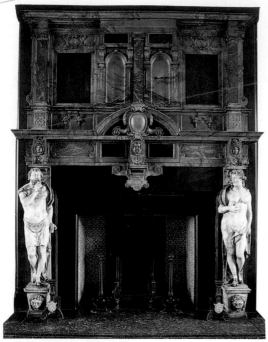

A Jacobean fireplace at Charlton House

Charlton House ⑲

Charlton Rd SE7. **Tel** 020-8856 3951.
⊇ Charlton. **Open** 9am–10pm Mon–
Fri, 10am–5pm Sat; phone to arrange
a visit. **Closed** public hols. 📖 book
ahead. 🖐 limited. 🖵 9am–3pm
Mon–Fri.

The house was completed in
1612 for Adam Newton, tutor
to Prince Henry. It has good
river views and is the best-
preserved Jacobean mansion
in London – well worth the
tricky journey for enthusiasts
of that period. It is now used
as a community centre and
library, but many of the original ceilings and fireplaces
survive, as does the carved
main staircase, all with an
astonishing quantity of ornament. Parts of the wood panelling, too, are original, and
the ceilings have been restored
using the original moulds. The
summer house in the grounds
was reputedly designed by
Inigo Jones, and a mulberry
tree (probably the oldest in
England) is said to have been
planted by James I in 1608 as
part of his failed attempt to
start an English silk industry.

Eltham Palace ⑳

Court Yard SE9. **Tel** 020-8294 2548.
⊇ Eltham, then a 15-minute walk.
Open Sun–Wed. Apr–Oct: 10am–
5pm; Nov & Dec, Feb & Mar: 10am–
4pm. **Closed** 24 Dec–Jan. **Adm
charge.** 📷 🖐 🖵 🛈
www.english-heritage.org.uk

This unique property lets
visitors relive the grand life of
two very different eras. In the
14th century, English kings
spent Christmas in a splendid
palace here. The Tudors used
it as a base for deer-hunting
but it fell to ruin after the Civil
War (1642–8). In 1935 Stephen
Courtauld, of the wealthy
textile family, restored the
Great Hall which, apart from
the bridge over the moat, was
the only part of the medieval
palace to survive. Next to it
he built a house described as
"a wonderful combination of
Hollywood glamour and Art
Deco design". It has been
superbly restored and is
open, along with the Great
Hall, the carp-filled moat and
the 1930s garden.

Horniman Museum ㉑

100 London Rd SE23. **Tel** 020-8699
1872. ⊇ Forest Hill. **Gardens open**
8am–dusk daily. **Museum open**
10.30am–5.30pm daily. **Closed** 24–26
Dec. 🖵 🛈 🖐 **Events & activities**.
www.horniman.ac.uk

Frederick Horniman, the tea
merchant, had this museum
built in 1901 to house the
curios he had collected on his
travels. Recently transformed
in a £13 million development,
the museum now features a
music gallery, aquarium,
world culture displays and a
history gallery. There is a
good shop with toys that
represent the popular range
of the museum's collections.

Dulwich Picture Gallery ㉒

College Rd SE21. 🄵 020-8693
5254. ⊇ West Dulwich, North
Dulwich. **Open** 10am–5pm Tue–Fri,
11am–5pm Sat, Sun & bank hol
Mon. **Closed** all public hols (not
bank hol Mon). **Adm charge.** 📷
🖸 3pm Sat & Sun or by
arrangement. 🖐 🖵 🛈
www.dulwichpicturegallery.org.uk

England's oldest public art
gallery, it was opened in 1817
and designed by Sir John
Soane (see pp136–7). Its

**Rembrandt's Jacob II de Gheyn at
Dulwich Picture Gallery**

imaginative use of skylights made it the prototype of most art galleries built since. The gallery was originally commissioned to house the royal collection for the King of Poland. The superb collection has works by Rembrandt (his *Jacob II de Gheyn* has been stolen from here four times), Canaletto, Poussin, Watteau, Claude, Murillo and Raphael.

The building houses Soane's mausoleum to Desenfans and Bourgeois, who were the original founders of the collection.

Tennis racket and net from 1888, Wimbledon Lawn Tennis Museum

Battersea Park ㉓

Albert Bridge Rd SW11. **Map** 19 C5.
Tel 020-8871 7530. 🚇 *Sloane Sq then bus 137.* 🚌 *Battersea Pk.*
Open *dawn–dusk daily.* ♿ 🅿
Sports facilities.
See **Six Guided Walks** *pp266–7.*
www.batterseapark.org

Peace Pagoda, Battersea Park

This was the second public park created to relieve the growing urban stresses on Victorian Londoners (the first was Victoria Park in the East End). It opened in 1858 on the former Battersea Fields – a swampy area notorious for every kind of vice, centred around the Old Red House, a disreputable pub.

The new park immediately became popular, especially for its man-made boating lake, with its romantic rocks, gardens and waterfalls. Later it became a great site for the new craze of cycling.

In 1985 a peace pagoda was opened, a 35-m (100-ft) high monument built by Buddhist nuns and monks. There are also a small zoo, sports activities and an art gallery, the Pumphouse.

St Mary's, Battersea ㉔

Battersea Church Rd SW11. *Tel* 020-7228 9648. 🚇 *Sloane Sq then bus 19 or 219.* **Open** *daily by arrangement.* 🕐 *8.30am, 11am, 6.30pm Sun.* 📷 ♿ **Concerts.**
www.stmarysbattersea.org.uk

There has been a church here since at least the 10th century. The present brick building dates from 1775, but the 17th-century stained glass, commemorating Tudor monarchs, comes from the former church.

In 1782 the poet and artist William Blake was married in the church. Later J M W Turner was to paint some marvellous views of the Thames from the church tower. Benedict Arnold, who served George Washington in the American War of Independence, is buried in the crypt.

Wimbledon Lawn Tennis Museum ㉕

Church Rd SW19. *Tel* 020-8946 6131. 🚇 *Southfields.* **Open** *10.30am–5pm daily (not during championships except to ticket holders).* **Closed** *24–26 Dec, 1 Jan.* **Adm charge.** ♿ 📷 *call for times.* 🅿 🕐
www.wimbledon.org/museum

Even those with only a passing interest in the sport will find plenty to enjoy at this museum. It traces tennis's development from its invention in the 1860s as a diversion for country house parties, to the sport it is today. Alongside strange 19th-century equipment are

film clips showing the great players of the past. More recent matches may be viewed in the video theatre.

Wimbledon Windmill Museum ㉖

Windmill Rd SW19 *Tel* 020-8947 2825. 🚇 🚌 *Wimbledon then 30-min walk.* **Open** *Apr–Oct: 2–5pm Sat & public hols, 11am–5pm Sun (Nov–Mar: groups only, by arrangement).*
Adm charge. 📷 🅿 🕐 **www**.wimbledonwindmillmuseum.org.uk

The mill on Wimbledon Common was built in 1817. The building at its base was turned into cottages in 1864. Boy Scout founder Lord Baden-Powell lived in the mill house. Today the site is a museum.

St Mary's, Battersea

West of the Centre

Ham House

Richmond Park ⓲

Kingston Vale SW15. **Tel** 020-8948 3209. 🌐 🚇 Richmond then bus 65 or 71. **Open** daily until 30 mins before dusk. Oct–Feb: from 7.30am; Mar–Sep: from 7am. **www**.royalparks.gov.uk

Deer in Richmond Park

In 1637, Charles I built a wall 8 miles (13 km) round to enclose the royal park as a hunting ground. Today the park is a national nature reserve and deer still graze warily among the chestnuts, birches and oaks, no longer hunted but still discreetly culled. They have learned to co-exist with the thousands of human visitors who stroll here on fine weekends.

In late spring the highlight is the Isabella Plantation with its spectacular display of azaleas, while the nearby Pen Ponds are very popular with optimistic anglers. (Adam's Pond is for model boats.) The rest of the park is heath, bracken and trees (some of them hundreds of years old). Richmond Gate, in the north-west corner, was designed by the landscape gardener Capability Brown in 1798. Nearby is Henry VIII Mound,

where in 1536 the king, staying in Richmond Palace, awaited the signal that his former wife, Anne Boleyn, had been executed. The Palladian White Lodge, built in 1729, is home to the Royal Ballet School.

Hampton Court ⓲

See pp254–7.

Ham House ⓲

Ham St, Richmond. **Tel** 020-8940 1950. 🌐 🚇 Richmond then bus 65 or 371. **Open** Apr–Oct: 1–5pm Sat–Wed. **Adm charge.** 📷 by appt. ♿ 🚻 & 🏠 11am–5.30pm. **Gardens open** 11am–6pm. **www**.nationaltrust.org.uk

This magnificent house by the Thames was built in 1610 but had its heyday later, when it was the home of the Duke of Lauderdale, confidant to Charles II and Secretary of

Marble Hill House

State for Scotland. His wife, the Countess of Dysart, inherited the house from her father, who had been Charles I's "whipping boy" – meaning that he was punished for the future king's misdemeanours. From 1672 the Duke and Countess started to modernize the house, and it was soon regarded as one of the finest in Britain. The diarist John Evelyn admired their garden, which has now been restored to its 17th-century form.

On some days in summer, a foot passenger ferry runs from here to Marble Hill House and Orleans House at Twickenham.

Orleans House Gallery ⓲

Orleans Rd, Twickenham. **Tel** 020-8831 6000. 🌐 🚇 Richmond then bus 33, 90, 290, R68 or R70. **Open** Apr–Sep: 1–5.30pm Tue–Sat, 2–5.30pm Sun & bank hols; Oct–Mar: 1–4.30pm Tue–Sat, 2–4.30pm Sun & bank hols. **Closed** 24–26 Dec, 1 Jan, Good Fri. **Gardens open** 9am–dusk daily. ♿ limited. 🏠

This gallery is located on the site of the original Orleans House, named after Louis Philippe, Duke of Orleans, who lived there from 1815 to 1817. Adjacent is the Octagon Room, designed by James Gibbs for James Johnson in 1720. The gallery opened to the public in 1972, and shows temporary exhibitions, including local history displays.

Marble Hill House ⓲

Richmond Rd, Twickenham. **Tel** 020-8892 5115. 🌐 🚇 Richmond then bus 33, 90, 290, R68 or R70. **Open** Apr–Oct: 10am–2pm Sat, 10am–5pm Sun & bank hols; prebooked guided tours at other times (not Jan). ♿ restricted. 📷 🏠 🚻 🏠 **Concerts, fireworks** at weekends. See **Entertainment** p349. **www**.english-heritage.org.uk

Built in 1729 for George II's mistress, Henrietta Howard, the house and its grounds have been open to the public since 1903. It has now been fully restored to its Georgian appearance. There are paintings by William Hogarth and a view of the river and house in 1762 by Richard Wilson, who is regarded as the father of English landscape painting. The café is especially good.

Richmond ㉜

SW15. ☐ ☒ *Richmond.*

Richmond side street

This attractive London village took its name from the palace that Henry VII built here in 1500. Many early 18th-century houses survive near the river and off Richmond Hill, notably Maids of Honour Row, which was built in 1724. The beautiful view of the river from the top of the hill has been captured by many artists, and is largely unspoiled.

Syon House ㉝

London Rd, Brentford. **Tel** 020-8560 0881. ☐ *Gunnersbury then bus 237 or 267.* **House open** *mid-Mar–Oct: 11am–5pm Wed–Thu, Sun (last adm 4.15pm).* **House closed** *Nov–mid-Mar.* **Gardens open** *10.30am–5pm (or dusk, whichever is earlier) daily.* **Closed** *25–26 Dec.* **Adm charge**. ☐ ☐ ☐ ☐ ☐ ☐ *gardens only.* **www**.syonpark.co.uk

The Earls and Dukes of Northumberland have lived here for 400 years – it is the only large mansion in the London area still in its hereditary ownership. The interior of the house was remodelled in 1761 by Robert Adam, and is considered to be one of his masterpieces. The five Adam rooms house original furnishings and a significant collection of Old Master paintings. The 200 acre park was landscaped by Capability Brown, and includes a 40 acre garden with more than 200 species of rare trees. The Great Conservatory inspired Joseph Paxton's designs for the Crystal Palace.

Musical Museum ㉞

365 High St, Brentford. ☐ *020-8560 8108.* ☐ *Gunnersbury, South Ealing then bus 65, 237 or 267. Relocating to a building nearby in 2007. Call or check website for details.* **Adm charge**. ☐ ☐ ☐ ☐ **www** musicalmuseum.co.uk

The collection comprises chiefly large instruments, including player (or automatic) pianos and organs, miniature and cinema pianos, and what is thought to be the only surviving self-playing Wurlitzer organ in Europe.

Drawing room: Osterley Park House

Osterley Park House ㉟

Isleworth. ☐ *020-8232 5050.* ☐ *Osterley.* **Open** *Mar: 1–4.30pm Sat & Sun; Apr–Oct: 1–4.30pm Wed–Sun.* **Closed** *Good Fri.* **Adm charge**. ☐ ☐ **Garden open** *9am–dusk daily.* **www**.nationaltrust.org.uk

Osterley is ranked among Robert Adam's finest works, and its colonnaded portico and elegant library ceiling are the proof. Much of the furniture is by Adam, and the garden and temple are by William Chambers, architect of Somerset House. The garden house is by Adam.

Robert Adam's red drawing room at Syon House

Hampton Court ㉘

Ceiling decoration from the Queen's Drawing Room

Cardinal Wolsey, powerful Archbishop of York to Henry VIII, began building Hampton Court in 1514. Originally it was not a royal palace, but was intended as Wolsey's riverside country house. Later, in 1528, in the hope of retaining royal favour, Wolsey offered it to the king. After the royal takeover, Hampton Court was twice rebuilt and extended, first by Henry himself and then, in the 1690s, by William and Mary, who employed Christopher Wren as architect.

There is a striking contrast between Wren's Classical royal apartments and the Tudor turrets, gables and chimneys elsewhere. The inspiration for the gardens as they are today comes largely from the time of William and Mary, for whom Wren created a vast, formal Baroque landscape, with radiating avenues of majestic limes and many collections of exotic plants.

★ The Maze
Lose yourself in one of the garden's most popular features.

Royal tennis court

River boat pier

Main entrance

River Thames

Privy Garden

★ The Great Vine
The vine was planted in 1768, and, in the 19th century, produced up to 910 kg (2,000 lbs) of black grapes.

The Pond Garden
This sunken garden was once a pond to store fresh fish for Henry VIII's Court.

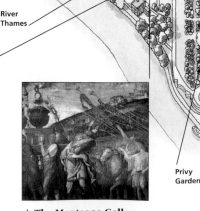

★ The Mantegna Gallery
Andrea Mantegna's nine canvases depicting The Triumphs of Caesar *(1490s) are housed here.*

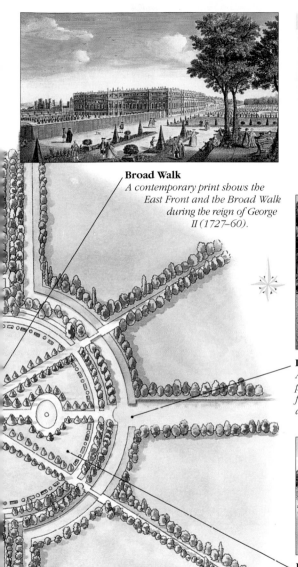

VISITORS' CHECKLIST

Surrey KT8 9AU. ☎ 0870-752
7777. 🚌 111, 216, 267, 411,
440. 🚆 Hampton Court.
🚤 Hampton Court pier. Open
Apr–Oct: 10am–6pm daily; Nov–
Mar: 10am–4.30pm daily (last
adm: 1 hour before closing).
Closed 24–26 Dec. Adm
charge. ♿ 🎫 📷 🍴 🎁
www.hrp.org.uk

Broad Walk
*A contemporary print shows the
East Front and the Broad Walk
during the reign of George
II (1727–60).*

Long Water
*A man-made lake runs
parallel to the Thames,
from the Fountain Garden
across the Home Park.*

Fountain Garden
*A few of the clipped yews
here were planted in the
reign of William and Mary.*

The East Front
*The windows of the
Queen's Drawing
Room, designed by
Wren, overlook the
central avenue of the
Fountain Garden.*

STAR FEATURES

★ The Great Vine

★ The Mantegna
    Gallery

★ The Maze

Exploring the Palace

Carving on the roof of the Great Hall

As an historic royal palace, Hampton Court bears traces of many of the kings and queens of England from Henry VIII to the present day. The building itself is a harmonious blend of Tudor and English Baroque architecture. Inside, visitors can see the Great Hall, built by Henry VIII, as well as state apartments of the Tudor court. Many of the Baroque state apartments, including those above Fountain Court by Christopher Wren, are decorated with furniture, tapestries and old masters from the Royal Collection.

Tudor Chimneys
Ornate chimneys, some original, some careful restorations, adorn the roof of the Tudor palace.

Queen's Presence Chamber

Queen's Guard Chamber

★ **Chapel Royal**
The Tudor chapel was re-fitted by Wren except for the carved and gilded vaulted ceiling.

Haunted Gallery

★ **Great Hall**
The stained-glass window in the Tudor Great Hall shows Henry VIII flanked by the coats of arms of his six wives.

STAR FEATURES

★ Great Hall

★ Fountain Court

★ Clock Court

★ Chapel Royal

★ **Clock Court**
Anne Boleyn's Gateway is at the entrance to Clock Court. The Astronomical Clock, created for Henry VIII in 1540, is also located here.

King's Great Bedchamber

William III bought the crimson bed from his Lord Chamberlain.

Wren's east facade

CARDINAL WOLSEY

Thomas Wolsey (c.1475–1530), simultaneously a cardinal, Archbishop of York and chancellor, was, after the king, the most powerful man in England. However, when he was unable to persuade the pope to allow Henry VIII to divorce his first wife, Catherine of Aragon, Wolsey fell from royal favour. He died while making his way to face trial for treason.

Queen's Gallery

This marble chimneypiece by John Nost adorns the Queen's Gallery, where entertainments were often staged.

★ Fountain Court

The windows of state apartments are visible above the cloisters of Fountain Court.

King's Staircase

Leading to the state apartments, the King's Staircase has wall paintings by Antonio Verrio.

TIMELINE

1514 Construction of palace begins		**1734** William Kent decorates the Queen's Staircase	**1838** Public first admitted to the palace	**1986** State apartments partly damaged by fire
1532 Henry starts new hall	**1647** Charles I imprisoned by Cromwell			
1500	1600	1700	1800	1900
1528 Wolsey gives the palace to Henry VIII	**1689** William and Mary move to Hampton Court	**1773** Great Gatehouse reduced by two storeys	**1992** Damaged apartments are reopened	
Henry VIII painted by Hans Holbein	**c. 1727** Queen's apartments are finally completed			

PM Gallery and House ㊱

Mattock Lane W5. **Tel** *020-8567 1227.* ⊖ *Ealing Broadway.* **Open** *1–5pm Tue–Fri, 11am–5pm Sat (also May–Sep: 1–5pm Sun).* **Closed** *public hols.* ⊙ ⓓ **Exhibitions**.

Sir John Soane, architect of the Bank of England *(see p147)*, designed this house, Pitzhanger Manor, on the site of an earlier one. Completed in 1803, it was to become his own country residence. There are clear echoes of his elaborately constructed town house in Lincoln's Inn Fields *(see pp136–7)*, especially in the library, with its imaginative use of mirrors, in the darkly-painted breakfast room opposite and in the "monk's dining room" which is located on the basement level.

Soane retained two of the principal formal rooms: the drawing room and the dining room. These were designed in 1768 by George Dance the Younger, with whom Soane had worked before establishing his own reputation.

A sympathetic 20th-century extension has been refurbished as a gallery offering a wide range of contemporary art exhibitions and associated events. The house also contains a large exhibition of Martinware, highly decorated glazed pottery made in nearby Southall between 1877 and 1915 and fashionable in late Victorian times. The gardens of Pitzhanger Manor are now a pleasant public park and offer a welcome contrast to the bustle of nearby Ealing.

Martinware bird at PM Gallery

Kew Bridge Steam Museum ㊲

Green Dragon Lane, Brentford. **Tel** *020-8568 4757.* ⊖ *Kew Bridge, Gunnersbury then bus 237 or 267.* **Open** *11am–5pm Tue–Sat.* **Closed** *two weeks at Christmas, Good Fri.* **Adm charge.** ⊠ *book ahead.* ⊡ *Sat & Sun.* ⊡ ⓓ www.kbsm.org

The 19th-century water pumping station, near the north end of Kew Bridge, is now a museum of steam power and water in London. Its main exhibits are five giant Cornish beam engines, which used to pump the water here from the river, to be distributed in London. The earliest engines, dating from 1820, are similar to those designed to pump water out of the Cornish mines. See them in operation at weekends and on public holidays.

Kew Gardens ㊳

See pp260–61.

City Barge: Strand on the Green

Strand on the Green ㊴

W4. ⊖ *Gunnersbury then bus 237 or 267.* ⊟ *Kew Bridge.*

This charming Thames-side walk passes some fine 18th-century houses as well as rows of more modest cottages once inhabited by fishermen. The oldest of its three pubs is the City Barge *(see pp316–19)*, parts of which date from the 15th century: the name is older and derives from the time when the Lord Mayor's barge was moored on the Thames outside.

Chiswick House ㊵

Burlington Lane W4. **Tel** *020-8995 0508.* ⊖ *Chiswick.* **Open** *Apr–Oct: 10am–5pm Wed–Sun & bank hols (till 2pm Sat); Nov–Mar: pre-booked visits only.* **Adm charge.** ⓓ *phone ahead.* ⊡ ⓗ www.english-heritage.org.uk

Completed in 1729 to the design of its owner, the third Earl of Burlington, this is a fine example of a Palladian villa. Burlington revered both

Chiswick House

Palladio and his disciple Inigo Jones, and their statues stand outside. Built round a central octagonal room, the house is packed with references to ancient Rome and Renaissance Italy, as is the garden.

Chiswick was Burlington's country residence and this house was built as an annexe to a larger, older house (since demolished). It was designed for recreation and entertaining – Lord Hervey, Burlington's enemy, dismissed it as "too little to live in and too big to hang on a watch chain". Some of the ceiling paintings are by William Kent, who also contributed to the garden design.

The house was a private mental home from 1892 until 1928, when a long process of restoration began. The restorers are continually searching for pieces of its original furniture, but the layout of the garden, now a public park, is much as Burlington designed it.

Plaque on Hogarth's House

Hogarth's House ④

Hogarth Lane, W4. **Tel** *020-8994 6757.* 🚇 *Turnham Green.* **Open** *Apr–Oct: 1–5pm Tue–Fri, 1–6pm Sat, Sun; Nov–Dec & Feb–Mar: 1–4pm Tue–Fri, 1–5pm Sat, Sun.* **Closed** *Jan.* 📷 🚫 & *ground floor only.* 🏠

When the painter William Hogarth lived here from 1749 until his death in 1764, he called it "a little country box by the Thames" and painted bucolic views from its windows – he had moved from Leicester Square (*see p103*). Today heavy traffic roars by along the Great West Road, on its way to and from Heathrow Airport – rush hour traffic is also notoriously bad here. In an environment as

hostile as this, and following years of neglect and then bombing during World War II, the house has done well to survive. It has now been turned into a small museum and gallery, which is filled mostly with a collection of engraved copies of the moralistic cartoon-style pictures with which Hogarth made his name. Salutary tales, such as *The Rake's Progress* (in Sir John Soane's Museum – *see pp136–7*), *Marriage à la Mode, An Election Entertainment* and many others, can all be seen here.

Fulham Palace ②

Bishops Ave SW6. **Tel** *020-7736 3233.* 🚇 *Putney Bridge.* **Open** *(phone to check due to restoration works) Mar–Oct: 2–5pm Wed–Sun, public hol Mon; Nov–Mar: 1–4pm Thu–Sun.* **Closed** *Good Fri, 25 & 26 Dec.* **Park open** *daylight hrs.* & 🚫 🏠 *Events, concerts, lectures.*

The home of the Bishops of London from the 8th century until 1973, the oldest surviving parts of Fulham Palace date from the 15th century. The palace stands in its own landscaped gardens northwest of Putney Bridge. Restoration work on a grand 18th-century Rococo room is due for completion during 2006.

Attractive residential and leisure development in Chelsea Harbour

Chelsea Harbour ㊽

SW10. 🚇 *Fulham Broadway.* & *Exhibitions.* 🖼 🏠

This is an impressive development of modern apartments, shops, offices, restaurants, a hotel and a marina. It is near the site of Cremorne Pleasure Gardens, which closed in 1877 after more than 40 years as a venue for dances and circuses. The centrepiece is the Belvedere, a 20-storey apartment tower with an external glass lift and pyramid roof, topped with a golden ball on a rod that rises and falls with the tide.

Eye-catching entrance to Fulham Palace dating from Tudor times

Kew Gardens ㊳

The Royal Botanic Gardens at Kew are a World Heritage Site and the most complete public gardens in the world. Their reputation was first established by Sir Joseph Banks, the British naturalist and plant hunter, who worked here in the late 18th century. In 1841 the former royal gardens were given to the nation and now display about 40,000 different kinds of plants. Kew is also a centre for scholarly research and garden enthusiasts will want a full day for their visit.

Princess Augusta
King George III's mother established the first garden on a nine-acre (3.6 ha) site here in 1759.

Queen Charlotte's Cottage

River Thames

HIGHLIGHTS

Spring
Cherry Walk ①
Crocus "carpet" ②

Summer
Rock Garden ③
Rose Garden ④

Autumn
Autumn foliage ⑤

Winter
Winter Garden ⑥
Witch Hazels ⑦

★ Pagoda
Britain's fascination with the Orient influenced William Chambers's pagoda, built in 1762.

Lion Gate entrance

Evolution House
gives a detailed history of plant life on Earth.

Flagpole

STAR SIGHTS

★ Temperate House

★ Pagoda

★ Palm House

★ Temperate House
The building dates from 1899. Delicate woody plants are arranged here according to their geographical origins.

Minka House
This minka (traditional wooden Japanese house), built around 1900, was shipped from Japan and reconstructed in the Bamboo Garden in 2001.

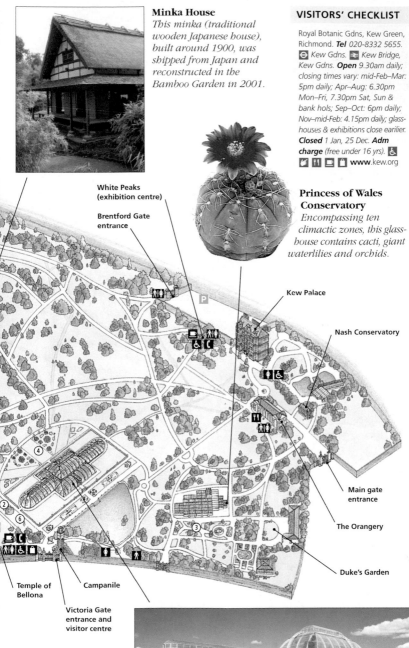

Princess of Wales Conservatory
Encompassing ten climactic zones, this glasshouse contains cacti, giant waterlilies and orchids.

White Peaks (exhibition centre)

Brentford Gate entrance

Kew Palace

Nash Conservatory

Main gate entrance

The Orangery

Duke's Garden

Temple of Bellona

Campanile

Victoria Gate entrance and visitor centre

★ Palm House
Designed by Decimus Burton in the 1840s, this famous jewel of Victorian engineering houses exotic plants in tropical conditions.

SIX GUIDED WALKS

London is an excellent city for walkers. Although it is much more spread out than most European capitals, many of the main tourist attractions are fairly close to each other *(see pp14–15)*. Central London is full of parks and gardens *(see pp48–51)*, and there are also several walk routes planned by the tourist board and local history societies. These include footpaths along canals and the Thames, and the Silver Jubilee Walk. Planned in 1977 to commemorate the Queen's Silver Jubilee, the walk runs for 12 miles (19 km) between Lambeth Bridge in the west and Tower Bridge in the east; the London Tourist Board *(see p363)* has maps of the route, which is marked by silver-coloured plaques placed at intervals on the pavement.

Statue of boy and dolphin in Regent's Park

Each of the 16 areas described in the *Area-by-Area* section of this book has a short walk marked on its *Street-by-Street* map. These walks will take you past many of the most interesting sights in that area. On the following twelve pages are routes for six walks that take you through areas of London not covered in detail elsewhere. These range from the bustling, fashionable King's Road *(see pp266–7)* to the wide open spaces of riverside Richmond and Kew *(see pp268–9)*.

Several companies offer guided walks *(see below)*. Most of these have themes, such as ghosts or Shakespeare's London. Look in listings magazines *(see p342)* for details.

USEFUL NUMBERS The Original London Walks
Tel 020-7624 3978. **www**.walks.com

CHOOSING A WALK

The Six Walks
This map shows the location of the six guided walks in relation to the main sightseeing areas of London.

King's Road, Chelsea

Regent's Canal *(pp264–5)*

Mayfair *(pp270–1)*

Strand on the Green, Kew

Notting Hill *(pp274–5)*

South Bank *(pp272–3)*

Chelsea and Battersea *(pp266–7)*

Richmond and Kew *(pp268–9)*

0 kilometres 4

0 miles 2

KEY

.... Walk route

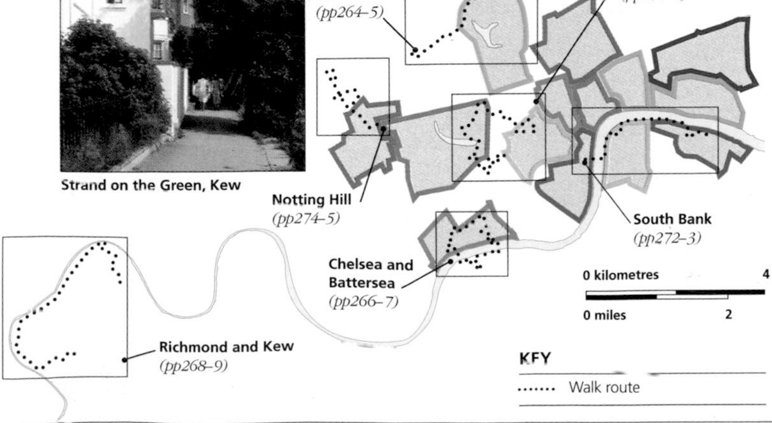

◁ Houseboats on Regent's Canal, Little Venice

A Two-Hour Walk along the Regent's Canal

Master builder John Nash wanted the Regent's Canal to pass through Regent's Park, but instead it circles north of the park. Opened in 1820, it is long defunct as a commercial waterway but is today a valuable leisure amenity. This walk starts at Little Venice and ends at Camden Lock market, diverting briefly to take in the view from Primrose Hill. For more details on the sights near the Regent's Canal, see pages 220–27.

Houseboat on the canal ③

From Little Venice to Lisson Grove

At Warwick Avenue station ① take the left-hand exit and walk straight to the traffic lights by the canal bridge at Blomfield Road. Turn right and descend to the canal through an iron gate ② opposite No. 42, marked "Lady Rose of Regent". The pretty basin with moored narrow boats is Little Venice ③. At the foot of the steps turn left to walk back beneath the blue iron bridge ④. You soon have to climb up to street level again because this stretch of the towpath is reserved for access to the

The Warwick Castle, near Warwick Avenue

barges. Cross Edgware Road and walk down Aberdeen Place. When the road turns to the left by a pub, Crockers ⑤, follow the signposted Canal Way down to the right of some modern flats. Continue your route along the canal towpath, crossing Park Road at street level. The scenery along this stretch is unremarkable, but it is not long before a splash of green to your right announces that you are now walking alongside Regent's Park ⑥.

Houseboats moored at Little Venice ③

KEY

••• Walk route
🌿 Good viewing point
Ⓔ Underground station
🚉 Railway station

TIPS FOR WALKERS

Starting point: Warwick Avenue Underground station.
Length: 3 miles (5 km).
Getting there: Warwick Avenue and Camden Town Underground stations are at either end of the walk. Buses 16, 16A and 98 go to Warwick Avenue; 24, 29 and 31 go to Camden Town.
Stopping-off points: Crockers, Queens and The Princess of Wales (corner of Fitzroy and Chalcot Roads) are good pubs. At the junction of Edgware Road and Aberdeen Place is Café La Ville. Camden Town has many cafés, restaurants and sandwich shops.

Regent's Park

Soon you see four mansions ⑦. A bridge on huge pillars marked "Coalbrookdale" ⑧ carries Avenue Road into the park. Cross the next bridge, with London Zoo ⑨ on your right, then turn left up a slope. A few steps later, take the right fork, and turn left to cross Prince Albert Road. Turn right before entering Primrose Hill through a gate ⑩ on your left.

Mansion with riverside gardens ⑦

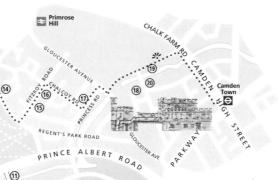

Indoor market, Camden Lock ⑲

Towards Camden
Almost opposite the gate is the Queens ⑬, a Victorian pub and, just to the left, is No. 122 Regent's Park Road ⑭. This was for 24 years the home of the communist philosopher Friedrich Engels; he was often visited there by his friend Karl Marx.

Turn right and walk down Regent's Park Road for 135 m (150 yd) then turn left up Fitzroy Road. On the right, between Nos. 41 and 39, is the entrance to Primrose Hill Studios ⑮, built in 1882. Residents have included the musician Sir Henry Wood and illustrator Arthur Rackham, famous for his fairy pictures.

Continue down Fitzroy Road past No. 23 ⑯, once home to the poet W B Yeats, then go right into Chalcot Road and left down Princess Road, past a Victorian board school ⑰. Turn right and rejoin the canal down steps across Gloucester Avenue. Turn left under the railway bridge and past the Pirate Castle ⑱, a water sports centre. Cross a hump bridge and enter Camden Lock Market ⑲ (see p332) through an arch on your left. After browsing there you can take the water bus ⑳ back to Little Venice or turn right into Chalk Farm Road and walk up to Camden Town Underground station.

Primrose Lodge, Primrose Hill ⑩

Primrose Hill
From here there is a view of the zoo aviary ⑪, designed by Lord Snowdon and opened in 1965. Inside the park, keep to the left-hand path that climbs to the top of the hill. Soon you fork right to the summit, which offers a fine view of the city skyline. A viewing panel ⑫ helps identify the landmarks but it does not include the 1990 skyscraper at Canary Wharf, with its pyramid crown, on the left. Descend on the left, making for the park gate at the junction of Regent's Park Road and Primrose Hill Road.

Pedestrian bridge over the canal at Camden Lock ⑲

A Three-Hour Walk in Chelsea and Battersea

This delightful circular walk ambles through the grounds of the Royal Hospital and across the river to Battersea Park, with its romantic Victorian landscaping. It then returns to the narrow village streets of Chelsea and the stylish shops on the King's Road. For more details on the sights in Chelsea see pages 192–7.

Royal Hospital ③

Sloane Square to Battersea Park

From the station ①, turn left and walk down Holbein Place. The Renaissance painter's connection with Chelsea stems from his friendship with Sir Thomas More who lived nearby. Pass the cluster of good antique shops ② as

you turn on to Royal Hospital Road. Enter the grounds of the Royal Hospital ③, designed by Christopher Wren, and turn left into the informal Ranelagh Gardens ④. The small pavilion by John Soane ⑤ displays a history of the gardens as a Georgian pleasure resort – it was the most fashionable meeting place for London society.

Charles II statue in Royal Hospital ⑥

Galleon on Chelsea Bridge

Leave the gardens for fine views of the hospital and Grinling Gibbons's bronze of Charles II ⑥. The granite obelisk ⑦ commemorates the 1849 battle at Chilianwalla, in what is now Pakistan, and forms the centre-piece of the main marquee at the Chelsea Flower Show (see p56).

Battersea Park

When crossing the Chelsea Bridge ⑧ (1937), look up at the four gilded galleons on top of the pillars at each end. Turn into Battersea Park ⑨ (see p251), one of London's liveliest, and follow the main path along the river to enjoy the excellent views of Chelsea. Turn left at the exotic Buddhist Peace Pagoda ⑩ to the main part of the park.

Past the bowling greens lies Henry Moore's carving of *Three Standing Figures* ⑪ (1948) and the lake, a favoured spot for wildfowl. (There are boats for hire.) Just beyond the sculpture head northwest and, after crossing the central avenue, fork right and make for the wooden gate into the rustic Old English Garden ⑫. Leave the garden by the metal gate and return to Chelsea via the Victorian Albert Bridge ⑬.

TIPS FOR WALKERS

Starting point: Sloane Square.
Length: 4 miles (6.5 km).
Getting there: Sloane Square is the nearest tube. There are frequent buses 11, 19, 22 and 349 to Sloane Square and along the King's Road.
Royal Hospital Grounds are open only 10am–6pm Mon–Sat, 2–6pm Sun.
Stopping-off points: There is a café in Battersea Park, by the lake. The Eight Bells, on Cheyne Walk, is a well-known local pub. There are several other pubs, restaurants and sandwich shops to be found along the King's Road. The Chelsea Farmers' Market on Sydney Street has several cafés.

Three Standing Figures by Henry Moore ⑪

KEY

••• Walk route

✹ Good viewing point

Ⓔ Underground station

Old English Garden in Battersea Park ⑫

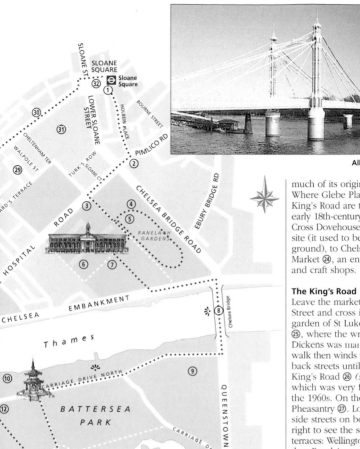

Albert Bridge ⑬

much of its original character. Where Glebe Place meets the King's Road are three pretty, early 18th-century houses ㉓. Cross Dovehouse Green opposite (it used to be a burial ground), to Chelsea Farmers' Market ㉔, an enclave of cafés and craft shops.

The King's Road

Leave the market on Sydney Street and cross into the garden of St Luke's Church ㉕, where the writer Charles Dickens was married. The walk then winds through pretty back streets until it rejoins the King's Road ㉖ (see p196), which was very fashionable in the 1960s. On the left is The Pheasantry ㉗. Look down the side streets on both left and right to see the squares and terraces: Wellington Square ㉘, then Royal Avenue ㉙, intended as a triumphal way to the Royal Hospital, and Blacklands Terrace ㉚, where book-lovers will want to visit John Sandoe's shop. The Duke of York's Territorial Headquarters ㉛ (1803) on the right – now home to the Saatchi Gallery – marks the approach to Sloane Square ㉜ and the Royal Court Theatre (see Sloane Square p197).

its carving by Jacob Epstein. Just beyond these is the old, medieval Crosby Hall ⑲. Justice Walk ⑳ has a nice view of two early Georgian houses – Duke's House and Monmouth House. Turn left to pass the site of the Chelsea porcelain factory ㉑, which used to make highly fashionable (and today very highly collectable) wares in the late 18th century. Glebe Place ㉒ has retained

Thomas Carlyle statue ⑮

The Back Streets of Chelsea

Over the bridge is David Wynne's sculpture of a boy and dolphin ⑭ (1975). Pass the sought-after residences on Cheyne Walk and the statues of historian Thomas Carlyle ⑮, and Sir Thomas More ⑯. The area was renowned for gatherings of intellectuals. Past Chelsea Old Church ⑰ is Roper's Gardens ⑱ with

Royal Court Theatre ㉜

A 90-Minute Walk around Richmond and Kew

This delightful riverside walk begins in historic Richmond by the remains of Henry VII's once-splendid palace and ends at Kew, Britain's premier botanic garden. For more details on the sights in Richmond and Kew, turn to pages 252–8.

The river at low tide

Richmond Green

From Richmond station ①, proceed to Oriel House ②, which is practically opposite. Take the alleyway beneath it, and turn left towards the red-brick and terracotta Richmond Theatre ③, built in 1899. The remarkable Edmund Kean, whose brief, meteoric career in the early 19th century had a lasting impact on English acting, was closely associated with the previous theatre on the site. Opposite is Richmond Green ④. Cross it diagonally and go through the entrance arch ⑤ of the old Tudor palace, which is adorned with the arms of Henry VII.

Old Palace: carving over entrance ⑤

contain remnants, much modified, of the 16th-century buildings.

Leave Old Palace Yard at the right-hand corner ⑥, following a sign "To the River", and turn left to pass the White Swan pub ⑦. At the river, go right along the towpath under the iron railway bridge and then the concrete Twickenham Bridge ⑧, completed in 1933, to reach Richmond Lock ⑨, with its cast-iron footbridge built in 1894. The Thames is tidal as far as Teddington, some 3 miles (5 km) upstream, and the lock is used to make the river continuously navigable.

The Riverside

Do not cross the bridge but continue along the wooded path by the river to Isleworth Ait ⑩, a large island where herons may be standing warily on the river bank. Just beyond it, on the far shore, is All Saints' Church ⑪, where the 15th-century tower has survived several rebuildings, most recently in the 1960s. Further round the inlet, Isleworth ⑫, once a small riverside village with a busy harbour, is now a dormitory for central London. Here there is river traffic to watch: barges, yachts and, in summer, the passenger boats that ply up-river to Hampton Court (see pp254–7). Rowers are out at most times of year, training for races. The most prestigious occasions are the Henley Regatta in July and the Oxford v Cambridge boat race, every spring from Putney to Mortlake (see p56).

Richmond Theatre ③

Richmond

Richmond owes much of its importance – as well as its name – to Henry, victor of the Wars of the Roses and the first Tudor monarch. On becoming king in 1485 he spent a lot of time at an earlier residence on this site, Sheen Palace, dating from the 12th century. The palace burned down in 1499 and Henry had it rebuilt, naming it Richmond after the town in Yorkshire where he held an earldom. In 1603 Henry's granddaughter, Elizabeth I, died here. The houses inside the archway on the left

Herons fish the river

HIGH ST

LONDON ROAD

SYON PARK

Thames

King's Observatory

OL

TWICKEN

Twickenham Bridge

THE AVENUE

KEY

•••	Walk route
⚐	Good viewing point
⊖	Underground station
🚆	Railway station

Kew

After a while the appearance of iron railings on your right marks where Old Deer Park ⑬ turns into Kew Gardens ⑭ (officially known as the Royal Botanic Gardens – *see pp260–61*). There used to be a riverside entrance for visitors arriving on foot or by water, but the gate ⑮ is now

Kew Palace in Kew Gardens ⑲

Just beyond are modern waterside apartments at Brentford ⑰. This was originally an industrial suburb, sited where the Grand Union Canal runs into the Thames, and its residential potential has only recently been exploited. You can pick out the tall chimney of the waterworks ⑱, now a museum dedicated to steam power. On the right, behind the Kew Gardens car park, there is soon a view of Kew Palace ⑲, now fully restored and open to the public.

Beyond the car park, leave the river by Ferry Lane on to Kew Green ⑳. Now you could spend the rest of the day in Kew Gardens or cross Kew Bridge and turn right on to Strand on the Green ㉑, a fine riverside walkway with atmospheric pubs, the oldest of them the City Barge ㉒. Head south down Kew Road if you need to get back, then turn left at Kew Gardens Road to depart from Kew Gardens Underground station (District line).

TIPS FOR WALKERS

Starting point: Richmond station, District Line.
Length: 3 miles (5 km).
Getting there: Richmond Underground or railway station. Bus 415 comes from Victoria; 391 and R68 from Kew.
Stopping-off points: There are many cafés, pubs and tearooms in Richmond. The famous Maids of Honour tearoom is at Kew, as is Jasper's Bun in the Oven, a good restaurant.

Steam Museum ⑱

| 0 metres | 500 |
| 0 yards | 500 |

closed and the nearest entrance is to the north, near the car park.

Across the river, there are magnificent views of Syon House ⑯, seat of the Dukes of Northumberland since 1594. Part of the present house dates from the 16th century but it was largely redesigned by Robert Adam in the 1760s. You are looking at it across the garden Capability Brown laid out in the 18th century.

The river bank between Richmond and Kew

A Two-Hour Walk Through Mayfair to Belgravia

This walk takes you from Green Park to Hyde Park, through the hearts of Mayfair and Belgravia, two of London's most elegant Georgian residential districts. It includes a bracing stroll through Hyde Park and, if you're feeling energetic, a row on the Serpentine.

L'Artiste Musclé restaurant, Shepherd Market, Mayfair

Green Park to Berkeley Square

Exit Green Park station ① following the signs for Piccadilly North. With Green Park opposite you, turn left. Pass Devonshire House ②, a 1920s office block that replaced the 18th-century mansion designed by William Kent. Only Kent's gates survive, now at the park entrance across Piccadilly. Turn left and walk up Berkeley Street to Berkeley Square ③. To the south, Lansdowne House by Robert Adam has been replaced by an advertising agency ④.

Berkeley Square statue ③

TIPS FOR WALKERS

Starting point: *Green Park Underground station.*
Length: *3 miles (5 km)*
Getting there: *Green Park is on the Victoria, Jubilee and Piccadilly Underground Lines. Or take bus Nos. 9, 14, 19, 22, 25 and 38 and go to Green Park underground station entrance.*
Stopping-off points: *There are numerous pubs, cafés and eateries in the area. Dell Café on the Serpentine is open 8am–8pm.*

There are still a few splendid 18th-century houses to the west, including No. 45 ⑤, home of the soldier and governor, Lord Clive of India.

Mayfair

Keep to the south of the square and turn into Charles Street, noting the evocative lampholders at Nos. 40 and 41 ⑥. Turn left into Queen Street and cross Curzon Street to enter Shepherd Market ⑦ *(see p97)* through Curzonfield House alleyway. Turn right up a pedestrian-only street then right onto Hertford Street, passing the Curzon Cinema ⑧ on the corner of Curzon Street. Here you are almost facing Crewe House ⑨, built in 1730 by Edward Shepherd who also laid out the market.

Turn left and walk up Curzon Street, then turn right onto Chesterfield Street. A left turn at Charles Street brings you to Red Lion Yard ⑩, where a pub stands opposite one of the few weatherboarded buildings in the West End. Turn right into Hay's Mews and left up Chesterfield Hill. Cross Hill Street and South Street and head left until you reach an alley leading to the peaceful haven of Mount Street Gardens ⑪. The gardens back on to the Church of the Immaculate Conception ⑫. Cross the garden and turn left

Berkeley Square, with its ancient plane trees and Georgian houses

| 0 metres | 400 |
| 0 yards | 400 |

Memorial in Grosvenor Square ⑬

General of the Army
Dwight D. Eisenhower
Commander in Chief
Allied Force
June–November 1942
Supreme Commander
Allied Expeditionary Force
January–March 1944

onto Mount Street; then right onto South Audley Street and left at Grosvenor Square ⑬ into Upper Grosvenor Street, passing to the left of the US Embassy. Look out for the statue of Franklin D Roosevelt. Turn right up Park

Official supplier to the royal family: royal coat of arms above the door

Lane and walk past houses that are the remnants of what used to be the city's most desirable residential street before the traffic got so heavy ⑭. At the end you can see Marble Arch *(see p211)*.

Hyde Park

Enter the pedestrian subway ⑮ at exit No. 6 and follow signs for Park Lane West Side, exit No. 5. You will emerge at Speakers' Corner ⑯ *(see p211)*, where on Sundays anyone can make a speech on any topic. Cross Hyde Park *(see p211)* south-

southwest, enjoying the views on all sides, and make for the boat house ⑰ on the Serpentine (an artificial lake created by Queen Caroline in 1730), where you rent a rowing boat. Turn left and follow the path to the Dell Café ⑱ for some refreshments. From there, take the stone bridge ⑲ and cross Rotten Row ⑳, where the very fashionable exercise their horses. Leave the park at Edinburgh Gate ㉑.

Speakers' Corner ⑯

eccentric structure fronted by colossal Doric columns, built in 1830. A path beside it leads to Halkin Arcade ㉔, built in the 1830s and adorned by Geoffrey Wickham's fountain built in 1971.

Belgravia

Turn left out of the arcade onto Kinnerton Street, which boasts one of London's smallest pubs, the Nag's Head ㉕. A street of pretty mews houses runs off to the left of this street at its northern end: look for Ann's Close and Kinnerton Place North. Almost opposite the latter, the street makes a sharp right turn to emerge into Wilton Place opposite St Paul's Church (1843). Turn right here and follow Wilton Crescent round to the left before turning left into Wilton Row, where there is another small pub, the Grenadier ㉖, once the officers' mess of the Guards' barracks and reputedly frequented by the Duke of Wellington. Up Old Barracks Yard to its right there are some old officers' billets and a worn stone said to have been used by the Iron Duke when mounting his horses. The alley leads to a T junction. To finish the walk, turn right onto Grosvenor Crescent Mews, then left onto Grosvenor Crescent, which leads you to Hyde Park Corner Underground station.

The Serpentine, on a fine day ⑰

Knightsbridge

Cross Knightsbridge and, resisting the temptations of two of London's great department stores – Harvey Nichols ㉒ and Harrods ㉓ *(see p207)* on Brompton Road – head down Sloane Street to turn left at Harriet Street. At Lowndes Square turn right and leave the square on the far side, turning left into Motcomb Street. On your left is the Pantechnicon, an

Once the officers' mess, now the Grenadier pub, Belgravia ㉖

A 90-Minute Walk Along the South Bank

The Riverside Walk along the South Bank from
Westminster Bridge (see page 186) via Bankside to
Southwark Cathedral is one of the most entertaining
excursions in town. From County Hall to Shakespeare's
Globe, with the South Bank's well-known music,
theatre and film venues, the shops and galleries of
Gabriel's Wharf and the Oxo Tower, there's something
for everyone. For more details on the sights in
Southwark and Bankside, see pages 173–83.

The Saatchi Gallery in County Hall ③

Westminster

Begin at Westminster station
① by the statue of Queen
Boudica (or Boadicea), and
walk over Westminster
Bridge. Once on the south
side ②, there is a fine view
back over the river to the
Houses of Parliament (see
pp72–3). The main
building on this side is
the former County
Hall ③, now offering
a range of
entertainment (see
p188). There's the
Saatchi Gallery for
cutting-edge British
Art, Dalí Universe for
a glimpse of the Surreal,
the Aquarium ④ to see the
underwater world, and
Namco Station, a games hall
with computer games, cars

what's showing at the
Hayward Gallery ⑩ (see
p188) too, just beyond, on
the level above. Moving on
along the Riverside Walk, past
Waterloo Bridge, you reach the
National Film Theatre ⑪ (see
p347) where films are shown
throughout the day. Outside
its lively café, rows of tables
stacked with second-hand
books shelter beneath the
bridge. The Royal National
Theatre ⑫ (see p188) also
has exhibitions and musical
events as well as

and pool tables. Outside the
Saatchi Gallery, bungee
bouncing on trampolines can
be tried. For the best city view,
British Airways London Eye
⑤ (see p189) is beside
Jubilee Gardens ⑥, where
buskers and mime artists
perform. Walk past
Hungerford Bridge ⑦ with its
modern walkways and trains
to Charing Cross Station, on
the site of the former
Hungerford market. Ahead is
the South Bank Centre ⑧ (see
pp186–7), the capital's main
arts showcase. Music and
exhibitions fill the Royal
Festival Hall ⑨ (see p188),
created for the Festival of
Britain in 1951. Check to see

View from the Oxo Tower ⑮

a good bookshop, while in
summer there are free
outdoor performances. Past
London Television Centre ⑬
is Gabriel's Wharf ⑭ (see
p191), a pleasant diversion of
art and craft shops.

The Oxo Tower

The next landmark you come
to is the Oxo Tower ⑮, a red-

TIPS FOR WALKERS

Starting point: Westminster
Bridge.
Length: 1.75 miles (2.75 km)
Getting there: Westminster
Underground station on the
District, Circle and Jubilee lines.
Stopping off points: All the
South Bank's art centres have
cafés, bars and restaurants. Also:
Gourmet Pizza, Gabriel's Wharf;
EAT, Riverside House (snacks and
sandwiches); Anchor pub with
river terrace (bars and restaurant).

Art at the Hayward Gallery, South Bank ⑩

Christopher Wren had a house by Cardinal Cap Alley in Cardinal's Wharf ㉓, where he had a good view of it. Next door to his house now is the exhibition and tour centre for Shakespeare's Globe ㉔ *(see p177)*. A tour around the theatre is the next best thing to attending a performance.

Bankside

Bankside becomes more cramped here, as the historic streets pass The Anchor ㉕ riverside pub and Vinopolis ㉖ to reach the Clink Prison Museum ㉗ *(see p182)*, on the site of one of London's

0 metres   200

0 yards   200

KEY

• • • Walk route

🄴 Underground station

🚊 Train station

brick industrial building, with contemporary designer shops and galleries, such as gallery@. Take the lift to the top of the tower for an excellent, free view of the city: the Inner Temple and Fleet Street lie opposite. Once down again, the Riverside Walk passes by Sea Containers House ⑯, with gold trimmings (built as a hotel, but now offices) and Doggett's Coat and Badge pub ⑰ *(see p63)*, then continue under Blackfriars Bridge ⑱, emerging by the remaining piers and railway emblem of a former bridge. On the right, opposite the Founders Arms ⑲, is the esteemed Bankside Gallery ⑳ *(see p177)*, which has regular exhibitions of its members' work and a shop. Behind it, opposite Falcon Point Piazza is Marcus Campbell, an

The Anchor pub, Bankside ㉕

excellent art bookshop, a stone's throw from Tate Modern ㉑ *(see pp178–81)*, the best free show on the river. Drop in for a coffee if nothing else. The Millennium Bridge ㉒ leads over to St Paul's *(see pp148–9)* and the City. Its architect Sir

first lock-ups. At St Mary Ovarie Dock, climb aboard a replica (1973) of *Golden Hinde* ㉘, in which the Elizabethan buccaneer Sir Francis Drake became the second man to circumnavigate the world. Southwark Cathedral ㉙ *(see p176)*, is a quiet place to end the walk - there is a good tea shop here. Or, if you still feel energetic, browse around Borough Market *(see p176)* before heading to the tube or train at London Bridge station ㉛.

Tate Modern: a vast space for contemporary British art ㉑

A Two-Hour Walk Around Notting Hill

This walk centres around Portobello Road, the city's most famous antiques and bric-a-brac shopping area in one of the ultra-fashionable parts of London. Great for original souvenirs, the neighbourhood is fascinating at any time, though the streets are busiest on Fridays and Saturdays, when all the shops are open and the market stalls laid out *(see page 333)*. This is the heart of Notting Hill, renowned for its carnival and, in recent years, favoured as a film setting and a smart address.

Odd bric-a-brac at a market stall

Sun in Splendour pub frontage ⑤

Portobello Road

Leaving Notting Hill Gate tube station ①, follow the signs to Portobello Road *(see p219)*, taking Pembridge Road ②. Intriguing shops here include Retro Woman ③ (Nos. 20 and 32) and Retro Man ④ (No. 34) for period clothes and accessories. At the Sun in Splendour pub ⑤, turn left into Portobello Road. No. 22, among the attractively painted terraced houses on the right, was where George Orwell lived in 1927 before his writing career began ⑥. Cross Chepstow Villas ⑦ and

the serious antique shops begin. Near the Portobello Arcade ⑧, signposted with a large teapot, is Portobello Gold (Nos. 95–7), a guest house where Bill, Hillary and Chelsea Clinton dropped in for a beer and a snack in 2000. At No. 115 ⑨ is a plaque to June Aylward who

opened the first antique shop in the street. At Colville Terrace ⑩ the daily fruit and vegetable market begins. On the left is the Electric Cinema ⑪, said to be the oldest working cinema in Britain (1910),

TIPS FOR WALKERS

Starting point: *Notting Hill Gate Underground station.*
Length: *1.85 miles (3 km)*
Getting there: *Notting Hill Underground station on Central, District and Circle lines.*
Stopping-off points: *The area is known for its pubs and restaurants. Try Grove Café at 253a Portobello Road; Eve's Market Café at 222 Portobello Road; Toms at 127 Westbourne Grove (great sandwiches and snacks); Ottolernghi's Patisserie at 62 Ledbury Road (superb pastries).*

The Electric Cinema, the UK's oldest working cinema ⑪

and certainly one of the most delightful. If there is not a film showing, you can go in and try the comfortable armchair seats and sofas.

The Travel Bookshop

Turn left down Blenheim Crescent to find The Travel Bookshop ⑫, inspiration for the location of the 1999 film *Notting Hill*, in which Hugh Grant was the assistant. Books for Cooks ⑬ (No. 4) is where recipes from the latest books are prepared and sold. Head back to Portobello Road and pass the local Salvation Army centre ⑭. Amble for several blocks to Grove Café ⑮ (No. 253a) on the corner (opposite the Market Bar ⑯). If you can find a table on the

Notting Hill's Travel Bookshop ⑫

Bevington Road, right along Blagrove Road and right again into Acklam Road to bring you back to Portobello Road. Continue for several blocks, turning left on Talbot Road, where All Saints' Church ⑲ has a glassed-in shrine to Our Lady of Walsingham – an unusual feature in a Protestant church. Just beyond the red-brick Tabernacle Centre for Arts and Education ⑳, where Pink Floyd made their debut

in 1966, is My Beautiful Laundrette ㉑, named after the successful 1986 film. Turn right into Ledbury Road to find high fashion shops, and also, at its end in the still-functioning Westbourne Grove Church ㉒. As you are passing No. 62, try the pastries in Ottolernghi Patisserie ㉓ for a snack to hit the spot. Turn right into Westbourne Grove for more stylish shopping. Nicole Farhi has a shop ㉔ (No. 202) of new and second-hand clothes. Detour to Toms deli and café ㉕ at 127, which claims the best toasted sandwiches in town, and is run by Tom Conran, son of the style guru Terence Conran. The Wild at Heart flower stall on Turquoise Island ㉖ opposite, won awards for its designer, Piers Gough, in 1993. On the far side is the Oxfam thrift shop ㉗, where its bargains reflect the good taste of the locals. Head back to Portobello Road ㉘ and Notting Hill Gate tube.

Award-winning Wild at Heart flower stall ㉖

upstairs terrace, you'll have a good view of the street. All-day breakfasts are a specialty. Excitement dwindles once you pass under the Westway flyover, except on Fridays and Saturdays when Tent City ⑰ and the Golborne Road Flea Market ⑱ are fully active, and the Portuguese cafés (especially the Lisboa at 55) are bustling. From Golborne Road, turn right into

The clock tower on All Saints Church ⑲

KEY

••• Walk route

🔵 Underground station

0 metres 200
0 yards 200

TRAVELLERS' NEEDS

WHERE TO STAY 278–91

RESTAURANTS AND PUBS 292–319

SHOPS AND MARKETS 320–41

ENTERTAINMENT IN LONDON 342–55

CHILDREN'S LONDON 356–9

WHERE TO STAY

The high cost of accommodation in London is one of the biggest drawbacks for visitors. At the top end of the market, there is no shortage of expensive pedigree hotels, such as the Savoy and the Ritz. Mid-range hotels, while there are many, tend to be slightly further out of the centre of town. Sadly, most of the budget hotels are seedy and unappealing, a problem exacerbated by rising land and property prices. However, there are ways to stay in the capital without breaking the bank. Low-cost hotel chains such as Travel Inn, Express by Holiday Inn and Ibis have

Hilton doorman

been established in many convenient locations throughout the city, offering good-quality if standardized accommodation at affordable prices. We have inspected more than 250 hotels and apartment complexes across a range of price brackets and localities and have more than 120 of the best of their kind. For further details on these, turn to the listings on pages 278–91. Self-catering apartments and private homes (see pp280–81) are available at a wide range of prices. Student halls and hostels, even a few camping sites on London's outskirts, are additional possibilities for budget travellers (see p281).

WHERE TO LOOK

The most expensive hotels tend to be in smart West End areas such as Mayfair and Belgravia. Often large and opulent, with uniformed staff, they are not always the most relaxing places to stay. For smaller, more personal, but still luxurious hotels, try South Kensington or Holland Park.

The streets off Earl's Court Road are full of hotels at the lower end of the price range. Several of the big railway stations are well served with budget hotels too. Try Ebury Street near Victoria, or Sussex

Gardens near Paddington. Close to Euston or Waterloo and in the City and Docklands, well-known hotels chain cater for travellers at a range of prices. The area immediately north of King's Cross is best avoided at night.

There are also inexpensive hotels in the suburbs, such as Ealing, Hendon, Wembley, Bromley or Harrow. From here you can get into town on public transport. Take care not to miss the last train back.

If you get stranded at an airport or have to catch a very early morning flight, consult the list on page 377.

For further information, advice and reservation services, contact **Visit London**, which publishes several annually updated booklets on accommodation in Greater London.

DISCOUNT RATES

Prices in the capital tend to stay high all year round, but there are bargains. Many hotels, especially the groups, offer reduced rates for weekends and special breaks (see p280). Others work on a more ad hoc basis, depending on how busy they are. If a hotel isn't full, it is always worth trying to negotiate a discount (see Booking On-line below). Older budget hotels may have rooms without showers or private bathrooms. These usually cost less than those with private facilities.

HIDDEN EXTRAS

Read the small print carefully. Most hotels quote room rates rather than rates per person, but not all. Service charges are usually included in the quoted price but in some cases they are added on later. Beware of high mark-ups on telephone calls. A hotel with a high room tariff may be even more expensive than at first appears, which means that the final bill can come as a shock to many visitors.

Imaginative design at One Aldwych hotel (see p289)

The Radisson Edwardian Hampshire hotel (see p287)

Breakfast may not be included in room rates, though it generally is in cheaper hotels. The definition of breakfast ranges from "full English" (a hearty, traditional fry-up which will see you through the most hectic sightseeing programme), to a "Continental" cup of coffee and a roll or croissant. Buffet breakfasts with lavish spreads of fruit, muesli and yoghurt are increasingly popular with health-conscious visitors.

Tipping is expected in the more expensive hotels, but there is no need to tip staff other than porters, except perhaps a helpful concierge for arranging theatre tickets or phoning for taxis.

Single travellers are usually charged a "supplement" and end up paying about 80 per cent of the double room rate, even if they are occupying a "single" room – so don't accept anything substandard.

The elegant hallway of The Gore hotel in Kensington (see p283)

FACILITIES

Room sizes in London hotels at all price ranges tend to be on the small side, but the majority of hotels now provide telephones, televisions and private baths or showers in all their rooms. At the top end of the scale, hotels compete to provide the very latest sound-and-video systems, computer equipment and high-tech gadgetry. A recent luxury craze is mini-television screens in the bathroom. Whatever the hotel, you will be expected to vacate your room by noon on the day you leave, sometimes earlier.

HOW TO BOOK

It is always advisable to book well in advance, as room availability fluctuates and better quality hotels are in constant demand. Direct bookings can be made by letter, phone, fax, or increasingly, via the internet. This generally entails giving some kind of guarantee: either a credit card number from which a cancellation fee can be deducted, or remitting a one-night deposit (some hotels will expect more for longer stays). Don't forget that if you subsequently cancel for any reason, part or all of the room price may be charged unless the hotel can relet the accommodation. Insurance cover is advised.

Travellers can phone the Visit London Accommodation Booking Service on 0845-644 3010 (also at www.superbreak.com). There is a £5 booking fee and customers will need to give a credit card number. During high season there may be a one-night deposit to pay, but that is at the discretion of the hotel. The Booking Service will advise, of course, if there is a deposit to pay. alternatively, travellers can use a similar booking service on the London Tourist Board's web-site (www.visitlondon.com) or they can e-mail the service directly at admin@superbreak. com. There is no booking fee if booking online.

Tourists can also book in person at the London Visitor

One of the stylish bathrooms at the Portobello Hotel (see p283)

Centre at No. 1 Regent Street, and can order a brochure, "Where to Stay on a Budget", from the Visit London brochure line on 0870-240 4326.

Accommodating booking services are also available at the British Travel Centre on Regent Street. A number of non-LTB booking agencies operate from booths in the major railway stations, charging a small fee to personal callers. Unidentified touts, who hang around at railway and coach stations offering cheap accommodation to tourists, should be avoided.

BOOKING ON-LINE

Many hotels have their own websites and the information available on these is often more regularly updated than the hotel brochure. If you are familiar with the technology, internet bookings can be quick and efficient. There are also some good deals available by booking online, especially at larger hotels. Accommodation agencies and travel websites also use the internet as a cost-effective way of doing business and, in most cases, at least some of the savings are passed on to customers. Increasingly, the internet demonstrates the fluidity of many hotel "rack rates" (i.e. the prices printed on the tariff sheet), which, far from being fixed in stone, fluctuate widely according to the laws of supply and demand.

SPECIAL BREAKS

Many travel agencies carry brochures from the major hotel chains listing special offers, which are usually costed on a minimum two-night stay. Some are extraordinarily good value compared to the usual tariff. For most leisure travellers or families with children, this is the best way to get value for money out of London hotels so that you can spend time in the city without breaking the bank.

City-break packages are organized by specialist operators, ferry companies and some privately owned hotels too. Sometimes the same hotel may be featured in several brochures at widely differing prices and with different perks. It's worth asking the hotel directly what special rates they offer, and checking their websites too.

DISABLED TRAVELLERS

Information about wheelchair access is based largely on hotels' own assessments, but travellers with special needs should always confirm when booking whether an establishment is suitable. If forewarned, many hotels will go out of their way to help disabled visitors. The nationwide *Tourism for All*

1920s Savoy poster

scheme provides details on accommodation standards and facilities for visitors with mobility problems. For more information on hotels that meet the three-tier "National Accessible Standard", contact **Visit London** or **Holiday Care**. A booklet, *Access in London*, can be obtained from **RADAR**.

TRAVELLING WITH CHILDREN

London hotels are no longer the notorious child-free zones they used to be. A large number now make a concerted effort to cater for the needs of people travelling with children, providing cots, high-chairs, baby-sitting services and special meal arrangements. Always ask whether the hotel offers special deals for children – some have special rates, or allow children to stay free of charge if they sleep in their parents' room. The hotel recommendations in our listing *(see pp282–91)* point out whether particular hotels offer child facilities, or whether on the other hand they have age restrictions.

SELF-CATERING FLATS

Many agencies offer self-catering accommodation in flats, usually for stays of a week or more. Prices,

depending on size and location, start at about £300 per week. Some luxury complexes are fully serviced, so you don't need to cook, shop or clean. **Bridge Street Accommodations** has over 550 London apartments in smart locations. It caters mainly for corporate and professional travellers, but its properties can be rented for short-term lets whenever they are available.

The **Landmark Trust** rents apartments in historic or unusual buildings. These include apartments in Hampton Court *(see pp254–7)* and in a pretty 18th-century terrace in the City: one of them was the home of the late poet laureate, Sir John Betjeman. A handbook of Landmark Trust properties is available for a small charge.

STAYING IN PRIVATE HOMES

A number of agencies organize stays in private homes; several are registered with Visit London. Credit card reservations can be made through Visit London's telephone booking service *(see box)*. Several agencies have minimum stays of anything up to a week. Prices depend on location, starting at around £20 per person per night. Sometimes you will enjoy family hospitality, but this isn't guaranteed, so enquire when you book. Deposits may be requested and cancellation fees imposed. The **Bed & Breakfast and Homestay Association (BBHA)** is an umbrella organization for several reputable agencies whose properties are inspected regularly. Several BBHA members are listed in the Directory *(see box)*.

Uptown Reservations arranges upmarket B&B in interesting, well-located London homes which have been inspected for their welcome, security and comfort. Prices start at £85 per night for a double room. It works in tandem with **Wolsey Lodges**, a nationwide consortium of distinctive private

Classical opulence at Claridge's Hotel *(see p286)*

homes, often of historic or architectural interest, offering individual hospitality and a good dinner. Wolsey Lodges lists a couple of charming London properties.

BUDGET ACCOMMODATION

Despite the high cost of many London hotels, budget accommodation does exist, and not only for young travellers.

Dormitory accommodation and youth hostels

These can be booked through the LTB's information centre at Victoria Station for a small fee plus a refundable deposit. Some private hostels near Earl's Court charge little more than £10 a night for a dormitory bed with breakfast. The **London Hostel Association** has a selection of very reasonably priced accommodation throughout central London.

City of London Youth Hostel

The **Youth Hostels Association (YHA)** runs seven hostels in London. There is no age limit, though non-members pay a small joining fee and adults also pay a little more to stay in them. Of the seven, two are located in the heart of London. The Oxford Street hostel (actually located in Noel Street, Soho) is within walking distance of many

attractions, and at the hub of London's nightlife. The City hostel is located in an atmospheric street near St Paul's Cathedral (*see pp148–51*).

There is an online booking service, the **International Booking Network**, run by the International Youth Hostel Federation, that is the easiest way to book a bed. One of the most popular hostels is Holland House, a Jacobean mansion in Holland Park.

Halls of residence

Many student rooms are available at Easter and from July to September at very reasonable prices. Some of these are in central locations such as South Kensington. Advance booking is a good idea, but places are sometimes available at short notice. Try **City University**, or, if you need a room in a hurry, **King's College** or **Imperial College** may be able to find you one.

DIRECTORY

RESERVATIONS AND INFORMATION

British Hotel Reservation Centre
15 Monck St
SW1 2BJ.
Tel 0800 282888.
www.bhrconline.com

Visit London
1 Warwick Row SW1E 5ER.
Tel 08456-443010.
www.visitlondon.com

DISABLED TRAVELLERS

Holiday Care
7th Floor, Sunley House, 4 Bedford Park, Croydon CR0 2AP
Tel 0845-124 9974.
www.holidaycare.org

RADAR
Unit 12, City Forum, 250 City Road EC1V 8AF.
Tel 020-7250 3222.
www.radar.org.uk

SELF-CATERING AGENCIES

Bridge Street Accommodations
Compass House, 22 Redan Place W2 4SA.
Tel 020-7792 2222.
www.bridgestreet.com

Landmark Trust
Shottesbrooke, Maidenhead, Berks SL6 3SW.
Tel 01628 825925.
www.landmarktrust.org.uk

AGENCIES FOR STAYS IN PRIVATE HOMES

At Home in London
70 Black Lion Lane W6 9BE.
Tel 020-8748 1943.
www.at-home-in-london.com

Bed & Breakfast & Homestay Assoc.
www.bbha.org.uk

Host & Guest Services
103 Dawes Road SW6 7DU
Tel 020-7385 9922.
www.host-guest.co.uk

London Bed and Breakfast Agency
71 Fellows Road NW3 3JY
Tel 020-7586 2768.
www.londonbb.com

Uptown Reservations
8 Kelso Place W8 5QD
Tel 020-7351 3445.
www.uptownres.co.uk

Wolsey Lodges
9 Market Place, Hadleigh, Ipswich, Suffolk, IP7 5DL.
Tel 01473 822058.
www.wolsey-lodges.com

HOSTEL BOOKING

International Booking Network (IBN)
Tel 01707 324170.
www.hostelbooking.com

London Hostel Association
54 Eccleston Sq SW1V 1PG.
Tel 020-7834 1545.
www.london-hostels.co.uk

Youth Hostels Association
Dimple Rd, Matlock, Derbyshire DE4 3YH.
Tel 01629 592600.
www.yha.org.uk

BOOKING ADDRESSES FOR RESIDENCE HALLS

City University Accommodation and Conference Service
Northampton Sq EC1V 0HB.
Tel 020-7040 5060.

Imperial College Summer Accommodation Centre
58 Princes Gate, Exhibition Road SW7 2PG.
Tel 020-7594 9507.
www.imperial-accommodationlink.com

King's Conference & Vacation Bureau
King's College London, Strand Bridge House, 3rd floor, Strand WC2R 1HH.
Tel 020-7848 1700.
www.kcl.ac.uk/kcvb

Choosing a Hotel

These hotels have been selected across a wide price range for their good value, facilities and location; they are listed by area. Starting with west and southwestern districts of London, the guide moves through central parts of the city and on to eastern districts, eventually looking at hotels further outside the city.

PRICE CATEGORIES
For a standard double room per night, inclusive of breakfast, service charges and any additional taxes such as VAT.

£ under £80
££ £80–£120
£££ £120–£180
££££ £180–£220
£££££ £220 plus

BAYSWATER, PADDINGTON

Stylotel
160–162 Sussex Gardens, W2 **Tel** 020 7723 1026 **Fax** 020 7262 2983 **Rooms** 40   **Map** 11 A2   £

Offering some of the cheapest rates in central London, Stylotel is true to its name, although the high-tech style may not suit all tastes. Rooms have wooden floors, aluminium walls, light-box bedside tables and futuristic bathrooms. There's a groovy lounge with curved stainless steel bar and blue leather seats. **www.stylotel.com**

Garden Court Hotel
30–31 Kensington Gardens Square, W2 **Tel** 020 7229 2553 **Fax** 020 7 727 2749 **Rooms** 34   **Map** 10 D2   ££

An antique beefeater guards the airy lobby of this good-value hotel on a lovely garden square. The Garden Court celebrated its 50th anniversary in 2004 with a facelift; rooms have tasteful modern wallpaper and new wooden furniture. To keep the cost down even further, you can opt for shared facilities. **www.gardencourthotel.co.uk**

Kyriad Princes Square
23–25 Prince's Square, W2 **Tel** 020 7229 9876 **Fax** 020 7229 4664 **Rooms** 50   **Map** 10 D2   ££

Behind the grand Victorian façade is a friendly, modern hotel. The recently-refurbished pastel rooms may have standard hotel furnishings, but they are neat and cheerful, and the bathrooms are spotless. There's a handy bar in the lobby and special deals bring the price down considerably. **www.princessquarehotel.co.uk**

Mornington
12 Lancaster Gate, W2 **Tel** 020 7262 7361 **Fax** 020 7706 1028 **Rooms** 66   **Map** 10 F2   ££

This formerly Swedish-owned hotel is now part of the quality Best Western chain. Bedrooms in the grand Victorian building near Hyde Park maintain a light, airy Scandinavian feel and a buffet *smorgasbord*-style breakfast caters to the many Swedish clientele. Inquire about special rates. **www.bw-morningtonhotel.co.uk**

Pavilion Hotel
34–36 Sussex Gardens, W2 **Tel** 020 7262 0905 **Fax** 020 7262 1324 **Rooms** 30   **Map** 11 A1   ££

The Pavilion's understated brick exterior may not stand out in this hotel-lined strip, but inside it's a world away from boring B&Bs. The fabulously themed rooms, from the rich panelling and tartan of *Highland Fling* to the antique Chinese chests and silks of *Enter the Dragon* are favoured by rock stars. **www.pavilionhoteluk.com**

Vancouver Studios
30 Prince's Square, W2 **Tel** 020 7243 1270 **Fax** 020 7221 8678 **Rooms** 45   **Map** 10 D2   ££

These stylishly decorated studios in three 19th-century terraced houses have fully-equipped kitchenettes, flatscreen TVs and DVD players. Resident cat Panther presides over the living room with a view onto the secluded garden. Coin-op Internet and laundry complete the home-from-home package. **www.vancouverstudios.co.uk**

The Delmere
130 Sussex Gardens, W2 **Tel** 020 7706 3344 **Fax** 020 7262 1863 **Rooms** 36   **Map** 11 A2   £££

Part of the Best Western chain, the Delmere offers accommodation a stone's throw away from Paddington Station. Rooms are well proportioned and attractively decorated, bathrooms are small yet stylish and there's a pleasant dining room and lounge where you can relax with the day's papers. **www.delmerehotels.com**

The Hempel
31–35 Craven Hill Gardens, W2 **Tel** 020 7298 9000 **Fax** 020 7402 4666 **Rooms** 46   **Map** 10 E2   ££££

Fans of the minimalist aesthetic will be in their element in Anouska Hempel's serene white hotel. Each room, complete with candles and all the requisite gadgetry, is unique. There is a striking geometric landscaped garden and an Italian-Thai fusion restaurant. **www.the-hempel.co.uk**

The Royal Park
3 Westbourne Terrace, W2 **Tel** 020 7479 6600 **Fax** 020 7479 6601 **Rooms** 48   **Map** 10 F2   £££££

This new townhouse hotel near Hyde Park has a discreet luxury, which has attracted celebrity guests. Classic, unfussy rooms are furnished with exquisite fabrics, original prints and stone-tiled bathrooms. All the usual gadgetry, plus free afternoon tea and evening champagne in the gracious drawing room. **www.theroyalpark.com**

Key to Symbols *see back cover flap*

KENSINGTON, EARL'S COURT

Abbey House

11 Vicarage Gate, W8 **Tel** *020 7727 2594* **Fax** *020 7727 1873* **Rooms** *16* ⓔ

Map *10 D4*

Occupying a prime position between Kensington High Street and Notting Hill Gate, this Victorian B&B on an exclusive square maintains an air of grandeur. Shared facilities keep the rates down, but these are scrupulously clean and the comfortable rooms have orthopaedic mattresses and colour TVs. **www.abbeyhousekensington.com**

Rushmore

11 Trebovir Road, SW5 **Tel** *020 7370 3839* **Fax** *020 7370 0274* **Rooms** *22* ⓔ

Map *17 C2*

Like the nearby Mayflower, the Rushmore is proof that accommodation doesn't have to be expensive to be stylish. Each room in this Victorian townhouse has been designed in a different style; even the bathrooms have been customized to fit in with the mood. Breakfast is served in a chic conservatory. **www.rushmore-hotel.co.uk**

Mayflower Hotel

26–28 Trebovir Road, SW5 **Tel** *020 7370 0991* **Fax** *020 7370 0994* **Rooms** *48* ⓔⓔ

Map *18 D2*

This beautifully furnished, budget-boutique hotel is a cut above the rest. The spacious, contemporary rooms have wooden floors and Eastern elements such as elaborately carved beds and rich silks. Marble bathrooms, ceiling fans and CD players are luxurious perks. There are also 35 tasteful apartments nearby. **www.mayflower-group.co.uk**

Twenty Nevern Square

20 Nevern Square, SW5 **Tel** *020 7565 9555* **Fax** *020 7565 9444* **Rooms** *20* ⓔⓔ

Map *17 C2*

This townhouse overlooking a private garden square combines unique decor with reasonable rates. Rooms are furnished with gorgeous silks and spectacular beds such as Eastern-carved wooden styles or four-posters. Widescreen TVs, CD players and 24-hour room service are further attractions. **www.twentynevernsquare.co.uk**

The Gore

190 Queen's Gate, SW7 **Tel** *020 7584 6601* **Fax** *020 7589 8127* **Rooms** *49* ⓔⓔⓔⓔ

Map *10 F5*

The Gore has been in operation for more than 110 years and, while it has recently been refurbished, it preserves the atmosphere of a bygone age. Rooms feature four-poster beds, framed pictures, luxurious draperies and opulent fabrics. There's a panelled bar and casual bistro as well. **www.gorehotel.com**

The Milestone Hotel

1 Kensington Court, W8 **Tel** *020 7917 1000* **Fax** *020 7917 1010* **Rooms** *57 + 6 apartments* ⓔⓔⓔⓔⓔ

Map *10 E5*

This plush hotel opposite Kensington Palace features originally designed rooms, from the smart "Savile Row" to the Colonial-style "Safari Suite". Extras include gym and resistance pool, broadband Internet and Penhaligon's toiletries in rooms, 24-hour butler and use of the hotel Bentley. **www.milestonehotel.com**

NOTTING HILL, HOLLAND PARK

The Main House

6 Colville Road, W11 **Tel** *020 7221 9691* **Rooms** *4* ⓔⓔ

Map *9 B2*

In the heart of hip Notting Hill, Caroline Main's chic guesthouse features airy, wooden-floored suites, each one fills an entire floor. The decor combines modern elements and antiques, and there are thoughtful extras such as bicycles to borrow and morning coffee brought to your room on a silver tray. **www.themainhouse.co.uk**

Guesthouse West

163–165 Westbourne Grove, W11 **Tel** *020 7792 9800* **Fax** *020 7792 9797* **Rooms** *20* ⓔⓔⓔ

Map *9 C2*

Formerly the Westbourne, Guesthouse West is a budget-conscious design hotel in an Edwardian house. Minimalist dark wood and beige rooms boast high-tech entertainment systems and Molton Brown toiletries. The hip restaurant has terrace tables and Westbourne Grove's bars and boutiques are on the doorstep. **www.guesthousewest.com**

Miller's Residence

111a Westbourne Grove, W2 **Tel** *020 7243 1024* **Fax** *020 7243 1064* **Rooms** *8* ⓔⓔⓔ

Map *10 D2*

Owned by antiques expert Martin Miller and a short stroll from Portobello Road's famous market, this hotel is a bric-a-brac-hunter's fantasy. Rooms are individually furnished with his finds, and free drinks and snacks are served in the eccentrically cluttered drawing room, which is candlelit in the evening. **www.millersuk.com**

The Portobello Hotel

22 Stanley Gardens, W11 **Tel** *020 7727 2777* **Fax** *020 7792 9641* **Rooms** *24* ⓔⓔⓔ

Map *9 B2*

This divinely decadent Notting Hill mansion has lured rock royalty for over 30 years with its hip location and extravagantly decorated rooms. Choose from such exotic retreats as the serene Japanese room with private grotto garden and the notorious "Round Bed Room" with its freestanding Victorian bath. **www.portobello-hotel.co.uk**

The Lennox
🖥️ P 🚶 🛗 🗎   ⓔⓔⓔⓔ

34 Pembridge Gardens, W2 **Tel** *0870 850 3317* **Fax** *020 7727 4982* **Rooms** *20*   **Map** *9 C3*

This elegant, detached 19th-century townhouse is furnished in classic modern style. All rooms incorporate a high-quality plasma TV screen and DVD player. There is 24-hour room service for drinks and snacks. **www.thelennox.com**

KNIGHTSBRIDGE, BROMPTON, BELGRAVIA

Knightsbridge Green Hotel
🖥️ 🚶 🛗 🗎   ⓔⓔⓔ

159 Knightsbridge, SW1 **Tel** *020 7584 6274* **Fax** *020 7225 1635* **Rooms** *28*   **Map** *11 C5*

A shopaholic's dream, this well-kept hotel is right on Knightsbridge and rates are reasonable for more spending power in Harrods and Harvey Nichols. The tidy, modern rooms are regularly upgraded and feature air conditioning and satellite TVs. There's also a small business centre on-site. **www.thekghotel.co.uk**

Willett
🚶   ⓔⓔⓔ

32 Sloane Gardens, SW11 **Tel** *020 7824 8415* **Fax** *020 7730 4830* **Rooms** *19*   **Map** *20 D2*

In a handsome Victorian property just off Sloane Square, the Willett retains many original features and regular guests return for its inexpensive yet characterful accommodation. Breakfast is served on white tablecloths in the breakfast room. Only the deluxe rooms are air conditioned. **www.eeh.co.uk**

The Franklin Hotel
🖥️ P 🍴 🚶 🛗 🗎   ⓔⓔⓔⓔ

28 Egerton Gardens, SW3 **Tel** *020 7584 5533* **Fax** *020 7584 5449* **Rooms** *47*   **Map** *19 B1*

Occupying four 19th-century townhouses in a quiet Knightsbridge street, the Franklin creates the pleasant illusion of staying with an aristocratic relation. Rooms are decorated with antiques and fine English fabrics. Best of all is the large, secluded gardens in the back, shared with well-heeled residents. **www.franklinhotel.co.uk**

The Knightsbridge
🖥️ 🚶 🗎   ⓔⓔⓔⓔ

10 Beaufort Gardens, SW3 **Tel** *020 7584 6300* **Fax** *020 7584 6355* **Rooms** *44*   **Map** *19 B1*

With its book-lined library and drawing room full of modern artworks, the Knightsbridge feels like the home of a well-travelled intellectual. A bit cheaper than the other Firmdale hotels, this one offers the same lovely, updated English-style bedrooms and faultless attention to detail. **www.firmdalehotels.com**

The Berkeley
🖥️ P 🍴 🏊 🚶 🛗 🗎   ⓔⓔⓔⓔⓔ

Wilton Place, SW1 **Tel** *020 7235 6000* **Fax** *020 7235 4330* **Rooms** *214*   **Map** *12 D5*

Although this glamorous hotel was established in the 19th century, its classical structure dates from the 1960s. The crowning glory is the spa's fabulous pool with retractable roof. A range of dining and drinking options includes acclaimed Pétrus and Boxwood Café, Gordon Ramsay's New York-style eateries. **www.the-berkeley.co.uk**

The Cadogan
🖥️ 🍴 🚶 🛗 🗎   ⓔⓔⓔⓔⓔ

75 Sloane Street, SW1 **Tel** *020 7235 7141* **Fax** *020 7245 0994* **Rooms** *65*   **Map** *19 C1*

Opened in 1888, the Cadogan has welcomed such famous guests as Lillie Langtry and Oscar Wilde, the latter was arrested in room 118. It has a traditional British character, and guests have access to the private Cadogan Place gardens and tennis courts across. **www.cadogan.com**

The Capital Hotel and Apartments
🖥️ P 🍴 🚶 🗎   ⓔⓔⓔⓔ

22–24 Basil Street, SW3 **Tel** *020 7589 5171* **Fax** *020 7225 0011* **Rooms** *49*   **Map** *11 C5*

Situated between Harrods and Harvey Nichols, this service-oriented hotel even offers personal shoppers and jogging partners. Its Michelin two-starred restaurant has been refurbished in 1940s-influenced style. Bedrooms feature king-size beds, designer fabrics and the latest technology. **www.capitalhotel.co.uk**

The Halkin
🖥️ 🍴 🚶 🛗 🗎   ⓔⓔⓔⓔⓔ

Halkin Street, SW1 **Tel** *020 7333 1000* **Fax** *020 7333 1100* **Rooms** *41*   **Map** *12 D5*

Modern comforts meet Eastern serenity at this gracious luxury hotel. Warm wood, curving lines and creamy bed linen are accented by Southest Asian art handpicked by the Singaporean owner. Be sure to have a meal at Nahm, it's the only Michelin-starred Thai restaurant outside Thailand. **www.halkin.como.bz**

SOUTH KENSINGTON, CHELSEA

Hotel 167
ⓔⓔ

167 Old Brompton Road, SW5 **Tel** *020 7373 0672* **Fax** *020 7373 3360* **Rooms** *19*   **Map** *18 E3*

This affordable, funky hotel in a capacious Victorian house certainly makes an impact, it's brimming with unusual works of art and colourful decorative touches. Every interior-designed bedroom is in a different style, so you can opt for modern or more traditional, depending on your taste. **www.hotel167.com**

Key to Price Guide *see p282* **Key to Symbols** *see back cover flap*

Swiss House

171 Old Brompton Road, SW5 **Tel** *020 7373 2769* **Fax** *020 7373 4983* **Rooms** *15*   **Map** *18 E3*

This charming, small hotel is especially good for families. Rooms are pretty without being fussy. Well placed for South Kensington's museums, the Swiss House prides itself on its child-friendly attitude and the concierge can suggest activities and restaurants geared towards little kids. **www.swisshousehotel.com**

Aster House

3 Sumner Place, SW7 **Tel** *020 7581 5888* **Fax** *020 7584 4925* **Rooms** *13*   **Map** *19 A2*

Three-time winner of the Tourist Board's best B&B award, this friendly hotel in a grand white stucco house has immaculate bedrooms in a typical English-floral style. A superior breakfast served in the palm-filled conservatory and a pretty garden complete with pond and resident ducks attracts guests. **www.asterhouse.com**

Five Sumner Place

5 Sumner Place, SW7 **Tel** *020 7584 7586* **Fax** *020 7823 9962* **Rooms** *13*   **Map** *19 A2*

This small hotel in a white stucco Victorian house, convenient for the shops and museums of South Kensington, has won several awards for its consistent high quality. Larger than average rooms are simply furnished in understated English style and breakfast is served in a pretty conservatory. **www.sumnerplace.com**

Sydney House

9–11 Sydney Street, SW3 **Tel** *020 7376 7711* **Fax** *020 7376 4233* **Rooms** *21*   **Map** *19 A2*

This small hotel, steps away from the chic shops of Brompton Cross, was given a contemporary revamp in 2003. Airy rooms are furnished with blond wood furniture, Frette linen, contemporary art and thoughtful features such as American wall sockets and water softener in the ultra-modern bathrooms. **www.sydneyhousechelsea.com**

Blakes Hotel

33 Roland Gardens, SW7 **Tel** *020 7370 6701* **Fax** *020 7373 0442* **Rooms** *45*   **Map** *18 F2*

Blakes is the original "boutique hotel", created by designer Anouska Hempel over two decades ago. Rooms range in style from baronial manor to opulent Oriental and contain pieces collected on her travels. The discreet residential location has made it a favourite celeb hideaway. Only some suites are air conditioned. **www.blakeshotels.com**

Myhotel Chelsea

35 Ixworth Place, SW3 **Tel** *020 7225 7500* **Fax** *020 7225 7555* **Rooms** *45*   **Map** *19 B2*

Opened in 2003 in a former police station, this hotel has the feel of a contemporary country house – modern but traditional. It has a library with complimentary drinks and Internet access, and the hotel's location is handy for Brompton Cross. **www.myhotels.com**

VICTORIA, WESTMINSTER, PIMLICO

Dover Hotel

42–44 Belgrave Road, SW1 **Tel** *020 7821 9085* **Fax** *020 7834 6425* **Rooms** *34*   **Map** *20 F2*

This well-maintained hotel is terrific value for money. It may not be luxurious once past the grand stucco façade, but the decor is refreshingly modern and every room has satellite TV and pristine en suite shower and WC. It's handy for Victoria Station and Pimlico's many pubs and cafés. **www.dover-hotel.co.uk**

Elizabeth Hotel and Apartments

37 Eccleston Square, SW1 **Tel** *020 7828 6812* **Fax** *020 7828 6814* **Rooms** *37 + 5 apartments*   **Map** *20 E2*

The rates are surprisingly reasonable in this elegant townhouse hotel on a grand garden square; Winston Churchill used to live a couple of doors down. Rooms are simple yet tastefully furnished and guests have access to the private gardens and stately drawing room with newspapers, tea, coffee and biscuits. **www.elizabethhotel.com**

Morgan Guest House

120 Ebury Street, SW1 **Tel** *020 7730 2384* **Fax** *020 7730 8442* **Rooms** *11*   **Map** *20 E2*

This comfortable guesthouse in a listed Georgian building offers excellent value for money, especially if you opt for a room without facilites, or one of the spacious family rooms that sleeps four. The decor is light and airy and many rooms contain original fireplaces. There is also a pretty garden. **www.morganhouse.co.uk**

Windermere

142–144 Warwick Way, SW1 **Tel** *020 7834 5163* **Fax** *020 7630 8831* **Rooms** *20*   **Map** *20 E2*

This Victorian house has a long history of hospitality, it was the site of one of the area's earliest B&Bs in 1881. Rooms are spacious with large windows and done in tasteful, traditional chintz, with extras such as satellite TV and safe; all have en suite facilities. The basement restaurant serves evening meals. **www.windermere-hotel.co.uk**

Tophams

28 Ebury Street, SW1 **Tel** *020 7730 8147* **Fax** *020 7823 5966* **Rooms** *51*   **Map** *20 E1*

Changes have been afoot at this endearingly eccentric hotel comprising five adjoining houses in an affluent street near Victoria Station. Formerly run by the Topham family since 1937, it has recently been bought by a British chain and has been extensively refurbished. There is a pleasant bar. **www.zolahotels.com**

Dolphin Square
Chichester Street, SW1 **Tel** *020 7834 3800* **Fax** *020 7798 8735* **Rooms** *148*   **Map** *21 A3*

Set in 3.5 acres of parkland, this 1930s development combines residential flats with suite hotel. Choose from classic, deluxe, admiral or master-style studios to three bedrooms with kitchens. Health club with pool, croquet lawn, shops and several restaurants complete the microcosm. **www.dolphinsquarehotel.co.uk**

41
41 Buckingham Palace Road, SW1 **Tel** *020 7300 0041* **Fax** *020 7 300 0141* **Rooms** *20*   **Map** *12 5F*

A boutique hotel with the feel of a private club. Guests are assigned a personal butler for their stay. The classic rooms have a smart, black-and-white colour scheme, state-of-the-art technology and marble bathrooms. Some have views of the Royal Mews, where the Queen's horses and carriages are kept. **www.41hotel.com**

City Inn Westminster
30 John Islip Street, SW1 **Tel** *020 7630 1000* **Fax** *020 7233 7575* **Rooms** *460*   **Map** *21 B2*

Around the corner from Tate Britain, City Inn is unpretentiously modern. Rooms have floor-to-ceiling windows (some of which command Thames views) and luxuries such as robes, flatscreen TVs and DVD players. There's a red cocktail lounge and café with outside tables. Enquire about cheap weekend deals. **www.cityinn.com**

Goring
Beeston Place, SW1 **Tel** *020 7396 9000* **Fax** *020 7834 4393* **Rooms** *71*   **Map** *20 E1*

O R Goring opened his eponymous hotel in 1910, and it's run by his great grandson today. Its comfortable rooms and marble bathrooms have a traditional charm, there's an airy, elegant restaurant and two bars, one in an enclosed terrace overlooking the lovely private garden. **www.goringhotel.co.uk**

MAYFAIR, ST JAMES'S

Brown's Hotel
Albemarle Street, W1 **Tel** *020 7493 6020* **Fax** *020 7493 9381* **Rooms** *117*   **Map** *12 F3*

This historic hotel, composed of 11 Georgian townhouses, has undergone extensive refurbishment, which respects its heritage while introducing contemporary furniture, British art and the latest technology. The bar, English Tea Room and restaurant have been updated and there's a health club. **www.brownshotel.com**

Chesterfield
35 Charles Street, W1 **Tel** *020 7491 2622* **Fax** *020 7491 4793* **Rooms** *110*   **Map** *12 E3*

A welcoming luxury hotel near Berkeley Square, the Chesterfield offers a variety of rooms, from the understated pinstriped "Savile Row" to the fun-themed "Garden Suite" with trellises and wicker furniture. There's underfloor heating in the marble bathrooms and free use of a nearby health club. **www.chesterfieldmayfair.com**

Claridges
Brook Street, W1 **Tel** *020 7629 8860* **Fax** *020 7499 2210* **Rooms** *203*   **Map** *12 E2*

Favoured by the European aristocracy in the 19th century (Empress Eugenie wintered here), Mayfair's Art Deco jewel attracts showbusiness, glitterati and corporate guests. Rooms range from Victorian to contemporary by way of fabulous Art Deco suites. Gordon Ramsay's fêted restaurant and a smart bar are further draws. **www.claridges.co.uk**

Metropolitan
Old Park Lane, W1 **Tel** *020 7447 1047* **Fax** *020 7447 1147* **Rooms** *150*   **Map** *12 E1*

The Metropolitan redefined the London luxury hotel when it opened in 1997 and its blond wood, pale fabrics and large plate-glass windows still epitomise modern chic. With holistic spa treatments, a top Japanese restaurant upstairs and entry to the exclusive Met Bar, you won't have to stray far. **www.metropolitan.como.bz**

No.5 Maddox
5 Maddox Street, W1 **Tel** *020 7647 0200* **Fax** *020 7647 0300* **Rooms** *12*   **Map** *12 F2*

Beautiful, contemporary one- to three-bedroom suites, complete with kitchens, hidden in an unmarked townhouse off Regent Street. Many have terraces or balconies. Among the many treats are welcome trays of goodies, linen kimonos, CD and DVD library and in-rooms holistic treatments. **www.no5maddoxst.com**

Ritz
150 Piccadilly, W1 **Tel** *020 7493 8181* **Fax** *020 7493 2687* **Rooms** *133*   **Map** *12 F3*

There are two staff for every room in this famous grand hotel on the edge of Green Park. You can even have your luggage unpacked for you. Rooms are in lavish Louis XVI style with antique furnishings and gold leaf, plus all mod cons. The Rivoli Bar has been restored to its Art Deco splendour. **www.theritzlondon.com**

Stafford
16–18 St James's Place, SW1 **Tel** *020 7493 0111* **Fax** *020 7493 7121* **Rooms** *81*   **Map** *12 F4*

This long-established townhouse hotel near Green Park has won a slew of awards and spends more than £1 million a year keeping up its refined period-style interior. Guests can stay in the main house or the atmospheric restored 17th-century stable yard. The American Bar is a cosy favourite. **www.thestaffordhotel.co.uk**

Key to Price Guide *see p282* **Key to Symbols** *see back cover flap*

The Connaught

Carlos Place, W1   **Tel** *020 7499 7070*   **Fax** *020 7495 3262*   **Rooms** *92*   **Map** *12 E3*

The Connaught maintains its traditional charm while moving with the times. Facilities include butler service and state-of-the-art gym. The interior feels less stuffy since many of the public rooms, including the Grill and the Connaught Bar, were restyled by renowned designer Nina Campbell. **www.theconnaught.co.uk**

The Dorchester

Park Lane, W1   **Tel** *020 7629 8888*   **Fax** *020 7409 0114*   **Rooms** *250*   **Map** *12 D3*

The epitome of the glamorous luxury hotel, with an outrageously lavish lobby and a star-studded history, the Dorchester has recently revamped its tasteful floral bedrooms. The Art Deco-style marble baths are probably the deepest in London. For even more pampering, pop down to the fabulous Art Deco spa. **www.thedorchester.com**

OXFORD STREET, SOHO

Edward Lear

28-30 Seymour Street, W1   **Tel** *020 7402 5401*   **Fax** *020 7706 3766*   **Rooms** *31*   **Map** *11 C2*

This characterful small hotel is in the former home of Victorian poet and artist Edward Lear. Rooms are tidy and spacious with satellite TVs. Opt for en suite or shared facilities to keep the cost down. There's a computer with free Internet access and leather seating in the pleasant guests' lounge. **www.edlear.com**

10 Manchester Street

10 Manchester Street, W1   **Tel** *020 7486 6669*   **Fax** *020 7224 0348*   **Rooms** *46*   **Map** *12 D1*

This grand 1919 former nursing home is equipped with many mod cons, including Internet access and satellite TV. Steps away from the Wallace Collection, the Wigmore Hall and the shops and restaurants of Marylebone High Street. There's a spacious guests' lounge as well. The hotel has recently been refurbished. **www.nichehotels.com**

Durrants Hotel

George Street, W1   **Tel** *020 7935 8131*   **Fax** *020 7487 3510*   **Rooms** *92*   **Map** *12 D1*

Established in 1790, Durrants occupies a row of terraced houses and its warren of creaky rooms is delightfully old fashioned. Decor is traditional, old prints and antiques, but TVs are hidden in cabinets and bathrooms are modern. The restaurant and bar are period pieces. Only a few rooms are air conditioned. **www.durrantshotel.co.uk**

Hazlitt's

6 Frith Street, W1   **Tel** *020 7434 1771*   **Fax** *020 7439 1524*   **Rooms** *23*   **Map** *13 A2*

The 18th-century essayist William Hazlitt was just one of the interesting figures to have resided here. Hazlitt's is as close to time travel as you can get: its period rooms feature fireplaces, antique beds and claw-footed baths, with mod cons such as Internet points and DVD players hidden discreetly away. **www.hazlittshotel.com**

Radisson Edwardian Hampshire

31-36 Leicester Square, WC2   **Tel** *020 7839 9399*   **Fax** *020 7930 8122*   **Rooms** *124*   **Map** *11 C2*

Colourful, cinema-lined Leicester Square is a good base if you want to make the most of London's nightlife, as it's well placed for the theatre district, bars, clubs and restaurants. This luxurious Radisson has designer bedrooms with Philippe Starck bathrooms and Bose sound systems in the suites. **www.radissonedwardian.com**

Sanderson

50 Berners Street, W1   **Tel** *020 7300 1400*   **Fax** *0207 300 1401*   **Rooms** *150*   **Map** *12 F1*

The Sanderson's witty decor, red lips sofa, a framed portrait that seems to hang in mid-air, is like a surreal stage set. Rooms have every comfort and the Alain Ducasse Spoon restaurant and two sophisticated cocktail bars are destinations in their own right. Agua spa offers holistic pampering. **www.morganshotelgroup.com**

The Cumberland

Great Cumberland Place, W1   **Tel** *0870 333 9280*   **Fax** *0870 333 9281*   **Rooms** *1019*   **Map** *11 C2*

This once-drab large hotel over Oxford Street has been reinvented as a spectacular showpiece. The vast lobby looks like a gallery in Tate Modern with large-scale avant-garde British works, rooms are modern without being clinical and fitted with the latest technology. Several chic dining and drinking spots nearby. **www.guoman.com**

The Leonard

15 Seymour Street, W1   **Tel** *020 7935 2010*   **Fax** *020 7935 6700*   **Rooms** *44*   **Map** *11 C1*

A gracious hotel comprising four 19th-century townhouses, minutes from bustling Oxford Street and Hyde Park. Rooms are in updated period style. There's free wireless Internet access throughout the hotel and staff will supply the latest DVDs to view in room. **www.theleonard.com**

The Soho Hotel

4 Richmond Mews, W1   **Tel** *020 7559 3000*   **Fax** *020 7559 3003*   **Rooms** *85 + 6 apartments*   **Map** *13 A2*

Firmdale Hotels' latest venture combines the light and space of a warehouse-style building with its signature modern English style. Two screening rooms, gym with personal trainer and exclusive Miller Harris products in the granite walk-in showers complete the sophisticated urban experience. **www.firmdalehotels.com**

REGENT'S PARK, MARYLEBONE

22 York Street   🚶   ££
22–24 York Street, W1 **Tel** *020 7224 2990* **Fax** *020 7224 1990* **Rooms** *20*   **Map** *3 C5*

This beautiful property is a cut above most B&Bs. Liz and Michael Callis ensure rooms in these two immaculately preserved Georgian houses are spotless and stylishly furnished with antiques and French quilts. A gourmet Continental breakfast is served in the rustic kitchen. Nonsmoking. **www.22yorkstreet.co.uk**

Hart House Hotel   🚶   ££
51 Gloucester Place, W1 **Tel** *020 7935 2288* **Fax** *020 7935 8516* **Rooms** *15*   **Map** *11 C1*

A well-maintained Georgian townhouse hotel with huge windows and high ceilings in some rooms. The dark wood furniture and bold tartan curtains make a refreshing change from frills and florals. The modern tiled bathrooms are spotless. Gloucester Place is a busy road, so you may prefer a back-facing room. **www.harthouse.co.uk**

Hotel La Place   🖥️🍴🚶📋   £££
17 Nottingham Place, W1 **Tel** *020 7486 2323* **Fax** *020 7486 4335* **Rooms** *20*   **Map** *4 D5*

In a pretty street in fashionable Marylebone, this small hotel is perfectly placed for shopping, dining and strolling in lovely Regent's Park. The en suite rooms are spacious with large windows and sweeping drapes, and the decor is regularly updated. There's also a chic bar, Internet room and restaurant. **www.hotellaplace.com**

Dorset Square   🖥️🍴🚶📋   ££££
39 Dorset Square, NW1 **Tel** *020 7723 7874* **Fax** *020 7724 3328* **Rooms** *37*   **Map** *3 C5*

Near Marylebone and Regent's Park, this Regency townhouse overlooks a tree-lined private square, the site of the first cricket ground (it later moved a mile north to Lord's). The hotel is decorated in English-country style, including romantic four-poster suites, and equipped with luxury amenities. **www.dorsetsquare.co.uk**

Sherlock Holmes Hotel   🖥️🍴📺📋   ££££
108 Baker Street, W1 **Tel** *020 7486 6161* **Fax** *020 7958 5211* **Rooms** *119*   **Map** *3 C5*

The name may suggest a tacky theme hotel, yet this is anything but that. You enter this Baker Street boutique hotel via its urban-chic bar. Contemporary rooms (many with wood floors) are softened with tactile throws and cushions; there are thoughtful details such as European and US sockets. The gym has spa facilities. **www.sherlockholmes.com**

Jury's Clifton Ford   🖥️🍴🛏️🚶📺📋   £££££
47 Welbeck Street, W1 **Tel** *020 7486 6600* **Fax** *020 7486 7492* **Rooms** *256*   **Map** *12 D1*

A classically furnished modern hotel in the heart of Marylebone village, the Clifton Ford offers spacious accommodation and great facilities, including its own health club with a swimming pool, whirlpool and sauna, a bar and restaurant. Very cheap seasonal offers are advertised on the website. **www.jurysdoyle.com**

The Langham   🖥️🍴🛏️🚶📺📋   £££££
1C Portland Place, W1 **Tel** *020 7636 1000* **Fax** *020 7323 2340* **Rooms** *427*   **Map** *12 E1*

The Langham was London's first grand hotel when it opened in 1865 and still offers an ultra-luxurious experience behind its sprawling Victorian façade. Rooms achieve a tasteful middle ground between modern and traditional and there are extensive spa facilities including a swimming pool. Near Regent's Park. **www.langhamhotels.com**

BLOOMSBURY, FITZROVIA

Arosfa   £
83 Gower Street, WC1 **Tel** *020 7636 2115* **Fax** *020 7636 2115* **Rooms** *15*   **Map** *5 A5*

The rooms are plainly furnished, but pristine, in this Georgian townhouse near London University. Every room has a tiny but spotless en suite shower and WC, making this one of the best deals in central London. True to its name, which means "resting place" in Welsh, there's a lounge with books and comfy sofas. **www.arosfalondon.com**

Hotel Cavendish   £
75 Gower Street, WC1 **Tel** *020 7636 9079* **Fax** *020 7580 3609* **Rooms** *31*   **Map** *5 A5*

This characterful B&B near London University has a fascinating history, DH Lawrence and the Beatles stayed here once. Rooms are simple yet comfortably furnished, and some have original fireplaces. Original artworks brighten up the breakfast room and there's a pretty garden as well. Shared facilities available. **www.hotelcavendish.com**

Crescent Hotel   🚶   ££
49–50 Cartwright Gardens, WC1 **Tel** *020 7387 1515* **Fax** *020 7 383 2054* **Rooms** *27*   **Map** *5 B4*

One of several hotels in this striking Regency street, the Crescent has been run by the same family since the 1950s. Most of the well-kept bedrooms have en suite facilities. Soft drinks and snacks are served in the homely lounge, and guests can use the tennis courts in the private gardens across. **www.crescenthoteloflondon.com**

Key to Price Guide *see p282* **Key to Symbols** *see back cover flap*

Euston Square Hotel

152–156 North Gower Street, NW1 **Tel** *020 7388 0099* **Fax** *020 7383 7165* **Rooms** *75*   **Map** *5 A4*

A chic stopover close to Euston Station. Rooms may be on the small side, but they are stylishly kitted out in dark wood and cream leather, with flatscreen TVs, a music library and tasteful tiled bathrooms. Complimentary papers and squashy sofas are on offer in the airy lounge and there's a restaurant/café. **www.euston-square-hotel.com**

Academy

21 Gower Street, WC1 **Tel** *020 7631 4115* **Fax** *020 7636 3442* **Rooms** *49*   **Map** *5 A5*

This discreet hotel comprising five interconnecting Georgian townhouses near London University is tastefully furnished in refined classic style, with modern features such as wireless broadband Internet and CD players. The lush private gardens are a lovely place to relax with a drink in the summer. **www.theetoncollection.com**

Bonnington Hotel

92 Southhampton Row, WC1 **Tel** *020 7242 2828* **Fax** *020 7831 9170* **Rooms** *247*   **Map** *5 C5*

An imposing early 20th-century hotel in a central location, offering comfortable, corporate-style accommodation at reasonable rates. Rooms are cheaper at weekends and there are discounts online. There's a chic executive wing with extra amenities. **www.bonnington.com**

Charlotte Street Hotel

15–17 Charlotte Street, W1 **Tel** *020 7806 2000* **Fax** *020 7806 2002* **Rooms** *52*   **Map** *13 A1*

The ground floor bar is always buzzing with local workers as well as guests in this exquisitely designed hotel in a street full of restaurants. Reflecting the area's history, its decor nods to the Bloomsbury set period with original artworks by Vanessa Bell and others. Weekend films in the screening room. **www.charlottestreethotel.com**

Myhotel Bloomsbury

11–13 Bayley Street, W1 **Tel** *020 7667 6000* **Fax** *020 7667 6044* **Rooms** *77*   **Map** *5 A5*

East meets West at this stylish contemporary hotel designed according to feng shui principles. The simple, serene rooms have low, Oriental-style beds and Aveda products. On-site facilities include a branch of Yo! Sushi, a buzzy public bar plus guests' library with Internet access, and holistic spa treatments. **www.myhotels.com**

The Montague on the Gardens

15 Montague Street, WC1 **Tel** *0845 634 2665* **Fax** *020 7612 8430* **Rooms** *104*   **Map** *5 B5*

This traditional townhouse hotel near the British Museum has high-tech amenities and newly-refurbished bathrooms in its classic, predominantly floral-print rooms and a well-equipped gym with sauna. There are two restaurants, a conservatory and a terrace bar on the secluded gardens. **www.montaguehotel.com**

COVENT GARDEN, STRAND, HOLBORN

Citadines Covent Garden/Holborn

94–99 High Holborn, WC1 **Tel** *020 7395 8800* **Fax** *0207 395 8799* **Rooms** *192*   **Map** *13 C1*

This centrally located branch of the French "apart'hotel" chain offers pleasant, good-value accommodation for up to four people. Studios or one-bedroom apartments have kitchenettes, dining tables, satellite TVs and hi-fis. There are also handy business facilities and breakfast room on-site. **www.citadines.com**

Fielding

4 Broad Court, Bow Street, WC2 **Tel** *020 7836 8305* **Fax** *020 7497 0064* **Rooms** *24*   **Map** *12 C2*

Situated in a historic pedestrianized area near Covent Garden, the Fielding is right across the street from the Royal Opera House. The decor may not make it into any interior design books, but rooms have en suite facilities and prices are keen given the area. **www.the-fielding-hotel.co.uk**

Covent Garden Hotel

10 Monmouth Street, WC2 **Tel** *020 7806 1000* **Fax** *020 7806 1100* **Rooms** *58*   **Map** *13 B2*

This exquisite hotel's Covent Garden location is one reason why it's popular with thespians. Part of the Firmdale chain, it is decorated in contemporary-English style with antiques and fresh fabrics. Brasserie Max is a popular meeting spot and films are shown in the luxurious screening room at weekends. **www.firmdalehotels.com**

One Aldwych
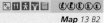

1 Aldwych, WC2 **Tel** *020 7300 1000* **Fax** *020 7300 1001* **Rooms** *105*   **Map** *13 C2*

A grand contemporary hotel in former Edwardian newspaper offices. Impressive details include original art and tarazzo-stone bathrooms with heated floors and mini TVs. There's a spacious health club with a swimming pool, several chic restaurants and the buzzing, high-ceilinged Lobby Bar. **www.onealdwych.com**

Renaissance Chancery Court

252 High Holborn, WC1 **Tel** *020 7829 9888* **Fax** *020 7829 9889* **Rooms** *356*   **Map** *13 C1*

A large, swanky hotel in the stately former Pearl Assurance headquarters. The decor is a modern spin on tradition with rich colours, clean lines and proper wooden headboards. There's a glamorous French restaurant, plus a spa with sauna and steam room, offering indulgent E'SPA treatments. **www.renaissancechancerycourt.com**

Savoy

£££££

Strand, WC2 **Tel** *020 7836 4343* **Fax** *020 7240 6040* **Rooms** *263*   **Map** *13 C2*

This legendary hotel was an afterthought, Richard D'Oyly Carte capitalized on the success of his Savoy Theatre by providing a place to stay. The rest is history. Monet painted the Thames view from his window, Elton John flooded a bathroom and the dry martini was invented in the bar. There's a rooftop pool as well. **www.fairmont.com/savoy**

SOUTHWARK, LAMBETH

Comfort Inn

££

87 South Lambeth Road, SW8 **Tel** *020 7735 9494* **Fax** *020 7735 1001* **Rooms** *94*   **Map** *21 5C*

The interior of this modern low-rise chain hotel is surprisingly cool and there are often very cheap offers on the website. Simple, contemporary rooms have en suite power showers and satellite TVs with pay Internet and games, while executive suites come with fridge, microwave and Jacuzzi. **www.comfortinnvx.co.uk**

Travel Inn London County Hall

££

Belvedere Road, SE1 **Tel** *0870 238 3300* **Fax** *020 7902 1619* **Rooms** *313*   **Map** *14 D5*

This branch of the budget premier Travel Inn chain is housed in the massive former County Hall on the Thames. The more expensive Marriott, which shares the building, has all the river views, but it's a good-value option next to the London Eye, near Waterloo and the South Bank arts complex. Wireless Internet on-site. **www.premiertravelinn.com**

Novotel London City South

£££

53–61 Southwark Bridge Road, SE1 **Tel** *020 7089 0400* **Fax** *020 7089 0410* **Rooms** *182*   **Map** *15 A3*

Billed as a "New Generation" Novotel, the interior has an airy, minimalist feel. Rooms are equipped with extras such as wireless Internet, mini bar and even a radio in the bathroom. The fitness centre has a sauna and steam room, and the location is convenient for the venues and galleries of the South Bank. **www.novotel.com**

Southwark Rose Hotel

£££

43–47 Southwark Bridge Road, SE1 **Tel** *020 7015 1480* **Fax** *020 7015 1481* **Rooms** *84*   **Map** *15 A3*

The name may conjure up images of an old-English inn, but this is a budget version of a modern luxury hotel near Tate Modern and Shakespeare's Globe. Rooms, in a different colour scheme on each floor, are kitted out with modern leather headboards, slick mosaic-tiled bathrooms and wireless Internet. **www.southwarkrosehotel.co.uk**

London Bridge Hotel

£££££

8–18 London Bridge Street, SE1 **Tel** *020 7855 2200* **Fax** *020 7855 2233* **Rooms** *138*   **Map** *15 B4*

A classic, if somewhat mainstream, hotel near foodie's paradise Borough Market, executive rooms are more styish. On-site Malaysian restaurant Georgetown makes a change from the usual bland hotel fare, and guests are given free entry to the adjoining Fitness First health club. **www.londonbridgehotel.com**

Marriott County Hall

£££££

Westminster Bridge Road, SE1 **Tel** *020 7928 5200* **Fax** *020 7928 5300* **Rooms** *200*   **Map** *13 C5*

Housed in the vast former County Hall building on the Thames, this Marriott is on a grand scale, with a magnificent library, new gym and spa and one of the largest pools in London. Rooms are in keeping with the period style; some boast four-poster beds and amazing views of Big Ben. **www.marriott.co.uk**

CITY, CLERKENWELL

The Zetter

£££

86–88 Clerkenwell Road, EC1 **Tel** *020 7324 4444* **Fax** *020 7324 4445* **Rooms** *59*   **Map** *6 F4*

In an area known for its loft apartments, this is a loft dining in a 19th-century warehouse. Rooms have exposed brick, quirky 1970s furniture, old Penguin books, hot-water bottles and high-tech extras, while vending machines on each floor dispense necessities. Hip-Italian restaurant at street level. **www.thezetter.com**

Great Eastern

£££££

Liverpool Street, EC2 **Tel** *020 7618 5000* **Fax** *020 7618 5001* **Rooms** *267*   **Map** *15 C1*

This magnificent 19th-century railway hotel was given a makeover by design guru Conran, juxtaposing dramatic modern elements with the original-Victorian features. Cutting-edge art is displayed throughout, bedrooms are furnished with Eames and Jacobson pieces and there are five fabulous eateries. **www.great-eastern-hotel.co.uk**

Hotel St Gregory

£££££

100 Shoreditch High Street, E1 **Tel** *020 7613 9800* **Fax** *020 7613 9811* **Rooms** *196*   **Map** *8 D4*

This swanky new hotel is the first to colonise this up-and-coming area, perfect for the arty boutiques off Brick Lane and the bars and galleries of Hoxton. There are interesting large-scale artworks in the cool white lobby, luxurious warm-toned rooms with Villeroy & Boch bathrooms and a 1970s-influenced bar. **www.saintgregoryhotel.com**

Key to Price Guide *see p282* **Key to Symbols** *see back cover flap*

Malmaison

Charterhouse Square, EC1 **Tel** *020 7012 3700* **Fax** *020 7012 3207* **Rooms** *97*   **Map** *6 F5*

The London outpost of this chic chain is in a red-brick Victorian building on a historic cobbled square; inside is a striking modern, art-filled interior and trendy brasserie. Rooms are spacious and comfortable with upholstered headboards, CD players and French wines. **www.malmaison-london.com**

Rookery

Peter's Lane, Cowcross Street, EC1 **Tel** *020 7336 0931* **Fax** *020 7336 0932* **Rooms** *33*   **Map** *6 F5*

Occupying six-Georgian houses and shops (with faded butcher's and baker's signs still visible on some), this Dickensian hideaway retains many original features, such as flagstone floors in the hall and ceiling beams in some of the rooms. Decorated with antiques throughout, it also offers all the latest technology. **www.rookeryhotel.com**

FURTHER AFIELD

Fulham Guest House

55 Wandsworth Bridge Road, SW6 **Tel** *020 7731 1662* **Rooms** *5*

Sam and George Doubledee run this friendly B&B from their Victorian home on a wide tree-lined street in affluent Fulham. Rooms are simple and comfortable and shared facilities are clean and up-to-date. The laidback atmosphere makes it a good choice for families; highchairs and toys are available. **www.fulhamguesthouse.com**

The Mitre

291 Greenwich High Street, SE10 **Tel** *020 8355 6760* **Fax** *020 8355 6761* **Rooms** *15*   **Map** *23 B2*

Bustling pub with rooms close to sights and transport links. The protected 18th-century building was originally a coffee house, and interior-designed, en suite rooms are traditional in pastel colour schemes. There's a weekday bar menu and carvery meals at weekends and bank holidays in the pub.

Hampstead Village Guesthouse

2 Kemplay Road, NW3 **Tel** *020 7435 8679* **Fax** *020 7794 0254* **Rooms** *9*   **Map** *1 B5*

This Victorian home, in the picturesque village and a short walk from the heath, is intriguingly cluttered with antiques and curios. Breakfast is served in the garden in summer, English weather permitting. Rooms are equipped with a hot-water bottle and fridge. The rates are cheaper if you forgo en suite facilities. **www.hampsteadguesthouse.com**

Novotel Greenwich

173–175 Greenwich High Road, SE10 **Tel** *020 8312 6800* **Fax** *020 8312 6810* **Rooms** *151*   **Map** *23 A3*

Opened in 2005, this modern hotel is conveniently located next to Greenwich station. It is light and airy and has a stylish decor created from wood, stone and richly coloured furnishings. 24-hour room service is available. **www.novotel.com**

The Petersham

Nightingale Lane, Richmond, Surrey, TW10 **Tel** *020 8940 7471* **Fax** *020 8939 1098* **Rooms** *61*

This sprawling Victorian hotel perches on Richmond Hill overlooking the Thames. The elegant rooms are in keeping with the building's period grandeur, while integrating modern elements; some have spectacular views of the Thames. Unsurprisingly given its romantic location, it's popular for weddings. **www.petershamhotel.co.uk**

Colonnade

2 Warrington Crescent, W9 **Tel** *020 7286 1052* **Fax** *020 7286 1057* **Rooms** *43*

Near the picturesque canals of Little Venice, this hotel in two Victorian mansions has been operating since the 1930s. Freud stayed here while his house was being redecorated, and JFK paid a visit in the 60s. The interior is grand yet unintimidating and every luxurious room has a different feel. **www.theetoncollection.com**

Hilton London Docklands
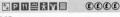

265 Rotherhithe Street, SE16 **Tel** *020 7231 1001* **Fax** *020 7231 0599* **Rooms** *365*

A modern hotel with great views of Canary Wharf, the Hilton is both family friendly and geared up for business travellers. Many of the spacious rooms have balconies, there's a fitness centre with a pool and a restaurant on a ship moored on the hotel's dry dock. Cheap rates are often available. **www.hilton.com**

K West

Richmond Way, W14 **Tel** *08700 274343* **Fax** *08708 112612* **Rooms** *220*

Off the beaten track near BBC HQ, this striking steel and glass hotel is popular with high-profile guests, and often offers amazingly cheap deals on the website. Sleek rooms are soothingly neutral, there's a cool bar and, best of all, a luxurious spa with gym, marble Jacuzzi room and E'SPA treatments. **www.k-west.co.uk**

Cannizaro House

West Side, Wimbledon Common, SW19 **Tel** *0870 333 9124* **Fax** *0870 333 9224* **Rooms** *45*

This Georgian mansion on the edge of Wimbledon Common is an ideal base for keen tennis fans. Rooms are decorated in a country-house style; some have four-poster beds and air conditioning. There is a restaurant, cocktail bar and extensive grounds, where you can play croquet. **www.cannizarohouse.com**

RESTAURANTS AND PUBS

Hailed as the world's dining capital, London thrives on an extraordinary culinary diversity. From a traditional forte of Indian, Chinese, French and Italian restaurants, eating out in London now enables your palate to take a gastronomic journey around the world, from America to Africa, taking in a pan-European tour, as well as the Middle East, Asia, and the Pacific Rim.

A pre-theatre menu board

included. More details are in the listings on pages 296–311, where restaurants are grouped by district. Restaurants have been selected for their good value or exceptional food and are listed alphabetically within each price category.

London's café scene has become much more dynamic over the past few years, with good coffee and snacks readily available throughout the day. Pubs have also evolved, with many modernizing their decor and placing far more emphasis on serving good food, ranging from classic British snacks to ethnic dishes. For a selection of mainly informal places to eat and drink, including pubs, see pages 312–19.

CHOOSING YOUR TABLE

The restaurants listed in this guide represent a comprehensive range of styles and prices. They are spread across the main tourist areas, although some that merit a special trip further afield are also

LONDON RESTAURANTS

The broadest choice of restaurants can be found in Covent Garden, Piccadilly, Mayfair, Soho and Leicester Square. Knightsbridge, Kensington and Chelsea also offer a good range of restaurants. Central London has few riverside restaurants, but there is a cluster along Chelsea Harbour, in Chelsea, and Butler's Wharf on the south bank of the Thames. While traditional British food can be enjoyed, the style is not so readily available. Chefs such as Fergus Henderson at St

Commissionaire at the Hard Rock Café *(see p315)*

John are revitalizing British dishes, but the emphasis is on Modern British cooking which combines a variety of culinary influences and techniques from around the world. Home-grown chefs such as Sally Clarke, Alastair Little and Marco Pierre White have been instrumental in helping to elevate restaurant dining over the past two decades.

Alongside great improvements in cuisine, the standard of service has risen, and there has never been so much focus on interior design. This has added to the "diversity" of London's restaurants, which offer anything from classically ornate and romantic decor, to modern and post-modern minimalism. London has long been a paradise for Indian, Chinese, French and Italian food, with more restaurants specializing in regional cuisine. Asian food is increasingly popular, particularly Thai and Japanese, with Soho offering plenty of choice.

Most restaurants provide at least one vegetarian option, and some have a separate vegetarian menu. A growing number of specialist vegetarian restaurants offer more adventurous dishes. Fish and seafood is another speciality, with both traditional and modern-style restaurants.

Great Eastern Dining Room *(see p311)*

OTHER PLACES TO EAT

Many hotels have excellent restaurants open to non-residents, which in some cases include a menu composed by, or even the actual dishes prepared by, a star chef. These restaurants range from the very formal to the fun and flamboyant, and prices tend to be at the top end of the scale. There are also increasing numbers of pizza, pasta and brasserie chains serving reliable, good-value food across the city.

Among these dramatic improvements are also "gastro-pubs" and wine bars that serve anything from standard staples to Thai curries, accompanied by global wine lists. Otherwise, you can grab a quick snack from one of the many sandwich bars or cafés.

Hakkasan *(see p305)*

TIPS ON EATING OUT

Most London restaurants serve lunch between noon and 2.30pm, with dinner from 6.30pm until 11pm, which usually means that last orders are taken at 11pm. Ethnic restaurants may stay open slightly longer, until midnight or even later. Some restaurants may close for either lunch or dinner during the weekend, and it is always best to check opening times first. All-day cafés and brasseries may now serve alcohol without restriction during licensing hours (11am–11pm).

The traditional British Sunday lunch appears in many pubs and restaurants, although more informal brunches are increasingly popular. It is worth checking beforehand, however, unless traditional Sunday lunch is what you particularly want, as even high-class restaurants may suspend their normal menu on Sundays.

Some of the most formal restaurants insist on a jacket and tie, or a jacket. Booking is advisable, especially at recently opened or celebrity-chef-run restaurants.

PRICE AND SERVICE

As London is one of the world's most expensive cities, restaurant prices can often seem exorbitant to visitors, with an average three-course meal and a few glasses of house wine, at a medium-priced central London restaurant costing around £25–35 per person. Many restaurants have set-price menus which are generally significantly less expensive than ordering à la carte and, in some instances, the price includes coffee and service.

Similarly, various West End restaurants serve pre-theatre set menus (typically from around 5.30–6pm). Although geared towards a quick turn-around, this provides an opportunity to eat at quality restaurants at a competitive price. Lower prices (around £10–15 a head) apply at smaller, more modest ethnic and vegetarian restaurants, wine bars and pubs, where the food can nevertheless be well prepared and offer good value. However, some of these establishments will only accept cash or cheques, not credit cards.

Before ordering, check the small print at the bottom of the menu. Prices will include Value Added Tax (VAT) and may add an optional service charge (between 10 and 15 per cent). Some restaurants may also impose a cover charge (£1–£2 a head), or a minimum charge during the busiest periods, while some do not accept certain credit cards. Beware of the old trick where service is included in the bill but staff leave the "total" box on your credit slip blank, hoping you will add another 10 per cent. Expect different types of service in different types of restaurant. This can range from cheerful and breezy in fast-food joints to discreet yet attentive in more expensive venues. At peak dining times you will usually have to wait longer to be served.

St John *(see p308)*

EATING WITH CHILDREN

Except in Italian restaurants, fast-food establishments, branches of Wagamama and a few other venues such as The Rainforest Café on Shaftesbury Avenue (a tropical haven for young diners), children tend to be simply tolerated in London restaurants rather than warmly welcomed.

However, with the growing trend for a more informal style of dining, more and more restaurants are learning to become child-friendly, offering a special children's menu or smaller portions and high chairs, while some provide colouring books and even put on live entertainment to keep the little diners happy. See page 357 for suggested places that cater for children of a wide range of ages.

London's top Hungarian restaurant *(see p305)*

The Flavours of London

"Modern European cooking" describes much of what's on offer in London, a reflection of the capital's cosmopolitan nature. However, as competitive restaurateurs vie for customers, they often look to traditional foods, from once-unfashionable beetroot to pig's trotters and offal, while increasing concern about what goes into the growing and rearing of food is also reflected on London menus. Even pub food, once limited to Sunday roasts, the ubiquitous "ploughman's lunch" (cheese or ham with bread and pickles) or sandwiches has been given fresh slant by "gastropubs" and a new breed of sandwich bars offering fresh, top-quality snacks.

Chef and customer at Clerkenwell's St John restaurant

LONDON'S LARDER

Nowhere better exemplifies the city's blossoming love affair with good food than Borough Market *(see p339)*. Its busy stalls of both regional and continental food are a microcosm of what Londoners today like to eat. There is produce from all over Britain – English and Irish cheeses; Scottish beef; Welsh lamb; Devon cider; Suffolk oysters – as well as from the rest of the world. Visitors can snack as they browse, on anything from Cornish scallops to grilled Spanish chorizo.

MODERN BRITISH FOOD

London menus increasingly detail the provenance of ingredients with obvious pride. Ancient or "rare" breeds of cattle are name-checked, such as Gloucester Old Spot pork. Once-overlooked, old-fashioned ingredients like rhubarb and black (blood) pudding are being used in creative new ways. Seasonal and organic produce is also taking more of a centre stage. The new breed of "gastropubs" were among the first to adopt these trends, offering good, imaginative, well-prepared,

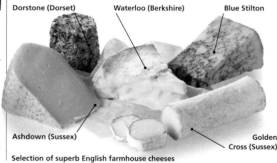

Dorstone (Dorset)   Waterloo (Berkshire)   Blue Stilton

Ashdown (Sussex)   Golden Cross (Sussex)

Selection of superb English farmhouse cheeses

TRADITIONAL ENGLISH FOOD

You can still find traditional dishes, such as jugged hare, roast beef or brown Windsor soup, but even fish 'n' chips can be harder to hunt down than tapas, pizza or chicken tikka masala. A "full English breakfast" is a fry-up of sausages, eggs, bacon, tomatoes, mushrooms and bread, perhaps with black (blood) pudding. Baked beans and fried potatoes may be included, as can bubble and squeak (re-fried cabbage and potato). There is an English heritage of heavy "nursery" puddings. These are a favourite of gentlemen's clubs and include such treats as treacle tart, roly-poly (suet and jam) pudding, spotted dick (suet and currants) and fruit crumbles with custard. Teatime may be a thing of the past but some top hotels still offer "cream teas" with scones, cakes and perhaps cucumber sandwiches.

Celery and Stilton soup *The king of English cheeses makes an excellent winter soup when combined with celery.*

Bountiful vegetable stall at south London's Borough Market

sensibly-priced food, as well as fine wines and beers, in the relaxed surroundings of the traditional London pub.

Chef Fergus Henderson of St John *(see p308)* is a pioneer of "head-to-toe" eating, espousing anything from ox cheek and tail to entire roast suckling pig.

London's historic seafood favourites, such as cockles and whelks, are increasingly hard to find at present but, as capital of an island nation, the city offers many fine fish restaurants. Concerns about over-fishing and farmed fish means that you are likely to see less cod and haddock and more of such local catch as bream, bass, sole and gurnard, as well as salmon being billed as wild, and scallops as diver-caught.

EASTERN FLAVOURS

Britain has long had a love affair with both Oriental and Indian food, and some of the best examples of each can be found in London. While

A mouthwatering pint of traditional London bitter beer

chicken tikka masala has been voted the nation's favourite dish (invented here, the legend goes, to satisfy the national passion for gravy by pairing tandoori dry-roasted meat with a mild, creamy sauce), regional Indian food is now to the fore, notably southern cuisine strong on coconut, fish and fruits. The balti is another British take on the food of the subcontinent – named for the bowl-shaped dish in which they are cooked and served, fresh-tasting stews are served alongside vast naan breads for dunking.

In Chinatown, you can enjoy everything from a simple bowl of noodles to gourmet dishes featuring rare ingredients such as razorshell clams and sea urchins.

WHAT TO DRINK

Beers There are two large brewers in London – Young's and Fuller's – and some micro-brewers, too. The main varieties found in Britain are:
Bitter Brewed from malted barley, hops, yeast and water; drunk at room temperature.
Mild ale Sweeter than bitter.
Lager Hundreds of varieties of this pale carbonated beer are available. Served chilled.
Stout Thick, dark, creamy Guinness is the most famous.

Cider English cider has undergone a revival, with producers often featuring single old English apple varieties and using traditional methods.

Dover sole *This is the most tasty flatfish, best served simply grilled with lemon, spinach and new potatoes.*

Roast beef *Horseradish sauce is a traditional accompaniment, as are crisp Yorkshire puddings made of batter.*

Summer pudding *Lightly cooked fruits fill a basin lined with bread, which absorbs the sweet juices.*

Choosing a Restaurant

These restaurants have been selected for their good value or exceptional food and are listed alphabetically within each price category. Starting with west and southwestern districts of London, the guide moves through central parts and on to eastern districts, eventually looking at restaurants further outside the city.

BAYSWATER

Alounak   £
44 Westbourne Grove, W2 5SH **Tel** *020 7229 4158*   **Map** 10 D2

A typical Iranian restaurant, which means it isn't exactly the same as Persian or any other related cuisine. The food is a little lighter and less rich. The style verges on a bazaar café, simple bare wood tables, with no wine on sale and soft drinks served in the can. The price reflects this simplicity and the presence of so many Iranians proves the authenticity.

Aphrodite Taverna   ££
15 Hereford Road, W2 4AB **Tel** *020 7229 2206*   **Map** 10 D2

Small and unpretentious, this little tavern tries hard and succeeds. Halloumi, kleftiko, moussaka, baklava and all the Greek greats are delicious, and their stuffed vine leaves aren't bathed in vicious brine. If not homemade, they are at least made by someone who cares. Aphrodite excels at starters and is popular with guests from nearby hotels.

Inaho   ££
4 Hereford Road, W2 4AA **Tel** *020 7221 8495*   **Map** 10 D2

Fish is a speciality in this small Japanese restaurant, and can include eel and top-quality tuna. Yakitori is delicious. Many people find it a strange little place and it certainly is not for the "trendies," but the chef really knows his stuff. Japanese restaurants attract heavy smokers though, so be warned.

Saigon Mekong Restaurant   ££
48 Queensway, W2 3RY **Tel** *020 7229 9111*   **Map** 10 E3

Very authentic is the verdict of regulars at this Vietnamese eatery. While Thai food has taken off in the capital, it's hard to find real Vietnamese cuisine that isn't a disgrace. This restaurant can hold its head up and point to zingy flavours in well-balanced dishes served by charming staff who are happy to help and advise.

Tawana   ££
3 Westbourne Grove, W2 4UA **Tel** *020 7229 3785*   **Map** 10 D1

A restaurant that has been established in the area for many years. A commitment to authentic Thai cuisine (and not the camouflaged Chinese that so many "Thai" restaurants try to get away with) means it has a loyal clientele. Ingredients are fresh and the balance of hot and sour is always perfect.

KENSINGTON, HOLLAND PARK, NOTTING HILL

Angies   ££
381 Harrow Road, W9 3NA **Tel** *020 8962 8761*   **Map** 9 B1

Angies offers a collection of dishes from the different regions of Africa and the Caribbean, with specials such as whole guinea fowl and grilled spiced rabbit. Friday nights are particularly busy, as are the family-orientated Sunday buffets.

Karma   ££
44 Blythe Road, W14 0HA **Tel** *020 7602 9333*   **Map** 17 A1

Karma takes you on a culinary journey of the Indian sub-continent, exploring the many regional styles of cooking that India has to offer and adding a modern twist to the dishes. The restaurant's wine list has been specially created to complement the food.

La Maja   ££
43–45 Porchester Road, W2 5DP **Tel** *020 7792 5885*   **Map** 10 D1

Loads of lovely tapas, as well as generous main courses, keep locals coming back for more. La Maja really feels authentic in an unforced way and the variety of dishes is mouthwatering. A great range of robust Riojas wash down the food, which is hearty and garlicky and just perfect for accompanying lively conversation.

Key to Symbols *see back cover flap*

Rodizio Rico

111 Westbourne Grove, W2 4UW **Tel** *020 7792 4035*   **Map** *9 D2*

Brazilian-style eating and great fun. Go for the buffet where you pick up your salad yourself and let the waiters bring you different bits of variously grilled meats at regular intervals. *Rodizio* is a concept in Brazil, which translates pretty much as "all you can eat". Really not a place for non-carnivores, but most will never leave hungry.

The Belvedere

Holland House, Abbotsbury Road, W8 6LU **Tel** *020 7602 1238*   **Map** *9 B5*

Tucked away in leafy Holland Park, The Belvedere is in a perfect location. The opulence of the main room might make you think you're in for a big bill, but it effortlessly combines a brilliant variety of dishes at a very fair price. "Gastro-pub" type food means hearty and heartening meals that comfort the senses while tickling the palate.

Yas

7 Hammersmith Road, Kensington Olympia, W14 8XJ **Tel** *020 7603 9148*   **Map** *17 A1*

Persian food means plenty of meat on the main course, although vegetarians can fill up on a great variety of dips. The bread here is baked on the premises. What's really remarkable is that this place is still open well past midnight. In fact, it doesn't begin to get busy until really rather late. On a warm night, sit outside and watch the world go by.

Assaggi

39 Chepstow Place, W2 4TS **Tel** *020 7792 5501*   **Map** *9 C2*

A short walk east from Bayswater tube gets you to this small restaurant. The menu is in Italian, but you can guess most dishes and the waiters will explain the rest. It's all smiles from the staff, but then they know you might easily break your bank. Good food, but be careful what you spend.

Cibo

3 Russell Gardens, W14 8EZ **Tel** *020 7371 6271*   **Map** *9 A5*

You get plenty of bread and olives to pack in while you wait for excellent Northern Italian food here. It's been on this site so long it's an institution, whilst its clever mix of tried and trusted Italian favourites combined with more adventurous dishes never fails to satisfy its young crowd. A good wine list completes its appeal.

The Ark

122 Palace Gardens Terrace, W8 4RT **Tel** *020 7229 4024*   **Map** *9 D3*

This restaurant has a stylish, intimate feel and serves superb Italian food to match, with impressive dishes such as butternut squash ravioli in a hazelnut and sage butter sauce. The wine list is excellent and informative, with imaginative cocktails and a truffle-tasting menu (winter only) adding to the Ark's considerable charm.

SOUTH KENSINGTON, KNIGHTSBRIDGE

Bugis Street Brasserie

The Millennium Gloucester Hotel, Ashburn Place, SW7 4LH **Tel** *020 7331 6211*   **Map** *18 E2*

It's called a brasserie but it's not French food. Expat Singapore natives say it's the best in London for their kind of food. Dishes are robust, extremely tasty and come in gigantic portions. Plus, for the area, it's not very expensive. For starters the salt and pepper squid is exceptional.

Maggie Jones

6 Old Court Place, W8 4PL **Tel** *020 7937 6462*   **Map** *10 D5*

A quirky ambience and the intimate dining atmosphere make this a peculiarly British-dining experience. Huge portions mean no one has left Maggie's hungry for over 16 years now. Service can be eccentric, but just sit back and enjoy. The steak and kidney pie is a must.

One

1 Kensington High Street, W8 5NP **Tel** *020 7937 0393*   **Map** *10 E5*

Persian and Greek food par excellence with perfect kebabs grilled to smoky brilliance. Try their tasty, moist pieces of marinated lamb and/or chicken over saffron-scented, buttery rice. Friendly staff are happy to advise on choice of dishes and to stop you from over-ordering, as you may be tempted to do so. Good value, too.

Amaya

Halkin Arcade, 19 Motcomb Street, SW1 8JT **Tel** *020 7823 1166*   **Map** *12 D5*

A very different Indian restaurant indeed. Spacious, stylish and with the kitchen on honest display. The speciality here is grills and you can see the three stations – tandoori, sigra and tawa – in action all evening. The range of meats and vegetables is brilliant and the presentation and service faultless. Expensive, but worth dining here.

Nahm

The Halkin, 5 Halkin Street, SW1X 7DJ **Tel** *020 7333 1234*   **Map** *12 D5*

A remarkable Thai restaurant that has a Michelin star so you can arrive with high hopes. The set menu offers not a dull moment. Try the appetiser *ma hor* – minced prawns and chicken simmered in palm sugar with deep fried shallots, garlic and peanuts, served on pineapple and mandarin orange. Not cheap but good.

One 0 One
101 William Street, SW1X 7RN **Tel** *020 7290 7101*   *Map 11 C5*

Fish, fish and shellfish. King crab risotto with scallops and razor clams is just a starter. Move on to freshwater black tiger prawns a la planta served with royal seafood paella and chorizo sauce and then keep going. This really is top-of-the-class cooking and the prices also reflect this. But it's not overpriced, just fair.

Pasha
1 Gloucester Road, SW7 4PP **Tel** *020 7589 7969*   *Map 18 E1*

North Africans love lamb, and here it comes at its best in a spicy tagine with loads of couscous to mop the lovely juices. The tables are rather tiny and it can be tricky keeping all your dishes from tumbling to the floor, but it's all good fun. Breads and mezza are delicious and there are occasional live music evenings with belly dancing.

Whits
21 Abingdon Road, W8 6AH **Tel** *020 7938 1122*   *Map 17 C1*

A neighbourhood restaurant on a side lane off busy High Street Kensington. Because of its position it does not attract the masses. Try whole roast sea bass with rocket and artichoke salad. Other mains include pork with crackling and Elwy Valley lamb. Food is consistently good and very seasonal, but always very affordable.

Foliage
Mandarin Oriental Hyde Park, 66 Knightsbridge, SW1X 7LA **Tel** *020 7235 2000*   *Map 11 C5*

A fantastic restaurant, which seems able to serve the most remarkable food at very reasonable prices. Foliage offers spectacular views of Hyde Park but don't let that distract you from the menu. Your three-course set meal is normally five when you include the little tasters in between and the service is faultless. A real jewel.

Mju
Millennium Knightsbridge, 17 Sloane Street, SW1X 9NU **Tel** *020 7201 6330*   *Map 19 C1*

The food is a bit hard to categorize at Mju but the restaurant isn't. In this location you expect style and you get it. The best way to appreciate the food is to go for the multicourse tasting menu. Each small dish is assembled with a smart precision. Try oysters with ginger and mirin as well as sea urchin and *foie gras* custard served in a shot glass!

The Conservatory
The Lanesborough, Hyde Park Corner, SW1X 7TA **Tel** *020 7259 5599*   *Map 12 D4*

Rather expensive but no one seems to be complaining. Colonial-style decor but a strong global menu. A jolly pianist knocks out some middle of the road swing and little dishes punctuate the main events. This is a luxury hotel and the service and food confirm this. Hard to go wrong and Sunday lunch is quite a bargain.

Zuma
5 Raphael Street, SW7 1DL **Tel** *020 7584 1010*   *Map 11 C5*

Very cool, very trendy and bang opposite Harrods. Celebrities can be spotted here but they come for the great food just like everyone else. Great sashimi, nigiri, sushi and tempura with fancy service and fancy prices. It's definitely an experience, but be prepared to dig deep into your holiday money.

Zafferano
15 Lowndes Street, SW1X 9EY **Tel** *020 7235 5800*   *Map 20 D1*

Zafferano has long been recognised as one of the capital's premier Italian restaurants. It's a discreet place, where the emphasis is firmly on the food. Dishes such as risotto with white truffle and char-grilled lamb with aubergine (eggplant) allow the quality of the ingredients to shine through.

CHELSEA, FULHAM

Lomo
222 Fulham Road, SW10 9NB **Tel** *020 7349 8848*   *Map 18 F4*

A bit of Barcelona in London, its patrons say. Look at the giant TV screens showing Spanish football, hear the roar of the crowd as it tucks into delicious tapas, sherry and Riojas. You can eat as a couple or go as a group, the ambience is always fine and you will always find that new dish you never had before as well as ones that are firm favourites.

1492 Latin Fusion
404 North End Road, SW6 1LU **Tel** *020 7381 3810*   *Map 17 C5*

Fusion food from South America means all kinds of interesting dishes in this nice welcoming restaurant. Warmly decorated with brown leather chairs, wooden floors and burnt Sienna walls, the South American feel is reflected in the art on the walls. The big steaks are as popular as the spicy combinations.

Borscht 'n' Tears
46 Beauchamp Place, SW3 1NX **Tel** *020 7584 9911*   *Map 19 B1*

This place has been here since before the Berlin Wall came down, doing its very best bit for Anglo-Russian relations. The vodka flows pretty freely and the tables can become dance floors. The food is traditional, so it's a bit heavy but the tastes are all there. You'll have a fun night, if you can remember anything afterwards!

Key to Price Guide *see p296* **Key to Symbols** *see back cover flap*

Buona Sera at the Jam

289a Kings Road, SW3 5EW **Tel** *020 7352 8827*

Map *19 A4*

Top-deck dining, literally. At this restaurant there are tables stacked up high like bunk beds. Shimmy up the ladder and settle down. It's not just a novelty restaurant; the food really is rather good and being perched on top only adds to the fun. A place for a night out with a difference. Try and call ahead to book yourself a top table!

Nirvana

430 Kings Road, SW10 0LJ **Tel** *020 7352 7771*

Map *18 F4*

Easy to walk past (a rather concealed entrance), Nirvana achieves high standards in a basement room. It's a family affair and it shows in the casual and unstressed way the team deal with a lot of people in quite a small space. Stir-fried baby squid with chilli and ginger is rather special. Some local celebrities like to dine here too.

Randall & Aubin

329–331 Fulham Road, SW10 9QL **Tel** *020 7823 3515*

Map *18 F4*

This is a place for fish fanatics, though meat including steaks is also on the menu. Oysters, scallops and whole brick-red lobsters are just a few dishes served at big tables or in small, intimate booths. Waiting staff are charming and extremely helpful.

The Painted Heron

112 Cheyne Walk, SW10 0DJ **Tel** *020 7351 5232*

Map *19 A5*

A nice Indian bistro in a pleasant part of Chelsea. Flavours are fresh with meat and poultry scoring highly for complex spices without overpowering chilli burn. Seafood, like so many Indian restaurants, is not so special although the crabcake starters are very good. It's a good deal classier than many Indian places in every way. One to try and enjoy.

Il Convivio

143 Ebury Street, SW1W 9QN **Tel** *020 7730 4099*

Map *20 E2*

It's a cliché to say that an Italian restaurant is "welcoming" but this one really is. Plus, it has that aroma that makes you feel extra hungry. Couples, groups, children and everyone else cram in to fill up on very good and honest Italian food. No one seems to have a bad word for this place so if you're in the area, get inside.

Racine

239 Brompton Road, SW3 2EP **Tel** *020 7584 4477*

Map *19 B1*

A restaurant that sets out to showcase French cuisine (*racine* means "roots") and succeeds very well. Genuine French food, French waiters and great atmosphere all combine to keep locals coming back for more. The venison when in season is excellent and the menu changes regularly. The service has improved considerably.

L'Etranger

36 Gloucester Road, SW7 4QT **Tel** *020 7584 1118*

Map *18 E1*

A gem of a place serving extremely good French-Japanese fusion food in very stylish surroundings. People rave about the caramelized black cod with miso and with good reason. But then every dish on this menu is delectable and there's a massive wine list that has been created with passion and love. And you can dance in the club downstairs.

Tom Aikens

43 Elystan Street, SW3 3NT **Tel** *020 7584 2003*

Map *19 B2*

At the time of writing, chef Aikens is the twinkliest star in the cooking firmament with other chefs praising his Modern-French creations no end. That said, some people find it a bit rich but everyone loves the experience. Dishes are lovingly constructed and beautifully plated with flavours finely balanced with a watchmaker's care. Book ahead.

1880 at The Bentley

27–33 Harrington Gardens, SW7 4JX **Tel** *020 7244 5555*

Map *18 F2*

This restaurant is very expensive, but you won't get much better in London. Exquisitely prepared Modern-European cuisine is showcased in the seven-, eight- and nine-course "grazing menus". And for once, an opulent interior has not bred snooty staff. They enjoy your gastronomic journey with you and the sommelier is a joy.

Gordon Ramsay At 68 Royal Hospital Road

68 Royal Hospital Road, SW3 4HP **Tel** *020 7352 4441*

Map *19 C4*

For an astonishing £100 per person (on average), this is probably the best restaurant in London, the UK and, Ramsay might tell you, the world. Everything is perfect from place settings to service. No restaurant gets three Michelin stars for nothing and this place deserves them all. As a souvenir of London, your meal memories here will last a lifetime.

WESTMINSTER, ST JAMES'S

Bigun's Ribs

2 Warwick Way, SW1V 1RU **Tel** *020 7834 7350*

Map *20 F2*

This is what you might expect, cheapish food served briskly in a noisy and unromantic ambience. Nothing wrong with that because the prices reflect the ambition. You don't have to like ribs either, as dishes such as rack of lamb are really very good for the money. A place to save cash so that you can indulge somewhere special another night.

Il Vicolo

3–4 Crown Passage, SW1Y 6PP **Tel** *020 7839 3960*   **Map** *13 A4*

Easily overlooked in its quiet location, this charming little Italian restaurant still has no problems filling tables. Be prepared to bump elbows with your neighbours as you tuck into lots of favourites prepared with skill. It's the sort of place you tell people about and which you return to again and again for an honest meal at a fair price.

Atrium

4 Millbank, SW1P 3JA **Tel** *020 7233 0032*   **Map** *21 B1*

The name says it all, this is a vast glass-covered space that has a real "wow" factor. The menu mixes and matches to largely good effect – salted cod and white bean soup with leeks and truffle oil for starters and paprika smoked monkfish tail with anchovies for main course, both come reasonably priced. Bright and modern in a conservative area.

Brasserie Roux

8 Pall Mall, SW1Y 5NG **Tel** *020 7968 2900*   **Map** *13 A3*

Another converted bank, so it's out with the old suspended ceilings and in with the designers. It looks great and more expensive than it actually turns out to be. Obviously Michel Roux is not in the kitchen but his influence is felt across the wide range of generally no nonsense French brasserie dishes. Ideal for pre-theatre dining.

Mango Tree

46 Grosvenor Place, SW1X 7AW **Tel** *020 7823 1888*   **Map** *12 E5*

Just opposite the back gate of Buckingham Palace, this restaurant takes Thai cuisine to a new level. The service, the decor and, of course, the food are all impeccable. Performing fresh twists with Thai standards, the chefs here create remarkable tastes and effects. Not cheap, but worth a trip.

Saharaween

3 Panton Street, SW1Y 4DL **Tel** *020 7930 2777*   **Map** *13 A3*

Floor cushions, low tables and colourful rugs make this a very Moroccan place indeed. Tajines, or stews, are the speciality here and most contain tender, moist and spiced lamb set off by juicy fruits such as plums. The couscous accompaniment lets you soak up the gravy without spilling a drop. This is a "bring your own bottle" restaurant.

Just St James

12 St James Street, SW1A 1ER **Tel** *020 7976 2222*   **Map** *12 F4*

Plush surroundings as befits a restaurant in St James. Built from a former Edwardian banking hall it's a restaurant that constantly surprises with its far-reaching, but not overambitious, menu. Strong British favourites such as calves' liver and bacon sit alongside steak and chips and dishes of more global provenance. Impressive.

London Showboat

Westminster Pier, SW1A 2JR **Tel** *020 7740 0400*   **Map** *13 C5*

Something different: a meal and a Thames boat trip combined. As you sail out majestically past London's landmarks you'll be entertained with cabaret performance of songs from London's top shows. On the way back, the decks are cleared for dancing. Food is a lot better than you might expect and all in all it's a good evening for everyone.

Quilon

41 Buckingham Gate, SW1E 6AF **Tel** *020 7821 1899*   **Map** *13 A5*

Southwest coastal cooking here, so stand by for more coconut than you find in North Indian restaurants. In general it's lighter, subtler and fish features far more on the menu. It is expensive compared to other run-of-the-mill Indian restaurants, but given its location and its quality this is not a criticism.

L'Oranger

5 St James's Street, SW1A 1EF **Tel** *020 7839 3774*   **Map** *12 F4*

A very formal French restaurant at the heart of the British Empire. Do dress up. The decor is heavy with timeless quality and the dishes for the most part are traditional too. Tables are beautifully laid with expensive linen, high-quality glasses and plates and the food is rather expensive, too. You get what you pay for, though.

Wilton's

55 Jermyn Street, SW1Y 6LX **Tel** *020 7629 9955*   **Map** *13 A3*

A landmark institution, there has been a Wilton's in London since 1742. A quintessential expensive club-dining experience. Morecambe Bay potted shrimps, grilled Dover sole, Scottish lobster thermidor, and West Mersey oysters are the main attractions here, but you will also want to bask in the atmosphere and in the attentive service.

SOUTH BANK

Baltic

74 Blackfriars Road, SE1 8HA **Tel** *020 7928 1111*   **Map** *14 F4*

Crayfish in vodka? Well that's Eastern European for sure. This restaurant exudes charm and is located inside a former coach house, which gives it exciting high ceilings. There's a massive range of vodkas and the food constantly surprises with dishes such as beef and venison meatballs. The kitchen is on show and there is often live jazz, too.

Key to Price Guide *see p296* **Key to Symbols** *see back cover flap*

Kennington Tandoori

313 Kennington Road, SE11 4QE **Tel** *020 7735 9247*

Map *22 E3*

One of the best Indian curry houses in London according to many. As it is a short drive from Westminster, many curry-loving MPs can be found debating a policy over a chicken jalfreezi. There are classic dishes and quite a few unique ones with nice innovations such as their own Nilgiri murgh. Reliable food in a calm oasis.

Mar I Terra

14 Gambia Street, Waterloo, SE1 0XH **Tel** *020 7928 7628*

Map *14 F4*

Described as a little gem by its fans, this local Spanish restaurant has also been steadily building custom from people living and working miles away. The quality of the ingredients is one of its secrets as is its location off the main drag. This means the diners are discerning gourmets who have come for the food and the cheerful atmosphere.

Troia Bar and Restaurant †

3F Belvedere Road, County Hall, SE1 7GQ **Tel** *020 7633 9309*

Map *14 D4*

Covering a lot more of Turkey's national dishes than many similar restaurants in London, Troia lets you explore on your own or let the set menus do all the hard work for you. *Kisir*, a cold starter of nuts, bulgar wheat, herbs and spring onions feels healthy and allows you the space to tuck in to the very hearty main dishes on offer.

County Hall

London Marriott County Hall, Queens Walk, SE1 7PB **Tel** *020 7902 8000*

Map *13 C4*

A great view of the Thames is just one reason to dine here, close to the Houses of Parliament. Prices are reasonable for the location and the cooking assured if not terribly inventive. That said, the food never fails to do a good job with dishes such as slow-cooked pork with a chorizo and pea risotto and enjoyable smoked duck.

Ozu

County Hall, Riverside Building, Westminster Bridge Road, SE1 7PB **Tel** *020 7928 7766*

Map *14 D5*

French owner, whose classic taste in Japanese food has been inspired from Japanese director Yasujiru Ozu. There is exquisite attention to detail here. Relaxed ambience, a big flat screen used for projecting movies and the 1940s- and 50s-style decor are worth it. A perfect place to enjoy the French-Japanese dishes with a glass of wine.

The Lobster Pot

3 Kennington Lane, SE11 4RG **Tel** *020 7582 5556*

Map *22 F2*

A remarkable little restaurant in an unprepossessing location. The French owners set out to recreate Brittany (even down to seagull soundtracks) and succeed brilliantly. The eight-course "surprise" menu is fantastic and the fish is always superbly fresh. Do book in advance, as it's not very big.

MAYFAIR

L'Autre

5b Shepherd Street, W1J 7HP **Tel** *020 7499 4680*

Map *12 E4*

A rather unique mix of Polish and Mexican/Spanish food makes this restaurant unusual. Some say the Polish dishes are usually better and more interesting than the standard Mexican fare of nachos and enchiladas. Tiny means intimate, but it's good value. Try the flavoured vodkas.

Chor Bizarre

16 Albemarle Street, W1S 4HW **Tel** *020 7629 9802*

Map *12 F3*

Serving dishes from Kashmir to the deep South this restaurant is always busy. Try the lamb with spinach and ginger and the aubergine with peanut sauce. Waiters can lose interest so keep them on their toes if you don't want to be forgotten. But they are friendly and willing to help you choose from the large menu.

Fakhreldine

85 Piccadilly, W1J 7NE **Tel** *020 7493 3424*

Map *12 E4*

An excellent view over the park partly explains the high prices. You can get cheaper Lebanese food but not like this. The interior offers a choice of tables or sofas and the kitchen has a *meze* selection up in the twenties. Some say it's not authentic, but if you are not Lebanese yourself that probably won't bother you.

Green's Restaurant & Oyster Bar

36 Duke Street, SW1Y 6DF **Tel** *020 7930 4566*

Map *12 F3*

Wonderful old-world ambience and extensive champagne list, this is a great establishment. Excellent lobster salads, first-class chips (fries) and, of course, a nice choice of oysters most of them down from Scotland that very day. If you don't fancy fish, how about Green's steak tartare? Closed on Sundays from May to September.

Kiku

17 Half Moon Street, W1J 7BE **Tel** *020 7499 4208*

Map *12 E4*

A low-key Japanese restaurant that doesn't try to attract trendy Westerners. It's a calm place. Good food and service in relaxed surroundings. A good sushi bar, a great selection of set meals and fast service if you need it. A place to really enjoy Japanese food as it should be served and prepared.

Langan's Brasserie

Stratton Street, W1J 8LB **Tel** *020 7491 8822*   **Map** *12 F3*

The original and perhaps still the best Langan's. The eponymous owner went to see the great chef in the sky a while back now, but his style lives on. Service is discreetly attentive and the staff are friendly. Try and get downstairs where they serve the soufflé with anchovy sauce. Upstairs they won't, it's too far from the kitchen.

Matsuri

15 Bury Street, SW1Y 6AL **Tel** *020 7839 1101*   **Map** *12 F3*

Excellent sushi and sashimi, but it's easy to spend a lot of money here if you get stuck into teppanyaki. However, the money is well spent as this is high-quality Japanese food pleasantly served to a discerning clientele. The pre-theatre deals are worth choosing if you can order before 7pm. Overall a superior place.

Tiger Green Brasserie

Half Moon Street, W1J 7BN **Tel** *020 7629 7522*   **Map** *12 E4*

Located in the recently refurbished Hilton London Green Park hotel, this restaurant welcomes all with an arresting menu. The classic combination of contemporary and modern design with an eclectic mix of traditional English and Mediterranean cuisine is well worth the experience. They also have a wide range of cocktails to choose from.

Zen Central

20 Queen Street, W1J 5P **Tel** *020 7629 8103*   **Map** *12 E3*

As with most Chinese restaurants centred in Soho, this one has wandered far. Of course in this area the decor and general ambience and service are far superior to the relatives back in Chinatown. The food however is much the same, you pay for the location but the menu is perfectly okay.

Mirabelle

56 Curzon Street, W1J 8PA **Tel** *020 7499 4636*   **Map** *12 E3*

Once the haunt of fashionable pre-war London, this underground restaurant still pulls in the well-heeled for a Michelin starred meal. Of course it's not cheap but it is good value with attentive staff and excellent, classic French cooking. Standards are set pretty high here and there's a pleasantly old-fashioned feel to the place.

Umu

14–16 Bruton Place, W1J 6L **Tel** *020 7499 8881*   **Map** *12 E3*

Seriously expensive (especially the tasting menu) but extremely stylish as well – the futuristic front door will make you gasp. The beautiful interior and impeccable service provided by great staff will also impress. As for the food, the sake list is remarkable, and this is one of the few places in London where you can find genuine Japanese kaiseki.

MARYLEBONE

Eat and Two Veg

50 Marylebone High Street, W1U 5HN **Tel** *020 7258 8595*   **Map** *4 D5*

When you see the imaginative menu here, it's clear that Vegetarian cuisine has come a long way from the days of nut cutlets. A funky interior and attractive staff contribute to the buzzy atmosphere. This is creative vegetarian cooking, so while lentils do make an appearance, you don't have to be an ageing hippy to enjoy the fine flavours.

Garangers Restaurant Bar

114–115 Crawford Street, W1H 2JQ **Tel** *020 7935 8447*   **Map** *3 C5*

Regulars rave over the chocolate desserts, but really the whole restaurant deserves wider praise. A cool and well-designed interior is well served by jolly, upbeat staff. Try warm octopus salad with sautéed squid and Charlotte potato or the chef's creation of the day. Why not drink at the bar downstairs, or even have a dance?

Ishtar

10–12 Crawford Street, W1U 6AZ **Tel** *020 7224 2446*   **Map** *3 C5*

Modern Turkish, so no plate throwing and no exotic dancers. You can dine on two levels, including under some romantic cellar arches and the dishes are familiar but updated. Go for grilled sea bass with potatoes and saffron sauce or some well-marinated kebabs. Leave room for some pastries too!

La Galette

56 Paddington Street, W1U 4HY **Tel** *020 7935 1554*   **Map** *4 D5*

La Galette takes its name from the delicious savoury buckwheat pancakes typical of Brittany and France. Choose from a simple filling such as spinach and cheese or something more substantial such as Toulouse sausage and caramelized onion. Breton cider comes in porcelain cups and French country wines and calvados are also served.

Langan's Bistro

26 Devonshire Street, W1G 6PJ **Tel** *020 7935 4531*   **Map** *4 D5*

They don't like change at Langan's so everything remains in a small time warp. Menus are still handwritten and once modern pictures and sketches by famous artists adorn the walls. Try goose liver and tarragon parfait followed by stuffed squid with romesco sauce. Good food and reasonable priced.

Key to Price Guide *see p296* **Key to Symbols** *see back cover flap*

Phoenix Palace

5 Glentworth Street, NW1 5PG **Tel** *020 7486 3515*   **Map** *3 C5*

A lot of Cantonese customers on show tell the discerning visitor that this must be an authentic place. Dim sum is very popular here although you may have to be quite "aggressive" to get served. Not that the staff are rude, it's just the Cantonese way – serve the loudest customers first and let the shy ones look after themselves. Good value.

Reubens

79 Baker Street, W1H 2JR **Tel** *020 7486 0035*   **Map** *3 C5*

You don't have to be Jewish for a wonderful dining experience. A great restaurant for the gentiles too, with all the Jewish classics on the menu like latkes and salt beef sandwiches. It is, of course, officially kosher and the portions are big and well priced. Children are taken under the staff's wings and kept happy while parents eat.

Caffe Caldesi

118 Marylebone Lane, W1U 2NE **Tel** *020 7935 1144*   **Map** *12 D1*

This airy Italian restaurant offers classic dishes and a very reasonable wine list, with a slightly more formal dinning space upstairs. Tuck into a big Tuscan breakfast or sit down to a traditional home-cooked dinner. There is also a patisserie, a delicatessen and a bar.

Defune

34 George Street, W1U 7DP **Tel** *020 7935 8311*   **Map** *12 D1*

Top-class sushi at a high price, which the experts say is well worth it. A charming minimalist decor is matched by an atmosphere that some find austere but is really just a cool appreciation of the food. This is a decent place and the service is superb. When you're eating raw fish you expect the highest standards and you pay for them.

Michael Moore

19 Blandford Street, W1U 3DG **Tel** *0871 223 8107*   **Map** *12 D1*

Perennially popular restaurant that mixes excellent food with a genuinely friendly ambience. Michael Moore (no relation to the American film-maker) is there virtually every night and tours the tables for a chat. A very accomplished chef, he changes his delightful menu regularly and keeps his regulars flocking back for more of Moore.

SOHO, FITZROVIA

Bam-Bou

1 Percy Street, W1T 1DB **Tel** *020 7323 9130*   **Map** *13 A1*

A nice bar upstairs lures you to a few drinks before you descend to the restaurant proper. Seated at a low table with just candlelight playing off dark wood, you feel a million miles from London. This is not your average Vietnamese restaurant. The food is excellent and the atmosphere relaxed and warm.

Busaba Eathai

106–110 Wardour Street, W1F 0TR **Tel** *020 7255 8686*   **Map** *13 A2*

Certainly cheap enough, this little restaurant meets demand for value and speed of service. As a result, there can be a queue of legendary proportions after 8pm, so get there early. You're going to share a table whatever time you arrive, so don't go for a romantic occasion. Food is good, try Thai calamari and the rose apple curry.

Chinese Experience

118 Shaftesbury Avenue, W1D 5EP **Tel** *020 7437 0377*   **Map** *13 A2*

A newcomer in 2004 and very welcome. Stylish modern interior – sit at bar type tables or ordinary square ones – and enjoy extra special food. This restaurant plates in the manner of a top-class hotel, which is a first for Chinatown and the prices are extremely fair. That's why you may find a queue outside. Persevere.

Chowki

2–3 Denman Street, W1D 7HA **Tel** *020 7439 1330*   **Map** *13 A2*

A modern and stylish looking place but with emphasis on traditional home Indian cooking. Very reasonable prices and without the Anglified dishes you find on the high street or the fusion style that has become rather too popular elsewhere. The menu changes every month, concentrating on three different regions of India.

ECapital

8 Gerrard Street, W1D 5PJ **Tel** *020 7434 3838*   **Map** *13 A2*

Sunglasses on for the pink interior but heads down for the food. It specialises in Shanghai-style cooking and, if you look for this section of the menu, you will have a special meal that's different to most around here. "Cubed Belly of Pork in the Poet's Style", for example. Service is unusually unhurried and the set menus can be a bargain.

Fung Shing

15 Lisle Street, WC2H 7BE **Tel** *020 7437 1539*   **Map** *13 B2*

A true Chinatown Chinese, it has been here since the 1970s. Try roasted garlic and chilli spare ribs and the sizzling eel, or soft-shelled crab, barbecue beef and deep-fried squid with chili. This is one of the places that local Michelin starred chefs come to after work for consistently high-quality cooking and reasonable prices.

Harbour City

46 Gerrard Street, W1D 5QJ **Tel** *020 7439 7859*

Map *13 B2*

The pedestrianized centre of Chinatown is home to many restaurants and wonderful grocers. This restaurant doesn't have staff outside trying to lure you in, it relies on regulars. And the food, which is consistently good. The decor is bright, colourful and cheerful after a recent refurbishment.

L'Escargot Marco Pierre White

48 Greek Street, W1D 3RS **Tel** *020 7437 6828*

Map *13 A1*

Another Soho institution now run by a legendary chef. Expect very high standards but be surprised by the really quite reasonable prices. In the Picasso Room you can look on some of the master's works while eating artistically crafted fine food. Closed on Sundays.

New Mayflower

68–70 Shaftesbury Avenue, W1B 6LY **Tel** *020 7734 9207*

Map *13 A2*

This genuine Cantonese restaurant proves that Shaftesbury Avenue is not just for theatre-goers. Dishes such as bean curd stuffed with shrimp, and deep-fried crab are appetizing and fresh. Service is efficient and free juicy oranges are given at the end of your meal (a Hong Kong tradition).

Signor Zilli

41 Dean Street, W1D 4PY **Tel** *020 7734 3924*

Map *13 A2*

Mr Zilli is often in attendance and that's what makes this restaurant somewhat special. The food is first rate, if unadventurous, but the atmosphere is always worth the admission. You won't break the bank here but will have an enjoyable meal and emerge feeling sated and pampered. Closed on Sundays.

St Moritz

161 Wardour Street, W1F 8WL **Tel** *020 7734 3324*

Map *13 A2*

Fondue is the speciality at this Swiss restaurant. Cook your meat at the table in boiling oil or dip your bread in molten cheese. Take your pick. The raclette, mini hot plates where you design your own mix of ingredients, is not quite so lethal. The Swiss say this place is authentic and it's good fun to try.

Thai Metro

38 Charlotte Street, W1T 2NL **Tel** *020 7436 4201*

Map *5 A5*

Top-class Thai cuisine that won't break your bank. Go for green curry but be warned, if you aren't hot for chillies you could come out in a sweat. The zingy flavours that characterize Thai food are all here in abundance and if the weather is warm you can enjoy your food in the fresh air. Service is fast, which may not be to everyone's taste.

Tomato

54 Frith Street, W1D 4SL **Tel** *020 7437 0666*

Map *13 A2*

A gourmet Italian restaurant. Tomato is reliable and friendly and still fairly good value – quite a rare combination in the West End. Tidily presented inside, it carries its style into properly cooked and served Italian food that mixes old favourites with a few new kids on the block.

Vasco & Piero's Pavilion

15 Poland Street, W1F 8QE **Tel** *020 7437 8774*

Map *13 A2*

Most of the dishes on the menu are Italian and the owner's Umbrian heritage ensures that chickpeas and lentils feature frequently. The pasta is made in house, with the finest quality ingredients, and a menu that changes twice daily. If you like truffles come visit – in season black and white truffles are imported from Umbria.

Veeraswamy

99–101 Regent Street, W1B 4RS **Tel** *020 7734 1401*

Map *12 F3*

A touch of the old Empire. Slide into London's oldest Indian restaurant and try some rather unique and genuine Indian cuisine. It is elegant and expensive but the presence of so many people from the subcontinent clearly enjoying themselves speaks for itself.

Yming

35–36 Greek Street, W1D 5DL **Tel** *020 7734 2721*

Map *13 B2*

Yming? Well Ynot? This is actually a rather stylish Chinese eatery with decor that won't send you blind and high standards of cooking. Tibetan lamb and empress' beef are excellent, snow peas and broccoli stir fried with garlic are a meal in itself. Nicely air conditioned, which not all around here can claim.

Elena's L'Etoile

30 Charlotte Street, W1T 2NA **Tel** *020 7636 7189*

Map *13 A1*

Another local institution, at lunchtime it fills up with power media people from surrounding ad agencies and TV companies. They know what they want and Elena's delivers classic French bistro food under the gaze of celebrity pictures that cover the walls. It's not cheap but you do get what you pay for and that indefinable extra – real atmosphere.

Elysee

13 Percy Street, W1T 1DT **Tel** *020 7636 4804*

Map *13 A1*

A legend among London's Greek restaurants, this is a noisy place that's not ideal for romantic couples. That said, it's great fun for a night out with belly dancers, bands and singers all delivering an impressive show. The food does take second billing to the entertainment but it's perfectly good grub at a fair price.

Key to Price Guide *see p296* **Key to Symbols** *see back cover flap*

Gay Hussar
2 Greek Street, W1D 4NB **Tel** *020 7437 0973*

Map 13 A1

Once the place of choice for cherry-nosed old journalists to meet and gossip and enjoy second-rate food that reminded them of their private schools (on expenses). However, now it provides a proper insight into Eastern European cuisine, wines and spirits, albeit at quite a high price.

Hong Kong
6–7 Lisle Street, WC2H 7BG **Tel** *020 7287 0324*

Map 13 A2

Best known for its excellent range of dim sums, although pork with orange is tender, flavoursome with a perfect sweetness. Nice modern decor and it's worth checking out the chef's special menu of the day for some surprises. Sensible prices and a good selection of wines as well.

Little Italy
21 Frith Street, W1D 4RN **Tel** *020 7734 4737*

Map 13 A2

The name says it all. A busy and vibrant place with a late licence until 4am. A page full of pasta dishes is always a safe bet, but if you feel like splashing out, the main courses are good too. You might miss the unassuming doorway so back up and look again, it's there. Some live music and dancing most nights.

Opium
1a Dean Street, W1D 3RB **Tel** *020 7287 9608*

Map 13 A1

A basement venue that's always busy, Opium sates the senses with very nice Vietnamese food, a bar that's open late and a dance floor. Portions aren't exactly enormous but the price is fair enough for Soho. Gets louder and madder as the night wears on, so be warned.

Pescatori
57 Charlotte Street, W1T 4PD **Tel** *020 7580 3289*

Map 5 A5

The cooking always smells great when you pass this place and, because patrons will try to sit outside in just about any weather, you get to gaze jealously at their food too. It's easy to go a bit mad and end up with a large bill here so be careful. Grilled squid is always good and garlicky, while pasta and seafood dishes are consistently tasty.

Quo Vadis
26–29 Dean Street, W1D 3LL **Tel** *020 7437 9585*

Map 13 A2

It's been here so long, Karl Marx once lived in the attic (according to the plaque outside). The food here is accomplished and correspondingly in a reasonably high-price bracket. The only real complaints seem to be about the small portions, but that's modern cuisine for you.

Hakkasan
8 Hanway Place, W1T 1HF **Tel** *020 7927 7000*

Map 13 A1

A very expensive Chinese restaurant, but one which has had no problems filling its tables from day one. The decor is superbly stylish and the food even more so. No windows mean you can't peer in to check it out before entering. It's busy and it's a bit smoky, but if you have the money and love good food you won't leave disappointed.

COVENT GARDEN

Café Med
57 & 59 Endell Street, WC2H 9AJ **Tel** *020 7240 8085*

Map 13 C2

Always great value and very popular, Café Med's great salads, family-sized pizzas, gourmet burgers and warm, friendly staff all contribute to a winning formula. Lone diners don't feel out of place and the downstairs Moroccan-themed lounge is a cool retreat from the hustle and bustle of Covent Garden.

Kulu Kulu Sushi
51–53 Shelton Street, WC2H 9HE **Tel** *020 7240 5687*

Map 13 C2

Fresh raw fish at a price that's right. Simple decor belies the attention to detail that goes into the creation and presentation of dishes. Salmon sashimi comes recommended by regulars and there's always a queue forming at lunchtime as health conscious office workers choose fish over sandwiches.

Abeno Okonomi-Yaki
47 Museum Street, WC1A 1LY **Tel** *020 7405 3211*

Map 13 B1

Healthy, warm and fun Japanese food to entertain the eyes and satisfy the palate is served here. Okonomi-Yaki is actually the name of the style of food cooked. Staff exhibit the exquisite politeness that is so much a part of Japanese culture and they are genuinely happy to help out the novice Japanese food-eater.

Belgo Centraal
50 Earlham Street, WC2H 9HP **Tel** *020 7813 2233*

Map 13 B2

Flagship of a small chain, this remains popular every night. Cool young staff whip up a great variety of mussels dishes, from *moules marinieres* to more exotic creations featuring Belgium's famous beers. Meat-eaters are also catered for. Eat at the long refectory tables and enjoy the fun.

Beotys

79 St. Martin's Lane, WC2N 4AA **Tel** *020 7836 8768*   **Map** *13 B2*

No dancing on tables or plate-smashing here and to many people this is now the best Greek restaurant in London. All the Greek favourites are available, including a bewildering yet tasty variety of *meze* (small portioned dishes). Always great fun with a crowd and the atmosphere is very friendly. Closed on Sundays.

Café Pacifico

5 Langley Street, WC2H 9JA **Tel** *020 7379 7728*   **Map** *13 B2*

If you like a lively night, you'll like it here. Mexican live music, a buzzy atmosphere and, if you're young, or young at heart, a few cocktails followed by some filling and reasonably priced food will send you singing out into the piazza.

Chez Gerard at the Opera Terrace

The Opera Terrace, The Market, Covent Garden Piazza, WC2E 8RF **Tel** *020 7379 0666*   **Map** *13 C2*

A prime location in Covent Garden makes up for the sometimes less than inspiring food. The usual brasserie menu is normally well done, with steak and frites hard to fault. Sitting outside on a sunny evening is a joy, although if it rains you may be stuck out there if inside is fully booked!

Le Deuxieme

65a Long Acre, WC2E 9JD **Tel** *020 7379 0033*   **Map** *13 C2*

Special pre-theatre meals mean you can enjoy your food confident you'll be on to your coffee in plenty of time before the curtain is raised. A large dining area and a warm team contribute to family-friendly dining. A good choice of dishes with tuna steak being a popular item. The set menu is good value for the area.

Loch Fyne

2–4 Catherine Street, WC2B 5JS **Tel** *020 7240 4999*   **Map** *13 C2*

The fish and shellfish come here fresh from Scotland with a wine list suitably chosen to match the crustaceans and other finny things on offer. Portions are generous whether you go for a platter of oysters or a large plate of poached smoked haddock.

Navajo Joe

34 King Street, WC2E 8JD **Tel** *020 7395 5802*   **Map** *13 B2*

A lively atmosphere, a busy bar and a good mix of food under the umbrella American, make this a popular Covent Garden eatery. Dishes come from South of the Border (down Mexico way) as well as from the heartland so it's hard not to find something to enjoy on the menu. Biggish portions and fairly speedy service.

Palm Court Brasserie

39 King Street, WC2E 8JS **Tel** *020 7395 5803*   **Map** *13 C2*

A good location and a sophisticated interior make Palm Court Brasserie a firm favourite with the locals. Mediterranean gutsy flavours with the southern sunshine well infused. Sharing platters are good fun and great value, whilst a roast rump of lamb will fill you up nicely. Like most restaurants in this area, there are special pre-theatre deals.

Porter's English Restaurant

17 Henrietta Street, WC2E 8QH **Tel** *020 7836 6466*   **Map** *13 C2*

Porter's do warm, hearty, traditional British "grub" with tasty pie dishes such as steak and Guinness, haddock and salmon or prawn. Desserts are equally large and not for anyone dieting. You'll get a proper fish and chips here too and all served by cheerful staff and at a good price for the location.

Rock Garden

4–6 The Piazza, WC2E 8HB **Tel** *020 7257 8613*   **Map** *13 C2*

Don't be fooled, this is not a tacky themed restaurant. The Rock Garden serves modern European cuisine with a wide variety of meat, fish and vegetarian dishes. It is ideal for children and has a good pre-theatre menu. The location is one of the best in Covent Garden, especially in summer.

Sarastro

126 Drury Lane, WC2B 5QG **Tel** *020 7836 0101*   **Map** *13 C2*

A remarkable decor likened to a gypsy encampment is just one of the delights in store. A very theatrical venue where the staff can be every bit as dramatic as the actors who like to come here. Be prepared for a very different night out and ready for anything. Some people love it, a few loathe it but it's hard not to have an opinion one way or another.

Sofra

36 Tavistock Street, WC2E 7PB **Tel** *020 7240 3773*   **Map** *13 C2*

Another London institution, Sofra has been serving superior Turkish food for many years. The speciality is the "healthy" option involving lots of little dishes to share. Bread and olives come free throughout the meal and dips such as hummus and tsatsiki always taste fresh and clean.

The Punjab

80 Neal Street, WC2H 9PA **Tel** *020 7836 9787*   **Map** *13 B1*

Punjab serves authentic Punjabi cuisine. It's important as most Indian restaurants serve Bangladeshi food. This is a restaurant where Punjab Indians come to eat to enjoy genuine tastes of home in a friendly atmosphere. Spicy and full of flavour, dishes here are definitely a cut above the average curry.

Key to Price Guide *see p296* **Key to Symbols** *see back cover flap*

Bertorelli's

44a Floral Street, WC2E 9DA **Tel** *020 7836 3969*

Map 13 C2

An Italian institution in Covent Garden, Bertorelli's Roman empire now extends further afield. This is the flagship, though not the one you may have seen in the film *Sliding Doors*. You always feel looked after here and the cooking is like mamma used to make. It's not crude but it's kept simple to bring out the flavours. Good value, too.

Christopher's The American Grill

18 Wellington Street, WC2E 7DD **Tel** *020 7240 4222*

Map 13 C2

Rather more formal than you might expect from an American grill, but then this is a superior establishment. And there are plenty of other American favourites to choose from, including delicious ham hocks, large steaks, excellent lobsters and New York cheesecake. Good value and unpretentious.

Indigo

1 Aldwych, WC2B 4BZ **Tel** *020 7300 0400*

Map 13 C2

This is a calm, modern and stylish restaurant with an eclectic mixture of dishes beautifully presented and attentively served. Enjoy a drink in the grand bar upstairs before descending in the lift to the plush dining room. Plenty of choice for all tastes and a useful "mix and match" salad and pasta course.

Le Palais du Jardin

136 Long Acre, WC2E 9AD **Tel** *020 7379 5353*

Map 13 B2

Very French with classic service delivering an ever-changing selection of smart French fare. Service is on the formal side, but cool jazz music playing in the background lightens the ambience. Excellent seafood as well as some very good *steak et frites*. A romantic destination.

Origin

24 Endell Street, WC2H 9RD **Tel** *020 7170 9200*

Map 13 C2

Beautifully crafted dishes and grown up surroundings in this fashionable restaurant. The transfer of this highly-acclaimed restaurant team from South London to Covent Garden has transformed this operation into an altogether more sophisticated affair. With excellent service, Origin delivers elegant, modern European cuisine.

Asia de Cuba

5 St. Martin's Lane, WC2N 4HX **Tel** *020 7300 5588*

Map 13 B2

Perhaps fusing Cuban and Chinese food is an experiment too far, and Asia de Cuba seems to be doing well on it. It's not cheap but the portions are massive and the service and attention to detail justify the cost. Calamari salad is popular as is the Hunan fish, but it's the aptly named "Bay of Pigs" dessert that will finish you off!

HOLBORN

Abbaye

55 Charterhouse Street, EC1M 6H **Tel** *020 7253 1612*

Map 6 F5

Close to Farringdon Station in the hinterland between Holborn and the City, Abbaye offers good Belgian fare. And, of course, an awful lot of beers to choose from many of which will lay you out flat. Go for mussels done in many different ways in variety of beers. There are steaks, too. Can be full of office workers drinking hard.

Chez Gerard

119 Chancery Lane, WC2A 1PP **Tel** *020 7405 0290*

Map 14 E1

Part of quite a large London chain, this is as good as its cousins. Which is to say decent food reasonable priced. Gerard is quite small so you can put your elbow in your neighbour's Bearnaise sauce, but then perhaps you can also steal some of his nice chips! A good place if you want a meal you can trust.

Ming Court

54–56 Ludgate Hill, EC4M 7HX **Tel** *020 7248 4303*

Map 14 F2

Just into the City but close to China in quality and style. Slightly more expensive than comparable Soho places but ahead of them too in decor, ambience and service. Peking duck scores highly here, and if you dislike brutish Chinese restaurants with harsh waiters, you will definitely approve of the Ming Court approach.

The Chancery

9 Cursitor Street, EC4A 1LL **Tel** *020 7831 4000*

Map 14 E1

A little gem of a new wave restaurant tucked away down a side street. Adventurous, modern and very good cooking in a stylish establishment. Try the ham hock and piccalilli with *foie gras* and green beans, potage of baby monkfish and oysters with summer truffle shavings. It's all very good and well priced.

The Gaucho Grill

125–126 Chancery Lane, WC2A 1PU **Tel** *020 7242 7727*

Map 14 E1

There are a few Gauchos around London and they remain consistent value. Of course the thing to eat is the steak – big ones. A large wine list helps wash down your enormous meal and the cocktails aren't bad either. For a pleasant no-nonsense feed it's a well-priced place in a reasonably expensive area.

Pearl

252 High Holborn, WC1V 7EN **Tel** *020 7829 7000*

Map 14 D1

Go for the multicourse-tasting menu and you won't go wrong. They also score high by offering a very large selection of wines by the glass. The decor is very cool, very Scandinavian using the old high-ceilinged banking hall that it used to be to good effect. The pre-theatre prices are a bargain.

SPITALFIELDS, CLERKENWELL

Bengal Cuisine

12 Brick Lane, E1 6RF **Tel** *020 7377 8405*

Map 8 E5

Just about every building in Brick Lane is an Indian restaurant, but the quality varies. It's certainly a lot cleaner and more modern here than some we daren't mention. Very good value and the cook goes easy on the chilli to suit the more Western customers. Staff are happy to advise on dishes if asked. Good Sunday buffet as well.

Corvino

7 Middlesex Street, E1 7AA **Tel** *020 7247 6461*

Map 16 D1

Nice atmosphere, spacious and good portions. Pasta is a nice choice, but the steaks go down well too. Monkfish is also well cooked and not dried out like some. They manage to keep it friendly even when under pressure and the prices are more than reasonable for what's on offer.

East is East

230 Commercial Road, E1 2NB **Tel** *020 7702 7222*

A very decent Indian restaurant that doesn't serve Bangladeshi dishes like some do. Of course you are spoiled for choice in this part of London for "an Indian" but this one seems to get top marks every time for its authentic cuisine and friendly service. And it's very low priced, which is always a bonus.

The Lane Restaurant

12–20 Osborn Street, E1 6TE **Tel** *020 7456 1067*

Map 16 E1

Down at the south end of famous Brick Lane but it's not an Indian restaurant. It's actually a rather cool and trendy place doing a variety of innovative world dishes at very reasonable prices. The cocktail bar area is nice too. It's in an up-and-coming area, so you may find yourself surrounded by young people with crazy clothes and a disposable income.

St John

26 St John Street, EC1M 4AY **Tel** *020 7251 0848*

Map 6 F5

Here they like to eat the bits of animals you barely hear about so don't bring squeamish eaters. You're a kidney stone's throw away from the meat markets, and the decor is hard and unyielding. The food is fantastic if you have the guts to try something different.

Moro

34–36 Exmouth Market, EC1R 4QE **Tel** *0871 223 8071*

Map 6 E4

Moro is well known for its Spanish/Moroccan cuisine and serves up consistently good food to regulars. Courgette (zacchini) and mint tortilla is an example of light, flavoursome food and there are some very good breads. Buy ingredients next door and take their famous cookbook home with you.

The Spitz

109 Commercial Street, E1 6BG **Tel** *020 7392 9032*

Map 8 D5

The live background music sets the tone for a friendly place. Food is diverse and imaginative – goat's cheese with pecans on a salad, for example. There are also gluten-free menu choices. Near Smithfield Market, it attracts a mixed crowd. The live music is diverse, from jazz to acoustic, and includes many up-and-coming artists.

CITY OF LONDON

Haz

9 Cutler Street, E1 7DJ **Tel** *020 7929 7923*

Map 16 D1

Lively, fun and a little posh too, this is a touch of true Turkey in the city. Go for a mixed *meze* starter. They just keep coming and they're all delicious. Go for the well-marinated meat dishes and kebabs and mop up the juice with the lovely flat bread. The office workers throng into Haz at lunchtime so get here before noon.

Noto

2–3 Basinghall Highwalk, EC2V 5DS **Tel** *020 7256 9433*

Map 15 B1

Authentic and great value is the decision of local Londoners as well as visiting Japanese. Fresh sushi for sure but also a fine selection of curries that you won't find elsewhere. There's good sashimi, crispy tempura and well-priced teriyaki. Small and inclined to be packed and, as usual with Japanese restaurants, home to a lot of smokers.

Key to Price Guide *see p296* **Key to Symbols** *see back cover flap*

Rajasthan

49 Monument Street, Monument, EC3R 8BU **Tel** *020 7626 1920*   **Map** *15 C3*

A newly-built Indian restaurant that avoids the obvious. Bright and airy, with fresh flowers on show and not a Bengal tiger or Taj Mahal in sight. The staff are happy to help you avoid the usual curry cliché dishes, but are equally happy to give you chicken tikka masala if that's what you want. Try something extra special such as a whole poussin.

Scu-zi

2 Creechurch Lane, EC3A 5AY **Tel** *020 7623 3444*   **Map** *16 D2*

Terrible punny name, but fresh and tasty pizzas. People say it has a "club underground feel to it" and rave about the service, food and atmosphere. It's not all pizza either, there are lots of your Italian favourites on the menu. Live bands. You get charged £1 extra for the band, which must make it the cheapest cabaret in town.

The Don

The Courtyard, 20 St Swithin's Lane, EC4N 8AD **Tel** *020 7626 2606*   **Map** *15 B2*

This used to be a wine warehouse so it's no surprise that it has an excellent wine list. It also has very attentive staff, who go out of their way to be helpful. A good sommelier and a range of interesting and unique dishes make this a very popular restaurant indeed and reservations are pretty much obligatory.

Abacus

24 Cornhill, EC3V 3ND **Tel** *020 7337 6767*   **Map** *15 B2*

A rather special place and you pay accordingly. Meals are punctuated by small *amuse-bouches* tiny, tasty creations that are so delicious they could be courses on their own. Hidden away in a basement near Bank Station it boasts a modern European seasonal menu with superior levels of service and presentation. A real treat. Daytime only.

HAMPSTEAD

Safir

116 Heath Street, NW3 1DR **Tel** *020 7431 9888*   **Map** *1 A4*

A Moroccan restaurant popular with a mixed crowd, especially at weekends when there is live music and belly dancers. Safir delivers simple, traditional cuisine with dishes such as couscous with chicken, caramelized onions and sultanas, and lamb tagine with prunes.

The Gaucho Grill

64 Heath Street, NW3 1DN **Tel** *020 7431 8222*   **Map** *1 A4*

Part of a chain serving hearty steaks for the larger appetite. A good family place with a lively atmosphere too. Can get a little boisterous when large groups come in, but you can normally have a pleasant calm meal here. On fine days, the outside seating is worth making an effort to secure.

Weng Wah House

240 Haverstock Hill, NW3 2AE **Tel** *020 7794 5123*

Highly regarded by locals for reliably good Chinese food at great prices. Be warned that there is karaoke, which isn't everyone's cup of tea, but it's not too intrusive and can actually be quite fun. Families will feel at home here. The food is actually very tasty so it's worth listening to the amateur Frank Sinatras accompanying it.

Base

3a Downshire Hill, 71 Hampstead High Street, NW3 1QP **Tel** *020 7431 2224*   **Map** *1 B5*

During the day Base is a bistro, which covers all bases (no pun intended!) from breakfast, coffee, pastries and snacks. In the evening it becomes a fine-dining Mediterranean fusion restaurant, offering sumptuous food with an emphasis on fresh ingredients. The menu changes regularly and is complemented by an extensive wine list.

Villa Bianca

1 Perrin's Court, NW3 1QS **Tel** *020 7435 3131*   **Map** *1 B5*

Tucked away from the crowd, and both family and local friendly, this Italian restaurant seems to make most visitors happy. The charming bow windows invite you in and it has a traditional feel about it. They have set menus and a great wine list. Service can be a bit erratic, but the owners know this and are making good efforts to improve it.

SOUTHWARK

Fusebox

12 Stoney Street, SE1 9AD **Tel** *020 7407 9888*   **Map** *15 B4*

Not so much a restaurant as a good place to eat when exploring Borough Market. Asian is the main food style with dishes such as tea smoked salmon or aubergine and oyster mushroom dish. There's a great selection of hot and cold things to try and the price is right too.

Tito's

4–6 London Bridge Street, SE1 9SG **Tel** *020 7407 7787*

Map *15 B4*

Tito's serves Peruvian staples like seafood, fish soups, fried yucca and rice, and its portions are extremely generous. Try the king prawn *chupe* – a milky soup with rice, peas and egg – or one of the restaurant's *pisco*-based cocktails.

Bermondsey Kitchen

194 Bermondsey Street, SE1 3TQ **Tel** *020 7407 5719*

Map *15 D5*

A great place for brunch such as eggs Florentine. There is a Spanish flavour to many of the options, with fresh ingredients from nearby Borough Market and tapas also on the menu. Global wines and an easy-going atmosphere complete the appeal.

Cantina Vinopolis

1 Bank End, SE1 9BU **Tel** *020 7940 8333*

Map *15 B3*

This is part of the massive wine museum so you know you are going to have a good wine list. The food isn't bad either with a wide choice ranging to suit most tastes. Try the monkfish and sea bass, beef carpaccio or tuna salad. Can be a little lacking in atmosphere but if you're a wine buff visiting the museum it's an ideal place to lunch.

Delfina Studio Café

50 Bermondsey Street, SE1 3UD **Tel** *020 7357 0244*

Map *15 C4*

Don't let the word "café" put you off. A former chocolate factory, it has a light gallery space, charming service and an interesting, balanced menu. Chew while admiring that week's pictures. Fish of the day might be from Australia, or you may see springbok. The menu is short but always interesting and there is a good wine list as well.

el Vergel

8 Lant Street, SE1 1QR **Tel** *020 7357 0057*

Map *15 A5*

Perhaps the only restaurant in town for Chilean food and it does it well. Home-cooked empanadas, and *pastel de choclo* are very popular. A small place and not really styled for fine dining, it has a very friendly atmosphere and portions can be huge. Rather charming and very Chilean.

Georgetown Restaurant

10 London Bridge Street, SE1 9SG **Tel** *020 7357 7359*

Map *15 B4*

Colonial look and feel with Singapore Sling cocktails to further the illusion. There are all kinds of Asian dishes on the menu from dim sums to curries with chicken and prawn dumplings, a lamb curry with beans standing out. Look out for special deals as it's a little overpriced otherwise.

Silka

6–8 Southwark Street, London Bridge, SE1 1RQ **Tel** *020 7378 7777*

Map *15 B4*

Ayurvedic food is a speciality here, which is basically food balanced for body and soul, and is particularly good for vegetarians. Of course, there are also all the usual Indian dishes too. There is some reluctance on the staff's part to write down your order so do check what arrives is actually what you asked for.

Tentazioni

2 Mill Street, SE1 2BD **Tel** *020 7237 1100*

Map *16 E5*

A bit more expensive than your average Italian, so should you be tempted by Tentazioni? Yes indeed. Very good food is on offer and the five-course tasting menu is a delight, especially at the very reasonable price. A busy and friendly restaurant that's well worth making the walk from Tower Bridge.

GREENWICH

Inside

19 Greenwich South Street, SE10 8NW **Tel** *020 8265 5060*

Map *23 B3*

Modern European cuisine in a clean minimalist setting and ideally placed to take in a pre-theatre meal. The menu keeps fresh by constantly changing and the staff exudes confidence in their kitchen. This is a restaurant which could comfortably charge more for your meals, but which so far, thankfully doesn't.

The Spread Eagle

1–2 Stockwell Street, SE10 9JN **Tel** *020 8853 2333*

Map *23 B2*

Fiercely championed by locals, this place radiates confidence with its innovative French cuisine. Small snuggly booths to dine in and a real, roaring fire in winter all conspire to make you want to stay long after the coffee has been cleared away. The food is rich and satisfying and the whole experience is a lot better than West End at half the price.

Thyme

1–3 Station Crescent, Westcombe Park, SE3 7EQ **Tel** *020 8293 9183*

Map *24 F1*

Small. Intimate. Minimalist. That's Thyme in Greenwich, a neighbourhood restaurant that remains perennially popular. There are a lot of places catering to tourists in Greenwich and most are substandard. Take the trouble to find Thyme and you'll get a very decent meal for a reasonable price.

Key to Price Guide *see p296* **Key to Symbols** *see back cover flap*

North Pole ⓔⓔⓔ

131 Greenwich High Road, SE10 8JA **Tel** *020 8853 3020* **Map 23 B3**

A nice bar downstairs and fire in the grate upstairs means North Pole is not a chilly place. A small piano tinkles away in the background. Food is of a very high standard and caters for all. It has a Michelin rating but the prices don't reflect this too badly. Another little Greenwich gem.

FURTHER AFIELD

Amerigo Vespucci ⓔⓔ

25 Cabot Square, Canary Wharf, E14 4QA **Tel** *020 7513 0288*

If you're lost among the towering spires of Docklands, pop in here for a reasonable riverside Italian lunch at a fair price. It was one of the first Italian restaurants to arrive in the area, and has an extensive á la carte menu with daily specials.

Babalou ⓔⓔ

The Crypt, St Matthew's Church, SW2 **Tel** *020 7738 3366*

With Brixton still trying to live up to its hype and out grow its past, Babalou is a new bar, restaurant and club offering a global fusion of dishes to suit the eclectic multiracial area. It's in a basement, but in summer you can comfortably sit outside and chill out.

Brown's Kew ⓔⓔ

3–5 Kew Green, Richmond, TW9 3AA **Tel** *020 8948 4838*

From its first beginning in Brighton the Brown's empire has spread out. It's solid British cooking. Sitting amid dark wooden café chairs and palms and whirling fans, you get quite a colonial feel. A lovely part of town deserves a pretty restaurant like this. Alfresco dining is possible in the summer.

Ginger ⓔⓔ

115 Westbourne Grove, W2 4UP **Tel** *020 7908 1990* **Map 10 D2**

A proper Bangladeshi restaurant, nicely modern and airy. Bangladeshis love their fish and a surmai macher biryani is something unique – a subtle fragrant rice dish with delicately spiced fish. All the dishes have something extra to the ordinary curry house fodder. Reasonably priced.

Great Eastern Dining Room ⓔⓔ

54 Great Eastern Street, EC2A 3QR **Tel** *020 7613 4545* **Map 7 C4**

Very tasty and popular, Great Eastern has been a raging success since day one. There are all kinds of dishes on the menu, many of which don't normally make it over to the UK, for example "Son In Law's Eggs!" Dim sums are filling and the curries balanced and spicy. And for once, service is impeccable and friendly.

Mezedepolio ⓔⓔ

14–15 Hoxton Market, N1 6HG **Tel** *020 7739 8212* **Map 7 C3**

Join the crowd in Hoxton and take in a massive selection of Greek dishes. They're all very tempting but keep an eye on the prices or you could end up with financial indigestion. The food is home-style cooking, therefore many of the dishes on the menu have never been seen in the UK before. The Real Greek wine bar serves Greek wines as well.

The Pelican ⓔⓔ

45 All Saints Road, W11 1HE **Tel** *020 7727 6126* **Map 9 B1**

Roasted beef, roasted suckling pig and other meaty delights in this rather genteelly tattered-around the edges place. The menu is full of British-type staples, including cod and chips. Normally jammed full with a funky hip crowd. Interestingly it features the first Marine Conservation Society approved menu.

Balham Kitchen and Bar ⓔⓔⓔ

15-19 Bedford Hill, Balham, SW12 9EX **Tel** *020 8675 6900*

Not the greatest of areas, rather grubby but getting better all the time. This restaurant is in the vanguard of delivering cool food to an increasingly well-heeled young crowd. Modern European flavours and a good selection of dishes means it's hard to leave unsatisfied with your meal.

Chez Bruce ⓔⓔⓔ

2 Bellevue Road, Wandsworth Common, SW17 7EG **Tel** *020 8672 0114*

The menu is a fusion of classic French dishes and more exotic flavours and after 10 years here, Bruce has got it right. Lots of emphasis on offal, so not a veggie paradise but otherwise a very good restaurant indeed. Great flavour combinations and a sure hand at the stove means it's worth its money.

Le Vacherin ⓔⓔⓔ

76–77 South Parade, W4 5LF **Tel** *020 8742 2121*

A chef-patron restaurant in deepest Chiswick, a lovely suburb of London. Here they have recreated a charming Parisian bistro serving top-notch food in a nice unpretentious way to a loyal local clientele. Sunday brunch is particularly popular. October to March, they serve Le Vacherin speciality cheese, baked with black truffles, almonds and white wine.

Light Meals and Snacks

When you want to make the most of the available sightseeing time, it doesn't always make sense to sit down for a lengthy restaurant meal. Or, perhaps you don't have the budget or the appetite for a full-course affair. London has several eateries for every taste and occasion – many of them unmissable institutions – from traditional fish-and-chip and pie-and-mash shops to elegant tearooms and cool cafés.

BREAKFAST

A good breakfast prepares you for a solid day's sightseeing, with the traditional British breakfast including staples such as bacon and eggs, smoked salmon and grilled kippers. Many hotels (see pp282–91) serve traditional breakfasts to non-residents, but to start the day like a 19th-century lord, head for **Simpson's-in-the-Strand**, which on weekdays offers an old-fashioned breakfast menu (as well as classic lunchtime and dinner roasts) in a historic panelled dining room. Porridge, lamb's kidneys, Cumberland sausage and black pudding are just part of the multicourse "10 deadly sins" set breakfast.

Several pubs around Smithfield serve the all-night meat market workers. The most famous of these is the **Cock Tavern**, dishing up good-value fare from 6am onwards. Traditional cafés also fry up artery-clogging working-men's morning meals including egg, sausage, mushrooms and baked beans.

For Continental breakfasts such as pastries and a cappuccino, there are many cafés to choose from. **The Wolseley** serves croissants, brioches and cooked breakfasts in opulent surroundings. Brunch has become increasingly popular in London. The spacious, modern restaurant in the back of popular French grocer/delicatessen, **Villandry**, serves one of the best on Saturday and Sunday. American restaurants such as **Joe Allen** and **Christopher's** also offer brunch, or head for well-heeled Westbourne Grove, where it's a weekend ritual at relaxed eateries such as **202** and **Tom's**.

COFFEE AND TEA

For a cappuccino or espresso at any time of day, step into round-the-clock Soho stalwart **Bar Italia**, which also serves a range of pastries and paninis. It's a legendary late-night pitstop, full of colourful characters (but do keep a hand on your bag/wallet). There is no shortage of coffee-bar chains, but one of the best is **Caffè Nero**, which dispenses authentic Italian coffee at reasonable prices across town.

If you're out shopping, many of London's department stores have their own cafés; Harvey Nichols' is one of the most stylish, while Selfridges has a branch of the cool Moroccan tearoom **Momo** among its many eating options. Designer stores such as Emporio Armani, Nicole Farhi and Joseph have trendy cafés – from the outside **202** looks like a chic French-style café, but it showcases Nicole Farhi's fashion and home designs downstairs. **Joe's Café**, surrounded by Joseph's three boutiques at Brompton Cross, is a small yet slick refreshment option; there are a few branches around town. In Portobello Market, quaint tearoom **Still Too Few**, below the antique kitchenalia shop of the same name, serves tea, sandwiches and cakes to bric-a-brac hunters on Saturdays.

Patisseries such as **Maison Bertaux** and **Patisserie Valerie** are a delight, with mouth-watering window displays of French pastries. **Richoux** in Piccadilly is another popular refreshment spot. Smart French bakery/patisserie **Paul** offers delicious tarts and other treats in a Parisian-café atmosphere. The elegantly old-world **The Wolseley** in

Piccadilly has an all-day café menu of sandwiches and salads. If you're strolling in picturesque Little Venice, **Café Laville** commands a spectacular view over Regent's Canal. **Bluebird**, Terence Conran's multi-faceted food centre in the converted 1920s Bluebird motor garage on the King's Road, has a café with tables on its cobbled forecourt as well as a more formal restaurant, bar and market.

No visit to London would be complete without taking afternoon tea. Top hotels such as the **Ritz** and **Brown's** (see p286) offer pots of your choice of tea, scones with jam and cream, delicious, thin cucumber sandwiches and cakes galore. For a relaxed place in beautiful Kensington Gardens, there's nothing to beat **The Orangery**. Its selection of English teas and cakes tastes even better in the elegant surroundings of Sir John Vanbrugh's 18th-century building. Good coffee (and cakes) can also be found at the **Monmouth Coffee House** in Covent Garden. **Fortnum and Mason** (see p321) serves both afternoon and high teas. In Kew, the **Maids of Honour** tearoom offers pastries, reputedly enjoyed by Henry VIII. For a more modern experience, **Sketch** offers exquisite contemporary confections in a restyled Georgian room.

TRADITIONAL CAFÉS

These basic greasy spoons all over the city are a London institution, serving up fried breakfasts and such British staples as sausages, pies and grills. They are usually only open until about 5pm; some close earlier. Granddaddy of them all is East End legend **E Pellicci**, with its wonderful Art Deco interior. A recent vogue for simple British fare spawned some modern versions of the "caff", including the mini chain **S&M Café** – sausage and mash before you get any funny ideas.

MUSEUM AND THEATRE CAFÉS

Most museums and galleries have cafés, including the Royal Academy, Tate Modern (with wonderful views over the Thames), the National Portrait Gallery and the British Museum. The National Film Theatre on the South Bank has a buzzing bar/café frequented by film fanatics, while St Martin-in-the-Fields church in Trafalgar Square, famous for its concerts, has a capacious self-service café in its vaulted crypt.

SANDWICH BARS

A leading sandwich chain in London is **Prêt à Manger**, with branches throughout the centre decked out with metalwork features and serving a range of delicious pre-packed sandwiches, salads, cakes and soft drinks. Another popular sandwich chain is **Eat**, which offers a daily changing menu of innovative soups and salads using seasonal ingredients as well as sandwiches made with homemade breads and tortilla wraps. Quality Italian sandwich fillings in focaccia and ciabatta breads can be had at Soho's **Carlton Coffee House**. For a quick bite in Fitzrovia, **Squat & Gobble** does great freshly made doorstep sandwiches, healthy salads and home-cooked dishes, as well as breakfasts.

DELIS

With Londoners becoming more and more interested in high-quality foods from small producers in Britain and abroad, there has been a boom in stylish delis, many of which provide seating so that you can sample their wares on site. **Tom's** is a one-stop deli and café. The chic **Grocer on Warwick Café** offers breakfast and light Oriental-influenced dishes as well as ready-prepared foods to take away, while deli/cheese shop **La Fromagerie** has a large communal table in the back for light bites. Nearby, is the 100-year-old family-run delicatessen/lunchroom **Paul Rothe & Son**, which serves sandwiches and soups among the shelves of "British and foreign provisions".

DINERS

London is full of American-style fast-food joints, serving burgers, fries, fried chicken, apple pie, milk shakes and cola, particularly around Soho, Leicester Square, Shaftesbury Avenue and Covent Garden. Some time-honoured establishments include family favourite **Maxwell's**, in Covent Garden, the **Hard Rock Café**, and the fun, 1950s kitsch **Ed's Easy Diner**, but thanks to the recent vogue for retro burger restaurants, new ones are popping up all over town. **Hamburger Union**, where you order at the grill before sitting down, is one of the best, while the **Lucky 7** near Notting Hill serves up burgers and breakfasts in a dice-and-cards-themed diner, complete with vinyl-seated booths and blaring rock 'n' roll.

PIZZA AND PASTA

Italian food has now become a staple of the British diet. Street-side stands offer variable quality, while there are well-established chains with several branches, including **Ask**. **Pizza Express** is another very popular choice, offering thin-crust pizzas that are a step up from the norm. Try the elegant Georgian townhouse outlet on Chelsea's King's Road, or the branch in a converted dairy in Soho where there's also live jazz. **Kettners**, also part of the group, offers casual, inexpensive eating in a legendary old dining room (there's also a champagne bar). The **Carluccio's Caffè** chain, which has a branch with al fresco tables in pedestrianized St Christopher's Place, serves good-quality, freshly made pastas and salads. **Marine Ices** near Camden Market serves great pizza and pasta in addition to its famous ice cream (see Street Food pp314–5). Among the other reliable pasta chains are **Spaghetti House** and **Café Pasta**. Inexpensive pasta is generally served at bustling trattorias such as **Pollo** in Soho.

FOOD IN PUBS

Traditional British "pub grub" is simple, hearty fare such as ploughman's lunch (cheese, salad, pickles and bread), shepherd's pie and roast beef with Yorkshire pudding on Sundays. Many pubs, such as the Fuller's Ale and Pie House chain, and **Dickens Inn**, housed in an old spice warehouse in St Katharine's Dock, still serve the classics.

But, in line with London's culinary revival, pub food has also undergone a complete evolution in the last decade. "Gastropubs" today serve the sort of food you would expect to find in a contemporary restaurant, with a mix of British, Mediterranean and Oriental influences; the difference is the relaxed setting and reasonable prices. Some pubs have a devoted dining room, while at others you eat in the main bar. **The Chapel**, **The Eagle**, **The Engineer**, **The Lansdowne** and **The Seven Stars** are among the best of the so-called gastropubs. It is usually essential to book in advance. (See also pp316–9).

FISH AND CHIPS

Fish and chips is typically considered the national dish of Britain, with a "chippy" serving a choice of fish (typically cod or plaice) deep-fried in batter, accompanied by chips (thicker cut than French fries). A range of accompaniments includes bread baps (rolls) for a "chip buttie" (a chip sandwich), mushy peas, pickled eggs or onions. Four of the best places for such fare are the **North Sea Fish Restaurant**, **Rock & Sole Plaice**, **Faulkner's** and **Fish Central**. Fish and chips is now considered very "trendy" and is increasingly available on the menu in various smart restaurants and chains such as **Fish!**

BARS AND WINE BARS

The range and quality of London's bars has grown over the past five years. There are numerous wine bars in the centre, such as **Café des Amis du Vin** in Covent Garden (downstairs from its ground-floor brasserie), and the legendary **El Vino**, as well as chains such as **Corney & Barrow** and **Balls Bros**, which also serve good food. The cosy **Tapa Room** on the ground floor of acclaimed **The Providores** restaurant serves globally influenced tapas. Good-value food is also part of the success of such chain bars as **All Bar One**. Capitalizing on young Londoners' habit of spending an entire evening out drinking, many style-conscious, modern bars serve food, such as the sleek **Eagle Bar Diner** off Oxford Street, which has a wide-ranging menu encompassing breakfast, burgers, pasta and grills, and the **Alphabet Bar** in Soho. *(See also pp317–9)*.

BRASSERIES

Now that informal dining is an integral aspect of life in London, brasseries have become part of the landscape. These are based on the classic French blueprint, with its Parisian ambience and decor, serving such favourites as steak frites and seafood platters – a classic example is long-established **La Brasserie** in South Kensington. Among the chains are the chandelier-embellished **Dôme** and **Café Rouge**. **Randall & Aubin** is a buzzy oyster and lobster (plus champagne) bar in a former delicatessen that has retained its period charm and overlooks Soho's lively Brewer Street. Relative newcomer **The Electric Brasserie**, next to Portobello's luxurious art-house cinema of the same name, is a popular update on the traditional model.

JUICE BARS AND ORGANIC CAFÉS

The healthy diet trend has made juice bars and organic food shops very popular. Longstanding Lebanese favourite **Ranoush Juice** has added new outlets to its original Edgware Road location, and there are more recent arrivals such as **Crussh** and **Bean Juice**. Organic food chains such as **Planet Organic** and **Fresh & Wild** do a roaring trade in hot and cold fare and freshly squeezed juices along side their groceries, baked goods and vitamins, with tables on the premises.

NOODLE BARS

Popular chain **Wagamama** still draws queues for its good-value noodles and other Oriental dishes in airy yet basic environs; customers sit at long communal tables. **Dim T Café** serves dim sum and mix-and-match noodles, meat and toppings in a modern café setting. **Taro** is a busy Japanese diner offering cheap sushi, ramen and teriyaki.

STREET FOOD

During summer, many parks have ice-cream vans parked by the entrances, with **Marine Ices** serving some of the town's best ice cream. Hot roasted chestnuts, made on mini-barbecues, are a winter delight found along Oxford Street. Shellfish stalls, selling ready-to-eat potted shrimps, crab, whelks and jellied eels are a feature of many street markets. At Camden Lock and Old Spitalfields Market, you can wander among the stalls choosing from falafel, satay chicken, vegeburgers and honey balls. In the East End, Jewish bakeries such as **Brick Lane Beigel Bake** are open 24 hours a day. Fresh plain bagels as well as ones with a wide range of fillings are available here.

The East End also has the largest number of pie and mash shops, which provide an inexpensive and satisfying "nosh-up" of jellied eels and potatoes, or meat pie with mash and liquor (green parsley sauce). Two classic venues, both on Bethnal Green Road, are **G Kelly** and **S&R Kelly**. Or try **Goddard's Pie & Mash** in Greenwich. For the real East End experience, you should drench your food in vinegar and wash it all down with a couple of mugs of strong, hot tea. Modern pie-maker **The Square Pie Company** sells superior pies with gourmet fillings in Old Spitalfields Market and Selfridges.

DIRECTORY

BREAKFAST

202
202 Westbourne Grove W11.
Map 9 C2.

Christopher's
18 Wellington St WC2.
Map 13 C2.

Cock Tavern
East Poultry Avenue, Smithfield Market EC1.
Map 6 F5.

Joe Allen
13 Exeter St WC2.
Map 13 C2.

Simpson's-in-the-Strand
100 Strand WC2.
Map 13 C2.

Tom's
226 Westbourne Grove W11. **Map** 9 B2.

Villandry
170 Great Portland Street W1. **Map** 4 F5.

The Wolseley
160 Piccadilly W1.
Map 12 F3.

COFFEE AND TEA

Bar Italia
22 Frith St W1.
Map 13 A2.

Bluebird Café
350 King's Rd SW3.
Map 19 A4.

Café Laville
Little Venice Parade, 453 Edgware Rd W2.

Emporio Armani Caffè
191 Brompton Rd SW3.
Map 19 B1.

Joe's Café
126 Draycott Ave SW3.
Map 19 B2.

Maids of Honour
288 Kew Rd Richmond, Surrey.

DIRECTORY

Maison Bertaux
28 Greek St W1.
Map 13 A1.

Monmouth Coffee House
27 Monmouth St WC2.
Map 13 B2.

The Orangery
Kensington Palace, Kensington Gardens W8.
Map 10 D3.

Patisserie Valerie
215 Brompton Rd SW3.
Map 19 B1.

Paul
29 Bedford St WC2.
Map 13 B2.

Richoux
172 Piccadilly W1.
Map 12 F3.

Sketch
9 Conduit St W1.
Map 12 F2.

Still Too Few
300 Westbourne Grove
W11. **Map** 9 B2.

TRADITIONAL CAFÉS

E Pellicci
332 Bethnal Green Rd E2.

S&M Café
268 Portobello Rd W11.
Map 9 A1.

MUSEUM AND THEATRE CAFÉS

Café in the Crypt
St Martin-in-the-Fields,
Duncannon St WC2.
Map 13 B3.

Film Café
National Film Theatre, S
Bank SE1. **Map** 14 D3.

SANDWICH BARS

Carlton Coffee House
41 Broadwick St W1.
Map 13 A2.

Eat
12 Oxo Tower Wharf,
Barge House St SE1
Map 14 E3.

Prêt à Manger
421 Strand WC2.
Map 13 C3.

Squat & Gobble
69 Charlotte Street W1.
Map 5 A5.

DELIS

La Fromagerie
2-4 Moxon St W1.
Map 4 D5.

Grocer on Warwick Café
21 Warwick St W1.
Map 12 F2.

Paul Rothe & Son
35 Marylebone Lane W1.
Map 12 D1.

DINERS

Ed's Easy Diner
12 Moor St W1.
Map 13 B2.

Hamburger Union
4-6 Garrick St WC2.
Map 13 B2.

Hard Rock Café
150 Old Park Lane W1.
Map 12 E4.

Lucky 7
127 Westbourne Park Rd
W2. **Map** 9 C1.

Maxwell's
89 James St WC2.
Map 13 C2.

PIZZA AND PASTA

Ask
103 St John St EC1.
Map 16 E2.

Café Pasta
184 Shaftesbury Avenue
WC2.
Map 13 2B.

Carluccio's Caffè
St Christopher's Place W1.
Map 12 E2.
One of several branches.

Kettner's
29 Romilly St W1.
Map 13 A2.

Pizza Express
30 Coptic St WC1.
Map 13 B1.
One of many branches.

Pollo
20 Old Compton St W1.
Map 13 A2.

FISH AND CHIPS

Faulkner's
424–426 Kingsland Rd E8.

Fish!
Borough Mkt SE1.
Map 15 B4.

Fish Central
149–151 Central St EC1.
Map 7 A3.

North Sea Fish Restaurant
7–8 Leigh St WC1.
Map 5 B4.

Rock & Sole Plaice
47 Endell St WC2.
Map 13 B1.

WINE BARS

All Bar One
103 Cannon St EC4.
Map 15 A2.

Alphabet Bar
61 Beak Street W1.
Map 12 F2.

Balls Bros
Hays Galleria Tooley Street
SE1. **Map** 15 B3.

Café des Amis du Vin
11–14 Hanover Place
WC2. **Map** 13 C2.

Corney & Barrow
19 Broadgate Circle EC2.
Map 7 C5.

Dickens Inn
St Katharine's Dock E1.
Map 16 E3.

Eagle Bar Diner
3-5 Rathbone Place W1.
Map 13 A1.

Providores Tapa Room
109 Marylebone High St
W1. **Map** 4 D5.

El Vino
47 Fleet Street EC4.
Map 14 E1.

BRASSERIES

La Brasserie
272 Brompton Rd SW3.
Map 19 B2.

Café Rouge
27 Basil St SW3.
Map 11 C5.

Dôme
57–59 Old Compton St
W1. **Map** 13 A2.

The Electric Brasserie
191 Portobello Rd W11.
Map 9 B2.

Randall & Aubin
16 Brewer St W1
Map 13 A2.

JUICE BARS AND ORGANIC CAFÉS

Bean Juice
10A St Christopher's Place
W1. **Map** 12 E2.

Crussh
Unit 1 1 Curzon Street
W1. **Map** 12 E3.

Fluid Juice Bar
208 Fulham Rd SW3.
Map 19 A2.

Fresh & Wild
208-212 Westbourne
Grove W11. **Map** 9 B2.

Planet Organic
22 Torrington Place WC1.
Map 5 A5.

Ranoush Juice
43 Edgware Rd W2.
Map 11 C2.

NOODLE BARS

Dim T Café
32 Charlotte St W1.
Map 13 A1.

Taro
59-61 Brewer St W1.
Map 13 A2.

Wagamama
101 Wigmore Street W1.
Map 12 D1.

STREET FOOD

Brick Lane Beigel Bake
159 Brick La E1.
Map 8 E5.

G Kelly S&R Kelly
Bethnal Green Road E1.
Map 8 D4.

Goddard's Eel & Pie
45 Greenwich Church
St SE10.
Map 23 B2.

Marine Ices
8 Haverstock Hill NW3.

London Pubs and Bars

Affectionately known as a "pub" as well as "boozer" and "the local", a public house was originally just that – a house in which the public could eat, drink, and even stay the night. Large inns with courtyards, such as The George Inn, were originally stopping points for horse-drawn coach services. Some pubs stand on historic public house sites, for instance the Ship, the Lamb and Flag and the City Barge. However, many of the finest ones date from the emergence of "gin palaces" in the late 1800s, where Londoners took refuge from the misery of their poverty amid lavish interiors, often with stunning mirrors (The Salisbury) and elaborate decorations. Since the 1990s cocktail-bar boom, the traditional pub has been given an image makeover, restoring the British institution's popularity with a fashionable crowd.

RULES AND CONVENTIONS

Visitors to London have long been bemused by early pub closing times, which made a night out a bit tricky – an after-theatre nightcap, for example, was usually out of the question outside of your hotel. In theory, reforms to the licensing laws, which came into effect in November 2005, mean pubs can now stay open up to 24 hours, as long as they obtain permission from their local authority, but it remains to be seen how many will extend their hours beyond the 11am–11pm standard. Some may close in the afternoon or early evening and also at weekends. You must be at least 18 to buy or drink alcohol, and at least 14 to enter a pub without an adult. Children can be taken into pubs that serve food, or can use outside areas. Order at the bar, and pay when you are served; tips are not usual unless you are served food and drink at a table. "Last orders" are usually called 10 minutes before closing, then "time" is called, and a further 20 minutes is then allowed for finishing up drinks. From summer 2007, smoking will be banned from pubs and clubs.

BRITISH BEER

The most traditional beers are available in various different strengths and styles, and are flat (not fizzy), and served only lightly cooled. The spectrum of bottled beers goes from "light" ale, through "pale", "brown", "bitter" and the strong "old". A sweeter, lower alcohol alternative is shandy, a classic mixture of draught beer or lager and lemonade. Many traditional methods of brewing and serving beer have been preserved over the years, and there is a great variety of "real ale" in London pubs. Serious beer drinkers should look for "Free Houses", pubs that are not tied to any particular brewery. The main London brewers are Young's (try their strong "Winter Warmer" beer) and Fuller's. The **Orange Brewery** serves a good pint and excellent food, and offers tours of the brewery.

OTHER PUB DRINKS

Cider is another traditional English drink found in every pub. Made from apples, it comes in a range of strengths and degrees of dryness. Blended Scotch whisky and malt whiskies are also staples, together with gin, usually drunk with tonic water. During the winter, mulled wine (warm and spicy) or hot toddies (brandy or whisky with hot water and sugar) may be served. Non-alcoholic drinks are also always available.

HISTORIC PUBS

Many pubs have a fascinating history and decor, whether it is a beamed medieval snug, Victorian fantasy, or an extraordinary Arts-and-Crafts interior, as at the **Black Friar**, a must-see temple to imbibing, featuring bronze bas reliefs, and an intimate, marble-and-mosaic chamber at the back. While many of the "gin palaces" of the 19th century have been revamped or abandoned, there are some notable survivors. At the **Prince Alfred** in Maida Vale the bar is divided by "snobscreens", a feature that enabled the upper set to enjoy a drink without mixing with their servants. The semi-circular **Viaduct Tavern**, opposite the Old Bailey, is a suitably stately setting for distinguished barristers and judges, ablaze with mirrors, chandeliers and etched glass, while the **Princess Louise** retains its magnificent central mahogany bar, complete with original clock, moulded ceiling and vivid wall tiles. Less grand but just as lovingly decorated is the tiny, tiled **Dog & Duck** in Soho – but you may have to battle for a seat or (in warm weather) stand outside with its many devotees.

Many pubs have strong literary associations, such as the **Fitzroy Tavern**, a meeting place for writers and artists in the 1930s and 40s, including Dylan Thomas, George Orwell and Augustus John, **Ye Olde Cheshire Cheese** is associated with Dr Johnson, Charles Dickens frequented the **Trafalgar Tavern**, while Oscar Wilde often went to **The Salisbury**. Samuel Pepys witnessed the Great Fire of London from the **Anchor**, on the river at Bankside. The less literary **Old Bull and Bush** in north London was the subject of a well known old music-hall song, while the 17th-century **Lamb and Flag** – one of central London's few surviving timber-framed buildings down an alleyway – was known as the Bucket of Blood because it was the venue for bare-knuckle prize fights. Some pubs have sinister associations, for example some of Jack the Ripper's victims were found near the **Ten Bells**. Dick

Turpin, the 18th-century highwayman, took refreshment at the **Spaniards Inn** in north London, and the **French House** in Soho was a meeting point for the French Resistance during World War II.

PUB NAMES

Signs have hung outside public houses since 1393, when King Richard II decreed they should replace the usual bush outside the door. As most people were illiterate, names that could easily be illustrated were chosen, such as the Rose & Crown, coats of arms (Freemasons' Arms), historical figures (Princess Louise) or heraldic animals (White Lion).

PUB ENTERTAINMENT

Fringe theatre productions (*see p346*) are staged at the **King's Head**, the **Latchmere**, and at the **Gate Theatre** above the Prince Albert. Some pubs have live music: there is excellent modern jazz at the **Bull's Head** in Barnes and a wide variety of music styles at the popular **Mean Fiddler** (*see pp350–3*). The diminutive **Golden Eagle**, on a winding backstreet in Marylebone, is a rare central London piano pub with nostalgic singalongs a few nights a week.

OUTDOOR DRINKING

Most pubs with outdoor seating tend to be located slightly outside the city centre. The **Freemason's Arms** for example, near Hampstead Heath, has a very pleasant garden. Some pubs enjoy riverside locations with fine views, from the **Prospect of Whitby** in Wapping and the **Grapes** in Limehouse to the **White Cross** in Richmond.

MICROBREWERIES

Delicious beer is brewed on the premises at microbreweries such as **Mash** where a space-age interior makes you forget that real ale tends to be the domain of older drinkers. This bar is frequented by a young and trendy crowd. Huge orange vats indicate where the actual brewing takes place. The **Bünker Bier Hall Bar and Kitchen** in Covent Garden has three signature beers, and a good atmosphere.

THEMED PUBS AND BARS

Big, brash Irish pubs such as **Filthy McNasty's** and **Waxy O'Connor's** (mocked up like a Catholic church, complete with confessional) attract a young, fun-loving crowd, as does Australian bar chain **Walkabout**. Sports bars are popular as well. The **Sports Café**, near Piccadilly, has three bars, a dance floor — and 120 television sets showing global sporting events on satellite TV. More low-key is "footie" bar **Kick** in Shoreditch (there's a smaller sister establishment, **Café Kick**, in Exmouth Market), which features table-soccer games and organic food in a relaxed setting. Pool players can take their cue at a branch of slick pool-bar chain the **Elbow Room**.

GASTROPUBS

Over the past decade, many old pubs have been given gleaming makeovers and kitchens turning out superior fare. Among the first "gastropubs" was the **Eagle**, frequented by journalists from the nearby *Guardian* newspaper offices. Many, like **The Lansdowne** and **The Engineer** have dedicated dining rooms as well as laid-back pub rooms where you can eat, drink or do both. TV foodie Roxy Beaujolais serves simple bistro dishes in tiny, quirky old pub the **Seven Stars** near the Royal Courts of Justice. **The Cow** is known for its oysters and Guinness, while the **Chapel**, the **Fire Station** and the **Dusk** are popular with both drinkers and diners. (*See also p313–15*)

BARS

London's bar scene has been transformed since the mid-1990s, when the choice was limited to either hotel bars, wine bars or pubs (*see p314–5*). Propelled by a cocktail revival, as well as the fact that eating and drinking out is now deeply ingrained in daily London life, new bars are opening all the time.

Eagerly sought out by style-conscious connoisseurs, the latest watering holes are now as much a talking point as new restaurants. Soho and Covent Garden are brimming with bars, but to sample the hottest nightspots, head either east or west. In the past decade, Shoreditch has been transformed from no-go area to an evening destination, which is spilling into neighbouring Bethnal Green.

Two of the earliest pioneers – basement lounge **Home** and the no-frills **The Shoreditch Electricity Showrooms** – are still hopping. They've recently been joined by, among others, the 1970s-styled warehouse space **T**, which is so vast it will never get too crowded, and, slightly further afield, the gloriously camp **Loungelover**, decorated with crystal chandeliers, vintage handbags and stuffed animals.

Across town in Notting Hill, sip good-value Scorpion Bowls and Zombies in the kitsch tiki-lounge ambience of **Trailer Happiness** or go for classic or more inventive cocktails at the **Lonsdale** with its bronze bubble-studded walls and hazy violet lighting. The area's style bars are in contrast with down-to-earth pubs frequented by the market traders, such as the bustling **Portobello Star**.

If you want to stick to the centre of town, fashionable options include the **Lab Bar**, which serves excellent cocktails, especially Central American drinks such as caprinhas and mojitos, or **Match**, which has a branch in Oxford Circus as well as Clerkenwell. Heading south, the **Fridge Bar** in Brixton has DJs playing decent hip hop and deep house with lots of dancing and drinking. Many restaurants feature excellent bars. The bar at **Green's Restaurant and Oyster Bar** (*see p301*) is a very special place to go, to drink champagne and eat oysters and lobster in elegant surroundings. **Smiths of Smithfield**, opposite the famous meat market, has a large, industrial-style café/bar at ground level, a sleek cocktail and champagne bar on the next floor, topped by two restaurants upstairs; nearby, **St John** *(see p308)* has a stylish bar serving excellent wine and bar food. A drink in the bar is the less-expensive way to experience the **Criterion** brasserie's sumptuous, gilded neo-Byzantine decor. Contemporary Chinese restaurant **Hakkasan** *(see p305)* serves exotic cocktails flavoured with the likes of ginger and lemongrass in its glamorous Oriental-style bar.

SPECIALIST BARS

Aficionados of particular spirits are well served. Modern Russian bar (and restaurant) **Potemkin** has over 130 vodkas in every conceivable flavour, plus imported Russian beers. Scottish restaurant Boisdale's **Macdonald Bar** boasts 170 Scotch malt whiskies (and an impressive selection of Cuban cigars), while the recently refurbished **Rockwell Bar** in the Trafalgar Hotel is London's largest bourbon selection. **Salt** is a slick, modern whisky bar, and **$**, in the basement of a glitzed-up former pub, serves a lengthy martini "library" in

a sexy setting. Mexican bar/restaurant **La Perla** in Covent Garden has an extensive range of tequilas.

CHAIN BARS

They may not be the most exciting places to drink, but London's chain bars are a reliable option. Halfway between a bar and a pub, with large windows and white walls, they are also far more female-friendly than dark, smokey pubs. **All Bar One** is very popular, with chunky wood furniture. **Pitcher & Piano** has sofas and blonde wood surrounds, while the **Slug & Lettuce** chain features paintings on the walls and quiet rooms for talking.

HOTEL BARS

London's hotel bars continue to offer an elegant setting for classic and innovative cocktails, with **The Blue Bar** at the Berkeley Hotel and the **Long Bar** at the Sanderson Hotel prime examples. The **American Bar** at The Savoy, decorated in an Art Deco style, has a pianist, a terrific atmosphere and classic cocktails (try the signature White Lady or the Dry Martini, which the bar introduced to Britain), while another Jazz Age gem, the **Rivoli Bar** at the Ritz, has been resplendently restored. **Claridge's Bar** offers excellent champagne cocktails (among other

concoctions) in a glamorous, contemporary-classic setting. **Trader Vic's** in the Park Lane Hilton offers an exotically tropical setting in which to enjoy an amazing range of rum cocktails. **Pearl Restaurant Bar**, in the Renaissance Chancery Court Hotel, brings sleek, contemporary style to the capacious former banking hall of the Pearl Assurance Building, serving fabulous fruity cocktails and 32 wines by the glass in the glow of striking pearl chandeliers. **Brasserie Max** in the Covent Garden Hotel is always buzzing and is very popular with theatre and film people.

GAY BARS

Old Compton Street in Soho has a well-established gay scene. Tables spill out on to the pavements and there is a lively atmosphere tolerant of all sexual preferences. **Compton's of Soho**, a busy pub, is across the road from the gay bar and eatery **Balans** and close to the well-known gay pub, **The Admiral Duncan**. **The Edge** is a sprawling bar and club over four floors, while **Rupert Street** is a stylishly low-key option for a relaxed drink. The **Candy Bar** is a popular lesbian bar, while, away from the West End, the **Royal Vauxhall Tavern** hosts Duckie's outrageous cabaret and DJs on Saturday nights.

DIRECTORY

SOHO, PICCADILLY

Admiral Duncan
Old Compton St W1.
Map 13 A2.

Balans
60 Old Compton St W1.
Map 13 A2.

Candy Bar
4 Carlisle St W1.
Map 13 A2.

Coach and Horses
29 Greek St WC2.
Map 14 F2.

Compton's of Soho
51–53 Old Compton St
W1. **Map** 13 A2.

Criterion
224 Piccadilly W1.
Map 13 A3.

Dog & Duck
18 Bateman St W1.
Map 13 A2.

Edge
11 Soho Sq W1.
Map 13 A1.

French House
49 Dean St W1.
Map 13 A2.

Lab Bar
12 Old Compton St
W1. **Map** 13 A2.

Long Bar
50 Berners Street.
Map 12 F1.

Mash
19–21 Great Portland St
W1. **Map** 12 F1.

Pitcher & Piano
70 Dean St W1.
Map 13 A1.

Rupert Street
50 Rupert St W1.
Map 13 A2.

Sports Café
80 Haymarket SW1.
Map 13 A3.

Waxy O'Connor's
14-16 Rupert St W1.
Map 13 A2.

MAYFAIR, ST JAMES'S

Claridge's
Brook St W1.
Map 12 E2.

Rivoli Bar
Ritz Hotel
150 Piccadilly W1.
Map 12 F3.

DIRECTORY

Salt
82 Seymour St W2.
Map 11 C2.

Slug & Lettuce
19 Hanover St W1
Map 12 F2.

Trader Vic's
22 Park Lane. **Map** 12 D3.

COVENT GARDEN, STRAND

American Bar
The Savoy, Strand WC2.
Map 13 C2.

Bünker Bier Hall Bar and Kitchen
41 Earlham St WC2.
Map 13 B2.

Lamb and Flag
33 Rose St WC2.
Map 13 B2.

La Perla
28 Maiden Lane WC2.
Map 13 C2.

Rockwell Bar
The Trafalgar
2 Spring Gardens SW1.
Map 13 B3.

The Salisbury
90 St Martin's Lane WC2.
Map 13 B2.

Seven Stars
53-54 Carey St WC2.
Map 14 D1.

Walkabout
11 Henrietta St WC2.
Map 13 C2.

BLOOMSBURY, HOLBORN

Fitzroy Tavern
16 Charlotte St W1.
Map 13 A1.

Princess Louise
208 High Holborn WC1.
Map 13 C1.

Pearl Restaurant Bar
Renaissance Chancery
Court Hotel
252 High Holborn WC1.
Map 13 C1.

THE CITY, CLERKENWELL

All Bar One
103 Cannon St EC4.
Map 15 A2.

Balls Brothers
11 Blomfield St EC2.
Map 15 C1.

Black Friar
174 Queen Victoria St
EC4.
Map 14 F2.

Corney & Barrow
19 Broadgate Circle EC2.
Map 7 C5.

$
2 Exmouth Market EC1.
Map 6 E4.

Eagle
159 Farringdon Rd EC1.
Map 6 E4.

Elbow Room
97-113 Curtain Rd EC2.
Map 7 C4.

Filthy McNasty's
68 Amwell St EC1.
Map 6 E3.

Home
100-106 Leonard St EC2.
Map 7 C4.

Kick
127 Shoreditch High St E1.
Map 8 D3.

Match
45–47 Clerkenwell Rd EC1.
Map 6 E5.

Loungelover
1 Whitby St E1.
Map 8 D4.

Potemkin
144 Clerkenwell Rd EC1.
Map 6 E5.

Ship Tavern
23 Lime St EC3.
Map 15 C2.

The Shoreditch Electricity Showrooms
39a Hoxton Sq N1.
Map 7 C3.

Smiths of Smithfield
67-77 Charterhouse St
EC1.
Map 6 F5.

T
The Tea Building
56 Shoreditch High St E1.
Map 8 D4.

Ten Bells
84 Commercial St E1.
Map 8 D5.

Viaduct Tavern
126 Newgate St EC1.
Map 14 F1.

Ye Olde Cheshire Cheese
145 Fleet St EC4.
Map 14 E1.

SOUTHWARK AND SOUTH BANK

Anchor
34 Park Street SE1.
Map 15 A3.

Fire Station
150 Waterloo Rd SE1.
Map 14 E4.

George Inn
77 Borough High St SE1.
Map 15 B4.

HAMPSTEAD

Freemasons Arms
32 Downshire Hill NW3.
Map 1 C5.

Old Bull and Bush
North End Way NW3.
Map 1 A3.

Spaniards Inn
Spaniards Way NW3.
Map 1 A3.

KNIGHTSBRIDGE, BELGRAVIA

Blue Bar
Wilton Pl SW1.
Map 12 D5.

Boisdale
15 Eccleston St SW1.
Map 20 E1.

The Lansdowne
90 Gloucester Ave NW1.
Map 4 D1.

PRIMROSE HILL, MARYLEBONE

Chapel
48 Chapel St NW1.
Map 3 B5.

Dusk
79 Marylebone High St W1.
Map 4 D5.

Golden Eagle
59 Marylebone Lane W1.
Map 12 D1.

The Engineer
65 Gloucester Ave NW1.
Map 4 D1.

BAYSWATER, NOTTING HILL

The Cow
89 Westbourne Park
Rd W11.
Map 23 C1.

Lonsdale
44-48 Lonsdale Rd W11.
Map 9 B2.

Portobello Star
171 Portobello Rd W11.
Map 9 B2.

Prince Albert
11 Pembridge Rd W11.
Map 9 C3.

Trailer Happiness
177 Portobello Rd W11.
Map 9 B2.

FURTHER AFIELD

Bull's Head
373 Lonsdale Rd SW13.

City Barge
27 Strand-o-t-Green W4.

Fridge Bar
1 Town Hill Parade SW2.

Grapes
76 Narrow St E14.

King's Head
115 Upper St N1.
Map 6 F1.

Latchmere
503 Battersea Pk Rd
SW11.

Prince Alfred
5a Formosa St W9.

Prospect of Whitby
57 Wapping Wall E1.

Royal Vauxhall Tavern
372 Kennington Lane
SE11.
Map 22 D3.

Trafalgar Tavern
Park Row SE10.

White Cross
Water Lane, Richmond,
Surrey.

SHOPS AND MARKETS

London is still one of the most lively shopping cities in the world. Here ultramodern stores sit alongside the old-fashioned emporia presided over by tailcoated staff. You can buy anything here, as long as you're prepared to pay. Luxury goods are expensive, although bargain-hunters will find a wealth of cheap goods in the thriving markets, which simply exude a carnival atmosphere. Explore the famous department stores, which encompass a huge breadth of merchandise, or seek out specialist shops. In general, you'll find upmarket designer stores around Knightsbridge, Regent Street and Bond Street, while Oxford Street is the frenetic centre for mid-priced labels as well as mainstream department stores. Notting Hill, Islington, Soho and the vicinity of Covent Garden are all rich in small, independent shops. Specialities include clothes from raincoats and traditional tweeds to cutting-edge design and catwalk copies; books and records; toiletries; art and antiques; and craft goods such as jewellery, ceramics and leather.

Bags from two of the most famous West End shops

WHEN TO SHOP

In central London, most shops open from 10am and close between 5.30pm–6pm from Monday to Saturday; many department stores have longer hours. The "late night" shopping until 7 or 8pm is on Thursdays and Fridays in Oxford Street and the rest of the West End, and on Wednesdays in Knightsbridge and Chelsea. Some shops in tourist areas, such as Covent Garden (see pp110–19) and the Trocadero, are open until 7pm or later every day and on Sundays. Some street markets (see pp339–41) and a number of other shops are usually open on Sundays as well.

HOW TO PAY

Most shops accept all major credit cards, including Master-Card, AmericanExpress, Diners Club, Japanese Credit Bureau and Visa. However, smaller shops and street markets do not. Some of the stores also accept traveller's cheques, especially if they're in sterling; for other currencies the rate of exchange is less favourable than in a bank. You need your passport. Most shops will accept a personal cheque, but only if drawn on a UK account and accompanied by a cheque guarantee card. Debit cards are accepted in many major stores, as are euros.

RIGHTS AND SERVICES

On a defective purchase, you usually get a refund, if proof of purchase is produced and the goods are returned. This isn't always the case with sales goods, so inspect them carefully. Most large stores, and some small ones, will pack goods up for you and send them anywhere in the world..

VAT EXEMPTION

VAT (Value Added Tax) is a sales tax of 17.5% which is charged on virtually all goods sold in Britain. The exceptions are books, food and children's clothes. VAT is mostly included in the advertised or marked price, although business suppliers, including some stationers and electrical goods shops, often charge separately.
 Non-European Union visitors to Britain who stay no longer than three months may claim back VAT. If you plan to do so, carry your passport when shopping. You must complete a form in the store when you buy the goods and then give a copy to Customs while leaving the country. The tax refund may be returned by cheque or attributed to your credit card, but then a service charge will be deducted and most stores have a minimum purchase threshold (often £50 or £75). If you arrange to have your goods shipped directly home from the store, VAT should be deducted before you pay.

Harrods' elaborate Edwardian tiled food halls

TWICE-YEARLY SALES

The traditional sale season is from January to February and June to July, when shops slash their prices and sell off imperfect or unwanted stock. The department stores have some of the best reductions; for the famous **Harrods** *(see p211)* sale queues start to form outside long before opening.

BEST OF THE DEPARTMENT STORES

The king of London's department stores, by tradition is **Harrods**, with over 300 departments and a staff of 5,000. The spectacular food hall with Edwardian tiles displays fish, cheese, fruit and vegetables. The specialities also include fashions for all ages, china and glass, kitchenware and electronics. Though Harrods is still just as popular, Londoners often head instead for nearby, **Harvey Nichols**, which aims to stock the best of everything. Clothes are particularly strong on high fashion, with emphasis on talented British, European as well as American names. There's also an impressive menswear section. The food hall, opened in 1992, is one of London's most stylish.

Selfridges on Oxford Street has expanded its range in recent years; it now has arguably the widest choice of labels, a great lingerie department and a section devoted to emerging designers. A melange of high-street concessions on the ground-floor caters to young women. It also has a food hall featuring global delicacies.

The original **John Lewis** was a draper, and even today his shop has a good selection of fabrics and haberdashery. Its china, glass and household items make John Lewis, and its popular Sloane Square partner, Peter Jones, equally popular with Londoners. **Liberty** *(see*

p109) near Carnaby Street still sells beautiful silks and other Oriental goods, for which it was famed after opening in 1875. Look out for the famous scarf department.

Fortnum and Mason's ground-floor food department is so engrossing that the upper floors of classic fashion and luxury items often remain free of crowds. The food section has everything from Fortnum's tins of biscuits and tea to the lovely wicker hampers.

MARKS AND SPENCER

Marks and Spencer has come a long way since 1882, when the Russian emigré, Michael Marks had a single stall in Leeds' Kirkgate market with the sign, "Don't ask the price – it's a penny!" It now has more than 680 stores worldwide and everything in them is "own label"- Marks and Spencer's underwear in particular is a staple of the British wardrobe. The food department mostly stores convenience foods. The main Oxford Street branches at the Pantheon (near Oxford Circus) and Marble Arch are best for clothes and household goods.

SHOPPING AREAS

London's best shopping areas range from the elegance of Knightsbridge, where porcelain, jewellery and couture come at the highest prices, to the colourful markets such as Brick Lane, Spitalfields and Portobello. Meccas for those seeking a bargain, London's markets reflect a vibrant street life engendered by its multi-racial community. The city is fertile ground for specialist shoppers; there are streets crammed with antique shops, antiquarian booksellers and art galleries. *(See also pp324–41.)*

Doorman at
Fortnum and Mason

DEPARTMENT STORES

Fortnum and Mason
181 Piccadilly W1. **Map** 12 F3.
Tel 020-7734 8040.

Harrods
87–135 Brompton Rd SW1.
Map 11 C5.
Tel 020-7730 1234.

Harvey Nichols
109–125 Knightsbridge SW1.
Map 11 C5.
Tel 020-7235 5000.

John Lewis
278–306 Oxford St W1. **Map** 12 E1.
Tel 020-7629 7711.

Liberty
210 220 Regent St W1. **Map** 12 F2.
Tel 020-7734 1234.

Selfridges
400 Oxford St W1. **Map** 12 D2.
Tel 0870-837 7377.

Some well-known names in British clothes design

Penhaligon's for scents *(see p332)*

London's Best: Shopping Streets and Markets

London's best shopping areas range from the elegance of Knightsbridge, where porcelain, jewellery and *couture* clothes come at the highest prices, to colourful markets such as Brick Lane, Spitalfields and Portobello. Meccas for those who enjoy searching for a bargain, London's markets also reflect the vibrant street life engendered by its enterprising multi-racial community. The city is fertile ground for specialist shoppers: there are streets crammed with antique shops, antiquarian booksellers and art galleries. Turn to pages 322–41 for more details of shops, grouped according to category.

Kensington Church Street
The small book and furniture shops on this winding street still provide old-fashioned service. (See p331.)

Regent's Park and Marylebone

See inset map

The Royal Borough of Kensington and Chelsea
PORTOBELLO ROAD, W.11.

Portobello Road Market
Over 1,000 stalls sell objets d'art, jewellery, medals, paintings and silverware – plus fresh fruit and vegetables. (See p333.)

Kensington and Holland Park

South Kensington and Knightsbridge

Piccadilly and St James's

Knightsbridge
Exclusive designer-wear is on sale here, at Harrods as well as smaller stores. (See p211.)

Chelsea

King's Road
Once a centre for avant-garde fashion in the 1960s and 1970s, the street is now home to chain-stores and designer shops. There is also a good antiques market. (See p196.)

Marks and Spencer

Selfridges

OXFORD ST

BERWICK ST

REGENT ST

NEW BOND ST

Liberty

OLD BOND ST

Tower Records

PICCADILLY

JERMYN ST

Fortnum & Mason

LONDON'S WEST END SHOPS

Oxford Street is sometimes called London's High Street and many of the shops that line it are branches of national or international chains. The big department stores such as Selfridges and John Lewis also loom along this street, as do smaller shops selling clothes and tourist souvenirs. South of Oxford Street, on Regent Street, Piccadilly and Bond Street, prices rise and shoppers search for specialized purchases among the designer clothes and accessories shops, jewellers and art and antique dealers.

Bloomsbury and Fitzrovia

Smithfield and Spitalfields

Soho and Trafalgar Square

Holborn and the Inns of Court

Covent Garden and the Strand

The City

South Bank

Southwark and Bankside

Whitehall and Westminster

RIVER THAMES

0 kilometres 1

0 miles 0.5

Brick Lane Market
In this East End street, everything from old books to new trainers is on sale. (See p332.)

Gabriel's Wharf
The wharf has been con-verted into small shops selling art, jewellery and crafts. (See p191.)

Petticoat Lane
London's most famous market has leather, clothes, watches, jewellery and toys. (See p333.)

Charing Cross Road
Crammed shops selling old and new books line this long street. (See pp326–7.)

Covent Garden and Neal Street
Street enter-tainers perform in this lively and historic market. The specialist shops of Neal Street are nearby. (See p115.)

Clothes

London has never been better for clothes shopping, offering a virtually inexhaustible range of styles, price levels and quality, across a far-reaching and varied geographical area. Besides the traditional British-style famous the world over, you'll also find international designers, global and home-grown chains and an ever increasing number of independent boutiques catering to every taste. While old-fashioned tailors, shirt-makers and cobblers still thrive, often in their original premises, shops are increasingly design-led. The hugely popular high-street chains have perfected the art of producing good-quality catwalk knock-offs, while a new generation of British design talent has revitalized the fashion scene.

TRADITIONAL CLOTHING

British tailoring and fabrics are world-renowned for their high quality. In Savile Row, you can follow in the sartorial footsteps of Winston Churchill and the Duke of Windsor, among other dapper luminaries, and have a suit made to measure or buy one off the peg. Established in 1806, **Henry Poole** was the first tailor in the Row. At **H Huntsman & Sons** each suit is painstakingly hand-stitched on the premises, which partly explains the exorbitant £3,000-plus price tag. They also design Alexander McQueen's bespoke line, which is available from the designer's Bond Street shop. In addition to making suits to order, **Gieves & Hawkes** has two ready-to-wear lines.

Over the past 10 years, a new breed of fashion-conscious tailor, known for modern cuts and vibrant fabrics, has joined the distinguished line-up, including **Ozwald Boateng** and **Richard James**. Jermyn Street is famous for smart shirts. At venerable shops such as **Turnbull & Asser** or the family-run **Harvie & Hudson**, you can either have them custom-made or choose the less expensive standard-sized options. Many manufacturers, including the popular shirt chain **Pink**, now also sell a wide variety of classic women's blouses.

In the past few years, several bastions of classic British style have completely reinvented themselves as fashion labels. **Burberry** is the best

example of this, although it still does a brisk trade in its famous trenchcoats, checked clothing (for children too) and distinctive accessories. **Aquascutum** is also a good choice for classic raincoats, suits and accessories for both sexes, as is **Daks**, which produces high-fashion takes on traditional British looks. **Dunhill** specializes in immaculate, if expensive, menswear and accessories, while at the

Crombie outlet, you can buy the famous fitted overcoat which came to be known by the company's name. The famous menswear emporium, **Hackett**, caters to a younger, yet still conservative, clientele. Designers **Margaret Howell** and **Nicole Farhi** create updated versions of relaxed British country garments for men and women, such as knitwear, tweeds and sheepskin coats. You can still find a more traditional, smart country look in the Regent Street, Piccadilly or Knightsbridge areas. Waxed Barbour jackets are on sale Harrods *(see p321)*. **Cordings**, established 1839, is good for country-gent/-lady gear, such as check shirts, moleskin trousers and Covert coats.

While **Liberty** *(see p109)* now has a good selection of contemporary designers, it still uses its famous patterned prints to make blouses and stylish men's shirts as well as scarves and ties. Floral print "English rose" dresses and feminine blouses can be found

SIZE CHART

For Australian sizes follow British and American convention

Children's clothing

British	2–3	4–5	6–7	8–9	10–11	12	14	14+ (years)
American	2–3	4–5	6–6X	7–8	10–12	14	16 (size)	
Continental	2–3	4–5	6–7	8–9	10–11	12	14	14+ (years)

Children's shoes

British	7½	8	9	10	11	12	13	1	2
American	7½	8½	9½	10½	11½	12½	13½	1½	2½
Continental	24	25½	27	28	29	30	32	33	34

Women's dresses, coats and skirts

British	6	8	10	12	14	16	18	20
American	4	6	8	10	12	14	16	18
Continental	38	40	42	44	46	48	50	52

Women's blouses and sweaters

British	30	32	34	36	38	40	42
American	6	8	10	12	14	16	18
Continental	40	42	44	46	48	50	52

Women's shoes

British	3	4	5	6	7	8
American	5	6	7	8	9	10
Continental	36	37	38	39	40	41

Men's suits

British	34	36	38	40	42	44	46	48
American	34	36	38	40	42	44	46	48
Continental	44	46	48	50	52	54	56	58

Men's shirts

British	14	15	15½	16	16½	17	17½	18
American	14	15	15½	16	16½	17	17½	18
Continental	36	38	39	41	42	43	44	45

Men's shoes

British	7	7½	8	9	10	11	12
American	7½	8	8½	9½	10½	11	11½
Continental	40	41	42	43	44	45	46

at **Laura Ashley**, although the store has introduced more contemporary looks as well.

MODERN BRITISH DESIGN AND STREET FASHION

London designers are known for their eclectic, irreverent style. Grand dames Vivienne Westwood and Zandra Rhodes have been on the scene since the 1970s – the latter opened the **Fashion and Textile Museum** in south-east London in 2003. It features 3,000 of her own garments as well as examples by other influential fashion figures. Many British designers of international stature have their flagship stores in the capital, including the popular **Paul Smith** and **Stella McCartney**, both of whom showcase their collections in fabulous townhouses. **Alexander McQueen** and **Matthew Williamson** also have stand-alone stores. Young home-grown talent such as Alice Temperley, whose feminine frocks are beloved of the London party set, Eley Kishimoto, characterized by bold prints, and avant-garde design duo Boudicca, can be found in most of the capital's boutiques.

Selfridges (see p321) also has an impressive selection of emerging designers. **Dover Street Market**, conceived by Comme des Garçons' Rei Kawakubo, revives the age-old London tradition of the covered clothes market, but in a much more upmarket milieu. Its four minimalist floors showcase a varied array of goods, from glitzy shoes by king of the platform, Terry de Havilland to cool art books and vintage and contemporary designer clothes.

If you want to take home a bit of British design, but can't afford the high prices, it's worth visiting **Debenhams**, which has harnessed the talents of numerous leading designers, including Jasper Conran, Julien Macdonald and Ben De Lisi, to create cheaper collections exclusive to the store. Young designers often start out with a stall on Portobello Road or Old Spitalfields Market (see p341), both

good sources of interesting clothing. There are also a few good designer sale shops: **Paul Smith Sale Shop** and **Browns Labels for Less** are both in central London. While those looking for **Burberry** bargains at its factory outlet will have to travel a bit further afield to the East End.

BOUTIQUES

Over the past few years, London has seen a boutique boom – hot new shops crop up and, it must be said, close down with dizzying regularity. The mother of them all is **Browns**. Established in the 1970s, it occupies several storefronts in South Molton Street and stocks a wide selection of international labels. But the highest concentration of boutiques is in Notting Hill, near the intersection of Westbourne Grove and Ledbury Road. Because of the numerous cafés in the area, and the relaxed, affluent atmosphere away from the crowded West End shopping districts, it's an extremely pleasant place to browse.

JW Beeton embodies quirky British style, while **Matches**, which also has outposts in Richmond and Wimbledon, dominates Ledbury Road with three separate shops – one for both sexes, another just for women plus one specializing in frocks by Diane von Furstenberg. Like Browns in the West End, **Matches** stocks international designer labels, including Balenciaga, Prada and Chloé, interspersed with a variety of British talent such as Temperley, Bella Freud, Matthew Williamson and Georgina Goodman. **Question Air** and **Feathers** also stock designer labels, while **Aimé** specializes in French clothes and homewares. A short walk away in a quiet residential street, celebrity favourite, **The Cross** is a delightfully understated little shop, packed with women's fashion, cute childrens clothes and toys, toiletries and varied displays of unusual accessories. **Cross The Road**, located right opposite, caters to chic

interiors. Primrose Hill, Islington, Soho and the streets radiating off Seven Dials near Covent Garden are also dotted with independent fashion shops. Some, such as **Labour of Love** and **Saloon** in Islington, combine clothes with a careful selection of interior items, lingerie, art books and CDs. Much of the stock at both boutiques is produced by brilliant, young British designers.

CHAIN STORES AND STREET FASHION

Britain has recently undergone a fashion revolution: designer looks are no longer the preserve of the rich. National fashion chains have never been better, both in terms of quality and design. Moreover, the cheaper versions of all the latest styles appear in the shops, almost as soon as they have been sashayed down the catwalk. **Oasis** and **Topshop** have both won celebrity fans for their up-to-the-minute, young womenswear. The latter, which proudly claims to be, "the world's largest fashion store" is a complete mine of inexpensive clothes and beautiful accessories, there is even an in-store "boutique" with latest collections by hip designers, and a vintage section as well.

Vintage fashion (see p326) has become so popular, many high-street chains either sell it or feature collections which recreate the style.

The upmarket chains, **Jigsaw** and **Whistles** are more expensive with the emphasis on beautiful fabrics and shapes which, while stylish, don't slavishly copy the catwalk. **Jigsaw Junior**, available in larger branches, offers delectable mini versions of its designs for little girls. **Reiss** and **Ted Baker** are more popular with the trend-conscious young men, though they also have good women's collections. More streetwise shops can be found in and around Newburgh Street, behind Carnaby Street, including **The Dispensary**, which caters to both sexes. The **Duffer of St George** near Covent Garden is among the trail-blazers for men.

VINTAGE FASHION

The city offers a vast hunting ground for the aficionados of vintage style, from market stalls to the exclusive shops showcasing immaculately preserved designerwear. Head east for funky emporia such as **Rokit**, which also has other branches in Camden and Covent Garden, in addition to the huge warehouse, **Beyond Retro**. Grays Antique Market *(see p340)* covers all the bases with the award-winning Vintage Modes, spanning the styles of the past century as well as fashion-conscious Advintage, run by a former department-store personal shopper. Glamorous evening gowns and pin-up lingerie for the girls, flashy Hawaiian shirts and novelty bar accessories for the guys, can be found at Sparkle Moore's gloriously kitsch string of stalls, **The Girl Can't Help It** in Alfies Antique Market, which also houses excellent vintage shop **Biba Lives**.

For mint-condition 1930s bias-cut silk slips and 1920s flapper dresses, head to **Annie's Vintage Clothes** in Camden Passage. Those looking for old designer gems should pay a visit to **Appleby** in West London, which is pretty much strong on the 1950s through 80s. Be warned, neither of these excellent shops is cheap, they both charge quite handsomely.

KNITWEAR

From the sought-after Fair Isle jumpers to Aran knits, the traditional British knitwear is famous. The best places for these are in Piccadilly, Regent Street and Knightsbridge. Heritage labels **Pringle** and **Ballantyne** have recently been revitalized with more contemporary shapes and vivid colours. Luxurious, casual label, **Joseph** features modern chunky knits, while **John Smedley** concentrates on more simple designs in fine-gauge wool and sea island cotton. For cashmere, **N Peal**, which has both men's and women's shops at opposite ends of the Burlington Arcade, has a great

selection – including a fairly cheaper, fashion-conscious line, npealworks. While the popular chain, **Brora** offers an affordable range of contemporary, Scottish cashmere for the entire family. **Marilyn Moore**, designs hip interpretations of classic knitwear.

UNDERWEAR AND LINGERIE

Marks & Spencer *(see p321)* is the most popular source of reasonably priced basics, it now has several fashionable lingerie lines as well. **Agent Provocateur**, owned by the famous designer, Vivienne Westwood's son and his wife, oozes retro pin-up glamour, from the slightly kinky, pink-uniforms worn by the staff to its nostalgically seductive bra sets. **Myla** sells contemporary lingerie and designer sex toys, that can pass for objets d'art. **Miss Lala's Boudoir** located in Primrose Hill, is an exquisitely feminine shop. Its collection includes, wispy negligées and hand-made, frilled undergarments, mixed in with items of clothing such as kitsch sequinned T-shirts, pretty tutu skirts and some vintage pieces.

CHILDREN'S CLOTHES

You can get traditional hand-smocked dresses and romper suits from Liberty, **Young England** and **Rachel Riley**, which stock smocks, gowns and tweed coats. Burberry's New Bond Street store has a children's section showcasing adorable mini macs, kilts and other items featuring the famous check. **Trotters** offers everything from shoes and clothes to haircuts, while **Daisy and Tom** is a large children's store, selling a wide variety of toys and clothing. For the very special, quintessentially English girls' clothes in pretty, patterned vintage fabrics, as seen on Madonna's daughter Lourdes, visit **Bunny London**, in the Oxo Tower Wharf.

SHOES

Some of the most famous names in the footwear industry are based in Britain. If you

have a few thousand pounds to spare, you can have a pair custom-made by the Royal Family's shoemaker, **John Lobb**. In the East End, ex-Lobb shoemaker, **Jason Amesbury** creates a bespoke range of footwear for considerably less, but you will still end up paying over £1,500. Ready-made, traditional brogues and Oxfords are the mainstay of **Church's Shoes**, while **Oliver Sweeney** gives classics a contemporary edge. For traditional, bench-made shoes at bargain prices, it's worth travelling further afield to Battersea, and splurge at the **Shipton & Heneage** outlet. It offers an exceptionally wide range of Oxfords, Derbys, loafers and boots crafted in the same Northamptonshire factories as some of the most celebrated names, for considerably lower prices, the out-of-the-way location keeps costs down.

Fans of the Fab Four can step into their idols' shoes; **Anello & Davide** designed the original Beatle Boot and still sells them for men and women in a range of materials. **The British Boot Company** in funky Camden has the widest range of Dr Martens, which were originally designed as hard-wearing work boots and appropriated by the rock 'n' rollers. **Jimmy Choo** and **Manolo Blahnik** are certainly, two beloved designers of most fashionable women worldwide. Their sophisticated high heels and cutting-edge designs are much sought-after.

While **Gina** emulates its namesake, Gina Lolobrigida with super-sexy designs, such as jewelled stiletto sandals, **Emma Hope** in Sloane Square is best known for simple, time-less shapes embellished with embroidery or beadwork. Less expensive, yet good quality designs can be found in **Hobbs** or **Pied à Terre**, while **Faith** and **Office** turn out young fashion-led styles, the latter also sells men's shoes. If you are on a look out for something that's a bit different, it's worth visiting London designer, **Georgina Goodman's** shop in the picturesque Shepherd Market, where she showcases her unique ready-to-wear range.

DIRECTORY

TRADITIONAL CLOTHING

Aquascutum
100 Regent St W1.
Map 12 F3.
Tel 020-7675 8200.

Burberry
21–23 New Bond St W1.
Map 12 F2.
Tel 020-7930 3343.
One of several branches.

Cordings
19 Piccadilly W1.
Map 13 A3.
Tel 020-7734 0830.

Crombie
105 New Bond St W1.
Map 12 E2.
Tel 020-7408 1583.
One of two branches.

Daks
10 Old Bond St W1.
Map 12 F3.
Tel 020-7409 4040.

Dunhill
48 Jermyn St W1.
Map 12 F3.
Tel 020-7290 8622.

Gieves & Hawkes
1 Savile Row W1.
Map 12 E3.
Tel 020-7434 2001.

H Huntsman & Sons
11 Savile Row W1.
Map 12 F3.
Tel 020-7734 7441.

Hackett
87 Jermyn St SW1.
Map 13 A3.
Tel 020-7930 1300.
One of several branches.

Harvie & Hudson
77 Jermyn St SW1.
Map 12 F3.
Tel 020-7930 3949.
One of three branches.

Henry Poole & Co
15 Savile Row W1.
Map 12 F3.
Tel 020-7734 5985.

Jaeger
200-206 Regent St W1.
Map 12 F2.
Tel 020-7200 4000.

Laura Ashley
451 Oxford St W1.
Map 12 F1.
Tel 0871-223 1425.
One of several branches.

Liberty
Regent St W1.
Map 12 F2.
Tel 020 7734 1234.

Margaret Howell
34 Wigmore St W1.
Map 12 E1.
Tel 020-7009 9009.

Nicole Farhi
158 New Bond St W1.
Map 12 E2.
Tel 020-7499 8368.
One of several branches.

Ozwald Boateng
12A Savile Row & 9 Vigo St W1.
Map 12 F3.
Tel 020-7437 0620.

Pink
85 Jermyn St SW1.
Map 12 F3.
Tel 020-7930 6364.
One of several branches.

Richard James
29 Savile Row W1.
Map 12 F2.
Tel 020-7434 0605.

Turnbull & Asser
71-72 Jermyn St SW1.
Map 12 F3.
Tel 020-7808 3000.

MODERN BRITISH DESIGN AND STREET FASHION

Alexander McQueen
4-5 Old Bond St W1.
Map 12 F3.
Tel 020-7355 0088.

Browns Labels for Less
50 South Molton St W1.
Map 12 E2.
Tel 020-7514 0052.

Burberry Factory Shop
29-53 Chatham Place E9.
Tel 020-8328 4320.

Debenhams
334-348 Oxford St W1.
Map 12 E2.
Tel 020-7580 3000.

Dover Street Market
17-18 Dover Street W1.
Map 12 F3.
Tel 020-7518 0680.

Fashion and Textile Museum
83 Bermondsey St SE1.
Map 15 C4.
Tel 020-7403 0222.

Matthew Williamson
28 Bruton St W1.
Map 12 E3.
Tel 020-7629 6200.

Paul Smith
Westbourne House
120 & 122 Kensington Park Rd W11.
Map 9 B2.
Tel 020-7727 3553.
One of several branches.

Paul Smith Sale Shop
23 Avery Row W1.
Map 12 E2.
Tel 020-7493 1287.

Stella McCartney
30 Bruton St W1.
Map 12 E3.
Tel 020-7518 3100.

Vivienne Westwood
6 Davies St W1.
Map 12 E2.
Tel 020-7629 3757.

BOUTIQUES

Aimé
32 Ledbury Rd W11.
Map 9 C2.
Tel 020-7221 7070.

Anna
126 Regent's Park Rd NW1.
Tel 020-7483 0411.

b Store
6 Conduit St W1.
Map 12 F2.
Tel 020-7499 6628.

Browns
23–27 South Molton St W1.
Map 12 E2.
Tel 020-7514 0000.

The Cross
141 Portland Rd W11.
Map 9 A3.
Tel 020-7727 6760.

Feathers
176 Westbourne Grove W11.
Map 9 C2.
Tel 020-7243 8800.

JW Beeton
48-50 Ledbury Road W11.
Map 9 C2.
Tel 020-7229 8874.

Koh Samui
65-67 Monmouth St WC2.
Map 13 B2.
Tel 020-7240 4280.

Labour of Love
193 Upper St N1.
Map 6 F1.
Tel 020-7354 9333.

Matches
60-64, 83 & 85 Ledbury Rd W11.
Map 9 C2.
Tel 020-7221 0255.

Saloon
23 Arlington Way EC1.
Map 6 E3.
(Off Rosebery Ave)
Tel 020-7278 4497.

Question Air
229 Westbourne Grove W11.
Map 9 C2.
Tel 020-7221 8163.

CHAIN STORES AND STREET FASHION

The Dispensary
8-9 Newburgh St W1.
Map 12 F2.
Tel 020-7287 8145.

Duffer of St George
29 Shorts Gardens W2.
Map 13 B2.
Tel 020-7379 4660.

Jigsaw
6 Duke of York Sq, Kings Rd SW3. **Map** 19 C2.
Tel 020-7730 4404.
One of several branches.

Hobbs
84–88 King's Rd SW3.
Map 19 C2.
Tel 020-7581 2914.
One of several branches.

Karen Millen
262-264 Regent St W1.
Map 12 F1.
Tel 020-7287 6158.
One of several branches.

DIRECTORY

Oasis
12-14 Argyll St W1.
Map 12 F2.
Tel 020-7434 1799.
One of several branches.

Reiss
Kent House, 14-17 Market Place W1.
Map 12 F1.
Tel 020-7637 9113.
One of several branches.

Ted Baker
9-10 Floral St WC2.
Map 13 C2.
Tel 020-7836 7808.
One of several branches.

Topshop
Oxford Circus W1.
Map 12 F1.
Tel 020-7636 7700.
One of several branches.

Whistles
12–14 St Christopher's Pl W1.
Map 12 D1.
Tel 020-7487 4484.
One of several branches.

VINTAGE FASHION

Annie's Vintage Clothes
12 Camden Passage N1.
Map 6 F1.
Tel 020-7359 0796.

Appleby
95 Westbourne Park Villas W2.
Map 9 C1.
Tel 020-7229 7772.

Beyond Retro
110–112 Cheshire St E2.
Map 8 E4.
Tel 020-7613 3636.

Biba Lives
Alfies Antiques Market, 13–25 Church St NW8.
Map 3 A5.
Tel 020-7258 7999.

The Girl Can't Help It
Alfies Antiques Market, 13–25 Church Street NW8.
Map 3 A5.
Tel 020-7724 8384.

Rokit
101 & 107 Brick Lane E1.
Map 8 E4.
Tel 020-7247 3777.
One of three branches.

KNITWEAR

Ballantyne
303 Westbourne Grove W11.
Map 9B2.
Tel 020-7493 4718.

Brora
81 Marylebone High St W1.
Map 4 D5.
Tel 020-7224 5040.
One of several branches.

John Smedley
24 Brook St W1.
Map 12 E2.
Tel 020-7495 2222.

Joseph
77 Fulham Rd SW3.
Map 19 B2.
Tel 020-7823 9500.
One of several branches.

Marilyn Moore
7 Elgin Crescent W11.
Map 9 B2.
Tel 020-7727 5577.

N Peal
Burlington Arcade, Piccadilly, W1.
Map 12 F3.
Tel 020-7493 9220.

Pringle Scotland
112 New Bond St W1.
Map 12 E2.
Tel 020-7297 4580.

UNDERWEAR AND LINGERIE

Agent Provocateur
6 Broadwick St W1.
Map 13 A2.
Tel 020-7439 0229.
One of several branches.

Miss Lala's Boudoir
144 Gloucester Ave NW1.
Map 4 D1.
Tel 020-7483 1888.

Myla
77 Lonsdale Rd W11.
Map 9 B2.
Tel 020-7221 9222.
One of several branches.

Rigby & Peller
22A Conduit St W1.
Map 12 F2.
Tel 020-7491 2200.

CHILDREN'S CLOTHES

Bunny London
Oxo Tower Wharf SE1.
Map 14 E3.
Tel 020-7928 6269.

Daisy and Tom
181–3 King's Road SW3.
Map 19 A4.
Tel 020-7352 5000.

Rachel Riley
82 Marylebone High St W1.
Map 4 D5.
Tel 020-7935 7007.
One of two branches.

Trotters
34 King's Rd SW3.
Map 19 C2.
Tel 20-7259 9620.
One of two branches.

Young England
47 Elizabeth St SW1.
Map 20 E2.
Tel 020-7259 9003.

SHOES

Anello & Davide
20-21 St Christopher's Place W1. **Map** 12 D1.
Tel 020-7935 7959.

The British Boot Company
5 Kentish Town Rd NW1.
Map 4 F1.
Tel 020-7485 8505.

Church's Shoes
201 Regent St W1.
Map 12 F2.
Tel 020-7734 2438.

Emma Hope
53 Sloane Sq SW1.
Map 19 C2.
Tel 020-7259 9566.
One of three branches.

Faith
192-194 Oxford St W1.
Map 12 F1.
Tel 020-7580 9561.
One of several branches.

Georgina Goodman
12-14 Shepherd St W1.
Map 12 E4.
Tel 020-7499 8599.

Gina
189 Sloane St SW1.
Map 19 C1.
Tel 020-7235 2932.

Hobbs
47–48 South Molton St W1.
Map 12 E2.
Tel 020-7629 0750.
One of several branches.

Jason Amesbury
32 Elder St E1.
Map 8 D5.
Tel 020-7377 2006.

Jimmy Choo
169 Draycott Ave SW3.
Map 19 B2.
Tel 020-7584 6111.

John Lobb
9 St James's St SW1.
Map 12 F4.
Tel 020-7930 3664.

Kate Kuba
22 Duke of York Square, King's Rd SW3.
Map 19 C2.
Tel 020-7259 0011.

Manolo Blahnik
49–51 Old Church St, Kings Road SW3.
Map 19 A4.
Tel 020-7352 3863.

Office
57 Neal St WC2.
Map 13 B1.
Tel 020-7379 1896.
One of several branches.

Oliver Sweeney
29 King's Rd SW3.
Map 19 C2.
Tel 020-7730 3666.

Pied à Terre
19 South Molton St W1.
Map 12 E2.
Tel 020-7629 1362.

Shelly's
266-270 Regent St W1.
Map 12 F1.
Tel 020-7287 0939.
One of several branches.

Shipton & Heneage
177 Queenstown Rd SW8.
Map 20 E5.
Tel 020-7738 8484.

Specialist Shops

London may be famed for the grand department stores such as Harrods, but there are many specialist shops which should also figure on the visitor's itinerary. Some have expertise built up over a century or more, while others are new and fashionable or cater to the whims of eccentric collectors. Whether you are looking for traditional British products and food, high-tech gadgets, or the latest trends in music, London has a wide range of stores to suite everyone's tastes.

FOOD

Britain's reputation for terrible food is proving hard to shake off, but over the past decade, not only has the national cuisine improved immeasurably, London has become one of the culinary capitals of the world. There is an unprecedented interest in local and organic produce as well as delicacies imported from all over Europe. This is reflected in the growing number of food markets, the main one being Borough Market *(see p339)*. Specialities that are well worth sampling, include a variety of chocolates, biscuits, preserves, cheeses and teas *(see pp294–5)*.

The food halls of Fortnum & Mason, Harrods and Harvey Nichols *(see p321)* are good outlets for all of these, but it's also worth visiting the gastronomic gems dotted around town. Of these, **A Gold**, housed in an atmospheric old milliner's shop near Spitalfields Market, specializes in traditional foods from across Britain. Its wares, including cheeses, sausages, jams, baked goods, English wines and mead, are advertised on chalkboards. **Paxton & Whitfield**, a delightful shop dating from 1830, stocks more than 300 cheeses, including baby Stiltons and Cheshire truckles, along with pork pies, biscuits, oils and preserves.

The shelves of tiny **Neal's Yard Dairy** groan with huge British farmhouse cheeses. **Paul Rothe & Son** is a family-run deli that has hardly changed since it opened more than a century ago. Besides selling "British and foreign provisions", such as preserves, old-fashioned sweets and biscuits, the white-coated proprietors also serve morning toast and sandwiches on proper china. For traditional English chocs, such as violet or rose creams and after-dinner mints in beautiful gift boxes, head for **Charbonnel et Walker** which has been in business for more than 100 years, and holds Royal warrants. True chocoholics will be in their element at one of **The Chocolate Society's** two shop/cafés, where only the finest pure chocolate is available. Also committed to "real" chocolate, **Rococo** is well-known for its unique blue-and-white Victorian-esque packaging.

DRINKS

Tea, the most British of drinks, comes in all kinds of flavours. Fortnum & Mason's traditional teas come in appealingly refined gift selections. **The Tea House** is packed with myriad varieties from classic to creative (such as "summer pudding"), colourful tourist-oriented tins and teapots. The quaint 19th-century **Algerian Coffee Stores** manages to pack more than 140 varieties of coffee and 200 teas into its small shop. Family business **HR Higgins**, sells fine coffees and teas from around the world. There are many attractive gift boxes and you can try before you buy in the coffee room downstairs.

For whisky lovers, **The Vintage House** displays the widest array of single malts in England, including some very old bottles. While beer drinkers after a souvenir brew will find hundreds from Britain and Europe, including some made on the premises, at **The Beer Shop**. **Berry Bros & Rudd** is one of the oldest wine merchants in the world, still trading in wines, fortified wines and spirits from its ancient, panelled shop in St James's. In contrast, **Vinopolis** *(see p182)*, Bankside's "wine city", which charges admission, has a vast range of wines to choose from once you been on their interactive world wine tour and enjoyed five tastings. You can continue to imbibe in the restaurant or wine bar.

ONE-OFFS

Sadly, many of London's quirky old specialist shops have closed, but there are still some fascinating anachronisms, as well as interesting newcomers, to be found across the city. A large number of specialist traders operate from stalls in antiques markets such as Alfies and Portobello Road *(see p341)*, where you can find everything from old military medals to commemorative china and vintage luggage. A notable survivor is **James Smith & Sons**, the largest and oldest umbrella shop in Europe. It first opened for business in 1830. Behind its mahogany and glass-panelled façade lies an array of high-quality umbrellas and walking sticks, including the once ubiquitous city gent brolly.

Halcyon Days specializes in little enamelled copper boxes, the delightful products of a revived English 18th-century craft. Past designs are also available from **Michael's Boxes**, whose stock in trade is hand-painted Limoges boxes, including London-themed ones such as red phone boxes or black taxis. **VV Rouleaux**, on the other hand, is festooned with every imaginable type of ribbon and flamboyant trimming.

For serious collectors of model-making kits and historic TV character dolls and toys, **Comet Miniatures** has the largest selection in London. While **Under Two Flags** deploys extensive armies of old-fashioned soldiers. Without a Gameboy in sight, **Benjamin Pollock's Toyshop** does a nifty line in miniature self-assembly paper theatres as well as other traditional toys and antique teddies. **Vertigo** deals in original movie posters, past and present.

At **Anything Left-Handed** in Soho, everything is designed to make life easier for the left-hander. Scissors, corkscrews, cutlery, pens and kitchen and garden tools are the main sellers. The tasteful erotic boutique **Coco de Mer**, banishes the seedy sex shop cliché with its exquisite hand-made lingerie and aesthetically pleasing sex toys. James Bond wannabes will love **Spymaster**, which stocks such indispensable items as shark repellent and a bug-detector "pen". Although it's a serious stockist to the military and law-enforcement agencies, amateur sleuths are always welcome to browse.

BOOKS AND MAGAZINES

Bookshops are high among London's specialities. Charing Cross Road (see p108) is undoubtedly the focal point for those searching for new, antiquarian and second-hand volumes. Although film buffs won't be able to browse in the shop that inspired the book and film, *84 Charing Cross Road*, they will be consoled by a commemorative plaque marking the site of the now defunct Marks & Co, which bore the celebrated address. On the strip there are plenty of other antiquarian booksellers, shelves groaning with dusty finds. Many shops offer a book-finding service if the title you want is no longer in print.

Charing Cross Road is famously the home of **Foyles**, known for its massive but notoriously badly organized stock; however, it was recently given a facelift and is now much easier to navigate. Here, you'll find everything from the latest bestsellers to academic tomes. London's largest women's interest bookshop, **Silver Moon**, is on the third floor, there's a jazz shop and a very cool café (see below), plus an art gallery and real live piranhas in the children's department. As well as large branches of

chains **Waterstone's** and **Borders**, many specialist bookshops are based here. Some of the popular ones are **Murder One** for crime books and **Sportspages** for all kinds of sports writing. Just around the corner is **Magma**, which is excellent for design subjects and avant-garde illustrated books.

Stanfords *(see p112)*, which stocks maps and guides to cover the globe, is in Long Acre; more travel books can be found at the **Travel Bookshop** in Notting Hill. Nearby is **Books for Cooks**, complete with café and test kitchen. The beautiful Edwardian **Daunt Books** in Marylebone has a soaring, galleried back room devoted entirely to travel titles and, unusually, related fiction organized by country. Graphic novels and American and European comics are the speciality at **Comic Showcase**, while fantasy and science fiction abound at **Forbidden Planet**. For gay writing, visit the pioneering **Gay's The Word**, near Russell Square. The best selection of books on movies is found at the **Cinema Store**.

London's oldest bookshop, **Hatchards** in Piccadilly, is also one of the best, offering a well-organized and extensive choice. **Grant & Cutler** is an unrivalled source of foreign books and videos, while **The Banana Bookshop** in Covent Garden must be London's most endearing remainder shop, artistically decorated with jungle murals.

Cecil Court *(see p101)* is a charming pedestrian alleyway lined with dealers specializing in everything from illustrated children's books to modern first editions. There are also shops selling old prints covering every theme – great for gifts – and especially theatrical memorabilia.

If you are looking for newspapers and magazines from abroad, Borders has an extremely wide selection, to keep you abreast with the latest. **Capital Newsagents** stocks among others, American, Italian, French, Spanish and Middle Eastern

publications. **Gray's Inn News** is also worth a visit for European press. For those with a keen interest in vintage magazines, there are more than 200,000 in the basement of **Vintage Magazines** in Soho, dating from the early 1900s through to the present. There are also all manner of movie and popular-culture memorabilia and gifts on the ground floor of the shop.

CDS AND RECORDS

As one of the world's greatest centres of recorded music, London has a huge and excellent selection of record shops catering to fans of all musical styles. Stores such as **HMV** and **Virgin Megastore** have a very comprehensive range of classical music and are the best source of mainstream platters from pop to punk to peaceful easy listening.

Small specialist shops, on the other hand, tend to cater to the more esoteric tastes. **Rough Trade** was at the centre of the emerging punk scene and still sniffs out interesting indie talent today. For jazz, check out **Ray's Jazz**, which is now housed in Foyle's bookshop along with a cool café where you can chill out to the vibe. Even if you're not a collector of rare vinyl, if you happen to be in the area, it's worth having a look at the kitsch Hawaiian hut interior of **Intoxica!**. It offers almost everything, from the 1960s surf pop to funk, punk and independent rock.

Reggae fans should head for **Dub Vendor Record Shack** in Ladbroke Grove for imports hot from Jamaica. **Stern's** has long been without an equal when it comes to exclusive collection of African music, and has recently broadened its scope to cover all world music. There is a high concentration of indie vinyl and CD shops in and around Berwick Street. For 12-inch singles, the medium of club and dance music, **Trax** and **Black Market** are certainly two of the most central places to visit.

DIRECTORY

FOODS

A Gold
42 Brushfield St E1.
Map 8 D5.
Tel 020-7247 2487.

Charbonnel et Walker
1 Royal Arcade, 28 Old Bond St W1. **Map** 12 F3.
Tel 020-7491 0939.

The Chocolate Society
32-34 Shepherd Market W1. **Map** 12 E4.
Tel 020-7495 0302.

Neal's Yard Dairy
17 Short's Gardens WC2.
Map 13 B2.
Tel 020-7240 5700.

Paul Rothe & Son
35 Marylebone Lane W1.
Map 12 E1.
Tel 020-7935 6783.

Paxton & Whitfield
93 Jermyn St SW1.
Map 12 F3.
Tel 020-7930 0259.

Rococo
321 King's Rd SW3.
Map 19 A4.
Tel 020-7352 5857.

DRINKS

Algerian Coffee Stores
52 Old Compton St W1.
Map 13 A2.
Tel 020-7437 2480.

The Beer Shop
14 Pitfield St N1.
Map 7 C3.
Tel 020-7739 3701.

Berry Bros & Rudd
3 St James's St SW1.
Map 12 F4.
Tel 020-7396 9600.

HR Higgins
79 Duke St W1.
Map 12 D2.
Tel 020-7629 3913.

The Tea House
15 Neal St WC2.
Map 13 B2.
Tel 020-7240 7539.

Vinopolis
1 Bank End SE1.
Map 15 B3.
Tel 0870-444 4777.

The Vintage House
42 Old Compton St W1.
Map 13 A2.
Tel 020-7437 2592.

ONE-OFFS

Anything Left-Handed
57 Brewer St W1. **Map** 13 A2. *Tel 020-7437 3910.*

Benjamin Pollock's Toyshop
44 The Market, Covent Garden Piazza WC2.
Map 13 C2.
Tel 020-7379 7866.

Coco de Mer
23 Monmouth St WC2.
Map 13 B2.
Tel 020-7836 8882.

Comet Miniatures
44-48 Lavender Hill SW11.
Tel 020-7228 3702.

Halcyon Days
14 Brook St W1. **Map** 12 E2.*Tel 020-7629 8811.*

James Smith & Son
53 New Oxford St W1.
Map 13 B1.
Tel 020-7836 4731.

Michael's Boxes
Grays Mews, 58 Davies St W1. **Map** 12 E2.
Tel 020-7629 5716.

Spymaster
3 Portman Square W1.**Map** 12 D1.
Tel 020-7486 3885.

Under Two Flags
4 St Christopher's Place W1. **Map** 12 D1.
Tel 020-7935 6934.

Vertigo
22 Wellington St WC2.
Map 13 C2.
Tel 020-7836 9252.

VV Rouleaux
6 Marylebone High St W1.
Map 4 D5.
Tel 020-7224 5179.

BOOKS AND MAGAZINES

The Banana Bookshop
10 The Market, Covent Garden Piazza WC2.
Map 13 C2.
Tel 020-7379 7475.

Books for Cooks
4 Blenheim Crescent W11.
Map 9 B2.
Tel 020-7221 1992.

Borders
120 Charing Cross Rd WC2. **Map** 13 B1.
Tel 020-7379 8877.

Capital Newsagents
48 Old Compton St W1.
Map 13 A2.
Tel 020-7437 2479.

Cinema Store
Unit 4B, Upper St Martin's Lane WC1. **Map** 13 B2.
Tel 020-7379 7838.

Comic Showcase
63 Charing Cross Rd WC1.
Map 13 B1.
Tel 020-7434 4349.

Daunt Books
83-84 Marylebone High St W1. **Map** 4 D5.
Tel 020-7224 2295.

Forbidden Planet
179 Shaftesbury Ave W1. **Map** 13 A2.
Tel 020-7836 4179.

Foyles
113-119 Charing Cross Rd WC2. **Map** 13 B1.
Tel 020-7437 5660.

Gay's The Word
66 Marchmont St WC1.
Map 5 B4.
Tel 020-7278 7654.

Gray's Inn News
50 Theobalds Rd WC1.
Map 6 D5.
Tel 020-7405 5241.

Hatchards
187 Piccadilly W1.
Map 12 F3.
Tel 020-7439 9921.

Magma
8 Earlham St WC2.
Map 13 B2.
Tel 020-7240 8498.

Murder One
71-73 Charing Cross Rd WC2. **Map** 13 B2.
Tel 020-7734 3485.

Sportspages
94-96 Charing Cross Rd WC2. **Map** 13 B2.
Tel 020-7240 9604.

Stanfords
12-14 Long Acre WC2.
Map 13 B2.
Tel 020-7836 1321.

Travel Bookshop
13 Blenheim Crescent W11. **Map** 9 B2.
Tel 020-7229 5260.

Waterstone's
19-23 Oxford St W1.
Map 13 A1.
Tel 020-7434 9759.

Vintage Magazines
39-43 Brewer St W1.
Map 13 A2.
Tel 020-7439 8525.

CDS AND RECORDS

Black Market
25 D'Arblay St W1.
Map 13 A2.
Tel 020-7437 0478.

Dub Vendor Record Shack
150 Ladbroke Grove W10.
Map 9 A1.
Tel 020-8969 3375.

HMV
150 Oxford St W1.
Map 13 A1.
Tel 020-7631 3423.

Intoxica!
231 Portobello Rd W11.
Map 9 B2.
Tel 020-7229 8010.

Ray's Jazz
(See Foyles).
Tel 020-7440 3205.

Rough Trade
130 Talbot Rd W11.
Map 9 C1.
Tel 020-7229 8541.

Stern's
293 Euston Rd NW1.
Map 5 A4.
Tel 020-7387 5550.

Trax
55 Greek St W1.
Map 13 A2.
Tel 020-7734 0795.

Virgin Megastore
14-30 Oxford St W1.
Map 13 A1.
Tel 020-7631 1234.

Gifts and Souvenirs

London is a wonderful place to shop for gifts. It presents an impressive array of original ceramics, jewellery, perfume and glassware, exotic merchandise from around the world including jewellery from India and Africa, stationery from Europe and kitchenware from France and Italy. The elegant, Regency-period Burlington Arcade (see p91), the largest of several covered shopping arcades in the area, is popular for its high-quality clothes, antique and new jewellery, leather goods and other items, many of which are made in the UK. It is also a real boon when the famously unpredictable weather turns nasty.

The shops at big museums, such as the Victoria and Albert (see pp202–5), the Natural History (see pp208–9) and the Science Museum (see pp212–13) often have unusual items to take home as mementoes, while Contemporary Applied Arts and the market in Covent Garden Piazza (see p114) sell a range of British pottery, knitwear, pictures, clothing and other crafts. To buy all your gifts under one roof, go to Liberty (see p109), where beautiful stock from the world over fills every department, and the classic Liberty print features on many goods.

GIFT SHOPS

If the phrase "gift shop" conjures up images of tacky tourist souvenirs, think again. A number of interesting shops bringing together a variety of present-friendly goods under one roof, has sprung up in the capital in recent years. Just off Brick Lane, one-room **Shelf** showcases stationery, prints, ceramics and other objects by local and European artists and designers. It's only open Friday to Sunday; call hours before making a special trip. There are several other quirky, small shops in this street good for gift-hunting, including **Labour & Wait**.

A short walk away, **Story**, in a beautifully preserved 18th-century residential street looks more like a gallery space than a shop. The fascinating mix of wares unites vintage dresses, organic bath products and modern and classic furnishings.

Across town in Notting Hill, **Coco Ribbon** is a girly emporium, kitted out with antique armoires and chandeliers, selling everything from 1950s-influenced embroidered cushions and scented candles to prettily packaged toiletries, hand-made lingerie and Australian designer fashion. The **Design Museum Shop** is a museum gift shop with a difference. It displays post-modern toys, games and innovative – and in some cases surprisingly affordable – accessories for home and office by big design names such as Arne Jacobsen, Tord Boontje and Eames. There are some wonderfully witty items, such as shoe-shaped shoe brushes and a doorstop in the form of a figure holding it open. Boutiques, **Saloon** and **Labour of Love** (see p326) also sell an eclectic range of items.

JEWELLERY

There are styles to suit every taste, from the fine, traditional jewellery found in the exclusive shops of Bond Street to unusual pieces by independent designers in areas like Covent Garden (see pp110–19), Gabriel's Wharf (see p191), and Camden Lock (see p339). Antique jewellery can be found in Hatton Garden and the Silver Vaults (see p141). The Crown Jeweller, **Garrard** in Albemarle Street, has been brought bang up-to-date under creative director Jade Jagger. Be warned, the spectacular creations have pricetags to match. Its former business partner, **Asprey** sells updated classics. While **Butler & Wilson** specializes in reproductions of vintage jewellery and accessories, **Electrum Gallery** next door showcases striking contemporary pieces. **Jess James's** unusual shop design, featuring a tropical fish tank and display cabinets that illuminate as you step in front of them, match the original stock. Popular London design house **Erickson Beamon**, which is also sold in Harrods (see p321), typically features dramatic chokers and earrings dripping with beads. The husband and wife duo, **Wright & Teague** design covetable modern silver and gold charm bracelets and necklaces, among other things.

The **Victoria & Albert shop** sells modern replicas of ancient British designs, as does the shop at the British Museum (see pp126–9). The **Lesley Craze Gallery**, which also deals in other handmade accessories and crafts, sells jewellery by designers from around the globe. Liberty (see p109) stocks a wide range of attractive jewellery as well.

HATS

Traditional men's headgear, from flat caps to trilbies and toppers, can be found at **Edward Bates**. Venerable hatter **Lock & Co**, established in 1672, caters for both men and women, while Swaine Adeney Brigg sells hats for both sexes by well-known name **Herbert Johnson**.

Philip Treacy is Britain's most celebrated milliner and his fabulous creations are on display at his shop on Elizabeth Street and in upmarket department stores. Established name **Stephen Jones** also has some very eye-catching looks, while **Rachel Skinner's** beautifully made, slightly nostalgic designs range from cute cloches to extravagant Ascot confections, which are less expensive than more famous names. **Fred Bare's** funky, affordable designs can be bought from the shop in Columbia Road on Sundays when the weekly flower market is in bloom, or from high-end department stores.

BAGS AND LEATHER GOODS

Traditional British luggage, bags and small leather goods can be found in the streets and arcades off Piccadilly. **Swaine Adeney Brigg** sells umbrellas, hats, classic bridle-leather bags, old-fashioned walking sticks and other accoutrements for the country gent and lady. Well known for its classic, hard-wearing bags and luggage, **Mulberry** was recently given an image overhaul. Its modern interpretations of English country clothes and accessories are sought after by fashion folk as well as anyone who appreciates fine quality.

The ultimate luxury is **Connolly**, a name famous for crafting sleek leather interiors for Rolls-Royce. Its two swish shops sell items that hark back to the golden age of motoring, such as leather driving jackets and shoes, magnificent tool cases and smart luggage, bound diaries and other extravagant home accessories and clothes. **J&M Davidson**, owned by an Anglo-French couple, produces beautifully crafted, slightly retro bags, belts and small leather goods, often in unusual colours or skins. The shop in Notting Hill also stocks a line of clothes and interior items. Not far away is **Bill Amberg's** shop, which sells simple, contemporary bags in various types of leather, suede and other skins, plus gloves, wallets, leather boxes and unusual items such as a sheepskin baby "papoose".

Lulu Guinness and **Anya Hindmarch** both bring British wit and eccentricity to their handbags. Guinness's elaborate designs include a bag in the shape of a flowerpot topped with red roses and a circular purse resembling an old fashioned rotary telephone dial and there are also many London-themed items. Hindmarch is famous for personalised, digitally printed photo bags, but also produces classic leather ones. For less expensive updated classics, try **Osprey**.

SCARVES

Textile designer **Georgina von Etzdorf** is the undisputed queen of richly decorative scarves and shawls in sumptuous fabrics such as silk and velvet. **Ginka by Neisha Crosland** is tiny shop crammed with items bearing the designer's signature colourful, graphic prints, besides scarves there are bags, gloves, hats, clothes and stationery. Of course, Liberty's famous print scarves are perennially popular. Small, stylish **Fenwick** is also known for its accessories department, which includes a wide array of interesting scarves by the likes of Pucci and Missoni, as well as bags, hats and a huge range of hair accessories. N Peal *(see p328)* has an extensive choice of cashmere scarves and shawls.

PERFUMES AND TOILETRIES

Many British perfumeries use recipes that are hundreds of years old. **Floris** and **Penhaligon's**, for example, still manufacture the same flower-based scents and toiletries for men and women that they sold in the 19th century. The same goes for men's specialists **Truefitt & Hill** and **George F Trumper**, where you can buy some wonderful reproductions of antique shaving equipment as well. Chemist and perfumer **DR Harris** has been making its own range of toiletries for over two centuries, it's worth stopping in just to see the old-fashioned shop.

Both **Culpeper Ltd** and **Neal's Yard Remedies** employ traditional herbal and floral remedies as bases for their natural, therapeutic products. Former facialist **Jo Malone** uses such delicious aromas as herbs, fruit, even coffee, as well as traditional floral essences in her fragrances, skincare and candles, which come in simple yet sophisticated packaging. If you're looking for an unusual scent, head for **Miller Harris**; young Grasse-trained perfumer Lyn Harris creates fragrances with remarkable depth, which come in boxes decorated with botanical prints. **Scent Systems** is a contender for the smallest shop in the capital, but its fragrances are worn by some of London's biggest names. The tiny shop near Carnaby Street brings together an exclusive selection of marvelously packaged perfumes from Europe and the US, including Mandy Aftel's Pink Lotus, which was specially commissioned for Madonna.

Space NK stocks the best and the most up-to-date collection of beauty products from around the world, along with its popular own-brand range. **The Body Shop** uses recyclable plastic packaging for its affordable natural cosmetics and toiletries, and encourages staff and customers alike to take an interest in environmental issues. **Molton Brown** sells a range of natural cosmetics, body and haircare products in branches throughout London. Relative newcomer, **REN** produces divine-smelling hair and body products based on pure plant oils.

STATIONERY

For luxurious writing paper and desk accessories, try the Queen's stationer, **Smythson** of Bond Street. The little bound notebooks and address books embossed with a wide selection of amusing and practical titles, such as "Travel Notes" and "Blondes, Brunettes, Redheads" make great gifts and souvenirs. Fortnum and Mason *(see p321)* does handsome leather-bound diaries, blotters and pencil holders, while Liberty embellishes desk accessories with its famous Art Nouveau prints. For personal organizers covered in anything from vinyl to iguana skin, try **The Filofax Centre**. Asprey also does a chic line of pocket diaries, organizers, key fobs and jewellery boxes in a variety of eye-catching skins.

Tessa Fantoni's attractive, paper-covered photo albums used to be sold at the **Conran Shop** and Harrods, but nowadays they are only available from her shop in

Clapham, where you will also find an appealing selection of gifts, cards and wrapping paper. Neisha Crosland's striking contemporary prints adorn wrapping paper and notebooks. **Papyrus** has an attractive selection of note-books, desk organisers and photo albums covered in leather or marbled paper.

Falkiner Fine Papers stocks a range of handmade and deco-rative papers. Its marbled paper, can make a glorious giftwrap for that very special present. Finally, for greeting cards, pens, gift wrapping paper and general stationery, pop into one of the branches of **Paperchase**.

INTERIORS

Wedgwood still makes the famous pale blue Jasper china that Josiah Wedgwood designed in the 18th century. You can buy this and the Irish Waterford crystal, at **Waterford Wedgwood** on Piccadilly. For a fine variety of original pottery, visit **Contemporary Ceramics**, the gallery of the Craft Potters Association, or go to **Contemporary Applied Arts**. **Mint's** hand-picked selection of unique furniture, home accessories, china and glassware by established names and up-and-coming design talent is a pleasure to

browse. Large interior stores, **Heal's** and the **Conran Shop** have a great display of stylish, modern accessories for the home. Those with more traditional tastes may prefer **Thomas Goode**, presided over by courteous tail-coated staff, which sells exquisite china, glassware, crystal, linen and gifts, including some antique pieces. The **Nicole Farhi Home** line exudes the same laid-back luxury as her clothes. If you're on a tighter budget, check out **Graham & Green**, which stocks a huge array of attractive items from around the globe, ranging from Moroccan tea glasses to Mongolian cushions and pretty nightwear.

Labour & Wait is a wonder-ful source of solid, functional British items for home and garden, such as old-fashioned stainless steel kettles, Welsh blankets and Guernsey sweaters. **David Mellor** is famous for his streamlined modern cutlery designs, while **Divertimenti** sells all manner of kitchen equipment and has a pleasant cafe at the back.

Bridgewater Pottery has chunky mugs, crockery and tea towels, which are decorated with traditional motifs and amusing mottoes. The **Irish Linen Company** has everything from lacy hankies and appliquéd guest

towels to tablecloths. **Cath Kidston** designs fresh, nostalgic, English-style prints which adorn everything from humble household items to fashion accessories. There's a huge range of pretty, giftable goods such as ironing-board covers, laundry bags, eiderdowns, clothes for women and children, bags, china and stationery.

Several interiors stores on Upper Street in the affluent Islington offer an impressive cache of gifts. **After Noah** is a big warehouse-like space bursting with vintage and retro-look items which also include, Bakelite rotary telephones, nostalgic toiletries, old metal tins and street signs, classic board games and a huge assortment of children's toys. There is another branch in King's Road and a conces-sion in Harvey Nichols *(see p321)*.

The modern interiors emporium **Aria** has two stores in the same vicinity. One of these concentrates entirely on furniture and housewares by designers such as Alessi and Philippe Starck, while its satellite across the street sells gifts, including stationery, frames, bags and jewellery. Also on the same stretch is the contemporary-design heavyweight **twentytwentyone**.

DIRECTORY

GIFT SHOPS

Coco Ribbon
21 Kensington Park Rd W11.
Map 9 B2.
Tel 020-7229 4904.

Design Museum Shop
Shad Thames SE1.
Map 16 E4.
Tel 020-7940 8753.

Labour & Wait
18 Cheshire Street,
Brick Lane.
Map 8 E4.
Tel 020-7729 6253.

Shelf
40 Cheshire St E2.
Map 8 E4.
Tel 020-7739 9444.

Story
4 Wilkes St E1. **Map** 8 E5.
Tel 020-7377 0313.

JEWELLERY

Asprey
165–169 New Bond St
W1. **Map** 12 F3.
Tel 020-7493 6767.

Butler & Wilson
20 South Molton St W1.
Map 12 E2.
Tel 020-7409 2955.

Electrum Gallery
21 South Molton St W1.
Map 12 E2.
Tel 020-7629 6325.

Erickson Beamon
38 Elizabeth St SW1.
Map 20 E2.
Tel 020-7259 0202.

Garrard
24 Albemarle St W1.
Map 12 F3.
Tel 020-7758 8520.

Jess James
3 Newburgh St W1.
Map 12 F2.
Tel 020-7437 0199.

Lesley Craze Gallery
34 Clerkenwell Green
EC1. **Map** 6 E4.
Tel 020-7608 0393.

Wright & Teague
14 Grafton St W1. **Map** 12 F3.
Tel 020-7629 2777.

HATS

Edward Bates
21a Jermyn St SW1.
Map 13 A3.
Tel 020-7734 2722.

Fred Bare
118 Columbia Rd E2.
Map 8 E3.
Tel 020-7729 6962.

Herbert Johnson
54 St James's Street.
Map 12 F3.
Tel 020-7408 1174.

Lock & Co
6 St James's St SW1.
Map 12 F4.
Tel 020-7930 8874.

Philip Treacy
69 Elizabeth Street SW1.
Map 20 E2.
Tel 020-7730 3992.

Rachel Skinner
13 Princess Rd NW1.
Map 4 D1.
Tel 020-7209 0066.

DIRECTORY

Rachel Skinner
13 Princess Rd NW1.
Map 4 D1.
Tel 020-7209 0066.

Stephen Jones
36 Great Queen St WC2.
Map 13 C1.
Tel 020-7242 0770.

BAGS AND LEATHER GOODS

Anya Hindmarch
15-17 Pont St SW1.
Map 20 D1.
Tel 020-7838 9177.

Bill Amberg
10 Chepstow Rd W2.
Map 9 C2.
Tel 020-7727 3560.

Connolly
41 Conduit St W1.
Map 12 F2.
Tel 020-7439 2510.

J&M Davidson
42 Ledbury Rd W11.
Map 9 C2.
Tel 020-7313 9532.

Lulu Guinness
3 Ellis St SW1.
Map 19 C2 .
Tel 020-7823 4828.

Mulberry
11–12 Gees Court, St
Christopher's Pl W1.
Map 12 D1.
Tel 020-7493 2546.

Swaine Adeney Brigg
54 St James's St SW1.
Map 12 F3.
Tel 020-7409 7277.

Osprey
11 St Christopher's Place
W1. **Map** 12 D1.
Tel 020-7935 2824.

SCARVES

Fenwick
63 New Bond St W1.
Map 12 E2.
Tel 020-7629 9161.

Georgina von Etzdorf
4 Ellis St SW1.
Map 19 C2.
Tel 020-7259 9715.

Ginka by Neisha Crosland
137 Fulham Rd SW3.
Map 19 B2.
Tel 020-7589 4866.

PERFUMES AND TOILETRIES

The Body Shop
64, 360 & 374, Oxford St
W1. **Map** 12 D2–F1.
Tel 020-7631 0027.

Culpeper Ltd
The Market, Covent Gdn
WC2. **Map** 13 C2.
Tel 020-7629 4559.

DR Harris
29 St James's St SW1.
Map 12 F3.
Tel 020-7930 3915.

Floris
89 Jermyn St SW1.
Map 13 A3.
Tel 020-7930 2885.

George F Trumper
9 Curzon St W1.
Map 12 E3.
Tel 020-7499 1850.

Jo Malone
23 Brook St W1.
Map 12 E2.
Tel 020-7491 9104.

Molton Brown
58 South Molton St W1.
Map 12 E2.
Tel 020-7499 6474.

Miller Harris
21 Bruton St W1.
Map 12 E3
Tel 020-7629 7750.

Neal's Yard Remedies
15 Neal's Yard WC2.
Map 13 B1.
Tel 020-7379 7222.

Penhaligon's
41 Wellington St WC2.
Map 13 C2.
Tel 020-7836 2150.

REN
19 Shepherd Market W1.
Map 12 E4.
Tel 020-7495 5960.

Scent Systems
11 Newburgh St W1.
Map 12 F2.
Tel 020-7434 1166.

Space NK
131 Westbourne Grove
W2.
Map 9 C2.
Tel 020-7727 8063.

Truefitt & Hill
71 St James's St SW1.
Map 12 F3.
Tel 020-7493 2961.

STATIONERY

Falkiner Fine Papers
76 Southampton Row
WC1. **Map** 5 C5.
Tel 020-7831 1151.

The Filofax Centre
21 Conduit St W1.
Map 12 F2.
Tel 020-7499 0457.

Paperchase
213 Tottenham Court Rd
W1.
Map 5 A5.
Tel 020-7467 6200.

Papyrus
48 Fulham Rd SW3.
Map 19 A2.
Tel 020-7584 8022.

Smythson
40 New Bond St W1.
Map 12 E2.
Tel 020-7629 8558.

Tessa Fantoni
77 Abbeville Rd SW4.
Tel 020-8673 1253.

INTERIORS

After Noah
121 Upper Street N1.
Map 6 F1.
Tel 020-7359 4281.

Aria
133 & 295–6 Upper St N1.
Map 6 F1.
Tel 020-7226 1021/
7704 1999.

Bridgewater Pottery
81a Marylebone High St.
Map 4 D5.
Tel 020-7486 6897
Also: 739 Fulham Road
Map 17 C5.
Tel 020-7371 5264.

Cath Kidston
51 Marylebone High St
W1.
Map 4 D5.
Tel 020-7935 6555.

Conran Shop
Michelin House, 81
Fulham Rd SW3.
Map 19 A2.
Tel 020-7589 7401.

Contemporary Applied Arts
2 Percy St WC1.
Map 13 A1.
Tel 020-7436 2344.

Contemporary Ceramics
7 Marshall St W1.
Map 12 F2.
Tel 020-7437 7605.

David Mellor
4 Sloane Sq SW1.
Map 20 D2.
Tel 020-7730 4259.

Divertimenti
33–34 Marylebone High St
W1.
Map 4 D5.
Tel 020-7935 0689.

Graham & Green
4 & 10 Elgin Crescent
W11.
Map 9 B2.
Tel 020-7727 4594.

Heal's
196 Tottenham Court Rd
W1. **Map** 5 A5.
Tel 020-7636 1666.

Irish Linen Company
Burlington Arcade W1.
Map 12 F3.
Tel 020-7493 8949.

Mint
70 Wigmore St W1.
Map 12 D1.
Tel 020-7224 4406.

Nicole Farhi Home
17 Clifford St W1.
Map 12 F3.
Tel 020-7494 9051.

Thomas Goode
19 South Audley St W1.
Map 12 D3.
Tel 020-7499 2823.

twentytwentyone
274 Upper St N1.
Map 6 F1.
Tel 020-7288 1996.

Waterford Wedgwood
173–174 Piccadilly W1.
Map 12 F3.
Tel 020-7629 2614.

Art and Antiques

London's art and antique shops are spread across the length and breadth of the capital city. While the more fashionable and more expensive dealers are mainly concentrated in a relatively small area bounded by Mayfair and St James's, other shops and galleries catering to a relatively modest budget are scattered over the rest of the city. Whether your taste is for Old Masters or young modern artists, Boule or Bauhaus, you are bound to find something of beauty in London that is within your financial means.

MAYFAIR

Cork Street is the centre of the British contemporary art world. The huge line-up of galleries offers work in varying degrees of the avant-garde. The biggest name to look out for is **Waddington Galleries**, and if you want to discover the flavour of the month, a stop here is a must. However, purchasing is only for the serious and rich collector. The **Mayor Gallery**, famous for Dada and Surrealism, was the first gallery to open in the street. **Redfern Art Gallery** shows mainstream modern art while **Flowers Central**, part of a growing modern-gallery chain, has some unusual British pieces. A couple of doors down, **Browse and Darby Gallery** sells 19th- and 20th-century British and French paintings as well as contemporary works.

Also look into Clifford Street, where **Maas Gallery** excels in Victorian masters, Sackville Street for **Henry Sotheran's** rare books and prints, and Maddox Street for the **Eyestorm/Britart Gallery**, which shows the work of both leading and emerging artists. Walk down Dover Street towards Piccadilly and, on your right you'll see a discreet sign for the **Piccadilly Gallery**, which sells modern British pictures. Although it's tucked away in the building's basement, casual visitors are always welcome.

Nearby, New Bond Street is the centre of the fine antiques trade in London. If it's Turner watercolours or Louis XV furniture you're after, this is the place. A walk up from Piccadilly takes you past the lush portals of **Richard Green** (which also has a gallery in Dover Street) and the **Fine Art Society**, among other extremely smart galleries. For jewellery and objets d'art visit **Bond Street Antiques Centre** and **Grays Antique Market**; for silver go to **S J Phillips**; and for 18th-century British furniture and art, try **Mallet Antiques**.

Even if you are not a buyer, these galleries are fascinating places to visit, so don't be afraid to walk in – you can learn more from an hour spent here than you can from weeks of studying text books. Also on New Bond Street are two of the big London auction houses, Bonhams and Sotheby's.

ST. JAMES'S

South of Piccadilly lies a maze of 18th-century streets. This is gentlemen's club country (*see Pall Mall p92*) and the galleries mostly reflect the traditional nature of the area. The centre is Duke Street, home of Old Master dealers, **Johnny van Haeften** and **Derek Johns**. Nearby, on King Street, you will find the main salerooms of **Christie's**, the well-known auction house where Van Goghs and Picassos change hands for millions. On the corner of Bury Street, celebrating past masculine pleasures is the sophisticated **Pullman Gallery**, which specialises in automobile art and collectables, vintage cocktail shakers, racy cigarette cases and other bar accessories.

Walk back up Bury Street past several interesting galleries, including the **Tryon Gallery** for traditional British sporting pictures and fine sculptures. Also duck into Ryder Street to take in **Chris Beetle's** gallery of works by illustrators and caricaturists.

KNIGHTSBRIDGE

If you walk around to the back of **Harrods** *(see p321)*, you'll find the beginning of pretty Walton Street, which is lined with art galleries, traditional interior shops and boutiques. As you would expect in this exclusive area, prices are high. On nearby Brompton Road the **Crane Kalman** gallery shows an enticing variety of contemporary art. Not far from Knightsbridge's other swish department store, **Harvey Nichols** *(see p321)* is located. Motcomb Street houses some notable galleries, including the fascinating **Mathaf Gallery**, which features 19th-century British and European paintings of the Arab world.

PIMLICO ROAD

The antique shops that line this road tend to cater predominantly for the pricey requirements of the interior decorator. This is where to come if you are searching for an Italian leather screen or a silver-encrusted ram's skull. Of particular fascination is **Westenholz**. While he doesn't deal in antiques, the Queen's nephew, furniture designer **Viscount Linley** produces some beautiful pieces that could pass as such, as well as contemporary designs. The finely crafted accessories, such as inlaid wooden boxes and frames, make great gifts.

EAST AND WEST

London's East End is a growth area for contemporary art. In addition to the famous **White Cube Gallery** in Hoxton Square and **Flowers East** in Kingsland Road, there is a cluster of galleries in **The Tea Building** on nearby Shoreditch High Street. The **Approach Tavern** combines an upstairs gallery with a good pub, frequented by local artists. On the other side of the river in south east London, **Purdy**

Hicks, based in a converted warehouse near Tate Modern, is great for contemporary British painting. The **Oxo Tower Wharf**, in a landmark Thameside building topped by a good restaurant, is a hive of creativity, housing over 30 design and craft studios. You can find everything from handwoven textiles and jewellery to homewares and fashion. Among the highlights are Black + Blum's innovative, affordable interior designs – for example, a lamp in the shape of a reading figure, made up of a lightbulb "holding" a book shade. Bodo Sperlain's delicate modern china and Studio Fusion's striking enamel pieces are also a draw for the visitors.

There are also some very interesting contemporary galleries in the vicinity of Portobello Road and Westbourne Grove. Some of the popular names include, **East West Gallery** for contemporary art, **Themes & Variations**, which combines striking post-war and contemporary furniture and decorative art, and **J&M Davidson Gallery**, owned by the couple behind the bag and clothing label. **Wolseley Fine Art** near Westbourne Grove specializes in British and French prints, drawings and watercolours by the likes of David Jones, Eric Gill – even the occasional Bonnard or Vuillard. A browse along Kensington Church Street in west London will reveal everything from Arts and Crafts furniture to Staffordshire dogs in a concentration of small antiques emporia.

NORTH

High-profile American dealer Larry Gagosian has been at the forefront of the regeneration of famously sleazy King's Cross by opening his second gallery here, in a capacious former garage. Expect world-class contemporary names as well as lesser-known artists at **Gagosian Gallery**. **Victoria Miro's** massive Victorian warehouse in Islington is a showcase for British as well as young

international talent. At its two spaces in the same quiet Marylebone Street, the **Lisson Gallery** often features cutting-edge installations. **Thompson's Gallery** has locations in Marylebone and the City, selling a diverse mix of appealing if somewhat mainstream current British art.

AFFORDABLE ART

For the chance to acquire a work by what could become one of the big names of the future, visit the **Contemporary Art Society**. Its annual ARTFutures market showcases the work of more than 100 artists, their prices run from £100 into the thousands. Open all year round, **Will's Art Warehouse** sells pieces from £50–£3,000. The owner founded the aptly named Affordable Art Fair, which takes place twice a year in Battersea Park.

PHOTOGRAPHY

The largest collection of original photographs for sale in the country is at the **Photographers' Gallery**. **Special Photographers Company** is well known for selling top-quality work by unknown artists as well as some famous photographic names. **Hamiltons Gallery** is worth visiting, especially during its major exhibitions.

Michael Hoppen's new three-floor space in Chelsea shows both vintage and current works. If you want to take home a piece of London's rock 'n' roll heritage, the **Rock Archive**, near Camden Passage in Islington, is a great source of limited-edition prints of British music legends such as Paul Weller posing with Pete Townshend or Mick Jagger jamming with Ronnie Wood. To pick up an interesting work on a budget, head to **55 Max**, where limited-edition framed prints often cost £55. It showcases a range of subjects and styles by young photographers and photojournalists, from moody London cityscapes and abstractions to fashion and celebrity shots.

BRIC-À-BRAC AND COLLECTABLES

For smaller, more affordable pieces, it's worth going to one of the established London markets, such as Portobello Road, Alfies Antique Market, Camden Passage *(see p340)* or Bermondsey *(see p339)*, which is the main antiques market, catering to the trade. Conveniently situated in the city's main shopping district, Grays Antique Markets *(see p340)* have some great specialist dealers, but the prices are a bit higher than elsewhere given the location, while further afield, Greenwich Market *(see p340)* is well worth a rummage and may throw up some bargains. Many high streets out of the centre of town have covered markets of specialist stalls.

Cary Grant's small shop hidden on a side street near Sadlers Wells contains a collector's cache of immaculate post-war ceramics by the modern designers of the day, including the young Terence Conran.

AUCTIONS

If you are confident enough, auctions are a much cheaper way to buy art or antiques, but be sure to read the small print in the catalogue, which usually costs around £15. Bidding is simple – you need to register, take a number, then raise your hand when the lot you want comes up. The auctioneer will see your bid. It's as easy as that, and can be great fun.

The main auction houses in London are **Christie's Fine Art Auctioneers**, **Sotheby's Auctioneers** and **Bonhams**. Don't forget Christie's saleroom in Kensington, and Sotheby's new premises in Olympia, both offer art and antiques for the modest budget. Bonhams' second London saleroom in Knightsbridge holds weekly auctions of affordable antiques and collectables.

DIRECTORY

MAYFAIR

Bond Street Antiques Centre
124 New Bond St W1.
Map 12 F3.
Tel 020-7351 5353.

Browse and Darby Gallery
19 Cork St W1.
Map 12 F3.
Tel 020-7734 7984.

Eyestorm/Britart Gallery
18 Maddox St W1.
Map 12 F2.
Tel 020-7659 0860.

Fine Art Society
148 New Bond St W1.
Map 12 E2.
Tel 020-7629 5116.

Flowers Central
21 Cork St W1.
Map 12 F3.
Tel 020-7439 7766.

Grays Antique Markets
58 Davies St & 1-7 Davies Mews W1.
Map 12 E2.
Tel 020-7629 7034.

Henry Sotheran
2–5 Sackville St W1.
Map 12 F3.
Tel 020-7439 6151.

Maas Gallery
15a Clifford St W1.
Map 12 F3.
Tel 020-7734 2302.

Mallet Antiques
141 New Bond St W1.
Map 12 E2.
Tel 020-7499 7411.

Mayor Gallery
22a Cork St W1.
Map 12 F3.
Tel 020-7734 3558.

Piccadilly Gallery
43 Dover St W1.
Map 12 F3.
Tel 020-7629 2875.

Redfern Art Gallery
20 Cork St W1.
Map 12 F3.
Tel 020-7734 1732.

Richard Green
33 & 147 New Bond St.
Also: 39 Dover St W1.
Map 12 E2.
Tel 020-7491 3277.

S J Phillips
139 New Bond St W1.
Map 12 E2.
Tel 020-7629 6261.

Waddington Galleries
11, 12, 34 Cork St W1.
Map 12 F3.
Tel 020-7437 8611.

ST. JAMES'S

Chris Beetle
8 & 10 Ryder St SW1.
Map 12 F3.
Tel 020-7839 7551.

Derek Johns
12 Duke St SW1.
Map 12 F3.
Tel 020-7839 7671.

Johnny van Haeften
13 Duke St SW1.
Map 12 F3.
Tel 020-7930 3062.

Pullman Gallery
14 King St SW1.
Map 12 F4.
Tel 020-7930 9595.

Tryon Gallery
7 Bury St SW1.
Map 12 F3.
Tel 020-7839 8083.

KNIGHTSBRIDGE

Crane Kalman
178 Brompton Rd SW3.
Map 19 B1.
Tel 020-7584 7566.

Mathaf Gallery
24 Motcomb St SW1.
Map 12 D5.
Tel 020-7235 0010.

PIMLICO ROAD

Viscount Linley
60 Pimlico Rd SW1.
Map 20 D2.
Tel 020-7730 7300.

Westenholz
76 Pimlico Rd SW1.
Map 20 D2.
Tel 020-7824 8090.

EAST AND WEST

Approach Tavern
1st Floor, 47 Approach Rd E2.
Tel 020-8983 3878.

East West Gallery
8 Blenheim Cres W11.
Map 8 D4.
Tel 020-7229 2973.

Flowers East
82 Kingsland Rd E2.
Tel 020-7920 7777.

J&M Davidson Gallery
97 Golborne Rd W10.
Tel 020-8969 2244.

Oxo Tower Wharf
Bargehouse St SE1.
Map 14 E3.
Tel 020-7401 2255.

Purdy Hicks
65 Hopton St SE1.
Map 14 F3.
Tel 020-7401 9229.

The Tea Building
56 Shoreditch High St E1.
Map 8 D4.
Tel 020-7729 2973.

Themes & Variations
231 Westbourne Grove W11. **Map** 9 B2.
Tel 020-7727 5531.

White Cube Gallery
Hoxton Square N1.
Map 7 C3.
Tel 020-7930 5373.

Wolseley Fine Art
12 Needham Rd W11.
Map 9 C2.
Tel 020-7792 2788.

NORTH

Gagosian Gallery
6–24 Britannia St WC1.
Map 5 C3.
Tel 020-7841 9960.

Lisson Gallery
29 & 52-54 Bell St.
Map 3 B5.
Tel 020-7724 2739.

Thompson's Gallery
76 Marylebone High St W1. **Map** 4 D5.
Tel 020-7935 3595.

Victoria Miro
16 Wharf Rd N1.
Map 7 A2.
Tel 020-7336 8109.

AFFORDABLE ART

Contemporary Art Society
Bloomsbury House, 74–77 Great Russell Street.
Map 13 B1.
Tel 020-7612 0730.

Will's Art Warehouse
Unit 3, Heathmans Rd SW6. *Tel 020-7371 8787.*

PHOTOGRAPHY

Hamiltons Gallery
13 Carlos Place London W1. **Map** 12 E3.
Tel 020-7499 9493.

55 Max
105 Boundary Rd NW8.
Tel 020-7625 3774.

Michael Hoppen
3 Jubilee Place SW3.
Map 19 B3.
Tel 020-7352 4499.

Photographers' Gallery
5 & 8 Great Newport St WC2. **Map** 13 B2.
Tel 020-7831 1772.

Rock Archive
110 Islington High St N1.
Map 6 F2.
Tel 020-7704 0598.

Special Photographers Company
236 Westbourne Park Rd W11. **Map** 9 B1.
Tel 020-7221 3489.

BRIC-A-BRAC AND COLLECTABLES

Cary Grant
18 Arlington Way EC1.
Map 6 E3.
Tel 020-7713 1122.

AUCTIONS

Bonhams, W & FC, Auctioneers
Montpelier St SW7.
Map 11 B5.
Tel 020-7393 3900.
Also: 101 New Bond St W1. **Map** 12 E2.
Tel 020-7629 6602.

Christie's Fine Art Auctioneers
8 King St SW1. **Map** 12 F4.
Tel 020-7839 9060.
Also: 85 Old Brompton Road SW7. **Map** 18 F2.
Tel 020-7930 6074.

Sotheby's Auctioneers
34–35 New Bond St W1.
Map 12 E2.
Tel 020-7293 5000.
Also: Hammersmith Rd W14.
Map 17 A1.
Tel 020-7293 5555

Markets

Even if you're not looking for cut-priced cabbages or a length of silk sari, it's worth paying a visit to one of London's crowded, colourful markets. Many mix English traditions with those of more recent immigrants, creating an exotic atmosphere and a fascinating patchwork quilt of merchandise. At some, the seasoned cockney hawkers have honed their sales patter to an entertaining art, which reaches fever pitch just before closing time as they advertise ever-plummeting prices. Keep your wits about you and your hand on your purse and join in the fun.

Antiquarius

131–141 King's Road SW3.
Map 19 B3. ⊖ *Sloane Sq.*
▥ *19, 22.* **Open** *10am–6pm Mon–Sat.*

This former 1920s gentlemen's club and pool hall claims to be London's oldest antique centre, which has been in operation since the 1960s. Behind its smart, green awnings are more or less 100 stalls. The dynamic merchants of the market include specialists in vintage Louis Vuitton luggage, sporting and equestrian antiques, Art Deco furniture, costume and fine jewellery.

Bermondsey Market
(New Caledonian Market)

Long Lane and Bermondsey St SE1.
Map 15 C5. ⊖ *London Bridge, Borough.* **Open** *5am–2pm Fri. Starts closing midday. See p182.*

Bermondsey is the gathering point for London's antique traders every Friday. Serious collectors start early and scrutinize the paintings, the silver and the vast array of old jewellery. Browsers might uncover some interesting curiosities but most bargains go before 9am.

Berwick Street Market

Berwick St W1. **Map** 13 A1.
⊖ *Piccadilly Circus, Leicester Sq.*
Open *9am–6pm Mon–Sat. See p108.*

The spirited costermongers of Soho's Berwick Street sell some of the cheapest and most attractive fruit and vegetables in the West End. Spanish black radish, star fruit and Italian plum tomatoes are among the produce you might find here, in addition to the various nuts and sweets. The market is good for fabrics and cheap household goods too, as well as for leather handbags and delicatessen. Separated from Berwick Street by a seedy passageway is the quieter Rupert Street market, where stallholders sell cheap street fashion.

Borough Market

Southwark St SE1. **Map** 14 F3.
⊖ *London Bridge.* **Open** *noon–6pm Fri, 9am–4pm Sat. See p176.*

On one of London's most ancient trading sites, Borough has for many years been a wholesale market catering to the restaurant and hotel trade. Now open to the public at weekends, the award-winning market has a reputation as London's premier centre for fine foods, selling a vast array of British and international foodstuffs. Among the cornucopia is organic meat and produce, top-quality handmade cheeses, breads, sweets, chocolates, coffees and teas and also soaps. It's a favourite foraging ground for the city's celebrity chefs.

Brick Lane Market

Brick Lane E1. **Map** 8 E5.
⊖ *Shoreditch, Liverpool St, Aldgate East.* **Open** *daybreak to 1pm Sun. See pp170–1.*

This massively popular East End jamboree is at its best around its gloriously frayed edges. Pick through the mish-mash of junk sold on Bethnal Green Road or head east on Cheshire Street, past the new outcrop of fashionable home-design and gift shops, to explore the indoor stalls, packed with tatty furniture and old books. Much of the action takes place in cobbled Sclater Street and the lots on either side. Here you'll find everything from fresh shellfish and trainers to old power tools and new bicycles. Further south on Brick Lane itself, the trendy boutiques and cafés give way to spice shops and curry restaurants in this centre for London's Bangladeshi community.

Brixton Market

Electric Ave SW9. ⊖ *Brixton.*
Open *8.30am–5.30pm Mon, Tue, Thu–Sat; 8.30am–1pm Wed.*

This market offers a wonderful assortment of Afro-Caribbean food, from goats' meat, pigs' feet and salt fish to plantain, yams and breadfruit. There is an abundance of produce in the large Brixton Village (formerly Granville) and Market Row arcades, where exotic fish are a highlight. You'll also find Afro-style wigs, strange herbs and potions, traditional African ensembles and fabrics, and children's toys. From record stalls, the bass of raw reggae pounds through this cosmopolitan market like a heartbeat.

Broadway Market

Broadway Market, between Andrews Rd & Westgate St E8. ▥ *394* .
Open *8am–6pm Sat.*

Although this market is a bit tricky to get to because it's not served by the tube, it's worth getting a bus from Islington or walking from Bethnal Green tube. One of London's oldest, Broadway Market had gone into decline until its recent rebirth as an organic farmers' market. On Saturdays the historic street running between London Fields and the Regent's Canal, comes alive with around 40 stalls selling fruit and vegetables, cheeses, baked goods, meats and confectionery. Also lining Broadway Market are some interesting, arty shops, catering to the young creative types who have been colonizing this part of Hackney over the past couple of decades. Black Truffle (No.74), owned by shoemaker Melissa Needham, stocks a range of accessories made by independent designers – both local and international – while textile designer Barley Massey sells her own unusual designs and those of others at Fabrications (No.7). L'Eau à la Bouche (No.49) is a superior deli offering everthing from charcuterie to fruit tarts. There are also a couple of contemporary galleries such as Flaca (No.69) and Seven Seven (No.75–77). When it's time to refuel, duck into the Dove pub (No.24–28) for a Belgian brew.

Camden Lock Market

Chalk Farm Road NW1. ⊖ *Camden Town.* **Open** *9.30am–5.30pm Mon–Fri, 10am–6pm Sat and Sun.*

Camden Lock Market has grown swiftly since its opening in 1974, spreading along Chalk Farm Road and Camden High Street. Crafts, new and second-hand street fashion, wholefoods, books, records and antiques, form the bulk of the goods that a shopper can choose from. Often, thousands of young people come here simply to enjoy the vibrant atmosphere, especially at weekends when Camden Lock is abuzz with activity *(see p246).*

Camden Passage Market

Camden Passage N1. **Map** 6 F1.
🚇 *Angel.* **Open** *10am–2pm Wed,
10am–5pm Sat.*

Camden Passage is a quiet walkway where cafés nestle among
bijou antique shops. Prints, silverware, 19th-century magazines,
jewellery and toys are among the
many collectables that are on show.
Don't miss the tiny shops tucked
away in the atmospherically poky
Pierrepont Arcade; one is precari-
ously stacked with 18th and 19th-
century porcelain; another specializes in antique puzzles and
games. Jubilee Photographica deals
in photographs from the 19th
century onwards. The passage is
also lined with shops – Annie's
Vintage Clothes is known for
pristine 1920s–40s frocks, while
Origin sells classic 20th-century
furniture. There's a specialist
book market on Thursdays.

Chapel Market

Chapel Market N1. **Map** 6 E2.
🚇 *Angel.* **Open** *9am–3.30pm Tue,
Wed, Fri, Sat; 9am–1pm Thu, Sun.*

This is one of London's most
traditional and exuberant street
markets. Weekends are best; the
fruit and vegetables are varied and
cheap, the fish stalls are the finest
in the area, there are also stalls selling European delicacies and
cheeses and a wealth of bargain
household goods and clothes.

Church Street Market

Church St NW8 and Bell St NW1.
Map 3 A5. 🚇 *Edgware Rd.*
Open *8.30am–4pm Mon–Thu,
8.30am–5pm Fri, Sat.*

Like many of London's markets,
Church Street reaches a crescendo
at the weekend. On Friday and
Saturday, stalls selling cheap
clothes, household goods, fish,
cheese and antiques join the
everyday fruit and vegetable stalls.
Alfies Antique Market (No.13–25)
houses around 100 dealers selling
everything from jewellery to
furniture. There is also a cluster of
interesting stand-alone antique
furniture shops, plus the fascinating
Gallery of Antique Costume and
Textiles (No.2), which showcases
immaculate garments dating back
as far as the 17th century.

Columbia Road Market

Columbia Rd E2. **Map** 8 D3.
🚇 *Shoreditch, Old St.*
Open *8am– 2pm Sun. See p171.*

This is the place to come to buy
greenery and blossoms or just to
enjoy the fragrances and colours.
Cut flowers, plants, shrubs,

seedlings and pots are all sold at
about half their normal prices on
a Sunday morning in this charming
Victorian street. There are also
some lovely shops that keep market hours, such as Angela Flanders'
pretty perfumerie (No.96), Salon for
vintage jewellery and cufflinks
(No.142) and hip hatter, Fred Bare
(No.118). When you're shopped
out, take tea at Treacle (No.160),
which turns out cute retro
cupcakes and classic jam sponge
cakes, plus cups of proper tea to
wash them down. There is also a
selection of vintage and modern
china for sale. People with a
sweet tooth can snack on deep-
fried prawns from hole in the
wall, Lee's Seafoods (No.134).

East Street Market

East St SE17. 🚇 *Elephant and Castle.*
Open *8am–5pm Tue, Wed, Fri, Sat;
8am–2pm Thu, Sun.*

East Street Market's high spot is
Sunday, when more than 250
stalls fill the narrow street and a
small plant and flower market is
set up on Blackwood Street. The
majority of traders sell clothes,
accessories and household goods,
although there is plenty of British
and Afro-Caribbean produce, fish
and other delicacies. Charlie
Chaplin *(see p37)* was born in this
street and sought inspiration for
his characters in the area.

Gabriel's Wharf and Riverside Walk Markets

56 Upper Ground and Riverside Walk
SE1. **Map** 14 E3. 🚇 *Waterloo.*
Gabriel's Wharf Open *9.30am–6pm
Fri–Sun;* **Riverside Walk open**
*10am–5pm Sat, Sun and irregular
weekdays. See p191.*

Little shops filled with ceramics,
paintings and jewellery surround a
bandstand in Gabriel's Wharf
where jazz groups sometimes play
in the summer. A few stalls are set
up around the courtyard, selling
ethnic clothing and handmade
jewellery and pottery. The book
market under Waterloo Bridge
includes a good selection of new
and old Penguin paperbacks.

Grays Antique Markets

58 Davies St & 1–7 Davies Mews W1.
Map 12 E2. 🚇 *Bond Street.* **Open**
10am–6pm Mon–Fri.

Conveniently placed in the West
End, Grays probably isn't the
place to bag a bargain – the
liveried doorman is a tip-off that
this place is posh – but it makes a
pleasant place to browse. There
are some lovely pieces here, from
costume jewellery and fabulous

vintage fashion to enamel boxes
and modern first editions from
Biblion bookseller.

Greenwich Market

College Approach SE10. **Map** 23 B2.
🚆 *Greenwich.* 🚇 *Cutty Sark DLR.*
Open *9am–5pm Sat, Sun.*

At weekends, the area west of
Hotel Ibis accommodates dozens
of trestle tables piled with coins,
medals, banknotes, second-hand
books, Art Deco furniture, and
assorted bric-à-brac. The covered
crafts market specializes in
wooden toys, clothes made by
young designers, handmade
jewellery and accessories.

Jubilee and Apple Markets

Covent Gdn Piazza WC2. **Map** 13 C2.
🚇 *Covent Gdn.* **Open** *9am–5pm daily.*

Covent Garden has become the
centre of London streetlife, with
some of the capital's best busking.
Both these markets sell crafts and
designs. The Apple Market, inside
the Piazza where the famous fruit
and vegetable market was housed
(see p114), has knitwear, jewellery
and novelty goods. Jubilee Hall
sells antiques on Monday, crafts at
the weekend, and a large selection
of clothes, handbags, cosmetics
and tacky mementoes in between.
During the first weekend of
November, the Covent Garden
Market is the venue for renowned
food writer, Henrietta Green's
Food Lovers' Fair. During that time
it comes alive with around 100
speciality food producers from all
over Britain . The event also
features cookery demonstrations
and celebrity chefs.

Leadenhall Market

Whittington Ave EC3. **Map** 15 C2.
🚇 *Bank, Monument.* **Open**
7am–4pm Mon–Fri. See p159.

There has been a marketplace
on this site since medieval times,
but the present spectacular, glass-
roofed structure was built in
1881. Leadenhall Market was
traditionally famous for fish, meat
and poultry, but only fishmonger
HS Linwood & Sons remains. The
smart, red and green façades now
bear the names of upmarket
clothing chains, restaurants, pubs
and gift shops. Recently, however,
Leadenhall has been somewhat
revived as a centre of fine food.
More than a dozen stalls set up
shop on the cobblestones
beneath this dramatic structure
every Friday from 10am to 4pm.
Wares include European cheeses,
cured meats, baked goods,
condiments and other gourmet
goods as well.

Leather Lane Market

Leather Lane EC1. **Map** 6 E5.
🚇 *Farringdon, Chancery Lane.*
Open *10.30am–2pm Mon–Fri.*

This ancient street, originally called Leveroun Lane, has played host to a market for over 300 years. The history of the Lane, however, has nothing to do with leather. Stalls here sell cut-price high-street clothes, plus shoes, bags, jewellery and accessories. All are well worth having a browse through.

Marylebone Farmers' Market

Cramer St carpark, behind Marylebone High St W1. **Map** 4 D5.
🚇 *Baker Street, Bond Street.*
Open *10am–2pm Sun.*

In response to the recent interest in local organic produce, weekly markets have sprung up all over the city. This enables farmers and other producers to sell directly to the public. Marylebone is the largest and most central, offering seasonal fruit and veg, dairy products, fish, meat, breads, preserves and sauces. There is also a line-up of excellent gourmet shops in adjacent Moxon Street, including a renowned rare-breed pork butcher, the Ginger Pig, and La Fromagerie delicatessen with its extensive cheese cave. Other locations include Islington Green and the carpark behind Waterstone's, Notting Hill.

Old Spitalfields Market

Commercial St E1. **Map** 8 E5.
🚇 *Aldgate East, Liverpool Street.*
Open *11am–3pm Mon–Fri, 9.30–5.30pm Sun. See p170.*

The main market is on a Sunday, and is a mecca for those interested in the latest street fashion trends. Many young designers have stalls, and prices are also reasonable. The stalls are of mixed quality, so you have to really search for the gems. The organic food stalls and a selection of cafés make it a good brunch venue any day. A varying number of stalls are open during the week.

Petticoat Lane Market

Middlesex St E1. **Map** 16 D1.
🚇 *Liverpool St, Aldgate, Aldgate East.* **Open** *9am–2pm Sun (Wentworth St 10am–2.30pm Mon–Fri). See p169.*

Probably the most famous of all London's street markets, Petticoat Lane continues to attract many thousands of visitors and locals every Sunday. The prices may not be as cheap as some of those to be found elsewhere, but the sheer

volume of leather goods, clothes (the Lane's traditional strong point), watches, cheap jewellery and toys more than make up for that. A variety of fast-food sellers do a brisk trade catering for the bustling crowds that throng the market on a weekend.

Piccadilly Crafts Market

St James's Church, Piccadilly W1.
Map 13 A3. 🚇 *Piccadilly Circus, Green Park.* **Open** *9am–6pm Wed–Sat.*

Many of the markets in the Middle Ages were held in churchyards and Piccadilly Crafts Market is rekindling that ancient tradition. It is aimed mostly at visitors to London rather than locals, and the merchandise on display ranges from tacky T-shirts to wooden toys. All are spread out in the shadow of Wren's beautiful church *(see p90).*

Portobello Road Market

Portobello Rd W10. **Map** 9 C3.
🚇 *Notting Hill Gate, Ladbroke Grove.* **Open** *antiques and junk: 5.30am–5.30pm Sat. General market: 9am–5pm Mon–Wed, Fri, Sat; 9am–1pm Thu. See p219.*

Portobello Road is really three or four markets rolled into one. The Notting Hill end has more than 1,000 stalls in numerous arcades and on the street, displaying a compendium of objets d'art, jewellery, old medals, paintings and silverware. Most stalls are managed by experts, so bargains are very rare. Further down the gentle hill, antiques give way to fruit and vegetables.

The next transformation comes under the Westway flyover, where young fashion designers sell inexpensive creations alongside second-hand clothes, record and food stalls on Fridays and Saturdays. It's also worth venturing into the covered Portobello Green market, which has an interesting mix of small shops selling everything from avant-garde fashion to kitsch cushions and lingerie. From this point on, the market becomes increasingly shabby.

Ridley Road Market

Ridley Rd E8. 🚈 *Dalston.* **Open** *9am–3pm Mon–Wed. 9am–noon Thu. 9am–5pm Fri, Sat.*

Early last century Ridley Road was a centre of the Jewish community. Since then, Asians, Greeks, Turks and West Indians have also settled in the area and the market is a lively celebration

of this cultural mix. Highlights include the 24-hour bagel bakery, shanty-town shacks selling green bananas and reggae records, colourful drapery stalls and cheap fruit and vegetables.

Roman Road Market

Roman Rd, between Parnell Rd and St Stephen's Rd E3. 🚇 *Bethnal Green.*
🚌 *8.* **Open** *8am–2pm Tue & Thu. 10am–5pm Sat.*

This lively market established in the 19th century has a real East End flavour and traditionally sells everything from cheap bedding and fashion to cut-price cleaning products and fruit and veg. Chances are that you'll be treated to some colourful cockney patter from the stallholders trying to drum up custom. Recently, some more unusual vendors have been added to the mix, thus offering a unique variety to please the customers. When you pay a visit to the Roman Road Market, you may just be tempted to buy some of the handmade jewellery, vintage clothes or antiques being sold at the stalls.

St Martin-in-the-Fields Market

St Martin-in-the-Fields Churchyard WC2. **Map** 13 B3. 🚇 *Charing Cross.*
Open *11am–5pm Mon–Sat; noon–5pm Sun. See p102.*

This crafts market was started in the late 1980s. T-shirts, football scarves and funny hats are among the unremarkable selection of London mementoes. However, more interesting are the Eastern carved wooden boxes, handmade soaps and inexpensive, yet unique ethnic jewellery.

Shepherd's Bush Market

Goldhawk Rd W12. 🚇 *Goldhawk Road, Shepherd's Bush.* **Open** *9.30am–5pm Mon–Wed, Fri, Sat. 9.30am–2.30pm Thu.*

A focal point for many of the local ethnic communities, this rambling market contains an impressive volume of eclectic wares.

West Indian food, Afro wigs, Asian spices, exotic fish, rugs and other household goods are just some of the major attractions. There are acres of cheap clothing for every occasion, from floral flannel nighties and men's suits to clubwear and elaborately beaded wedding gowns. Cheap fabric stalls are a highlight of the Shepherd's Bush Market, and there is even an on-site tailor and barber, if you please.

ENTERTAINMENT IN LONDON

London has the enormous, multi-layered variety of entertainment that only the great cities of the world can provide, and, as always, the city's historical backdrop adds depth to the experience. While few things could be more contemporary than dancing the night away in style at a famed disco such as Stringfellows or Heaven, you could also choose to spend the evening picturing the ghosts of long-dead Hamlets pacing ancient boards in the shadow of one of the living legends that grace the West End theatres today. There's a healthy, innovative fringe theatre scene too, plus world-class ballet and opera in fabled venues such as Sadler's Wells, the Royal Opera House and the Coliseum. In London you'll be able to hear the

Café sign advertising free live music

best music, ranging from classical, jazz and rock to rhythm and blues, while dedicated movie buffs can choose from hundreds of different films each night, both in large, multi-screen complexes and excellent small independent cinemas. Sports fans can watch a game of cricket at Lords, cheer on oarsmen on the Thames or eat strawberries and cream at Wimbledon. Should you be feeling adventurous and sporty yourself, you could try going for a horse ride along Rotten Row in Hyde Park. There are festivals, celebrations and sports to attend, and there's plenty for children to do, too – in fact, there's plenty for everyone to do. Whatever you want, you'll be sure to find it on offer in London; it's just a question of knowing where to look.

Cultural classics: a concert at Kenwood House *(top)*; open-air theatre at Regent's Park *(above left)*; performers at the Coliseum *(above right)*

INFORMATION SOURCES

For details of events in London, check the comprehensive weekly listings and review magazine *Time Out* (published every Tuesday), sold at most newsagents and many bookshops. The weekly

What's On (Wednesdays) is also useful, and London's evening newspaper, the *Evening Standard*, gives brief daily listings. The *Independent* has daily listings and also reviews a different arts sector every day, plus a weekly round-up section, "The Information"; the

Guardian has arts reviews in its G2 section every day and weekly listings on Saturday. The *Independent, Guardian* and *The Times* all have lists of ticket availability.

Specialized news sheets, brochures and advance listings are distributed free in the foyers of theatres, concert halls, cinemas and arts complexes such as the South Bank and Barbican. Tourist information offices and hotel foyers often have the same publications. Fly posters advertise forthcoming events on billboards everywhere.

The Society of London Theatre (SOLT) publishes an informative free broadsheet every fortnight, available in many theatre foyers. It tends to concentrate on mainstream theatres, but does provide invaluable information about what's on. The National Theatre and the Royal Shakespeare Company also publish free broadsheets detailing future performances, distributed at the theatres.

SOLT's website (www. officiallondontheatre.co.uk) provides full details of current productions. It also has news and updates, but not seat availability. For this, there is a faxback service (09069-111 311). Many theatres also operate a faxback service which enables you to see a seating plan showing the unsold seats for any performance.

Line-up from the Royal Ballet, on stage at Covent Garden

BOOKING TICKETS

Some of the more popular shows and plays in London's West End – the latest Lloyd Webber musical for instance – can be totally booked out for weeks and even months ahead and you will find it impossible to purchase any tickets. This is not the norm, though, and most tickets will be available on the night, especially if you would be prepared to queue in front of the theatre for returns. However, for a stress-free holiday it helps to book tickets in advance; this will ensure that you get the day, time and seats that you want. You can book tickets from the box office in person, by telephone or by post. Quite a few hotels have concierges or porters who will give advice on where to go and arrange tickets for you.

Box offices are usually open from about 10am–8pm, and accept payment by cash, credit card, traveller's cheque or else a personal UK cheque

Palace Theatre plaque

when supported by a cheque guarantee card. Many venues will now sell unclaimed or returned tickets just before the performance; ask at the box office for the queuing times. To reserve seats by telephone, call the box office and either pay on arrival or send payment – seats are usually held for three days. Some venues now have separate phone numbers for your credit card bookings – check before you call. Reserve your seat, and always take your credit card with you when you collect your ticket. Some smaller venues do not accept credit cards.

DISABLED VISITORS

Many London venues are old buildings and were not originally designed with disabled visitors in mind, but

recently many facilities have been updated, particularly to give access to those using wheelchairs, or for those with hearing difficulties.

Telephone the box office prior to your visit to reserve the special seating places or equipment, which are often limited. Special discounts may be available: for details and information on facilities call Artsline (020-7388 2227, www.artslineonline.com).

TRANSPORT

Night buses (see p383) are now the preferred late-night mode of transport, or phone for a cab from the venue. If you find yourself outside the city centre late at night, do not rely on being able to hail a black taxi quickly in the street. Never take a mini-cab. The Underground usually runs until just after midnight, but check the timetables displayed in the stations (see pp380–81).

BOOKING AGENCIES

Tickets are also available from agencies. Try the theatre box office first; if no seats are available there, find out the standard prices before going to an agency. Most, but not all, are reputable. Agencies advertising top show tickets for "tonight" may really have them, and they may be a fair price. If you order by phone, tickets will be posted to you or sent to the theatre for you to collect. Commission should be a standard 22%. Some shows waive the agency fee by paying the commission themselves; this is usually advertised, and agencies should then charge standard box office prices. Always compare prices, try to avoid agencies in bureaux de change, and buy from ticket touts in the street only in desperation.

The major listings magazines

Ticket booth in Shaftesbury Avenue

London's Theatres

London offers an extraordinary range of theatrical entertainment – this is one of the world's great stages, and, at its best, standards of quality are extremely high. Despite their legendary reputation for reserve, the British are passionate about theatre and London's theatres reflect every nuance of this passion. You can stroll along a street of West End theatres and find a sombre Samuel Beckett, Brecht or Chekhov play showing next door to some absurdly frothy farce like *No Sex Please, We're British!* Amid such diversity there is always something to appeal to everyone.

WEST END THEATRE

There is a distinct glamour to the West End theatres. Perhaps it is the glittering lights of the foyer and the impressively ornate interiors, or maybe it is their hallowed reputations – but whatever it is, the old theatres retain a magic all of their own.

The West End billboards always feature a generous sprinkling of world-famous performers such as Judi Dench, Vanessa Redgrave, John Malkovich and Kevin Spacey.

The major commercial theatres cluster along Shaftesbury Avenue and the Haymarket and around Covent Garden and Charing Cross Road. Unlike the national theatres, most West End theatres survive only on profits; they do not receive any state subsidy. They rely on an army of ever-hopeful "angels" (financial backers) and producers to keep the old traditions alive.

Many theatres are historical landmarks, such as the classic **Theatre Royal Drury Lane**, established in 1663 *(see p115)*, and the elegant **Theatre Royal Haymarket** – both superb examples of early 19th-century buildings. Another to note is the **Palace** *(see p108)*, with its terracotta exterior and imposing position right on Cambridge Circus.

NATIONAL THEATRE

The **National Theatre** is based in the South Bank Centre *(see p188)*. Here, the large, open-staged Olivier, the proscenium-staged Lyttelton and the small, flexible Cottesloe offer a range of size and style, making it possible to produce every kind of theatre from large, extravagant works to miniature masterpieces. The complex is also a lively social centre. Enjoy a drink with your friends before your play begins; watch the crowds and the river drift by; wander around the many free art exhibitions; relax during the free early evening concerts in the foyer or browse through the theatre bookshop.

The **Royal Shakespeare Company** is Britain's national theatre company, one of the worlds' great theatre ensembles, with an unparalleled reputation for its dramatic interpretation of Shakespeare and other leading dramatists. Although its official home since the 19th century has been in Stratford-upon-Avon, it has maintained a regular London presence since the 1960s. Its London base used to be the Barbican Centre, but the RSC has for the moment decided to end its position as resident theatre company there, which leaves it free to put on plays at West End theatres too. If you want to find out where the RSC is performing in London call their ticket hotline.

NATIONAL THEATRE BOOKING ADDRESSES

National Theatre
(Lyttelton, Cottesloe, Olivier)
South Bank SE1. **Map** 14 D3.
Tel 020-7452 3000.
www.nationaltheatre.org.uk

Royal Shakespeare Company
Tel 0870-609 1110.

PANTOMIME

Should you happen to be visiting London between December and February, one unmissable experience for the whole family is pantomime. "Panto" is an absurd tradition in which major female characters are played by men and male characters by women, and the audience has to participate, shouting encouragement according to a set formula. Whatever adults may think of it, children love the experience.

OPEN-AIR THEATRE

A performance of one of Shakespeare's airier creations, such as *A Midsummer Night's Dream*, takes on an atmosphere of pure enchantment among the green vistas of **Regent's Park** *(see p224)*. Lavish opera productions are staged during the summer months in **Holland Park** *(see p218)*. Take a blanket and, to be safe, an umbrella. Refreshments are available, or you can take a picnic.

Open-air performances of a different kind are to be had at **Shakespeare's Globe** *(see p177)*, an exciting recent arrival on London's theatre circuit. This authentic reproduction of an Elizabethan playhouse, open to the skies – but with protected seating – is open to visitors all year round but only puts on performances in the summer months.

OPEN-AIR THEATRE BOOKING ADDRESSES

Holland Park Theatre
Holland Park. **Map** 9 B4.
Tel 020-7602 7856.
Open Jun–Aug.
www.operahollandpark.com

Open-Air Theatre
Inner Circle, Regent's Park NW1.
Map 4 D3. *Open* May–Sep.
Tel 0870-060 1811.

Shakespeare's Globe
New Globe Walk SE1. **Map** 15 A3.
Tel 020-7401 9919.
Performances May–Sep.
www.shakespeares-globe.org

WEST END THEATRES

Adelphi ⑬
Strand WC2.
Tel 0870-403 0303.

Albery ❶
St Martin's Lane WC2.
Tel 0870-060 6621.

Aldwych ⑱
Aldwych WC2.
Tel 020-7379 3367.

Apollo ㉜
Shaftesbury Ave W1.
Tel 020-7494 5050.

Cambridge ㉔
Earlham St WC2.
Tel 0870-264 3333.

Comedy ❽
Panton St SW1.
Tel 0870-060 6622.

Criterion ❼
Piccadilly Circus W1.
Tel 020-7413 1437.

Dominion Theatre ㉓
Tottenham Court Rd.
Tel 0870-607 7460.

Duchess ⑯
Catherine St WC2.
Tel 020-7494 5050.

Duke of York's ❸
St Martin's Lane WC2.
Tel 0870-060 6623.

Fortune ⑳
Russell St WC2.
Tel 0870-060 6626.

Garrick ❹
Charing Cross Rd WC2.
Tel 0870-264 3333.

Gielgud ㉛
Shaftesbury Ave W1.
Tel 0870-264 3333.

Her Majesty's ❿
Haymarket SW1.
Tel 0870-264 3333.

Lyceum Theatre ⑮
Wellington St WC2.
Tel 0870-243 9000.

Lyric ㉝
Shaftesbury Ave W1.
Tel 0870-890 1107.

New Ambassadors ㉖
West St WC2.
Tel 0870-060 6627.

New London ㉑
Drury Lane WC2.
Tel 0870-264 3333.

Palace ㉘
Shaftesbury Ave W1.
Tel 020-7494 5050.

Phoenix ㉗
Charing Cross Rd WC2.
Tel 0870-060 6629.

Piccadilly ㉞
Denman St W1.
Tel 0870-060 6630.

Playhouse ⑫
Northumberland Ave WC2.
Tel 0870-060 6631.

Prince Edward ㉙
Old Compton St W1.
Tel 0870-850 9191.

Prince of Wales ❻
Coventry St W1.
Tel 0870-850 0393.

Queen's ㉚
Shaftesbury Ave W1.
Tel 020-7494 5040.

Shaftesbury ㉒
Shaftesbury Ave WC2.
Tel 020-7379 3345.

Strand ⑰
Aldwych WC2.
Tel 0870-060 2335.

St Martin's ㉕
West St WC2.
Tel 0870-162 8787.

Theatre Royal Drury Lane ⑲
Catherine St WC2.
Tel 0870-264 3333.

Theatre Royal Haymarket ❾
Haymarket SW1.
Tel 0870-901 3356..

Vaudeville ⑭
Strand WC2.
Tel 020-7494 5050.

The Venue ❺
Leicester Pl W1.
Tel 020-7494 5050.

Whitehall ⑪
Trafalgar Studios
Whitehall SW1.
Tel 0870-060 6632.

Wyndham's ❷
Charing Cross Rd WC2.
Tel 0870-950 0920.

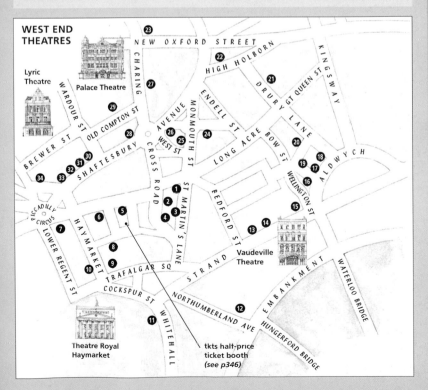

WEST END THEATRES

Lyric Theatre
Palace Theatre
Vaudeville Theatre
Theatre Royal Haymarket
tkts half-price ticket booth (see p346)

FRINGE THEATRE

London's fringe theatre acts as an outlet for new, adventurous writing and for writers from other cultures and lifestyles – works by Irish writers appear regularly, as do plays by Caribbean and Latin American authors and feminist and gay writers.

The plays are usually staged in tiny theatres based in pubs, such as the **Gate Theatre** above the Prince Albert pub in Notting Hill, the **King's Head** in Islington and the **Latchmere** pub in Battersea, or in warehouses and spare space in larger theatres, such as the **Donmar Warehouse** and the **Studio** in the Lyric.

Venues like the **Bush**, the **Almeida** and the **Theatre Upstairs** at the Royal Court have earned their reputations for discovering outstanding new works, some of which have subsequently transferred successfully to the West End.

Foreign-language plays are sometimes performed at national cultural institutes; for example you might be able to catch Molière at the **Institut Français** or Brecht at the **Goethe Institute**; check the listings magazines.

For alternative stand-up comedy and cabaret, where you can encounter the sharp edge of satire with its brash, newsy style, try the **Comedy Store**, the birthplace of so-called "alternative" comedy, or the **Hackney Empire**, a former Victorian music hall, completely refurbished in 2003 to its former glory to host a variety of shows.

BUDGET TICKETS

There is a wide range of prices for seats in London theatres. The cheaper West End tickets, for example, can cost under £10, whereas the best seats for musicals hover around the £30 mark. However, it is usually quite possible to obtain cheaper tickets.

"tkts" (see p345) is the only official discount theatre ticket shop in London, and sells tickets on the day of the performance for a wide range of mainstream shows. Located on the south side of Leicester Square, the booth is open Monday to Saturday (10am–7pm) for matinee and evening shows, and Sunday (noon–3:30pm) for matinees only. Payment is by cash or credit card, and there is a strict limit of up to four tickets per purchase, and a small service charge.

You can sometimes get reduced price seats for matinee performances, press and preview nights – it is always worth checking with the box office to see what they currently have on offer.

CHOOSING SEATS

If you go to the theatre in person, you will be able to see its seating plan and note where you can get a good view at an affordable price. If you book by telephone, you should note the following: stalls are in front of the stage and expensive. The back stalls are slightly cheaper; dress, grand or royal circles are above the stalls and cheaper again; the upper circle or balcony are the cheapest seats

but you will have to climb several flights of stairs; the slips are seats that run along the edges of the theatre; boxes are the most expensive option.

It is also as well to bear in mind that some of the cheap seats have a restricted view.

THEATRE-RELATED ACTIVITIES

If you are curious about how the mechanics of the theatre work, you will probably enjoy a back-stage tour. The National Theatre organizes tours (contact the box office – see p344 – for details). The tour includes the Lyttleton, Olivier and Cottesloe auditoria, as well as the workshops and dressing rooms. The Theatre Museum (see p115) is well worth a visit.

IRATE GHOSTS

Many London theatres are reputed to have ghosts; however, the two most famous spectres haunt the environs of the Garrick and the Duke of York's (see p345). The Garrick is heavily atmospheric and the ghost of Arthur Bourchier, a manager at the turn of the 20th century, is reputed to make fairly regular appearances. He hated critics and many believe he is still trying to frighten them away. The ghost occupying the Duke of York's theatre was Violet Melnotte, an actress manager during the 1890s, who was famed for her extremely fiery temper.

FRINGE THEATRE

Almeida
Almeida St N1.
Tel 020-7359 4404.

Bush
Shepherds Bush Green
W12.
Tel 020-7602 3703.

Comedy Store
28a Leicester Sq WC2.
Map 13 B3.
Tel 020-7344 0234.

Donmar Warehouse
41 Earlham St WC2.
Map 13 B2.
Tel 0870-060 6624.

Gate Theatre
The Prince Albert,
11 Pembridge Rd W11.
Map 9 C3.
Tel 020-7229 0706.

Goethe Institute
50 Prince's Gate, Exhibition
Rd SW7. **Map** 11 A5.
Tel 020-7596 4000.

Hackney Empire
291 Mare St E8.
Tel 020-8985 2424.

Institut Français
17 Queensberry Pl SW7.
Map 18 F2.
Tel 020-7073 1350.

King's Head
115 Upper St N1.
Map 6 F1.
Tel 020-7226 1916.

Latchmere
503 Battersea Park Rd
SW11.
Tel 020-7978 7040.

Royal Court Theatre Upstairs
Sloane Sq SW1.
Map 19 C2.
Tel 020-7565 5000.

Studio
Lyric, Hammersmith,
King St W6.
Tel 0870-0500 511.

Cinemas

If you can't find a movie you like in London, then you don't like movies. The huge choice of British, American, foreign-language, new, classic, popular and special-interest films makes London a major international film centre, with about 250 different films showing at any one time. There are about 50 cinemas in the central district of London alone, many of them ultra-modern multi-screened complexes. The big commercial chains show current smash-hits and a healthy number of independent cinemas offer some inventive programmes drawing on the whole history of film. London's listings magazines carry full details of what's on where.

WEST END CINEMAS

West End is a loose term for the main cinemas in the West End of London which show new releases, such as the **Odeon Leicester Square** and the **UGC** Shaftesbury Avenue at the Trocadero, but it also includes the cinemas found in Chelsea, Fulham and Notting Hill. Programmes begin around midday and are then repeated every two or three hours, with the last show around 8.30pm; there are often late-night screenings on Fridays and Saturdays.

West End cinemas are very expensive, but admission is often cheaper for afternoon performances or on Mondays. Reserve your seats well in advance for screenings of the more popular films on Friday and Saturday evenings and Sunday afternoon.

BFI LONDON IMAX

The largest IMAX screen in Britain shows specially created movies accompanied by surround sound. Subjects like spaceflight or the undersea world suit this breathtaking format well, as do animations.

REPERTORY CINEMAS

These cinemas often show foreign-language and slightly more "off-beat" art films and sometimes change programmes daily or even several times each day. Some cinemas show two or three films, often on the same theme, for one entrance charge.

These include the **Prince Charles**, which is situated centrally, close to Leicester Square, the **Everyman** in north London, the ICA in the Mall, the newly refurbished **Ritzy** in South London and the National Film Theatre.

NATIONAL FILM THEATRE

The National Film Theatre (NFT) is located in the South Bank Arts Complex, near Waterloo Station. The NFT has two cinemas of its own, both of which offer a huge and diverse selection of films, both British and international. The NFT also holds regular screenings of rare and restored films and television programmes taken from the National Film Archive. It is absolutely essential for movie buffs to pay a visit.

FOREIGN-LANGUAGE FILMS

These are screened at a number of repertory and independent cinemas, including the **Renoir**, the **Prince Charles**, the **Curzon Soho** in Shaftesbury Avenue, the **Other Cinema** and the **Screen** cinemas chain. Films are shown in the original language, with English subtitles.

FILM CERTIFICATES

Children are allowed to go to a cinema unaccompanied by an adult to films which have been awarded either a U (universal) or a PG (parental guidance advised) certificate for viewing.

With other films, the numbers 12, 15 or 18 quite simply denote the minimum ages allowed for admission to the cinema. These classifications are always clearly advertised in the publicity for the film.

LONDON FILM FESTIVAL

The most important cinema event in Britain is held every November, when over 100 films – some of which will have already won awards abroad – from a number of countries are screened. The NFT, several of the repertory cinemas and some of the big West End cinemas will have special showings of these films. Details are published in the listings magazines. Tickets are quite hard to come by but some "standby" tickets will generally be available to the public 30 minutes before the start of a performance.

CINEMA ADDRESSES

BFI London IMAX
Waterloo Rd SE1.
Map 14 D4.
☎ 0870-787 2525.

Curzon Soho
93–107 Shaftesbury Ave
W1. **Map** 13 B2.
☎ 020-7734 2255.

Everyman
Hollybush Vale NW3. **Map** 1 A5.
☎ 0870-066 4777.

NFT
South Bank Centre, SE1.
Map 14 D3.
Tel 020-7928 3232.

Odeon Leicester Sq
Leicester Sq, WC2. **Map** 13 B2.
☎ 0871-224 4007.

Other Cinema
Rupert St W1. **Map** 13 A2.
Tel 020-7437 0757.

Prince Charles
Leicester Pl, WC2.
Map 13 B2
Tel 020-7494 3654.

Renoir
Brunswick Sq WC1.
Map 5 C4.
☎ 020-7837 8402.

Ritzy
Brixton Rd SW2.
Tel 020-7733 2229.

Screen Cinemas
96 Baker St NW1
Map 3 C5.
Tel 020-7935 2772.

UGC (at the Trocadero)
Coventry St W1.
Map 13 A3.
☎ 0871-200 2000.

Opera, Classical and Contemporary Music

Until recently, opera enjoyed a somewhat elitist reputation. However, televised concerts and free outdoor concerts in Hyde Park and the Piazza, Covent Garden, have greatly increased its popularity. London is home to five world-class orchestras and a veritable host of smaller music companies and contemporary music ensembles; it also houses three permanent opera companies and numerous smaller opera groups and leads the world with its period orchestras. It is a major centre for the classical recording industry, which helps to support a large community of musicians and singers. Mainstream, obscure, traditional and innovative music are all to be found in profusion. Time Out magazine (see p342) has the most comprehensive listings of the classical music on offer around the capital.

Royal Opera House

Floral Street WC2. **Map** 13 C2.
Tel 020-7304 4000. See p115.
www.royaloperahouse.org

The building, with its elaborate red, white and gold interior, is opulent; it looks, and is, expensive. It is the home of the Royal Opera and the Royal Ballet, but visiting opera and ballet companies also perform here. Many productions are shared with foreign opera houses, so check that you haven't already seen the same production at home. Works are always performed in the original language, but English translations are flashed up above the stage.

Seats are usually booked well in advance, particularly if major stars such as Placido Domingo or Kiri Te Kanawa are performing. The sound is best in the seats centre of stage, right in the front. Tickets range from about £5 to £200 or more for a world-class star. The cheapest seats tend to go first, although a number of these tickets are reserved for sale on the day. Some of the cheaper seats have extremely restricted views. Standing passes can often be obtained right up to the time of a performance. Standby information is available on the day, and there are often concessions on tickets. It is worthwhile queuing for last-minute returns.

London Coliseum

St Martin's Lane WC2. **Map** 13 B3.
Tel 020-7836 0111. 📠 020-7632 8300. See p119. www.eno.org

The Coliseum, home of the English National Opera (ENO), has recently been restored. Founded in 1961, the company's hallmarks are performances in English, high musical standards and a permanent ensemble complemented by guest appearances. Productions range from the classic to the adventurous.

They are often praised for their contemporary interpretations. The audiences tend to be younger than at the Royal Opera House, the seats are much cheaper and there is less corporate entertaining. For weekday performances, there are 500 prebookable seats at £10 and under.

South Bank Centre

South Bank Centre SE1. **Map** 14 D4.
Tel 020-7921 0600. See pp186–7.
www.southbanklondon.com

The South Bank Centre includes the **Royal Festival Hall (RFH)**, the **Queen Elizabeth Hall**, the **Purcell Room** and the **Hayward Gallery**. There are nightly performances, mostly of classical music, interspersed with opera, jazz, ballet and modern dance seasons, as well as festivals of contemporary and ethnic music. The largest concert hall on the South Bank is the RFH. Built in the 1950s, it is now considered one of the best modernist structures in London. The RFH is ideal for major orchestras and large-scale choral works. The airy halls outside the auditorium are also used to house exhibitions, a number of cafés, a book and music shop, and the occasional free performance. It has recently been refurbished.

The Purcell Room is comparatively small and tends to host chamber and contemporary music in addition to many debut recitals of young artists. The Queen Elizabeth Hall lies somewhere in between. It stages medium-sized ensembles whose audiences, while too large for the Purcell Room, would not fill the Festival Hall. Jazz and ethnic music are performed here and the innovative and often controversial Opera Factory makes several appearances throughout the year. It performs a range of modern interpretations of the classics, and often commissions

new works. The London Philharmonic Orchestra and the Philharmonia are resident at the South Bank. The Royal Philharmonic and the BBC Symphony Orchestra are frequent visitors, along with leading ensembles and soloists such as Angela Gheorghiu, Mitsuko Uchida, Stephen Kovacevich and Anne-Sofie von Mutter. Visiting international musicians cover a wide repertoire of music from the Kronos Quartet to the Vienna Symphony Orchestra. World-class conductors who have played here include Daniel Barenboim, Kurt Masur and Simon Rattle.

The Academy of St Martin-in-the-Fields, the London Festival Orchestra, Opera Factory, the London Classical Players and the London Mozart Players all have regular seasons. There are also frequent free foyer concerts, and throughout the summer the centre is well worth visiting as musical events take place on the terraces when the weather permits.

LONDON MUSIC FESTIVALS

The BBC run Promenade concerts are mostly held at the Royal Albert Hall (see p349) between July and September. More than 70 concerts feature soloists, orchestras and conductors from around the world, performing a wide repertoire from much-loved classics to newly commissioned pieces. Every concert is broadcast live both on the radio and online. Tickets are best bought in advance, but 500 standing or 'promming' places are sold on the day, one and a half hours before the performance. The City of London Festival is held annually in June and July, when churches and public buildings in the City host a range of varied musical events. Venues such as the Tower of London (see p154) and Goldsmiths' Hall lend a special atmosphere to the events. Many concerts are free. For more details, apply to the information office (020-7377 0540) from May onwards.

Barbican Concert Hall

Silk Street EC2. **Map** 7 A5.
Tel 0845-120 7500. *See p165.*
www.barbican.org.uk

The Barbican is the home of the London Symphony Orchestra (LSO). Classical concerts are performed by the resident LSO and the BBC Symphony Orchestra, as well as many other visiting orchestras and ensembles, as part of the Barbican's own international concert seasons. The concert hall is also renowned for its performances of contemporary music, including jazz, blues and world music, which attract the top musicians in their field.

Royal Albert Hall

Kensington Gore SW7. **Map** 10 F5.
Tel 020-7589 8212. *See p207.*
www.royalalberthall.com

Each year the Royal Albert Hall hosts over 300 concerts, from ballet to rock, pop, opera and national events. From mid-July to mid-September it is devoted to the Henry Wood Promenade Concerts, the "Proms". Organized by the BBC, the season features the BBC Symphony Orchestra performing modern symphonies and other works as well as classics. Visiting orchestras make up a varied pro-gramme. Tickets for the Proms can be bought on the day of perform-ance or booked in advance, but long queues build up early in the day, so experienced Promenaders take cushions to sit on. Tickets sell out weeks ahead for the "Last Night of the Proms", which has become a national institution.

The hall is also open for tours that take you on a journey of its extraordinary history, and give you the chance to experience the workings of this performing arts venue.

Handel House Museum

25 Brook St W1. **Map** 12 E2.
Tel 020-7495 1685. **Open** 10am–6pm Tue–Sat (until 8pm Thu), noon–6pm Sun.
www.handelhouse.org

Located in the finely restored Georgian house where George Frideric Handel lived from 1723 until his death in 1759, the Handel House Museum provides an intimate venue for performances. Thursday night recitals of baroque music on period instruments are held in the panelled rehearsal and performance room, where Handel himself would have entertained his guests. Concert tickets include access to the museum. Check the website for more concerts, lectures and workshops.

OUTDOOR MUSIC

London has many outdoor musical events in summer. At Kenwood House on Hampstead Heath *(see p234)*, a grassy hill leads down to a lake, beyond which is the concert platform. Arrive early as the concerts are popular, particularly if fireworks are to accompany the music. Deck-chairs tend to be booked up early, so most people sit on the grass. Take a sweater and a picnic. Purists beware – people walk around, eat and talk throughout and the music is amplified so it can be a little distorted. You don't get your money back if it rains, as they have never abandoned a performance yet.

Other venues include Marble Hill House in Twickenham *(see p252)*, with practices similar to Kenwood, Crystal Palace Park and Holland Park.

Wigmore Hall

36 Wigmore St W1. **Map** 12 E1.
Tel 020-7935 2141. *See p226.*
www.wigmore-hall.org.uk

Because of its excellent acoustics the Wigmore Hall is a favourite with visiting artists, and attracts international names such as Andreas Scholl and András Schiff for a wide-ranging programme of events. It presents seven evening concerts a week, BBC Monday lunchtime concerts, and a Sunday morning concert from September to July.

St Martin-in-the-Fields

Trafalgar Sq WC2. **Map** 13 B3.
Tel 020-7766 1100. *See p102.*
www.smitf.org

This elegant Gibbs church is where the famous Academy of St Martin-in-the-Fields and the famous choir of the same name began life. Orchestras as disparate as the Delmont Ensemble and the London Oriana Choir provide evening concerts. The choice of each pro-gramme is partly dictated by the religious year; for example, Bach's *St John Passion* is played at Ascen-siontide. Free lunchtime concerts are held on Mondays, Tuesdays and Fridays by young artists.

St John's, Smith Square

Smith Sq SW1. **Map** 21 B1.
Tel 020-7222 1061. *See p81.*
www.sjss.org.uk

This converted Baroque church has good acoustics and comfortable seating. It hosts varied concerts by groups such as the Academy of Ancient Music, the London Mozart Players, the Monteverdi Choir and Polyphony. The concert period runs from September to mid-July.

Broadgate Arena

3 Broadgate EC2. **Map** 7 C5.
Tel 020-7505 4000. *See p169.*

This is the new City-based venue for a summer season of lunchtime concerts offering varied prog-rammes, often from up-and-coming musicians.

MUSIC VENUES

Orchestral
Barbican Concert Hall
Broadgate Arena
Queen Elizabeth Hall
Royal Albert Hall
Royal Festival Hall
St Martin-in-the-Fields
St John's, Smith Square

Chamber and Ensemble
Barbican Concert Hall
Broadgate Arena
Handel House Museum
LSO St Luke's
Purcell Room
Royal Festival Hall foyer
St Martin-in-the-Fields
St John's, Smith Square
Wigmore Hall

Soloists and Recitals
Barbican Concert Hall
Handel House Museum
Purcell Room
Royal Albert Hall
St Martin-in-the-Fields
St John's, Smith Square
Wigmore Hall

Children's
Barbican Concert Hall
Royal Festival Hall

Free
Barbican Concert Hall
Royal Festival Hall foyer
Royal National Theatre foyer (see p344)
St Martin-in-the-Fields (lunchtime)

Early Music
Purcell Room
Wigmore Hall

Contemporary Music
Barbican Concert Hall
South Bank Complex

Dance

London-based dance companies present a range of styles from classical ballet to mime, jazz, experimental and ethnic dance. London is also host to visiting companies as diverse as the classic Bolshoi Ballet and the innovative Jaleo Flamenco. Most dance companies (with the exception of the resident ballets) have short seasons that seldom last longer than a fortnight and often less than a week – check the listings magazines for details *(see p342)*. Theatres that regularly feature dance are the **Royal Opera House**, the **London Coliseum, Sadler's Wells** and **The Place Theatre**. There are also performances at the **South Bank Centre** and other arts centres throughout the city.

BALLET

The **Royal Opera House** *(see p115)* and the **London Coliseum** in St Martin's Lane are by far the best venues for classical ballet, providing the stage for foreign companies when they visit London. The Opera House is home to the Royal Ballet, which usually invites major international guest artists to take up residence. Book well in advance for classics such as *Swan Lake* and *Giselle*. The company also has an unusual repertoire of modern ballet; triple bills provide a mixture of new and old and seats are normally quite readily available.

The English National Ballet holds its summer season at the **London Coliseum**. It has a similar repertoire to the Royal Ballet and stages some very popular productions.

Visiting companies also perform at **Sadler's Wells**, which, although it is London's premier venue for contemporary dance, also hosts a few companies with a classical repertoire.

CONTEMPORARY

A plethora of new and young companies is flourishing in London, each one with a distinctive style. **Sadler's Wells** has a proud reputation as the host of contemporary dance companies from around the world. There are regular visits from such luminaries of dance as the Nederlands Dance Theatre and the Alvin Ailey Company from New York. The innovative English ensemble, the Rambert Dance Company, have a regular, twice-a-year slot at the theatre – usually in May and November. A stunning new building, opened in October 1998, replaced the historic site of the Sadler's Wells Ballet. The **Peacock Theatre** (the West End home of Sadler's Wells) also features contemporary dance as part of its programme.

The Place is the home of contemporary and ethnic dance companies and has a year-round programme of performances from these and a number of visiting dancers.

Jacksons Lane community centre in Highgate has become an acclaimed venue for innovative dance, often from international dance groups. Other venues include the **Institute of Contemporary Arts** (ICA) *(see p92)* and the **Chisenhale Dance Space**, a centre for small companies currently regarded as being on the experimental fringes.

ETHNIC

There is a constant stream of visiting groups coming to perform traditional dance from all over the world. Both **Sadler's Wells** and the **Riverside Studios** are major venues, while classical ethnic dance companies, including Indian and Far Eastern, have seasons at the South Bank Centre, often in the **Queen Elizabeth Hall**. Check the listings magazines for details.

DANCE FESTIVALS

There are two major contemporary dance festivals each year in London, featuring many different companies. Spring Loaded runs from February to April, while Dance Umbrella runs from early October to early November. The listings magazines carry all details.

Other smaller festivals include Almeida Dance, from the end of April to the first week of May at the **Almeida Theatre**, and The Turning World, a festival running in April and May offering dance from all over the world.

DANCE VENUES

Almeida Theatre
Almeida St N1.
Tel 020-7226 7432.

Chisenhale Dance Space
64 Chisenhale Rd E3.
Tel 020-8981 6617.

ICA
Nash House,
Carlton House Terrace,
The Mall SW1.
Map 13 A4.
Tel 020-7930 0493.

Jacksons Lane
269a Archway Rd N6.
Tel 020-8341 4421.

London Coliseum
St Martin's Lane WC2.
Map 13 B3.
Tel 020-7836 0111 or 020-7632 8300.

Peacock Theatre
Portugal St WC2.
Map 14 D1.
Tel 020-7863 8000.

The Place
17 Duke's Rd WC1.
Map 5 B3.
Tel 020-7387 0031.

Queen Elizabeth Hall
South Bank Centre SE1.
Map 14 D4.
Tel 0870-380 0400.

Riverside Studios
Crisp Rd W6.
Tel 020-8237 1111.

Royal Opera House
Floral St WC2.
Map 13 C2.
Tel 020-7304 4000.

Sadler's Wells
Rosebery Ave EC1.
Map 6 E3.
Tel 020-7863 8000.

Rock, Pop, Jazz, Reggae and World Music

You will find the whole range of popular music being strummed and hummed, howled, growled or synthesized in London. There may be as many as 80 listed concerts on an ordinary weeknight, featuring rock, reggae, soul, folk, country, jazz, Latin and world music. In addition to the gigs, there are music festivals in the summer at parks, pubs, halls and stadiums throughout the capital (see p353). Check the listings magazines and keep your eyes open for publicity posters (see p342).

MAJOR VENUES

The largest venues in London are host to an extraordinary variety of music.

Places where pop idols hope to draw enormous crowds of adoring fans include the cavernous indoor **Wembley Arena**, the **Hammersmith Apollo**, or, if they take themselves rather seriously, the grand **Royal Albert Hall**.

The **Brixton Academy** and the **Town and Country Club** are next in prominence and size. Each can take well over 1,000 people, and for many Londoners these former cinemas are the capital's best venues, with seating upstairs, large dance-floors downstairs and accessible bars.

ROCK AND POP

Indie music is one of the mainstays of London's live music output. Following the leads of Manchester and Bristol, the capital has a healthy, cross-fertilized rock scene: venues all over town offer Britpop, bratpop, hip-hop, trip-hop and the many other variations on pop which have yet to be labelled for the mass market. The **Union Chapel** in Islington hosts a variety of bands. Kentish Town's **Bull and Gate** is good for goth, and rock is the order of the day at venues such as the **Astoria** and **The Shepherd's Bush Empire** among others.

The **Mean Fiddler** in Charing Cross Road is one of the best of the mid-sized venues and is famous for being the place that bands play twice – once on the way up, and again on the way down. London is the home of pub-rock, which is a vibrant blend of rhythm and blues, rock and punk that has been evolving since the 1960s as a genre in which bands frequently develop before finding their real musical identity. Such diverse bands as the Clash, Dr Feelgood and Dire Straits all started as pub rockers. While there's usually no entrance fee to pub gigs, drinks tend to be surcharged.

New bands have a popular showcase at the **Rock Garden** in Covent Garden most week nights, while **Borderline**, near to Leicester Square, is frequented by record company talent scouts.

The **Barfly** in Chalk Farm delivers a good range of indie acts. The **Camden Palace** is very good value for money, especially on Tuesdays, when you can listen to the finest established indie pop both before and after live performances from up-and-coming indie bands. Another good venue for stimulating rock bands in North London is **The Garage** at Highbury Corner.

JAZZ

The number of jazz venues in London has grown in the last few years – both the music and the lifestyle which is romantically imagined to go with it are officially hip once again. **Ronnie Scott's** in the West End is still the pick of the vintage crop, and since the 1950s many of the finest performers in the world have come to play here. The **100 Club** in Oxford Street is another very popular venue for confirmed jazzniks.

Jazz and food have formed a partnership at venues such as the **Palookaville** in Covent Garden, the **Dover Street Wine Bar** and the largely vegetarian **Jazz Café**. Others include the **Pizza Express** on Dean Street and the **Pizza on the Park**, by Hyde Park Corner.

The **South Bank Centre** (see pp186–7) and also the **Barbican** (see p165) feature formal jazz concerts and free jazz in the foyers.

REGGAE

London's large West Indian community has made the city the European reggae capital. At the **Notting Hill Carnival** (see p57), late in August, many top bands perform free.

Reggae has now become integrated with the mainstream rock music scene, and bands appear at most of London's rock venues.

WORLD MUSIC

Musicians from every corner of the globe live in London. "World music" includes African, Latin, South American, anything exotic, and its popularity has sparked a revitalization of British and Irish folk music. **Cecil Sharp House** has regular shows for folk purists, while the **ICA** (see p92) hosts innovative acts. **Spitz**, in Spitalfields Market, has a reputation for hosting African and Latin American music nights. Hot Latin nights can be found at **Cuba Libre** in Islington, and laid-back vibes pervade the **Notting Hill Arts Club**. For all French Caribbean and African sounds you could check **Le Café de Piaf** inside Waterloo Station, and for the widest selection of African sounds and food in town, try visiting the **Africa Centre** in Covent Garden. The **Barbican Centre**, the **Royal Festival Hall** and the **Queen Elizabeth Hall** at the South Bank Centre all offer plenty of world music.

Clubs

The old cliché that London dies when the pubs shut no longer holds true. Europe has long scoffed at Londoners going to bed at 11pm when the night is only just beginning in Paris, Madrid and Rome, but London has caught on at last and you can revel all night if you want to. The best clubs are not all confined to the city's centre – initial disappointment that your hotel is a half-hour tube-ride from Leicester Square can be offset by the discovery of a trendy club right on your doorstep.

ETIQUETTE

Fashions and club nights change very rapidly and nightspots open and close down all the time. Some of the best club nights are one-nighters – check the listings magazines (see p342). Be aware that there are some-times bouncers on the door, enforcing a variety of dress or other appearance codes for a particular club. If you are set on visiting one of these, do some research before you go.

A few clubs require that you arrange membership 48 hours in advance, and you may also find that you have to be introduced by a member. Again, check these details in the listings magazines. Groups of men may not be welcome, so split up and find a woman to go in with; expect to queue to get in. Entrance fees may seem reasonable, but drinks tend to be over-priced.

Opening times are usually 10pm–3am Monday to Satur-day, although many clubs stay open until 6am at the weekend and some open on Sunday from about 8pm to midnight.

MAINSTREAM

London is home to one of the best-known discos in the world: **Stringfellows** is as much a part of the tourist circuit as Madame Tussaud's. It's glitzy and expensive so jeans are out of the question. The nearby **Hippodrome** is similar. One of the world's largest discos, it has stunning lighting, several bars and also serves food.

Most of the more upmarket nightclubs in London, for example **Annabel's**, have a strict members-only policy; they require nominations

by current members and have long waiting lists, so unless you mix in privileged circles you are unlikely to get in.

Traditional disco-type clubs which are easier to enter include the **Café de Paris**, where you can dine and boogie the night away.

Further north, the **Forum** hosts popular club nights, which feature classic soul, funk and rhythm and blues. Similar clubs are **Equinox** in Leicester Square and the **Tattershall Castle**, a disco boat moored on the Thames.

FASHIONABLE VENUES AND CLUB NIGHTS

Over the last few years London has become one of the most innovative and sought-after club capitals in the world. It is now a major stage where trends are set. **Heaven** hosts England's premier "house" night. With its huge dance floor, excellent lasers, sound systems and lightshows it's very popular, so start queuing early. The **Ministry of Sound** is a New York-style club that set the pattern for others to follow. However, it is notoriously difficult to get into. If you are feeling energetic, house nights are also run at the **Gardening Club** and **Woody's**, which is home to garage as well as hardcore house, and there's always the music-loving **Fabric**.

As with many clubs, **Bar Rumba** has different themes on different evenings, but if you like your dancing with a dash of spice and a lot of sauce, sashay along to its salsa night with dance classes also available. **Cargo**, the pioneering live/mixed music

venue, features some of London's funkiest sounds.

Turnmills is London's first 24-hour club; it's cheap, plays funky jazz and also boasts a decent restaurant. **The End** has one of the best sound systems in the West End. Dress in uniform for the "School Disco Night" with 70s, 80s and 90s sounds (check listings for the venue, as it moves regularly).

Disappointingly, there are surprisingly few regular reggae nights. **Soho Lounge** has the best dance reggae on Saturday nights and a tremendous toe-tapping tripartite rhythm riot of ska, classic soul and R 'n' B sounds on Thursdays.

GAY

London has a number of gay nightclubs. The best-known and most popular is **Heaven**, with its huge dance floor and bar and video lounge. The **Fridge** and the **Gardening Club** host mixed gay nights, and the Fridge holds women-only nights.

TRANSVESTITE

Watch for the occasional "Kinky Gerlinky" night in the listings magazines, an outrageously kitsch collection of drag queens and assorted exotica. In Soho, **Madame Jojo**'s revue is a fabulous whirl of glittering colour and extreme high camp.

CASINOS

To gamble in London you must be a member, or at least the guest of a member, of a licensed gaming club. Most clubs are happy to let you join but membership must be arranged 48 hours in advance. Many will let you in to use facilities other than the gambling tables until about 4am, when most close. Try the excellent restaurants and bars, which are often subject to the usual licensing laws (see p318). Many clubs also have "hostesses" – beware the cost of their company.

DIRECTORY

MAJOR MUSIC VENUES

Brixton Academy
211 Stockwell Rd SW9.
Tel 0870-771 2000.

Forum
9–17 Highgate Rd NW5.
Tel 020-7284 1001.

Hammersmith Apollo
Queen Caroline St W6.
Tel 0870-606 3400.

Royal Albert Hall
See p203.

Wembley Arena
Empire Way, Wembley,
Middlesex HA9.
Tel 0870-739 0739.

ROCK AND POP VENUES

Astoria
157 Charing Cross Rd
WC2. **Map** 13 B1.
Tel 020-7434 9592.

Barfly
49 Chalk Farm Rd NW1.
Map 4 F1.
Tel 020 7691 4244.

Borderline
Orange Yard, Manette St
WC2. **Map** 13 B1.
Tel 020-7434 9592.

Bull and Gate
389 Kentish Town Rd
NW5.
Tel 020-7485 5358.

Camden Palace
1a Camden High St NW1.
Map 4 F2.
Tel 0906-210 0200.

The Garage
20–22 Highbury Corner,
N5.
Tel 0870-150 0044.

Mean Fiddler
157 Charing Cross Rd
WC2. **Map** 13 B2.
Tel 0870-150 0044.

Rock Garden
6–7 The Piazza, Covent
Garden WC2.
Map 13 C2.
Tel 020-7836 4052.
www.rockgarden.uk

Shepherd's Bush Empire
Shepherd's Bush Green
W12.
Tel 0870-771 2000.

Union Chapel
The Vestry, Compton
Ave N1.
Tel 0870-120 1349.

Woody's
41–43 Woodfield Rd
W9.
Tel 020-7266 3030.

JAZZ VENUES

100 Club
100 Oxford St W1.
Map 13 A1.
Tel 020-7636 0933.

Barbican Hall
See p165.

Dover Street Wine Bar
8–10 Dover St W1.
Map 12 F3.
Tel 020-7629 9813.

Jazz Café
5 Parkway NW1.
Map 4 E1.
Tel 020-7916 6060.

Pizza Express
10 Dean St W1.
Map 13 A1.
Tel 020 7437 9595.

Pizza on the Park
11 Knightsbridge SW1.
Map 12 D5.
Tel 020-7235 5550.

Ronnie Scott's
47 Frith St W1.
Map 13 A2.
Tel 020-7439 0747.
www.ronniescotts.co.uk

Royal Festival Hall
See p348.

Vortex Jazz Club
Dalston Culture House
Gillett St, N16.
Map 8 1D.
Tel 020-7254 6516.

WORLD MUSIC

Africa Centre
38 King St WC2.
Map 13 C2.
Tel 020-7836 1973.

Barbican Centre
See p349.

Cecil Sharp House
2 Regent's Park Rd NW1.
Map 4 D1.
Tel 020-7485 2206.

Cuba Libre
72 Upper St N1.
Map 6 F1.
Tel 020-7354 9998.

ICA *See p350.*

Notting Hill Arts Club
21 Notting Hill Gate W11.
Map 9 C3.
Tel 020-7460 4459.

Queen Elizabeth Hall
South Bank Centre SE1.
Map 14 D4.
Tel 0870-380 0400.

Royal Festival Hall
See p348.

Spitz
109 Commercial St E2.
Tel 020-7392 9032.

CLUBS

Annabel's
44 Berkeley Sq W1.
Map 12 E3.
Tel 020-7629 1096.

Bar Rumba
36 Shaftesbury Ave
WC2.
Map 6 E2.
Tel 020-7287 2715.

Café de Paris
3 Coventry St W1.
Map 13 A3.
Tel 020-7734 7700.

Cargo
83 Rivington St EC2.
Map 7 C3.
Tel 020-7739 3440.

The End
16a West Central St WC1.
Map 13 B2.
Tel 020-7419 9199.

Equinox
Leicester Sq WC2.
Map 13 B2.
Tel 020-7437 1446.

Fabric
77a Charterhouse St EC1.
Map 6 F5.
Tel 020-7336 8898.

Fridge
Town Hall Parade,
Brixton Hill SW2.
Tel 020-7326 5100.

Gardening Club
4 The Piazza, Covent Gdn
WC2. **Map** 13 C2.
Tel 020-7497 3154.

Heaven
Under the Arches,
Villiers St WC2.
Map 13 C3.
Tel 020-7930 2020.

Hippodrome
Cranbourn St WC2.
Map 13 B2.
Tel 020-7437 4311.

Madame Jojo
8–10 Brewer St W1.
Map 13 A2.
Tel 020-7734 3040.

Ministry of Sound
103 Gaunt St SE1.
Tel 020-7378 6528.

Soho Lounge
69 Dean St W1.
Map 13 A2.
Tel 020-7434 4480.

Stringfellows
16 Upper St Martin's Lane
WC2.
Map 13 B2.
Tel 020-7240 5534.
www.stringfellows.uk

Tattershall Castle
Victoria Embankment,
SW1.
Map 13 C3.
Tel 020-7839 6548.

Turnmills
63 Clerkenwell Rd EC1.
Map 6 E5.
Tel 020-7250 3409.

Sport

The range of sports on offer in London is quite phenomenal. Should you feel the urge to watch a game of medieval tennis or go scuba-diving in the city centre, you've come to the right place. More likely, you'll just want to watch a football or rugby match, or play a set of tennis in a park. With far more public facilities than most European capitals, London is the place to enjoy cheap, accessible sport. What the city lacks, however, is a national stadium. The new Wembley Stadium is being built, and should be completed by the middle of 2007. The project is intended to be a design and engineering masterpiece, with perfect views for all events.

ATHLETICS

Athletes will find a good choice of running tracks, often with free admission. **West London Stadium** has good facilities; **Regent's Park** is free; try also **Parliament Hill Fields**. For a sociable jog, meet the Bow Street Runners at **Jubilee Hall** on Tuesdays at 6pm.

CRICKET

Five-day test matches and one-day internationals are played in summer at **Lord's** (see p246) and the Oval, near Vauxhall. Tickets for the first four days of tests and for one-day games are hard to get, but you may get in on the last day and see a thrilling finish. When Middlesex and Surrey play county games at these grounds there are always seats.

FOOTBALL (SOCCER)

This is the most popular spectator sport in Britain, its season running from August to May, with matches on weekends and weekday evenings. It is the most common topic of conversation in pubs, where games are often shown live on TV. Premier League and FA Cup games are frequently sold out in advance. London's top clubs include **Arsenal, Chelsea, West Ham** and **Tottenham Hotspur**.

GOLF

There are no golf courses in central London, but a few are scattered around the outskirts. The most accessible public courses are **Hounslow Heath, Chessington** (nine holes, train from Waterloo) and **Richmond Park** (two courses, computerized indoor teaching room). If you didn't pack your clubs, sets can be hired at a reasonable price.

GREYHOUND RACING

At a night "down the dogs", you can follow the races on a screen in the bar, stand by the track or watch from the comfort of the restaurant (book in advance) at **Walthamstow Stadium or Wimbledon Stadium**.

HORSE RACING

High class flat racing in summer and steeplechasing in winter can be seen at **Ascot, Kempton Park** and **Sandown Park**, which are all less than an hour from central London by train. Britain's most famous flat race, the Derby, is run at **Epsom** in June.

HORSE-RIDING

For centuries, fashionable riders have exercised their steeds in Hyde Park; **Ross Nye** will provide you with a horse so that you can follow a long tradition.

ICE-SKATING

Ice-skaters should head for London's best-known rink, **Queens**. The most attractive ice rinks, open only in winter, are in the **Broadgate** complex in the City, and at **Somerset House** (see p117).

RUGBY FOOTBALL

Rugby union, or rugger, is a 15-a-side game, once played only by amateurs, but now a professional sport. International matches are played at **Twickenham Rugby Football Ground**. The season runs from September to April and you can watch "friendly" weekend games at local grounds. Top London teams **Saracens** and **Rosslyn Park** can be seen at their own grounds outside the centre of town.

SQUASH

Squash courts tend to be busy, so try to book at least two days ahead. Many sports centres have squash facilities and will hire out equipment, including **Swiss Cottage Sports Centre** and the **Oasis Sports Centre**.

SWIMMING

Best indoor pools include **Chelsea Sports Centre**, the **Oasis** and **Porchester Baths**; for outdoor, try **Highgate** (separate ponds for men and women), **Hampstead** and the **Oasis**.

TENNIS

There are hundreds of tennis courts in London's public parks, most of them cheap to hire and easily reserved. It can be busy in the summer, so book your court two or three days ahead. You must supply your own racquet and balls. Good public tennis courts include **Holland Park** and **Parliament Hill**.

Tickets for the Centre Court of the **All England Lawn Tennis Club** at Wimbledon are hard to obtain – it is possibly easier to enter the tournament as a player than to obtain tickets for Centre Court; try queueing overnight, or queue for return tickets after lunch on the day – for a bargain price, you can still enjoy a good four hours of tennis (see p57).

TRADITIONAL SPORTS

An old London tradition is the University Boat Race, held in March or April, when teams from Oxford and Cambridge row from Putney to Mortlake *(see p56)*; a newer tradition is the London Marathon, which is run from Greenwich to The Mall at Westminster *(see p56)* on an April Sunday. You can watch croquet at the **Hurlingham Club** and medieval (real) tennis at **Queen's Club**.

WATER SPORTS

There are facilities for a wide variety of water sports at the **Docklands Sailing and Water Sports Centre**. You can choose from sports such as windsurfing, dinghy sailing, powerboating, waterskiing and canoeing. Rowing boats are also available for hire by the hour on the calmer, central London waters of the **Serpentine** in Hyde Park and **Regent's Park Lake**.

WORKING OUT

Most sports centres have gymnasiums, work-out studios and health clubs. If you are a member of the YMCA, you'll be able to use the excellent facilities at the **Central YMCA. Jubilee Hall Clubs** and the **Oasis Sports Centre** both offer a variety of aerobic classes, keep-fit and weight training. For those who have overdone it, the **Chelsea Sports Centre** has a sports injury clinic.

DIRECTORY

Sport England
Tel 020-7273 1500. For info on London facilities: www.sportengland.org

All England Lawn Tennis and Croquet Club
Church Rd, Wimbledon SW19. *Tel* 020-8946 2244.

Arsenal Stadium
Avenell Rd, Highbury N5. *Tel* 020-7704 4000.

Ascot Racecourse
Ascot, Berkshire. *Tel* 01344 622211.

Broadgate Ice Rink
Broadgate Circle EC2. **Map** 7 C5. *Tel* 020-7505 4068.

Central YMCA
112 Great Russell St WC1. **Map** 13 B1. *Tel* 020-7343 1844.

Chelsea Football Club
Stamford Bridge SW6. *Tel* 0870-300 1212.

Chelsea Sports Centre
Chelsea Manor St SW3. **Map** 19 B3. *Tel* 020-7352 6985.

Chessington Golf Course
Garrison Lane, Surrey. *Tel* 020-8391 0948.

Docklands Sailing and Watersports Centre
235a Westferry Rd, E14. *Tel* 020-7537 2626. www.dswc.org

Epsom Racecourse
Epsom Downs, Surrey. *Tel* 01372 726311.

Hampstead Ponds
off East Heath Rd NW3. **Map** 1 C4. *Tel* 020-7482 7073.

Highgate Ponds
Millfield Lane N6. **Map** 2 E3. *Tel* 020-7482 7073.

Holland Park Public Tennis Courts
1 Ilchester Place W8. **Map** 9 B5. *Tel* 020-7602 2226.

Hounslow Heath Golf Course
Staines Rd, Hounslow, Middlesex. *Tel* 020-8570 5271.

Hurlingham Club
Ranelagh Gdns SW6. *Tel* 020-7736 8411.

Jubilee Hall Clubs
30 The Piazza, Covent Garden WC2. **Map** 13 C2. *Tel* 020-7836 4835.

Kempton Park
Sunbury on Thames, Middx. *Tel* 01932 782292.

Linford Christie Stadium
Du Cane Rd W12. *Tel* 020-8740 7379.

Lord's Cricket Ground
St John's Wood NW8. **Map** 3 A3. *Tel* 020-7289 1611.

Oasis Swimming Pool & Sports Centre
32 Endell St WC2. **Map** 13 B1. *Tel* 020-7831 1804.

Oval Cricket Ground
Kennington Oval SE11. **Map** 22 D4. *Tel* 020-7582 6660.

Parliament Hill
Highgate Rd NW5. **Map** 2 E5. *Tel* 020-7485 4491.

Porchester Centre
Queensway W2. **Map** 10 D1. *Tel* 020-7792 2919.

Queen's Club (Real Tennis)
Palliser Rd W14. **Map** 17 A3. *Tel* 020-7385 3421.

Queens Ice Skating Club
17 Queensway W2. **Map** 10 E2. *Tel* 020-7229 0172.

Regent's Park and Lake
Regent's Park NW1. **Map** 3 C3. *Tel* 020-7486 7905. *Tel* 020-7724 4069 (boat hire).

Richmond Park Golf
Roehampton Gate, Priory Lane SW15. *Tel* 020-8876 3205.

Rosslyn Park Rugby
Priory Lane, Upper Richmond Rd SW15. *Tel* 020-8876 1879.

Ross Nye Stables
8 Bathurst Mews W2. **Map** 11 A2. *Tel* 020-7262 3791.

Sandown Park Racecourse
Esher, Surrey. *Tel* 01372 463072.

Saracens Rugby Football Club
5 Vicarage Rd, Watford, Hertfordshire, WD1. *Tel* 01923 475222.

Serpentine
Hyde Park W2. **Map** 11 B4. *Tel* 020-7298 2100 *(boat hire).*

Somerset House Ice Rink
Strand WC2. **Map** 14 D2. *Tel* 020-7845 4600.

Tottenham Hotspur FC
White Hart Lane, 748 High Rd N17. *Tel* 020-8365 5050.

Twickenham Rugby Ground
Whitton Rd, Twickenham, Middlesex. *Tel* 020-8892 2000.

Walthamstow Stadium
Chingford Rd E4. *Tel* 020-8498 3300.

West Ham United
Boleyn Ground, Green St, Upton Park E13. *Tel* 0870-112 2700.

CHILDREN'S LONDON

London offers children a potential goldmine of fun, excitement and adventure. Each year finds new attractions and sights opening up and older ones being updated.

First-time visitors may want to watch traditional ceremonies (see pp52–5) or visit famous buildings (see p37), but these are merely the tip of the iceberg. While London's parks, zoos and

Humpty Dumpty doll

adventure playgrounds provide outdoor activities there are also loads of workshops, activity centres and museums providing quizzes, hands-on experiments and interactive displays. A day out need not be costly: children are entitled to reduced fares on London Transport and lower admission prices at museums. Some of London's star attractions, for instance all the ceremonies, are free.

PRACTICAL ADVICE

A little planning is the key to a successful outing. You may want to check the opening hours of the places you plan to visit in advance, by telephone. Work out your journey thoroughly using the tube map at the end of this book. If you are travelling with very young children remember that there will be queues at the Underground stations or bus stops near popular sights. These will be long during peak hours, so buy your tickets or a Travelcard in advance (see p378).

Children under 5 can travel free on buses and tubes and child fares operate for all children between the ages of 5 and 15. (Children of 14 and 15, and those who look older than they are, need to have a Photocard.) Children very often enjoy using public transport, especially when it's

Punch and Judy show in the Piazza, Covent Garden

a novelty, so plan your outing carefully using one form of transport for the outward journey and another for the journey home. You can get around London easily by bus, Underground, taxi, train and riverboat (see pp378–85). Visiting all the exhibitions and museums as a family doesn't have to be

Covent Garden clowns

as expensive as it sounds. An annual family season ticket, usually for two adults and up to four children, is available at many of the museums and often costs only marginally more than the initial visit. In some cases you can buy a family ticket that covers a group of museums; for instance the Science, Natural History and Victoria and Albert Museums in South Kensington (see pp198–213). Being able to visit a sight more than once means that you won't exhaust your children and put them off museums for life by trying to see absolutely everything over one long, tiring day.

If your children want a break from sightseeing, most borough councils provide information on activities for children such as playgroups, theatres, fun-fairs and activity centres in their area. Leaflets are usually available from libraries and leisure centres, as well as local town halls. During the long summer school holidays (July to the beginning of September) there are organized activity programmes all over London.

CHILDREN AND THE LAW

Children under 14 are not allowed into British pubs and wine bars (unless there is a special family room or garden) and only people over 18 can drink or buy any alcohol. In restaurants, the law is a little more relaxed. Those over 16 can drink wine or beer with their meal, but you

EATING OUT WITH CHILDREN

The restaurant listings *(see pp296–311)* have symbols to indicate which establishments welcome children (see back cover flap for key to symbols). But as long as your offspring are reasonably well-behaved, most of London's more informal and ethnic restaurants will be happy to serve a family. Some can also provide highchairs and booster cushions, as well as colouring mats to keep children quiet while waiting for their food to arrive. Many will also offer special children's menus with small helpings which, although fairly unadventurous, will cut the cost of your meal.

Over the weekend some restaurants (such as **Smollensky's On The Strand** and **Sticky Fingers**) provide live entertainment for children in the form of clowns, face painters and magicians. A number accept bookings for children's parties. It is always worth trying to book in advance (especially for Sunday lunch), so that you don't have to hang around waiting with tired and hungry children.

Coming up for air at Smollensky's On The Strand

London has a number of restaurants ideal for older children. Among these are the **Rainforest Café** and the **Hard Rock Café** on Old Park Lane.

For budget eating, try the Café in the Crypt, St Martin-in-the-Fields *(see p102)*.

Dine with the elephants at the Rainforest Cafe

USEFUL ADDRESSES

Hard Rock Café
150 Old Park Lane W1. **Map** 12 E4.
Tel 020-7629 0382.

Rainforest Café
20 Shaftesbury Ave W1. **Map** 13 A2.
Tel 020-7434 3111.

Smollensky's On The Strand
105 Strand WC2.
Map 14 D2. *Tel 020-7497 2101.*

Sticky Fingers
1a Phillimore Gdns, W8. **Map** 9 C5.
Tel 020-7938 5338.

still have to be over 18 to be served spirits. In general, young children are rarely welcome anywhere they might create a nuisance. Some films are classed as unsuitable for children *(see p347)*.

If you want to take your children by car, you must use seat belts wherever they are provided. Babies will need a special child seat. If you are in doubt, ask at any police station.

GETTING THEM OFF YOUR HANDS

Many of London's great museums *(see pp40–43)* and theatres *(see pp344–6)* provide weekend and holiday activities and workshops where you can leave children over a certain age for a few hours or even for a whole day, and the children's theatres are a great way to spend a rainy afternoon. A day at the fair is always a success – try Hampstead fair on summer bank holidays.

London has a great many sports centres *(see pp354–5)*, which usually open daily and often have special clubs and activities to occupy children of every age.

If you want a total break, contact **Childminders**, **Annies Nannies**, **Kensington Nannies**, or **Pippa Pop-Ins**, a nursery school offering full-day childcare.

CHILDMINDING

Annies Nannies
19 Webbs Rd, SW11.
Tel 0870-013 2944.

Childminders
9 Nottingham St W1. **Map** 4 D5. *Tel 020-7487 5040.* www.babysitter.co.uk

Kensington Nannies
3 Hornton Place, W8.
Map 10 D5. *Tel 020-7937 2333.*
www.kensington-nannies.com

Pippa Pop-Ins
430 Fulham Road SW6 **Map** 18 D5.
Tel 020-7385 2458.
Also at 165 New King's Rd SW6.

Airborne at the Hampstead fair

Holiday fun at Pippa Pop-Ins

SHOPPING

All children love a visit to **Hamleys** toy shop or Harrods toy department *(see p321)*. **Davenport's Magic Shop** and **The Disney Store** are smaller and more specialized.

Both the **Early Learning Centre** (many branches) and the **Children's Book Centre** have good selections of books. Some shops organize readings and signings by children's authors, especially during Children's Book Week, held in October.

USEFUL NUMBERS Children's Book Centre *Tel* 020-7937 7497; Davenport's Magic Shop *Tel* 020-7836 0408; The Disney Store *Tel* 020-7491 9136; Early Learning Centre *Tel* 020-7581 5764; Hamleys *Tel* 0870-333 2455.

Bears at Hamleys toy shop

MUSEUMS AND GALLERIES

London has a wealth of museums, exhibitions and galleries; more information on those listed here is to be found on pages 40–43. Most have been updated over the last few years to incorporate some exciting modern display techniques. It's unlikely that you'll have to drag reluctant children around an assortment of lifeless, stuffy exhibits.

The Bethnal Green Museum of Childhood *(p248)*, the children's branch of the V&A in East London, and Pollock's Toy Museum *(p131)* are both especially good for young children.

For older children try one of London's Brass Rubbing Centres: the great Brass Rubbing Centre in the Crypt of St Martin-in-the-Fields *(p102)* or at St James's Church on Piccadilly *(p90)*. Madame Tussauds *(p224)* and Tower Bridge *(p153)* are firm favourites with children.

The British Museum *(pp126–9)* has fabulous treasures from all over the world, and the Horniman Museum *(p250)* has colourful displays from many different cultures. The Science Museum *(pp212–13)*, with over 600 working exhibits, is one of London's best attractions for children – its hands-on galleries in the basement, including the much-loved Launch Pad, will help keep them amused for hours. The interactive displays in the high-tech Wellcome Wing are also entertaining. If you have the stamina, the Natural History Museum *(pp208–9)* next door contains hundreds of amazing objects and animals from the world of nature. Included is a Dinosaur Exhibition. Suits of armour built for knights and monarchs can be seen at the

Shirley Temple doll at Bethnal Green Museum

Tower of London *(pp154–7)*. More up-to-date armoury and weapons, including aircraft and the tools of modern warfare, can be seen at the National Army Museum *(p197)* and the Imperial War Museum *(pp190–91)*. Also worth a visit is the Guards' Museum *(p80)* located on Birdcage Walk. London's colourful past is brought alive at the Museum of London. The superb London Aquarium *(p188)*, on the bank of the Thames, offers close-up encounters with sea life from starfish to sharks.

THE GREAT OUTDOORS

London is fortunate in having many parks and open spaces *(see pp48–51)*. Most local parks contain conventional playgrounds for children, many with modern, safe equipment. Some parks also have One O'Clock Clubs (enclosed areas for children under 5 with activities supervised by play-workers) as well as adventure playgrounds, nature trails, boating ponds and athletic tracks for older children and energetic adults.

Puppets at the Little Angel Theatre, Islington

Playground at Gunnersbury Park

A delightful children's park in Bloomsbury is Coram's Fields (p125), where grassy areas, sand-pits and playgrounds make it perfect for picnics. Kite-flying on Blackheath (p243), Hampstead Heath or Parliament Hill can be fun, as can boating in Regent's Park. A trip to Primrose Hill (pp266–7) can be combined with a visit to the Zoo and Regent's Canal (p227). The large parks are one of London's greatest assets for parents who have energetic children. For a good walk or cycle ride, there are parks all over London. For instance, there's Hyde Park in the city centre; Hampstead Heath up in the north; Wimbledon Common in southwest London; and Gunnersbury Park in west London. Cyclists should be sure to watch out for pedestrians and remember that some paths may be out of bounds.

Battersea Park has a children's zoo and Crystal Palace Park (Penge SE20) has a children's farm and a dinosaur park. Richmond Park has a deer herd. For a relaxing trip, go and feed the ducks in St James's Park.

Tuojiangasaurus
skeleton at
the Natural
History
Museum

CHILDREN'S THEATRE

Introducing children to the theatre can be great fun for adults too. Get involved at the **Little Angel Theatre,** or the **Puppet Theatre Barge** in Little Venice. The **Unicorn Theatre** offers the best range of children's theatre and the **Polka Children's Theatre** has some good shows.
USEFUL NUMBERS Little Angel Theatre **Tel** 020-7359 8581. Polka Children's Theatre **Tel** 020-8543 4888. **www.**polkatheatre.com Puppet Theatre Barge Marionette Performers **Tel** 020-7249 6876. Unicorn Theatre **Tel** 0870-534534 or **www.**unicorntheatre.com

Deer in Richmond Park

SIGHTSEEING

For seeing the sights of London you can't beat the top of a double-decker bus (see pp382–3). It's a cheap and easy way of entertaining children, and if they get restless you can always jump off the bus at the next stop. London's colourful ceremonies are detailed on pages 52–5. Children will also enjoy such spectacles as the summer fun-fairs in London's parks, the firework displays throughout London on

Boating lake near Winfield House in Regent's Park

Guy Fawkes Night (every 5 November) and the Christmas decorations in Oxford Street and Regent Street and Trafalgar Square's Christmas tree.

BEHIND THE SCENES

Older children in particular will love the opportunity to look "behind the scenes" and see how famous events or institutions are run.

If you have a brood of sports enthusiasts, you should visit Twickenham Rugby Football Ground (see p355), Lord's Cricket Ground (p246), the Wimbledon Lawn Tennis Museum (p251), and Chelsea Football Stadium (p339).

For budding theatre buffs, the Royal National Theatre (p188), the Royal Opera House (p115), Sadler's Wells (p334), and the Theatre Royal Drury Lane (p115) all offer tours.

Other good buildings for children to visit include the Tower of London (pp154–7), the Old Bailey law courts (p147) and the Houses of Parliament (pp72–3).

If none of the above satisfies the children, the London Fire Brigade (020-7587 4063) offers more unusual guided tours.

SURVIVAL
GUIDE

PRACTICAL INFORMATION 362–71
GETTING TO LONDON 372–7
GETTING AROUND LONDON 378–85

PRACTICAL INFORMATION

London has responded well to the demands of tourism. The range of facilities on offer to travellers, from cashpoint machines and bureaux de change to medical care and late-night transport, has expanded very quickly over the last few years. Whether or not you find London an expensive city will depend on the prevailing exchange rate between the pound and your own cur-

rency. It is known for its high hotel prices but even here there are budget options *(see pp278–81)*. Nor need you spend a lot on food if you choose carefully: for the price of a single meal at some Mayfair restaurants you could feed yourself, albeit modestly, for several days *(see pp312–15)*. The following tips will help you to make the most of your visit.

A walking tour of the City

AVOIDING THE CROWDS

Museums and galleries can be crowded with school parties, particularly at the end of terms, so it might be best to plan your visit to start after 2.30pm during term-time. At other times of the year, visit early in the day and try and avoid weekends if you can.

Coach parties are another source of congestion. They do, however, tend to follow a predictable path. To miss them, it is wise to steer well clear of Westminster Abbey in the

morning, and St Paul's around the afternoon. The Tower of London is usually busy all day.

A lot of London can be seen on foot. Brown signs indicate sights and facilities of interest to tourists. Look out, too, for the blue plaques attached to many buildings *(see p39)* showing where famous citizens have lived in the past.

GUIDED TOURS

A good way to enjoy London, weather permitting, is from the top of a traditional open-topped double-decker bus. The **Original Tour** and the **Big Bus** companies offer a 24-hour ticket that includes a hop-on-hop-off service and a river cruise. Tours leave from various central locations. Commercial rivals, such as **Back Roads Touring**, offer tours lasting anything from an hour to a full day. You can buy tickets just before boarding, or in advance at Tourist Information Centres. Private tours can also be arranged with many companies, such as **Tour Guides Ltd** or **British Tours**. The best tour guides receive a Blue Badge qualification from the London Tourist Board.

You can also explore London by joining a walking tour *(see p263)*. Check for details at tourist offices or in listings magazines *(see p342)*.

Cruises operate on the river *(pp60–65)*. **London Duck Tours** travel on land and water in amphibious craft from World War II, a great way of seeing London.

USEFUL NUMBERS
British Tours **Tel** 020-7734 8734; **www**.britishtours.com
Back Roads Touring **Tel** 020-8566 5312; The Original Tour **Tel** 020-8877 1722; Tour Guides Ltd **Tel** 020-7495 5504; Big Bus Co. **Tel** 020-7233 9533; London Duck Tours **Tel** 020-7928 3132; **www**.londonducktours.co.uk

OPENING HOURS

Opening times for sights have been listed in the *Area by Area* section of this book. Core visiting times in London are 10am to 5pm daily, though many places stay open longer, especially in summer. Some major sights, like the British Museum, also stay open late on certain evenings. There are variations at weekends and public holidays. Opening times on Sundays are often restricted and a few museums close on Mondays.

Double-decker sightseeing bus with an open top

Queueing for a bus

ADMISSION CHARGES

Many major sights, including London's cathedrals and some churches, either charge for admission or ask for a voluntary contribution upon entry. Charges vary greatly. The *Area by Area* listings tell you which museums charge for admission. Some sights have reduced-price visiting times and offer concessions. Telephone if you think you might be eligible.

The GoSee Card is a saver pass to 17 of London's major museums and galleries. Valid for either three or seven days, it is available from a wide range of tourist and travel centres.

Signposted information

ETIQUETTE

Smoking is now forbidden in many of London's public places. These include the bus and Underground transport systems, taxis, some railway stations, all theatres and most cinemas. Many London restaurants now have no-smoking sections. The great exception to the anti-smoking trend is pubs. ASH (Action on Smoking and Health) can give advice on smoke-free venues (020-7739 5902, www.ash.org.uk). Consult the Hotels and Restaurants listings *(pp282– 91 and pp300– 11)* for details of places that cater for non-smokers.

Londoners queue for anything from shops, buses and post offices to theatre tickets,

takeaway food and taxis. Anyone barging in will encounter frosty glares and acid comments. The exceptions are commuter rail and rush-hour tube services, when the laws of the jungle prevail.

The words "please", "thank you" and "sorry" are used regularly in London; people sometimes apologize if you step on their feet. It may seem unnecessary to thank a barman for simply doing his job, but it should improve your chances of decent service.

Like any big city, London can seem alienating to newcomers, but Londoners are usually helpful, and most will respond generously to your request for directions. The stalwart British bobby (police constable on the beat) is also always patiently ready to help stranded tourists *(see p364)*.

DISABLED VISITORS

Many sights have access for wheelchairs. Again, this information is listed in the *Area by Area* section of this book, but phone first to check that your needs are catered for. Useful guides to buy include *Access in London*, published by Nicholson, *London for All*, published by the London Tourist Board, and a booklet called *Access to the Underground*, available at main tube stations. **Artsline** gives free information on facilities at cultural events and venues. **Holiday Care Service** offers many facts on hotel facilities. **Tripscope** has free information on transport for the elderly and the disabled. **USEFUL NUMBERS** Artsline *Tel 020-7388 2227;* **www**.artslineonline. com; Holiday Care Service *Tel 0845-124 9974,* **www**.holidaycare.org.uk; Tripscope *Tel 0845-758 5641;* **www**.tripscope.org.uk

Box for voluntary contributions in lieu of admission charges

TOURIST INFORMATION CENTRES

These offer advice on anything from day trips and guided tours to accommodation.

Tourist information symbol

If you need tourist information, look for the large blue symbol at the following locations:

Britain and London Visitor Centre
1 Regent St, Piccadilly Circus SW1. **Map** 13 A3. ⊖ *Piccadilly Circus.* **Open** *Mon 9.30am–6.30pm, Tue–Fri 9am–6.30pm, Sat & Sun 10am–4pm (Jun–Oct: Sat 9am–5pm). Personal callers only.*

City of London Tourist Information Centre
For information about the City of London area only (see pp143–59). St Paul's Churchyard EC4. **Map** 15 A1. *Tel 020-7332 1456.* ⊖ *St Paul's.* **Open** *Faster– Sep: 9.30am–5pm daily; Oct–Mar: 9.30am–12.30pm Sat only.*

Greenwich Tourist Information Centre
Pepys House, 2 Cutty Sark Gardens, Greenwich SE10 (next to Cutty Sark ship) ⊖ *Cutty Sark DLR.* ⊉ *Greenwich.* **Map** 23 B2. **Open** *10am–5pm daily. Tel 0870-608 2000. Fax 020-8853 4607.*

London Information Centre
Leicester Sq W1. **Map** 13 B2. ⊖ *Leicester Sq.* **Open** *8am–11pm daily. Tel 020-7292 2333. Free maps & hotel booking service.*

Southwark Tourist Information Centre
Vinopolis, 1 Bank End, SE1. **Map** 15 B3. ⊖ *London Bridge.* **Open** *10am–6pm Tue–Sun.*

You can also contact Visit London: *Tel 020-7234 5800.* **www**.visitlondon.com

Personal Security and Health

London is a large city which, like any other, has had its recent share of urban problems. It has also often been a terrorist target, and London life is sometimes disrupted by security alerts. Nearly all of these turn out to be false alarms, but they should always still be taken seriously. Never hesitate to approach one of London's many police constables for assistance – they are trained to help the public with any of their problems.

SUITABLE PRECAUTIONS

There is little likelihood that your stay in London will be blighted at all by the spectre of violent crime. Even in the run-down and rougher parts of the town, the risk of having your pocket picked, or your bag stolen, is not very great. It is far more likely to happen right in the middle of heaving shopping crowds in areas like Oxford Street or Camden Lock, or perhaps on a very busy tube platform.

Muggers and rapists prefer poorly lit or isolated places like back-streets, parks and unmanned railway stations. If you avoid these, especially at night, or travel round in a group, you should manage to stay out of danger.

Pickpockets and thieves pose a much more immediate problem. Keep your valuables securely concealed. If you carry a handbag or a case, never let it out of your sight – particularly in restaurants, theatres and cinemas, where it is not unknown for bags to vanish from between the feet of their owners.

Although London has a small population of homeless people, they do not present a threat. The very worst they are likely to trouble you with is a request for spare change.

WOMEN TRAVELLING ALONE

Unlike some European cities, it is considered quite normal in London for women to eat out on their own or go out in a group, perhaps to a pub or a bar. However, risks do exist, and caution is essential. Stick to well-lit streets with plenty of traffic. Many women avoid travelling on the tube late at night, and it is

Mounted police

best not to travel alone on trains. If you have no companions, try to find an occupied carriage – preferably with more than one group of people. Best of all, take a licensed taxi *(see p385)*.

Many forms of self-defence are restricted in the UK, and it is illegal for anyone to carry various offensive weapons in public places. These include knives, coshes, guns and tear-gas canisters, all of which are strictly prohibited. Personal alarm systems are permitted.

PERSONAL PROPERTY

Take sensible precautions with personal property at all times. Make sure that your possessions are adequately insured before you arrive, since it is difficult for visitors to arrange once in the UK.

Do not carry your valuables around with you; take just as much cash as you need, and leave the rest in a hotel safe or lock it up in your suitcase. Traveller's cheques are the safest method of carrying large amounts of money *(see p367)*. Never leave bags or briefcases unattended in tube or train stations – they will either be stolen or suspected of being bombs and therefore cause a security alert.

Report all lost items to the nearest police station (get the necessary paperwork if you plan an insurance claim). Each of the main rail stations has a lost property office on the premises. If you do leave something on a bus or tube, it may be better to call in at the address given below rather than to telephone.

Lost Property

Lost Property Offices
Transport For London Lost Property Office, 200 Baker Street NW1.
Open weekdays 8.30am–4pm.
Tel 020-7918 2000.
020-7486 2496.
www.tfl.gov.uk/lpo

Woman Police Constable   **Traffic Police Officer**   **Police Constable**

Typical London police car

London ambulance

London fire engine

EMERGENCIES

London's emergency police, ambulance and fire services are on call 24 hours a day. These, like the London hospital casualty services, are strictly for emergencies only.

Services are also available to offer help in emergencies, for instance in case of rape. If there is no appropriate number in the Crisis Information box *(see right)* you may be able to obtain one from the British Telecom directory enquiries service (dial 118 500). Police stations and also hospitals with casualty wards are shown on the Street Finder maps *(see pp386–7)*.

MEDICAL TREATMENT

Visitors to London from all countries outside the European Union (EU) are strongly advised to take out medical insurance. Any good insurance policy should cover against the cost of any emergency hospital care, specialists' fees and repatriation to your home country. Emergency treatment in a British casualty ward in a public hospital is free, but any additional medical care may be costly.

Residents of the EU and nationals of other European and Commonwealth countries are entitled to receive free medical treatment under the National Health Service (NHS). Before travelling, you should obtain a form confirming that your country of origin has adequate reciprocal health arrangements with Britain. However, even without this form, free medical treatment can still be obtained if you offer proof of your nationality, but there are exceptions for certain kinds of treatment which is why taking out medical insurance is always advisable.

If you need to see a dentist while staying in London, you will have to pay at least a small amount as dentist care is not normally free. This will vary, depending on your entitlement to NHS treatment, and whether you can find an NHS dentist. Various institutions offer emergency dental treatment *(see addresses right)*, but if you wish to visit a private dental surgeon, you should try looking in the Yellow Pages *(see p368)* or seek advice from your hotel.

MEDICINES

You can buy most medical supplies from chemists and supermarkets throughout London. However, many medicines are available only with a doctor's prescription. If you are likely to require drugs, you should either bring your own supplies or get your doctor to write out the generic name of the drug, as opposed to the brand name. If you are not eligible to receive NHS treatment, you will be charged at the medicine's cost price; remember to get a receipt to support any medical insurance claim you may wish to make after your trip.

Boots, a chain of chemists' shops

CRISIS INFORMATION

Police, fire & ambulance services
Tel Dial 999 or 112. Calls are free.

Emergency Dental Care
Tel 020-7837 3646. Children only.

Samaritans
Tel 08457-909090 (24-hr help-line). For all emotional problems.

Women's Counselling Service *Tel 0845-123 2324.*

Chelsea & Westminster Hospital
369 Fulham Rd SW10. **Map** 18 F4. *Tel 020-8746 8999.
Tel 020-8746 8013 (24 hrs) for Accident & Emergency*

St Thomas' Hospital
Lambeth Palace Rd SE1.
Map 13 C5. *Tel 020-7188 7188.*

University College Hospital
Outpatients, Accident & Emergency, 235 Euston Road NW1.
Map 5 A4. *Tel 0845-155 5000.*

Medical Express (Private Casualty Clinic)
117A Harley St W1. **Map** 4 E5.
Tel 020-7486 0516. Open 9am–6pm Mon–Fri, 9.30am–2.30pm Sat. Treatment within 30 mins, but fee for consultations and tests.

NHS Direct
Tel 0845-4647 (24-hr health information and nurse-led advice).

Eastman Dental School
256 Gray's Inn Rd WC1.
Map 6 D4. *Tel 020-7915 1000. Private and NHS dental care.*

Guy's Hospital Dental School
St Thomas's St SE1. Map 15 B4.
Tel 020-7188 7188. Daytime only.

King's College Hospital
Denmark Hill SE5. *Tel 020-7737 4000. Dental emergencies 6–11pm.*

Late-opening chemists
Contact your local London police station for a comprehensive list.

Bliss Chemist
5–6 Marble Arch W1. Map 11 C2.
*Tel 020-7723 6116.
Open until midnight daily.*

Boots the Chemist
Piccadilly Circus W1. **Map** 13 A3.
*Tel 020-7734 6126.
Open 9am–midnight Mon–Sat, noon–6pm Sun.*

Banking and Local Currency

Visitors to London will find that banks usually offer them the best rates of exchange. Privately owned bureaux de change have variable exchange rates, and care should be taken to check the small print details relating to commission and minimum charges before completing any transaction. Bureaux de change do, however, have the advantage of staying open long after the banks have closed.

Cashpoint machine

BANKING

Banking hours vary in London. The minimum opening hours are, without exception, 9.30am–3.30pm Mon–Fri, but many stay open longer than this, especially those in the centre of London. Saturday morning opening is also more common now. All banks are closed on public holidays (known as bank holidays in the UK, *see p59*), and some may close early on the day before a holiday.

Many major banks in London have cashpoint machines that will allow you to obtain money by using your credit card and a PIN (personal identification number); some machines have clear computerized instructions in several languages. American Express cards may be used at all ATM cash machines in London, but you must arrange to have your PIN linked by code to your personal account before you leave home. There is a 2% charge for each transaction.

Besides the main clearing banks, good places to change your traveller's cheques are **Travelex** and **American Express** offices, or the bank-operated bureaux de change, which can usually be found at airports and major railway stations. Don't forget to bring along a passport if you want to change cheques.

see p59

BUREAUX DE CHANGE

American Express
30 Haymarket SW1. **Map** 13 A3.
Tel 020-7484 9610.
www.americanexpress.com

Chequepoint
548 Oxford St W1.
Map 13 A1. *Tel* 020-7723 1005.

Exchange International
Victoria Station SW1.
Map 20 E1. *Tel* 020-7630 1107.

Travelex
65 Kingsway
WC2. **Map**
13C2.
Tel 020-7400
4000.

Ways of paying accepted at bureaux de change

You can find facilities for changing money all over the city centre, at main stations and tourist information offices, and in most large stores. **Chequepoint** is one of the largest bureaux de change in Britain; **Exchange International** has a number of useful late-opening branches. Since, in London, there is no consumer organization to regulate the activities of the privately run bureaux de change, their prices need to be examined carefully.

CREDIT CARDS

It is worth bringing a credit card with you, particularly for hotel and restaurant bills, shopping, car hire and booking tickets by telephone. Visa is the most widely accepted card in London, followed by Mastercard (its local name is Access), American Express, Diners Club and JCB.

It is possible to obtain cash advances (up to your credit limit) with an internationally recognized credit card at any London bank displaying the appropriate card sign. You will be charged the credit card company's interest rate, which appears on your statement with the amount advanced.

MAIN BANKS IN LONDON

England's main clearing banks (those whose dealings are processed through a single clearing house) are Barclays, Lloyds TSB, HSBC (formerly the Midland Bank) and National Westminster (NatWest). The Royal Bank of Scotland also has a number of branches in London with exchange facilities. The commission charged by each bank for changing money can vary, so check before going ahead with your transaction.

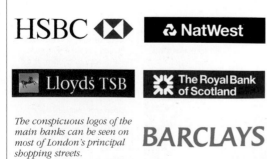

The conspicuous logos of the main banks can be seen on most of London's principal shopping streets.

CASH AND TRAVELLER'S CHEQUES

Britain's currency is the pound sterling (£), which is divided into 100 pence (p). Since there are no exchange controls in Britain, there is no limit to how much cash you may import or export.

Traveller's cheques are the safest alternative to carrying large amounts of cash. Keep receipts from your traveller's cheques separately, and also make a note of offices where you will be able to obtain a refund if the cheques are lost or stolen. Some banks issue traveller's cheques free of commission to established customers, but the normal rate is about 1%. It is sensible to change some money into sterling before arriving in Britain, as queues at airport exchange offices can be very long. Do obtain some smaller denominations. shopkeepers may refuse to accept larger notes for small purchases.

English bank notes of all denominations always feature the Queen's head on one side

Bank Notes

English notes used in the UK are £5, £10, £20 and £50. Scotland has its own notes which, despite being legal tender throughout the UK, are not always accepted.

£50 note

£20 note

£10 note

£5 note

Coins of the Realm

Coins in circulation are £2, £1, 50p, 20p, 10p, 5p, 2p and 1p (shown here slightly smaller than actual size). They all have the Queen's head on one side.

2 pounds (£2)	1 pound (£1)	50 pence (50p)	20 pence (20p)

10 pence (10p)	5 pence (5p)	2 pence (2p)	1 penny (1p)

Using London's Phones

You will find a phonebox on many street corners in central London and in main bus stations and every railway station. You can use coins, buy prepaid phonecards or use your credit card in most payphones. The telephone system in Britain is efficient and inexpensive. Charges depend on when, where and for how long you talk. Inland calls are most expensive from 9am to 1pm on weekdays. Cheap rate applies before 8am or after 6pm on weekdays, and all day at weekends. Cheap times for overseas calls vary from country to country, but tend to be at weekends and in the evening.

PHONEBOXES

There are several different types of BT phoneboxes in London, ranging from old-style red phoneboxes to a modern style, some of which are multimedia. The payphones take coins and/or cards. Phones accept 10p, 20p, 50p and £1 coins. The minimum cost of a call is 20p. If making a short call, use 10p or 20p pieces, as payphones only return unused coins. Phonecards are convenient if you wish to make a number

Old BT phonebox   **Modern BT phonebox**

of calls. When using a credit card, bear in mind that a higher rate will be charged.

TELEPHONE DIRECTORIES

Should you require any services that are not listed in this guide, try consulting one of London's telephone directories. The *Yellow Pages* comprehensively lists services throughout London, while *The Thomson Local* is area-specific. Both of these can be found at Post Offices, libraries, and often at your hotel. *Yellow Pages* (118 247) is a telephone service that gives you the telephone number of anyone who offers the service you require in any part of London or the UK.

BT Directory enquiries (dial 118 500) can be dialled for a small charge and will give you any telephone number in the directory. You need to know the name and address of the person or business you wish to contact.

The *Yellow Pages* logo

USING A CARD AND COIN PHONE

1 Lift the receiver and wait for the dial tone.

2 Insert your phone card into the slot or deposit any of the following coins: 10p, 20p, 50p, £1, £2. The minimum amount is 20p.

3 Dial the number and wait to be connected.

4 The display indicates how much credit you have left. A rapid bleeping noise means your money has run out. Deposit more coins or insert another phone card.

5 If you want to make another call and you have money left in credit, do not replace the receiver, press the follow-on-call button.

6 When you have finished speaking, replace the receiver and retrieve your card or collect your change. Only wholly unused coins are refunded.

£1   **50p**   **20p**   **10p**

REACHING THE RIGHT NUMBER

- All London codes were changed in April 2000.
- The area code for London is 020.
- Phone numbers in central London start with 7 and in outer areas with 8. The 020 prefix must be used if dialling from outside these two areas.
- British Telecom directory enquiries is 118 500.
- If you have any problems contacting a number, call the operator on 100.
- To make an international call, dial 00 followed by the country code (USA and Canada: 1; Australia: 61; New Zealand: 64), the area code and the number. The international operator number is 155 (freephone).
- A phonecard needs at least £2 credit for an international call.
- **In an emergency, dial 999 or 112.**

Postal and Internet Services

Red and gold Post Office logo

Besides main Post Office branches that offer all the postal services available, London has many Post Office branches which double as newsagents. Branches are usually open from 9am to 5.30pm Monday to Friday, and until 12.30pm on Saturday. First- and second-class stamps are available either individually or in books of six or twelve. Other stamps can be used for letters and cards to the European Union. Post boxes – in all shapes and sizes but always red – are found throughout the city.

Old-style pillar box

POSTAL SERVICES

Stamps can be bought at any outlet which displays the sign "Stamps sold here". Hotels often have post boxes in their reception areas. When writing to a UK address always make sure to include the postcode, which can be obtained from either the **Royal Mail** enquiry line or website. Letters posted within the UK can be sent first or second class. The first-class service is quicker, but more expensive, with letters usually

Air letters are all 1st class

1st-class stamp

2nd-class stamp

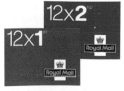

Books of twelve 1st- and 2nd-class stamps

reaching their destination the following day (except on Sunday); second-class mail takes a day or two longer.

Royal Mail
Tel 0845 7740740.
www.royalmail.com

POSTE RESTANTE

It is possible to receive mail in London by *poste restante*. This is a service where letters can be sent for collection. To use the service be sure to print the surname clearly so it will be filed away correctly. Send it to *Poste Restante* followed by the address of the post office. To collect your post you will have to show your existing passport or another form of identification. Post will be kept for one month. London's main post office branch is in William IV Street, WC2. Also, the American Express office at 30 Haymarket, London SW1 provides a *poste restante* service for its customers.

POST BOXES

These may be either freestanding "pillar boxes" or wall safes, both painted bright red. Some pillar boxes have separate slots, which are clearly labelled, one slot for overseas and first-class mail, another for second-class mail. Initials found on the outside of the older style post boxes indicate the monarch at the time it was erected. Collections are usually made several times a day during weekdays (less often on Saturdays and Sundays); times are marked on the box.

ACCESSING THE INTERNET

London has plenty of public access to computers and the Internet. Free Internet access is often available at public libraries, but you may have to book in advance. Internet cafés usually charge by the minute for computer use, and charges build up quickly, especially when including the cost of printed pages. EasyEverything, a chain of massive Internet cafés, has four main branches in central London: 9–16 Tottenham Court Road, 358 Oxford Street, 7 Strand (Trafalgar Square), and 9–13 Wilton Road (Victoria). Internet access is cheapest during off-peak times.

24-hour Internet access at the Europe-wide chain EasyEverything

POSTING ABROAD

Air letters go by Royal Mail's airmail service anywhere in the world. On average, it takes 3 days for them to reach cities in Europe, and 4–6 days for other destinations. Sending post by surface mail is more economical, but it can take up to 8 weeks to reach its destination. For express deliveries use the Royal Mail's **Airsure** service. **Parcelforce Worldwide**, the national courier service, is comparable in price to **DHL**, **Crossflight** or **Expressair**.

Airsure (Royal Mail)
Tel 0845 774 0740.

Crossflight
Tel 01753 776000.
www.crossflight.co.uk

DHL
Tel 0870 110 0300.

Expressair
Tel 020-8897 6568.
www.expressair.co.uk

Parcelforce Worldwide
Tel 08708 501150.

INSURANCE

It is sensible to take out travel insurance to cover cancellation or curtailment of your trip, theft or loss of money and possessions and the cost of any medical treatment *(see p365)*. If your country has a reciprocal medical arrangement with Britain (for example, Australia, New Zealand, and the EU), you can obtain free treatment under the National Health Service, but there are a number of forms to fill out. North American and Canadian health plans or student identity cards may give you some protection against costs, but check the small print.

If you want to drive a car in London it is advisable to take out fully comprehensive insurance, and you must always carry a valid driver's licence.

CUSTOMS AND IMMIGRATION

A valid passport is needed to enter the UK. Visitors from the EU, the US, Canada, Australia and New Zealand do not require a visa to enter, nor are any inoculations or vaccinations necessary.

When you arrive at one of Britain's ports you will find separate queues at immigration control – one for EU nationals, others for everyone else.

European union has led to changes in UK customs and immigration policy. Travellers entering the UK from outside the EU still have to pass through customs channels: red exit routes for people carrying goods on which duty has to be paid; green routes for those with no payment to make (nothing to "declare"). If, however, you are travelling from within the EU you will find that these have been replaced by a blue channel – EU residents no longer have to "declare" goods. Random checks are made to guard against drugs traffickers.

EU residents are no longer entitled to a Value Added Tax refund on goods bought in the UK. Travellers from outside the EU can obtain one if they leave the UK within three months of the purchase.

International Student Identity Card

STUDENT TRAVELLERS

An ISIC card (International Student Identity Card) entitles full-time students to discounts on things from travel to sports events. For students from the US, the ISIC also includes some medical cover, though this may not be sufficient on its own. If you don't have an ISIC, it can be obtained (with proof of student status) from the **University of London Students' Union** (ULSU) or branches of **STA Travel**. ULSU offers many social and sports facilities to valid union card holders and reciprocating educational establishments. **International Youth Hostel Federation** membership is also worth having for cheap accommodation in London.

EU nationals do not need a permit to work in the UK. Commonwealth citizens under the age of 27 can work in the UK for up to two years. Visiting students from the US can get a blue card that enables them to work for up to six months (obtain before you arrive). **BUNAC** is a student club organizing work exchange for students from Australia, the US, Canada, New Zealand, South Africa, Ghana, Costa Rica and Peru.

USEFUL ADDRESSES AND TELEPHONE NUMBERS

BUNAC
16 Bowling Green Lane EC1.
Map 6 E4. *Tel* 020-7251 3472.
www.bunac.org

International Youth Hostel Federation
Tel 0870-770 8868.
www.hihostels.com

STA Travel
52 Grosvenor Gdns SW1 (main store).
Map 20 E1. *Tel* 020-7828 3526.

ULSU
Malet St WC1. **Map** 5 A5. *Tel* 020-7664 2000. **www**.isiccard.com

NEWSPAPERS, TELEVISION AND RADIO

London's principal newspaper is the *Evening Standard*, which is available from about midday, Monday to Friday – as well as all the city's news, it has a listings section and reviews.

PUBLIC TOILETS

Although many older-style, supervised public conveniences still exist, these have largely been replaced by coin-operated "Superloos". Young children should never use these devices on their own – they will find it almost impossible to operate the inner door handle.

1 If the green "vacant" light is shown, insert the required fee. The door located on your left will slide open.

"Vacant" light   Coin slot

2 Once inside, the door slides closed and locks.

3 To exit, pull down the inner door handle.

London newspaper stand

International newspapers are sold in many newsagents. The *International Herald Tribune* is available on the day of issue; others may appear a day or more later. Five TV channels can be seen with conventional receiving equipment: two run by the BBC (BBC1 and BBC2), and three independent (ITV and Channels 4 and 5). Satellite and cable networks are both available in the UK, and many hotels have these facilities for their guests.

The BBC's local and national radio stations are supplemented by many independent local companies, like London's Capital Radio (95.8 FM), a pop music station, and easy-listening Classic FM (101.9 FM).

EMBASSIES AND CONSULATES

Australian High Commission
Australia House, Strand WC2.
Map 13 C2. *Tel* 020-7379 4334.
www.australia.org.uk

Canadian High Commission
1 Grosvenor Square W1.
Map 12 D2.*Tel* 020-7258 6600.
www.canada.org.uk

New Zealand High Commission
80 Haymarket SW1. **Map** 13 A3.
Tel 020-7930 8422.
www.nzembassy.com/uk

United States Embassy
24 Grosvenor Square W1.
Map 12 D2. *Tel* 020-7499 9000.
www.usembassy.org.uk

INTERNATIONAL NEWSAGENTS

Gray's Inn News
50 Theobalds Rd WC1.
Map 5 C5.
Tel 020-7405 5241.

D S Radford
61 Fleet St EC4. **Map** 14 E1.
Tel 020-7583 7166.

LONDON TIME

London is on Greenwich Mean Time (GMT) during the winter months, five hours ahead of Eastern Standard Time and ten hours behind Sydney. From late March to late October, clocks are set forward one hour to British Summer Time (equivalent to Central European Time). At any time of year you can check the correct time by dialling 123 to contact the 24-hour **Speaking Clock** service (there is a charge for this service).

Standard British plug

ELECTRICAL ADAPTORS

The voltage in London is 240V AC. Plugs have three square pins and take fuses of 3, 5 or 13 amps. Visitors will need an adaptor for appliances.

CONVERSION CHART

Officially the metric system is used, but imperial measures are still common.

Imperial to metric
1 inch = 2.5 centimetres
1 foot = 30 centimetres
1 mile = 1.6 kilometres
1 ounce = 28 grams
1 pound = 454 grams
1 pint = 0.6 litre
1 gallon = 4.6 litres

Metric to imperial
1 millimetre = 0.04 inch
1 centimetre = 0.4 inch
1 metre = 3 feet 3 inches
1 kilometre = 0.6 mile
1 gram = 0.04 ounce
1 kilogram = 2.2 pounds

RELIGIOUS SERVICES

The following organizations can help you find a place to worship.

Anglican (Episcopalian)
St. Paul's Cathedral EC4.
Map 15 A2. *Tel* 020-7236 4128.

Baptist
London Baptist Association, 235 Shaftesbury Ave WC2.
Map 13 B1. *Tel* 020-7692 5592.

Catholic
Westminster Cathedral, Victoria St SW1. **Map** 20 F1.
Tel 020-7798 9055.

Evangelical Alliance
Whitefield House, 186 Kennington Park Rd SE11. **Map** 22 E4. *Tel* 020-7207 2100.
www.eauk.org

Quaker
Religious Society of Friends, 173–7 Euston Rd NW1.
Map 5 A4. *Tel* 020-7663 1000.

Buddhist
The Buddhist Society, 58 Eccleston Sq SW1.**Map** 20 F2.
Tel 020-7834 5858.
www.thebuddhistsociety.org.uk

Jewish
Liberal Jewish Synagogue, 28 St. John's Wood Rd NW8. **Map** 3 A3. *Tel* 020-7286 5181. United Synagogue (Orthodox), 735 High Rd N12. *Tel* 020-8343 8989.

Muslim
Islamic Cultural Centre, 146 Park Rd NW8. **Map** 3 B3. *Tel* 020-7724 3363. **www**.iccuk.org

St Martin-in-the-Fields, Trafalgar Square (see p102)

GETTING TO LONDON

London is one of Europe's central routing points for international air and sea travel. By air, travellers face a bewildering choice of carriers serving Europe, North America, Australasia and the Far East. Stiff competition on some routes means that low fares are occasionally introduced to attract new passengers, but after a while fares always seem to level out again. Long-distance sea travel is a different proposition as few transatlantic liners operate these days. Cunard offers the only regular services on the *Queen* *Elizabeth 2*. There are efficient and regular ferry services from Europe. About 20 passenger and car ferry routes, served by large ferries, jetfoils and catamarans, cross the North Sea and the English Channel to Britain. Since 1995 the Channel Tunnel has provided a new, efficient high-speed train link – Eurostar – running between Europe and the UK, although work on the new rail line on the English side of the Channel will not be complete for some years. The tunnel also enables drivers to cross the Channel in a little over half an hour.

British Airways 737

AIR TRAVEL

The main United States airlines offering scheduled flights to London include Delta, **United**, **American Airlines** and USAir. Two major British operators are **British Airways** and **Virgin Atlantic**. From Canada, the main carriers are British Airways and **Air Canada**. The flight time from New York is about six and a half hours, and from Los Angeles about 10 hours.

There are regular scheduled flights to London from all the major European cities, as well as from numerous other parts of the UK itself, including northern England, Scotland and Northern Ireland.

The choice of carriers from Australasia is enormous. Well over 20 airlines share around two dozen different routes. The more indirect your route, the cheaper the fare; but remember that lengthy jet travel is bound to be stressful. **Qantas**, **Air New Zealand** and British Airways may be your

Passenger jet landing at Luton

first thoughts for comfort and speed, but all the Far Eastern operators and several European airlines offer interesting alternatives.

Getting a good deal
Cheap deals are available from good travel agents and package operators, and are advertised in newspapers and travel magazines. Students, senior citizens and regular or business travellers may well be able to obtain a discount. Children under two (who do not occupy a separate seat) pay 10% of the adult fare; older children up to 12 also travel at lower fares.

Ticket types
Excursion tickets can be good buys, but they need to be booked up to a month in advance. They are subject to restrictions and cannot be changed without penalty. There are usually minimum (and maximum) length of stay requirements. Fares on scheduled flights are available through specialist agents at much lower rates. Charter flights offer even cheaper seats, but have less flexible departure times and can be less punctual.

If you book a cheap deal with a discount agent, check whether you will get a refund if the agent or operator ceases trading, and do not part with the full fare until you see the ticket; you will have to pay a deposit to hold it. Do not forget to check with the relevant airline to ensure that your seat has been confirmed.

AIRLINE INFORMATION

Major Carriers
Air Canada
www.aircanada.com

Air New Zealand
www.airnewzealand.com

American Airlines
www.aa.com

British Airways
www.britishairways.com

Qantas
www.qantas.com.au

Singapore Airlines
www.singaporeair.com

United Airlines
www.united.com

Virgin Atlantic
www.virgin-atlantic.com

Discount ticket agents
Lupus Travel (Air Travel Advisory Bureau).
Tel 0870-737 0020.
www.atab.co.uk

Trailfinders *(European and worldwide travel)*
Tel 020-7937 5400.
www.trailfinders.com

Flight Centre *(worldwide travel)*
Tel 020-7434 1919.
www.flightcentre.com

TRAVELLING BY RAIL

London has eight main rail stations at which trains terminate. These are scattered in a ring around the city centre. Paddington in west London serves the West Country, Wales and the South Midlands; Liverpool Street in the City covers East Anglia and Essex. In north London, Euston, St Pancras and King's Cross serve northern and central Britain. In the south, Charing Cross, Victoria and Waterloo serve southern England and are also the termini for travel by ferry and train from Europe. Since 1995, **Eurostar** has operated the Channel Tunnel rail service, with trains running from St Pancras International to Paris, Brussels, Lille, Avignon, Calais, the Disneyland resort in Paris and the French Alps.

London's stations are now smart and modern with many

Station concourse at Liverpool Street

facilities for the traveller, such as bureaux de change and shops selling food, books and confectionery.

Information about rail services is quite easy to find; most rail stations have an information point detailing times, prices and destinations. In addition, constantly updated details of services are screened on monitors dotted around the stations Railway staff are usually helpful and courteous.

If your ferry ticket does not include the price of rail travel to the centre of London, tickets can be bought at the clearly signed ticket offices or automatic machines *(see p384)*. You may decide to buy a Travelcard from the first day you are in London *(see p378)*.
Eurostar London St Pancras International **Tel** *0870 518 6186*. **www**.eurostar.com
National Rail Enquiries Tel *0845-748 4950.* **www**.nationalrail.co.uk

Rail information point *(see p363)*

COACH SERVICES

The main coach station in London is on Buckingham Palace Road (about 10 minutes' walk from Victoria railway station). You can travel to London by coach from many European cities, but the majority of services travelling to London are from within the UK. **National Express** runs to about 1,200 UK destinations, but other companies depart from this station, too. Coach travel is cheaper than the railway, but journeys are longer and arrival times can be unpredictable. National Express coaches are comfortable with good facilities. **Greenline** buses travel between London and Luton and Hemel Hempstead.
Coach companies
Greenline **Tel** *0870- 608 7261*, **www**.greenline.co.uk
National Express **Tel** *0870-580 8080;* **www**.nationalexpress.com

CROSSING THE CHANNEL

Britain's sea links with Europe were finally joined by a landlink in 1995, when the Channel Tunnel opened. **Eurotunnel** operates a drive-on-drive-off ferry service for cars between Folkestone and Calais which runs about three times an hour with a journey time of 35 minutes.

A network of ferry services also operates between British and Continental ports. Ferry crossings to and from the Continent are operated by **P&O Ferries, SeaFrance** and **Brittany Ferries**.

Fast catamaran Seacat services between Dover and Calais are run by **Hoverspeed**, which also operates between Newhaven and Dieppe. The shortest crossings are not necessarily the cheapest; you pay both for the speed of your journey and the convenience.

Cross-channel ferry

Contact Brittany Ferries **www**.brittany-ferries.com **Tel** *0870-536 0360;*
Eurotunnel **www**.eurotunnel.co.uk **Tel** *0870-535 3535;*
Hoverspeed **www**.hoverspeed.com **Tel** *0870-524 0241;*
P&O Ferries **www**.poferries.com **Tel** *0870-600 0600;*
SeaFrance **www**.seafrance.com **Tel** *0870-571 1711.*

London's Airports

London's two main airports, Heathrow and Gatwick, are supported by Luton, Stansted and London City airports (*see p377*). Heathrow is well connected to London by tube and train, and the other airports have train or coach links. Each airport has facilities from bureaux de change to shops and nearby hotels. Check which airport you are landing at so you can plan your journey from there. www.baa.com has more details on the airports.

Access to the Underground in the arrival terminal at Heathrow

British Airways passenger jet at Heathrow airport

HEATHROW (LHR)

Heathrow in West London (airport information 0870-000 0123) is the world's busiest international airport. Mainly scheduled long-haul aircraft land here, and a fifth terminal is opening in 2008, along with a new tube station, to handle increased air traffic. Money exchange, left-luggage facilities, shops and restaurants are found in all terminals.

All terminals are linked to the Underground system by a variety of moving walkways, passageways and lifts. There are clear directions in each terminal. London Underground runs a good service on the Piccadilly line. The tube journey into central London takes about 40 minutes, but generally add 10 minutes more from Terminal 4. However, until early 2007, the tube stop for Terminal 4 is closed, while a new Terminal 5 tube station is being constructed. If travelling from central London to Terminal 4, you can either take the replacement bus service from Hatton Cross tube station (depart every 5 mins), or take the Heathrow Express (*see below*) for no charge from Terminals 1 to 3 (depart every 15 mins).

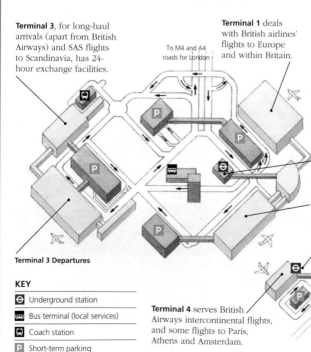

Terminal 3, for long-haul arrivals (apart from British Airways) and SAS flights to Scandinavia, has 24-hour exchange facilities.

Terminal 1 deals with British airlines' flights to Europe and within Britain.

To M4 and A4 roads for London

Terminal 3 Departures

Terminal 4 serves British Airways intercontinental flights, and some flights to Paris, Athens and Amsterdam.

Plan of Heathrow Airport
When leaving London be sure to check which terminal you need. Terminal 4 is some way from the others and the Underground station is closed until early 2007 – see main text above.

Heathrow terminals 1, 2 and 3 station

Terminal 2 handles most European services of non-British airlines.

Heathrow Terminal 4 station (closed until early 2007 – see above)

A30 road

Hilton London Heathrow

KEY

⊖	Underground station
🚌	Bus terminal (local services)
Ⓒ	Coach station
P	Short-term parking
⇌	Direction of traffic flow

This closure does not affect the Heathrow Express (*see below*).

The best way between London and Heathrow is the Heathrow Express to Paddington (www.heathrowexpress.com). Trains run every 15 minutes from 5am to midnight. The journey takes 15 minutes (8 minutes more for Terminal 4). A new service called Heathrow Connect stops at Ealing Broadway, which is closer to London and on the tube.

Road links for Heathrow can be congested, although the M4 motorway has a taxi lane for quick access to London.

Check-in is at least 2 hours before departure (1 hour with hand luggage only). Most

Distinctive logo of the Gatwick Express service

airlines' check-in desks open from 5am to 9pm daily.

GATWICK (LGW)

Gatwick airport (airport information: 0870-000 2468) is south of London. Unlike Heathrow, it handles scheduled, charter and low-cost flights. A large volume of package holiday traffic passes through Gatwick, so passengers should allow plenty of time to check in.

Remember to check from which terminal your flight home leaves.

Gatwick has 24-hour restaurants, bank facilities and shops in each terminal.

Gatwick has good rail links with the capital, including frequent services to London Bridge and Victoria. The Gatwick Express train (0845-850 1530, www.gatwickexpress.com) has a fast, regular service to Victoria station. Journey time is 30 minutes (departs every 15 mins; closed 1.30am–4.30am).

Driving from Gatwick to central London can take 2 hours. A taxi costs from £50 to £60.

KEY

![railway]	Railway station
![coach]	Coach station
P	Short-term parking
![police]	Police station
⇒	Direction of traffic flow

Gatwick's free monorail service linking the two terminals

Plan of Gatwick Airport

There are two terminals at Gatwick: north and south. They are linked by a free monorail service, and the journey between them takes only a couple of minutes. Near the railway station entrance (which, if you are not arriving by rail, is clearly marked) you will find boards that state which terminal serves your carrier.

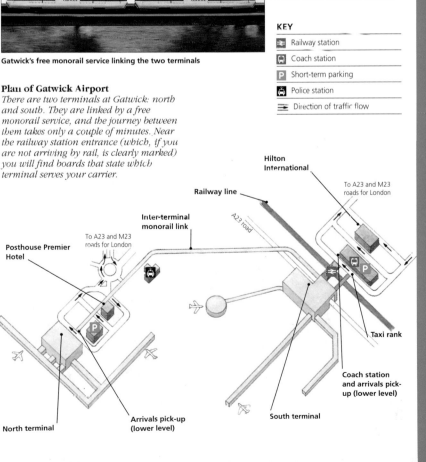

Hilton International

Railway line

To A23 and M23 roads for London

A23 road

Inter-terminal monorail link

To A23 and M23 roads for London

Posthouse Premier Hotel

Taxi rank

Coach station and arrivals pick-up (lower level)

Arrivals pick-up (lower level)

South terminal

North terminal

Entrance to Stansted's spacious modern passenger terminal

STANSTED (STN)

Stansted is in Essex (airport information 0870-000 0303; www.baa.com/stansted), to the northeast of London. It is the UK's fourth largest airport, and Europe's fastest growing, handling in excess of 20 million passengers per year. It is particularly successful as a base for the growing number of low-cost airlines, with over 120 destinations on offer operated by 20 scheduled airlines. Standard facilities are present including restaurants, retail shops and bureaux de change. Three satellite buildings help to serve the growing number of passengers. Rapid-transit driverless trains shuttle between the terminal and two satellites, the third being just a short walk from the Departures Lounge.

A rail link with London's Liverpool Street station, the Stansted Express (0845-850 0150, www.stanstedexpress.com), runs every 15 minutes (closed midnight to 5.30am). Journey time is 45 minutes. It stops at Tottenham Hale for access to the Victoria Line tube. Night coach services operate every 30 minutes Monday to Saturday between Stansted and Liverpool Street (journey time 1 hour). A coach station is next to the terminal. The M11 motorway links Stansted to London.

LUTON (LTN)

Luton airport (airport information 01582-405 100; www.london-luton.com) is to the north of London, close to junction 10 of the M1 motorway, the UK's main arterial road. Its passenger terminal has a dedicated train station, Luton Parkway, with frequent trains to King's Cross station (journey time about 40 minutes). A free shuttle bus links the airport with the station. Coach services also link it to London, with pick-up and set-down points directly outside the terminal. The airport deals with 5 million passengers each year. Luton Airport is used by the budget airline easyJet, as are Stansted and London City.

LONDON CITY AIRPORT (LCY)

London City Airport (information 020-7646 0088; www.londoncityairport.com) opened in 1987. It now serves over 1.7 million passengers each year. Not surprisingly, given its location just 10 km (6 miles) from the City, it is very popular with business travellers, a fact reflected in the standard of dedicated facilities (including meeting rooms, secretarial services and private dining rooms) in addition to the more usual airport essentials. An additional incentive is the check-in time: 10 minutes. While an estimated 70 per cent of passengers reach City Airport by private car or taxi (parking is adjacent to the terminal), public transport is also on hand. A new DLR station for London City Airport opened recently, and shuttle buses link the airport to the Jubilee Line (30 minutes to the West End).

London City airport, within sight of the city's Docklands area

AIRPORT	FROM CITY CENTRE	AVERAGE JOURNEY TIME	AVERAGE TAXI FARE
London City	10 km (6 miles)	Tube and DLR: 40 minutes	£20
Heathrow	23 km (14 miles)	Rail: 15 minutes Tube: 45 minutes	£35
Gatwick	45 km (28 miles)	Rail: 30 minutes Bus: 70 minutes	£55
Luton	51 km (32 miles)	Rail: 35 minutes Bus: 70 minutes	£55
Stansted	55 km (34 miles)	Rail: 45 minutes Bus: 75 minutes	£55

AIRPORT HOTELS

HEATHROW
Hilton London Heathrow
Tel 020-8759 7755.
www.hilton.com

Holiday Inn M4
Tel 0870-400 8595
www.holiday-inn.com

Crowne Plaza
Tel 0870-400 9140. **www.**london-heathrow.crowneplaza.com

Sheridan Skyline
Tel 020-8759 2535.
www.sheridan.com/skyline

GATWICK
Thistle Gatwick
Tel 01293-786992. **www.**thistlehotels.com/londongatwick

Hilton London Gatwick
Tel 01293-518080.
www.hilton.com

Le Meridien Gatwick Airport
Tel 0800 500 500 or (from abroad) 0870 050 0500. **www.**lemeridien.com

Gatwick Holiday Inn
Tel 0870-400 9030.
www.holiday-inn.com

STANSTED
Hilton London Stansted
Tel 01279-680800. www.hilton.com

Harlow Stansted Moat House
Tel 01279-829988.
www.moathousehotels.com

Radisson SAS Stansted Airport
Tel 01279-661012.
www.radissonsas.com

Swallow Churchgate
Tel 01279-420246.
www.swallowhotels.com

LUTON
Ibis Luton Airport
Tel 01582-424488.
www.ibishotel.com

Luton Regent Lodge Hotel
Tel 01582-575955.
www.regentlodgehotel.com

Hertfordshire Moat House
Tel 01582-449988.
www.moathousehotels.com

LONDON CITY
Four Seasons Canary Wharf
Tel 020-7510 1999.
www.fourseasons.com

Ibis Greenwich
Tel 020-8305 1177.
www.ibishotel.com

Relaxing bar of the popular Sheridan Skyline hotel

KEY

🚉	Railway stations
Ⓔ	Tube stations
✈	Airport
▬	Motorway
▬	'A' road

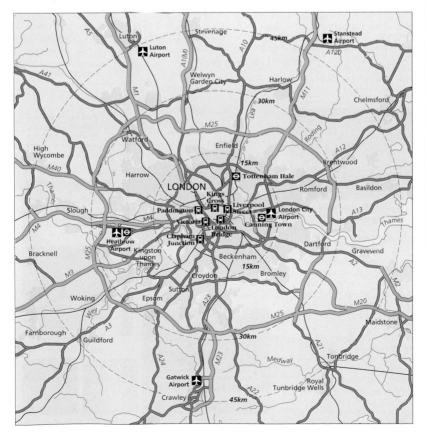

GETTING AROUND LONDON

London's public transport system is one of the busiest and largest in Europe, and has all the overcrowding problems to match. The worst and busiest times to travel are in the two rush hours, between 8am and 9.30am and from 4.30pm to 6.30pm. Within London and its suburbs, public transport is organized by Transport for London (TfL). This consists of various types of bus, the Underground system, and

Routemaster bus

the overground train system, run by several private companies. For any information you require about fares, routes and timings of the various transport services, ring 020-7222 1234, check TfL's website (www.tfl.gov.uk) or visit one of the Travel information Centres at Euston, King's Cross and Victoria mainline stations, as well as at Oxford Circus and Piccadilly Circus Underground stations and Heathrow Airport.

THE TRANSPORT SYSTEM

The Underground (the "tube") is usually the quickest way of travelling around London. Services are, however, prone to delays and the trains are often crowded. Changing lines may involve a longish walk at some stations. London is so large that some sights are a long way, even a bus journey, from any Underground station. There are also areas, often in the south, with no tube. Bus travel can be slow, and walking may be quicker.

Pre-paid Oyster card being placed on a card reader

TRAVELCARDS

Public transport in London is expensive compared with many cities in Europe. Short trips are relatively more expensive than the longer journeys; it is rarely worth getting on the tube to travel just one stop.

The most economic tickets are Travelcards – daily, family, weekly or monthly passes that allow unlimited travel on all forms of transport in the zones you require – and the new pre-pay Oyster cards, which you can credit with money before your journey.

(Six bands, called travel zones, extend outwards from the city centre; most of London's main sights are in Zone One.)

Travelcards and Oyster cards are bought in train or Underground stations (see p380) and at newsagents with a red "pass agent" sign. For monthly tickets you need a passport-sized photo. One-day Travelcards cannot be used before 9.30am

from Monday to Friday. There are no restrictions on weekend, weekly or monthly Travelcards. If you are in London for four days or more, a two-zone weekly Travelcard is advisable; for more than ten days, an Oyster card, but it is essential to place it on a card reader at the beginning and end of each bus or tube journey, or you will get charged much more.

LONDON ON FOOT

Once you get used to traffic driving on the left, London can be safely explored on foot but take care when crossing the road. There are two types of pedestrian crossing in London: striped zebra crossings marked by beacons, and push-button crossings at traffic lights. Traffic should stop for you if you are waiting at a zebra crossing, but at push-button crossings cars will not stop until the green man lights up. Look out for instructions written on the road; these tell you from which direction you can expect the traffic to come.

Zebra crossing

Beacons mark London's older-style zebra crossings

Pushing the button makes the red man, located on a pillar across the road, turn into a green man

Push-button control

Do not cross   Cross the road

Driving a Car in London

Sign for a car park

Most visitors are better off not driving in central London. Traffic moves at an average speed of about 11 mph (18 km/h) during the rush hour, and parking is hard to find. Many Londoners only take their car out at weekends and after 6.30pm on weekdays, when parking regulations are less restricted and congestion charges in the city centre are waived. Remember that you must drive on the left.

Double yellow lines on road, meaning no parking at any time

CONGESTION CHARGING

Congestion charging aims to reduce traffic and fund improvements to public transport. If you drive within the congestion zone (roughly bordered by Tower Bridge, Euston Road, Hyde Park and Vauxhall Bridge) from Monday to Friday, 7am to 6.30pm, you will need to pay an £8 fee that day at a newsagent, petrol station or Post Office. The charge rises to £10 between 10pm and 11.59pm. These fees are due to increase, and the zone is expanding westward in February 2007. Not paying the charge leads to a fine. (Call 0845-900 1234 or go to www.cclondon.com for further information.)

Parking meter

PARKING REGULATIONS

Parking in London is scarce, and you should check any restrictions (usually on adjacent posts). Meters are expensive during working hours (8.30am–6.30pm Mon–Sat) and two hours is the maximum stay. National Car Parks (NCP) are found centrally; to get their free guide showing car park locations, write to: St George House, 32–34 Hill St, Birmingham B5 4AN (0870-606 7050; www.ncp.co.uk).

There is strictly no parking on red routes or double yellow lines at any time. Parking on single yellow lines is generally allowed in the evenings or on Sundays. Resident permit zones are unenforced outside posted hours.

CLAMPING AND TOWING

If you park illegally or allow a meter to run out, you may well find your car has been clamped. A large notice should inform you which Payment Centre you need to visit to pay your fine and get your car released. If your car has vanished, it has probably been removed by London's feared and hated car impounders. Their efficiency is remarkable, the cost and inconvenience to drivers enormous: it is rarely worth the risk. Ring 020-7747 4747 (24 hrs) to find out where your car is being held.

Traffic Signs
Every driver should read the UK Highway Code *manual (available from bookshops) and familiarize themselves with London's traffic signs.*

No entry

GIVE WAY

Give way to all vehicles

One-way traffic

No right turn allowed

Illegally parked car immobilized by wheel clamp

CAR HIRE AGENCIES

Avis Rent a Car
Tel 0870 606 0100. www.avis.co.uk

Europcar
Tel 0870 607 5005.
www.europcar.co.uk

Hertz Rent a Car
Tel 0870 840 0084. www.hertz.com

Thrifty Car Rental
Tel 01494 751 600.
www.thrifty.co.uk

No stopping

30 mph (48 km/h) speed limit

Travelling by Underground

Underground sign
outside a station

The Underground system, known as the "tube" to Londoners, has 273 stations, each clearly marked with the Underground logo. Trains run every day, except Christmas Day, from about 5.30am until just after midnight, but a few lines or sections of lines have an irregular service. Check for running times and information on 020-7222 1234 (and www.tfl.gov.uk). Fewer trains run on Sundays. The Docklands Light Railway links the tube to much of east and southeast London.

London Underground train

PLANNING YOUR JOURNEY

The 12 Underground lines are colour-coded, and maps *(see inside cover)* called Journey Planners are posted at every station. Maps of the central section are displayed in the trains. The map shows how to change lines to travel from where you are to any station on the Underground system. Some lines, such as the Victoria and Jubilee, are simple single-branch routes; others, such as the Northern Line, have more than one branch. The Circle Line is a continuous loop around central London. Distances shown on the map are not to scale and the routes that lines are seen to take should not be relied upon for directions.

BUYING A TICKET

If you are likely to be making more than two trips a day on the Underground, the best ticket to buy is a Travelcard or an Oyster card *(see p378)*. You can also buy single tickets or return tickets which are available from ticket offices and automatic ticket machines.

All destinations fall within six specified London transport zones *(see p378)*. The zones you travel through determine the cost of your journey. Check the Journey Planner to determine which zone your destination is in. Most stations now have touch screen machines that give step-by-step instructions in a variety of languages. They accept coins, notes, credit and debit cards. You may come across an older push-button machine that takes coins and £5 or £10 notes only. Select the ticket type you need, such as single or return, then choose the station you are travelling to, and the cost of the fare will be displayed. Smaller ticket machines geared towards regular Underground users show a choice of fare prices from which you select the appropriate one for your journey. All of the ticket machines have a large red display indicating whether or not change is available.

HOW TO READ THE JOURNEY PLANNER MAPS
(see inside back cover)

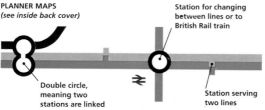

Station for changing between lines or to British Rail train

Double circle, meaning two stations are linked

Station serving two lines

TUBE ARCHITECTURE

The Underground's reputation for exciting architecture was established during its heyday in the 1930s. In 2000 the new Jubilee Line Extension opened to great acclaim. The line added six new stations, and five existing ones were redesigned by a group of respected architects including Lord Norman Foster (Canary Wharf), Matthew Hopkins (Westminster), and Will Alsop (North Greenwich). Light and space are the principles in these imposing, yet elegant structures.

Concourse at Canary Wharf Station, Jubilee Line

MAKING A JOURNEY BY UNDERGROUND

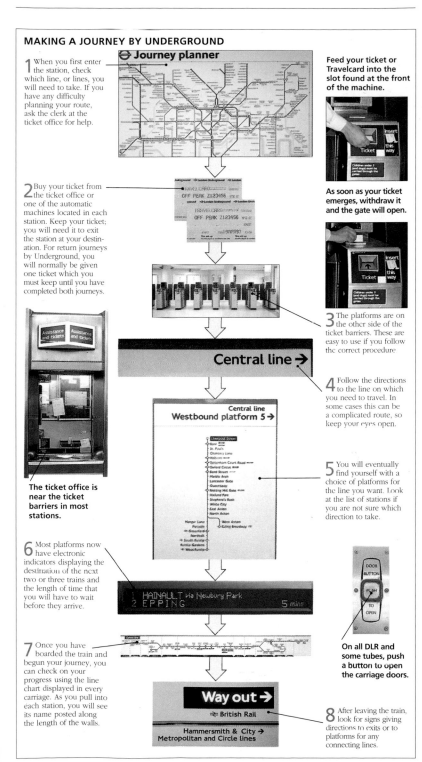

1 When you first enter the station, check which line, or lines, you will need to take. If you have any difficulty planning your route, ask the clerk at the ticket office for help.

⊖ Journey planner

Feed your ticket or Travelcard into the slot found at the front of the machine.

2 Buy your ticket from the ticket office or one of the automatic machines located in each station. Keep your ticket; you will need it to exit the station at your destination. For return journeys by Underground, you will normally be given one ticket which you must keep until you have completed both journeys.

As soon as your ticket emerges, withdraw it and the gate will open.

3 The platforms are on the other side of the ticket barriers. These are easy to use if you follow the correct procedure

The ticket office is near the ticket barriers in most stations.

Central line →

4 Follow the directions to the line on which you need to travel. In some cases this can be a complicated route, so keep your eyes open.

Central line
Westbound platform 5 →

5 You will eventually find yourself with a choice of platforms for the line you want. Look at the list of stations if you are not sure which direction to take.

6 Most platforms now have electronic indicators displaying the destination of the next two or three trains and the length of time that you will have to wait before they arrive.

1 HAINAULT via Newbury Park
2 EPPING   5 mins

7 Once you have boarded the train and begun your journey, you can check on your progress using the line chart displayed in every carriage. As you pull into each station, you will see its name posted along the length of the walls.

On all DLR and some tubes, push a button to open the carriage doors.

Way out →
⇌ British Rail

Hammersmith & City →
Metropolitan and Circle lines

8 After leaving the train, look for signs giving directions to exits or to platforms for any connecting lines.

London's Buses

Distinctive logo used on London bus stops

One of London's most recognizable symbols is the old-fashioned, red double-decker Routemaster bus, but it is a much less common sight now than it once was. Today, the need to modernize the buses has resulted in the production of many new vehicles which offer wheelchair access and more comfortable seating, such as the new long bendy bus. If you are able to get a seat, a bus journey is an undemanding and enjoyable way to see London. If you are in a hurry, however, it can be an extremely frustrating experience. London's traffic is often congested and bus journeys can take a long time, especially during the morning and evening rush hours (8–10am and 4–7pm).

Bus Stops
If you are boarding the bus at a yellow stop (below), you must pay for your ticket before boarding. At some stops, called request stops, the driver will not halt unless you signal that you want to get on or off. If you want to board, raise your arm as the bus approaches the stop; if you want to get off, ring the bell once before your stop.

FINDING THE RIGHT BUS

Each bus stop in central London has a list of main destinations showing which bus routes you need. There may also be a local street plan with each nearby bus stop letter-coded. Make sure you catch a bus going in the right direction; if in doubt, check with the driver. For details, contact **London Travel Information**.

London Travel Information
Tel 020-7222 1234.
www.tfl.gov.uk

USING LONDON'S BUSES

Buses always halt at bus stops marked with the London Buses symbol *(see above)*, unless they are label-led "request" stops. Destinations are displayed clearly on the front of the bus, but if you are unsure which stop you need, ask the driver to alert you and stay on the lower deck. Routemaster services have a conductor who collects fares and tickets during the journey. They will tell you the fare for your destination, but will not always accept notes, so try to keep a selection of coins handy. The Routemaster services now only operate on selected Heritage routes and the majority of buses in central London are new-style buses. These buses have no conductor and it is therefore essential to buy a ticket before

boarding. All single cash fare bus journeys in London cost £1.50. Buy a Bus Pass if you're making more than two bus journeys, or a Travelcard or Oyster card *(see p378)* for lower fares if you also plan on using the tube and are in London for more than four days. Ticket machines are located at most central bus stops, but tickets and passes can also be bought from newsagents and London Underground stations.

USEFUL BUS ROUTES

Several of London's bus routes are convenient for many of the capital's main sights and shops. If you arm yourself with a Travelcard or Bus Pass and are in no particular hurry, sight-seeing or shopping by bus can be great fun. The cost of a journey by public transport is far less than any of the charges levied by tour operators, but you won't have the commentary that tour companies give you as you pass sights *(see p362)*.

There are also some sights or areas in London that are inaccessible by Underground. Buses run regularly from the city centre to, for instance, the Albert Hall *(see p207)* and Chelsea *(see pp192–7)*.

Harrods

Marble Arch

Natural History Museum

Knightsbridge

Hyde Park Corner

South Kensington

Sloane Square

Victoria and Albert Museum

Destinations are shown on the front and rear of buses.

When approaching your stop, ring the bell near the stairs or doors to inform the driver.

Give your ticket or show your pass to the driver.

Routemaster Bus
These buses have been taken out of regular service and now only operate on two "Heritage" routes.

Night Buses
These services run through the night from stops with this logo. One-day Travelcards are valid on them until 4:30am.

New-Style Bus
These buses do not have a conductor. In central London, buy a ticket at a machine or newsagent before boarding.

NIGHT BUSES

London's night-time services run on many popular routes from 11pm until 6am. The routes are prefixed with the letter "N" before blue or yellow numbers. Some of these services pass through Trafalgar Square, so if you are out late, head there to get a ride at least part of the way. Be sure to plan your journey carefully; London is so big that even if you board a bus going in the right direction you could end up completely lost, or a long walk from your accommodation. As always, make sure that you employ a little common sense when travelling on a night bus. Sitting all alone on the top deck is not a good idea; be aware of your personal security. Travel information centres can supply you with details of routes and time-tables for night buses, which are also posted at bus stops.

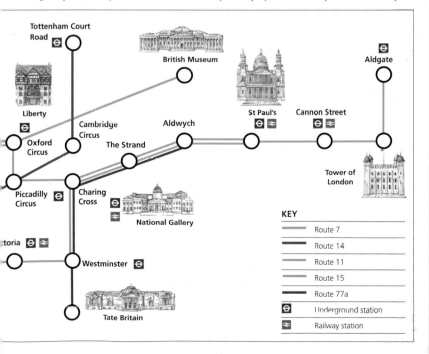

KEY

— Route 7
— Route 14
— Route 11
— Route 15
— Route 77a
⊖ Underground station
⇌ Railway station

Seeing London by Rail

Paddington

Railway station sign

London's train service is used by many hundreds of thousands of commuters daily. As far as tourists are concerned, rail services are useful for trips to the outskirts of the capital, especially south of the river where the Underground hardly extends. Trains are also ideal for day trips and longer excursions around Britain.

USEFUL ROUTES

Perhaps the most useful rail line for visitors to London is the one that starts off from Charing Cross or Cannon Street stations (services from here only run on weekdays) and goes via London Bridge to Greenwich (see pp236–43).

The Thameslink service also connects Luton Airport with south London, Gatwick Airport and Brighton via West Hampstead and Blackfriars.

USING THE TRAINS

London has eight main railway stations serving the whole of the southeast of England and beyond. Rail services travel overground and vary between slow stopping trains, express services to major towns and intercity trains which travel throughout the UK. Make sure that you study the platform indicators carefully so that you get on the most direct train to the correct destination.

Some train doors will open automatically, others at the touch of a button or else by means of a handle. To open the older-style manual doors from inside, you need to pull down the window and reach outside. Keep well away from the doors while the train is travelling, and if you have to stand, make sure you hold on firmly to a strap or hand-rail.

RAIL TICKETS

Tickets can be bought in person, either from a travel agent or from a railway station; by phone with a credit card (08457 484950); or on the internet (www.trainline.com). Most credit cards are accepted. Queues for ticket offices can often be long, so use the automatic machines.

A bewildering range of train tickets exists, but two main options stand out: for travel within Greater London, Travelcards (see p378) offer the most flexibility, while for longer journeys, Cheap Day Return tickets offer excellent value compared to the standard return fares. However, these are both only usable after 9.30am.

Cheap Day Return tickets

DAY TRIPS

Southeast England has a lot more besides the capital to offer visitors. Getting out of London is fast and easy by rail. For details of sights ring Visit Britain (020-8846 9000; www.visitbritain.com). Passenger Enquiries (0845 748 4950; www.trainline.com) has details of all rail services.

Boating on the River Thames at Windsor Castle

Audley End
Village with a stunning Jacobean mansion nearby.
from Liverpool Street. 40 miles (64 km); 1 hr.

Bath
Beautiful Georgian city which has escaped redevelopment. It also has Roman remains.
from Paddington. 107 miles (172 km); 1 hr 25 mins.

Brighton
Lively and attractive seaside resort. See the Royal Pavilion.
from Victoria. 53 miles (85 km); 1 hr.

Cambridge
University city with fine art gallery and ancient colleges.
from Liverpool Street or King's Cross. 54 miles (86 km); 1 hr.

Canterbury
Its cathedral is one of England's oldest and greatest sights.
from Victoria. 62 miles (100 km); 1 hr 25 mins.

Hatfield House
Elizabethan palace with remarkable contents.
from King's Cross or Moorgate. 21 miles (33 km); 20 mins.

Oxford
Like Cambridge, famous for its ancient university.
from Paddington. 56 miles (86 km); 1 hr.

Salisbury
Famous for its cathedral, Salisbury is within driving distance of Stonehenge.
from Waterloo. 84 miles (135 km); 1 hr 40 mins.

St Albans
Cathedral and Roman theatre.
from King's Cross or Moorgate. 25 miles (40km); 30 mins.

Windsor
Riverside town; royal castle restored after fire in 1992.
from Paddington, change Slough. 20 miles (32 km); approx. 30 mins.

Getting a Taxi

London's well-known black cabs are almost as much of an institution as its red buses. But they, too, are being modernized, and you may well see blue, green, red or even white cabs, with some carrying advertising. Black-cab drivers have to take a stringent test on their knowledge of London's streets and its quickest traffic routes before they are awarded a licence. Contrary to popular opinion, they are also among London's safest drivers, if only because they are forbidden to drive a cab with damaged bodywork.

The modern colours of traditional London cabs

London taxi rank

FINDING A CAB

Licensed cabs must carry a "For Hire" sign, which is lit up whenever they are free. You can ring for them, hail them on the streets or find them at ranks, especially near large stations and some major hotels. Raise your arm and wave purposefully. The cab will stop and you simply tell the driver your destination. If a cab stops, it must take you anywhere within a radius of 6 miles (9.6 km) as long as it is

in the Metropolitan Police district, which includes most of the Greater London area and Heathrow Airport.

An alternative to black cabs are mini-cabs, saloon cars summoned by ringing a firm or going into one of their offices, which are usually open 24 hours a day. Do not take a mini-cab in the street as they often operate illegally, without proper insurance, and can be dangerous. Negotiate your fare before setting off. Mini-cab firms are listed in the Yellow Pages (see p368).

TAXI FARES

All licensed cabs have meters which will start ticking at around £1.40 as soon as the taxidriver accepts your custom. The fare increases by minute or for each 311 m (340 yds) travelled. Surcharges are then added for every piece of luggage, for each extra

passenger and for any journeys after 8pm. Fares should be displayed in the vehicle.

USEFUL NUMBERS

Computer Cabs (licensed)
Tel 020-7286 0286.

Radio Taxis (licensed)
Tel 020-7272 0272.

Lady Minicabs (women-only drivers) *Tel* 020-7272 3300. www.ladyminicabs.com

Zingo *Tel* 0870-070 7000 (book from mobiles only).

Lost property *Tel* 020-7918 2000. *Open* 8.30am–4pm Mon–Fri. To log an enquiry www.tfl.gov.uk/lpo

Complaints (Public Carriage Office) *Tel* 020 7941 7800. www.tfl.gov.uk/pco You will need the cab's serial number.

The light, when lit, shows the cab is available and whether there is wheelchair access.

The meter displays your fare as it increases, and surcharges for extra passengers, luggage or unsocial hours. Fares are the same in all licensed cabs.

Fare / Surcharges /

Licensed Cabs
London's cabs are a safe way of travelling around the capital. They have two fold-down seats, can carry a maximum of five passengers and have ample luggage space.

STREET FINDER

The map references given with all sights, hotels, restaurants, shops and entertainment venues described in this book refer to the maps in this section *(see How Map References Work opposite)*. A complete index of street names and all the places of interest marked on the maps can be found on the following pages.

The key map shows the area of London covered by the *Street Finder*, with the postal codes of all the various districts. The maps include the sightseeing areas (which are colour-coded), as well as the whole of central London with all the districts important for hotels, restaurants, pubs and entertainment venues.

NW2   N2   N6

1   **2**

Hampstead

Postal districts are labelled and outlined in orange.

HOLLOWAY ROAD

NW3   NW7

CALEDONIAN ROAD

N1

0 kilometres   2

0 miles   1

FINCHLEY ROAD

MAIDA VALE

KING'S

3   **4** **5**   **6** **7**

Regent's Park and Marylebone   NW1

W9   NW8   EUSTON ROAD   *Bloomsbury and Fitzrovia*   EC1

WC1   *Smithfield and Spitalfields*

9   **10** **11**   **12** **13**   **14** **15** EC2

W11   W2   OXFORD ST   *Soho and Trafalgar Square*   *Covent Garden and the Strand*   *Holborn and the Inns of Court*   EC3   *The City*

BAYSWATER RD   W1

Kensington and Holland Park   *South Kensington and Knightsbridge*   *Piccadilly and St James's*   *South Bank*   SE1   *Southwark and Bankside*

17   W8   **18** **19**   **20** **21**   **22**

W14   SW7   SW3   SW1   *Whitehall and Westminster*   SE11   SE17

SW10   *Chelsea*   CHELSEA EMBANKMENT

SW6   THAMES   SW4   CLAPHAM ROAD   CAMBERWELL NEW ROAD   SW2

SW11   SW2

KEY

-- Postal district boundary

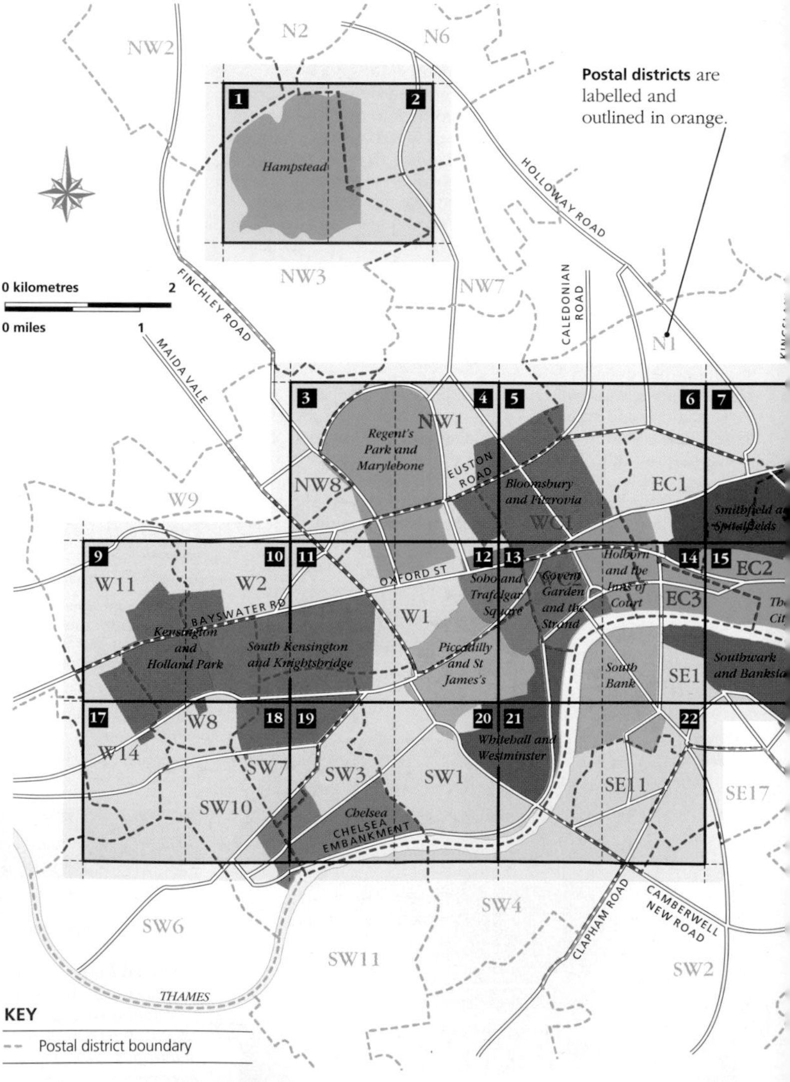

HOW THE MAP REFERENCES WORK

The first figure tells you which Street Finder map to turn to.

Wesley's Chapel-Leysian Mission ⓬

49 City Rd EC1. Map 7 B4.
Tel 020-7253 2262. ⊖ *Old St.*
House open 10am–4pm Mon–Sat,
12.30–1.45pm Sun. ⚫ *not house.* ✝
9.45am (not 1st Sun of month), 11am
Sun, 12.45pm Thu. ⚫ *groups book
ahead.* ⚫ *www.wesleyschapel.org.uk*

A letter and number give the grid reference. Letters go across the map's top and bottom; figures on its sides.

The map continues on map 15 of the Street Finder.

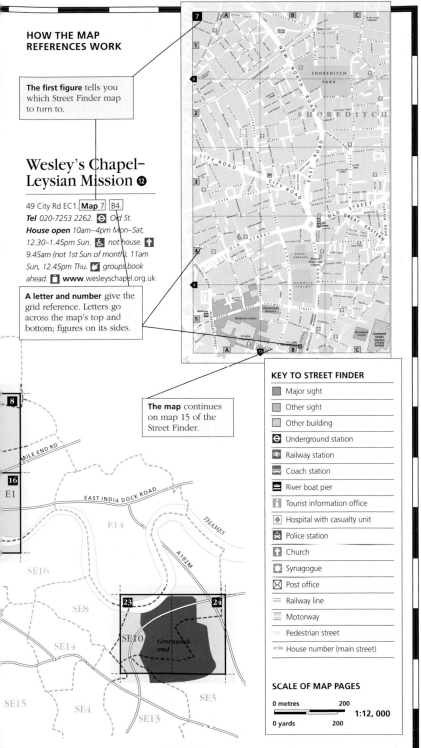

KEY TO STREET FINDER

🟥	Major sight
🟧	Other sight
⬜	Other building
⊖	Underground station
⬕	Railway station
🚌	Coach station
⛴	River boat pier
ℹ	Tourist information office
➕	Hospital with casualty unit
🚓	Police station
✝	Church
✡	Synagogue
⊠	Post office
＝	Railway line
≡	Motorway
	Pedestrian street
◄130	House number (main street)

SCALE OF MAP PAGES

0 metres   200
0 yards   200
                    1:12, 000

Street Finder Index

A

A102 (M) SE10   24 F1
A40 (M) Flyover W2   3 A5
Abbey Gdns W6   17 A4
Abbey Orchard St
SW1   13 B5
Abbey St SE1   16 D5
Abbot's La SE1   15 C4
Abbotsbury Clo W14   9 B5
Abbotsbury Rd W14   9 B5
Abchurch La EC4   15 B2
Aberdeen Ter SE3   23 C5
Abingdon Rd W8   17 C1
Abingdon St SW1   21 B1
Abingdon Vlls W8   17 C1
  18 D1
Acacia Rd NW8   3 A1
Acklam Rd W10   9 A1
Acton Ms E8   8 D1
Acton St WC1   5 C3
  6 D3
Ada Pl E2   8 F1
Ada St E8   8 F1
Adam St WC2   13 C3
Adam's Row W1   12 D3
Addington St SE1   14 D5
Addison Ave W11   9 A4
Addison Cres W14   9 A5
Addison Rd W14   9 A5
Addle Street EC2   15 A1
Adelphi Theatre
WC2   13 C3
Adler St E1   16 E1
Admiral's Wlk NW3   1 A4
Admiralty Arch SW1   13 B3
Admiralty, The SW1   13 B4
Agincourt Rd NW3   2 D5
Aintree St SW6   17 A5
Airlie Gdns W8   9 C4
Air St W1   13 A2
Aisgill Ave W14   17 C3
Albany Courtyard W1   12 F3
Albany St NW1   4 E2
Albemarle St W1   12 F3
Albert Bridge SW3   19 B4
Albert Bridge SW11   19 B5
Albert Bridge Rd
SW11   19 B5
Albert Ct SW7   10 F5
Albert Embankment
SE1   13 C5
Albert Embankment
SE1   21C2
Albert Memorial SW7   10 F5
Alberta St SE17   22 F3
Albion Pl EC1   6 F5
Albion St W2   11 B2
Aldenham St NW1   5 A2
Aldermanbury EC2   15 A1
Aldermanbury Sq
EC2   15 A1
Alderney St SW1   20 E2
Aldersgate St EC1   7 A5
Aldersgate St EC1   15 A1
Aldford St W1   12 D3
Aldgate EC3   16 D2
Aldgate High St EC3   16 D1
Aldridge Rd Vlls W11   9 B1
Aldwych WC2   14 D2
Alexander Pl SW7   19 A1
Alexander Sq SW3   19 B1
Alexander St W2   10 D1
Alfred Pl WC1   5 A5
Alie St E1   16 E1
All Hallows by the
Tower EC3   16 D3
All Saint's Dri SE3   24 E5
All Saint's Rd W11   9 B1
All Saint's St N1   5 C2
All Souls Church W1   12 F1
Allen St W8   18 D1
Allestree Rd SW6   17 A5
Allhallows La EC4   15 B3
Allingham St N1   7 A1

Allington St SW1   20 F1
Allitsen Rd NW8   3 A2
Allsop Pl NW1   3 C4
Alpha Pl SW3   19 B4
Ambergate St SE17   22 F3
Ambrosden Ave SW1   20 F1
Ampton St WC1   6 D3
Amwell St EC1   6 E3
Anderson St SW3   19 B2
Andrew's Rd E8   8 F1
Angel Ct EC2   15 B1
Angel Pas EC4   15 B3
Angel St EC1   15 A1
Angerstein La SE3   24 F4
Anhalt Rd SW11   19 B5
Ann La SW10   18 F5
Annandale Rd SE10   24 E1
Anselm Rd SW6   17 C4
Apothecaries' Hall
EC4   14 F2
Appleby St E2   8 D2
Appold St EC2   7 C5
Apsley House W1   12 D4
Aquinas St SE1   14 E4
Archbishop's Pk SE1   22 D1
Archel Rd W14   17 B4
Argyle Sq WC1   5 C3
Argyle St WC1   5 C3
Argyll Rd W8   9 C5
Argyll St W1   12 F2
Arlington Ave N1   7 A1
Arlington Rd NW1   4 E1
Arlington Sq N1   7 A1
Arlington St SW1   12 F3
Armadale Rd SW6   17 C5
Armitage Rd SE10   24 E1
Arnold Circus E2   8 D3
Artesian Rd W2   9 C2
Arthur St EC4   15 B2
Artillery La E1   8 D5
Artillery Row SW1   21 A1
Arundel Gdns W11   9 B2
Arundel St WC2   14 D2
Ashbridge St NW8   3 A4
Ashburn Gdns SW7   18 E2
Ashburn Pl SW7   18 E2
Ashburnham Gro SE10   23 A4
Ashburnham Pl SE10   23 A3
Ashburnham Rd SW10   18 F5
Ashby St EC1   6 F3
Asher Way E1   16 F3
Ashford St N1   7 C3
Ashley Pl SW1   20 F1
Ashmill St NW1   3 B5
Astell St SW3   19 B3
Atherstone Ms SW7   18 F1
Atterbury St SW1   21 B2
Attneave St WC1   6 D4
Aubrey Rd W8   9 B4
Aubrey Wlk W8   9 B4
Audley Sq W1   12 D3
Audrey St E2   8 F2
Augustus St NW1   4 F2
Auriol Rd W14   17 A2
Austin St E2   8 D3
Australia House WC2   14 D2
Austral St SE11   22 F1
Aveline St SE11   22 D3
Avenue Rd NW8   3 A1
Avenue, The SE10   23 C3
Avery Row W1   12 E2
Avonmore Rd W14   17 A1
Aybrook St W1   12 D1
Aylesbury St EC1   6 F4
Aylesford St SW1   21 A3
Ayres St SE1   15 A4

B

Babmaes St SW1   13 A3
Bache's St N1   7 C3
Back Church La E1   16 F2
Back Hill EC1   6 E4
Back La NW3   1 B5
Bacon St E1, E2   8 E4
Bainbridge St WC1   13 B1

Baker St NW1, W1   3 C5
  12 D1
Balcombe St NW1   3 B4
Balderton St W1   12 D2
Baldwin St EC1   7 B3
Baldwin's Gdns EC1   6 E5
Balfe St N1   5 C2
Ballast Quay SE10   23 C1
Ballast Quay SE10   24 D1
Balniel Gate SW1   21 B3
Baltic St EC1   7 A4
Bank End SE1   15 3B
Bank of England EC2   15 B1
Bankside SE1   15 A3
Bankside Gallery SE1   14 F3
Banner St EC1   7 A4
Banning St SE10   24 D1
Banqueting House
SW1   13 B4
Barbican Centre EC2   7 A5
Barclay Rd SW6   17 C5
Bardsley La SE10   23 A2
Barford St N1   6 E1
Barge House St SE1   14 E3
Baring St N1   7 B1
Bark Pl W2   10 D2
Barkston Gdns SW5   18 D2
Barnby St NW1   5 A2
Barnet Gro E2   8 E3
Barnham St E1   16 D4
Barnsbury Rd N1   6 E1
Baron St N1   6 E2
Baroness Rd E2   8 E3
Baron's Ct Rd W14   17 A3
Baron's Keep W14   17 A2
Baron's Pl SE1   14 E5
Barrow Hill Rd NW8   3 A2
Barter St WC1   13 C1
Bartholomew Clo
EC1   7 A5
Bartholomew La EC2   15 B1
Bartholomew Sq EC1   7 A4
Barton Rd W14   17 A3
Basil St SW3   11 C5
Basing St W11   9 B1
Basinghall Ave EC2   15 B1
Basinghall St EC2   15 B1
Basire St N1   7 A1
Bassett Rd W10   9 A1
Bastwick St EC1   7 A4
Batchelor St N1   6 E1
Bateman's Row EC2   8 D4
Bath St EC1   7 B3
Bathurst Ms W2   11 A2
Bathurst St W2   11 A2
Battersea Bridge
SW3, SW11   19 A5
Battersea Bridge
Rd SW11   19 A5
Battersea Park SW11   19 C5
  20 D5
Battersea Pk Rd
SW8, SW11   20 F5
Battersea Power
Station SW8   20 F4
Battle Bridge La SE1   15 C4
Battle Bridge Rd NW1   5 B2
Batty St E1   16 F1
Baxendale St E2   8 E3
Bayham St NW1   4 F1
Baylis Rd SE1   14 E5
Bayswater Rd W2   10 E3
Bayswater Rd W2   11 A2
Beaconsfield Clo SE3   24 F2
Beaconsfield Rd SE3   24 F2
Beak St W1   12 F2
Bear Gdns SE1   15 A3
Bear La SE1   14 F4
Beauchamp Pl SW3   19 B1
Beaufort Gdns SW3   19 B1
Beaufort St SW3   18 F3
  19 A4
Beaufoy Wlk SE11   22 D2
Beaumont Ave W14   17 B3
Beaumont Cres
W14   17 B3

Beaumont Pl W1   5 A4
Beaumont St W1   4 D5
Beck Clo SE13   23 A5
Bedale St SE1   15 B4
Bedford Ave WC1   13 B1
Bedford Gdns W8   9 C4
Bedford Pl WC1   5 B5
Bedford Row WC1   6 D5
Bedford Sq WC1   5 B5
Bedford St WC2   13 C3
Bedford Way WC1   5 B4
Bedfordbury WC2   13 B2
Beech St EC2   7 A5
Belfast Gdns SE3   24 E2
Belgrave Ms North
SW1   12 D5
Belgrave Ms West
SW1   20 D1
Belgrave Pl SW1   20 D1
Belgrave Rd SW1   20 F2
  21 A3
Belgrave Sq SW1   12 D5
Belgrove St WC1   5 C3
Bell La E1   16 D1
Bell St NW1   3 A5
Bell Wharf La EC4   15 B2
Bell Yd WC2   14 D1
Bellot St SE10   24 D1
Belvedere Rd SE1   14 D4
Bemerton St N1   5 C1
Bennett Gro SE13   23 A5
Bentinck St W1   12 D1
Berkeley Sq W1   12 E3
Berkeley St W1   12 E3
Bermondsey Antiques
Mkt SE1   15 C5
Bermondsey St SE1   15 C4
Bermondsey Wall
East SE16   16 F5
Bermondsey Wall
West SE16   16 E4
Bernard St WC1   5 C4
Berners St W1   12 F1
  13 A1
Berry St EC1   6 F4
Berwick St W1   13 A1
Bessborough Pl SW1   21 A3
Bessborough St SW1   21 A3
Bethnal Grn Rd E1   8 D4
Bethnal Grn Rd E2   8 F3
Bethwin Rd SE5   22 F5
Bevan St N1   7 A1
Bevenden St N1   7 C3
Bevington St SE16   16 F5
Bevis Marks EC3   16 D1
Bickenhall St W1   3 C5
Bidborough St WC1   5 B3
Big Ben SW1   13 C5
Billing Rd SW10   18 E5
Billingsgate EC3   15 C3
Bina Gdns SW5   18 E2
Binney St W1   12 D2
Birdcage Wlk SW1   12 F5
  13 A5
Birkenhead St WC1   5 C3
Bisham Gdns N6   2 F1
Bishop King's Rd
W14   17 A2
Bishop St N1   7 A1
Bishops Ave, The
NW2   1 B1
Bishop's Bridge Rd
W2   10 E1
Bishop's Rd SW11   19 B5
Bishopsgate EC2   8 D5
  15 C1
Bishopsgate Church
Yard EC2   15 C1
Bishopswood Rd N6   2 D1
Black Prince Rd SE1   21 C2
Black Prince Rd
SE11   22 D2
Blackall St EC2   7 C4
Blackfriars Bridge
EC4   14 F2
Blackfriars La EC4   14 F2

Blackfriars Rd SE1	14 F3	Bridport Pl N1	7 B1
Blackfriars		Bridstow Pl W2	9 C1
Underpass EC4	14 F2	Brill Pl NW1	5 B2
Blackheath SE3	24 D5	British Airways	
Blackheath Ave SE10	24 D3	London Eye SE1	13 4C
Blackheath Hill SE10	23 B4	Britannia Row N1	7 A1
Blackheath Rise		Britannia St WC1	5 C3
SE13	23 B5	Britannia Wlk N1	7 B3
Blackheath Rd SE10	23 A4	British Library WC1	5 B3
Blackheath Vale SE3	24 D5	British Museum WC1	5 B5
Blackwall La SE10	24 E1	British Telecom	
Blagrove Rd W10	9 A1	Tower N1	4 F5
Blandford Sq NW1	3 B5	Brittania Rd SW6	18 D5
Blandford St W1	12 D1	Britten St SW3	19 A3
Blantyre St SW10	18 F5	Britton St EC1	6 F5
Blenheim Cres W11	9 A2	Brixton Rd SW9	22 E5
Bletchley St N1	7 B2	Broad Sanctuary SW1	13 B5
Blewcoat School		Broad Wlk NW1	4 D2
SW1	13 A5	Broad Wlk, The W8	10 E4
Bliss Cres SE13	23 A5	Broadbridge Clo SE3	24 F3
Blisset St SE10	23 A4	Broadcasting House	
Blomfield St EC2	15 C1	W1	12 E1
Bloomfield Terr SW1	20 D3	Broadgate Centre	
Bloomsbury Pl WC1	5 C5	EC2	7 C5
Bloomsbury Sq WC1	5 C5	Broadley St NW8	3 A5
Bloomsbury St WC1	13 B1	Broadley Terr NW1	3 B4
Bloomsbury Way		Broadwall SE1	14 E3
WC1	13 C1	Broadway SW1	13 A5
Blue Anchor Yrd E1	16 E2	Broadway Mkt E8	8 F1
Blythe Rd W14	17 A1	Broadwick St W1	12 F2
Boadicea St N1	5 C1		13 A2
Boating Lake NW1	3 C3	Broken Wharf EC4	15 A2
Boating Lake SW11	20 D5	Brompton Cemetery	
Bolney St SW8	21 C5	SW10	18 D4
Bolsover St W1	4 F5	Brompton Oratory	
Bolton Gdns SW5	18 D3	SW7	19 A1
Bolton St W1	12 E3	Brompton Pk Cres	
Boltons, The SW10	18 E3	SW6	18 D4
Bond Way SW8	21 C4	Brompton Pl SW3	19 B1
Bonhill St EC2	7 C4	Brompton Rd SW3	11 B5
Bonnington Sq SW8	21 C4		19 B1
Boot St N1	7 C3	Brompton Sq SW3	19 B1
Borough High St SE1	15 B4	Bromwich Ave N6	2 F3
Borough Mkt SE1	15 B4	Bronsart Rd SW6	17 A5
Borough Rd SE1	14 F5	Brook Dri SE11	22 E1
Borough Rd SE1	15 A5	Brook Gate W1	11 C3
Boscobel St NW8	3 A5	Brook Ms North W2	10 F2
Boston Pl NW1	3 B4	Brook St W1	12 E2
Boswell St WC1	5 C5	Brook St W2	11 A2
Boundary St E2	8 D4	Brooke St EC1	6 E5
Bourdon St W1	12 E2	Brookmill Rd SE8	23 A5
Bourne St SW1	20 D2	Brook's Ms W1	12 E2
Bouverie Pl W2	11 A1	Brookville Rd SW6	17 B5
Bouverie St EC4	14 E2	Brougham Rd E8	8 F1
Bow La EC4	15 A2	Brown St W1	11 B1
Bow St WC2	13 C2	Brownlow Ms WC1	6 D4
Bower Ave SE10	24 D3	Brownlow St WC1	6 D5
Bowling Grn La EC1	6 E4	Brunswick Ct SE1	16 D5
Bowling Grn St SE11	22 E4	Brunswick Gdns W8	10 D4
Boyfield St SE1	14 F5	Brunswick Pl N1	7 B3
Brackley St EC1	7 A5	Brunswick Sq WC1	5 C4
Brad St SE1	14 E4	Brushfield St E1	8 D5
Braganza St SE17	22 F3	Bruton La W1	12 E3
Braham St E1	16 E1	Bruton Pl W1	12 E3
Braidwood St SE1	15 C4	Bruton St W1	12 E3
Bramber Rd W14	17 B4	Bryanston Ms East W1	11 C1
Bramerton St SW3	19 A4	Bryanston Pl W1	11 B1
Bramham Gdns SW5	18 D2	Bryanston Sq W1	11 C1
Branch Hill NW3	1 A4	Bryanston St W1	11 C2
Branch Pl N1	7 B1	Buck Hill Wlk W2	11 A3
Brand St SE10	23 B3	Buckingham Gate	
Bray Pl SW3	19 C2	SW1	12 F5
Bread St EC4	15 A2	Buckingham Gate	
Bream's Bldgs EC4	14 E1	SW1	13 A5
Brechin Pl SW7	18 F2	Buckingham Palace	
Brecon Rd W6	17 A4	SW1	12 F5
Bremner Rd SW7	10 F5	Buckingham Palace	
Brendon St W1	11 B1	Gardens SW1	12 E5
Bressenden Pl SW1	20 F1	Buckingham Palace	
Brewer St W1	13 A2	Rd SW1	20 E2
Brick La E1, E2	8 E5	Buckland St N1	7 C2
	8 E3	Bull Wharf La EC4	15 A2
Brick St W1	12 E4	Bulls Gdns SW3	19 B2
Bridge Pl SW1	20 F2	Bulmer Pl W11	9 C3
Bridge St SW1	13 C5	Bunhill Fields EC1	7 B4
Bridgefoot SE1	21 C3	Bunhill Row EC1	7 B4
Bridgeman St NW8	3 A2	Burdett Ms W2	10 D1
Bridgeway St NW1	5 A2		

Burgh House NW3	1 B4	Carlisle Pl SW1	20 F1
Burgh St N1	6 F2	Carlos Pl W1	12 E3
Burial Grounds EC1	7 B4	Carlow St NW1	4 F1
Burlington Arcade W1	12 F3	Carlton House Terr	
Burlington Gdns W1	12 F3	SW1	13 A4
Burnaby St SW10	18 F5	Carlyle Sq SW3	19 A3
Burney St SE10	23 B3	Carlyle's House SW3	19 B4
Burnsall St SW3	19 B3	Carmelite St EC4	14 E2
Burnthwaite Rd SW6	17 C5	Carnaby St W1	12 F2
Burrell St SE1	14 F3	Carnegie St N1	6 D1
Burslem St E1	16 F2	Carol St NW1	4 F1
Burton St WC1	5 B4	Caroline Gdns E2	8 D3
Burton's Ct SW3	19 C3	Caroline Pl W2	10 D2
Bury Pl WC1	13 C1	Caroline Terr SW1	20 D2
Bury St EC3	16 D1	Carriage Dri East	
Bury St SW1	12 F3	SW11	20 D5
Bush House WC2	14 D2	Carriage Dri North	
Buttesland St N1	7 C3	SW11	19 C5
Buxton St E1	8 E4		20 D4
Byward St EC3	16 D2	Carriage Dri West	
		SW11	19 C5
C		Carroun Rd SW8	22 D5
		Carter La EC4	14 F2
Cabinet War Rooms and		Cartwright Gdns WC1	5 B3
Churchill Museum SW1	13 B4	Cartwright St E1	16 E2
Cable St E1	16 F2	Casson St E1	8 E5
Cade Rd SE10	23 C4	Castle Baynard St	
Cadogan Gate SW1	19 C2	EC4	14 F2
Cadogan Gdns SW3	19 C2		15 A2
Cadogan La SW1	20 D1	Castle La SW1	12 F5
Cadogan Pier SW3	19 B4	Castletown Rd W14	17 A3
Cadogan Pl SW1	19 C1	Cathcart Rd SW10	18 E4
Cadogan Sq SW1	19 C1	Cathedral St SE1	15 B3
Cadogan St SW3	19 C2	Catherine Gro SE10	23 A4
Cale St SW3	19 A3	Catherine St WC2	13 C2
Caledonian Rd N1	5 C2	Catton St WC1	13 C1
	6 D1	Causton St SW1	21 B2
Callender Rd SW7	10 F5	Cavendish Ave NW8	3 A2
Callow St SW3	18 F4	Cavendish Pl W1	12 E1
Calshot St N1	6 D2	Cavendish Sq W1	12 E1
Calthorpe St WC1	6 D4	Cavendish St N1	7 B2
Calvert Ave E2	8 D3	Caversham St SW3	19 C4
Calvert Rd SE10	24 E1	Caxton St SW1	13 A5
Calvin St E1	8 D5	Cedarne Rd SW6	18 D5
Camberwell New Rd		Cenotaph SW1	13 B4
SE5	22 E5	Central Criminal	
Cambridge Circus		Court EC4	14 F1
WC2	13 B2	Central Mkt WC2	13 C2
Cambridge Gdns		Central St EC1	7 A3
W10	9 A1	Chadwell St EC1	6 E3
Cambridge Pl W8	10 E5	Chadwick St SW1	21 A1
Cambridge Sq W2	11 A1	Chagford St NW1	3 C4
Cambridge St SW1	20 F3	Chaldon Rd SW6	17 A5
Camden High St NW1	4 F1	Challoner St W14	17 B3
Camden St NW1	4 F1	Chalton St NW1	5 A2
	5 A1	Chamber St E1	16 E2
Camden Wlk N1	6 F1	Chambers St SE16	16 F5
Camera Pl SW10	18 F4	Chambord St E2	8 E3
Camlet St E2	8 D4	Chance St E1,E2	8 D4
Camley St NW1	5 A1	Chancel St SE1	14 F4
Campden Gro W8	9 C4	Chancery La WC2	14 D1
Campden Hill W8	9 C4	Chandos Pl WC2	13 B3
Campden Hill Rd		Chandos St W1	12 E1
W11	9 C4	Chapel Mkt N1	6 E2
Campden Hill Sq W8	9 B4	Chapel Side W2	10 D2
Campden St W8	9 C4	Chapel St NW1	3 B5
Canadian Embassy		Chapel St SW1	12 D5
SW1	13 B3	Chapter Rd SE17	22 F3
Canal Wlk N1	7 B1	Chapter St SW1	21 A2
Canning Pl W8	10 E5	Charing Cross	
Cannon La NW3	1 B4	Pier WC2	13 C3
Cannon Pl NW3	1 B4	Charing Cross Rd	
Cannon Row SW1	13 B5	WC2	13 B1
Cannon St EC4	15 A2	Charlbert St NW8	3 A2
Cannon St Rd E1	16 F1	Charles La NW8	3 A2
Canon St N1	7 A1	Charles Sq N1	7 C3
Canrobert St E2	8 F2	Charles St W1	12 E3
Canterbury Pl SE17	22 F2	Charles II St SW1	13 A3
Capland St NW8	3 A4	Charleville Rd W14	17 A3
Caradoc Clo W2	9 C1	Charlotte Rd EC2	7 C3
Caradoc St SE10	24 D1	Charlotte St W1	4 F5
Cardigan St SE11	22 D3		5 A5
Cardington St NW1	5 A3		13 A1
Carey St WC2	14 D1	Charlotte Terr N1	6 D1
Carlingford Rd NW3	1 B5	Charlton Pl N1	6 F1
Carlisle La SE1	14 D5	Charlton Way SE3	24 D4
	22 D1	Charlwood St SW1	20 F3
			21 A2

Each place name is followed by its postal district, and then by its Street Finder reference

Charrington St NW1 **5 A2**
Chart St N1 **7 C3**
Charterhouse Sq EC1 **6 F5**
Charterhouse St EC1 **6 F5**
Cheapside EC2 **15 A1**
Chelsea Bridge SW1 **20 E4**
Chelsea Bridge Rd
SW1, SW8 **20 D3**
Chelsea Embankment
SW3 **19 B4**
20 D4
Chelsea Manor St
SW3 **19 B3**
Chelsea Old Church
SW3 **19 A4**
Chelsea Physic
Garden SW3 **19 C4**
Chelsea Pk Gdns SW3 **18 F4**
Chelsea Royal
Hospital SW3 **20 D3**
Chelsea Sq SW3 **19 A3**
Cheltenham Terr SW3 **19 C3**
Chenies Ms WC1 **5 A4**
Chenies St WC1 **5 A5**
Cheniston Gdns W8 **18 D1**
Chepstow Cres W11 **9 C2**
Chepstow Pl W2 **9 C2**
Chepstow Rd W2 **9 C1**
Chepstow Vlls W11 **9 C2**
Chequer St EC1 **7 B4**
Cherbury St N1 **7 C2**
Chesham Pl SW1 **20 D1**
Chesham St SW1 **20 D1**
Cheshire St E2 **8 E4**
Chesson Rd W14 **17 B4**
Chester Gate NW1 **4 E3**
Chester Ms SW1 **12 E5**
Chester Rd NW1 **4 D3**
Chester Row SW1 **20 D2**
Chester Sq SW1 **20 E1**
Chester St SW1 **12 E5**
Chester Terr NW1 **4 E3**
Chester Way SE11 **22 E2**
Chesterfield Wlk
SE10 **23 C4**
Cheval Pl SW7 **19 B1**
Chevening Rd SE10 **24 F1**
Cheyne Gdns SW3 **19 B4**
Cheyne Wlk SW3,
SW10 **19 A5**
Chicheley St SE1 **14 D4**
Chichester St SW1 **21 A3**
Chicksand St E1 **8 E5**
Chiltern St W1 **4 D5**
12 D1
Chilton St E2 **8 E4**
Chilver St SE10 **24 F1**
Chilworth Ms W2 **10 F1**
Chilworth St W2 **10 F2**
Chiswell St EC1 **7 B5**
Christ Church,
Spitalfields E1 **8 E5**
Christchurch Hill
NW3 **1 B4**
Christchurch St SW3 **19 C4**
Christchurch Way
SE10 **24 D1**
Christian St E1 **16 F1**
Christopher St EC2 **7 C5**
Chryssell Rd SW9 **22 E5**
Church Row NW3 **1 A5**
Church St NW8 **3 A5**
Churchill Gardens
SW1 **20 F3**
Churchill Gardens
Rd SW1 **20 F3**
Churchway NW1 **5 A3**
Churchyard Row
SE11 **22 F2**
Churton St SW1 **20 F2**
Circus St SE10 **23 B3**
City Garden Row N1 **6 F2**
7 A2
City Rd EC1 **6 F2**
7 B3
City Rd Basin N1 **7 A2**
Clabon Ms SW1 **19 C1**
Clanricarde Gdns W2 **10 D3**

Clapham Rd SW9 **22 D5**
Claredale St E2 **8 F2**
Claremont Clo N1 **6 E2**
Claremont Sq N1 **6 E2**
Claremont St SE10 **23 A2**
Clarence Gdns NW1 **4 F3**
Clarence House SW1 **12 F4**
Clarendon Pl W2 **11 A2**
Clarendon Rd W11 **9 A2**
Clarendon St SW1 **20 F3**
Clareville Gro SW7 **18 F2**
Clareville St SW7 **18 F2**
Clarges St W1 **12 E3**
Clarissa St E8 **8 D1**
Claverton St SW1 **21 A3**
Claylands Rd SW8 **22 D4**
Clayton St SE11 **22 E4**
Cleaver Sq SE11 **22 E3**
Cleaver St SE11 **22 E3**
Clem Attlee Ct SW6 **17 B4**
Clement's La EC4 **15 C2**
Cleopatra's Needle
WC2 **13 C3**
Clere St EC2 **7 C4**
Clerkenwell Green
EC1 **6 E4**
Clerkenwell Rd EC1 **6 E5**
Cleveland Gdns W2 **10 E2**
Cleveland Sq W2 **10 E2**
Cleveland St W1 **4 F5**
Cleveland Terr W2 **10 F1**
Clifford St W1 **12 F2**
Clifton St EC2 **7 C4**
Clink Exhibition
SE1 **15 B3**
Clink St SE1 **15 B3**
Clipstone St W1 **4 F5**
Cliveden Pl SW1 **20 D2**
Cloth Fair EC1 **6 F5**
Cloudesley Pl N1 **6 E1**
Cloudesley Rd N1 **6 E1**
Cloudesley Sq N1 **6 E1**
Cloudesley St N1 **6 E1**
Club Row E1,E2 **8 D4**
Cluny Ms SW5 **17 C2**
Coate St E2 **8 F2**
Cochrane St NW8 **3 A2**
Cock La EC1 **14 F1**
Cockspur St SW1 **13 B3**
Coin St SE1 **14 E3**
Colbeck Ms SW7 **18 E2**
Coldbath St SE13 **23 A5**
Cole St SE1 **15 B5**
Colebrooke Row N1 **6 F2**
Coleherne Ct SW5 **18 E3**
Coleherne Rd SW10 **18 D3**
Coleman Fields N1 **7 A1**
Coleman St EC2 **15 B1**
Coleraine Rd SE3 **24 E2**
Coley St WC1 **6 D4**
College Pl NW1 **5 A1**
College St EC4 **15 B2**
Collier St N1 **5 C2**
6 D2
Collingham Gdns
SW5 **18 E2**
Collingham Pl SW5 **18 D2**
Collingham Rd SW5 **18 E2**
Colnbrook St SE1 **22 F1**
Colomb St SE10 **24 E1**
Colonnade WC1 **5 C4**
Columbia Rd E2 **8 D3**
Colville Gdns W11 **9 B2**
Colville Ms W11 **9 B2**
Colville Rd W11 **9 B2**
Colville Terr W11 **9 B2**
Combe Ave SE3 **24 E3**
Combe Ms SE3 **24 E3**
Combedale Rd
SE10 **24 F1**
Comeragh Rd W14 **17 A3**
Commercial Rd E1 **16 E1**
Commercial St E1 **8 D5**
Commerell St SE10 **24 D1**
Compton Ave N6 **1 C1**
Compton St EC1 **6 F4**
Concert Hall
Approach SE1 **14 D4**

Conduit Ms W2 **10 F2**
Conduit St W1 **12 F2**
Conington Rd SE13 **23 A5**
Conley St SE10 **24 E1**
Connaught Pl W2 **11 C2**
Connaught Sq W2 **11 B2**
Connaught St W2 **11 B2**
Constantine Rd NW3 **2 D5**
Constitution Hill SW1 **12 E5**
Cook's Rd SE17 **22 F4**
Coomer Pl SW6 **17 C4**
Coopers La NW1 **5 B2**
Cooper's Row EC3 **16 D2**
Cope Pl W8 **17 C1**
Copenhagen St N1 **5 C1**
Copenhagen St N1 **6 D1**
Copperas St SE8 **23 A2**
Copperfield St SE1 **14 F4**
15 A4
Copthall Ave EC2 **15 B1**
Coptic St WC1 **13 B1**
Coral St SE1 **14 E5**
Corams' Fields WC1 **5 C4**
Cork St W1 **12 F3**
Cornhill EC3 **15 C2**
Cornwall Cres W11 **9 A2**
Cornwall Gdns SW7 **18 E1**
Cornwall Rd SE1 **14 E4**
Cornwall Terr NW1 **3 C4**
Coronet St N1 **7 C3**
Corporation Row
EC1 **6 E4**
Corsham St N1 **7 B3**
Cosmo Pl WC1 **5 C5**
Cosser St SE1 **22 D1**
Cosway St NW1 **3 B5**
Cottage Pl SW3 **19 A1**
Cottesmore Gdns W8 **18 E1**
Cottington Clo SE11 **22 F2**
Cottington St SE11 **22 E2**
Coulson St SW3 **19 C2**
Counter St SE1 **15 C4**
County Hall SE1 **8 D5**
Courtauld Gallery WC2 **14 D2**
Courtenay St SE11 **22 D3**
Courtfield Gdns SW5 **18 E2**
Courtfield Rd SW7 **18 E2**
Courthope Rd NW3 **2 E5**
Courtnell St W2 **9 C1**
Cousin La EC4 **15 B3**
Coutt's Cres NW5 **2 F3**
Covent Garden WC2 **13 C2**
Coventry St WC1 **13 A3**
Cowcross St EC1 **6 F5**
Cowper St EC2 **7 B4**
Cramer St W1 **4 D5**
Crane St SE10 **23 C1**
Cranleigh St NW1 **5 A2**
Cranley Gdns SW7 **18 F3**
Cranley Ms SW7 **18 F3**
Cranley Pl SW7 **18 F2**
Cranmer Rd SW9 **22 E5**
Cranwood St EC1 **7 B3**
Craven Hill W2 **10 F2**
Craven Hill Gdns W2 **10 E2**
Craven Rd W2 **10 F2**
Craven St SW2 **13 B3**
Craven Terr W2 **10 F2**
Crawford Pas EC1 **6 E4**
Crawford Pl W1 **11 B1**
Crawford St W1 **3 C5**
Creechurch La EC3 **16 D1**
Creed St EC4 **14 F2**
Creek Rd SE8 **23 A2**
Cremer St E2 **8 D2**
Cremorne Rd SW10 **18 F5**
Cresswell Gdns SW5 **18 E3**
Cresswell Pl SW10 **18 E3**
Cressy Rd NW3 **2 D5**
Crestfield St WC1 **5 C3**
Crewdson Rd SW9 **22 D5**
Crimsworth Rd SW8 **21 B5**
Crinan St N1 **5 C2**
Cringle St SW8 **20 F5**
Crispin St E1 **8 D5**
Croftdown Rd NW5 **2 F4**
Cromer St WC1 **5 C3**
Cromwell Cres SW5 **17 C2**

Cromwell Gdns SW7 **19 A1**
Cromwell Pl SW7 **19 A1**
Cromwell Rd SW5,
SW7 **18 D2**
18 F1
Crondall St N1 **7 C2**
Croom's Hill SE10 **23 C3**
Croom's Hill Gro
SE10 **23 B3**
Cropley St N1 **7 B2**
Crosby Row SE1 **15 B5**
Croston St E8 **8 F1**
Crown Office Row
EC4 **14 E2**
Crowndale Rd NW1 **4 F2**
5 A1
Crucifix La SE1 **15 C4**
Cruden St N1 **6 F1**
Crutched Friars EC3 **16 D2**
Cubitt St WC1 **6 D3**
Culford Gdns SW3 **19 C2**
Culross St W1 **12 D3**
Culworth St NW8 **3 B2**
Cumberland Cres
W14 **17 A2**
Cumberland Gate W1 **11 C2**
Cumberland Mkt NW1 **4 F3**
Cumberland Place
NW1 **11 C2**
Cumberland St SW1 **20 F3**
Cumberland Terr NW1 **4 E2**
Cumberland Terr Ms
NW1 **4 E2**
Cumming St N1 **6 D2**
Cundy St SW1 **20 D2**
Cureton St SW1 **21 B2**
Curlew St SE1 **16 E4**
Cursitor St EC4 **14 E1**
Curtain Rd EC2 **7 C3**
Curzon St W1 **12 D4**
Cut, The SE1 **14 E4**
Cutlers Gdns E1 **16 D1**
Cutty Sark SE10 **23 B2**
Cynthia St N1 **6 D2**
Cyrus St EC1 **6 F4**

D

D'Arblay St W1 **13 A2**
Dabin Cres SE10 **23 A4**
Dacre St SW1 **13 A5**
Dallington St EC1 **6 F4**
Dame St N1 **7 A2**
Danbury St N1 **6 F2**
Dante Rd SE11 **22 F2**
Danube St SW3 **19 B3**
Danvers St SW3 **19 A4**
Dartmouth Clo W11 **9 C1**
Dartmouth Gro SE10 **23 B5**
Dartmouth Hill SE10 **23 B4**
Dartmouth Row
SE10 **23 B5**
Dartmouth St SW1 **13 A5**
Davidson Gdns SW8 **21 B5**
Davies St W1 **12 E2**
Dawes Rd SW6 **17 A5**
Dawson Pl W2 **9 C2**
Dawson St E2 **8 E2**
De Beauvoir Cres N1 **7 C1**
De Laune St SE17 **22 F3**
De Vere Gdns W8 **10 E5**
Deal St E1 **8 5F**
Dean Ryle St SW1 **21 B1**
Dean St W1 **13 A1**
Dean's Yd SW1 **13 B5**
Decima St SE1 **15 C5**
Delaford St SW6 **17 A5**
Delancey St NW1 **4 E1**
Denbigh Pl SW1 **20 F3**
Denbigh Rd W11 **9 B2**
Denbigh St SW1 **20 F2**
Denbigh Terr W11 **9 B2**
Denham St SE10 **24 F1**
Denman St W1 **13 A2**
Denning Rd NW3 **1 B5**
Dennis Severs
House E1 **8 D5**
Denny St SE11 **22 E2**

Denyer St SW3 19 B2
Derbyshire St E2 8 F3
Dereham Pl EC2 8 D4
Dericote St E8 8 F1
Derry St W8 10 D5
Design Museum SE1 16 E4
Devonshire Clo W1 4 E5
Devonshire Dri SE10 23 A4
Devonshire Pl W1 4 D5
Devonshire Sq EC2 16 D1
Devonshire St W1 4 E5
Devonshire Terr W2 10 F2
Dewey Rd N1 6 E1
Diamond Terr SE10 23 B4
Diana, Princess of
 Wales Memorial
 Playground W2 10 D3
Dickens House
 Museum WC1 6 D4
Dilke St SW3 19 C4
Dingley Rd EC1 7 A3
Dinsdale Rd SE3 24 E2
Disbrowe Rd W6 17 A4
Disney Pl SE1 15 A4
Diss St E2 8 E2
Ditch Alley SE10 23 A4
Dock St E1 16 E2
Dockhead SE1 16 E5
Dr Johnson's House
 EC4 14 E1
Doddington Gro
 SE17 22 F3
Doddington Pl SE17 22 F4
Dodson St SE1 14 E5
Dolben St SE1 14 F4
Dolphin Sq SW1 21 A3
Dombey St WC1 5 C5
Donegal St N1 6 D2
Donne Pl SW3 19 B2
Doon St SE1 14 E3
Doric Way NW1 5 A3
Dorset Rd SW8 21 C5
 22 D5
Dorset St NW1, W1 3 C5
Doughty Ms WC1 6 D4
Doughty St WC1 6 D4
Douglas St SW1 21 A2
Douro Pl W8 10 E5
Dove House St SW3 19 A3
Dove Row E2 8 F1
Dover St W1 12 F3
Down St W1 12 E4
Downing St SW1 13 B4
Downshire Hill NW3 1 C5
Draycott Ave SW3 19 B2
Draycott Pl SW3 19 C2
Draycott Terr SW3 19 C2
Drayton Gdns SW10 18 F3
Druid St SE1 16 D4
Drummond Cres
 NW1 5 A3
Drummond Gate
 SW1 21 B3
Drummond St NW1 4 F4
 5 A3
Drury La WC2 13 C1
Drysdale St N1 8 D3
Duchess of Bedford's
 Wlk W8 9 C5
Duchess St W1 4 E5
Duchy St SE1 14 E3
Dufferin St EC1 7 B4
Duke Humphrey
 Rd SE3 24 D5
Duke of Wellington
 Pl SW1 12 D5
Duke of York St
 SW1 13 A3
Duke St SW1 12 F3
Duke St W1 12 D2
Duke St Hill SE1 15 B3
Duke's La W8 10 D4
Duke's Rd WC1 5 B3
Duke's Pl EC3 16 D1
Dunbridge St E2 8 F4
Duncan Rd E8 8 F1
Duncan St N1 6 F2
Duncan Terr N1 6 F2

Dunloe St E2 8 E2
Dunraven St W1 11 C2
Dunston Rd E8 8 D1
Dunston St E8 8 D1
Durant St E2 8 F2
Durham St SE11 22 D3
Durham Terr W2 10 D1
Durward St E1 8 F5
Dutton St SE10 23 B4
Dyott St WC1 13 B1

E
Eagle Ct EC1 6 F5
Eagle St WC1 13 C1
Eagle Wharf Rd N1 7 A2
Eamont St NW8 3 B2
Earl St EC2 7 C5
Earlham St WC2 13 B2
Earl's Court Exhibition
 Centre SW5 17 C3
Earl's Court Gdns
 SW5 18 D2
Earl's Court Rd SW5,
 W8 18 D2
Earl's Court Sq SW5 18 D3
Earl's Terr W8 17 B1
Earl's Wlk W8 17 C1
Earlswood St SE10 24 D1
Earsby St W14 17 A2
East Ferry Rd E14 23 A1
East Heath NW3 1 B3
East Heath Rd NW3 1 B4
East Pier E1 16 F4
East Rd N1 7 B3
East Smithfield E1 16 E3
East Tenter St E1 16 E2
Eastbourne Ms W2 10 F1
Eastbourne Terr W2 10 F1
Eastcastle St W1 12 F1
 13 A1
Eastcheap EC3 15 C2
Eastney St SE10 23 C1
Eaton Gate SW1 20 D2
Eaton La SW1 20 E1
Eaton Ms SW1 20 D1
Eaton Ms North SW1 20 D1
Eaton Ms West SW1 20 D2
Eaton Pl SW1 20 D1
Eaton Sq SW1 20 D1
Eaton Terr SW1 20 D2
Ebbisham Dri SW8 22 D4
Ebor St E1 8 D4
Ebury Bridge SW1 20 E2
Ebury Bridge Rd
 SW1 20 E3
Ebury Ms SW1 20 E1
Ebury Sq SW1 20 E2
Ebury St SW1 20 E2
Eccleston Bridge
 SW1 20 E2
Eccleston Ms SW1 20 D1
Eccleston Pl SW1 20 E2
Eccleston Sq SW1 20 F2
Eccleston St SW1 20 E1
Edge St W8 9 C4
Edgware Rd W2 3 A5
 11 B1
Edith Gro SW10 18 E4
Edith Rd W14 17 A2
Edith Terr SW10 18 E5
Edith Vlls W14 17 B2
Edwardes Sq W8 17 C1
Effie Rd SW6 17 C5
Egerton Cres SW3 19 B1
Egerton Dri SE10 23 A4
Egerton Gdns SW3 19 B1
Egerton Pl SW3 19 B1
Egerton Terr SW3 19 B1
Elaine Gro NW5 2 E5
Elcho St SW11 19 B5
Elder St E1 8 D5
Eldon Gro NW3 1 B5
Eldon Rd W8 18 E1
Eldon St EC2 7 C5
Elgin Cres W11 9 A2
Elia St N1 6 F2

Eliot Hill SE13 23 B5
Eliot Pl SE3 24 D5
Eliot Vale SE3 23 C5
Elizabeth Bridge SW1 20 E2
Elizabeth St SW1 20 E2
Ellen St E1 16 F2
Ellerdale Clo NW3 1 A5
Ellerdale Rd NW3 1 A5
Elliott's Row SE11 22 F1
Elm Pk Gdns SW10 18 F3
 19 A3
Elm Pk Rd SW3 18 F4
 19 A3
Elm Pl SW7 18 F3
Elm St WC1 6 D4
Elsham Rd W14 9 A5
Elvaston Pl SW7 18 E1
Elverson Rd SE8 23 A5
Elverton St SW1 21 A1
Elwin St E2 8 E3
Elystan Pl SW3 19 B2
Elystan St SW3 19 B2
Emba St SE16 16 F5
Embankment Gdns
 SW3 19 C4
Emerald St WC1 6 D5
Emerson St SE1 15 A3
Emma St E2 8 F2
Emperor's Gate SW7 18 E1
Endell St WC2 13 B1
Enderby St SE10 24 D1
Endsleigh Gdns WC1 5 A4
Endsleigh St WC1 5 A4
Enford St W1 3 B5
English Grounds SE1 15 C4
Enid St SE16 16 E5
Ennismore Gdns
 SW7 11 A5
Ennismore Gdns
 Ms SW7 11 A5
Ensign St E1 16 F2
Epirus Rd SW6 17 C5
Epworth St EC2 7 C4
Erasmus St SW1 21 B2
Errol St EC1 7 B4
Essex Rd N1 6 F1
Essex St WC2 14 D2
Essex Vlls W8 9 C5
Estcourt Rd SW6 17 B5
Estelle Rd NW3 2 E5
Esterbrooke St SW1 21 A2
Eustace Rd SW6 17 C5
Euston Rd NW1 4 F4
 5 A4
Euston Sq NW1 5 A3
Euston St NW1 5 A4
Evelyn Gdns SW7 18 F3
Evelyn Wlk N1 7 B2
Eversholt St NW1 4 F2
Eversholt St NW1 5 A3
Ewer St SE1 15 A4
Exeter St WC2 13 C2
Exhibition Rd SW7 11 A5
 19 A1
Exton St SE1 14 E4
Eyre St Hill EC1 6 E4
Ezra St E2 8 E3

F
Fabian Rd SW6 17 B5
Fair St SE1 16 D4
Fairclough St E1 16 F1
Fairholme Rd W14 17 A3
Fakruddin St E1 8 F4
Falconwood Ct SE3 24 E5
Falkirk St N1 8 D2
Fan Museum SE10 23 B3
Fane St W14 17 B4
Fann St EC1 7 A5
Fanshaw St N1 7 C3
Faraday Museum W1 12 F3
Farm La SW6 17 C5
Farm St W1 12 E3
Farmer's Rd SE5 22 F5
Farncombe St SE16 16 F5
Farnham Royal SE11 22 D3
Farringdon La EC1 6 E4

Farringdon Rd EC1 6 E4
Farringdon St EC4 14 F1
Fashion and Textile
 Museum SE1 15 C4
Fashion St E1 8 E5
Faunce St SE17 22 F3
Fawcett St SW10 18 E4
Feathers Pl SE10 23 C2
Featherstone St EC1 7 B4
Felton St N1 7 B1
Fenchurch Ave EC3 15 C2
Fenchurch Bldgs EC3 16 D2
Fenchurch St EC3 15 C2
 16 D2
Fentiman Rd SW8 21 C4
 22 D5
Fenton House NW3 1 A4
Fernshaw Rd SW10 18 E4
Ferry St E14 23 B1
Festival/South
 Bank Pier SE1 14 D3
Fetter La EC4 14 E1
Field Rd W6 17 A4
Fieldgate St E1 16 F1
Filmer Rd SW6 17 B5
Finborough Rd SW10 18 E4
Fingal St SE10 24 F1
Finsbury Circus EC2 7 B5
 15 B1
Finsbury Mkt EC2 7 C5
Finsbury Pavement
 EC2 7 B5
Finsbury Sq EC2 7 B5
Finsbury St EC2 7 B5
First St SW3 19 B1
Fisherton St NW8 3 A4
Fishmongers' Hall
 EC3 15 B2
Fitzalan St SE11 22 D2
Fitzgeorge Ave W14 17 A2
Fitzjames Ave W14 17 A2
Fitzjohn's Ave NW3 1 B5
Fitzroy Pk N6 2 E1
Fitzroy Sq W1 4 F4
Fitzroy St W1 4 F5
Flask Wlk NW3 1 B5
Flaxman Terr WC1 5 B3
Fleet Rd NW3 2 D5
Fleet St EC4 14 E1
Fleming Rd SE17 22 F4
Fleur de Lis St E1 8 D5
Flitcroft St WC2 13 B1
Flood St SW3 19 B3
Flood Wlk SW3 19 B3
Floral St WC2 13 C2
Florence Nightingale
 Museum SE1 14 D5
Florida St E2 8 F3
Flower Wlk, The
 SW7 10 F5
Foley St W1 4 F5
Folgate St E1 8 D5
Forbes St E1 16 F2
Fordham St E1 16 F1
Fore St EC2 7 B5
Foreign & Common-
 wealth Office SW1 13 B4
Forset St W1 11 B1
Forston St N1 7 B2
Forsyth Gdns SE17 22 F4
Fortune St EC1 7 A4
Foster La EC2 15 A1
Foubert's Pl W1 12 F2
Foulis Terr SW7 19 A2
Fount St SW8 21 B5
Fountains, The W2 10 F3
Fournier St E1 8 E5
Foxley Rd SW9 22 E5
Foyle Rd SE3 24 E2
Frampton St NW8 3 A4
Francis St SW1 20 F1
 21 A1
Franklins Row SW3 19 C3
Frazier St SE1 14 E5
Frederick St WC1 6 D3
Friend St EC1 6 F3
Frith St W1 13 A2
Frognal NW3 1 A5

Each place name is followed by its postal district, and then by its Street Finder reference

Frognal Gdns NW3	1 A5
Frognal La NW3	1 A5
Frognal Rise NW3	1 A4
Frognal Way NW3	1 A5
Frome St N1	7 A2
Fulham Broadway SW6	17 C5
Fulham Rd SW6	17 C5
Fulham Rd SW10	18 F4
Fulham Rd SW3	19 A2
Fulthorp Rd SE3	24 F5
Fulwood Pl WC1	6 D5
Furnival St EC4	14 E1

G

Gabriel's Wharf SE1	14 E2
Gainsborough Gdns NW3	1 B4
Gainsford St SE1	16 D4
Galway St EC1	7 A3
Gambia St SE1	14 F4
Ganton St W1	12 F2
Garden History, Museum of SE1	21 C1
Garden Ms W2	11 A2
Garden Row SE1	22 F1
Garden Wlk EC2	7 C4
Gardners La EC4	15 A2
Garlick Hill EC4	15 A2
Garrett St EC1	7 A4
Garrick St WC2	13 B2
Garway Rd W2	10 D2
Gascoigne Pl E2	8 D3
Gasholder Pl SE11	22 D3
Gaskin St N1	6 F1
Gatliff Rd SW1	20 E3
Gayfere St SW1	21 B1
Gayton Cres NW3	1 B5
Gayton Rd NW3	1 B5
Gaza St SE17	22 F3
Gee St EC1	7 A4
Geffrye Museum E2	8 D2
Geffrye St E2	8 D2
General Wolfe Rd SE10	23 C4
George Row SE16	16 E5
George St W1	12 D1
Georgette Pl SE10	23 B3
Gerald Rd SW1	20 D2
Geraldine Mary Harmsworth Park SE11	22 E1
Geraldine St SE11	22 F1
Gerrard Pl WC2	13 B2
Gerrard St W1	13 A2
Gerridge St SE1	14 E5
Gertrude St SW10	18 F4
Gibbs Grn W14	17 B3
Gibson Rd SE11	22 D2
Gibson Sq N1	6 E1
Gibson St SE10	24 D1
Gilbert Rd SE11	22 E2
Gilbert St W1	12 D2
Gillingham St SW1	20 F2
Gilston Rd SW10	18 F3
Giltspur St EC1	14 F1
Gipsy Moth IV SE10	23 B2
GLA Headquarters SE1	16 D4
Gladstone St SE1	22 F1
Glasgow Terr SW1	20 F3
Glasshill St SE1	14 F4
Glasshouse St W1	13 A3
Glasshouse Wlk SE11	21 C3
Glaz'bury Rd W14	17 A2
Glebe Pl SW3	19 B4
Gledhow Gdns SW5	18 E2
Gledstanes Rd W14	17 A3
Glenhurst Ave NW5	2 F5
Glenister Rd SE10	24 E1
Glentworth St NW1	3 C4
Gliddon Rd W14	17 A2
Globe St SE1	15 B5
Gloucester Ave NW1	4 D1
Gloucester Circus SE10	23 B3
Gloucester Cres NW1	4 E1
Gloucester Gate NW1	4 E2
Gloucester Ms W2	10 F2
Gloucester Ms West W2	10 E1
Gloucester Pl NW1	3 C4
Gloucester Pl W1	11 C1
Gloucester Pl Ms W1	11 C1
Gloucester Rd SW7	18 E1
Gloucester Sq W2	11 A2
Gloucester St SW1	20 F3
Gloucester Terr W2	10 E1
Gloucester Wlk W8	9 C4
Godfrey St SW3	19 B3
Goding St SE11	21 C3
Godson St N1	6 E2
Goffers Rd SE3	24 D5
Golden La EC1	7 A4
Goldington Cres NW1	5 A1
Goldington St NW1	5 A2
Goldsmith's Row E2	8 F2
Goldsmith's Sq E2	8 F2
Goodge Pl W1	5 A5
Goodge St W1	5 A5
Goodmans Yd E1	16 E2
Goods Way NW1	5 B2
Gopsall St N1	7 B1
Gordon House Rd NW5	2 F5
Gordon Sq WC1	5 A4
Gordon St WC1	5 A4
Gorleston St W14	17 A2
Gorsuch St E2	8 D2
Gosfield St W1	4 F5
Gosset St E2	8 E3
Goswell Rd EC1	6 F3 / 7 A4
Gough St WC1	6 D4
Goulston St E1	16 D1
Gower Pl WC1	5 A4
Gower St WC1	5 A4
Gower's Wlk E1	16 E1
Gracechurch St EC3	15 C2
Grafton Pl NW1	5 A3
Grafton St W1	12 F3
Grafton Way W1	4 F4
Grafton Way WC1	5 A4
Graham St N1	6 F2 / 7 A2
Graham Terr SW1	20 D2
Granary St NW1	5 A1
Granby St E2	8 E4
Granby Terr NW1	4 F2
Grand Union Canal N1	7 A1
Grand Union Canal NW1	
Grant St N1	6 E2
Grantbridge St N1	6 F1
Granville Pk SE13	23 C5
Granville Sq WC1	6 D3
Gratton Rd W14	17 A1
Gravel La E1	16 D1
Gray St SE1	14 E5
Gray's Inn WC1	6 D5
Gray's Inn Gardens WC1	6 D5
Gray's Inn Rd WC1	5 C3 / 6 D4
Great Castle St W1	12 F1
Great College St SW1	21 B1
Great Cumberland Pl W1	11 C2
Great Dover St SE1	15 B5
Great Eastern St EC2	7 C4
Great George St SW1	13 B5
Great Guildford St SE1	15 A4
Great James St WC1	6 D5
Great Malborough St W1	12 F2
Great Maze Pond SE1	15 B4
Great Newport St WC2	13 B2
Great Ormond St WC1	5 C5
Great Percy St WC1	6 D3
Great Peter St SW1	21 B1
Great Portland St W1	4 F5 / 12 F1
Great Pulteney St W1	13 A2
Great Queen St WC2	13 C1
Great Russell St WC1	13 B1
Great Scotland Yd SW1	13 B3
Great Smith St SW1	13 B5
Great St Helen's EC3	15 C1
Great Suffolk St SE1	14 F4
Great Sutton St EC1	6 F4
Great Titchfield St W1	4 F5 / 12 F1
Great Tower St EC3	15 C2
Great Western Rd W11	9 C1
Great Winchester St EC2	15 C1
Great Windmill St W1	13 A2
Greatorex St E1	8 E5
Greek St W1	13 A2
Green Hill NW3	1 B4
Green Park SW1	12 E4
Green St W1	12 D2
Greencoat Pl SW1	21 A1
Greenfield Rd E1	16 F1
Greenwell St W1	4 F5
Greenwich Church St SE10	23 B2
Greenwich District Hospital SE10	24 E1
Greenwich Foot Tunnel E14, SE10	23 B1
Greenwich High Rd SE10	23 A3
Greenwich Park SE10	23 C3 / 24 D3
Greenwich Pier SE10	23 B1
Greenwich South St SE10	23 A4
Greet St SE1	14 E4
Grendon St NW8	3 A4
Grenville Pl SW7	18 E1
Grenville St WC1	5 C4
Gresham St EC2	15 A1
Greville St EC1	6 E5
Grey Eagle St E1	8 D5
Greycoat Pl SW1	21 A1
Greycoat St SW1	21 A1
Greyhound Rd W14	17 A4
Grosvenor Cres SW1	12 D5
Grosvenor Cres Ms SW1	12 D5
Grosvenor Gdns SW1	20 E1
Grosvenor Gate W1	11 C3
Grosvenor Pl SW1	12 D5
Grosvenor Rd SW1	20 E4 / 21 A4
Grosvenor Sq W1	12 D2
Grosvenor St W1	12 E2
Grote's Pl SE3	24 D5
Grove Terr NW5	2 F4
Grove, The N6	2 F1
Guards' Museum SW1	13 A5
Guildford Gro SE10	23 A4
Guildhall EC2	15 B1
Guildhouse St SW1	20 F2
Guilford St WC1	5 C4
Gunter Gro SW10	18 E4
Gunterstone Rd W14	17 A2
Gunthorpe St E1	16 E1
Gutter La EC2	15 A1
Guy St SE1	15 C4
Guy's Hospital EC1	15 B4
Gwendwr Rd W14	17 A3

H

Haberdasher St N1	7 B3
Hackford Rd SW9	22 D5
Hackney Rd E2	8 E2
Haddo St SE10	23 A2
Hadrian St SE10	24 D1
Haggerston Park E2	8 E2
Haggerston Rd E8	8 E1
Halcombe St N1	7 C1
Haldane Rd SW6	17 B5
Half Moon St W1	12 E4
Halfmoon Cres N1	6 D1
Halford Rd SW6	17 C4
Halkin St SW1	12 D5
Hall Pl W2	3 A5
Hall St EC1	6 F3
Hallam St W1	4 E5
Hallfield Estate W2	10 E1
Halsey St SW3	19 C2
Halstow Rd SE10	24 F1
Hamilton Pl W1	12 D4
Hammersmith Rd W14	17 A2
Hampstead Gro NW3	1 A4
Hampstead Heath N6	1 C2
Hampstead High St NW3	1 B5
Hampstead Hill Gdns NW3	1 C5
Hampstead La NW3	1 B1
Hampstead La N6	2 D1
Hampstead Ponds NW3	1 C4
Hampstead Rd NW1	4 F2
Hampstead Way NW11	1 A1
Hanbury St E1	8 E5
Handel St WC1	5 C4
Handforth Rd SW9	22 D5
Hankey Pl EC1	15 B5
Hannell Rd SW6	17 A5
Hanover Gate NW1	3 B3
Hanover Pl WC2	13 C2
Hanover Sq W1	12 E2
Hanover St W1	12 F2
Hanover Terr NW1	3 B3
Hans Cres SW1	11 C5
Hans Pl SW1	19 C1
Hans Rd SW3	11 C5 / 19 C1
Hans St SW1	19 C1
Hanson St W1	4 F5
Hanway Pl W1	13 A1
Hanway St W1	13 A1
Harcourt St W1	3 B5
Harcourt Ter SW10	18 E3
Hardwick St EC1	6 E3
Hardwidge St SE1	15 C4
Hardy Rd SE3	24 F3
Hare & Billet Rd SE3	23 C5 / 24 D5
Hare Wlk N1	8 D2
Harewood Ave NW1	3 B4
Harley Gdns SW10	18 F3
Harley Pl W1	12 E1
Harley St W1	4 E5 / 12 E1
Harleyford Rd SE11	21 C3 / 22 D4
Harmsworth St SE17	22 F3
Harper Rd SE1	15 A5
Harpur St WC1	5 C5
Harriet Wlk SW1	11 C5
Harrington Gdns SW7	18 E2
Harrington Rd SW7	18 F2 / 19 A2
Harrington Sq NW1	4 F2
Harrington St NW1	4 F3
Harrison St WC1	5 C3
Harrow Rd W2	3 A5
Harrowby St W1	11 B1
Hart St EC3	16 D2
Hartington Rd SW8	21 B5
Hartismere Rd SW6	17 B5
Harvey St N1	7 C1
Harwood Rd SW6	18 D5
Hasker St SW3	19 B1
Hastings St WC1	5 B3
Hatfields SE1	14 E3
Hatton Pl EC1	6 E5
Havelock St N1	5 C1
Hay Hill W1	12 F3
Hay St E2	8 F1
Haydon St EC3	16 D2
Hayles St SE11	22 F1
Haymarket SW1	13 A3

Hay's La SE1 15 C3
Hay's Ms W1 12 E3
Hayward Gallery SE1 14 D3
Hazlitt Rd W14 17 A1
Headfort Pl SW1 12 D5
Hearn St EC2 7 C4
Heath Brow NW3 1 A3
Heath Hurst Rd NW3 1 C5
Heath Side NW3 1 A4
Heath St NW3 1 A4
Heath Way SE3 24 F3
Heathcote St WC1 5 C4
Heddon St W1 12 F2
Helmet Row EC1 7 A4
Hemans St SW8 21 B5
Hemingford Rd N1 6 D1
Hemming St E1 8 F4
Hemsworth St N1 7 C2
Heneage St E1 8 E5
Henrietta Pl W1 12 E1
Henrietta St WC2 13 C2
Henriques St E1 16 F1
Herbal Hill EC1 6 E5
Herbrand St WC1 5 B4
Hercules Rd SE1 14 D5
Hercules St SE1 22 D1
Hereford Rd W2 9 C1, 10 D2
Hereford St E2 8 F4
Hermit St EC1 6 F3
Herrick St SW1 21 B2
Hertford St W1 12 E4
Hesper Ms SW5 18 D2
Hessel St E1 16 F1
Hester Rd SW11 19 B5
Hewett St EC2 8 D4
Hexagon, The N6 2 E2
Heyford Ave SW8 21 C5
Heysham La NW3 1 A4
Hide Pl SW1 21 A2
High Bridge SE10 23 C1
High Holborn WC1 6 D5, 13 B1, 14 D1
High Timber St EC4 15 A2
Highfields Grn N6 2 E2
Highgate Cemetery N6 2 F2
Highgate Clo N6 2 E1
Highgate High St N6 2 F1
Highgate Ponds N6 2 E3
Highgate Rd NW5 2 F4
Highgate West Hill N6 2 E2
Highmore Rd SE3 24 E3
Highway, The E1 16 F2
Hilary Clo SW6 18 D5
Hill St W1 12 E3
Hill, The NW3 1 A2
Hillgate Pl W8 9 C3
Hillgate St W8 9 C3
Hillingdon St SE5 22 F5
Hillsleigh Rd W8 9 B4
Hillway N6 2 F2
Hindmarsh Clo E1 16 F2
HMS Belfast SE1 16 D3
Hobart Pl SW1 20 E1
Hobury St SW10 18 F4
Hogarth Rd SW5 18 D2
Holbein Pl SW1 20 D2
Holborn EC1 14 E1
Holborn Circus E4 14 E1
Holborn Viaduct EC1 14 F1
Holford Rd NW3 1 B4
Holford St WC1 6 D3
Holland Gdns W14 17 A1
Holland Gro SW9 22 E5
Holland House W8 9 B5
Holland Park W8 9 B4
Holland Pk W11 9 A4
Holland Pk Ave W11 9 A4
Holland Pk Gdns W14 9 A4
Holland Pk Ms W11 9 A4
Holland Pk Rd W14 17 B1
Holland Rd W14 9 A5, 17 A1
Holland St SE1 14 F3
Holland St W8 10 D5
Holland Vlls Rd W14 9 A5
Holland Wlk W8 9 B4

Holles St W1 12 E1
Holly Bush Vale NW3 1 A5
Holly Hill NW3 1 A4
Holly Lodge Gdns N6 2 E2
Holly Wlk NW3 1 A5
Hollymount Clo SE10 23 B4
Hollywood Rd SW10 18 E4
Holmead Rd SW6 18 E5
Holwell La EC2 8 D4
Holyoak Rd SE11 22 F2
Holyrood St SE1 15 C4
Homer Row W1 11 B1
Homestead Rd SW6 17 B5
Hooper St E1 16 E2
Hop Exchange EC1 15 B4
Hopetown St E1 8 E5
Hopton St SE1 14 F3
Horatio St E2 8 E2
Horbury Cres W11 9 C3
Hornton St W8 10 D5
Horse Guards SW1 13 B4
Horse Guards Rd SW1 13 B4
Horseferry Pl SE10 23 A2
Horseferry Rd SW1 21 B1
Horseguards Ave SW1 13 B4
Hortensia Rd SW10 18 E5
Hosier La EC1 14 F1
Hoskins St SE10 23 C1
Houghton St WC2 14 D2
Houndsditch EC3 16 D1
Houses of Parliament SW1 13 C5
Howick Pl SW1 21 A1
Howie St SW11 19 B5
Howland St W1 4 F5
Hows St E2 8 D2
Hoxton Sq N1 7 C3
Hoxton St N1 7 C1
Hugh St SW1 20 E2
Humber Rd SE3 24 E2
Humbolt Rd W6 17 A4
Hungerford Foot Bridge SE1 13 C3
Hunter St WC1 5 C4
Huntley St WC1 5 A4
Hunton St E1 8 E5
Hyde Park W2 11 B3
Hyde Pk Corner W1 12 D4
Hyde Pk Cres W2 11 A1
Hyde Pk Gate SW7 10 E5
Hyde Pk Gdns W2 11 A2
Hyde Pk Sq W2 11 A2
Hyde Pk St W2 11 B2
Hyde Rd N1 7 C1
Hyde Vale SE10 23 C4

I
Ifield Rd SW10 18 E4
Ilchester Gdns W2 10 D2
Ilchester Pl W14 9 B5
Imperial College Rd SW7 18 F1
Imperial War Museum SE11 22 E1
Ingelbert St EC1 6 E3
Ingleside Gro SE3 24 F2
Ingram Ave NW11 1 B1
Inner Circle NW1 4 D3
Inner Temple Gdns EC4 14 E2
Institute of Contemporary Arts SW1 13 B3
Instruments, Museum of SW7 10 F5
Inverforth Clo NW3 1 A3
Inverness Ms W2 10 E2
Inverness Pl W2 10 E2
Inverness Terr W2 10 E2
Ironmonger La EC2 15 B1
Ironmonger Row EC1 7 A3
Island Gardens E14 23 B1
Islington Grn Gdns N1 6 F1
Islington High St N1 6 E2
Iverna Ct W8 10 D5

Iverna Gdns W8 18 D1
Ives St SW3 19 B2
Ivor Pl NW1 3 B4
Ivy St N1 7 C2
Ixworth Pl SW3 19 B2

J
Jackman St E8 8 F1
Jacob St SE1 16 E5
Jamaica Rd SE1 16 E5
Jamaica Rd SE16 16 F5
James St W1 12 D1
James St WC2 13 C2
Jameson St W8 9 C3
Jamme Masjid E1 8 E5
Janeway St SE16 16 F5
Jay Ms SW7 10 F5
Jermyn St SW1 12 F3, 13 A3
Jewel Tower SW1 13 B5
Jewish Museum NW1 4 E1
Jewry St EC3 16 D2
Joan St SE1 14 F4
Jockey's Fields WC1 6 D5
John Adam St WC2 13 C3
John Carpenter St EC4 14 E2
John Fisher St E1 16 E2
John Islip St SW1 21 B2
John Penn St SE13 23 A4
John Ruskin St SE5 22 F5
John's Ms WC1 6 D5
John's St WC1 6 D5
Johnson's Pl SW1 20 F3
Jonathan St SE11 22 D2
Jubilee Gardens SE1 14 D4
Jubilee Pl SW3 19 B3
Judd St WC1 5 B3
Judges Wlk NW3 1 A4
Juer St SW11 19 B5
Juxon St SE11 22 D1

K
Kay St E2 8 F2
Kean St WC2 13 C2
Keat's Gro NW3 1 C5
Keat's House NW3 1 C5
Keep, The SE3 24 F5
Keeton's Rd SE16 16 F5
Kelsey St E2 8 F4
Kelso Pl W8 18 D1
Kemble St WC2 13 C2
Kemplay Rd NW3 1 B5
Kempsford Gdns SW5 18 D3
Kempsford Rd SE11 22 E2
Kemsing Rd SE10 24 F1
Kenchester Clo SW9 21 C5
Kendal Clo SW9 22 F5
Kendal St W2 11 B2
Kenley Wlk W11 9 A3
Kennet St E1 16 F3
Kennington Gro SE11 22 D4
Kennington La SE11 22 D3
Kennington Oval SE11 22 D4
Kennington Park SE11 22 E4
Kennington Pk Gdns SE11 22 F4
Kennington Pk Rd SE11 22 E4
Kennington Rd SE1 22 E1
Kensington Church St W8 10 D4
Kensington Ct Pl W8 10 E5
Kensington Ct W8 10 E5
Kensington Gardens W2 10 E4
Kensington Gdns Sq W2 10 D2
Kensington Gate W8 10 E5
Kensington Gore SW7 10 F5

Kensington High St W8 9 C5, 10 D5
Kensington High St W14 17 B1
Kensington Palace W8 10 D4
Kensington Palace Gdns W8 10 D3
Kensington Pk Gdns W11 9 B3
Kensington Pk Rd W11 9 B2
Kensington Pl W8 9 C4
Kensington Rd W7, W8 10 E5
Kensington Rd SW7 11 A5
Kensington Roof Gardens W8 10 D5
Kensington Sq W8 10 D5
Kent Pas NW1 3 B4
Kent St E2 8 E2
Kentish Bldgs SE1 15 B4
Kenton St WC1 5 B4
Kenway Rd SW5 18 D2
Kenwood Clo NW3 1 B1
Kenwood House N6 1 C1
Keyworth St SE1 14 F5
Kidbrooke Gdns SE3 24 F5
Kildare Gdns W2 10 D1
Kildare Terr W2 10 D1
Killick St N1 5 C2
Kiln Pl NW5 2 F5
King St EC2 15 B1
King St SW1 12 F4, 13 A3
King St WC2 13 B2
King Charles St SW1 13 B5
King Edward St EC1 15 A1
King Edward Wlk SE1 22 E1
King George St SE10 23 B3
King James St SE1 14 F5
King William St EC4 15 B2
King William Wlk SE10 23 B2
Kingly St W1 12 F2
King's Bench Wlk EC4 14 E2
Kings Head Yd SE1 15 B4
Kings Rd SW3 19 A4
King's Rd SW6, SW10 18 E5
King's Scholars Pas SW1 20 F1
King's Terr NW1 4 F1
King's Cross Rd WC1 5 C2, 6 D3
Kingsland Basin N1 8 D1
Kingsland Rd E2 8 D1
Kingsmill Ter NW8 3 A2
Kingstown St NW1 4 D1
Kingsway WC2 13 C1
Kinnerton St SW1 11 C5
Kinnoul Rd W6 17 A4
Kipling St SE1 15 C5
Kirby Gro SE1 15 C4
Kirby St EC1 6 E5
Kirtling St SW8 20 F4
Kirton Gdns E2 8 E3
Knaresborough Pl SW5 18 D2
Knighten St E1 16 F4
Knightrider St EC4 14 F2
Knightsbridge SW1 12 D5
Knivet Rd SW6 17 C4
Knox St W1 3 C5
Kynance Pl SW7 18 E1

L
Laburnum St E2 8 D1
Lackington St EC2 7 B5
Ladbroke Cres W11 9 A1
Ladbroke Gdns W11 9 B2
Ladbroke Gro W11 9 A1
Ladbroke Rd W11 9 B3
Ladbroke Sq W11 9 B3

Each place name is followed by its postal district, and then by its Street Finder reference

Ladbroke Terr W11	9 B3	Lever St EC1	7 A3	Lothbury EC2	15 B1	Mark St EC2	7 C4

Ladbroke Terr W11 9 B3
Ladbroke Wlk W11 9 B3
Lafone St SE1 16 D4
Lamb St E1 8 D5
Lamb Wlk SE1 15 C5
Lamb's Conduit St WC1 5 C4
Lamb's Pas EC1 7 B5
Lambeth Bridge SE1 21 C1
Lambeth High St SE1 21 C2
Lambeth Palace Rd SE1 14 D5, 21 C1
Lambeth Palace SE1 21 C1
Lambeth Rd SE1 22 D1
Lambeth Wlk SE11 22 D1
Lamble St NW5 2 F5
Lamlash St SE11 22 F1
Lamont Rd SW10 18 F4
Lancaster Ct SW6 17 C5
Lancaster Gate W2 10 F2
Lancaster House SW1 12 F4
Lancaster Ms W2 10 F2
Lancaster Pl WC2 13 C2
Lancaster Rd W11 9 A1
Lancaster St SE1 14 F5
Lancaster Terr W2 10 F2
Lancaster Wlk W2 10 F3
Lancelot Pl SW7 11 B5
Langbourne Ave N6 2 F3
Langdale Rd SE10 23 A3
Langham Hilton Hotel W1 12 E1
Langham Pl W1 12 E1
Langham St W1 12 F1
Langley La SW8 21 C4
Langley St WC2 13 B2
Langton Rd SW9 22 F5
Langton St SW10 18 F4
Langton Way SE3 24 F4
Lansdowne Cres W11 9 A3
Lansdowne Rd W11 9 A2
Lansdowne Rise W11 9 A3
Lansdowne Terr WC1 5 C4
Lansdowne Wlk W11 9 B3
Lant St SE1 15 A5
Lassell St SE10 23 C1, 24 D1
Launceston Pl W8 18 E1
Laundry Rd W6 17 A4
Laurence Poutney La EC4 15 B2
Laverton Pl SW5 18 D2
Lavington St SE1 14 F4
Law Society WC2 14 E1
Lawn La SW8 21 C4
Lawrence St SW3 19 A4
Laystall St EC1 6 D4
Leadenhall Mkt EC3 15 C2
Leadenhall St EC3 15 C2, 16 D2
Leake St SE1 14 D4
Leamington Rd Vlls W11 9 B1
Leather La EC1 6 E5
Leathermarket St SE1 15 C5
Leathwell Rd SE13 23 A5
Ledbury Rd W11 9 C2
Leeke St WC1 5 C3
Lees Pl W1 12 D2
Leicester Pl WC2 13 B2
Leicester Sq WC2 13 B3
Leicester St WC2 13 A2
Leigh St WC1 5 B4
Leighton House W14 17 B1
Leinster Gdns W2 10 E2
Leinster Pl W2 10 E2
Leinster Sq W2 10 D2
Leinster Terr W2 10 E2
Leman St E1 16 E1
Lennox Gdns Ms SW1 19 B1
Lennox Gdns SW1 19 C1
Leonard St EC2 7 C4
Lethbridge Clo SE13 23 B5
Letterstone Rd SW6 17 B5

Lever St EC1 7 A3
Lewisham Hill SE13 73 B5
Lewisham Rd SE13 23 A4
Lexham Gdns W8 18 D1
Lexington St W1 13 A2
Leyden St E1 16 D1
Library St SE1 14 F5
Lidlington Pl NW1 4 F2
Lilestone St NW8 3 B4
Lillie Rd SW6 17 A5
Lime St EC3 15 C2
Limerston St SW10 18 F4
Lincoln's Inn Fields WC2 14 D1
Lincoln's Inn WC2 14 D1
Linden Gdns W2 9 C3
Linhope St NW1 3 B4
Linley Sambourne House W8 9 C5
Linton St N1 7 A1
Lisburne Rd NW3 2 E5
Lisgar Terr W14 17 B2
Lisle St WC2 13 A2
Lissenden Gdns NW5 2 F5
Lisson Gro NW1 3 B5
Lisson Gro NW8 3 A4
Lisson St NW1 3 A5
Little Boltons, The SW10 18 E3
Little Britain EC1 15 A1
Little Chester St SW1 12 E5
Little College St SW1 21 B1
Little Dorrit Ct SE1 15 A4
Little Portland St W1 12 F1
Liverpool Rd N1 6 E1
Liverpool St EC2 15 C1
Lizard St EC1 7 A3
Lloyd Baker St WC1 6 D3
Lloyd St WC1 6 D3
Lloyd's of London EC3 15 C2
Lloyd's Ave EC3 16 D2
Lloyd's Row EC1 6 E3
Lodge Rd NW8 3 A3
Logan Ms W8 17 C2
Logan Pl W8 17 C2
Lollard St SE11 22 D2
Loman St SE1 14 F4
Lombard St EC3 15 B2
London Aquarium SE1 14 C4
London Bridge SE1 15 B3
London Bridge City Pier SE1 15 C3
London Bridge St EC1 15 B4
London Central Mosque NW1 3 B3
London Coliseum WC2 13 B3
London Dungeon SE1 15 C3
London Rd SE1 14 F5, 22 F1
London St W2 10 F1, 11 A1
London Transport Museum WC2 13 C2
London Wall EC3 15 A1
London Zoo NW1 4 D2
London, Museum of EC2 15 A1
Long Acre WC1 13 B2
Long La EC1 6 F5, 7 A5
Long La SE1 15 B5
Long Pond Rd SE3 24 D4
Long St E2 8 D3
Longford St NW1 4 E4
Longridge Rd SW5 17 C2
Longville Rd SE11 22 F2
Lonsdale Rd W11 9 B2
Lord Hill Bridge W2 10 D1
Lord's Cricket Ground NW8 3 A3
Lorrimore Rd SE17 22 F4
Lorrimore Sq SE17 22 F4
Lot's Rd SW10 18 E5

Lothbury EC2 15 B1
Loughborough St SE11 22 D3
Lovat La EC3 15 C2
Love La EC2 15 A1
Lower Addison Gdns W14 9 A5
Lower Belgrave St SW1 20 E1
Lower Grosvenor Pl SW1 20 E1
Lower Marsh SE1 14 D5
Lower Sloane St SW1 20 D3
Lower Terr NW3 1 A4
Lower Thames St EC3 15 C3, 16 D3
Lowndes Pl SW1 20 D1
Lowndes Sq SW1 11 C5
Lowndes St SW1 20 D1
Lucan Pl SW3 19 B2
Ludgate Circus EC4 14 F1
Ludgate Hill EC4 14 F1
Luke St EC2 7 C4
Lupus St SW1 20 F3, 21 A3
Luscombe Way SW8 21 B5
Luton Pl SE10 23 B3
Luton St NW8 3 A4
Luxborough St W1 4 D5
Lyall St SW1 20 D1
Lyndale Clo SE3 24 E2

M

Mabledon Pl WC1 5 B3
Mablethorpe Rd SW6 17 A5
Macclesfield Rd EC1 7 A3
McGregor Rd W11 9 B1
Mackennal St NW8 3 B2
Mackeson Rd NW3 2 D5
Macklin St WC2 13 C1
Mackworth St NW1 4F3
McLeod's Ms SW7 18 E1
Maclise Rd W14 17 A1
Madame Tussauds' NW1 4 D5
Maddox St W1 12 F2
Maiden La WC2 13 C2
Maidenstone Hill SE10 23 B4
Makepeace Ave N6 2 F3
Malet St WC1 5 A5
Mall, The SW1 12 F4, 13 A4
Mallord St SW3 19 A4
Mallow St EC1 7 B4
Malta St EC1 6 F4
Maltby St SE1 16 D5
Malton Rd W10 9 A1
Manchester Rd E14 23 B1
Manchester Sq W1 12 D1
Manchester St W1 12 D1
Manciple St SE1 15 B5
Mandela St NW1 4 F1
Mandela St SW9 22 E5
Mandeville Clo SE3 24 F3
Mandeville Pl W1 12 D1
Manette St W1 13 B1
Manor Pl SE17 22 F3
Manresa Rd SW3 19 A3
Mansell St E1 16 E2
Mansfield Rd NW3 2 E5
Mansford St E2 8 F2
Mansion House EC4 15 B2
Manson Pl SW7 18 F2
Maple St E2 8 F4
Maple St W1 4 F5
Marble Arch W1 11 C2
Marchbank Rd W14 17 B4
Marchmont St WC1 5 B4
Margaret St W1 12 F1
Margaretta Terr SW3 19 B4
Margery St WC1 6 D3
Marigold St SE16 16 F5
Marine St SE16 16 E5

Mark St EC2 7 C4
Market Entrance SW8 21 A5
Market Ms W1 12 E4
Markham Sq SW3 19 B3
Markham St SW3 19 B3
Marlborough Bldgs SW3 19 B2
Marlborough House SW1 13 A4
Marlborough Rd SW1 13 A4
Marlborough St SW3 19 B2
Marloes Rd W8 18 D1
Marshall St W1 12 F2
Marshalsea Rd SE1 15 A4
Marsham St SW1 21 B1
Mary Pl W11 9 A3
Mary St N1 7 A1
Marylebone High St W1 4 D5
Marylebone La W1 12 E1
Marylebone Rd NW1 3 B5, 4 D5
Marylebone St W1 4 D5
Marylee Way SE11 22 D2
Maryon Ms NW3 1 C5
Mason's Pl EC1 7 A3
Matheson Rd W14 17 B2
Matilda St N1 6 D1
Maunsel St SW1 21 A1
Mawbey St SW8 21 B5
Maxwell Rd SW6 18 D5
Maygood St N1 6 D2
Maze Hill SE10 24 D2
Meadow Rd SW8 21 C5, 22 D4
Mecklenburgh Gardens WC1 5 C4
Medway St SW1 21 A1
Melbury Rd W14 17 B1
Mendora Rd SW6 17 A5
Mercer St WC2 13 B2
Meredith St EC1 6 F3
Mermaid Ct SE1 15 B4
Merrifield SE3 24 F5
Merton La N6 2 E2
Methley St SE11 22 E3
Mews St E1 16 E3
Meymott St SE1 14 E4
Micawber St N1 7 A3
Middle St EC1 7 A5
Middle Temple La EC4 14 E2
Middlesex St E1 16 D1
Midland Pl E14 23 B1
Midland Rd NW1 5 B2
Milborne Gro SW10 18 F3
Miles St SW8 21 B4
Milford La WC2 14 D2
Milk St EC2 15 A1
Mill Row N1 8 D1
Mill St SE1 16 E5
Millbank SW1 21 B1
Millfield La N6 1 C1
Millfield La N6 2 D1
Millfield Pl N6 2 E3
Millman St WC1 5 C4
Milmans St SW10 19 A4
Milner St SW3 19 C1
Milson Rd W14 17 A1
Milton St EC2 7 B5
Milverton St SE11 22 E3
Mincing La EC3 15 C2
Minera Ms SW1 20 D2
Ministry of Defence SW1 13 C4
Minories EC3 16 D2
Minories Hill EC3 16 D2
Mint St SE1 15 A4
Mintern St N1 7 C2
Mirabel Rd SW6 17 B5
Mitchell St EC1 7 A4
Mitre Rd SE1 14 E4
Mitre St EC3 16 D2
Molyneux St W1 11 B1
Monck St SW1 21 B1
Monkton St SE11 22 E2
Monmouth Rd W2 10 D2
Monmouth St WC2 13 B2
Montpelier St SW7 11 B1

Montagu Mansions
W1 3 C5
Montagu Pl W1 4 D5
11 C1
Montagu Sq W1 11 C1
Montagu St W1 11 C1
Montague Pl WC1 5 B5
Montague St WC1 5 B5
Montclare St E2 8 D4
Montford Pl SE11 22 D3
Montpelier Pl SW7 11 B5
Montpelier Row SE3 24 E5
Montpelier Sq SW7 11 B5
Montpelier Wlk SW7 11 B5
Montrose Ct SW7 11 A5
Montrose Pl SW1 12 D5
Monument EC3 15 C2
Monument St EC3 15 C2
Moorhouse Rd W2 9 C1
Moor La EC2 7 B5
Moore Pk Rd SW6 18 D5
Moore St SW3 19 C2
Moorfields EC2 7 B5
Moorgate EC2 7 B5
15 B1
Mora St EC1 7 A3
Moravian Pl SW10 19 A4
Morden Clo SE13 23 B5
Morden Hill SE13 23 B5
Morden Rd SE3 24 F5
Morden Rd Ms SE3 24 F5
Morden St SE13 23 A4
Moreland St EC1 6 F3
7 A3
Moreton Pl SW1 21 A3
Moreton St SW1 21 A3
Morgan's La SE1 15 C4
Morley St SE1 14 E5
Mornington Ave W14 17 B2
Mornington Cres NW1 4 F2
Mornington Pl NW1 4 F2
Mornington Terr NW1 4 E1
Morocco St SE1 15 C5
Morpeth Terr SW1 20 F1
Mortimer St W1 12 F1
Morwell St WC1 13 A1
Moscow Rd W2 10 D2
Mossop St SW3 19 B2
Motcomb St SW1 12 D5
Mount Pleasant WC1 6 D4
Mount Row W1 12 E3
Mount St W1 12 D3
Mount, The NW3 1 A4
Mounts Pond Rd SE3 23 C5
24 D5
Moving Image,
Museum of the
SE1 14 D3
Mowll St SW9 22 D5
Moylan Rd W6 17 A4
Mulberry St E1 16 F1
Mulberry Wlk SW3 19 A4
Mulgrave Rd SW6 17 B4
Mulvaney Way SE1 15 C5
Mund St W14 17 B3
Munden St W14 17 A2
Munster Rd SW6 17 A5
Munster Sq NW1 4 F4
Muriel St N1 6 D1
Murphy St SE1 14 E5
Murray Gro N1 7 B2
Musard Rd W6 17 A4
Museum St WC1 13 B1
Mycenae Rd SE3 24 F3
Myddelton Pas EC1 6 E3
Myddelton Sq EC1 6 E3
Myddelton St EC1 6 E4
Myrdle St E1 16 F1

N

Napier Gro N1 7 B2
Napier Pl W14 17 B1
Napier Rd W14 17 A1
Nash St NW1 4 E3
Nassington Rd NW3 2 D5
National Army
Museum SW3 19 C4

National Film
Theatre SE1 14 D3
National Gallery WC2 13 B3
National Maritime
Museum SE10 23 C2
National Portrait
Gallery WC2 13 B3
National Theatre SE1 14 D3
Natural History
Museum SW7 18 F1
19 A1
Navarre St E2 8 D4
Nazrul St E2 8 D2
Neal St WC2 13 B1
Neal's Yd WC2 13 B1
Neckinger St SE1 16 E5
Nectarine Way SE13 23 A5
Needham Rd W11 9 C2
Nelson Gdns E2 8 F3
Nelson Pl N1 6 F2
Nelson Rd SE10 23 B2
Nelson Sq SE1 14 F4
Nelson's Column
WC2 13 B3
Nesham St E1 16 F3
Netherton Gro SW10 18 F4
Nevada St SE10 23 B3
Nevern Pl SW5 17 C2
Nevern Rd SW5 17 C2
Nevern Sq SW5 17 C2
Neville St SW7 19 A3
New Bond St W1 12 E2
New Bridge St EC4 14 F2
New British Library
NW1 5 B3
New Broad St EC2 15 C1
New Cavendish St
W1 4 E5
New Change EC4 15 A2
New Compton St
WC2 13 B1
New Covent Garden
Mkt SW8 21 A5
New End NW3 1 B4
New End Sq NW3 1 B4
New Fetter La EC4 14 E1
New Inn Yd EC2 8 D4
New North Rd N1 7 B1
New North St WC1 5 C5
New Oxford St WC1 13 B1
New Palace Yd SW1 13 B5
New Rd E1 8 F5
16 F1
New Row WC2 13 B2
New Scotland Yd
SW1 13 A5
New Sq WC2 14 D1
New St EC2 16 D1
New Wharf Rd N1 5 C2
New Zealand House
SW1 13 A3
Newburn St SE11 22 D3
Newcomen St SE1 15 B4
Newcourt St NW8 3 A2
Newgate St EC1 14 F1
15 A1
Newington Butts
SE11 22 F2
Newington
Causeway SE1 15 A5
Newman St W1 13 A1
Newport St SE11 22 D2
Newton Rd W2 10 D1
Newton St WC2 13 C1
Nicholas La EC4 15 B2
Nile St N1 7 B3
Nine Elms La SW8 21 A4
Noble St EC2 15 A1
Noel Rd N1 6 F2
7 A2
Noel St W1 13 A1
Norfolk Cres W2 11 B1
Norfolk Pl W2 11 A1
Norfolk Rd NW8 3 A1
Norfolk Sq W2 11 A1
Norland Sq W11 9 A4
Norman Rd SE10 23 A3
Norman St EC1 7 A4

Normand Rd W14 17 B4
North Audley St W1 12 D2
North East Pier E1 16 F4
North End Ave NW3 1 A2
North End NW3 1 A2
North End Rd SW6 17 C3
North End Rd W14 17 A2
North End Way NW3 1 A2
North Gower St NW1 4 F3
North Gro N6 2 F1
North Rd N6 2 F1
North Row W1 11 C2
North Tenter St E1 16 E2
North Terr SW3 19 A1
North West Pier E1 16 F4
North Wharf Rd W2 10 F1
Northampton Rd EC1 6 E4
Northampton Sq EC1 6 F3
Northburgh St EC1 6 F4
Northdown St N1 5 C2
Northington St WC1 6 D5
Northumberland Ave
WC2 13 B3
Northumberland Pl
W2 9 C1
Norton Folgate E1 8 D5
Norway St SE10 23 A2
Notting Hill Gate
W11 9 C3
10 D3
Nottingham Pl W1 4 D5
Nottingham St W1 4 D5
Nutford Pl W1 11 B1
Nuttall St N1 7 C1
8 D1

O

Oak Hill Pk NW3 1 A5
Oak Hill Way NW3 1 A5
Oak Tree Rd NW8 3 A3
Oak Village NW5 2 F5
Oakcroft Rd SE13 23 C5
Oakden St SE11 22 E2
Oakeshott Ave N6 2 F2
Oakley Gdns SW3 19 B4
Oakley Sq NW1 5 A2
Oakley St SW3 19 B4
Oakwood Ct W14 9 B5
Oat La EC2 15 A1
Observatory Gdns
W8 9 C4
Offley Rd SW9 22 E5
Old Bailey EC4 14 F1
Old Bethnal Grn
Rd E2 8 F3
Old Bond St W1 12 F3
Old Brewery Ms
NW3 1 B5
Old Broad St EC2 15 C1
Old Brompton Rd
SW5 18 D3
Old Brompton Rd
SW7 19 A2
Old Castle St E1 16 D1
Old Cavendish St
W1 12 E1
Old Church St SW3 19 A3
Old Compton St
W1 13 A2
Old Ct Pl W8 10 D5
Old Gloucester St
WC1 5 C5
Old Jamaica Rd SE16 16 E5
Old Jewry EC2 15 B1
Old Marylebone
Rd NW1 3 B5
11 B1
Old Montague St
E1 8 E5
Old Nichol St E2 8 D4
Old Orchard, The
NW3 2 D5
Old Palace Yd SW1 13 B5
Old Paradise St
SE11 22 D2
Old Pk La W1 12 E4
Old Pye St SW1 21 A1

Old Quebec St W1 11 C2
Old Queen St SW1 13 B5
Old Royal
Observatory SE10 23 C3
Old St EC1 7 A4
Old St Thomas's
Operating Theatre
EC1 15 B4
Old Vic SE1 14 E5
Old Woolwich Rd
SE10 23 C1
24 D1
Olympia W14 17 A1
Olympia Way W14 17 A1
Ongar Rd SW6 17 C4
Onslow Gdns SW7 18 F2
Onslow Sq SW7 19 A2
Ontario St SE1 22 F1
Opal St SE11 22 F2
Orange St WC2 13 B3
Orbain Rd SW6 17 A5
Orchard Dri SE3 24 D5
Orchard Hill SE13 23 A5
Orchard Rd SE3 24 D5
Orchard St W1 12 D2
Orchard, The SE3 23 C5
Orchardson St NW8 3 A4
Orde Hall St WC1 5 C5
Ordnance Hill NW8 3 A1
Orlop St SE10 24 D1
Orme Ct W2 10 D3
Orme La W2 10 D3
Ormiston Rd SE10 24 F1
Ormonde Gate SW3 19 C3
Ormonde Terr NW8 3 C1
Ormsby St E2 8 D2
Orsett St SE11 22 D3
Orsett Terr W2 10 E1
Orsman Rd N1 7 C1
8 D1
Osborn St E1 16 E1
Ostaburgh St NW1 4 E4
Ossington St W2 10 D3
Ossulston St NW1 5 A2
Oswin St SE11 22 F1
Otto St SE17 22 F4
Outer Circle NW1 3 B2
4 D2
Oval Pl SW8 22 D5
Oval Rd NW1 4 E1
Oval, The SE11 22 D4
Oval Way SE11 22 D3
Ovington Gdns
SW3 19 B1
Ovington Sq SW3 19 B1
Ovington St SW3 19 B1
Owen St EC1 6 E2
Oxford Gdns W10 9 A1
Oxford Sq W2 11 B1
Oxford St W1 12 D2
13 A1

P

Pakenham St WC1 6 D4
Packington Sq N1 7 A1
Packington St N1 6 F1
7 A1
Paddington Basin
W2 11 A1
Paddington Garden
W2 3 A5
Paddington St W1 4 D5
Page St SW1 21 B2
Paget St EC1 6 F3
Pagoda Gdns SE3 23 C5
Palace Ave W8 10 D4
Palace Ct W2 10 D3
Palace Gate W8 10 E5
Palace Gdns Ms W8 10 D3
Palace Gdns Terr W8 10 D3
Palace Grn W8 10 D4
Palace St SW1 12 F5
Palace Theatre WC2 13 B2
Palfrey Pl SW8 22 D5
Pall Mall SW1 13 A3
Pall Mall East SW1 13 B3
Palliser Rd W14 17 A3

Palmer St SW1 **13 A5**
Pancras Rd NW1 **5 B2**
Panton St SW1 **13 A3**
Parade, The SW11 **19 C5**
Paradise Wlk SW3 **19 C4**
Paragon Pl SE3 **24 E5**
Paragon, The SE3 **24 F5**
Pardoner St SE1 **15 B5**
Paris Garden SE1 **14 E3**
Park Cres W1 **4 E5**
Park La W1 **11 C2**
12 D3
Park Pl SW1 **12 F4**
Park Rd NW1, NW8 **3 B3**
Park Row SE10 **23 C1**
Park Sq East NW1 **4 E4**
Park Sq Gdns NW1 **4 E4**
Park Sq West NW1 **4 E4**
Park St SE1 **15 A3**
Park St W1 **12 D2**
Park Village East
NW1 **4 E2**
Park Vista SE10 **23 C2**
24 D2
Park West Pl W2 **11 B1**
Park Wlk SW10 **18 F4**
Parker St WC2 **13 C1**
Parkfield St N1 **6 E2**
Parkgate Rd SW11 **19 B5**
Parkville Rd SW6 **17 B5**
Parkway NW1 **4 E1**
Parliament Hill N6 **2 D4**
2 E4
Parliament Sq SW1 **13 B5**
Parliament St SW1 **13 B4**
Parr St N1 **7 B2**
Parry St SW8 **21 C4**
Pascal St SW8 **21 B5**
Pater St W8 **17 C1**
Paul St EC2 **7 C4**
Paultons Sq SW3 **19 A4**
Paultons St SW3 **19 A4**
Paveley Dri SW11 **19 A5**
Paveley St NW8 **3 B4**
Pavilion Rd SW1 **11 C5**
19 C1
Peabody Ave SW1 **20 E3**
Peace Pagoda SW11 **19 C5**
Peachum Rd SE3 **24 F2**
Pear Tree St EC1 **7 A4**
Pearman St SE1 **14 E5**
Pearson St E2 **8 D2**
Pedley St E1 **8 E4**
Peel St W8 **9 C4**
Peerless St EC1 **7 B3**
Pelham Cres SW7 **19 A2**
Pelham Pl SW7 **19 A2**
Pelham St SW7 **19 A2**
Pellant Rd SW6 **17 A5**
Pelter St E2 **8 D3**
Pelton Rd SE10 **24 D1**
Pembridge Cres W11 **9 C2**
Pembridge Gdns W2 **9 C3**
Pembridge Pl W2 **9 C2**
Pembridge Rd W11 **9 C3**
Pembridge Sq W2 **9 C3**
Pembridge Vlls W11 **9 C2**
Pembroke Gdns W8 **17 C1**
Pembroke Gdns Clo
W8 **17 C1**
Pembroke Rd W8 **17 C1**
Pembroke Sq W8 **17 C1**
Pembroke Vlls W8 **17 C1**
Penfold St NW1,
NW8 **3 A4**
Penn St N1 **7 B1**
Pennant Ms W8 **18 D1**
Pennington St E1 **16 F3**
Penryn St NW1 **5 A2**
Penton Pl SE17 **22 F2**
Penton Rise WC1 **6 D3**
Penton St N1 **6 D2**
Pentonville Rd N1 **6 D2**
Penywern Rd SW5 **18 D3**
Penzance Pl W11 **9 A3**
Penzance St W11 **9 A3**
Pepper St SE1 **15 A4**
Pepys St EC3 **16 D2**

Percival David
Foundation WC1 **5 B4**
Percival St EC1 **6 F4**
Percy Circus WC1 **6 D3**
Percy St W1 **13 A1**
Perham Rd W14 **17 A3**
Perrin's La NW3 **1 B5**
Perrin's Wlk NW3 **1 A5**
Peter Jones SW3 **19 C2**
Peter Pan Statue
W2 **10 F3**
Petersham La SW7 **18 E1**
Petersham Pl SW7 **18 E1**
Peto Pl NW1 **4 E4**
Petticoat La E1 **16 D1**
Petticoat Sq E1 **16 D1**
Petty France SW1 **13 A5**
Petyward SW3 **19 B2**
Phene St SW3 **19 B4**
Philbeach Gdns SW5 **17 C2**
Phillimore Gdns W8 **9 C5**
Phillimore Pl W8 **9 C5**
Phillimore Wlk W8 **9 C5**
Phillipp St N1 **7 C1**
8 D1
Philpot La EC3 **15 C2**
Phoenix Pl WC1 **6 D4**
Phoenix Rd NW1 **5 A3**
Photographer's
Gallery WC2 **13 B2**
Piccadilly Circus W1 **13 A3**
Piccadilly W1 **12 E4**
13 A3
Pickard St EC1 **7 A3**
Pilgrim St EC4 **14 F2**
Pilgrim's La NW3 **1 C5**
Pilgrimage St EC1 **15 B5**
Pimlico Rd SW1 **20 D2**
Pinchin St E1 **16 F2**
Pindar St EC2 **7 C5**
Pitfield St N1 **7 C2**
Pitt St W8 **10 D4**
Pitt's Head Ms W1 **12 E4**
Planetarium NW1 **4 D5**
Platt St NW1 **5 A2**
Playing Fields SE11 **22 F2**
Plender St NW1 **4 F1**
5 A1
Plough Yd EC2 **8 D4**
Plumber's Row E1 **16 F1**
Pocock St SE1 **14 F4**
Point Hill SE10 **23 B4**
Pointers Clo E14 **23 A1**
Poland St W1 **12 F1**
Poland St W1 **13 A2**
Pollard Row E2 **8 F3**
Pollock's Toy
Museum W1 **5 A5**
Polygon Rd NW1 **5 A2**
Pond Pl SW3 **19 A2**
Pond Rd SE3 **24 F5**
Pond St NW3 **1 C5**
Ponler St E1 **16 F2**
Ponsonby Pl SW1 **21 B3**
Ponsonby Terr
SW1 **21 B3**
Pont St SW1 **19 C1**
20 D1
Ponton Rd SW8 **21 A4**
Poole St N1 **7 B1**
Pope Rd SE1 **16 D5**
Popham Rd N1 **7 A1**
Popham St N1 **7 A1**
Porchester Gdns W2 **10 D2**
Porchester Pl W2 **11 B1**
Porchester Rd W2 **10 D1**
Porchester Sq W2 **10 D1**
Porchester Terr W2 **10 E2**
Porlock St SE1 **15 B5**
Portland Pl W1 **4 E5**
Portland Rd W11 **9 A3**
Portman Clo W1 **11 C1**
Portman Ms South
W1 **12 D2**
Portman Sq W1 **12 D1**
Portobello Rd W10 **9 A1**
Portobello Rd W11 **9 B2**
Portpool La EC1 **6 D5**

Portsmouth St WC2 **14 D1**
Portsoken St E1 **16 D2**
Portugal St WC2 **14 D1**
Pottery La W11 **9 A3**
Poultry EC2 **15 B2**
Powis Gdns W11 **9 B1**
Powis Sq W11 **9 B1**
Powis Terr W11 **9 B1**
Pownall Rd E8 **8 E1**
Praed St W2 **10 F1**
11 A1
Pratt St NW1 **4 F1**
Pratt Wlk SE11 **22 D1**
Prebend St N1 **7 A1**
Prescot St E1 **16 E2**
Price's Yd N1 **6 D1**
Prideaux Pl WC1 **6 D3**
Prima Rd SW9 **22 E5**
Primrose Hill NW3,
NW8 **3 B1**
Primrose St EC2 **7 C5**
Prince Albert Rd
NW1, NW8 **3 B2**
4 D1
Prince Arthur Rd
NW3 **1 B5**
Prince Charles Rd
SE3 **24 E4**
Prince Consort Rd
SW7 **10 F5**
Prince of Wales Rd
SE3 **24 F4**
Prince's Gate SW7 **11 A5**
Prince's Gate Ms
SW7 **19 A1**
Prince's Gdns SW7 **11 A5**
Prince's Rise SE13 **23 B5**
Prince's Sq W2 **10 D2**
Prince's St EC2 **15 B1**
Princedale Rd W11 **9 A3**
Princelet St E1 **8 E5**
Princes Pl W11 **9 A3**
Princes St W1 **12 F2**
Princess Rd NW1 **4 D1**
Princeton St WC1 **6 D5**
Printer Sq EC4 **14 E1**
Prior St SE10 **23 B3**
Priory Wlk SW10 **18 F3**
Pritchard's Rd E2 **8 F1**
Protheroe Rd SW6 **17 A5**
Provence St N1 **7 A2**
Provost St N1 **7 B3**
Public Gardens W1 **4 D5**
Puddle Dock EC4 **14 F2**
Purbrook St SE1 **16 D5**
Purcell St N1 **7 C2**
Purchese St NW1 **5 A2**

Quaker St E1 **8 D4**
Queen Anne St W1 **12 E1**
Queen Anne's
Gate SW1 **13 A5**
Queen Elizabeth
St SE1 **16 D4**
Queen Mary's
Gardens NW1 **4 D3**
Queen Sq WC1 **5 C5**
Queen St EC4 **15 A2**
Queen St Pl EC4 **15 A2**
Queen Victoria St
EC4 **14 F2**
15 A2
Queen's Chapel SW1 **13 A4**
Queen's Club Gdns
W14 **17 A4**
Queen's Gallery
SW1 **12 F5**
Queen's Gdns SW1 **12 F5**
Queen's Gdns W2 **10 E2**
Queen's Gate SW7 **10 F5**
18 F1
Queen's Gate Gdns
SW7 **18 F1**
Queen's Gate Ms SW7 **10 F5**
Queen's Gate Pl SW7 **18 F1**
Queen's Gate Pl Ms
SW7 **18 F1**

Queen's Gate Terr
SW7 **18 E1**
Queen's Gro NW8 **3 A1**
Queen's House SE10 **23 C2**
Queen's Wlk SW1 **12 F4**
Queen's Wlk SE1 **14 E3**
16 E4
Queenhithe EC4 **15 A2**
Queensberry Pl SW7 **18 F1**
Queensborough Ms
W2 **10 E2**
Queensborough
Terr W2 **10 E2**
Queensbridge Rd
E2, E8 **8 E1**
Queensdale Rd W11 **9 A4**
Queenstown Rd SW8 **20 E4**
Queensway W2 **10 D2**
Quilter St E2 **8 E3**

R

Racton Rd SW6 **17 C4**
Radnor Ms W2 **11 A2**
Radnor Pl W2 **11 A1**
Radnor St EC1 **7 A3**
Radnor Terr W14 **17 B1**
Radnor Wlk SW3 **19 B3**
Radstock St SW11 **19 B5**
Railway Approach
SE1 **15 B3**
Railway St N1 **5 C2**
Raleigh St N1 **6 F1**
Rampayne St SW1 **21 A3**
Randall Pl SE10 **23 A3**
Randall Rd SE11 **21 C2**
Ranelagh Gardens
SW3 **20 D3**
Ranelagh Gro SW1 **20 D3**
Ranger's House SE10 **23 C4**
Raphael St SW7 **11 B5**
Rathbone Pl W1 **13 A1**
Rathbone St W1 **13 A1**
Ravensbourne Pl
SE13 **23 A5**
Ravenscroft St E2 **8 E2**
Ravensdon St SE11 **22 E3**
Ravent Rd SE11 **22 D2**
Rawlings St SW3 **19 B2**
Rawstorne St EC1 **6 F3**
Ray St EC1 **6 E4**
Raymond Bldgs WC1 **6 D5**
Rector St N1 **7 A1**
Red Lion Sq WC1 **5 C5**
Red Lion St WC1 **6 D5**
Redan Pl W2 **10 D2**
Redburn St SW3 **19 B4**
Redchurch St E2 **8 D4**
Redcliffe Gdns SW10 **18 E3**
Redcliffe Ms SW10 **18 E3**
Redcliffe Pl SW10 **18 E4**
Redcliffe Rd SW10 **18 4F**
Redcliffe Sq SW10 **18 D3**
Redcross Way SE1 **15 A4**
Redesdale St SW3 **19 B3**
Redfield La SW5 **18 D2**
Redhill St NW1 **4 E3**
Redington Rd NW3 **1 A5**
Redvers St N1 **8 D2**
Reedworth St SE11 **22 E2**
Rees St N1 **7 B1**
Reeves Ms W1 **12 D3**
Regan Way N1 **7 C2**
Regency St SW1 **21 A2**
Regent Sq WC1 **5 C3**
Regent St W1, SW1 **12 F1**
13 A3
Regent's Park NW1 **3 C2**
4 D2
Regent's Pk Terr
NW1 **4 E1**
Regent's Pl SE3 **24 F5**
Regent's Pk Rd NW1 **3 C1**
4 D1
Regent's Row E8 **8 E1**
Renfrew Rd SE11 **22 F2**
Rennie St SE1 **14 F3**
Restell Clo SE3 **24 E2**

Rheidol Terr N1	7 A1
Richard's Pl SW3	19 B2
Richborne Terr SW8	22 D5
Richmond Terr SW1	13 B4
Rick La SW5	18 D3
Rickett St SW6	17 C4
Ridgmount Gdns WC1	5 A5
Ridgmount St WC1	5 A5
Riding House St W1	12 F1
Riley Rd SE1	16 D5
Ring, The W2	11 A3
Risinghill St N1	6 D2
Rita Rd SW8	21 C5
Ritz Hotel SW1	12 F3
River St EC1	6 E3
Rivington St EC2	7 C5
Roan St SE10	23 A2
Robert St NW1	4 F3
Robert Adam St W1	12 D1
Roberta St E2	8 F3
Robin Gro N6	2 F2
Rochester Row SW1	21 A2
Roderick Rd NW3	2 E5
Rodmarton St W1	11 C1
Rodmere St SE10	24 E1
Rodney St N1	6 D2
Roger St WC1	6 D4
Roland Gdns SW7	18 F3
Roland Way SW7	18 F3
Romilly St W1	13 A2
Romney Clo NW11	1 A1
Romney Rd SE10	23 B2
Romney St SW1	21 B1
Rona Rd NW3	2 E5
Rood La EC3	15 C2
Ropemaker St EC2	7 B5
Roper's Garden SW3	19 A4
Rosaline Rd SW6	17 A5
Rosary Gdns SW7	18 E2
Rosaville Rd SW6	17 B5
Rose Alley SE1	15 A3
Rose St WC2	13 B2
Rose Theatre SE1	15 A3
Rosebery Ave EC1	6 E4
Rosemoor St SW3	19 B2
Rosewood Gdns SE13	23 A5
Rosmead Rd W11	9 A2
Rosslyn Hill NW3	1 C5
Rossmore Rd NW1	3 B4
Rotary St SE1	14 F5
Rotten Row SW7	11 A4
Roupell St SE1	14 E4
Rowallan Rd SW6	17 A5
Royal Academy of Arts W1	12 F3
Royal Academy of Music NW1	4 D4
Royal Albert Hall SW7	10 F5
Royal Ave SW3	19 C3
Royal College of Art SW7	10 F5
Royal College of Music SW7	10 F5
Royal College St NW1	5 A1
Royal Courts of Justice WC2	14 D2
Royal Exchange EC4	15 C2
Royal Festival Hall SE1	14 D4
Royal Free Hospital NW3	2 D5
Royal Hill SE10	23 B3
Royal Hospital Cemetery SE10	24 F1
Royal Hospital Rd SW3	19 C3
Royal Hospital Rd SW3	20 D3
Royal Mint St E1	16 E2
Royal Ms SW1	12 E5
Royal Naval College SE10	23 C2
Royal Opera House WC2	13 C2
Royal Parade SE3	24 E5
Royal Rd SE17	22 F4
Royal St SE1	14 D5
Rudall Cres NW3	1 B5
Rumbold Rd SW6	18 E5
Rupert St W1	13 A2
Rushton St N1	7 B2
Rushworth St SE1	14 F4
Russell Gdns W14	9 A5
Russell Gdns Ms W14	9 A5
Russell Rd W14	17 A1
Russell Sq WC1	5 B5
Russell St WC2	13 C2
Russett Way SE13	23 A5
Ruston Ms W11	9 A1
Rutherford St SW1	21 A2
Ruthin Rd SE3	24 F2
Rutland Gdns SW7	11 B5
Rutland Gate SW7	11 B5
Rycusf Sq SE3	24 F5
Ryder St SW1	12 F4
Rylston Rd SW6	17 B4

S

Saatchi Gallery SW3	19 C2
St Agnes Pl SE11	22 E4
St Alban's Rd NW5	2 F3
St Alban's St SW1	13 A3
St Alfege Passage SE10	23 B2
St Andrew's EC4	14 E1
St Andrew's Gdns WC1	6 D4
St Andrew's Pl NW1	4 E4
St Andrews St EC4	14 E1
St Anne's Clo N6	2 F3
St Ann's St SW1	21 B1
St Ann's Terr NW8	3 A2
St Austell Rd SE13	23 B5
St Barnabas St SW1	20 D2
St Bartholomew's Hospital EC1	14 F1
St Bartholomews-the-Great EC1	6 F5
St Botolph Church EC1	15 A1
St Botolph St EC3	16 D1
St Bride St EC4	14 E1
St Bride's EC4	14 F2
St Chad's Pl WC1	5 C3
St Chad's St WC1	5 C3
St Clement Danes WC2	14 D2
St Crispin Clo NW3	2 D5
St Cross St EC1	6 E5
St Edmund's Terr NW8	3 B1
St Ethelreda's EC1	6 E5
St George's Bloomsbury WC1	13 B1
St George's Cathedral SE1	14 E5
St George's Circus SE1	14 F5
St George's Dri SW1	20 F2
St George's Fields W2	11 B2
St George's Gdn SW1	12 D3
St George's Gdns WC1	5 C4
St George's Rd SE1	22 F1
St George's Sq SW1	21 A3
St German's Pl SE3	24 F4
St Giles EC2	7 A5
St Giles, Cripplegate High St WC2	13 B1
St Helen's Bishopsgate EC3	15 C1
St James's Church SW1	13 A3
St James's Palace SW1	12 F4
St James's Park SW1	13 A4
St James's Pk Lake SW1	13 A4
St James's Pl SW1	12 F4
St James's Rd SE16	16 F5
St James's Sq SW1	13 A3
St James's St SW1	12 F3
St John St EC1	6 E2
St John's SE1	14 E4
St John's Gdns SW1	21 B1
St John's Gdns W11	9 A3
St John's High St NW8	3 A2
St John's La EC1	6 F5
St John's Pk SE3	24 F3
St John's Smith Sq SW1	21 B1
St John's Sq EC1	6 F4
St John's Wood Church Gdns NW8	3 A3
St John's Wood High St NW8	3 A2
St John's Wood Rd NW8	3 A3
St John's Wood Terr NW8	3 A2
St Katherines Dock E1	16 E3
St Katherines Pier E1	16 E3
St Katharine's Way E1	16 E3
St Lawrence Terr W10	9 A1
St Leonard's Terr SW3	19 C3
St Loo Ave SW3	19 B4
St Luke's Ms W11	9 B1
St Luke's Rd W11	9 B1
St Luke's St SW3	19 B3
St Magnus the Martyr EC3	15 C3
St Margaret Pattens EC3	15 C2
St Margaret's Church SW1	13 B5
St Margaret St SW1	13 B5
St Mark St E1	16 E2
St Mark's Cres NW1	4 D1
St Mark's Rd W11	9 A2
St Martin's La WC2	13 B2
St Martin's Le Grand EC1	15 A1
St Martin's Pl WC2	13 B3
St Martin's St WC2	13 B3
St Martin-in-the-Fields WC2	13 B3
St Mary Abbots Terr W14	17 B1
St Mary at Hill EC3	15 C2
St Mary Axe EC3	15 C1
St Mary's Hospital W2	11 A1
St Mary Le Strand WC2	14 D2
St Mary's Path N1	6 F1
St Mary's Wlk SE11	22 E2
St Mary-le-Bow EC4	15 A2
St Marylebone Parish Church W1	4 D5
St Matthew's Row E2	8 E4
St Michael's St W2	11 A1
St Olaf's Rd SW6	17 A5
St Oswald's Pl SE11	22 D3
St Pancras Church WC1	5 B3
St Pancras Way NW1	5 A1
St Paul St N1	7 A1
St Paul's Cathedral EC4	15 A2
St Paul's Church WC2	13 C2
St Paul's Churchyard EC4	15 A1
St Peter's Clo E2	8 F2
St Peter's St N1	6 F1
St Petersburgh Pl W2	10 D3
St Stephen Walbrook EC4	15 B2
St Stephen's Gdns W2	9 C1
St Stephen's Terr SW8	21 C5
St Swithin's La EC4	15 B2
St Thomas St SE1	15 B4
St Thomas' Hospital SE1	13 C5
St Thomas' Way SW6	17 B5
Sackville St W1	12 F3
Saffron Hill EC1	6 E5
Sail St SE11	22 D1
Salamanca St SE11	21 C2
Sale Pl W2	11 A1
Salem Rd W2	10 D2
Salisbury Ct EC4	14 E2
Salisbury St NW8	3 A4
Sampson St E1	16 F4
Sancroft St SE11	22 D2
Sandwich St WC1	5 B3
Sandys Row E1	8 D5
Sans Wlk EC1	6 E4
Saunders Ness Rd E14	23 B1
Savernake Rd NW3	2 E5
Savile Row W1	12 F2
Savona St SW8	20 F5
Savoy Chapel WC2	13 C2
Savoy Hill WC2	13 C3
Savoy Pl WC2	13 C3
Savoy Row WC2	13 C3
Savoy St WC2	13 C2
Savoy, The WC2	13 C2
Scala St W1	5 A5
Scarborough St E1	16 E2
Scarsdale Vlls W8	17 C1
	18 D1
Science Museum SW7	18 F1
	19 A1
Sclater St E1	8 E4
Scott Lidgett Cres SE16	16 F5
Scott St E1	8 F4
Scovell Crescent SE1	15 A5
Scrutton St EC2	7 C4
Seagrave Rd SW6	17 C4
	18 D4
Sebastian St EC1	6 F3
Sedlescombe Rd SW6	17 C4
Seething La EC3	16 D2
Selby St E1	8 F4
Selfridge's W1	12 D2
Selwood Pl SW7	18 F3
Selwood Terr SW7	18 F3
Semley Pl SW1	20 E2
Serle St WC2	14 D1
Serpentine Gallery W2	11 A4
Serpentine Rd W2	11 C4
	12 D4
Serpentine, The W2	11 B4
Settles St E1	16 F1
Seven Dials WC2	13 B2
Seville St SW1	11 C5
Seward St EC1	7 A4
Seymour Ms W1	12 D1
Seymour Pl W1	3 B5
	11 B1
Seymour St W1,W2	11 C2
Seymour Wlk SW10	18 E4
Shad Thames SE1	16 E4
Shaftesbury Ave W1	13 A2
Shaftesbury Ave WC2	13 B1
Shaftesbury St N1	7 B2
Shafto Ms SW1	19 C1
Shafts Ct EC3	15 C1
Shakespeare's Globe SE1	15 A3
Shalcomb St SW10	18 F4
Sharsted St SE17	22 F3
Shawfield St SW3	19 B3
Sheffield Ter W8	9 C4
Sheldon Ave N6	2 D1
Sheldrake Pl W8	9 C5
Shelton St WC2	13 B2
Shenfield St N1	8 D2
Shepherd Mkt W1	12 E4
Shepherd St W1	12 E4
Shepherdess Wlk N1	7 A2
Shepherd's Wlk NW3	1 B5
Shepperton Rd N1	7 B1
Sherbourne La EC4	15 B2
Sherbrooke Rd SW6	18 D5

Each place name is followed by its postal district, and then by its Street Finder reference

Sherlock Holmes
Museum W1 — 3 C4
Sherwood St W1 — 13 A2
Shipton St E2 — 8 E2
Shirlock Rd NW3 — 2 E5
Shoe La EC4 — 14 E1
Shooters Hill Rd SE3 — 24 D4
Shooters Hill Rd
SE18 — 23 C4
Shoreditch High St
EC2, SE3 — 8 D3
Shoreditch Park E2 — 7 B1
Shorrold's Rd SW6 — 17 C5
Short St SE1 — 14 E4
Shouldham St W1 — 11 B1
Shroton St NW1 — 3 B5
Sidmouth St WC1 — 5 C3
Silk St EC2 — 7 B5
Sinclair Rd W14 — 17 A1
Singer St EC2 — 7 C4
Sir John Soane's
Museum WC2 — 14 D1
Skinner St EC1 — 6 E4
Slaidburn St SW10 — 18 F4
Sleaford St SW8 — 20 F5
Sloane Ave SW3 — 19 B2
Sloane Ct East SW3 — 20 D3
Sloane Gdns SW1 — 20 D2
Sloane Sq SW1 — 19 C2
— 20 D2
Sloane St SW1 — 11 C5
— 19 C1
Smith Sq SW1 — 21 B1
Smith St SW3 — 19 C3
Smith Terr SW3 — 19 C3
Smithfield Mkt EC1 — 6 F5
Snow Hill EC1 — 14 F1
Snowfields SE1 — 15 B4
Soho Sq W1 — 13 A1
Soho St W1 — 13 A1
Somers Cres W2 — 11 A1
South Audley St W1 — 12 D3
South Eaton Pl SW1 — 20 D2
South Edwardes Sq
W8 — 17 C1
South End Clo NW3 — 2 D5
South End Rd NW3 — 1 C5
South Gro N6 — 2 F1
South Hill Pk NW3 — 2 D5
South Hill Pk Gdns
NW3 — 2 D4
South Island Pl SW9 — 22 D5
South Lambeth Pl
SW8 — 21 C4
South Lambeth Rd
SW8 — 21 C4
South Molton La W1 — 12 E2
South Molton St W1 — 12 E2
South Parade SW3 — 19 A3
South Pl EC2 — 7 B5
South Row SE3 — 24 E5
South St W1 — 12 D3
South Tenter St E1 — 16 E2
South Terr SW7 — 19 A2
South Wharf Rd W2 — 11 A1
Southampton Pl WC1 — 13 C1
Southampton Row
WC1 — 5 C5
Southampton St WC2 — 13 C2
Southern St N1 — 5 C2
Southwark Bridge
SE1 — 15 A3
Southwark Bridge
Rd SE1 — 15 A4
Southwark Cathedral
EC1 — 15 B3
Southwark St SE1 — 14 F3
— 15 A3
Southwell Gdns SW7 — 18 E1
Southwick St W2 — 11 A1
Southwood La N6 — 2 F1
Spa Fields EC1 — 6 E4
Spaniards Clo NW11 — 1 B1
Spaniards End NW3 — 1 B1
Spaniards Rd NW3 — 1 A3
Sparta St SE10 — 23 A4
Speakers' Corner W2 — 11 C2
Spedan Clo NW3 — 1 A4

Spelman St E1 — 8 E5
Spencer House SW1 — 12 F4
Spencer St EC1 — 6 F3
Spenser St SW1 — 20 F1
Spital Sq E1 — 8 D5
Spital St E1 — 8 E5
Spitalfields Centre
Museum of
Immigration E1 — 8 E5
Spitalfields Market — 8 D5
Spring St W2 — 10 F2
Spur Rd SW1 — 12 F5
Squires Mount NW3 — 1 B4
Squirries St E2 — 8 F3
Stable Yd Rd SW1 — 12 F4
Stafford Terr W8 — 9 C5
Stag Pl SW1 — 20 F1
Stamford St SE1 — 14 E3
Stanford Rd W8 — 18 E1
Stanhope Gdns SW7 — 18 F2
Stanhope Gate W1 — 12 D4
Stanhope Ms East
SW7 — 18 F2
Stanhope Ms West
SW7 — 18 F2
Stanhope Pl W2 — 11 B2
Stanhope St NW1 — 4 F3
Stanhope Terr W2 — 11 A2
Stanley Cres W11 — 9 B2
Stanley Gdns W11 — 9 B2
Stannary St SE11 — 22 E3
Stanway St N1 — 8 D2
Stanwick Rd W14 — 17 B2
Staple Inn WC1 — 14 E1
Staple St SE1 — 15 B5
Star Rd W14 — 17 B4
Star St W2 — 11 A1
Starcross St NW1 — 4 F3
Stean St E8 — 8 D1
Stephen St W1 — 13 A1
Stephenson Way NW1 — 5 A4
Steward St E1 — 8 D5
Stewart's Rd SW8 — 20 F5
Stock Exchange EC2 — 15 B1
Stockwell St SE10 — 23 B2
Stone Bldgs WC2 — 14 D1
Stonefield St N1 — 6 E1
Stones End St SE1 — 15 A5
Stoney La E1 — 16 D1
Stoney St SE1 — 15 B3
Stonor Rd W14 — 17 B2
Store St WC1 — 5 A5
Storey's Gate SW1 — 13 B5
Stormont Rd N6 — 2 D1
Stowage SE8 — 23 A2
Straightsmouth St
SE10 — 23 B3
Strand WC2 — 13 B3
Strand La WC2 — 14 D2
Stratford Rd W8 — 18 D1
Stratheden Rd SE3 — 24 F4
Stratton St W1 — 12 E3
Streatham St WC1 — 13 B1
Streatley Pl NW3 — 1 B4
Strode Rd SW6 — 17 A5
Strutton Ground SW1 — 21 A1
Sturt St N1 — 7 A2
Stutfield St E1 — 16 F2
Sudeley St N1 — 6 F2
Suffolk La EC4 — 15 B2
Suffolk Pl SW1 — 13 A3
Suffolk St WC1 — 13 B3
Sumner Pl SW7 — 19 A2
Sumner St SE1 — 15 A3
Sun Rd W14 — 17 B3
Sun St EC2 — 7 C5
Sunderland Terr W2 — 10 D1
Surrey Row SE1 — 14 F4
Surrey St WC2 — 14 D2
Sussex Gdns W2 — 11 A1
Sussex Pl NW1 — 3 C4
Sussex Pl W2 — 11 A2
Sussex Sq W2 — 11 A2
Sussex St SW1 — 20 F3
Sutherland Pl W2 — 9 C1
Sutherland St SW1 — 20 E3
Sutton Row W1 — 13 A1
Swain's La N6 — 2 F1

Swallow St W1 — 12 F3
Swan La EC4 — 15 B3
Swan La Pier SE1 — 15 B3
Swan St SE1 — 15 A5
Swan Wlk SW3 — 19 C4
Swanfield St E2 — 8 E3
Swinton St WC1 — 5 C3
Sydney Pl SW3 — 19 A2
Sydney St SW3 — 19 A3
Symons St SW3 — 19 C2

T

Tabard St SE1 — 15 B5
Tabernacle St EC2 — 7 C4
Tachbrook St SW1 — 21 A2
Tadema Rd SW10 — 18 F5
Talbot Rd W2,W11 — 9 C1
Talbot Sq W2 — 11 A2
Talgarth Rd W6,W14 — 17 A3
Tallis St EC4 — 14 E2
Tanner St SE1 — 16 D5
Tamworth St SW6 — 17 C4
Tanza Rd NW3 — 2 D4
Taplow St N1 — 7 A2
Tarves Way SE10 — 23 A3
Tasso Rd W6 — 17 A4
Tate Britain SW1 — 21 B2
Tate Modern SE1 — 14 F3
— 15 A3
Tavistock Cres W11 — 9 B1
Tavistock Pl WC1 — 5 B4
Tavistock Rd W11 — 9 B1
Tavistock Sq WC1 — 5 B4
Tavistock St WC2 — 13 C2
Taviton St WC1 — 5 A4
Teale St E2 — 8 F2
Tedworth Sq SW3 — 19 C3
Teesdale Clo E2 — 8 F2
Teesdale St E2 — 8 F2
Telegraph St EC2 — 15 B1
Temple EC4 — 14 E2
Temple Ave EC4 — 14 E2
Temple Bar
Memorial WC2 — 14 D2
Temple La EC4 — 14 E2
Temple Pl WC2 — 14 D2
Temple St E2 — 8 F2
Templeton Pl SW5 — 17 C2
Tent St E1 — 8 F4
Tenterden St W1 — 12 E2
Terminus Pl SW1 — 20 F1
Tetcott Rd SW10 — 18 E5
Thames St SE10 — 23 A2
Thanet St WC1 — 5 B3
Thaxton Rd W14 — 17 B4
Thayer St W1 — 12 D1
Theatre Museum
WC2 — 13 C2
Theatre Royal WC2 — 13 C2
Theatre Royal
Haymarket WC2 — 13 A3
Theberton St N1 — 6 E1
Theed St SE1 — 14 E4
Theobald's Rd WC1 — 5 C5
— 6 D5
Thessaly Rd SW8 — 20 F5
Thirleby Rd SW1 — 20 F1
Thistle Gro SW7 — 18 F3
Thomas More St E1 — 16 E3
Thoresby St N1 — 7 A3
Thorncroft St SW8 — 21 B5
Thorney St SW1 — 21 B1
Thornham St SE10 — 23 A2
Thornhaugh St WC1 — 5 B5
Thrale St SE1 — 15 A4
Thrawl St E1 — 8 E5
Threadneedle St
EC4 — 15 B2
Throgmorton Ave
EC2 — 15 C1
Throgmorton St EC2 — 15 B1
Thurloe Pl SW7 — 19 A1
Thurloe Sq SW7 — 19 A1
Thurloe St SW7 — 19 A2
Thurlow Rd NW3 — 1 B5
Tiber Gdns N1 — 5 C1

Tilney St W1 — 12 D3
Tilton St SW6 — 17 B4
Tinworth St SE11 — 21 C3
Titchborne Row W2 — 11 B2
Titchfield Rd NW8 — 3 B1
Tite St SW3 — 19 C4
Tolpuddle St N1 — 6 E2
Tom Smith Clo SE3 — 24 D2
Tomlinson Clo E2 — 8 E3
Tompion St EC1 — 6 F3
Tonbridge St WC1 — 5 B3
Tooley St EC1 — 15 B3
Tooley St SE1 — 16 D4
Tor Gdns W8 — 9 C4
Torrington Pl WC1 — 5 A5
Torrington Sq WC1 — 5 A4
Tothill St SW1 — 13 B5
Tottenham Ct Rd W1 — 4 F4
— 5 A5
— 13 A1
Tottenham St W1 — 5 A5
Toulmin St SE1 — 15 A5
Tournay Rd SW6 — 17 C5
Tower Bridge E1 — 16 D3
Tower Bridge SE1 — 16 D4
Tower Bridge
Approach E1 — 16 E3
Tower Bridge Rd
SE1 — 16 D4
Tower Clo NW3 — 1 C5
Tower Hill EC3 — 16 D2
Tower of London
EC3 — 16 D3
Townshend Rd NW8 — 3 B1
Toynbee St E1 — 16 D1
Tradescant Rd SW8 — 21 C5
Trafalgar Rd SE10 — 24 D1
Trafalgar Sq SW1 — 13 B3
Trafalgar Sq WC2 — 13 B3
Tranquil Vale SE3 — 24 E5
Treasury, The SW1 — 13 B5
Treaty St N1 — 5 C1
Trebovir Rd SW5 — 17 C3
Tregunter Rd SW10 — 18 E4
Trevanion Rd W14 — 17 A2
Trevor Pl SW7 — 11 B5
Trevor Sq SW7 — 11 B5
Trevor St SW7 — 11 B5
Trinity Church Sq SE1 — 15 A5
Trinity Sq EC3 — 16 D2
Trinity St SE1 — 15 A5
Triton Sq NW1 — 4 F4
Trocadero Centre W1 — 13 A2
Tudor St EC4 — 14 E2
Tufton St SW1 — 21 B1
Turin St E2 — 8 E3
Turk's Row SW3 — 19 C3
— 20 D3
Turners Wood NW11 — 1 A1
Turneville Rd W14 — 17 B4
Turnmill St EC1 — 6 E5
Turpentine La SW1 — 20 E3
Thurtle Rd E2 — 8 E1
Tuskar St SE10 — 24 D1
Twyford St N1 — 5 C1
Tyers Gate SE1 — 15 C5
Tyers St SE11 — 22 D2
Tyers Terr SE11 — 22 D3
Tyler St SE10 — 24 E

U

Ufford St SE1 — 14 E4
Ulundi Rd SE3 — 24 E2
Underwood Rd E1 — 8 F5
Underwood St N1 — 7 B3
Unicorn Pass SE1 — 16 D3
Union Sq N1 — 7 A1
Union St SE1 — 14 F4
— 15 A4
Union Wlk E2 — 8 D3
University St WC1 — 5 A4
University College
WC1 — 5 A4
University College
Hospital WC1 — 5 A4
Upcerne Rd SW10 — 18 E5
Upper St N1 — 6 F1

Upper Terr NW3 — 1 A4
Upper Belgrave Street SW1 — 20 E1
Upper Berkeley St W1 — 11 C1
Upper Brook St W1 — 12 D2
Upper Cheyne Row SW3 — 19 B4
Upper Grosvenor St W1 — 12 D3
Upper Ground SE1 — 14 E3
Upper Marsh SE1 — 14 D5
Upper Montagu St W1 — 3 C5
Upper Phillimore Gdns W8 — 9 C5
Upper St Martin's La WC2 — 13 B2
Upper Thames St EC4 — 15 A2
Upper Wimpole St W1 — 4 D5
Upper Woburn Pl WC1 — 5 B4
US Embassy W1 — 12 D2
Uxbridge St W8 — 9 C3

Vale, The SW3 — 19 A4
Vale of Health NW3 — 1 B3
Valentine Pl SE1 — 14 F5
Vallance Rd E1,E2 — 8 F4
Vanbrugh Fields SE3 — 24 E3
Vanbrugh Hill SE3 — 24 E2
Vanbrugh Hill SE10 — 24 E1
Vanbrugh Pk SE3 — 24 E3
Vanbrugh Pk Rd SE3 — 24 F3
Vanbrugh Pk Rd West SE3 — 24 E3
Vanbrugh Terr SE3 — 24 F4
Vane Clo NW3 — 1 B5
Vanston Pl SW6 — 17 C5
Varndell St NW1 — 4 F3
Vassall Rd SW9 — 22 E5
Vaughan Way E1 — 16 F3
Vauxhall Bridge SW1 — 21 B3
Vauxhall Bridge Rd SW1, SE1 — 20 F1 / 21 A2
Vauxhall Gro SW8 — 21 C4
Vauxhall Park SW8 — 21 C4
Vauxhall St SE11 — 22 D3
Vauxhall Wlk SE11 — 21 C3
Vere St W1 — 12 E1
Vereker Rd W14 — 17 A3
Vernon Rise WC1 — 6 D3
Vernon St W14 — 17 A2
Vestry St N1 — 7 B3
Vicarage Gate W8 — 10 D4
Victoria & Albert Museum SW7 — 19 A1
Victoria Embankment EC4 — 14 E2
Victoria Embankment SW1 — 13 C4
Victoria Embankment WC2 — 13 C3
Victoria Embankment Gdns WC2 — 13 C3
Victoria Gro W8 — 18 E1
Victoria Rd W8 — 10 E5 / 18 E1
Victoria St SW1 — 13 B5 / 20 F1 / 21 A1
Victoria Tower Gardens SW1 — 21 C1
Villiers St WC2 — 13 C3
Vince St EC1 — 7 C3
Vincent Sq SW1 — 21 A2
Vincent St SW1 — 21 A2
Vincent Terr N1 — 6 F2
Vine La SE1 — 16 D4
Vine St EC3 — 16 D2
Vintner's Pl EC4 — 15 A2
Virginia Rd E2 — 8 D3
Voss St E2 — 8 F3

W
Wakefield St WC1 — 5 C4
Wakley St EC1 — 6 F3
Walbrook EC4 — 15 B2
Walcot Sq SE11 — 22 E1
Waldorf Hotel WC2 — 13 C2
Wallace Collection W1 — 12 D1
Walmer Rd W11 — 9 A3
Walnut Tree Rd SE10 — 24 E1
Walnut Tree Wlk SE11 — 22 D1
Walpole St SW3 — 19 C3
Walton Pl SW3 — 19 C1
Walton St SW3 — 19 B2
Wandon Rd SW6 — 18 E5
Wandsworth Rd SW8 — 21 B5
Wansdown Pl SW6 — 18 D5
Wapping High St E1 — 16 F4
Wardour St W1 — 13 A2
Warham St SE5 — 22 F5
Warner Pl E2 — 8 F2
Warner St EC1 — 6 E4
Warren St W1 — 4 F4
Warwick Gdns W14 — 17 B1
Warwick La EC4 — 14 F1
Warwick Rd SW5 — 18 D3
Warwick Rd W14 — 17 B1
Warwick Sq SW1 — 20 F2
Warwick St W1 — 12 F2
Warwick Way SW1 — 20 F2
Wat Tyler Rd SE10 — 23 B5
Waterford Rd SW6 — 18 D5
Waterloo Bridge SE1,WC2 — 14 D3
Waterloo Pl SW1 — 13 A3
Waterloo Rd SE1 — 14 F4
Waterson St E2 — 8 D3
Watling St EC4 — 15 A2
Weaver St E1 — 8 E4
Weavers La SE1 — 16 D4
Webb Rd SE3 — 24 E2
Webber Row SE1 — 14 E5
Webber St SE1 — 14 E4
Weighouse St W1 — 12 D2
Welbeck St W1 — 12 D1
Well Rd NW3 — 1 B4
Well Wlk NW3 — 1 B4
Welland St SE10 — 23 B2
Weller St SE1 — 15 A5
Wellesley Terr N1 — 7 A3
Wellington Arch W1 — 12 D5
Wellington Bldgs SW1 — 20 E3
Wellington Pl NW8 — 3 A3
Wellington Rd NW8 — 3 A2
Wellington Row E2 — 8 E3
Wellington Sq SW3 — 19 C3
Wellington St WC2 — 13 C2
Wells Rise NW8 — 3 C1
Wells St W1 — 12 F1
Wenlock Basin N1 — 7 A2
Wenlock Rd N1 — 7 A2
Wenlock St N1 — 7 B2
Wentworth St E1 — 16 D1
Werrington St NW1 — 5 A2
Wesley's House & Chapel EC1 — 7 B4
West Sq SE11 — 22 F1
West St WC2 — 13 B2
West Cromwell Rd SW5,W14 — 17 B3
West Eaton Pl SW1 — 20 D1
West Ferry Rd E14 — 23 A1
West Gro SE10 — 23 B4
West Harding St EC4 — 14 E1
West Heath NW3 — 1 A3
West Heath Rd NW3 — 1 A4
West Hill Ct N6 — 2 E3
West Hill Pk N6 — 2 E2
West Pier E1 — 16 F4
West Smithfield EC1 — 14 F1
West Tenter St E1 — 16 E2
Westbourne Cres W2 — 10 F2
Westbourne Gdns W2 — 10 D1
Westbourne Gro W2 — 10 D2
Westbourne Gro W11 — 9 B2
Westbourne Pk Rd W2 — 10 D1
Westbourne Pk Rd W11 — 9 B1
Westbourne Pk Vlls W2 — 10 D1
Westbourne St W2 — 11 A2
Westbourne Terr W2 — 10 E1
Westcombe Hill SE10 — 24 F1
Westcombe Pk Rd SE3 — 24 E2
Westcott Rd SE17 — 22 F4
Westerdale Rd SE10 — 24 F1
Westgate St E8 — 18 D3
Westgrove La SE10 — 23 B4
Westland Pl N1 — 7 B3
Westminster Abbey SW1 — 13 B5
Westminster Bridge SE1, SW1 — 13 C5
Westminster Bridge Rd SE1 — 14 D5
Westminster Cathedral SW1 — 20 F1
Westminster Hospital SW1 — 21 B1
Westminster School Playing Fields SW1 — 21 A2
Westmoreland Pl SW1 — 20 E3
Westmoreland St W1 — 4 D5
Westmoreland Terr SW1 — 20 E3
Weston Rise WC1 — 6 D3
Weston St SE1 — 15 C4
Westway A40(M) W10 — 9 A1
Wetherby Gdns SW5 — 18 E2
Wetherby Pl SW7 — 18 E2
Weymouth Ms W1 — 4 E5
Weymouth St W1 — 4 E5
Weymouth Terr E2 — 8 E2
Wharf Pl E2 — 8 F1
Wharf Rd N1 — 7 A2
Wharfdale Rd N1 — 5 C2
Wharton St WC1 — 6 D3
Wheatsheaf La SW8 — 21 C5
Wheler St E1 — 8 D4
Whetstone Pk WC2 — 14 D1
Whiston Rd E2 — 8 D1
Whitbread Brewery EC2 — 7 B5
Whitcomb St WC2 — 13 A3
White Lion St N1 — 6 E2
White's Row E1 — 8 D5
Whitechapel Art Gallery E1 — 16 E1
Whitechapel High St E1 — 16 E1
Whitechapel Rd E1 — 8 F5 / 16 E1
Whitechurch La E1 — 16 E1
Whitecross St EC1,EC2 — 7 A4
Whitefriars St EC4 — 14 E2
Whitehall SW1 — 13 B3
Whitehall Ct SW1 — 13 C4
Whitehall Pl SW1 — 13 B4
Whitehall Theatre SW1 — 13 B3
Whitehead's Gro SW3 — 19 B2
White's Grounds SE1 — 16 D4
Whitfield Rd SE3 — 23 C5
Whitfield St W1 — 5 A5
Whitgift St SE11 — 21 C2
Whitmore Rd N1 — 7 C1
Whitworth St SE10 — 24 D1
Wicker St E1 — 16 F2
Wickham St SE11 — 22 D3
Wicklow St WC1 — 5 C3
Wigmore Hall W1 — 12 E1
Wigmore St W1 — 12 D1
Wilcox Rd SW8 — 21 B5
Wild Ct WC2 — 13 C1
Wild St WC2 — 13 C1
Wild's Rents SE1 — 15 C5
Wildwood Gro NW3 — 1 A2
Wildwood Rise NW11 — 1 A1
Wildwood Rd NW11 — 1 A1
Wilfred St SW1 — 12 F5
Wilkinson St SW8 — 21 C5
William St SW1 — 11 C5
William IV St WC2 — 13 B3
William Rd NW1 — 4 F3
Willoughby Rd NW3 — 1 B5
Willow Pl SW1 — 20 F2
Willow Rd NW3 — 1 C4
Willow St EC2 — 7 C4
Wilmer Gdns N1 — 7 C1
Wilmer Gdns N1 — 8 D1
Wilmington Ms SW1 — 11 C5
Wilmington Sq WC1 — 6 E3
Wilsham St W11 — 9 A3
Wilkes St E1 — 8 E5
Wilson Gro SE16 — 16 F5
Wilson St EC2 — 7 C5
Wilton Cres SW1 — 12 D5
Wilton Pl SW1 — 12 D5
Wilton Rd SW1 — 20 F1
Wilton Row SW1 — 12 D5
Wilton Sq N1 — 7 B1
Wiltshire Row N1 — 7 B1
Wimborne St N1 — 7 B2
Wimpole Ms W1 — 4 E5
Wimpole St W1 — 4 E5 / 12 E1
Winchester Clo SE17 — 22 F2
Winchester St SW1 — 20 E3
Wincott St SE11 — 22 E2
Windmill Hill NW3 — 1 A4
Windmill Wlk SE1 — 14 E4
Windsor Terr N1 — 7 A3
Winfield House NW1 — 3 B3
Winforton St SE10 — 23 B4
Winnington Rd N2 — 1 B1
Winsland St W2 — 10 F1 / 11 A1
Woburn Pl WC1 — 5 B4
Woburn Sq WC1 — 5 B4
Woburn Wlk WC1 — 5 B4
Wolseley St SE1 — 16 E5
Wood Clo E2 — 8 F4
Wood St EC2 — 15 A1
Woodbridge St EC1 — 6 F4
Woodland Gro SE10 — 24 D1
Woodlands Pk Rd SE10 — 24 D2
Woods Ms W1 — 12 D2
Woodseer St E1 — 8 E5
Woodsford Sq W14 — 9 A4
Woodsome Rd NW5 — 2 F4
Woodstock St W1 — 12 E1
Woolwich Rd SE10 — 24 E1
Wootton St SE1 — 14 E4
Worfield St SW11 — 19 B5
World's End Pas SW10 — 18 F5
Wormwood St EC2 — 15 C1
Woronzow Rd NW8 — 3 A1
Worship St EC2 — 7 C4
Wren St WC1 — 6 D4
Wright's La W8 — 10 D5
Wycherley Clo SE3 — 24 E3
Wyclif St EC1 — 6 F3
Wyldes Clo NW11 — 1 A2
Wynan Rd E14 — 23 A1
Wyndham Rd SE5 — 22 F5
Wyndham St W1 — 3 C5
Wynford Rd N1 — 6 D2
Wynyatt St EC1 — 6 F3
Wyvil Rd SW8 — 21 B5

Y
Yardley St WC1 — 6 E4
Yeoman's Row SW3 — 19 B1
York Gate NW1 — 4 D4
York House Pl W8 — 10 D4
York Rd SE1 — 14 D4
York St W1 — 3 B5
York Ter East NW1 — 4 D4
York Ter West NW1 — 4 D4
York Way N1 — 5 C1
Yorkton St E2 — 8 E2
Young St W8 — 10 D5

Each place name is followed by its postal district, and then by its Street Finder reference

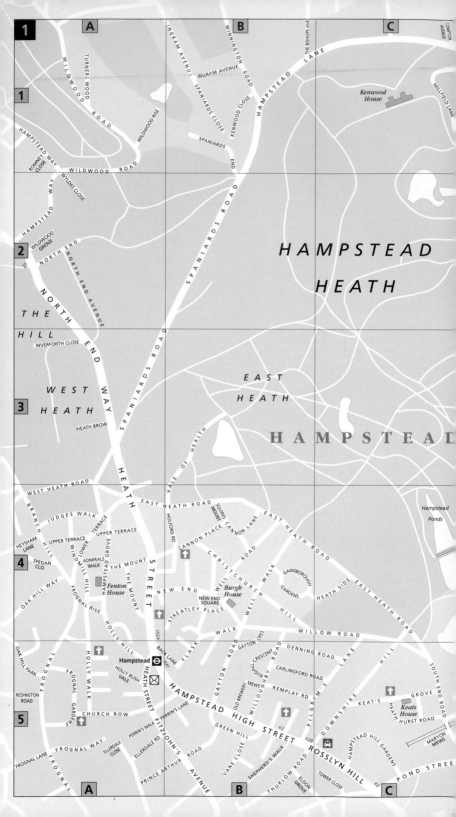

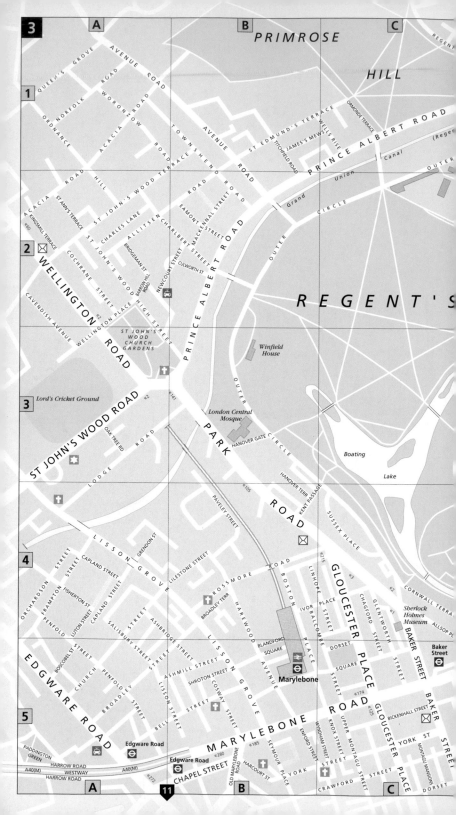

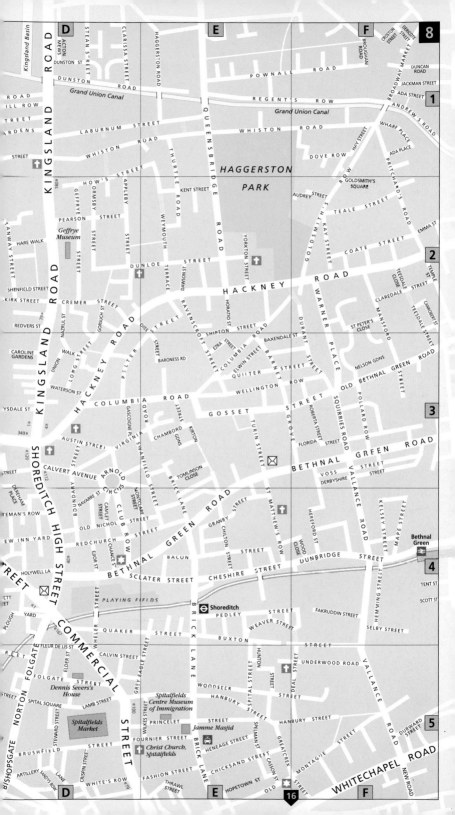

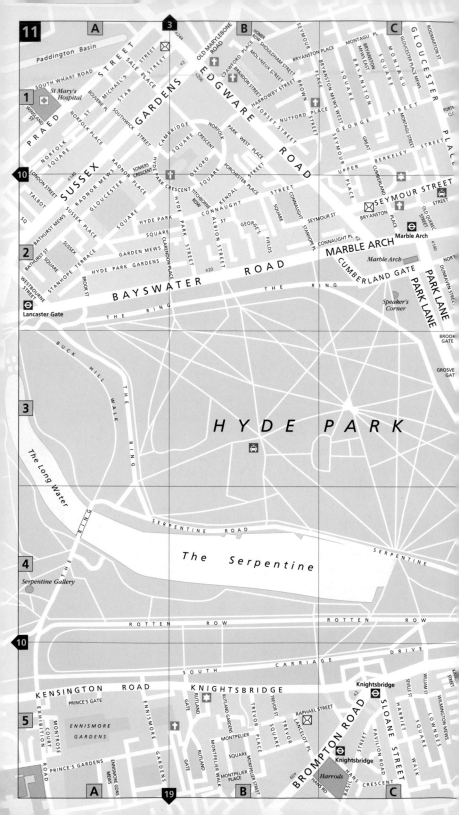

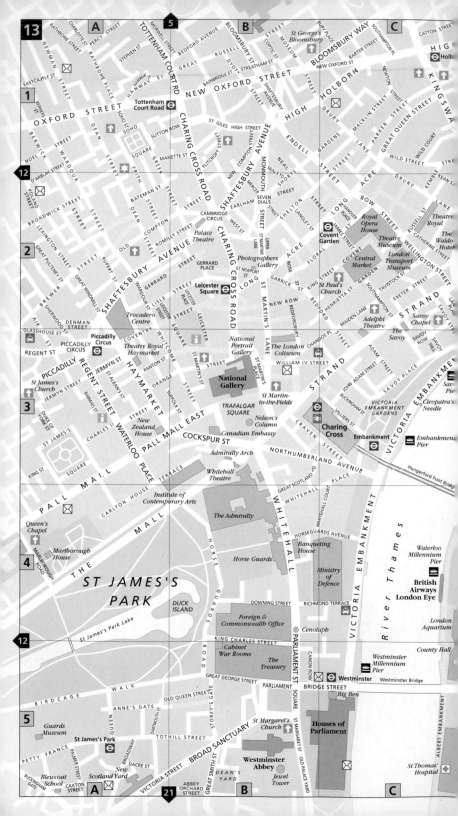

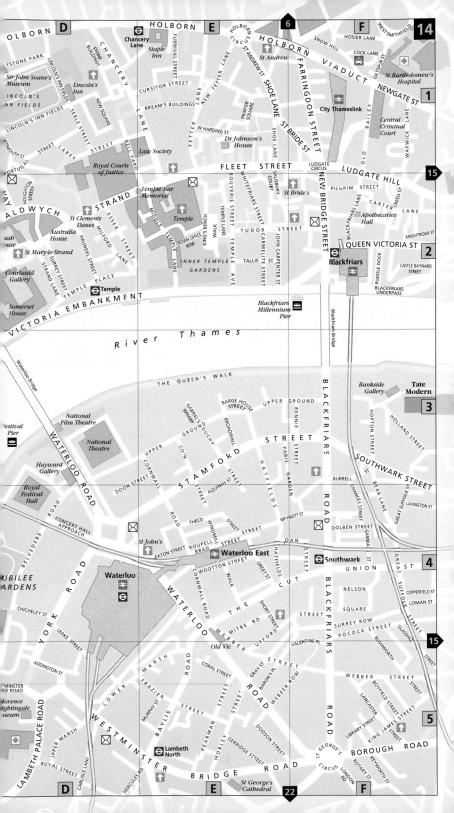

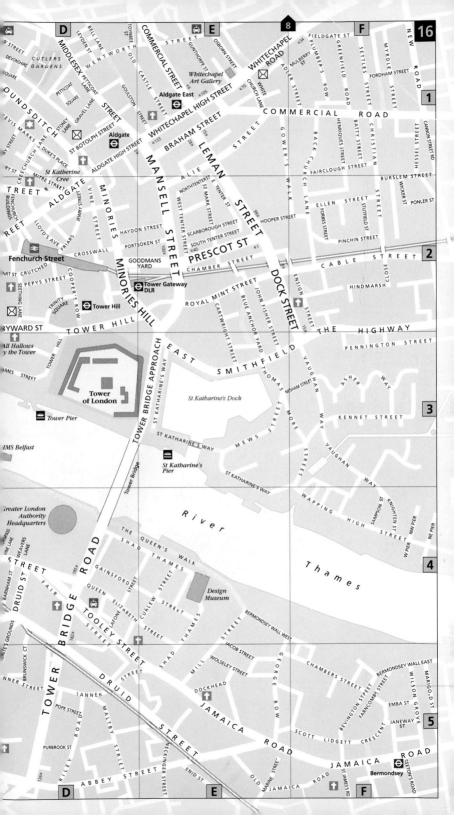

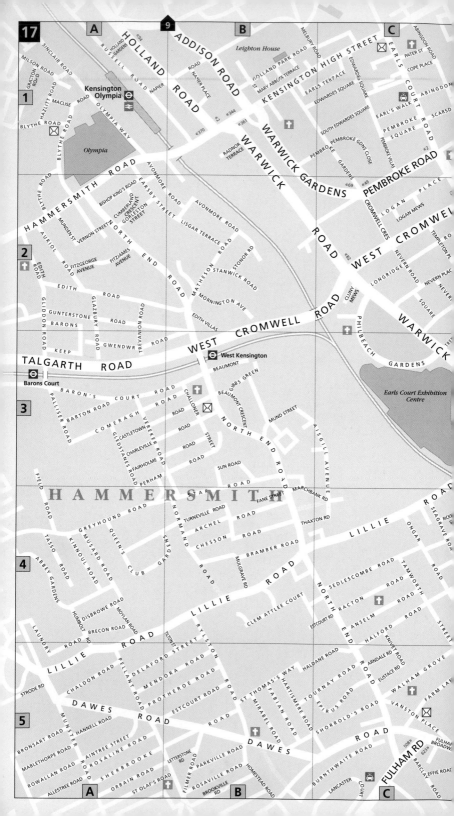

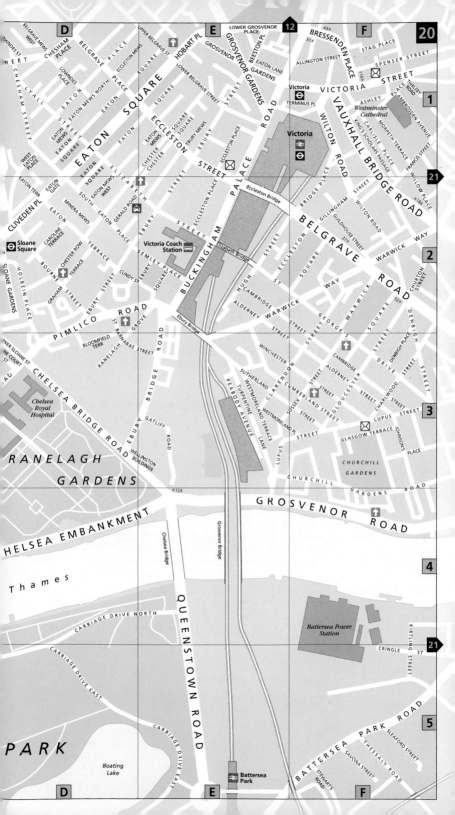

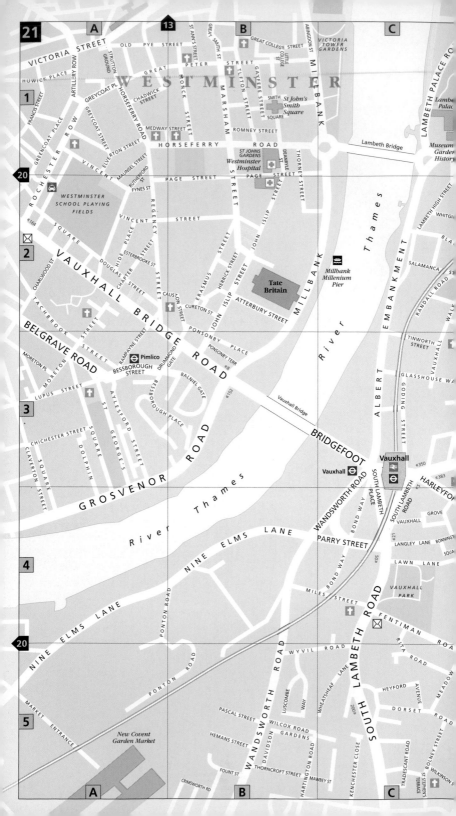

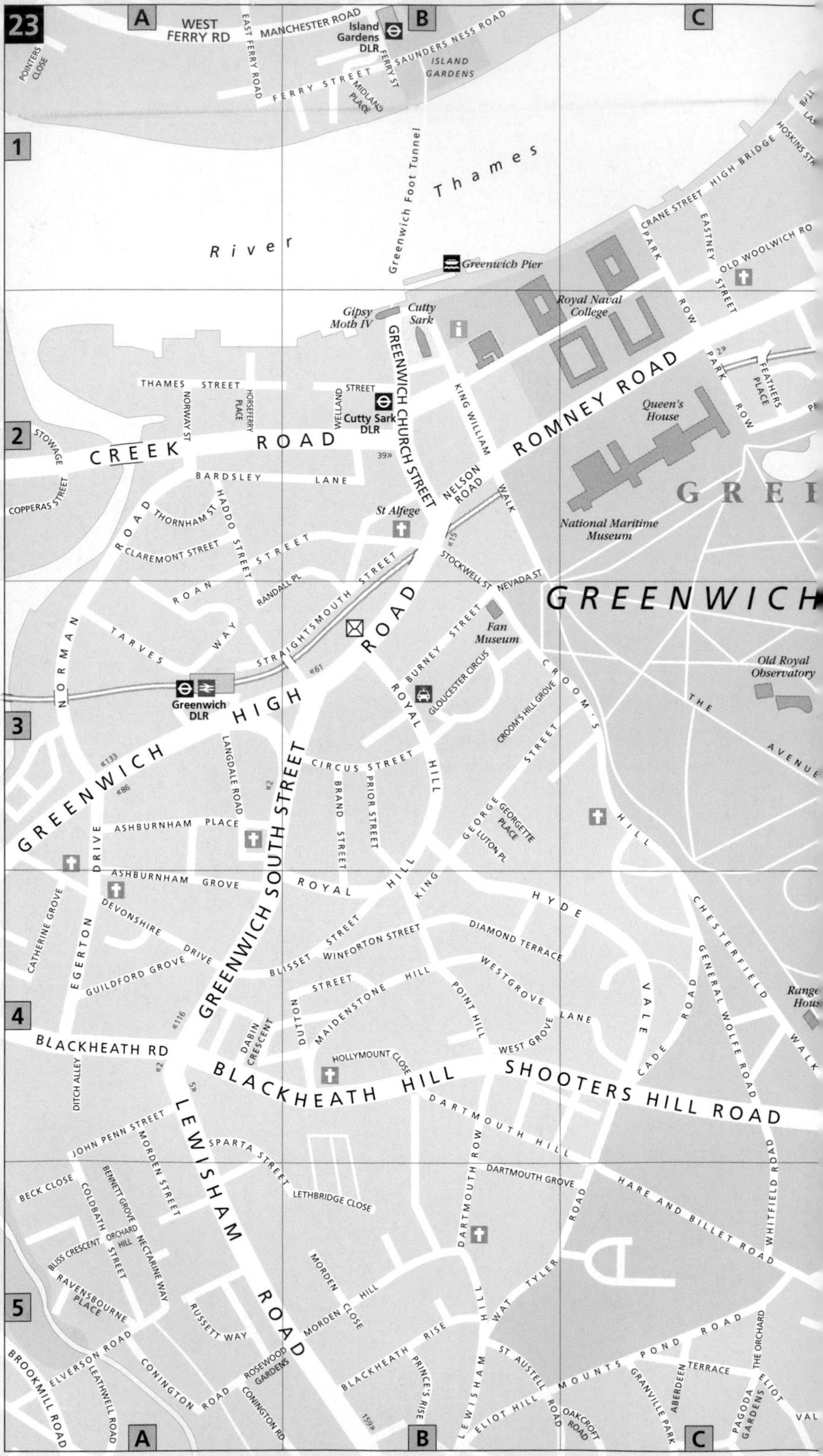

23

WEST FERRY RD

MANCHESTER ROAD

EAST FERRY ROAD

B

Island Gardens DLR

FERRY ST

SAUNDERS NESS ROAD

ISLAND GARDENS

C

POINTERS CLOSE

FERRY STREET

MIDLAND PLACE

1

Greenwich Foot Tunnel

Thames

BALL LAN

HOSKINS STR

CRANE STREET

HIGH BRIDGE

EASTNEY

OLD WOOLWICH RD

River

Greenwich Pier

PARK

STREET

Gipsy Moth IV

Cutty Sark

Royal Naval College

ROW

2

STOWAGE

THAMES STREET

NORWAY ST

HORSEFERRY PLACE

STREET

WELLAND

Cutty Sark DLR

GREENWICH CHURCH STREET

KING WILLIAM

ROMNEY ROAD

29

FEATHERS PLACE

ROW

CREEK ROAD

BARDSLEY

LANE

NELSON ROAD

WALK

Queen's House

COPPERAS STREET

ROAD

THORNHAM ST

HADDO STREET

STREET

St Alfege

National Maritime Museum

GREE

CLAREMONT STREET

ROAN

RANDALL PL

STRAIGHTSMOUTH STREET

STOCKWELL ST

NEVADA ST

GREENWICH

NORMAN

TARVES

WAY

STREET

HIGH

ROAD

BURNEY STREET

Fan Museum

CROOM'S

Old Royal Observatory

3

133

Greenwich DLR

86

LANGDALE ROAD

GREENWICH SOUTH STREET

CIRCUS STREET

ROYAL

HILL

GLOUCESTER CIRCUS

CROOM'S HILL GROVE

STREET

HILL

THE

AVENUE

GREENWICH

ASHBURNHAM PLACE

BRAND STREET

PRIOR STREET

GEORGETTE PLACE

LUTON PL.

GEORGE

DRIVE

ASHBURNHAM GROVE

ROYAL

HILL

KING

HYDE

CHESTERFIELD

CATHERINE GROVE

DEVONSHIRE

BLISSET STREET

WINFORTON STREET

DIAMOND TERRACE

WESTGROVE

VALE

GENERAL WOLFE ROAD

Range Hous

4

EGERTON

GUILDFORD GROVE

DRIVE

116

MAIDENSTONE HILL

POINT HILL

WEST GROVE

LANE

CADE ROAD

WALK

BLACKHEATH RD

2

DARIN CRESCENT

DUTTON STREET

STREET

Hollymount Close

BLACKHEATH HILL

DARTMOUTH HILL

SHOOTERS HILL ROAD

DITCH ALLEY

LEWISHAM

JOHN PENN STREET

MORDEN STREET

SPARTA STREET

LETHBRIDGE CLOSE

DARTMOUTH ROW

DARTMOUTH GROVE

ROAD

HARE AND BILLET ROAD

WHITFIELD ROAD

5

BECK CLOSE

COLDBATH

BENNETT GROVE

ORCHARD STREET

NECTARINE WAY

ROAD

BLISS CRESCENT

RAVENSBOURNE PLACE

ELVERSON ROAD

HEATHWELL ROAD

RUSSETT WAY

ROSEWOOD GARDENS

MORDEN HILL

MORDEN CLOSE

BLACKHEATH RISE

PRINCE'S RISE

DARTMOUTH HILL

LEWISHAM HILL

ST AUSTELL ROAD

WAT TYLER ROAD

MOUNTS POND ROAD

GRANVILLE PARK

ABERDEEN TERRACE

OAKCROFT ROAD

ELIOT HILL ROAD

PAGODA GARDENS

THE ORCHARD

ELIOT PLACE

VAL

BROOKMILL ROAD

CONINGTON ROAD

CONINGTON RD

159

A

B

C

General Index

Page numbers in **bold** type refer to main entries.

A

Abbeys
  Westminster Abbey 44, 46, 70, **76–9**
Accessories shops **328**, 329
Actors **39**
Adam, James 26, 38
  Portland Place 225
Adam, John 119
Adam, Robert 26, 38
  Adelphi 119
  Apsley House 97
  Fitzroy Square 130–31
  Kenwood House 234–5
  Lansdowne House 270
  Osterley Park House 253
  Portland Place 225
  Syon House 253, 269
Adams, John Quincy 153
Adelphi **119**
Adelphi Theatre **116**, 345
Admiral's House
  Street-by-Street map 230
Admiralty Arch **102**
  Street-by-Street map 101
The Adoration of the Kings (Brueghel) 106
Affordable art galleries (commercial) **337**, 338
Africa Centre 353
Agencies, booking tickets 343
Airsure 369
Air Canada 372
Air New Zealand 372
Air travel **372**
Air Travel Advisory Bureau *see* Lupus Travel
Airports **374–7**
  map 377
Albany **90**
  Street-by-Street map 88
Albert, Prince Consort 28
  Albert Memorial 201, **207**
  Lancaster House 96
  Royal Albert Hall 207
  Victoria and Albert Museum 202
Albert Bridge
  Chelsea and Battersea walk 266
  Street-by-Street map 195
Albert Hall Mansions
  Street-by-Street map 201
Albert Memorial 199, **207**
  Street-by-Street map 201
Albery Theatre 345
Aldwych Theatre 345
Alexander, Helene 243
Alexandra, Queen 93
Alfege, St, Archbishop of Canterbury 241
Alfred the Great, King of Wessex 19, 138
Algerian Coffee House 109

All England Lawn Tennis and Croquet Club 353
All Hallows by the Tower **153**
All Saints' Church
  Isleworth, Richmond and Kew walk 268
All Souls, Langham Place **225**
  London's Best: Churches 44, 47
Almeida Theatre 346, 350
Altdorfer, Albrecht 106
The Ambassadors (Holbein) **105**, 106
Ambulances 365
American Airlines 372
American Express 366
Anchor, The **182**
  Street-by-Street map 175
Annabel's 353
Anne, Princess Royal 95
Anne, Queen 35
  Kensington Palace 210
  Queen Square 124
  statues of 80, 148
Anne of Denmark 240
The Annunciation (Lippi) 106
Antiques
  Antiquarius **339**
  Bermondsey Antiques Market **182, 339**
  Chelsea Antiques Fair 58
  shops **336–8**
Antiquities
  London's Best: Museums and Galleries **42**
Antonello da Messina 106
Apollo Theatre 345
Apothecaries' Hall **152**
Apple Market **340**
Apsley, Baron 97
Apsley House **97**
Aquarium, London 62, 187, **188, 358**
Archaeology
  London's Best: Museums and Galleries **42**
Archbishops of Canterbury 190
Archer, Thomas 81
Architecture
  architects and engineers **38**
  Post-Modern architecture 33
  Tube Architecture 381
Arnolfini Portrait (van Eyck) **105**, 106
Arsenal Stadium 353
Art shops **336–8**
  fine art shops **336–8**
Arthur, Prince 74
Artists **38–9**
Artsline 363
Ascot Racecourse 353
Ashcroft, Dame Peggy 39
Astoria Theatre 353
At the Theatre (Renoir) 107
Athletics **354**

Auctions and auction houses **337**, 338
Audley End 384
August Bank Holiday 59
Augusta, Princess 260
Austen, Jane 39
Autumn in London **58**
Avis Rent a Car 379

B

Back Roads Touring 362
Bacon, Francis
  Tate Britain 85
  Tate Modern 180, 181
Baden-Powell, Lord 164, 251
Bag shops **333**, 334
Baird, John Logie 109
Ballet **350**
  Royal Opera House 115
Bank of England 25, 26
Bank of England Museum **147**
  Street-by-Street map 145
Bank notes **367**
Banking **366–7**
Banks, Sir Joseph 260
Bankside
  walks 272–3
  see also Southwark and Bankside
Bankside Gallery **177**
Bankside Power Station 180
Banqueting House 25, **80**
  Four Great Days in London 10
  A River View of London 62
  Street-by-Street map 71
Baptism of Christ (Piero della Francesca) 105
Baptist churches 371
Bar at the Folies Bergère (Manet) 41
Barbican **165**
  Street-by-Street map 163
Barbican Centre 50, 165
Barbican Concert Hall **349**
Barfly 351, 353
Barrie, J M 210, 219
Barry, Sir Charles 38
  Houses of Parliament 72
  Reform Club 92
  Royal College of Surgeons 134
  Travellers' Club 92
Barry, E M
  Charing Cross 119
  Royal Opera House 115
Bars **314**, 315, **316–19**
The Bath (Bonnard) 181
Bathers at Asnières (Seurat) **105**, 107
Battersea Park 50, 51, **251**
  London's Best: Parks and Gardens 49
  walks **266–7**
Battersea Power Station 189
Baylis, Lilian 191
Bayswater
  hotels **282**
  restaurants **296**

Bazalgette, Sir Joseph 28, 38
BBC 30
  All Souls, Langham Place 225
  Broadcasting House **225**
Beating the Bounds 56
Beating the Retreat 54, 56
Beatles, The 32
Beauchamp Tower 154
Becket, St Thomas à, Archbishop
  of Canterbury 20
Bed & Breakfast and Homestay
  Association 280, 281
Bedford, 5th Duke of
  statue of 123
Bedford, Earl of 111
Bedford Square 122
  Street-by-Street map 122
Beefeaters 154
Beer 295
  microbreweries **317**, 318
  pubs **316–19**
  Whitbread's Brewery **168**
Behind the scenes tours 346, **359**
Belfast, HMS **183**
  A River View of London 65
Belgravia
  hotels **284**
  walks **270–71**
Bell, Vanessa 39, 124
Bellini, Giovanni 106
  Courtauld Institute 117
  Doge Leonardo Loredan 104
  National Gallery 106
Bengalis 170–71
Bentley, John Francis 81
Berkeley Square 27, 50
  walks 270–71
Bermondsey Antique Market **182**, **339**
Berwick Street Market **108**, **339**
Bethnal Green Museum of
  Childhood **248**
  London's Best: Museums and
  Galleries 43
Betjeman, John 165
Beuys, Joseph 180
Bevis, L Cubitt 194
BFI London IMAX 185, **347**
Bicycles 379
Big Ben 69, 72, **74**
  Street-by-Street map 71
Billingsgate **152**
  A River View of London 64
Binning, Lady 233
Bird, Francis 148
Black Death (1348) 20, 21
Blackfriars Bridge
  A River View of London 63
Blackheath **243**
  see also Greenwich and
  Blackheath
Blacklands Terrace
  Chelsea and Battersea
  walk 267
Blake, Peter
  Royal College of Art 200, 207
  Tate Britain 85

Blake, William 84
  St James's Church, Piccadilly 90
  St Mary's, Battersea 251
  Satan Smiting Job with Sore Boils
  84
  tomb of 168
Blewcoat School **81**
Bligh, William
  tomb 190
Blitz 31, 32
Blomfield, Sir Arthur 206
"Blood, Colonel" 155
Bloody Tower 155
Bloomsbury and Fitzrovia **121–31**
  area map 121
  British Museum **126–9**
  hotels **288–9**
  pubs 319
  Street-by-Street map 122–3
Bloomsbury Group 39, 121, 124
Bloomsbury Square **124**
  Street-by-Street map 123
Blue Posts
  Street-by-Street map 100
Blunt, Anthony 96
Boadicea, Queen 18
  statue of 71
Boats
  Cutty Sark 238, **241**
  Gipsy Moth IV 238, **241**
  HMS *Belfast* 65, **183**
  National Maritime Museum 239,
  240
  Oxford v Cambridge boat
  race 56
Boccioni, Umberto
  *Unique Forms of Continuity in
  Space* 181
Boer War 29
Boleyn, Anne
  execution 22, 155, 252
  Hampton Court 256
Bond Street
  Four Great Days in London 11
Bonnard, Pierre
  The Bath 181
Bookshops **330**, 331
  Charing Cross Road 108
Boots the Chemist 365
Borderline 353
Borough Market **176**, **339**
  Street-by-Street map 175
Bosch, Hieronymus
  Christ Mocked 106
Boswell, James 113, 140
Boswells
  Street-by-Street map 113
Botticelli, Sandro
  Courtauld Institute 117
  National Gallery 106
Boucher, François 107
Bourchier, Arthur 346
Bourchier, Elizabeth 168
Bourgeois 251
Bourgeois, Louise 180, 181
  Maman 181

Bow Street Police Station
  Street-by-Street map 113
Boy and Dolphin (Wynne) **195**, 267
Brasseries **314**, 315
Brawne, Fanny 233
Breakfast **312**, 314
  in hotels 279
Brentford
  Richmond and Kew walk 269
Breweries
  microbreweries **317**, 318
  Whitbread's Brewery **168**
Bric-à-brac shops **337**, 338
Brick Lane **170–71**
Brick Lane Market 171, **339**
  London's Best: Shopping Streets
  and Markets 323
Bridge Street Accommodations 281
Bridges
  Albert Bridge 195
  Blackfriars Bridge 63
  Holborn Viaduct **140**
  Hungerford Bridge 186
  London Bridge 17, 20–21, 24, 175
  Millennium Bridge 173
  New London Bridge 32
  Southwark Bridge 174
  Tower Bridge 65, **153**
  Waterloo Bridge 187
Brighton 384
Britain Seen From the North
  (Cragg) 178
British Airways 372
British Airways London Eye 185, **189**
  Four Great Days in London 11
  A River View of London 62
  Street-by-Street map 186
British Hotel Reservation Centre
  281
British Library **125**
British Museum **126–9**
  floorplan 126–7
  Great Court and the Old Reading
  Room 129
  London's Best: Museums and
  Galleries 40, 42
  Street-by-Street map 122
  Visitors' checklist 127
British Tours 362
Brittany Ferries 373
Britten, Benjamin 206
Brixton Academy 353
Brixton Market **339**
Broadcasting House **225**
Broadgate Arena **349**
Broadgate Centre **169**
Broadgate Ice Rink 354, 355
Broadway Market **339**
Brompton
  hotels **284**
Brompton Oratory **206**
  London's Best: Churches 44, 47
  Street-by-Street map 201
Brompton Square
  Street-by-Street map 201
Brougham, Lord 134

Brown, Lancelot "Capability"
  Richmond Park 252
  Syon House 269
Browning, Elizabeth Barrett 222, 224
Browning, Robert 222, 224
Brueghel, Pieter the Elder
  The Adoration of the Kings 106
  Courtauld Institute 117
Buckingham, Duke of 118
Buckingham Palace **94–5**, 189
  Four Great Days in London 10
  London's Best: Ceremonies 52, 54
  The Mall **93**
Buddhism 371
Buddhist Peace Pagoda
  Chelsea and Battersea walk 266
BUNAC 370
Bunhill Fields 51, **168**
Bunyan, John
  tomb of 168
Bureaux de change 366
Burgh, Rev Allatson 232
Burgh House **232**
  Street-by-Street map 231
The Burghers of Calais (Rodin) 70
Burlington, 3rd Earl of 258–9
Burlington Arcade **91**
  Street-by-Street map 88
Burne-Jones, Edward 21
  Downshire Hill 233
  Kensington Square 219
  Linley Sambourne House 218
Burns, Robert 118
Burton, Decimus 40
  Athenaeum 92
  Palm House, Kew
    Gardens 261
  Wellington Arch 97
Buses 378, **382–3**
Bush, Irving T 118
Bush House **118**
Bush Theatre 346
Byfield, John 248
Byron, Lord
  Albany 90
  Holland House 218
  St Marylebone Parish Church 224
  Spaniards Inn 235
  Vale of Health 235

C

Cabinet War Rooms **75**
  Street-by-Street map 70
Caesar, Julius 17, 18
Café de Paris 353
Cafés **312–15**
  Organic **314**, 315
  Tate Britain 83
Cakes and Ale Sermon
  London's Best: Ceremonies 55
Calder, Alexander 180
Cambridge 384
Cambridge Theatre 345
Camden
  Regent's Canal walk 265
Camden Lock Market **339**

Camden Market **246**
Camden Palace 353
Camden Passage Market **340**
Camping 281
Canada Tower 33, 249
Canaletto
  Dulwich Picture Gallery 251
  National Gallery 107
  Rome: The Pantheon 94
Canals
  Regent's Canal **227**, 263, **264–5**
Canary Wharf 33, **249**, 381
  hotels 291
Canova, Antonio 97
Canterbury 384
Capon, William 139
Car travel **379**
  children 357
Caracci, Annibale 93
Caravaggio 107
Cardinal's Wharf **177**
Carlyle, Thomas
  Carlyle's House 38, **196**
  Chelsea 193
  London Library 92
  statue of 267
Carlyle's House 38, **196**
  Street-by-Street map 194
Carnaby Street **109**
Caro, Anthony 169
Carol services 59
Caroline, Queen 211, 271
Carracci, Annibale 107
Carrington, Dora 124
Carter, Gilbert 196
Casinos **352**
Casson, Sir Hugh 81, 207
Cathedrals
  St Paul's Cathedral 24, 45, 63,
    143, 144, **148–51**
  Southwark Cathedral 45, 46, 64,
    175, **176**
  Westminster Cathedral 44, 47, **81**
Catherine of Aragon 74, 257
Catholic Church
  Brompton Oratory **206**
  religious services 371
  Westminster Cathedral **81**
Caulfield, Patrick 180
  After Lunch 180
Cavendish, Lord 91
Caxton, William 21, 138
CD shops **330**, 331
Cecil Court
  Street-by-Street map 101
Cecil Sharp House 353
Cemeteries **51**
  Bunhill Fields **168**
  Highgate Cemetery **246**
Cenotaph **74–5**
  London's Best: Ceremonies 53, 54
  Street-by-Street map 71
Central Hall
  Street-by-Street map 70
Ceremonies
  London's Best **52–5**

Certificates, films 347
Cézanne, Paul 117, 180
Chain bars **318**, 319
Chamberlain, Neville 75
Chambers, Sir William
  Osterley Park House 253
  Pagoda, Kew Gardens 260
  Somerset House 117
Changing of the Guard 94
  London's Best: Ceremonies 54
Channel ferries **373**
Channel Tunnel 373
Chapel Market **340**
Chapel of St Thomas 20
Chaplin, Charlie 31, 39
  statue of 100, 103
Chardin, Jean-Baptiste-Siméon 107
Charing Cross 33, 108
  A River View of London 62
Charing Cross Pier 61
Charing Cross Road **108**
  London's Best: Shopping Streets
    and Markets 322–3
  Street-by-Street map 100
Charles Dickens Museum 38, 125
Charles, Prince of Wales 33, 107
  Clarence House 96
  Crown Jewels 156
  St Paul's Cathedral 149, 150
Charles I, King 35, 107
  Banqueting House 80
  Charles I Commemoration 59
  Crown Jewels 156
  execution 24
  Hampton Court 257
  Houses of Parliament 73
  Richmond Park 252
  Tower of London 157
Charles II, King 35, 116
  Banqueting House 80
  Crown Jewels 156
  Green Park 97
  The Mall 93
  Monument 152
  and Nell Gwynne 39
  Oak Apple Day 52, 55
  Greenwich Royal Observatory 242
  Restoration 24–5
  Royal Hospital 197
  St James's Park 93
  Soho Square 108
  statue of 197, 266
  Tower of London 157
Charles Street, Piccadilly 270
Charlotte, Queen
  Queen's Chapel 93
  statue of 124
  Whitbread's Brewery 168
Charlotte Street **131**
Charlton House **250**
Charterhouse **164**
  Street-by-Street map 163
Chaucer, Geoffrey 21, 39
Chelsea **193–7**
  area map 193
  hotels **284–5**

Charlton House **250**
Charterhouse **164**
  Street-by-Street map 163
Chaucer, Geoffrey 21, 39
Chelsea **193–7**
  area map 193
  hotels **284–5**
  pubs 319
  restaurants **298–9**
  Street-by-Street map 194–5
  walks **266–7**
Chelsea and Westminster Hospital 365
Chelsea Farmers' Market
  Chelsea and Battersea walk 267
Chelsea Flower Show 56
Chelsea Football Club 355, 359
Chelsea Harbour **259**
Chelsea Hospital 56
  London's Best: Ceremonies 52, 55
Chelsea Old Church **196**
  Chelsea and Battersea walk 267
  London's Best: Churches 46
  Street-by-Street map 194
Chelsea Pensioners 197
Chelsea Physic Garden 50, **197**
  Street-by-Street map 195
Chelsea porcelain factory 267
Chelsea Sports Centre 355
Chelsea Town Hall
  Street-by-Street map 195
Chemists 365
Chequepoint 366
Chessington Golf Course 355
Chesterfield Street, Mayfair 270
Chevalier, Maurice 109
Cheyne, Lady Jane 196
Cheyne Walk **196**
  Street-by-Street map 195
Childminders 357
Children **356–9**
  clothes shops **326**, 328
  in hotels 280
  in restaurants 293, **357**
Children's Book Centre 358
Chinatown **108**
  Four Great Days in London 11
  Street-by-Street map 100
Chinese New Year 59
Ching Court 112
Chisenhale Dance Space 350
Chiswick House 50, **258–9**
Christ Church, Spitalfields **170**
  London's Best: Churches 47
  Street-by-Street map 163
Christ Mocked (Bosch) 106
Christmas 58, 59
Church of England 371
Church Row **233**
  Street-by-Street map 231
Church Street Market **340**
Church Walk
  Street-by-Street map 217
Churches
  All Hallows by the Tower **153**
  All Saints' Church, Isleworth 268

Churches (cont.)
  All Souls, Langham Place 44, 47, **225**
  Brompton Oratory 44, 47, 201, **206**
  Chelsea Old Church 46, 194, **196**, 267
  Christ Church, Spitalfields 47, 163, **170**
  Holy Trinity 201
  Immaculate Conception, Mayfair 270
  London's Best **44–7**
  Notre Dame 101
  Queen's Chapel 46, **93**
  St Alfege 47, 238, **240–41**
  St Andrew, Holborn **140**
  St Anne's, Limehouse 47, **249**
  St Bartholomew-the-Great 46, 163, **165**
  St Bartholomew-the-Less 162
  St Botolph, Aldersgate **164**
  St Bride's 46, 47, **139**
  St Clement Danes 47, 135, **138**
  St Etheldreda's Chapel **140–41**
  St George's, Bloomsbury 46, 47, 123, **124**
  St Giles, Cripplegate **168**
  St Helen's Bishopsgate **158**
  St James Garlickhythe 47, 144
  St James's, Piccadilly 47, 89, **90**
  St John's, Smith Square **81**
  St Katherine Cree **158**
  St Luke's 267
  St Magnus the Martyr 47, **152**
  St Margaret's 71, **74**
  St Margaret Pattens **153**
  St Martin-in-the-Fields 44, 46, 47, 101, **102**
  St Mary Abchurch 145
  St Mary-at-Hill **152–3**
  St Mary-le-Bow 46, 47, 144, **147**
  St Mary-le-Strand 45, 47, **118**
  St Mary, Rotherhithe **248**
  St Mary Woolnoth 45, 47, 145
  St Marylebone Parish Church 222, **224–5**
  St Mary's, Battersea **251**
  St Nicholas Cole 144
  St Pancras 47, **130**
  St Paul's, Belgravia 271
  St Paul's, Covent Garden 44, 46, 113, **114**
  St Stephen Walbrook 45, 47, 145, **146**
  Savoy Chapel **116**
  spires 46
  Temple Church 45, 46
  Wesley's Chapel-Leysian Mission **168**
  see also Cathedrals
Churchill, Clementine 74
Churchill, Winston 31
  Cabinet War Rooms and Churchill Museum 70, 75
  St Margaret's Church 74
  St Paul's Cathedral 150
  statue of 71, 74

Cinema **347**
Cipriani, Giovanni 96
The City **143–59**
  area map 143
  Beating the Bounds 56
  hotels **290–91**
  London's Best: Ceremonies 53, 55
  pubs 319
  restaurants **308–9**
  St Paul's Cathedral **148–51**
  Street-by-Street map 144–5
  Tower of London **154–7**
City Hall 65
City of London Information Centre 363
City of London Festival 57
City University Accommodation and Conference Service 281
Civil War 24
Clamping cars 379
Clarence House **96**
Claude Lorrain 107, 251
Claudius, Emperor 18
Cleopatra's Needle **118**
  A River View of London 62
Clerkenwell
  hotels **290–91**
  pubs 319
  restaurants **308**
Climate **56–9**
Clink Prison Museum **182**
  Street-by-Street map 175
Clive of India 270
Clore Galleries, Tate Britain 82, **84**
Cloth Fair **165**
  Street-by-Street map 163
Clothes
  boutiques **325**, 327
  chain stores **325**, 327
  children's clothes **326**, 328
  knitwear **326**, 328
  lingerie **326**, 328
  modern British fashion **325**, 327
  shoes **326**, 328
  shops **324–7**
  size chart **324**
  street fashion **325**, 327
  traditional **324**, 326
  underwear **326**, 328
Clowns' Service 59
  London's Best: Ceremonies 55
Clubs **352**, 353
  Pall Mall 92
Coach and Horses 109, 318
Coach travel **373**
Cocteau, Jean 101
Coffee **312**, 314–15
Coins **367**
Cold Dark Matter: An Exploded View (Parker) 85
Coleridge, Sir John Taylor 135
Coleridge, Samuel Taylor 235
Collcutt, T E 226
Collectables shops **337**, 338
College of Arms
  Street-by-Street map 144

Columbia Road Market **171**, **340**
Comedy Store 346
Comedy Theatre 345
Commonwealth 24, 35
Company of Watermen
London's Best: Ceremonies 55
Composition (Man and Woman)
(Giacometti) 178
Computer Cabs 385
Congestion Charge 379
Constable, John 39
Burgh House 232
Charlotte Street 131
grave of 233
The Hay-Wain **105**, 107
National Gallery 107
Well Walk 231, 232
Contemporary dance **350**
Conversion chart, measurements 371
Cook, Captain James 27, 240
Copley, John Singleton 84, 159
Coram, Thomas 125
Coram's Fields 125, 359
Corinth, Lovis
*Magdalen with Pearls in
her Hair* 181
Coronations
Coronation Day gun
salutes 57
Crown Jewels **156**
Westminster Abbey **79**
Corot, Jean-Baptiste Camille 107
Costume and jewellery
London's Best: Museums and
Galleries **42**
County Hall **188**, 272
Four Great Days in London 11
A River View of London 62
Street-by-Street map 187
Courier services 369
Courtauld, Samuel 117
Courtauld, Stephen 250
Courtauld Institute of Art Gallery 117
London's Best: Museums and
Galleries 41, 43
Covent Garden and the Strand
111–19
area map 111
Four Great Days in London 11
Garden Flower Festival 57
hotels **289–90**
London's Best: Shopping Streets
and Markets 323
pubs 319
Punch and Judy Festival 58
restaurants **305–7**
Street-by-Street map 112–13
Crafts and design
London's Best: Museums and
Galleries **42**
shops 334, 335
Crafts Council Gallery **247**
London's Best: Museums and
Galleries 42
Cragg, Tony 85, 178
Britain Seen From the North 178

Credit cards **366**
in restaurants 293
in shops 320
Crewe House, Mayfair 270
Cricket **354**
Lord's Cricket Ground **246**
test matches 57
Crime 364
Crippen, Dr 224
Criterion Theatre 345
Cromwell, Oliver 35
Apothecaries' Hall 152
Banqueting House 80
Commonwealth 24
Hampton Court 257
Lincoln's Inn 134–5
Oak Apple Day 55
St Giles, Cripplegate 168
Croom's Hill **243**
Crosby Hall
Chelsea and Battersea walk 267
Crossflight 369
Crowds, avoiding 362
Crown Jewels 154, **156**
Crowne Plaza 377
Cruickshank, George 242
Crystal Palace **28–9**
open-air concerts 57
Cubitt, Thomas 130
Cumberland Terrace **227**
Currency **366–7**
Curzon Cinema 270
Curzonfield House 270
Curzon Street, Mayfair 270
Custom House
A River View of London 64
Customs and immigration **370**
Cutty Sark **241**
Street-by-Street map 238
Cycling 379

D

Dalí, Salvador 180, 188
Dance **350**
Dance, George the Elder 146
Dance, George the Younger 258
Darwin, Charles 196
Daubigny, Charles-François 107
Davenport's Magic Shop 358
David, Percival 130
Davison, Emily 124
Day Lewis, Daniel 243
Day trips **384**
Days in London, Four Great
10–11
Family Fun Day **11**
Great Outdoors **11**
History and Culture **10**
Shopping in Style **10**
De Gaulle, Charles
The French House 109
St James's Square 92
De Morgan, William
William Morris Gallery 249
Deacon, Richard 85
Dean, Tacita 85, 180

Dean's Yard **74**
Street-by-Street map 70
Death Hope Life Fear (Gilbert and
George) 178
Defoe, Daniel
tomb of 168
Degas, Edgar 117
Delacroix, Eugène 107
Delis **313**, 315
Dell Café, Hyde Park 270, 271
Dennis Severs House **171**
Dentists 365
Department stores **321**
Depression 30, 31
Derain, Andre 180
Desenfans 251
Design Museum **183**
London's Best: Museums and
Galleries 41, 42
A River View of London 65
Devonshire House, Piccadilly
walks 270–71
DHL 369
Dialling codes 368
Diana, Princess of Wales 33
Diana, Princess of Wales
Memorial Fountain 11, 215
Memorial Playground **219**
Kensington Gardens 210
Kensington Palace 210
St Paul's Cathedral 149, 150
Spencer House 91
Dickens, Charles
Carlyle's House 196
Charles Dickens Museum 38,
125
Gray's Inn 141
Old Curiosity Shop 137
St Luke's Church 267
Trafalgar Tavern 242
Westminster Abbey 79
Ye Olde Cheshire Cheese 140
Diners **313**, 315
Dion, Mark 180
Dior, Christian 205
Disabled visitors **363**
entertainment 343
in hotels **280**, 281
Discounts
air travel 372
in hotels 278
museum tickets 356
student travellers 370
theatre tickets 346
Disney Store, The 358
Disraeli, Benjamin
St Andrew, Holborn 140
statue of 71
Docklands Light Railway (DLR) 33
Docklands Museum 249
Docklands Sailing and Watersports
Centre 355
Docks 26
St Katharine's Dock **158**
Dr Johnson's House **140**
Doge Leonardo Loredan (Bellini) 104

Doggett's Coat and Badge
  A River View of London 63
Doggett's Coat and Badge Race 57
  London's Best: Ceremonies 55
Doll, Charles 124
Dome, The **249**
Domesday Book 20
Dominion Theatre 345
Donmar Warehouse 346
Donne, John 39
  Lincoln's Inn 134–5
  tomb of 151
Dormitory accommodation 281
Doubleday, John 103
Dover House
  Street-by-Street map 71
Downing, Sir George 75
Downing Street **75**
  Four Great Days in London 10
  Street-by-Street map 70
Downshire Hill **233**
Doyle, Sir Arthur Conan 38
  Sherlock Holmes Museum
  226
Drake, Sir Francis 23
Drayson Mews
  Street-by-Street map 217
Drink see Food and drink
Dryden, John
  Lamb and Flag 116
  Westminster School 74
Du Pré, Jacqueline 188
Dub Vendor (shop) 327
Duccio 106
Duchamp, Marcel 180
Duchess Theatre 345
Duke of York's Headquarters
  Chelsea and Battersea walk 267
Duke of York's Theatre 345
Dulwich Picture Gallery **250–51**
  London's Best: Museums and
  Galleries 43
Dunstan, St 78
Durham, Joseph 207
Dvořák, Antonín 225
Dysart, Countess of 252

E
Earl's Court
  hotels **283**
East End art galleries **336–7**, 338
East Street Market **340**
Easter 56, 59
Edinburgh, Duke of
  Buckingham Palace 95
  Duke of Edinburgh's Birthday
  gun salutes 57
Edward, Prince 95
Edward the Confessor, King 20
  coronation 156
  Crown Jewels 156
  Houses of Parliament 73
  Westminster Abbey 77, 79
Edward I, King 34
  Charing Cross 119
  Tower of London 155

Edward II, King 34
Edward III, King 34, 74
Edward IV, King 34, 157
Edward V, King 34
Edward VI, King 22, 35
Edward VII, King 29, 30, 35
  Crown Jewels 156
  Marlborough House 93
Edward VIII, King 31, 35
Egg, Augustus 84
Eisenhower, Dwight 92
El Vino
  Street-by-Street map 135
Eleanor of Castile 119
Electrical adaptors **371**
Elgin, Lord 126, 129
Eliot, George
  Cheyne Walk 196
  grave of 246
Eliot, T S
  Cheyne Walk 196
  Russell Square 124
Elizabeth, Queen Mother
  Crown Jewels 156
Elizabeth I, Queen 22, 35
  Greenwich 242
  National Portrait Gallery 103
  portrait of 23
  Richmond Palace 268
  Royal Exchange 147
  St James's Palace 91
  tomb of 79
Elizabeth II, Queen 32, 35
  Albert Memorial 207
  Buckingham Palace 95
  Celebrations 56, 57
  Ceremonies 52, 53, **54**, 59
  Coronation 77, 79, 156
  Jubilee Gardens 187
  Madame Tussauds 224
  Queen's Gallery 96
  St James's Palace 91
  Silver Jubilee 32
Elizabethan London **22–3**
Eltham Palace **250**
Embankment
  London's Best: Ceremonies
  53
Embankment Gardens
  A River View of London 62
Embassy, US, Mayfair 270
Emergencies **365**
End, The (club) 352, 353
Engels, Friedrich 265
Engineers **38**
English National Opera 119
Entertainment **342–55**
  booking tickets 343
  cinema **347**
  clubs **352**, 353
  dance **350**
  disabled visitors 343
  information sources 342–3
  opera, classical and
  contemporary music **348–9**
  in pubs **317**

Entertainment (cont.)
  rock, pop, jazz, reggae and
  world music **351**, 353
  sport **354–5**
  theatres **344–5**
Epsom Racecourse 355
Epstein, Sir Jacob 39
  Imperial War Museum 191
  Rima 210
  Roper's Garden 194, 196, 267
  St James's Park Station 81
  Tate Britain 85
Equinox 353
Eros, statue of 90, 103
Ethelbert, King 19
Ethnic dance **350**
Etiquette **363**
  in clubs 352
Eton College
  London's Best: Ceremonies 55
Europcar 379
Europe
  map 12
Eurostar 373
  St Pancras International 121, 130
Eurotunnel 373
Evangelical services 371
Evelyn, John 252
Everyman Cinema 347
  Street-by-Street map 231
Exchange International 366
Expressair 369

F
FA Cup Final 56
Faber, Father Frederick William 206
Fabric 353
Fan Museum **243**
Faraday, Michael 97
Faraday Museum **97**
  London's Best: Museums and
  Galleries 43
Farrell, Terry 33
  Charing Cross 33, 119
  Ching Court 112
Fashion see Clothes
Fashion and Textile Museum 182
Fawkes, Guy
  Gunpowder Plot 24, 73
  Parliament Hill 234
Fenton House 50, **233**
  Street-by-Street map 230
Ferries, cross-channel **373**
Festival of Britain (1951) 32, 185, 188
Festivals **56–9**
  dance **350**
  music **348**
Film **347**
Fine Art and Antiques fair 57
Fine art galleries (commercial) **336–8**
Fire services 365
Fireworks 58
Fish and chips **315**, 317
Fishmongers' Hall **152**
  A River View of London 64
Fitzalwin, Henry 20

Fitzrovia *see* Bloomsbury and
    Fitzrovia
Fitzroy Square **130–31**
Fitzroy Tavern **131**, 311
Flamsteed, John 242
Flamsteed House 242
Flanagan, Barry 169
Flask Walk **232**
    Street-by-Street map 231
Flats, self-catering **280**, 281
Flaxman, John 115
Fleet Street **138–9**
    Street-by-Street map 135
Fleming, Ian 196
Flight Centre 372
Florence Nightingale Museum **190**
    London's Best: Museums and
    Galleries 43
Foley, John 207
Food and drink
    light meals and snacks **312–15**
    pubs **316–19**
    shops **329**, 331
    What to Eat in London
    294–5
    see also Restaurants
Football **354**
Foreign-language films **347**
Forster, E M 39
Fortnum and Mason 321
Four Great Days in London 10
    Street-by-Street map 88
Fortune Theatre 345
Forum 353
Foster, Sir Norman
    British Museum 129
    Sackler Galleries 90
Foundling Museum **125**
Four Seasons Canary Wharf
    377
Fournier Street **170**
Fowke, Francis 207
Fowler, Charles 114
Fox, Charles James
    statue of 123
Fox and Anchor pub
    Street-by-Street map 162
Frampton, Sir George 210
Franklin, Benjamin 165
Frederick, Prince of Wales
    240
French House 109, 318
Freud, Anna 246
Freud, Lucien 85
Freud, Sigmund 38
    Freud Museum 42, **246**
Fringe theatre **346**
Frith, William Powell 84
Fry, Roger 39, 131
Fulham
    restaurants **298–9**
Fulham Palace **259**
Funfairs 56, 57
Furniture and interiors
    London's Best: Museums and
    Galleries **42**

G

Gabo, Naum 181
Gabriel's Wharf **191**, 272, **340**
    London's Best: Shopping Streets
    and Markets 323
    A River View of London 63
Gainsborough, Thomas 38
    Dulwich Picture Gallery 43
    Kenwood House 43
    National Gallery 107
    Tate Britain 84
    Wallace Collection 226
Galleries
    commercial **336–8**
    see also Museums and
    galleries
Galsworthy, John 230
Gandhi, Mahatma 129
Gardening Club 353
Gardens *see* Parks and gardens
Garnet, Henry 159
Garrick, David 235
Garrick Club
    Street-by-Street map 112
Garrick Theatre 345
Gate Theatre 346
Gatwick Airport **375**, 376
    hotels 377
Gaudier-Brzeska, Henri
    Stone Dancer 43
Gauguin, Paul 117
Gay bars **318**
Gay clubs **352**
Geffrye, Sir Robert 248
Geffrye Museum **248**
    London's Best: Museums and
    Galleries 42
General Sports Information Line 355
Gentile da Fabriano 106
George I, King 26, 35
    St George's Bloomsbury 46, 47, 124
George II, King 26, 35
    Downing Street 75
    Foundling Museum 125
    Hampton Court 255
    Henrietta Howard (mistress) 252
    Marble Hill House 252
    statue of 239
    White Lodge 252
George III, King 26, 35
    British Library 125
    Kew Palace 261
    Queen Square 124
    Queen's Chapel 93
    Royal Mews 96
    Whitbread's Brewery 168
George IV, King (Prince Regent)
    27, 35
    Buckingham Palace 94
    Cumberland Terrace 227
    National Gallery 104
George V, King 30, 35
George VI, King 32, 35
    Crown Jewels 156
    portrait of 31

George Inn **176**, 319
    Street-by-Street map 175
Georgian London **26–7**
Géricault, Théodore 107
Gertler, Mark 233
Ghosts, in theatres **346**
Giacometti, Alberto 181
    Composition (Man and Woman)
    178
Gibberd, Sir Frederick 226
Gibbons, Grinling
    All Hallows by the Tower 153
    St Alfege Church 241
    St James's Church, Piccadilly 90
    St Mary Abchurch 145
    St Paul's Cathedral 151
    St Paul's Church 114
    statue of Charles II 197, 266
    Tower of London 157
Gibbons, Dr William 232
Gibbs, James 38
    churches **47**
    Orleans House 252
    St Martin-in-the-Fields 44, 46,
    101, 102
    St Mary-le-Strand 45, 118
Gielgud, Sir John 39
Gielgud Theatre 345
Gift shops **332**, 334
Gilbert, Alfred
    statue of Eros 90
Gilbert, Arthur 117
Gilbert and George 85
    Death Hope Life Fear 178
    Tate Modern 181
Gilbert Collection 117
Gill, Eric
    Broadcasting House 225
    St James's Park Station 81
    Westminster Cathedral 81
Giotto 106
Gladstone, William
    Albany 90
    Harley Street 225
    statue of 134
Glebe Place
    Chelsea and Battersea walk
    267
Globe Theatre *see* Shakespeare's
    Globe
Goddard's Pie and Eel House
    Street-by-Street map 238
Goethe Institute 346
Goldsmith, Oliver 247
Golf **354**
Good Friday 56, 59
Goodwin's Court
    Street-by-Street map 112
Gordon, Douglas 85
Gormley, Antony 85
Grable, Betty 159
Grahame, Kenneth 217
Granges, David des
    The Saltonstall Family 82
Grant, Duncan 39, 124
Gray's Antique Markets **340**

Gray's Inn 50, **141**
Great Bed of Ware **204**
Great Cumberland Place 26
Great Exhibition (1851) **28–9**, 200, 207, 211
Great Fire of London (1666) 17, **24–5**
    Monument **152**
Great River Race 58
Great Stink (1858) 28
Greater London
    map 13
Greater London Council (GLC) 33
Greenline Buses 373
Green Park 50, **97**
    London's Best: Parks and Gardens 49
    walks 270–71
Greene, Graham 90
Greenwich and Blackheath **237–43**
    area map 237
    cruise highlights 61
    Four Great Days in London 11
    hotels **291**
    restaurants **310–11**
    Street-by-Street map 238–9
Greenwich Foot Tunnel **241**
    Street-by-Street map 238
Greenwich Market **340**
    Street-by-Street map 238
Greenwich Mean Time 242
Greenwich Park 51, **243**
    London's Best: Parks and Gardens 49
Greenwich Royal Observatory **242–3**
Greiflenhagen, Maurice
    A London Street Scene 30
Grenadier pub, Belgravia 271
Gresham, Sir Thomas 41, 147
    tomb of 158
Grey, Lady Jane 155
Greyhound racing **354**
Gribble, Herbert 206
Grimaldi, Joseph 55
Grosvenor Square 26
Grove, George 206
Grove Lodge
    Street-by-Street map 230
Guards Museum **81**
    London's Best: Museums and Galleries 42
Guided tours **362**
Guildhall 159
    London's Best: Ceremonies 55
Guildhall Art Gallery **159**
Guildhall School of Music and Drama 165
Gunpowder Plot (1605) 24, 73, 159, 234
Guy Fawkes Night 58
Guy's Hospital Dental School 365
Gwynne, Nell 39
    Theatre Royal 115
    tomb of 102
Gyms **355**

H

Hackney Empire 346
Haig, Earl
    statue of 70
Hall, Sir Benjamin 74
Hals, Frans 234
    Laughing Cavalier **40**, 226
Ham House 25, 50, **252**
Hamilton, Richard 85
Hamleys 358
Hammersmith Apollo 353
Hampstead **229–35**
    area map 229
    hotels **291**
    pubs 319
    restaurants **309**
    Street-by-Street map 230–31
Hampstead Heath 51, 229, **234**
    London's Best: Parks and Gardens 48
    open-air concerts 57
    Street-by-Street map 230
Hampstead Ponds 355
Hampton Court 50, **254–7**
    cruise highlights 61
    park **254–5**
    timeline 257
    Visitors' checklist 255
Hampton Court Flower Show 57
Handel, George Frideric
    Fenton House 233
    Handel House Museum 38, **349**
    Museum of Musical Instruments 206
    St Katharine Cree 158
Hanover Square 26
Hard Rock Café 313, 357
Hardiman, Alfred 70
Hardwick, Thomas 224–5
Harley Street **225**
    Street-by-Street map 223
Harlow Stansted Moat House 377
Harrison, John 242
Harrod, Henry Charles 211
Harrods **211**, 320–21
Harvard, John 176
Harvest of the Sea 58
Harvey Nichols 321
Hat shops **332**, 334–5
Hatfield House 384
Hatton, Sir Christopher 141
Hatton Garden **141**
Hawksmoor, Nicholas 38
    Christ Church, Spitalfields 170
    churches **46–7**
    St Alfege 240–41
    St Anne's, Limehouse 249
    St George's, Bloomsbury 46, 124
    St Mary Woolnoth 45, 145
    Westminster Abbey 76
Haydn, Joseph 206
Hay's Galleria
    A River View of London 64
Hay's Mews, Mayfair 270
The Hay-Wain (Constable) **105**, 107

Hayward Gallery 185, **188**
    London's Best: Museums and Galleries 43
    Street-by-Street map 186
Health care **365**
Heathrow Airport **374–5**, 376
    hotels 377
Heathrow Connect (train service) 374–5
Heathrow Express (train service) 374–5
Henrietta Maria, Queen
    Queen's Chapel 46, 93
    Queen's House 240
Henry, Prince of Wales 139
Henry I, King 34
Henry II, King 20, 34
Henry III, King 34
    Tower of London 155
    Westminster Abbey 78
Henry IV, King 34
Henry V, King 34
Henry VI, King 34
    Ceremonies 55, 56
Henry VII, King 34
    Richmond 253
    Richmond Palace 268
    Westminster Abbey 79
Henry VIII, King 22, 34
    Charterhouse 164
    Chelsea 193
    execution of Anne Boleyn 22, 252
    Green Park 97
    Greenwich 242
    Hampton Court 254–7
    Horse Guards 80
    Hyde Park 211
    Lincoln's Inn 134
    National Portrait Gallery 103
    portrait of 257
    Richmond Park 252
    St Alfege 241
    St Bartholomew-the-Great 165
    St James's Palace 88, 91
    St James's Park 93
    and Sir Thomas More 39
    Tower of London 157
    Victoria and Albert Museum 202
    Westminster Abbey 78
Henry of Rheims 77
Henry Wood Promenade Concerts 57, 58, 348, 349
Hepworth, Barbara 85
Hermitage Rooms 117
Hertford family 226
Hertfordshire Moat House 377
Hertz Rent a Car 379
Herzog and de Meuron 180
Hess, Rudolph 155
Highgate **246**
Highgate Cemetery 51, **246**
The Hill Garden 50, **235**
Hill, Rowland 28
    statue of 163
Hiller, Susan 180

Hilliard, Nicholas
  A Young Man Among Roses 205
Hilton London Gatwick 377
Hilton London Heathrow 377
Hilton London Stansted 377
Hippodrome 353
  Street-by-Street map 101
Hiring cars 379
Hirst, Damien 85, 180
History **17–35**
HMS Belfast **183**
Hockney, David 171
  Mr and Mrs Clark and Percy 85
  Tate Britain 85
  Royal College of Art 200, 207
  Whitechapel Art Gallery 169
Hodgkin, Howard 85
Hogarth, Mary 125
Hogarth, William 38
  Foundling Museum 125
  Hogarth's House **259**
  Leicester Square 103
  Marble Hill House 253
  Portrait of Captain Coram 125
  St Bartholomew-the-Great 165
  St John's Gate 247
  Sir John Soane's Museum 134
  Tate Britain 84
  tomb of 102
Holbein, Hans 266
  The Ambassadors **105**, 106
  Henry VIII 257
  National Portrait Gallery 103
Holborn and the Inns of Court
  133–41
  area map 133
  hotels **289–90**
  Lincoln's Inn: Street-by-Street
    map 134–5
  pubs 319
  restaurants **307–8**
Holborn Viaduct **140**
Holden, Charles 81, 137
Holiday Care 280, 281, 363
Holiday Inn, Gatwick 377
Holiday Inn M4 377
Holidays, public 59
Holland, Henry 90
Holland House **218**
  Street-by-Street map 216
Holland Park 50, **218**
  hotels **283–4**
  London's Best: Parks and
    Gardens 48
  open-air theatre season 57
  restaurants **296–7**
  Street-by-Street map 216
  see also Kensington
    and Holland Park
Holland Park Public Tennis
  Courts 355
Holman Hunt, William 84
Holmes, Sherlock 38
  Sherlock Holmes Museum **226**
Holy Trinity, Dalston
  Clowns' Service 55, 59

Holy Trinity, South Kensington
  Street-by-Street map 201
Hop Exchange **176**
Horniman, Frederick 250
Horniman Museum **250**
Horse Guards **80**
  London's Best: Ceremonies 52, 54
  Street-by-Street map 71
  Trooping the Colour 57
Horses
  Festival of Showjumping 59
  Horse of the Year Show 58
  racing **354**
  riding **354**
  Royal Mews **96**
Hospitals 365
  St Bartholomew's Hospital 162
Host & Guest Services 281
Hostels 281
Hotels **278–91**
  airport hotels 377
  bars 318, 319
  Bayswater and Paddington **282**
  Bloomsbury and Fitzrovia **288–9**
  booking on-line 279
  budget accommodation 281
  Canary Wharf and Greenwich **291**
  children in 280
  The City and Clerkenwell
    290–91
  Covent Garden, Strand and
    Holborn **289–90**
  disabled travellers **280**, 281
  discount rates 278
  East of Central London **291**
  facilities 279
  Further afield **291**
  Hampstead **291**
  hidden extras 278–9
  how to book 279
  Kensington and Earl's Court **283**
  Knightsbridge, Brompton and
    Belgravia **284**
  Mayfair and St James's **286–7**
  Notting Hill and Holland
    Park **283–4**
  Oxford Street and Soho **287**
  Regent's Park and
    Marylebone **288**
  Ritz Hotel **91**
  Savoy Hotel **116**
  self-catering flats **280**, 281
  South Kensington and Chelsea
    284–5
  Southwark and Lambeth **290**
  special breaks 280
  Victoria, Westminster and
    Pimlico **285–6**
  where to look 278
Houdon, Jean-Antoine 226
Hounslow Heath Golf Course 355
Houses, historic
  Apsley House **97**
  Burgh House 231, **232**
  Charlton House **250**
  Chiswick House **258–9**

Houses, historic (cont.)
  Clarence House **96**
  Fenton House 230, **233**
  Ham House **252**
  Hogarth's House **259**
  Holland House 216, **218**
  Keats House **233**
  Kenwood House **234–5**
  Lancaster House **96**
  Leighton House 216, **218**
  Linley Sambourne House 217, **218**
  Marble Hill House **252–3**
  Marlborough House **93**
  Orleans House Gallery **252**
  Osterley Park House **253**
  Pitzhanger Manor **258**
  Queen's House 239, **240**
  Ranger's House 241, 243
  Spencer House **91**
  Sutton House **248**
  Syon House **253**
  see also Palaces
Houses of Parliament **72–3**, 189
  Four Great Days in London 10
  London's Best: Ceremonies 53, 54
  State Opening of Parliament 54, 58
  Street-by-Street map 71
Hoverspeed 373
Hoyland, John 169
Huguenots 161, 170
Hungerford Bridge
  Street-by-Street map 186
Hurlingham Club 355
Hyde Park 50, 51, **211**
  Great Exhibition (1851) 29
  London's Best: Ceremonies 52, 54
  London's Best: Parks and
    Gardens 49
  walks 271

I

Ibis Greenwich 377
Ibis Luton Airport 377
Ice-skating **354**
IMAX cinema 185, **347**
Immigration **370**
Imperial College
  Street-by-Street map 201
  Summer Accommodation
    Centre 281
Imperial War Museum **190–91**
  London's Best: Museums and
    Galleries 41, 43
Ingres, Jean-Auguste-Dominique
  107
Inns of Court
  A River View of London 63
  see also Holborn and
    the Inns of Court
Institut Français 346
Institute of Contemporary Arts
  (ICA) **92**, 350
Insurance 364, 365, **370**
Interiors shops **334**, 335
International Festival of
  Showjumping 59

International Model Railway
  Exhibition 56
International Youth Hostel
  Federation 370
Internet services **369**
  booking hotel rooms 279
Irving, Henry 39
Irving, Washington 247
Isleworth
  Richmond and Kew walk 268
Islington **247**

J

Jacksons Lane 350
Jacob II de Gheyn (Rembrandt) 250, 251
James I, King 23, 24, 35, 139
  Banqueting House 80
  Blackheath 243
  Charlton House 250
  Greenwich Park 243
  Hyde Park 211
James II, King 25, 35, 204
James, Henry 196
Jazz **351**, 353
  Capital Radio Jazz
    Festival 57
Jazz Café 353
Jermyn Street 89
Jewel Tower **74**
  Street-by-Street map 70
Jewellery
  Crown Jewels 154, **156**
  Hatton Garden **141**
  London's Best: Museums and
    Galleries **42**
  shops **332**, 334
Jews
  Jewish Museum **247**
  religious services 371
John, King 20, 34
John, Augustus 39, 131
John Lewis 321
Johnson, James 252
Johnson, Dr Samuel 38, 182
  Boswells 113
  Dr Johnson's House **140**
  statue of 138
  Ye Olde Cheshire Cheese 140
Jones, Adrian 97
Jones, Christopher 248
Jones, Sir Horace
  Leadenhall Market 159
  Smithfield Market 162, 164
Jones, Inigo 38, 258–9
  Banqueting House 25, 62, 71, **80**
  Charlton House 250
  churches **46**
  Piazza and Central Market
    (Covent Garden) 111, 114
  Queen's Chapel 93
  Queen's House 239, **240**, 241
  St Paul's, Covent Garden 44, 113, **114**
Jonson, Ben
  Fleet Street 139
  Lincoln's Inn 134
  Westminster School 74

Jubilee Footbridge 64
Jubilee Gardens
  Street-by-Street map 187
Jubilee Hall Clubs 355
Jubilee Line 32
Jubilee Line Architecture 380
Jubilee Market **340**
  Street-by-Street map 113
Juice bars **314**, 315
Justice Walk
  Chelsea and Battersea walk 267

K

Kapoor, Anish 180
Kauffer, E McKnight 114
Kean, Edmund 39, 268
Keats, John 38
  Apothecaries' Hall 152
  Keats House **233**
  St John's, Hampstead 233
  Spaniards Inn 235
  Vale of Health 235
  Well Walk 232
Kelly, Ellsworth 180
Kempton Park Racecourse 355
Kensal Green Cemetery 51
Kensington and Holland Park
  215–19
  area map 215
  hotels **282**
  restaurants **296–7**
  Street-by-Street map 216–17
  see also South Kensington and
    Knightsbridge
Kensington Church Street
  London's Best: Shopping Streets
    and Markets 322
Kensington Civic Centre
  Street-by-Street map 217
Kensington Gardens 50,
  210–11
  Four Great Days in London 11
  London's Best: Parks and
    Gardens 48
Kensington Palace 50, **210**
  Four Great Days in London 11
  London's Best: Museums and
    Galleries 42
Kensington Palace Gardens **219**
Kensington Roof Gardens **218–19**
Kensington Square **219**
Kent, William 270
  Chiswick House 259
  Hampton Court 257
  Horse Guards 80
  Kensington Gardens 210
Kenwood House 50, **234–5**
  London's Best: Museums and
    Galleries 43
  open-air concerts 57
Kew
  cruise highlights 61
  walks **268–9**
Kew Bridge Steam Museum **258**
  London's Best: Museums and
    Galleries 43

Kew Gardens 26, 50, 51, **260–61**
  London's Best: Parks and
    Gardens 48
Kew Palace 261
  Richmond and Kew
    walk 269
Keynes, John Maynard 39
King, Martin Luther 224
King Street
  Street-by-Street map 89
Kings and queens **34–5**
King's College, Cambridge 55
King's Conference Vacation
  Bureau 281
King's Head 317, 346
King's Road **196**
  Chelsea and Battersea walk 267
  London's Best: Shopping Streets
    and Markets 322
  Street-by-Street map 194
Kipling, Rudyard 232
Kitaj, R B 85
Knights Templar
  Temple 135, 139
  Temple Church 45, 46
Knightsbridge
  art and antique shops **336**, 338
  hotels **284**
  London's Best: Shopping Streets
    and Markets 322
  restaurants **297–8**
  see also South Kensington and
    Knightsbridge
Knitwear shops **326**, 328

L

Lady of Shalott (Waterhouse)
  83
Lady Minicabs 385
Lamb and Flag **116**, 319
  Street-by-Street map 112
Lambeth
  hotels **290**
Lambeth Palace **190**
Lancaster, House of 34
Lancaster House **96**
Landmark Trust 280, 281
Lansdowne House 270
Landseer, Edwin 102
Landy, Michael
  Scrapheap Services 179
Lane, Danny 205
Langham Hotel **225**
Lasdun, Sir Denys 188
Last Night of the Proms 58
Latchmere Theatre 346
Latimer, Bishop 22
Lauderdale, Duke of 252
Laughing Cavalier (Hals) **40**, 226
Law Courts *see* Royal Courts
  of Justice
Law Society **137**
  Street-by-Street map 135
Lawrence, D H 232, 235
Lawrence, T E 151
Lawrence, Sir Thomas 196

Lawrence, Thomas 84
Le Neve, Ethel 224
Le Nôtre, André 243
Leach, Bernard 205
Leadenhall Market **159**, **340**
Leaders **39**
Leather goods shops **333**, 335
Leather Lane Market **341**
Legislation, children 356–7
Leicester Square **103**
  Street-by-Street map 100
Leigh, Vivien 41
Hunt, Leigh 193, 235
Leighton, Lord 216, 218
Leighton House **218**
  Street-by-Street map 216
Lely, Sir Peter 243
Lenin 224
Leonardo da Vinci
  Queen's Gallery 96
  Virgin and Child **104**, 106
Leverhulme, Lord 235
Lewis, Wyndham 85
Liberty, Arthur Lasenby 109
Liberty **109**, 321
Libraries
  British Library **125**
Light meals and snacks **312–15**
Light Red Over Black (Rothko) 179
Lincoln, Abraham
  statue of 74
Lincoln's Inn
  Street-by-Street map 134–5
Lincoln's Inn Fields 51, **137**
  Street-by-Street map 134
Linford Christie Stadium 355
Linley Sambourne House **218**
  London's Best: Museums and
    Galleries 42
  Street-by-Street map 217
Lippi, Filippo
  The Annunciation 106
Lisson Grove
  Regent's Canal walk 264
Little Angel Theatre 359
Little Venice 227, 263
  Regent's Canal walk 264
Live Aid 33
Livery Companies
  London's Best: Ceremonies 55
Livingstone, David 201
Livingstone, Ken 33
Lloyd Webber, Andrew 108
Lloyd's of London 25, 32, **159**
Lombard Street
  Street-by-Street map 145
London Aquarium **188**, 358
  Street-by-Street map 187
London Bed and Breakfast Agency 281
London Bridge 17, 20–21, 24
  Street-by-Street map 175
London to Brighton veteran car
  rally 58
London Central Mosque **226**
London City Airport **376**
  hotels 377

London Clinic
  Street-by-Street map 223
London Coliseum **119**, **348**, 350
London County Council (LCC) 29
London Duck Tours 362
London Dungeon **183**
London Eye *see* British Airways
  London Eye
London Film Festival **347**
London Hostel Association 281
London Jamme Masjid **170**
London Marathon 56
London Rape Crisis Centre 365
London Silver Vaults **141**
A London Street Scene
  (Greiflenhagen) 30
London Transport Lost Property
  Office 364
London Transport Sightseeing Tour
  362
London Travel Information 382
London Zoo 51, **227**
  Regent's Canal walk 264, 265
London's Transport Museum **114**
  London's Best: Museums and
    Galleries 43
  Street-by-Street map 113
Long, Richard 85
Longhi, Pietro 107
Lord, Thomas 246
Lord Mayor
  Lord Mayor's Show 53, 55, 58, 167
  Mansion House **146**
Lords, House of *see* Houses of
  Parliament
Lord's Cricket Ground **246**, 355
Loredan, Doge Leonardo (Bellini)
  104
Lost property 364, 385
Louis Philippe, Duke of Orleans 252
Lovat, Lord 157
LSO St Luke's 349
Lucas, Sarah 85
Lupus Travel (Air Travel Advisory
  Bureau) 372
Luton Airport **376**
  hotels 377
Luton Regent Lodge Hotel 377
Lutyens, Sir Edwin
  Cenotaph 71, 74
Lyceum Theatre 345
Lyric Theatre 345

M

Macarius, Joannes 213
McBean, Angus 41
Mackmurdo, A H 249
McQueen, Alexander 205
McQueen, Steve 85
Madame Jojo 353
Madame Tussauds **224**
  Street-by-Street map 222
Madonna and Child (Michelangelo) 90
Magazines, shops **330**, 331
Magdalen with Pearls in her Hair
  (Corinth) 181

Magnus, St 152
Magritte, René 180
Mahler, Gustav 115
Maida Vale
  pubs 319
Maison Bertaux 109, 312, 315
The Mall **93**
Maman (Bourgeois) 181
Manchester Square 26
Mandela, Nelson
  statue of 187
Manet, Édouard
  Bar at the Folies Bergère 41
  Courtauld Institute 117
Mansfield, Earl of 234, 235
Mansion House **146**
  Street-by-Street map 145
Mantegna, Andrea 106
  The Triumphs of Caesar 254
Maps
  airports 377
  Bloomsbury and Fitzrovia 121,
    122–3
  bus routes 382–3
  Central London 14–15
  Ceremonies: London's
    Best 52–3
  Chelsea 193, 194–5
  Churches: London's Best
    44–5
  The City 143, 144–5
  Covent Garden 112–13
  Covent Garden and
    the Strand 111
  Georgian London 26
  Greater London 13
  Greenwich 238–9
  Greenwich and Blackheath 237
  Hampstead 229, 230–31
  Holborn and the Inns of Court 133
  Kensington and Holland Park
    215, 216–17
  Lincoln's Inn 134–5
  London between
    the World Wars 30
  Marylebone 222–3
  Medieval London 20
  Museums and Galleries:
    London's Best 40–41
  Parks and Gardens:
    London's Best 48–9
  Piccadilly and St James's 87, 88–9
  Postwar London 32
  Regent's Park and Marylebone 221
  Restoration London 24
  Roman London 18
  Shopping Streets and Markets:
    London's Best 322–3
  Smithfield 162–3
  Smithfield and Spitalfields 161
  Soho and Trafalgar Square 99
  South Bank 185, 186–7
  South Kensington and
    Knightsbridge 199, 200–201
  Southwark and Bankside 173,
    174–5

Maps (cont.)
   Trafalgar Square 100–101
   Victorian London 28
   Walks in London 263–75
   West End theatres 345
   Western Europe 12
   Whitehall and Westminster 69, 70–71
Marble Arch **211**
Marble Hill House **252–3**
   open-air concerts 57
Marianne North Gallery 260
Markets **339–41**
   Antiquarius **339**
   Apple Market **340**
   Bermondsey Antique Market **182, 339**
   Berwick Street Market **108, 339**
   Billingsgate **152**
   Borough Market 175, **176, 339**
   Brick Lane Market 171, **339**
   Brixton Market **339**
   Camden Market **246**
   Camden Lock Market **339**
   Camden Passage Market **340**
   Chapel Market **340**
   Church Street Market **340**
   Columbia Road Market **171, 340**
   Covent Garden 114, 323
   East Street Market **340**
   Gabriel's Wharf Market **340**
   Greenwich Market 238, **340**
   Jubilee Market **340**
   Leadenhall Market **159, 340**
   Leather Lane Market **341**
   London's Best **322–3**
   Marylebone Farmers' Market **341**
   New Caledonian Market **340**
   Old Spitalfields Market **170, 341**
   Petticoat Lane **169**, 315, **341**
   Piccadilly Crafts Market **341**
   Portobello Road **219**, 314, **341**
   Ridley Road Market **341**
   Riverside Walk Market **340**
   Roman Road **341**
   St Martin-in-the-Fields Market **341**
   Shepherd's Bush Market **341**
   Smithfield Market 162, **164**
Marks and Spencer **321**
Marlborough, Duchess of 93
Marlborough House **93**
Marlowe, Christopher 39
Marochetti, Carlo 70
Martin, John 84
Martin, Sir Leslie 188
Marx, Karl 265
   British Museum 129
   grave of 246
Mary I, Queen 22, 23, 35
   Greenwich 242
   tomb of 79
Mary II, Queen 35
   Hampton Court 254, 255, 257
   Kensington Palace 210

Marylebone
   hotels **288**
   restaurants **302–3**
   Street-by-Street map 222–3
   see also Regent's Park and Marylebone
Marylebone Farmers' Market **341**
Masaccio 106
Matcham, Frank 119
Matisse, Henri 180
Matthew, Sir Robert 188
Maurice, Bishop of London 149
May Day 59
Mayfair
   art and antiques shops **336**, 338
   hotels **286–7**
   restaurants **301–2**
   walks **270–71**
Mayor Thames Festival 58
Maze, Hampton Court 254
Mean Fiddler 353
Measurements, conversion chart 371
Medical Express 365
Medical treatment **365**
Medicines 365
Medieval London **20–21**
   churches **46**
Meissen 205
Melbury Road
   Street-by-Street map 216
Meridian 242
Metropolitan Railway 28, 30
Michelangelo
   Madonna and Child 90
   National Gallery 106
Microbreweries **317**
Middle Temple 50–51
Military
   London's Best: Ceremonies **54**
   London's Best: Museums and Galleries **42–3**
Mill, John Stuart
   Kensington Square 219
Millais, John Everett 84, 218
Millennium Bridge 173
Milton, John 39
   Bunhill Fields 168
   tomb of 168
Ministry of Defence
   A River View of London 62
Ministry of Sound 353
Minogue, Kylie 224
Mitchell, Joan 180
Mr and Mrs Clark and Percy (Hockney) 85
Modigliani, Amedeo 117, 181
Mohammed Ali, Viceroy of Egypt 118
Mondrian, Piet 181
Monet, Claude 59
   Courtauld Institute 117
   National Gallery 107
   Tate Modern 180
Money **366–7**
Monuments

Cenotaph **74–5**
The Monument 64, **152**
Nelson's Column 102
Temple Bar Memorial 135, **138**
Victoria Monument 96
War Memorial 175
see also Statues
Moody, F W 200
Moore, Henry
   Arch 210
   Imperial War Museum 191
   Recumbent Figure 85
   St James's Park Station 81
   St Stephen Walbrook 45, 146
   Tate Britain 85
   Three Standing Figures 266
More, Sir Thomas 22, **39**, 266
   Chelsea 194
   Chelsea Old Church 196
   statues of 194, 196, 267
   Tower of London 155
Morris, William
   Liberty 109
   Linley Sambourne House 218
   Victoria and Albert Museum 204
   William Morris Gallery 42, **249**
Mosques
   London Central Mosque **226**
   London Jamme Masjid **170**
Mount Street, Mayfair 270
Mount Street Gardens 270
Moynihan, Rodrigo 102
Mozart, Wolfgang Amadeus 109
Murillo, Bartolomé Esteban 107, 251
Museum Street
   Street-by-Street map 122
Museums (general)
   admission charges 363
   avoiding crowds 362
   cafés **313**, 315
   children in 356, **358**
   London's Best **40–43**
Museums and galleries (individual)
   Apsley House 97
   Bank of England Museum 145, **147**
   Bankside Gallery **177**
   Bethnal Green Museum of Childhood 43, **248**
   British Museum 40, 42, **126–9**
   Broadcasting House 225
   Burgh House 231, **232**
   Carlyle's House **196**
   Charles Dickens Museum **125**
   Charlton House **250**
   Chiswick House **258–9**
   Clink Prison Museum 175, **182**
   Courtauld Institute of Art Gallery 41, 43, 117
   Crafts Council Gallery 42, **247**
   Cutty Sark 238, **241**
   Dennis Severs House **171**
   Design Museum 41, 42, 65, **183**
   Dr Johnson's House **140**
   Dulwich Picture Gallery 43, **250–51**

Museums and Galleries (ind.) (cont.)
Eltham Palace **250**
Fan Museum **243**
Faraday Museum 43, **97**
Fashion and Textiles Museum 182
Fenton House **233**
Florence Nightingale
Museum 43, **190**
Foundling Museum **125**
Freud Museum 42, **246**
Geffrye Museum 42, **248**
Gilbert Collection 117
Guards Museum 42, **81**
Guildhall Art Gallery **159**
Ham House **252**
Handel House Museum 38, **349**
Hayward Gallery 43, 185, 186, **188**
Hermitage Rooms 117
HMS Belfast **183**
Hogarth's House **259**
Horniman Museum **250**
Imperial War Museum 41, 43,
190–91
Institute of Contemporary Arts **92**
Jewel Tower 74
Jewish Museum **247**
Keats House **233**
Kensington Palace 42
Kenwood House 43, **234–5**
Kew Bridge Steam Museum 43,
258
Leighton House **218**
Linley Sambourne House 42, 217,
218
London Dungeon **183**
London's Transport Museum 43,
113, **114**
Lord's Cricket Ground 246
Madame Tussauds 222, **224**
Marble Hill House **252–3**
Museum in Docklands 249
Museum of Garden History 43,
50, **190**
Museum of London 41, 42, 43,
146, 163, **166–7**
Museum of Musical Instruments
206
Musical Museum **253**
National Army Museum 42, **197**
National Gallery 41, 43, 101,
104–7
National Maritime Museum 43,
239, **240**
National Portrait Gallery 41, 101,
102–3
National Postal Museum 163
Natural History Museum 40, 43,
200, **208–9**
Old Operating Theatre **176–7**
Greenwich Royal Observatory **242–3**
Osterley Park House **253**
Percival David Foundation of
Chinese Art **130**
Photographers' Gallery **116**
PM Gallery and House **258**
Pollock's Toy Museum 43, **131**

Museums and Galleries (ind.) (cont.)
Prince Henry's Room 139
Queen's Gallery **96**
Queen's House 239, **240**
Ranger's House, Greenwich 243
Royal Academy of Arts 40, 43,
88, **90**
Royal College of Surgeons 134
Royal Mews **96**
Royal Observatory 43
Saatchi Collection **246**
St John's Gate 247
Science Museum 40, 43, 200,
212–13
Serpentine Gallery **210**
Shakespeare's Globe **177**
Sherlock Holmes Museum **226**
Sir John Soane's Museum 42,
134, **136–7**
Somerset House **117**
Spitalfields Centre Museum of
Immigration & Diversity **170**
Syon House **253**
Tate Britain 41, 43, **82–5**
Tate Modern 41, 43, 63, **178–81**
Theatre Museum 42, 113, **115**
Tower Bridge Exhibition 153
Tower of London 41, 42–3, **154–7**
Victoria and Albert Museum 40,
42, 43, 201, **202–5**
Vinopolis **182**
Wallace Collection 40, 43, **226**
Wellington Arch 97
Wernher Collection **241**, 243
Wesley's Chapel-Leysian
Mission **168**
Whitechapel Art Gallery **169**
William Morris Gallery 42, **249**
Wimbledon Lawn Tennis
Museum **251**
Wimbledon Windmill Museum
251
Music
dance **350**
festivals **349**
Henry Wood Promenade
Concerts 57, 58
Museum of Musical
Instruments 206
Musical Museum **253**
open-air concerts **51**, 57
opera, classical and
contemporary music **349–50**
rock, pop, jazz, reggae and
world music **351**, 353
Royal College of Music 200, **206**
shops **330–31**
Muslims
London Central Mosque **226**
London Jamme Masjid **170**
religious services 371
Myddleton, Sir Hugh 247

N

Nag's Head pub, Belgravia 271
Name-day Ceremonies **55**

Napoleon I, Emperor 97, 102
Nash, John 26, 38
All Souls, Langham Place 44, 47,
225
Buckingham Palace 94
Carlton House Terrace 92
Clarence House 96
Cumberland Terrace 27, 227
Marble Arch 211
Park Crescent 223
Piccadilly Circus 90
Portland Place 225
Regent's Canal 227, 264
Regent's Park 221, 222, 224
Royal Mews 96
Royal Opera Arcade 92
Theatre Royal 38, 100, 103
Trafalgar Square 102
United Services Club 92
Nash, Paul
Imperial War Museum 191
London's Transport Museum 114
National Army Museum **197**
London's Best: Museums and
Galleries 42
National Film Theatre 185, **347**
Street-by-Street map 186
National Gallery **104–7**
floorplan 104–5
Four Great Days in London 10
London's Best: Museums and
Galleries 41, 43
Sainsbury Wing 104, **107**
Street-by-Street map 101
Visitors' checklist 105
National Maritime Museum **240**
London's Best: Museums and
Galleries 43
Street-by-Street map 239
National Portrait Gallery **102–3**
Four Great Days in London 10
London's Best: Museums and
Galleries 41
Street-by-Street map 101
National Postal Museum
Street-by-Street map 163
National Rail Enquiries 373
National Theatre 32, 185, 188, 344
National Trust
Blewcoat School 81
Fenton House 233
George Inn 176
Natural history
London's Best: Museums and
Galleries **43**
Natural History Museum **208–9**
London's Best: Museums and
Galleries 40, 43
Street-by-Street map 200
Navy Day 54, 58
Neal Street **115**
London's Best: Shopping Streets
and Markets 323
Street-by-Street map 112
Neal's Yard **115**
Four Great Days in London 11

Neal's Yard Dairy 115
Nelson, Admiral Lord
  National Maritime Museum 240
  Nelson's Column 102
  St Paul's Cathedral 151
Neri, St Philip 206
New Ambassadors Theatre 345
New Caledonian Market **339**
New End Theatre
  Street by-Street map 231
New London Bridge 32
New London Theatre 345
New Row
  Street-by-Street map 112
New Year's Day 59
New Year's Parade 59
Newcomen, Thomas 40
Newman, Barnett 180
Newman, John Henry 206
Newsagents, international 371
Newspapers 370–71
Newton, Adam 250
Newton, Sir Isaac 25
  Leicester Square 103
Newton, William 137
NHS Direct 365
Night buses 383
Nightingale, Florence
  Florence Nightingale
    Museum 43, **190**
  tomb of 150
Nightingale, Lady
  Lady Nightingale's Memorial 78
Noodle bars **314**, 315
Norman kings 34
Norman Shaw Buildings
  Street-by-Street map 71
North London
  art and antique shops **337**, 338
Northumberland, Dukes of 253, 269
Northumberland, Earls of 253
Nost, John 257
Notting Hill **219**
  hotels **283–4**
  pubs 319
  restaurants **296–7**
Notting Hill Arts Club 351, 353
Notting Hill Carnival 57

O
Oasis Sports Centre 354, 355
Observatories
  Greenwich Royal Observatory
    242–3
Odeon Leicester Square 347
Olaf II Haraldsson,
  King of Norway 19
Old Bailey **147**
Old Billingsgate **152**
  A River View of London 64
Old Bull and Bush 229, 230, **232**
Old Compton Street 109
Old Curiosity Shop **137**
  Street-by-Street map 134
Old Dairy
  Street-by-Street map 194

Old Deer Park
  Richmond and Kew walk 269
Old English Garden
  Chelsea and Battersea walk 266
Old Operating Theatre **176–7**
Old Spitalfields Market
  170, **341**
Old Vic, The 32, 39, 185, **191**
Ye Olde Cheshire Cheese **140**,
  319
Oldenburg, Claes
  Soft Drainpipe – Blue (Cool)
    Version 179
  Tate Modern 180
Olitski, Jules
  Instant Loveland 180
Olivier, Laurence 39
  Royal National Theatre 188
Olympic Games (1948) 32
100 Club 353
One-off shops **329**, 331
Open-air concerts **51**, 57, **349**
Open-air theatre 57, **344**
Opening hours **362**
  banks 366
  pubs 316
  restaurants 293
  shops 320
Opera **348–9**
  English National Opera 119
  Royal Opera House **115**
The Orangery
  Street-by-Street map 216
Oranges and Lemons service 56
  London's Best: Ceremonies 55
Oriel House
  Richmond and Kew walk 268
Orleans House Gallery **252**
Orton, Joe 247
Orwell, George 131, 247
Osterley Park 50
Osterley Park House **253**
Other Place cinema 347
Outdoor music **51**, 57, **349**
Outdoor drinking, pubs **317**
Oval Cricket Ground 355
Oxford 384
Oxford, Robert Harley, Earl of 221
Oxford v Cambridge boat race 56
Oxford v Cambridge rugby union
  match 59
Oxford Street
  hotels **287**
OXO Tower **191**, 272
  A River View of London 63
Oyster card (bus & tube ticket) 378

P
P&O Ferries 373
Paddington
  hotels **282**
Painted Hall 242
  Street-by-Street map 239
Palace Theatre **108**, 109, 345
Palace of Westminster *see* Houses
  of Parliament

Palaces
  Buckingham Palace **94–5**, 189
  Eltham Palace **250**
  Fulham Palace **259**
  Kensington Palace 42, 50, **210**
  Kew Palace 261, 269
  Lambeth Palace **190**
  Richmond Palace 268
  St James's Palace 88, **91**
  Whitehall Palace 80
  Winchester Palace 21
  see also Houses, historic
Pall Mall **92**
  Street-by-Street map 89
Palladio, Andrea 258–9
Palmerston, Lord
  Holland House 218
  Queen Anne's Gate 80
Pankhurst, Emmeline 146
Pantomime **344**
Paolozzi, Eduardo
  Design Museum 183
  Royal College of Art 207
Parcelforce Worldwide 369
Paris, Matthew 34
Park Crescent
  Street-by-Street map 223
Parker, Cornelia
  Cold Dark Matter: An Exploded
    View 85
Parking 379
Parks and gardens
  Barbican Centre 50
  Battersea Park 49, 50, 51, **251**,
    266
  Berkeley Square 50
  Blackheath **243**
  Chelsea Flower Show 56
  Chelsea Physic Garden 50,
    195, **197**
  children in **358–9**
  Chiswick House 50
  Coram's Fields 125, 359
  Diana, Princess of Wales
    Memorial Playground **219**
  Embankment Gardens 62
  Fenton House 50, 230
  Gray's Inn 50
  Green Park 49, 50, **97**
  Greenwich Park 49, 51, **243**
  Ham House 50, 252
  Hampstead Heath 48, 51, 229,
    230, **234**
  Hampton Court 50, **254–5**
  Hampton Court Flower Show
    57
  The Hill 50, **235**
  Holland Park 48, 50, 216, **218**
  Hyde Park 49, 50, 51, **211**
  Jubilee Gardens 187
  Kensington Gardens 48, 50, **210–11**
  Kensington Palace Gardens 50, **219**
  Kensington Roof Gardens **218–19**
  Kenwood 50
  Kew Gardens 26, 48, 50, 51,
    260–61

Parks and Gardens (cont.)
Lincoln's Inn Fields 51
London Zoo 51
London's Best **48–51**
Middle Temple 50–51
Museum of Garden History 43, 50, **190**
Osterley Park 50
Parliament Hill 51, **234–5**
PM Gallery and House 258
Ranelagh Gardens 266
Regent's Park 49, 50, 51, 222, **224**
Richmond Park 48, 51, **252**
Roper's Garden 194, **196**, 267
Russell Square 50
St James's Park 49, 50, 51, **93**
Soho Square 51
Syon House 51, 269
Victoria Embankment Gardens **118**
Parliament *see* Houses of Parliament
Parliament Hill 51, **234–5**, 355
Parliament Square **74**
Street-by-Street map 71
Partridge (Ruel) 117
Passports 370
Pasta **315**, 317
Paterson, William 25
Patisserie Valerie 109, 312, 315
Pavlova, Anna 108
Paxton, Joseph 29
Peabody Buildings 28
Peace – Burial at Sea (Turner) 83
Peacock Theatre 350
Pearly Harvest Festival 58
Pearly Kings and Queens
London's Best: Ceremonies 55
Peasants' Revolt (1381) 21, 232, 243
Peel, Sir Robert 39
Pelli, César 31, 249
Penn, William 135, 153
Pepys, Samuel 25, 39
All Hallows by the Tower 153
Museum of London 166
Piazza and Central Market (Covent Garden) 114
Prince Henry's Room 139
Ye Olde Cheshire Cheese 140
Percival David Foundation of Chinese Art **130**
Perfume shops **333**, 335
Peter Pan, statue of 210, 219
Petticoat Lane **169**, **341**
London's Best: Shopping Streets and Markets 323
The Pheasantry 196
Chelsea and Battersea walk 267
Phillimore Place
Street-by-Street map 217
Phoenix Theatre 345
Phoneboxes **368**
Photographers' Gallery **116**, 337, 338
Four Great Days in London 11
Photography shops **337**, 338
Piazotta, Enzo
The Young Dancer 111

Piazza and Central Market (Covent Garden) **114**
Street-by-Street map 113
Picasso, Pablo
Tate Modern 180, 181
Victoria and Albert Museum 205
Piccadilly and St James's **87–109**
area map 87
art and antiques shops **336**, 338
Buckingham Palace **94–5**
hotels **286–7**
pubs 319
restaurants **299–300**
Street-by-Street map 88–9
walks 270–71
Piccadilly Arcade 87
Piccadilly Circus **90**
Street-by-Street map 89
Piccadilly Crafts Market **341**
Piccadilly Theatre 345
Pickpockets 364
Piero della Francesca 106
Baptism of Christ 105
Piero di Cosimo 106
Pimlico
art and antiques shops **336**, 338
hotels **284–5**
Piombo, Sebastiano del 106
Pippa Pop-Ins 357
Pisanello 106
Pissarro, Camille 117
Pitt, William the Elder 90
Pitzhanger Manor and Gallery **258**
Pizza Express 353
Street-by-Street map 122
Pizza on the Park 353
Pizzas **313**, 315
The Place 350
Plague (1665) 24, 25
Planetarium **224**
Street-by-Street map 222
Plantagenets 34
Plaques, famous Londoners **39**
Playhouse Theatre 345
Poets' Corner, Westminster Abbey 79
Police 364, **365**
Polka Children's Theatre 359
Pollock, Benjamin 131
Pollock, Jackson
Summertime: Number 9A 181
Tate Modern 180
Whitechapel Art Gallery 169
Pollock's Toy Museum **131**
London's Best: Museums and Galleries 43
Pop music **351**, 353
Porchester Centre 355
Portland Place **225**
Street-by-Street map 223
Portman Square 26
Portobello Road **219**
walks 274–5
Portobello Road Market **341**
London's Best: Shopping Streets and Markets 322

Portrait of Captain Coram (Hogarth) 125
Portsmouth, Duchess of 116
Post-Modern architecture 33
Postal services **369**
Poste restante **369**
Postwar London **32–3**
Poussin, Nicolas
Dulwich Picture Gallery 43, 251
Wallace Collection 226
Pre-Raphaelite Brotherhood 84, 249
Priestley, J B 232
Prime Ministers
Downing Street **75**
Houses of Parliament 72
Primrose Hill
Regent's Canal walk 265
Prince Charles Cinema 347
Prince Edward Theatre 345
Prince Henry's Room **139**
Street-by-Street map 135
Prince of Wales Theatre 345
Princes in the Tower **157**
Private homes, staying in 280–81
Promenade Concerts 57, 58, 348, 349
Public holidays 59
Public Record Office 29
Public toilets 370
Pubs **316–19**
The Anchor **182**
children in 356
Fitzroy Tavern **131**
food in **313**, 315
Fox and Anchor 162
George Inn 175, **176**
Lamb and Flag **116**
Old Bull and Bush 229, 230, **232**
Prospect of Whitby 61
Saracen's Head 162
Spaniards Inn **235**
Trafalgar Tavern **242**
Ye Olde Cheshire Cheese **140**
Punch and Judy Festival 58
Puppet Theatre Barge 359
Purcell, Henry 158
Purcell Room 348
Puritans 24

Q
Qantas 372
Quakers 371
Queen Anne's Gate **80–81**
Queen Elizabeth Hall 348, 350, 353
Street-by-Street map 186
Queen Mary's Gardens, Regent's Park 224
Queen Square **124**
Queens **34–5**
Queen's Chapel **93**
London's Best: Churches 46
Queen's Club (Real Tennis) 355
Queen's Gallery **96**
Queen's House, Greenwich 237, **240**, 241
Street-by-Street map 239

Queen's House, Tower of London 154
Queens Ice Skating Club 355
Queen's Theatre 345
Queensway **219**
Queues 363

R

Racing
  greyhound **354**
  horse **354**
Rackham, Arthur 265
RADAR 275
Radford, D S 371
Radio 371
Radio Taxis 385
Radisson SAS Stansted
  Airport hotel 377
Rail travel **373**, **384**
Railway stations
  Charing Cross Station 119
  St Pancras Station **130**
  Waterloo Station **191**
Railways *see* Trains
Rainfall 58
Rainforest Café 357
Raleigh, Sir Walter 23, 155
Ranelagh Gardens
  Chelsea and Battersea walk 266
Ranger's House, Greenwich 241, 243
Raphael
  Dulwich Picture Gallery 251
  National Gallery 104, 106
Rauschenberg, Robert 169
Ravens
  Tower of London 154
Record shops **330**, 331
Recumbent Figure (Moore) 85
Red Lion Yard, Mayfair 270
Regency churches **47**
Regent's Canal **227**, 263
  walks **264–5**
Regent's Park **224**
  London's Best: Parks and
    Gardens 49, 50, 51
  open-air theatre season 57
  Regent's Canal walk 264
  Street-by-Street map 222
Regent's Park and
  Marylebone **221–7**
  area map 221
  hotels **288**
  Street-by-Street map: Marylebone
    222–3
Regent's Park Lake 355
Reggae **351**
Religious services 371
Rembrandt
  Dulwich Picture Gallery 43
  Jacob II de Gheyn 250, 251
  Kenwood House 234
  National Gallery 104, 107
  Wallace Collection 226
Remembrance Sunday 58
  London's Best: Ceremonies 53, 54
Rennie, John 187

Renoir, Pierre Auguste
  At the Theatre 107
  Courtauld Institute 117
Renoir Cinema 347
Repertory cinemas **347**
Restaurants **292–319**
  Bayswater **296**
  Chelsea and Fulham **298–9**
  children in 293, **357**
  Covent Garden **305–7**
  Hampstead **309**
  Kensington, Holland Park and
    Notting Hill **296–7**
  Mayfair **301–2**
  price and service 293
  Soho **303–5**
  South Bank **300–1**
  South Kensington **297–8**
  Spitalfields and Clerkenwell **308**
  What to Eat in London **294–5**
  see also Food and drink
Restoration London 24–5
Reynolds, Sir Joshua 38
  Kenwood House 43, 234
  Leicester Square 103
  National Gallery 107
  Photographers' Gallery 116
  Royal Academy of Arts 88
  Spaniards Inn 235
  Tate Britain 84
  tomb of 102
  Wallace Collection 226
RIBA (Royal Institute of British
Architects)
  Victoria and Albert 202, 204–5
Richard I, King 34
  Great Seal 21
  statue of 70
Richard II, King 106
Richard III, King 34
  College of Arms 144
  Princes in the Tower 157
Richardson, Sir Ralph 39
Richelieu, Cardinal 107
Richmond 60, **253**
  walks **268–9**
Richmond, William 150
Richmond House
  Street-by-Street map 71
Richmond Palace 268
Richmond Park 51, **252**
  London's Best: Parks and
    Gardens 48
Richmond Park Golf 355
Richmond Theatre 268
Ridley, Bishop 22
Ridley Road Market **333**
Ritz, César 88, 91
Ritz Hotel **91**
  Four Great Days in London 10
  Street-by-Street map 88
Ritzy Cinema 347
A River View of London **60–65**
River Cruises 61
Rivera, Diego 180
Riverside Studios 350

Riverside Walk Market **340**
Rock Garden 353
Rock music **351**, 353
Rodin, Auguste
  The Burghers of Calais 70
Rogers, Richard 33
  Lloyd's of London 32, 159
Rokeby Venus (Velázquez) 105
Roman Amphitheatre 19, 159
Roman Bath **118**
Roman Catholic Church 371
Roman London 17, **18–19**
  Amphitheatre 159
  Museum of London 166
  Temple of Mithras 144
Roman Road Market **341**
Rome: The Pantheon (Canaletto) 94
Romney, George 226, 234
Ronnie Scott's 109, 353
Roosevelt, Franklin D. 270
Roper, Margaret 196
Roper, William 196
Roper's Garden **196**
  Chelsea and Battersea walk 267
  Street-by-Street map 194
Rose Theatre 177
Ross Nye Stables 355
Rossetti, Dante Gabriel
  Cheyne Walk 193, 194
  Downshire Hill 233
  Liberty 109
  Venus Venticordia 38
Rosslyn Park Rugby 355
Rothko, Mark
  Light Red Over Black 179
  Tate Modern 180
Rothschild, Baron Ferdinand 128
Rotten Row, Hyde Park 271
Roubiliac, Louis François
  Lady Nightingale's Memorial 78
  Wallace Collection 226
Rough Trade 327
Rousseau, Henri (Le Douanier) 107
Royal Academy of Art 26, **90**
  Four Great Days in London 11
  London's Best: Museums and
    Galleries 40, 43
  Street-by-Street map 88
  Summer Exhibition 56
Royal Academy of Music
  Street-by-Street map 222
Royal Albert Hall **207**
  concerts **349**, 353
  Henry Wood Promenade
    Concerts 57, 58, 348, 349
  Street-by-Street map 200
Royal Avenue
  Chelsea and Battersea walk 267
Royal Botanic Gardens *see* Kew
  Gardens
Royal College of Art **207**
  Street-by-Street map 200
Royal College of Music **206**
  Street-by-Street map 200
Royal College of Organists
  Street-by-Street map 200

Royal College of Surgeons
  Street-by-Street map 134
Royal Court Theatre 197
Royal Courts of Justice (the Law
  Courts) 133, **138**
  Street-by-Street map 135
Royal Exchange **147**
  Street-by-Street map 145
Royal Festival Hall 32, 185, **188**
  concerts 348
  Street-by-Street map 186
Royal Geographical Society
  Street-by-Street map 201
Royal Hospital **197**
  Chelsea and Battersea walk 266
Royal Institute of British
  Architects 225
  Street-by-Street map 223
Royal Mail 369
Royal Mews **96**
Royal Naval College, Old 241, **242**
  Street-by-Street map 239
Royal Observatory Greenwich
  London's Best: Museums and
  Galleries 43
Royal Opera Arcade **92**
Royal Opera House 111, **115**
  ballet 350
  opera **348**
  Street-by-Street map 113
Royal Salutes
  London's Best: Ceremonies 54
Royal Shakespeare Company **344**
Royal Society of Painter-
  Printmakers 177
Royal Tournament 57
Royal Watercolour Society 177
Royal Worcester 205
Royalty **34–5**
  Buckingham Palace **94–5**
  coronations **79**
  London's Best: Ceremonies **54**
  Royal Mews **96**
Rubens, Peter Paul
  Banqueting House 25, 71, 80
  Courtauld Institute 117
  Dulwich Picture Gallery 43
  Kenwood House 43
  National Gallery 107
Ruel, Gorg
  Partridge 117
Rugby **354**
Rules (restaurant)
  Street-by-Street map 112
Ruskin, John 109
Russell Square 50, **124**
  Street-by-Street map 123
Rysbrack, John Michael
  George II Statue 239
  Wallace Collection 226

S

S J Phillips 331
Saatchi Gallery 197
  London's Best: Museums and
  Galleries 43

Sackler Galleries 90
Sadleir, Ralph 248
Sadler's Wells **350**
Safety **364–5**
St Albans 384
St Alfege **240–41**
  London's Best: Churches 47
  Street-by-Street map 238
St Andrew, Holborn **140**
  London's Best: Churches 47
St Anne's, Limehouse **249**
  London's Best: Churches 47
St Anne's Church Tower, Soho
  109
St Bartholomew-the-Great **165**
  London's Best: Churches 46
  Street-by-Street map 163
St Bartholomew-the-Less
  Street-by-Street map 162
St Bartholomew's Hospital
  Street-by-Street map 162
St Botolph, Aldersgate **164**
St Bride's **139**
  London's Best: Churches 47
  spire 46
St Clement Danes **138**
  London's Best: Churches 47
  Oranges and Lemons service 55,
  56
  Street-by-Street map 135
St Etheldreda's Chapel **140–41**
St George's, Bloomsbury **124**
  London's Best: Churches 47
  spire 46
  Street-by-Street map 123
St Giles, Cripplegate **168**
St Helen's Bishopsgate **158**
St James Garlickhythe
  London's Best: Churches 47
  Street-by-Street map 144
St James's
  hotels **286–7**
  restaurants **299–300**
  see also Piccadilly and St James's
St James's, Piccadilly **90**
  London's Best: Churches 47
  Street-by-Street map 89
St James's Palace **91**
  London's Best: Ceremonies 52
  Street-by-Street map 88
St James's Park 50, 51, **93**
  Four Great Days in London 10
  London's Best: Parks and
  Gardens 49
  open-air concerts 57
St James's Park Station **81**
St James's Square **92**
  Street-by-Street map 89
St James's Street
  Four Great Days in London 10
St John's, Smith Square **81**
  concerts **349**
St John's Gate **247**
St Katharine's Dock **158**
  Four Great Days in London 11
  A River View of London 65
St Katherine Cree **158**

St Luke's Church
  Chelsea and Battersea
  walk 267
St Magnus the Martyr **152**
  London's Best: Churches 47
St Margaret Pattens **153**
St Margaret's, Westminster **74**
  Street-by-Street map 71
St Martin-in-the-Fields **102**
  concerts **349**
  London's Best: Churches 44, 47
  Pearly Harvest Festival 58
  Pearly Kings and Queens 55
  spire 46
  Street-by-Street map 101
St Martin-in-the-Fields Market **341**
St Martin's Theatre 345
  Street-by-Street map 112
St Mary, Battersea **251**
St Mary of Lambeth (Museum
  of Garden History) **190**
St Mary, Rotherhithe **248**
St Mary Abchurch
  Street-by-Street map 145
St Mary-at-Hill **152–3**
  Harvest of the Sea 58
St Mary-le-Bow **147**
  London's Best: Churches 47
  spire 46
  Street-by-Street map 144
St Mary-le-Strand **118**
  London's Best: Churches 45, 47
St Mary Woolnoth
  London's Best: Churches 45, 47
  Street-by-Street map 145
St Marylebone Parish Church **224–5**
  Street-by-Street map 222
St Nicholas Cole
  Street-by-Street map 144
St Olave's House
  A River View of London 64
St Pancras Parish Church **130**
  London's Best: Churches 47
St Pancras International Station **130**
St Paul's Cathedral 143, **148–51**
  Cakes and Ale Sermon 55
  floorplan 150–51
  Great Fire 24
  London's Best: Churches 45
  A River View of London 63
  Street-by-Street map 144
  timeline 149
  views of 177, 179
  Visitors' checklist 149
St Paul's Church **114**
  London's Best: Churches 44, 46
  Street-by-Street map 113
St Stephen Walbrook **146**
  London's Best: Churches 45, 47
  Street-by-Street map 145
St Thomas' Hospital 365
  Old Operating Theatre **176–7**
Sales 57, 59, **321**
Salisbury 384
The Saltonstall Family (des Granges) 82
Samaritans 365

Samson and Delilah (Van Dyck) 43
Sandoe, John 267
Sandown Park Racecourse 355
Sandwich bars **313**, 315
Saracen's Head
  Street-by-Street map 162
Saracens Rugby Football Club 355
Sargent, John Singer 39, 82, 84
Satan Smiting Job with Sore Boils (Blake) 84
Saunders, Nicholas 115
Savoy Chapel **116**
Savoy Hotel **116**
  A River View of London 62
The Scale of Love (Watteau) 107
Le Scandale 353
Scarf shops **333**, 335
The Scarlet Sunset: A Town on a River (Turner) 84
Schad, Christian 180, 181
School of London painters 85
Schools
  Blewcoat School **81**
  Charterhouse **164**
  Westminster 74
Science
  London's Best: Museums and Galleries **43**
Science Museum **212–13**
  London's Best: Museums and Galleries 40, 43
  Street-by-Street map 200
Scott, Sir George Gilbert 38
  Albert Memorial 207
  Hereford Screen 205
  St Pancras Station 130
Scott, Sir Giles Gilbert
  Bankside Power Station 180
  Waterloo Bridge 187
Scott, John 116
Screen Cinemas 347
SeaFrance 373
Security **364–5**
Segal, George 169
Self-catering flats **280**, 281
Self-Portrait with Bandaged Ear (Van Gogh) 117
Selfridges 321
  Four Great Days in London 11
Senate House
  Street-by-Street map 122
The Serpentine 211, 339
Serpentine Gallery **210**
  Four Great Days in London 11
Seurat, Georges
  Bathers at Asnières **105**, 107
Seven Dials **116**
  Street-by-Street map 112
Severs, Dennis
  Dennis Severs House **171**
Shackleton, Sir Ernest 240
Shaftesbury, Earl of 90, 103
Shaftesbury Avenue **103**
  Street-by-Street map 100
Shaftesbury Theatre 345

Shakespeare, William 24, 39, 224
  British Library 125
  Fleet Street 139
  Gray's Inn 141
  Great Bed of Ware 204
  Madame Tussauds 224
  National Portrait Gallery 103
  Old Vic 191
  Southwark Cathedral 173
  Temple 139
  Twelfth Night 23
  Westminster Abbey 79
Shakespeare's Globe **22–3**, 64, **177**, 345
  A River View of London 64
  Street-by-Street map 174
Shaw, George Bernard 39
  British Museum 129
  Fitzroy Square 131
Shaw, Norman 38
  Albert Hall Mansions 201
Sheen Palace 268
Shell Building
  Street-by-Street map 187
Shell Mex House
  A River View of London 62
Shelley, Harriet 210
Shelley, Percy Bysshe 210, 235
Shepherd, Edward 97, 270
Shepherd Market **97**, 270
Shepherd's Bush Empire 353
Shepherd's Bush Market **341**
Sheridan Skyline Hotel 377
Sherlock Holmes
  Museum **226**
Sherman, Cindy 180
Shoe shops **325**
Shopping **320–41**
  art and antiques **322–3**
  bags and leather goods **333**, 335
  books **330**, 331
  CDs **330**, 331
  children **326**, 328, **358**
  clothes **324–8**
  drinks **329**, 331
  foods **329**, 331
  gifts **332**, 334
  hats **332**, 334–5
  interiors **334**, 335
  jewellery **332**, 334
  London's Best **322–3**
  magazines **330**, 331
  one-offs **329**, 331
  perfumes & toiletries **333**, 335
  records **330**, 331
  scarves **333**, 335
  souvenirs **332–5**
  specialist shops **329–31**
  stationery **333**, 335
Shoreditch Electricity Rooms 317
Sicilian Avenue
  Street-by-Street map 123
Sickert, Walter 181
Siddons, Sarah 39
Silent Change, Guildhall 58
  London's Best: Ceremonies 55

Silver
  London Silver Vaults **141**
Simpson, Wallis 31
Singapore Airlines 372
Sir John Soane's Museum **136–7**
  London's Best: Museums and Galleries 42
  Street-by-Street map 134
Skating **354**
Skinners' Hall
  Street-by-Street map 144
Sloane, Sir Hans
  British Museum 126
  Chelsea Physic Garden 197
  Sloane Square 197
  statue of 195, 197
Sloane Square **197**
  Chelsea and Battersea walk 266, 267
Smirke, Robert 126
Smithfield and Spitalfields **161–71**
  area map 161
  Museum of London **166–7**
  restaurants **294–5**
  Smithfield: Street-by-Street map 162–3
Smithfield Market **164**
  Street-by-Street map 162
  turkey auction 59
Smoking 316, 363
Smollensky's On The Strand 357
Snacks **312–15**
Soane, Sir John 26, 38
  Bank of England 147
  Dulwich Picture Gallery 250–51
  Pitzhanger Manor and Gallery 258
  Ranelagh Gardens 266
  Sir John Soane's Museum 134, **136–7**
Soft Drainpipe – Blue (Cool) Version (Oldenburg) 179
Soho and Trafalgar Square **99–109**
  area map 99
  The Heart of Soho **109**
  hotels **287**
  National Gallery **104–7**
  pubs 319
  restaurants **303–5**
  Trafalgar Square: Street-by-Street map 100–101
Soho Lounge 353
Soho Square 51, **108**
Solti, Georg 188
Somerset, Duke of 117
Somerset House **117**
  A River View of London 62
  ice rink 354, 355
South Bank **185–91**
  area map 185
  pubs 319
  restaurants **300–1**
  A River View of London 62
  Street-by-Street map 186–7
South Bank Centre **348–9**
  Street-by-Street map 186–7

South Kensington and
 Knightsbridge **199–211**
 area map 199
 hotels **284–5**
 pubs 319
 restaurants **297–8**
 Street-by-Street map 200–201
 Victoria and Albert Museum
 202–5
Southwark and Bankside **173–83**
 area map 173
 hotels **290**
 pubs 319
 restaurants **309–10**
 Street-by-Street map 174–5
 Tate Modern **178–81**
Southwark Bridge
 A River View of London 64
 Street-by-Street map 174
Southwark Cathedral **176**
 London's Best: Churches 45, 46
 A River View of London 64
 Street-by-Street map 175
Southwark Wharves
 A River View of London 65
Souvenir shops **332–5**
Spacey, Kevin 191
Spaniards Inn **235**, 319
Speakers' Corner **211**, 271
Specialist shops **329–31**
Spence, Sir Basil 80–81, 217
Spencer, Earl 91
Spencer, Stanley
 Burgh House 232
 Downshire Hill 233
 Tate Modern 181
 Vale of Health 235
Spencer House **91**
 Street-by-Street map 88
Spires, churches 46
Spitalfields
 restaurants **308**
 see also Smithfield and
 Spitalfields
Spitalfields Centre Museum of
 Immigration & Diversity **170**
Spitalfields Market see Old
 Spitalfields Market
Spitalfields Show 58
Spitz 353
Sports Cafe 317
Sport England 355
Sports **354–5**
 for children 357
 in parks **51**
Spread Eagle Yard
 Street-by-Street map 238
Spring Equinox celebration 56
Spring in London **56**
Squares
 Bedford Square 122
 Berkeley Square 27, 50
 Bloomsbury Square 123, **124**
 Brompton Square 201
 Fitzroy Square **130–31**
 Grosvenor Square 26

Squares (cont.)
 Hanover Square 26
 Kensington Square **219**
 Leicester Square **103**
 Manchester Square 26
 Parliament Square 71, **74**
 Piazza and Central Market
 (Covent Garden) 114
 Portman Square 26
 Queen Square **124**
 Russell Square 50, 123, **124**
 St James's Square 89, **92**
 Sloane Square **197**
 Soho Square 51, **108**
 Trafalgar Square **102**
Squash **354**
STA Travel 370
Stamps, postage 369
Standing by the Rags (Freud) 179
Stanfords 330. 331
 Street-by-Street map 112
Stansted Airport **376**
 hotels 377
 Stansted Express (rail) 376
Staple Inn **141**
State Opening of Parliament 58
 London's Best: Ceremonies 54
Stationery shops **333**, 335
Statues
 Abraham Lincoln 74
 Albert Memorial 207
 Benjamin Disraeli 71
 Boadicea 71
 Charles II 197, 266
 Charles James Fox 123
 Charlie Chaplin 100, 103
 Dr Samuel Johnson 138
 Duke of Bedford 123
 Earl Haig 70
 Eros 90, 103
 Field Marshal Sir George Stuart
 White 223
 Franklin D. Roosevelt 270
 George I 124
 George II 239
 Nelson Mandela 187
 Peter Pan 210, 219
 Queen Anne 80, 148
 Queen Charlotte 124
 Queen Victoria 210
 Richard I 70
 Rowland Hill 163
 Sir Hans Sloane 195, 197
 Sir Thomas More 267
 Thomas Carlyle 267
 Thomas More 194, 196
 William III 89, 92
 William Gladstone 134
 Winston Churchill 71, 74
 see also Monuments
Steer, Philip Wilson 38
Stella, Frank 246
Stevenson, Robert Louis 131
Sticky Fingers 357
 Street-by-Street map 217
De Stijl 181

Stirling, Sir James 82
Stock Exchange 27, **158**
Stone Dancer (Gaudier-Brzeska) 43
Strachey, Lytton 124
Strand see Covent Garden
 and the Strand
Strand on the Green **258**
Strand Theatre 345
Street food **314**, 315
Street theatre festival 57
Stringfellows 353
The Struggle is My Life (Walters) 187
Stuart, House of 35
Stuart, James 242
Student travellers **370**
Studio Theatre 346
Summer in London **57**
Summertime: Number 9A
 (Pollock) 181
Sunshine 57
Surrealists 180
Sutherland, Graham
 Imperial War Museum 191
 London's Transport Museum 114
Sutton House **248**
Swallow Churchgate 377
Swimming **354**
Swinburne, Algernon 193
Syon House 51, **253**
 Richmond and Kew walk 269

T

Tallis, Thomas
 tomb of 241
Tate Britain **82–5**
 Clore Galleries 82, **84**
 floorplan 82–3
 London's Best: Museums and
 Galleries 41, 43
 Visitors' checklist 83
Tate Modern **178–81**
 Bankside Power Station 180
 floorplan 178–9
 London's Best: Museums and
 Galleries 41, 43
 A River View of London 63
 Street-by-Street map 174
 Visitors' checklist 179
 walks 272–3
Tattershall Castle 353
Taxes
 in hotels 272–3
 VAT (Value Added Tax) 320–21, 370
Taxis **385**
Taylor-Wood, Sam 85
Tea **312**, 314–15
Telecom Tower 32, 131
Telephones **368**
Television 371
Telford, Thomas 158
Temperatures 59
Temple **139**
 A River View of London 63
 Street-by-Street map 135
Temple Bar Memorial **138**
 Street-by-Street map 135

Temple Church
London's Best: Churches 45, 46
Temple of Mithras 18
Street-by-Street map 144
Tennis **354**
Wimbledon Lawn Tennis
Championships 57
Wimbledon Lawn Tennis
Museum **251**
Tennyson, Alfred Lord
Carlyle's House 196
Terry, Ellen 39
Thackeray, William
Carlyle's House 196
Charterhouse 164
Thames, River
Great River Race 58
Great Stink (1858) 28
Richmond and Kew walk 268
A River View of London
60–65
Thames Barrier 33, 61, **249**
Thatcher, Margaret 32
Wesley's Chapel-Leysian
Mission 168
Theatre **344–6**
actors **39**
Adelphi Theatre **116**
cafés **313**, 315
children in **359**
London Coliseum **119**
Old Vic **191**
open-air theatre season 57
Palace Theatre **108**
Royal National Theatre **188**
Royal Opera House **115**
Shakespeare's Globe **22–3**, 64,
174, **177**
street theatre festival 57
Theatre Museum **115**
tkts half-price ticket booth 346
Whitehall Theatre **80**
Theatre Museum
London's Best: Museums and
Galleries 42
Street-by-Street map 113
Theatre Royal Drury Lane 115, 345,
359
Theatre Royal Haymarket 38, **103**,
345
Street-by-Street map 100, 113
Theatre Upstairs 346
Theft 364
Themed pubs and bars **317**
Thistle Gatwick 377
Thomas, Dylan 121, 131
Thomas Neal's **116**
Street-by-Street map 112
Thomson, James 227
Thornhill, Sir James
Painted Hall 239, 242
St Paul's Cathedral 151
Thornycroft, Thomas 71
Thrale, Henry 182
Thrale, Mrs 140
Three Standing Figures (Moore) 266

Thrifty Car Rental 379
Tiepolo, Giovanni Battista 107
Tijou, Jean
St Alfege Church 240, 241
St Paul's Cathedral 151
Time **371**
Tipping, in hotels 279
Tite, William 147
Titian
National Gallery 106
Wallace Collection 226
Toiletry shops **333**, 335
Toilets, public 370
Tottenham Hotspur 355
Tour Guides Ltd 362
Tourist Information
see Visit London
Tourist information centres 182, **363**
Tours, guided **362**
Tower Bridge **153**
A River View of London 65
Tower Green 154
Tower of London 17, 21, 25, **154–7**
Crown Jewels **156**
Four Great Days in London 11
Line of Kings **157**
London's Best: Ceremonies 53, 54
London's Best: Museums and
Galleries 41, 42–3
Ordnance Gallery **157**
The Princes in the Tower **157**
A River View of London 65
Royal Castle and Armour
Gallery **157**
Small Armoury and Crypt **157**
timeline 155
Visitors' checklist 155
White Tower 154, **157**
Townsend, C Harrison 169
Toys
Bethnal Green Museum of
Childhood **248**
London's Best: Museums and
Galleries **43**
Pollock's Toy Museum 43, **131**
Tradescant, John 190
Trafalgar Square **102**
Four Great Days in London 10
Street-by-Street map 100–101
see also Soho and Trafalgar Square
Trafalgar Studios *see*
Whitehall Theatre
Trafalgar Tavern 11, **242**, 319
Traffic signs 379
Trailfinders 372
Traitors' Gate, Tower of London 155
Transport for London (TfL) 364,
378, 380
Transvestite clubs **352**
Travel **372–85**
air **372**, **374–7**
Bloomsbury and Fitzrovia 121
buses **378**, **382–3**
cars **379**
Chelsea 193
children 356

Travel (cont.)
The City 143
coaches **373**
Covent Garden and the Strand 111
cycling 379
Greenwich and Blackheath 237
Hampstead 229
Holborn and the Inns of Court 133
Kensington and Holland Park 215
late-night 343
London's Transport Museum 43,
114
Piccadilly and St James's 87
rail **373**, **384**
Regent's Park and Marylebone 221
Smithfield and Spitalfields 161
Soho and Trafalgar Square 99
South Bank 185
South Kensington and
Knightsbridge 199
Southwark and Bankside 173
taxis **385**
Underground 378, **380–81**
walking 378
Whitehall and Westminster 69
Travelcards 378, 380
Travelex 366
Traveller's cheques 364, **367**
Treasury
Street-by-Street map 71
Trees
Green London **50–51**
Trent, N A 119
Tripscope 363
The Triumphs of Caesar (Mantegna)
254
Trocadero
Street-by-Street map 100
Trooping the Colour 57
London's Best: Ceremonies 52, 54
"Tube" *see* Underground
Tudor kings 34
Turkey auction 59
Turner, J M W 38, 248
Cheyne Walk 193, 194, **196**
Clore Galleries 82, **84**
Kenwood House 234
National Gallery 107
Peace – Burial at Sea 83
St Mary's, Battersea 251
*The Scarlet Sunset: A Town on a
River* 84
Tate Britain 41
Turnmills 353
Turpin, Dick 235
Tussaud, Madame *see* Madame
Tussauds
Twain, Mark
Langham Hilton Hotel 225
Ye Olde Cheshire Cheese 140
Twickenham 244
Twickenham Bridge
Richmond and Kew walk 268
Twickenham Rugby Ground 355
Twinings 134
Twombly, Cy 180

Tyler, Wat
  Blackheath 243
  death 152
  Smithfield 162

U

UGC 347
Uccello, Paolo 106
Underground 378, **380–81**
Unicorn Theatre 359
Union Chapel 353
Unique Forms of Continuity in Space (Boccioni) 181
United Airlines 372
Universities
  accommodation in 281
University College Hospital 365
University of London Students' Union 370
Uptown Reservations 281

V

Vale of Health **235**
Van Dyck, Sir Anthony
  Kenwood House 234
  National Gallery 107
  Samson and Delilah 43
Van Eyck, Jan
  Arnolfini Portrait **105**, 106
Van Gogh, Vincent
  National Gallery 107
  Self-Portrait with Bandaged Ear 117
Vanbrugh, Sir John 242
Varah, Rev Chad 146
VAT (Value Added Tax) 320–21, 370
Vaudeville Theatre 345
Vaughan Williams, Ralph 206
Velázquez, Diego
  Apsley House 97
  National Gallery 107
  Rokeby Venus 105
Venturi, Robert 107
The Venue 345
Venus Venticordia (Rossetti) 38
Vermeer, Jan
  Kenwood House 234
  Queen's Gallery 96
  Young Woman Standing at a Virginal 107
Verrio, Antonio 257
Victoria
  hotels **285–6**
Victoria, Queen 28, 29, 35, 102
  Albert Memorial 207
  Buckingham Palace 94
  Crown Jewels 156
  Guildhall Art Gallery 159
  Kensington Palace 210
  Lancaster House 96
  Old Vic 191
  Queensway 219
  Royal Albert Hall 207
  Royal Mews 96
  statue of 210

Victoria, Queen (cont.)
  Victoria and Albert Museum 202
  Victoria Monument 96
  Westminster Abbey 77
Victoria and Albert Museum **202–5**
  Bethnal Green Museum of Childhood **248**
  London's Best: Museums and Galleries 40, 42, 43
  Street-by-Street map 201
Victoria Embankment Gardens **118**
Victorian London **28–9**
  churches **47**
Vinopolis **182**
  Street-by-Street map 175
Vintage fashion 326, 328
Vintners' and Distillers' Wine Harvest 58
  London's Best: Ceremonies 55
Virgin and Child (Leonardo da Vinci) **104**, 106
Virgin Atlantic 372
Visit London 56, 57, 279–81
  Accommodation Booking Service 279
Visual arts
  London's Best: Museums and Galleries **43**
Vortex Jazz Club 353
Vorticist group 85

W

Wagner, Richard 115
Walks **262–75**, 378
  Chelsea and Battersea **266–7**
  Mayfair to Belgravia **270–71**
  Portobello **274–5**
  Regent's Canal **264–5**
  Richmond and Kew **268–9**
  South Bank **272–3**
Wallace Collection **226**
  London's Best: Museums and Galleries 40, 43
Walpole, Sir Robert 75
Walters, Ian
  The Struggle is My Life 187
Walthamstow Stadium 355
Walton Street
  art and antiques shops **330**
War Memorial
  Street-by-Street map 175
Warhol, Andy 246
Water sports **355**
Waterhouse, Alfred 38
  Natural History Museum 208
Waterhouse, J W
  Lady of Shalott 83
Waterloo Bridge
  Street-by-Street map 187
Waterloo Station **191**
Watteau, Jean Antoine
  Dulwich Picture Gallery 251
  The Scale of Love 107
Watts, George Frederick
  Kensington Gardens 210
  St Botolph, Aldersgate 164

Waugh, Evelyn 247
Weather **56–9**
Webb, Sir Aston
  Admiralty Arch 102
  The Mall 93
  Victoria and Albert Museum 203
Well Walk **232**
  Street-by-Street map 231
Wellington, Duke of 38, 92, 271
  Apsley House 97
  Lancaster House 96
Wellington Arch **97**
Wellington Square
  Chelsea and Battersea walk 267
Wembley Arena 353
Wernher Collection at Ranger's House **241**, 243
Wesley, John 26
  Charterhouse 163, 164
  Wesley's Chapel-Leysian Mission **168**
West, Benjamin 146
West End
  art and antiques **336–7**, 338
  cinemas **347**
  London's Best: Shopping Streets and Markets 323
  theatres **344–5**
West Ham United 355
Westminster
  hotels **285–6**
  restaurants **299–300**
  walks **272–3**
  see also Whitehall and Westminster
Westminster Abbey 20, **76–9**
  ceremonies 57
  Coronation ceremony 156
  Dr Johnson memorial service 59
  Easter procession and hymns 56
  floorplan 78–9
  Four Great Days in London 10
  London's Best: Churches 44, 46
  Street-by-Street map 70
  Visitors' checklist 77
Westminster Cathedral **81**
  London's Best: Churches 44, 47
Westminster Hall 21, 72
Westminster School 74
  Street-by-Street map 70
Weyden, Rogier van der 106
Wheelchair access *see* Disabled travellers
Wheeler's 109
Whistler, James McNeill 38
  Cheyne Walk 193, 194
  Liberty 109
Whistler, Rex 83
Whit Monday 59
Whitbread, Samuel 168
Whitbread's Brewery **168**
White, Field Marshal Sir George Stuart
  statue of 223

White Tower, Tower of London 154, **157**
Whitechapel Art Gallery **169**
Whitehall and Westminster **69–85**
  area map 69
  hotels **285–6**
  Houses of Parliament **72–3**
  Street-by-Street map 70–71
  Westminster Abbey **76–9**
  Tate Britain **82–5**
Whitehall Theatre
  Trafalgar Studios **80**, 345
Whitestone Pond
  Street-by-Street map 230
Whitfield, William 71
Whittington, Richard (Dick) 20, 21, **39**, 246
Wickham, Geoffrey
  fountain, Halkin Arcade 271
Wigmore Hall **226**, **349**
Wilde, Oscar 39, 225
Wildlife, in parks **51**
Wilkie, David 83
Wilkins, William 104
William I the Conqueror, King 20, 34
  Tower of London 155, 157
William II, King 34
William III, King 25, 35, 242
  Hampton Court 254, 255, 257
  Kensington Palace 210
  statue of 89, 92
  Tower of London 157
William IV, King 27, 35, 210
  Buckingham Palace 94
  Clarence House 96
William Morris Gallery **249**
Wilson, Sir Colin St John 125
Wilson, Richard 253
Wilson twins 85
Wimbledon Lawn Tennis Championships 57
Wimbledon Lawn Tennis Museum **251**
Wimbledon Windmill Museum **251**

Winchester, Bishops of 182
Winchester Palace 21
Windsor 384
Windsor, House of 35
Wine
  Vinopolis **182**
Winter in London **59**
Woburn Walk **130**
Wolsey, Cardinal **257**
  Cardinal's Wharf 177
  Hampton Court 254
Wolsey Lodges 280, 281
Wombwell, George 246
Women travellers 364
Women's Counselling Service 365
Wood, Sir Henry 265
Woodrow, Bill 85
Woody's 353
Woolf, Virginia 39
  Bloomsbury Square 124
  Fitzroy Square 131
World music **351**, 353
World War I 30
  Cenotaph 74–5
World War II 17, 30
  Blitz 31, 32
  Cabinet War Rooms 75
Wornum, Grey 223
Wren, Sir Christopher 38, 118
  Cardinal's Wharf 177
  Christ Church 163
  churches **47**
  Flamsteed House 242
  Hampton Court 254–6
  Kensington Palace 210
  Marlborough House 93
  The Monument 152
  Royal Hospital 197, 266
  Royal Naval College 239, 241, **242**
  St Andrew, Holborn 140
  St Bride's 46, 139
  St Clement Danes 135, 138
  St James Garlickhythe 144
  St James's, Piccadilly 89, 90

Wren, Sir Christopher (cont.)
  St Magnus the Martyr 152
  St Margaret Pattens 153
  St Mary Abchurch 145
  St Mary-at-Hill 152–3
  St Mary-le-Bow 46, 144, 147
  St Nicholas Cole 144
  St Paul's Cathedral 45, 63, **148–51**
  St Stephen Walbrook 45, 145, 146
  Theatre Royal 115
  tomb of 150
Wright, Frank Lloyd 202
Writers **39**
Wyatt, Benjamin Dean
  Apsley House 97
  Lancaster House 96
  Theatre Royal 115
Wyman, Bill 217
Wyndham's Theatre 345
Wynne, David
  Boy and Dolphin **195**, 267

Y

Ye Olde Cheshire Cheese **140**, 319
Yeats, W B 130
Yellow Pages 368
YMCA, Central 355
York, Prince Andrew, Duke of 95
York, Frederick, Duke of 96
York, House of 34
Young British Artists (YBAs) 85
The Young Dancer (Piazzotta) 111
Young Woman Standing at a Virginal (Vermeer) 107
Youth hostels 281
Youth Hostels Association 281

Z

Zingo (cab service) 385
Zoo 51, **227**

Acknowledgments

Dorling Kindersley would like to thank the following people whose help and assistance contributed to the preparation of this book.

Main Contributor

Michael Leapman was born in London in 1938 and has been a journalist since he was 20. He has worked for most British national newspapers and writes about travel and other subjects for several publications, among them *The Independent, Independent on Sunday, The Economist* and *Country Life*. He has written ten books, including *London's River* (1991) and the award-winning *Companion Guide to New York* (1983, revised 1991). In 1989 he edited the acclaimed *Book of London*.

Contributors

James Aufenast, Yvonne Deutch, Guy Dimond, George Foster, Iain Gale, Fiona Holman, Phil Harriss, Lindsay Hunt, Christopher Middleton, Steven Parissien, Christopher Pick, Bazyli Solowij, Matthew Tanner, Mark Wareham, Jude Welton, Ian Wisniewski.

DORLING KINDERSLEY wishes to thank the following editors and researchers at Webster's International Publishers: Sandy Carr, Matthew Barrell, Siobhan Bremner, Serena Cross, Annie Galpin, Miriam Lloyd, Ava-Lee Tanner.

Additional Photography

Max Alexander, Peter Anderson, Stephen Bere, June Buck, Peter Chadwick, Michael Dent, Philip Dowell, Mike Dunning, Philip Enticknap, Andreas Einsiedel, Steve Gorton, Christi Graham, Alison Harris, Peter Hayman, Stephen Hayward, Roger Hilton, Ed Ironside, Colin Keates, Dave King, Neil Mersh, Nick Nichols, Robert O'Dea, Ian O'Leary, Vincent Oliver, John Parker, Tim Ridley, Kim Sayer, Chris Stevens, James Stevenson, James Strachan, Doug Traverso, David Ward, Mathew Ward, Steven Wooster and Nick Wright.

Additional Illustrations

Ann Child, Gary Cross, Tim Hayward, Arghya Jyoti Hore, Fiona M Macpherson, Janos Marffy, David More, Chris D Orr, Richard Phipps, Michelle Ross and John Woodcock.

Cartography

Andrew Heritage, James Mills-Hicks, Chez Picthall, John Plumer (DK Cartography). Advanced Illustration (Cheshire), Contour Publishing (Derby), Euromap Ltd (Berkshire). Street Finder maps: ERA Maptec Ltd (Dublin) adapted with permission from original survey and mapping from Shobunsha (Japan).

Cartographic Research

James Anderson, Roger Bullen, Tony Chambers, Ruth Duxbury, Jason Gough, Ailsa Heritage, Jayne Parsons, Donna Rispoli, Jill Tinsley, Andrew Thompson, Iorwerth Watkins.

Design and Editorial

MANAGING EDITOR Douglas Amrine
MANAGING ART EDITOR Geoff Manders
SENIOR EDITOR Georgina Matthews
EDITORIAL DIRECTOR David Lamb
ART DIRECTOR Anne-Marie Bulat
PRODUCTION CONTROLLER Hilary Stephens
PICTURE RESEARCH Ellen Root
DTP EDITOR Siri Lowe
REVISIONS EDITOR Neil Lockley
ASSISTANT REVISIONS EDITOR Kate Molan

Keith Addison, Elizabeth Atherton, Sam Atkinson, Oliver Bennett, Julie Bowles Michelle Clark, Carey Combe, Vanessa Courtier, Lorna Damms, Jessica Doyle, Jane Ewart, Simon Farbrother, Gadi Farfour, Fay Franklin, Simon Hall, Marcus Hardy, Sasha Heseltine, Paul Hines, Stephanie Jackson, Gail Jones, Nancy Jones, Stephen Knowlden, Esther Labi, Michelle de Larrabeiti, Chris Lascelles, Jeanette Leung, Ferdie McDonald, Jane Middleton, Rebecca Milner, Fiona Morgan, Louise Parsons, Andrea Powell, Leigh Priest, Liz Rowe, Simon Ryder, Susannah Steel, Kathryn Steve, Anna Streiffert, Andrew Szudek, Hugh Thompson, Diana Vowles, Andy Wilkinson.

Special Assistance

Christine Brandt at Kew Gardens, Sheila Brown at The Bank of England, John Cattermole at London Buses Northern, the DK picture department, especially Jenny Rayner, Pippa Grimes at the V & A, Emma Healy at the Bethnal Green Museum of Childhood, Alan Hills at the British Museum, Emma Hutton and Cooling Brown Partnership, Gavin Morgan at the Musuem of London, Clare Murphy at Historic Royal Palaces, Ali Naqei at the Science Museum, Patrizio Semproni, Caroline Shaw at the Natural History Museum, Gary Smith at British Rail, Monica Thurnauer at Tate, Simon Wilson at Tate, and Alastair Wardle.

Photographic Reference

The London Aerial Photo Library, and P and P F James.

Photography Permissions

DORLING KINDERSLEY would like to thank all the museums, galleries, churches and other sights that allowed us to photograph at their establishments.

Picture Credits

t = top; tl = top left; tc = top centre; tr = top right; cla = centre left above; ca = centre above; cra = centre right above; cl = centre left; c = centre; cr = centre right; clb = centre left below; cb = centre below; crb = centre right below; bl = bottom left; b = bottom; bc = bottom centre; br = bottom right.

Works of art have been reproduced with the permission of the following copyright holders: *The Bath*, 1925, Pierre Bonnard © ADAGP, Paris and DACS, London 2001 181b; *After Lunch*, 1975 © Patrick Caulfield. All rights Reserved, DACS 2001 180t; *Lobster Telephone*, 1936 © Salvador Dali, Gala-Salvador Dali Foundation/DACS 2001 41cr; *Composition: Man and Woman*, 1927, Alberto Giacometti © ADAGP, Paris and DACS, London 2001 178tr; *Death* from *Death Hope Life Fear* (d) 1984 © Gilbert and George 178lb; *Mr. and Mrs. Clark and Percy* (1970–71) © David Hockney 85t; Bust of *Lawrence of Arabia* © The Family of Eric H. Kennington, RA 151bl; © Mario Merz 178la; *Cold Dark Matter: An Exploded View*, 1991 © Cornelia Parker 85b; The works by Henry Moore illustrated on the following pages have been reproduced by kind permission of the Henry Moore Foundation: 45c, 85c, 266cb. *Soft Drainpipe – Blue (Cool) version*, 1967 © Claes Oldenburg 179c; *Maman*, 2000 © Louise Bourgeois/VAGA, New York/DACS, London 2001 181cr; *Summertime: Number 9A*, 1948, Jackson Pollock © ARS, New York and DACS, London 2001 181t; *Light Red Over Black*, 1957 © 1998 Kate Rothko Prizel and Christopher Rothko/DACS 179cr.

The Publishers are grateful to the following individuals, companies and picture libraries for permission to reproduce their photographs: ALAMY.COM:Robert Harding World Imagery 100clb; THE ALBERMARLE CONNECTION: 91t; ARCAID: Richard Bryant, Architect Foster and Partners 126t; Richard Bryant 249cr; ARCBLUE: Peter Durant 189cl; THE ART ARCHIVE: 21bl, 28c, 28bc, 29bl, 30br, 31cra, 31clb, 35tc, 35cr, 188b, 188bl; British Library, London 20cr; Imperial War Museum, London 32bc; Museum of London 17b, 29br, 30bl; Science Museum, London 29cla; Stoke Museum Staffordshire Polytechnic 25bl, 27cl, 35bc; Victoria and Albert Museum, London 22c, 23bc, 27tr; AXIOM: James Morris 164tl.

GOVERNOR AND COMPANY OF THE BANK OF ENGLAND: 145tr; BRIDGEMAN ART LIBRARY, London: 23t, 30t; British Library, London 16, 21tr, (detail) 23br, 26cb, (detail) 34tl, 34bl; Courtesy of the Institute of Directors, London 31cla; Guildhall Art Gallery, Corporation of London (detail) 28t; Guildhall Library, Corporation of London 26br, 76c; ML Holmes Jamestown – Yorktown Educational Trust, VA (detail) 19bc; Master and Fellows, Magdalene College, Cambridge (detail) 25clb; Marylebone Cricket Club, London 246c; William Morris Gallery, Walthamstow 21tl, 249tl; Museum of London 24–5; O'Shea Gallery, London (detail) 24cl; Royal Holloway & Bedford New College 157bl; Russell Cotes Art Gallery and Museum, Bournemouth 38tr; Thyssen-Bornemisza Collection, Lugano Casta 257b; Westminster Abbey, London (detail) 34bc;

White House, Bond Street, London 30cb. BRITISH AIRWAYS: Adrian Meredith Photography: 372t, 374tl; reproduced with permission of the BRITISH LIBRARY BOARD: 125b; © THE BRITISH MUSEUM: 18t, 18ca, 19tl, 40t, 91c, 126–7 all pics except 126t, 128–9 all pics.

CAMERA PRESS, London: P. Abbey - LNS 73cb; Cecil Beaton 79tl; HRH Prince Andrew 95bl; Allan Warren 33cb; COLLECTIONS: Oliver Benn 60b; John Miller 163bl; COLORIFIC!: Steve Benbow 55t; David Levenson 66–7; CONRAN RESTAURANTS 293cl, 322bc; CORBIS: 259t; Bruce Burkhardt 289c; Tim Graham 3br, 95bl; Angelo Hornak 61c, 183b; London Aerial Photo Library 189bl, 189t; Kim Sayer 2br; Patrick Ward 61t; Courtesy of the CORPORATION OF LONDON: 55c, 146t; COURTAULD INSTITUTE GALLERIES, London: 41c, 117b.

PERCIVAL DAVID FOUNDATION OF CHINESE ART: 130c; Copyright: Dean & Chapter of Westminster 78bl, 79tr; DEPARTMENT OF TRANSPORT (Crown Copyright): 379b; Courtesy of the GOVERNORS AND THE DIRECTORS DULWICH PICTURE GALLERY: 43bl, 250bl.

EASYJET: 372b; EASY EVERYTHING: James Hamilton 369cr; ENGLISH HERITAGE: 252b, 258b; Jonathon Bailey 241clb; ENGLISH LIFE PUBLICATIONS LTD: 252b; PHILIP ENTICKNAP: 255tr; MARY EVANS PICTURE LIBRARY: 18bl, 18br, 19bl, 19br, 22bl, 24bl, 26t, 27bc, 27br, 29t, 29cb, 29bc, 32bl, 34br, 35tl, 35cl, 35bl, 35br, 38tl, 39bl, 72cb, 72b, 90b, 112b, 114b, 135t, 139t, 155bl, 159t, 162ca, 174ca, 177l, 207b, 216t, 226b.

Courtesy of the FAN MUSEUM (The Helene Alexander Collection) 243b; FREUD MUSEUM, London: 246t.

GATWICK EXPRESS: 375t; THE GORE HOTEL, London: 279b; GEFFRYE MUSEUM, London: 248tl; GILBERT COLLECTION: 117t.

ROBERT HARDING PICTURE LIBRARY: 33ca, 42c, 52ca, 169tl, 343t, 365cb, 384b; Philip Craven 210t; Sylvain Gradadam 289tl; Brian Hawkes 23clb; Michael Jenner 23cra, 242t; 58t, 227t; Mark Mawson 113tl; Nick Wood 63bl; HARRODS (printed by kind permission of Mohamed al Fayed): 320b; HAYES-DAVIDSON (computer generated images: 174bl; HAYWARD GALLERY: Richard Haughton 273tl; Reproduced with permission of HER MAJESTY'S STATIONERY OFFICE (Crown Copyright): 156 all pics; JOHN HESELTINE: 51tr, 63br, 98, 124b, 132, 142, 172, 220; FRIENDS OF HIGHGATE CEMETERY: 244, 246b; HISTORIC ROYAL PALACES (Crown Copyright): 7t, 37tc, 254–255 all except 254br, 256–7 all except 257b; THE HORNIMAN MUSEUM, London: 256br; HOVERSPEED LTD: 377b; HULTON GETTY: 26bl, 124tl, 135cr, 232t. THE IMAGE BANK, London: Gio Barto 55b; Derek Berwin 33t, 272t; Romilly Lockyer 12bl,

13br, 72t, 94br; Leo Mason 56t; Terry Williams 139b; Courtesy of ISIC, UK: 370t.

PETER JACKSON COLLECTION: 26–7; JEWISH MUSEUM, London: 247tl.

LEIGHTON HOUSE: 216b; LITTLE ANGEL MARIONETTE THEATRE: 359tl; LONDON AMBULANCE SERVICE: 365ca; LONDON AQUARIUM 3c, 188c, 188r; LONDON CITY AIRPORT: 376b; LONDON DUNGEON: 183t; LONDON PALLADIUM: 103; LONDON REGIONAL TRANSPORT: 380t; LONDON TRANSPORT MUSEUM: 30ca, 380–81 all maps and tickets.

MADAME TUSSAUDS: 222c, 224t; MANSELL COLLECTION: 21br, 22t, 22br, 23bl, 24t, 24cl, 25br, 29ca, 34tr; METROPOLITAN POLICE SERVICE: 364t, 365t; ROB MOORE: 115t; MUSEUM OF LONDON: 13bl, 18cb, 19tr, 19cb, 20t, 23crb, 41tc, 166–7 all pics.

NATIONAL EXPRESS LTD: 376; Reproduced by courtesy of the TRUSTEES, THE NATIONAL GALLERY, London: (detail) 37c, 104–5 all except 104t, 106–7 all except 107t; NATIONAL PORTRAIT GALLERY, London: 4t, 41tl, 101cb, 102br; NATIONAL POSTAL MUSEUM, London: 28bl; By permission of the KEEPER OF THE NATIONAL RAILWAY MUSEUM, York: 30–31; NATIONAL TRUST PHOTOGRAPHIC LIBRARY: Wendy Aldiss 25ca; John Bethell 252t, 253t; Michael Boys 38b; NATURAL HISTORY MUSEUM, LONDON: John Downs 12clb, 209t, 209cr; Derek Adams 208b, 208cl; NEW SHAKESPEARE THEATRE CO: 342bl.

P&O STENA LINE LTD: 353b; PA PHOTOS LTD: 33cr; PALACE THEATRE ARCHIVE: 108t; PERETTI COMMUNICA-TIONS: Chris Gascoigne & Lifshutz Davidson 292cr; PICTOR INTERNATIONAL, London: 60cl, 174br; PICTURES COLOUR LIBRARY: 54br; PIPPA POP-INS CHILDREN'S NURSERY, London: 357b; PITZHANGER MANOR MUSEUM: 258c; POPPERFOTO: 31tl, 31crb, 32tl, 32tr, 32c, 35tr, 39br; THE PORTOBELLO HOTEL: 279tr; POST HOUSE HEATHROW: Tim Young 377t; PRESS ASSOCIATION LTD: 31bl, 31br; PUBLIC RECORD OFFICE (Crown Copyright): 20b.

BILL RAFFERTY: 342br; RAINFOREST CAFE: 357cl; REX FEATURES LTD: 53tl; Peter Brooker 53tr; Andrew Laenen 54c; Jonathon Player 288cla; THE RITZ, London: 91b; ROYAL ACADEMY OF ARTS, London: 90tr; THE BOARD OF TRUSTEES OF THE ROYAL ARMOURIES: 41tr, 155tl, 157t, 157br;

ROYAL BOTANIC GARDENS, KEW: Andrew McRob 48cl, 56b, 260–61 all pics except 260t & 260br; ROYAL COLLECTION, ST JAMES'S PALACE © HM THE QUEEN: 8–9, 53b, 88t, 93t, 94–5 all pics except 94br & 95bl, 96t, 254br; ROYAL COLLEGE OF MUSIC, London: 200c, 206c.

THE SAVOY GROUP: 116cr, 274t, 274b; SCIENCE MUSEUM, London: 212–13 all pics; SCIENCE PHOTO LIBRARY: Maptec International Ltd 12b; SPENCER HOUSE LTD: 88b; SOUTHBANK PRESS OFFICE: 186bl; SYNDICATION INTERNATIONAL: 33bl, 37tr, 52cb, 53c, 58bl, 59t, 136; Library of Congress 27bl.

ST PAUL'S CATHEDRAL: Sampson Lloyd 148cl, 150cla, 151tr.

TATE LONDON 2001: 12br, 41cr, 43br, 82–3 all pics, 84–5 all pics, 178–9 all pics, 180–81 all pics; 273br. TRANSPORT FOR LONDON: 378cl; 482CL Courtesy of the BOARD OF TRUSTEES OF THE VICTORIA AND ALBERT MUSEUM: 12cl, 37br, 40b, 201cl; 202–3 all pics, 204–5 all pics, 254b, 358t; VIEW PICTURES: Dennis Gilbert 380br. THE WALDORF, London: 272b; By kind permission of the trustees of THE WALLACE COLLECTION, London: 40ca, 226cl; PHILIP WAY PHOTOGRAPHY: 64lb, 150clb, 177b; Courtesy of the TRUSTEES OF THE WEDGWOOD MUSEUM, Barlaston, Stoke-on-Trent, Staffs, England: 28br; VIVIENNE WESTWOOD: Patrick Fetherstonhaugh 33br; THE WIMBLEDON LAWN TENNIS MUSEUM: Micky White 251t; Photo © WOODMANSTERNE: Jeremy Marks 37tl, 149t; GREGORY WRONA 267r.
YOUTH HOSTEL ASSOCIATION: 277; ZEFA: 12t, 52b, 342c; Bob Croxford 57t; Clive Sawyer 57b. ZWEMMER MEDIA: David Bennett 323bl.

Front Endpaper: All special photography except JOHN HESELTINE: cl, cr, tr, crb, br.

JACKET
Front – ALAMY IMAGES: Robert Harding Picture Library bl; JON ARNOLD: Main Image. Back – DK IMAGES: Max Alexander tl, bl; Stephen Oliver cla; PERETTI COMMUNICATIONS: Chris Gasgoine and Liftschutz Davidson clb. Spine – JON ARNOLD: t; DK IMAGES: Max Alexander b.

All other images © DORLING KINDERSLEY
For further information see ww.DKimages.com

The London Underground